Minstrels Playing

MUSIC IN EARLY ENGLISH
RELIGIOUS DRAMA

Volume 2

Minstrels Playing

MUSIC IN EARLY ENGLISH
RELIGIOUS DRAMA

RICHARD RASTALL

Volume 2

D. S. BREWER

First published 2001
D. S. Brewer, Cambridge

ISBN 0 85991 585 9

D. S. Brewer is an imprint of Boydell & Brewer Ltd
PO Box 9, Woodbridge, Suffolk IP12 3DF, UK
and of Boydell & Brewer Inc.
PO Box 41026, Rochester, NY 14604–4126, USA
website: http://www.boydell.co.uk

A catalogue record for this title is available
from the British Library

Library of Congress Cataloging-in-Publication Data
applied for

This publication is printed on acid free paper

Printed in Great Britain by
Antony Rowe Ltd, Chippenham, Wiltshire

CONTENTS

PART 1
Historical Drama 1 : Biblical Plays

To
GORDON,
and in memory of
JEAN

PREFACE AND ACKNOWLEDGEMENTS

The title of this book does not indicate that it is particularly concerned with instrumental music, as opposed to a vocal or angelic bias in *The Heaven Singing*. Both titles, of course, are taken from well-known stage directions in the repertory under examination here: the former from **Chester 2** (see page 237, below) and the latter from **N-Town 9/245+sd** (see page 66, below). They do however serve to remind us of the rich diversity of musical provision that must have been found in productions of this repertory, a diversity that provides the reason both for the writing of this work and for its long gestation.

One reviewer of *The Heaven Singing* hoped that the second volume of *Music in Early English Religious Drama* 'will not be long – in either sense'. I have surely disappointed him on both counts. It has taken four years to produce this volume after the publication of the first, one result of a busy academic life: much as I enjoy my work, no-one regrets more than I do the erosion of the time available for reading, thinking and writing in my profession. I do not however regret the length of this volume, since the play-by-play discussions were always planned as the major part of the work.

These discussions are presented under the main headings of biblical, saint and moral plays, with incomplete and lost plays in each section following those for which texts survive.[1] Each play or cycle is discussed in an order that is common to all: an introductory section, followed by discussions of the dramatic directions, text references concerning music, the use of Latin and references to liturgy, the record evidence and, finally, a list of music and other aural cues. When a play or cycle has a chapter to itself, the sub-headings for the chapter reflect this organisation, so that X.4 is always the section on Latin and the liturgy in chapter X and the last section is always the cue-list. Only section X.5 is variable: where there is no possible record evidence for a play or cycle, that section is omitted and the cue-list becomes section X.5 rather than X.6.

It may be helpful to discuss briefly the purpose of each of these sections.

Introduction   This section gives a summary of the main historical and biblio-
graphical information for the play or cycle concerned. It also lists the numbers, titles, and (for the civic cycles) the guilds responsible for the plays concerned: this is the numbering used in all the discussions.

---

[1]   As noted in section 9.1, the Shrewsbury and Pepys fragments are not included here, being discussed in Volume I. I have also excluded *Everyman*, for reasons rehearsed in I, 4–5: that play is discussed in Rastall '*Everyman*' (see Bibliography).

Dramatic directions These are the most obvious indication of musical performance in the plays, and often the most precise. The musical directions can be interpreted only in the context of the dramatist's or scribe's overall treatment of directions, however, and a general study of directions is therefore necessary. In the light of this, the individual directions are assessed.

Text references References to music in the text can be as helpful as directions in giving information about where, and in what form, music cues should be provided. They may be anything from a specific description of music demanded by a direction to the most oblique metaphorical allusion to musical activity. Clear metaphorical usages are quoted but not usually discussed: when it is not clear whether a reference is literal or metaphorical, the text is examined. Although the information given by metaphorical references is indirect, it is helpful in assessing the author's interest in music and his attitude to it.

Surviving banns are treated here as texts, their nature and function having been assessed first in the Introduction. In the quotations, a speech-heading enclosed in brackets denotes a character already speaking; one without brackets shows a character starting to speak at the beginning of the quotation.

Latin and the liturgy The discussions of the use of Latin in the plays, and of the function of liturgical material, partly overlap the kind of material treated in the two previous sections. The questions to be answered belong to two areas:

1 Is a Latin word or phrase to be heard? If so, should it be sung or spoken? The first of these questions demands a consideration of the context of the Latin lines, the second an investigation of the Vulgate and possible liturgical versions of the text, including the precise wording and the relations between biblical and liturgical versions. There are in addition other possible sources of Latin texts, such as the various compilations of saints' lives and other devotional and exegetical writings. I have not thought it necessary to make positive identifications in these sources, although I have regularly consulted the *Legenda Aurea*, perhaps the most commonly used of these sources in the plays.

2 If it can be established that a Latin text is liturgical then there may be a presumption that it should be sung. In this case the precise version must be identified. Here one must assess any data to be gained from purely musical considerations, as well as the overall context of the Latin. Often the Latin *incipit* belongs to two or more liturgical items, in which case various factors must be considered:

(i) The type of piece: antiphon, respond verse, gradual, etc. (A 'liturgical item' in this book normally refers to a text with its own chant setting rather than one which is recited.)

(ii) Its sources and liturgical function: the service books in which it occurs and its place in the liturgy according to those sources. I have considered the Use of Salisbury to be the most sensible reference for secular uses unless the obviously relevant use is available. Clearly, it is necessary to compare items in the York plays with the York Use, and this is perfectly possible because the

York Use is easily available. Equally, however, items in the Chester and Shrewsbury plays should be compared with the Lichfield Use: but this is more problematic, since that use is not so easily available and few Lichfield books have been firmly identified. The Chester plays, too, raise the question of the Benedictine liturgy, and here the Worcester antiphoner provides an available and fairly comprehensive means of comparison, at least for the music and texts of the Office. It should be noted, however, that the liturgy varied considerably in its details from one house to another. Other religious uses need eventually to be considered, but a full investigation is outside the scope of this work. Bibliographic abbreviations for the liturgical sources consulted are listed below under Abbreviations: Works Frequently Cited.

(iii) The precise text. The various items beginning with a particular *incipit* do not necessarily continue in the same way, and there is also some variation in the amount of text set. These variations may affect the suitability of the item for the dramatic context.

(iv) The type of chant. Chant is roughly classified as syllabic (basically one note per syllable), neumatic (mainly two or three notes per syllable, but perhaps with the occasional short melisma), and melismatic (with many and/or long melismas). In many cases this classification confirms others: for example, syllabic chant is usually for the priest and/or the congregation, and is therefore notated low in pitch, whereas melismatic chant is for a soloist and is often notated high.

(v) Mode. Chant is classified according to the notated pitch of its final (or 'key-note') and reciting note.[2] This is not normally relevant to the present work, and I have not always noted the mode: but it may be important when two or more items are sung consecutively or when a polyphonic setting is chant-based.

(vi) Range. The vocal range helps to identify the kind of singer involved liturgically (priest, congregation, trained choir, soloist), and therefore the type of performer required in the drama.

(i)–(iii), above, relate to the piece's textual and liturgical propriety, while (iv)–(vi) relate to its musical suitability in the drama and to the performers required to sing it. The musical features indirectly give information on the difficulty of the music, which may be relevant to what we know of the casting for a particular performance.

Records These sections concentrate on the financial accounts of the guilds mounting the drama – that is, primarily the financing of the performances and only secondarily the organisation. This information is largely missing from the chapters of Parts 2 and 3, since it is only in the case of civic performances that the records can be matched with identifiable texts. Both of the possible

---

2 For a convenient list of the modes and their characteristics, see Robertson and Stevens *Pelican History of Music I*, 155.

exceptions to this general situation, the Cornish plays and those performed at Chelmsford in 1562 (discussed in I, 168–74), underline this problem: it is impossible to match play-texts to records with any degree of certainty.

Cue list The list of cues for music and other aural effects uses the information presented in the previous sections. We can rarely draw firm conclusions about the performance of music in a particular play, so that this section offers no easy answers. I have however tried to adjudicate objectively when the probabilities are finely balanced. The first item for each cue is a listing of the dynamic functions (for which see I, 225–32) of that cue:

- (a) Movement of character(s) around the acting areas;
- (b) Entrance of character(s);
- (c) Exit of character(s);
- (d) The passage of time;
- (e) Change of location;
- (f) Start of play;
- (g) End of play;
- (h) Scene-division; and
- (i) Tableau.

Representational functions are not noted in this way, although they may be discussed briefly: the reader is referred to I, chapter 5, for these.

Musical items are identified if possible. I have been concerned only with what the evidence suggests, however, and solutions are not offered if the evidence is insufficient.

In the cue-list I discuss individual pageants or play-sections in order. Music cues are numbered in the form N_m, where N is the number of the play (in a cycle) or section (of a play) and m is the number of the music cue in that play or section: thus 'York 45_2' is the second music cue in York play 45, discussed in the relevant place in section 1.6. Where the evidence for a cue seems too speculative for it to be certain that music should be heard, a letter takes the place of a cue-number, e.g. 'York 18_A'. This numbering of cues is used throughout the book.

It had been my intention to bring together here all the relevant information about each individual cue, but it is often not possible to draw firm conclusions. Sometimes this is because the evidence is inadequate, but sometimes because it seems probable that the play text itself offers alternatives to a producer. In such cases the discussion may be too unwieldy to be rehearsed in full. The reader is therefore warned that it may be necessary to backtrack over the previous sections in order to obtain the full picture of the evidence concerning any particular cue. I hope that my numbering-system and the running heads will make this an easy operation.

It may be worth while to generalise this last point. While we should like firm and unequivocal answers to the questions posed about the positioning and musical content of music cues, in practice the results of my investigation are often less simple. We should not regret this: it is a function of the richness and diversity of English dramatic life in the fifteenth and sixteenth centuries, and should be welcomed. Besides, it may be possible later, with more information and a clearer understanding of the issues, to arrive at firmer conclusions than are offered here.

It is also worth explaining why I have studied fragmentary texts and the records of lost texts, for which little positive result is obtainable. A musical study of these items is not necessarily pointless, for even tentative results may help to clarify the relationship between musical usage and the precise categories into which the plays fall. In such a complex and diffuse subject, we should collect and analyse the available information, even if no immediate use for it can be seen: but I have not tried to be comprehensive in my treatment of fragments, and not every survival is discussed in this book.

I return here to the ultimate aim of my work: to enable an appropriate use of music in performances of these plays. When the results of such investigation are sometimes so indefinite we have to draw on a wide range of evidence to arrive at solutions that are both practical and likely to be appropriate. My own experience in providing music for late medieval drama is that this is not always easy. The last part of this book therefore raises and examines some of the issues concerned. It is inevitably a very personal view, and for that reason it can hardly be a comprehensive practical guide for someone accepting musical responsibility for a play or cycle. It will, I hope, help to raise awareness of the issues concerned, not only in musical directors but in producers as well. It will be a long time yet before the provision of music in late medieval drama is given full consideration as a matter of course. If this book helps towards that end it will have fulfilled much of its purpose.

* * *

I should like to thank again all those whose help was acknowledged in *The Heaven Singing*: this second volume, which presents the evidence on which that one was based, has also gained from their expertise. I am particularly grateful to Richard Beadle, Philip Butterworth, Pamela King, David Klausner and Peter Meredith, whose continued advice has been invaluable. This volume has also benefitted from the advice of Clifford Davidson, Alan Kent, Graham Lyndon-Jones, Barbara Palmer and Denise Ryan, to all of whom I am very grateful.

To my family, I offer renewed thanks for opportunities to hide away and write this work. It has never been quite absent from the lives of Eleanor, Jim and Will, who have been kind in their comparisons of me with more normal dads. The support given by my mother and by my father-in-law is so deeply embedded in life's fabric that nothing I could say here would be adequate; and the dedication of this book is a long-overdue acknowledgement of my huge debt to Jane's parents. To Jane herself, as always, my work owes its existence.

Leeds: March 2001   GRR

BIBLIOGRAPHICAL NOTES

(i)   Any reference in the form 'I, xx' without title is a page-reference to Volume I, *The Heaven Singing* (1996).

(ii)   The abbreviations for play texts and frequently-cited works (below, xvi–xx) are largely the same as those listed in I, xiii–xvii. In this volume, however, I have used the edition by Stevens and Cawley for the Towneley cycle and that of King and Davidson for the Coventry plays. This causes some discrepancies between line-numbers here and those in *The Heaven Singing*, but it seemed wise to refer to what has become the standard texts. Further discussion of the editions used is at the start of each chapter in Parts 1–3.

(iii)   I have used the library *sigla* of the Répertoire Internationale des Sources Musicales (RISM) for manuscripts in the following libraries:

      British Library, London: Lbl

      The library of Christ Church, Oxford: Och

(iv)   The abbreviations SD, MD and SH (sd, md, sh) are used for 'stage direction', 'marginal direction' and 'speech heading', respectively.

(v)   Internal references in the form '9.3' are to chapter and section as given in the Contents and in the running heads. References in the form '**York 2/13**' or '**Mary Play 1224**' are to collection/cycle, pageant and line or to play and line, as appropriate; '**+sd**', '**+md**' and '**+lat**' indicate the stage direction, marginal direction or Latin text following the line in question in the relevant edition; the form '**1–**' and '**21+**' refers to whatever precedes or follows the line concerned. References in the form '**York 12₃**' are to music cues (in this case, cue number 3 in York play 12), so numbered in the cue-lists: cues using a letter subscript, '**York 18ᴀ**', are putative cues for which the evidence is reasonable but speculative.

(vi)   Plays are numbered according to the relevant modern edition or other authority: these are listed below, with their short references.

(vii)   Short bibliographical references other than these abbreviations take the form of the author's/editor's surname and a recognisable abbreviation: thus 'Spencer *Pilgrim Souvenirs*' refers to Brian Spencer's 1998 volume *Pilgrim Souvenirs and Secular Badges*, listed in the Bibliography. Page references are to the latest edition listed.

(viii) Some much-cited works have been given their own abbreviations, and these are included in the list below.

(ix) Translations of biblical texts are from the Authorized Version unless otherwise stated. References are given as Book Chapter/Verse, e.g. Hosea 4/16.

(x)   Liturgical texts are quoted from the relevant service books, listed in the Abbreviations below and in the Bibliography.

(xi) In the discussions of music unspecified pitches are given capital letters: for instance, C is the note C but not in any particular octave (unless it is obvious from the musical context). Specific pitches are referred to by the Helmholtz system, in which c'-b' is the octave from middle C upwards.

ABBREVIATIONS: PLAY TEXTS

In this work, a name in roman type (e.g. Chester) refers to a cycle; names in italic (e.g. *Chester*) refer specifically to the edition listed here unless another is specified, or to an individual play (e.g. *Wisdom*). References to specific parts of a play text are given in **bold** type (e.g. **Towneley 13/50** refers to line 50 of Towneley play 13; **Castle 156** refers to line 156 of *The Castle of Perseverance*).

Ashmole	'The Ashmole Fragment' in Norman Davis, ed. *Non-Cycle Plays and Fragments*. Early English Text Society, supplementary series, 1. London: Oxford University Press, 1970. 120.
Brome	'The Brome Play' in Norman Davis, ed. *Non-Cycle Plays and Fragments*. Early English Text Society, supplementary series, 1. London: Oxford University Press, 1970. 43–57.
Burial	'Christ's Burial' in Donald C. Baker, John L. Murphy and Louis B. Hall, Jr, eds. *The Late Religious Plays of Bodleian MSS Digby 133 and E Museo 160*. Early English Text Society, 283. London: Oxford University Press, 1982. 141–68.
Cambridge	'The Cambridge Prologue' in Norman Davis, ed. *Non-Cycle Plays and Fragments*. Early English Text Society, supplementary series, 1. London: Oxford University Press, 1970. 114–15.
Castle	'The Castle of Perseverance' in Mark Eccles, ed. *The Macro Plays*. Early English Text Society, 262. London: Oxford University Press, 1969. 1–111.
Chester	R.M. Lumiansky and David Mills, eds. *The Chester Mystery Cycle*. Early English Text Society, supplementary series, 3, 9. London: Oxford University Press, 1974 and 1986): references are to the first volume (Text) unless otherwise specified.
Coventry	Pamela M. King and Clifford Davidson, eds. *The Coventry Corpus Christi Plays*. Kalamazoo, MI: Medieval Institute Publications, 2000.
Creacion	Paula Neuss, ed. *The Creacion of the World*. New York: Garland, 1983.
Delight	'The Reynes Extracts: A. A Speech of "Delight"' in Norman Davis, ed. *Non-Cycle Plays and Fragments*. Early English Text Society, supplementary series, 1. London: Oxford University Press, 1970. 121–2.
Durham	'The Durham Prologue' in Norman Davis, ed. *Non-Cycle Plays and Fragments*. Early English Text Society, supplementary series, 1. London: Oxford University Press,

1970. 118–19.

Dux Moraud   'Dux Moraud' in Norman Davis, ed. *Non-Cycle Plays and Fragments*. Early English Text Society, supplementary series, 1. London: Oxford University Press, 1970. 106–13.

Epilogue   'The Reynes Extracts: B. An Epilogue' in Norman Davis, ed. *Non-Cycle Plays and Fragments*. Early English Text Society, supplementary series, 1. London: Oxford University Press, 1970. 123.

Killing   'Candlemas Day and the Killing of the Children of Israel' in Donald C. Baker, John L. Murphy and Louis B. Hall, Jr., eds. *The Late Religious Plays of Bodleian MSS Digby 133 and E Museo 160*. Early English Text Society, 283. London: Oxford University Press, 1982. 96–115. [This play is often called just 'The Killing of the Children'.]

Lucidus and Dubius   The Winchester Dialogues, 1. Winchester College, MS 33, ff. 54v–64v, in MDF 5.

Mankind   'Mankind' in Mark Eccles, ed. *The Macro Plays*. Early English Text Society, 262. London: Oxford University Press, 1969. 153–84.

Mary Magdalen   'Mary Magdalen' in Donald C. Baker, John L. Murphy and Louis B. Hall, Jr, eds. *The Late Religious Plays of Bodleian MSS Digby 133 and E Museo 160*. Early English Text Society, 283. London: Oxford University Press, 1982. 24–95.

Mary Play   Peter Meredith, ed. *The Mary Play from the N.town Manuscript*. London: Longman, 1987.

Meriasek   Whitley Stokes, ed. and trans. *Beunans Meriasek: The Life of St Meriasek*. London: Trübner, 1872.

Newcastle   'The Newcastle Play' in Norman Davis, ed. *Non-Cycle Plays and Fragments*. Early English Text Society, supplementary series, 1. London: Oxford University Press, 1970. 19–31.

Northampton   'The Northampton Play' in Norman Davis, ed. *Non-Cycle Plays and Fragments*. Early English Text Society, supplementary series, 1. London: Oxford University Press, 1970. 32–42.

Norwich   'The Norwich Grocers' Play' in Norman Davis, ed. *Non-Cycle Plays and Fragments*. Early English Text Society, supplementary series, 1. London: Oxford University Press, 1970. 8–18.

N-Town   Stephen Spector, ed. *The N-Town Play*. Early English Text Society, supplementary series, 11, 12. London: Oxford University Press, 1991.

Occupation and Idleness   The Winchester Dialogues, 2. Winchester College, MS 33, ff. 65r–73v, in MDF 5.

Ordinalia   Edwin Norris, ed. *The Ancient Cornish Drama*. Oxford: Oxford University Press, 1859. 2 vols. [The first and third days being called 'ordinale' in the manuscript, the Cornish cycle is often known as the Ordinalia.]

Passion Play   Peter Meredith, ed. *The Passion Play from the N.Town Manuscript*. London: Longman, 1990.

Pride of Life   'The Pride of Life' in Norman Davis, ed. *Non-Cycle Plays and Fragments*. Early English Text Society, supplementary series, 1. London: Oxford University Press, 1970. 90–105.

Resurrection   'Christ's Resurrection' in Donald C. Baker, John L. Murphy and Louis B. Hall, Jr., eds. *The Late Religious Plays of Bodleian MSS Digby 133 and E Museo 160*. Early English Text Society, 283. London: Oxford University Press, 1982. 169–93.

Reynes   'The Reynes Extracts' in Norman Davis, ed. *Non-Cycle Plays and Fragments*. Early English Text Society, supplementary series, 1. London: Oxford University Press, 1970. 121–3.

Rickinghall   'The Rickinghall (Bury St Edmunds) Fragment' in Norman Davis, ed. *Non-Cycle Plays and Fragments*. Early English Text Society, supplementary series, 1. London: Oxford University Press, 1970. 116–17.

Sacrament   'The Play of the Sacrament' in Norman Davis, ed. *Non-Cycle Plays and Fragments*. Early English Text Society, supplementary series, 1. London: Oxford University Press, 1970. 58–89. [This play is often known as the Croxton play.]

St Paul   'The Conversion of St Paul' in Donald C. Baker, John L. Murphy and Louis B. Hall, Jr., eds. *The Late Religious Plays of Bodleian MSS Digby 133 and E Museo 160*. Early English Text Society, 283. London: Oxford University Press, 1982. 1–23.

Towneley   Martin Stevens and A.C. Cawley, eds. *The Towneley Plays*. Early English Text Society. Oxford: Oxford University Press, 1994.

Winchester   'The Winchester Dialogues'. MDF 5, 133–208. Winchester College MS 33, ff. 54V–73v.

Wisdom   'Wisdom' in Mark Eccles, ed. *The Macro Plays*. Early English Text Society, 262. London: Oxford University Press, 1969. 113–52. [An incomplete version of the play is in the 'Digby' collection, pp. 116–40 in Baker, Murphy and Hall, eds. *The Late Religious Plays of Bodleian MSS Digby 133 and E Museo 160*. Early English Text Society, 283. London: Oxford University Press, 1982.]

York   Richard Beadle, ed. *The York Plays*. London: Edward Arnold, 1982.

ABBREVIATIONS:
WORKS FREQUENTLY CITED

AM *Antiphonale Monasticum*. Tournai: Desclée, 1934.

AR *Antiphonale Romanum*. Paris: Descleé, 1924.

AS *Antiphonale Sarisburiense*, ed. Walter H. Frere. London: Plainsong and Mediaeval Music Society, 1901–15; repr. Farnborough: Gregg Press, 1966.

Aspects Neuss, Paula, ed. *Aspects of Early English Drama*. Cambridge: D.S. Brewer; Totowa, NJ: Barnes and Noble,1983.

BE *Breviarium ad usum insignis ecclesie Eboracensis*, ed. Stephen W. Lawley. Durham: Surtees Society, 71 and 75, 1879 and 1883.

BH *The Hereford Breviary*, ed. Walter H. Frere and L.E.G. Brown. London: Henry Bradshaw Society, 1904–15.

BS *Breviarium ac usum insignis ecclesiae Sarum*, ed. Francis Procter and C. Wordsworth. Cambridge: 1879–86; repr. Farnborough: Gregg Press, 1970.

Contexts Marianne G. Briscoe and John C. Coldewey, eds. *Contexts for Early English Drama*. Bloomington, IN: Indiana University Press, 1989.

Essays R.M. Lumiansky and David Mills. *The Chester Mystery Cycle: Essays and Documents, with an Essay, 'Music in the Cycle', by Richard Rastall*. Chapel Hill, NC: University of North Carolina Press, 1983.

GL *The Golden Legend*, by Jacobus de Voragine, trans. Granger Ryan and Helmut Ripperger. 1941; repr. New York: Arno Press, 1969. [See also LA.]

GR *Graduale Sacrosancte Romanae Ecclesiae*. Solesmes: Abbatia Sancti Petri de Solesmes, 1974.

GS *Graduale Sarisburiense*, ed. Walter H. Frere. London: Plainsong and Mediaeval Music Society, 1891–4; repr. Farnborough: Gregg Press, 1966.

HS *Hymnarium Sarisburiense*. London: James Darling, 1851.

IMEV I Carlton Brown and Rossell Hope Robbins. *The Index of Middle English Verse*. New York: Columbia University Press for the Index Society, 1943.
   II Rossell Hope Robbins and John L. Cutler. *Supplement to the Index of Middle English Verse*. 1965.

LA *Legenda Aurea*, by Jacobus de Voragine, ed. Th. Graesse. Vratistlavia [Breslau]: 3rd edn, Koebner, 1890. [See also GL.]

LH *Liber Hymnarius*. Solesmes: Abbaye Saint-Pierre de Solesmes, 1983.

LMRP Donald C. Baker, J.L. Murphy and Louis B. Hall. *The Late Religious*

	Plays of Bodleian MSS Digby 133 and E Museo 160. Early English Text Society, 283. London: Oxford University Press, 1982.
LU	*The Liber Usualis, with introduction and rubrics in English,* edited by the Benedictines of Solesmes. Tournai: Desclée, 1938.
MDF	Leeds Texts and Monographs, Medieval Drama Facsimiles. Leeds: The University of Leeds School of English, 1973–. For a list, see the Bibliography under Medieval Drama Facsimiles.
MED	*The Middle English Dictionary.* Ann Arbor, MI: University of Michigan Press, 1952– .
MisE	*Missale ad usum insignis ecclesie Eboracensis,* ed. William G. Henderson. Durham: Surtees Society, 59 and 60, 1874.
MisS(D)	*Missale ad usum insignis et praeclarae ecclesiae Sarum,* ed. Francis H. Dickinson, 1861–83; repr. Farnborough: Gregg Press, 1969.
MisS(L)	*The Sarum Missal Edited from Three Early Manuscripts,* ed. J. Wickham Legg. Oxford: Clarendon Press, 1916; repr. 1969.
MPE	*Manuale et processionale ad usum insignis ecclesiae Eboracensis* [ed. William G. Henderson]. Durham: Surtees Society, 63, 1875.
MS	*Manuale ad usum percelebris ecclesiae Sarisburiensis,* ed. A. Jefferies Collins. London: Henry Bradshaw Society, 1960.
NCPF	Davis, Norman. *Non-Cycle Plays and Fragments.* Early English Text Society, supplementary series,1. London: Oxford University Press, 1970.
OE	*Ordinale Exoniense,* ed. J.N. Dalton. 4 vols. London: Henry Bradshaw Society, 1909–40.
OED	*The Oxford English Dictionary.* Oxford: Clarendon Press, 1884–1987.
OS	*Ordinale Sarum sive Directorium Sacerdotum,* by Clement Maydeston, ed. William Cooke and Christopher Wordsworth. London: Henry Bradshaw Society, 20 and 22, 1901–2.
PS(H)	*Processionale ad usum insignis ac praeclarae ecclesiae Sarum,* ed. William G. Henderson. Leeds: M'Corquodale and Co., 1882; repr. Farnborough: Gregg Press, 1969.
PS(P)	*Processionale ad Usum Sarum 1502.* Originally published by Richard Pynson. Facsimile repr.: The Use of Sarum 1. Kilkenny: Boethius Press, 1980.
Reed.York	For this and other REED volumes similarly abbreviated, see the Bibliography under Records of Early English Drama.
RMLWL	*The Revised Medieval Latin Word-List,* prepared by R.E. Latham. London: Oxford University Press for the British Academy, 1965; reprinted with Supplement, 1980.
Sandon	Nick Sandon, ed. *The Use of Salisbury.* 6 vols. Newton Abbot: Antico Edition, 1984– .
WA	[Worcester Antiphoner] *Antiphonaire Monastique ... de Worcester,* ed. André Mocquereau. Paléographie Musicale 12. Tournay: Desclée, 1922.

TABLES

MUSICAL EXAMPLES

PART 1

Historical Drama 1: Biblical Plays

1

The York Cycle

1.1   Introduction

The manuscript of the York cycle is the official civic copy of the plays, now
Additional MS 35290 at the British Library, London. It is available in mono-
chrome facsimile, with the music pages also printed separately in full colour, un
the Medieval Drama Facsimiles series (MDF 7). The plays were edited by Lucy
Toulmin Smith in 1885, a work that was a classic of its kind and remained the
standard (and only complete) edition until Richard Beadle's, published in 1982
(*York Plays*). Beadle includes a careful examination of the manuscript's physical
features as well as a close study of the text itself and a piecing-together of the
history of the cycle.

The composed polyphony of **York 45**, the Assumption play, is discussed in I,
121–37. As noted there, the body of the play contains settings of three Latin
texts, all in two voices, while another group of two-voiced settings of the same
texts is at the end of the play. The role of these settings in the numerical
construction of the play is discussed in I, 246–8. These six items of polyphony
are the most substantial body of notated music in the repertory.

The music was edited by W.H. Cummings in Smith's edition of 1885 (Smith
York Plays, 517–28), but his work is unusable and has probably been a major
factor in the neglect of the York music (see I, 137). Only in recent performances
in the streets of York (1988, 1994) has this music been allowed to show its
worth. Later editions were published by Ruth Steiner (in Wall 'York Pageant
XLVI', 698–711), JoAnna Dutka (*Music*, 38–42 and 44–50), John Stevens (in
Beadle *York Plays*, 465–74) and myself (Rastall *Six Songs*). All of these give an
acceptable account of the music, although some knotty problems of rhythm and
even of texture result in differences between them.[1]

The play, its music and the texts of the musical items were discussed also by
Hoffman ('Source of the Words'), Wall ('Apocryphal' and 'York Pageant XLVI'),

---

1   See especially I, 127–8 and 131–2, including n. 81.

3

and Rastall ('[York] Music' and 'Vocal Range and Tessitura').

Documentary evidence for the York cycle is published in *REED.York*. The earliest record of an apparent Corpus Christi play at York is in an item concerning the building in which three pageants were being stored in 1376 (*REED.York*, 3). As Beadle points out (*York Plays*, 20), this need not imply the existence of a cycle at that date, although the known involvement of several of the York trade guilds in the period from 1386 or 1387 to 1390 has been cited as evidence of it (*REED.York*, 4–7). This involvement, and York's position as a social and economic centre, are discussed by Beadle in his introduction (*York Plays*, 20–3). It is certain, however, that by 1399 there was some large-scale presentation involving several trade guilds, with stations through the city, many of which are recognisable as stations used for the cycle in the fifteenth century.[2]

In 1415 the then Common Clerk of York, Roger Burton, drew up an *ordo paginarum* that provides the first extant list and description of the pageants and the guilds responsible for them. This list was annotated at various times during the fifteenth century, and it therefore contains evidence of the development of the cycle between 1415 and the copying of the extant play-manuscript in the 1460s or 1470s. This matter has been much discussed, but need not concern us here (see Beadle *York Plays*, 23–8, for bibliography). A slightly later but undatable list of the plays follows the 1415 *ordo* in the city's A/Y Memorandum Book.[3] To some extent this existence of the 1415 *ordo paginarum* and the later list of pageants makes up for the lack of descriptive banns for the York cycle.

The text of the York cycle survives in a unique source, Lbl Add. MS 35290. This is the official register copy, no doubt commissioned by the Mayor and Corporation of York and apparently copied from the prompt-copies belonging to the individual guilds. The Register dates from the period 1463–77 (Beadle and Meredith 'Further External Evidence'), and presumably represents the text of the cycle as performed at that time. Three plays were not entered then, however: one of these (play 4) was entered probably between 1557 and 1559, but according to Beadle it is not the same as the relevant play described in the 1415 *ordo paginarum*; the other two never were entered, although an extra play (no. 17) was added some time after 1567 (Beadle *York Plays*, 12). Further evidence that the Register was still in use in the middle of the sixteenth century is provided by a number of late annotations.[4] To some extent these annotations give clues to the subsequent history of the cycle, but they also cause problems over the precise period of validity of the evidence concerned. The last recorded performance of the cycle was in 1569.

A single surviving guild-copy is for play **41**, mounted by the Scriveners

---

2 *REED.York*, 11–12, translated *ibid.*, 697–8 and in Beadle *York Plays*, 22f.

3 *REED.York*, 25f, translated *ibid.*, 710f and in Beadle *York Plays*, 25f: both documents are reproduced in MDF 7.

4 See especially Meredith 'John Clerke's Hand'. The Register was at that time referred to as 'the old Register': see *REED.York*, 351.

(Cawley 'Sykes Manuscript'). No music cues occur in that play.

The plays of the York cycle are listed below, together with the guilds mounting them at the time of the Register's copying. The numbering and titles are Beadle's.[5]

1	The Fall of the Angels	Barkers
2	The Creation	Plasterers
3	The Creation of Adam and Eve	Cardmakers
4	Adam and Eve in Eden	Fullers
5	The Fall of Man	Coopers
6	The Expulsion	Armourers
7	Cain and Abel	Glovers
8	The Building of the Ark	Shipwrights
9	The Flood	Fishers and Mariners
10	Abraham and Isaac	Parchmentmakers and Bookbinders
11	Moses and Pharaoh	Hosiers
12	The Annunciation and the Visitation	Spicers
13	Joseph's Trouble about Mary	Pewterers and Founders
14	The Nativity	Tilethatchers
15	The Shepherds	Chandlers
16	Herod and The Magi	Masons Goldsmiths
17	The Purification	Hatmakers, Masons and Labourers
18	The Flight into Egypt	Marshals
19	The Slaughter of the Innocents	Girdlers and Nailers
20	Christ and the Doctors	Spurriers and Lorimers
21	The Baptism	Barbers
22	The Temptation	Smiths
22A[6]	The Marriage at Cana	Vintners
23	The Transfiguration	Curriers
23A[7]	Jesus in the House of Simon the Leper	Ironmongers

---

5 Toulmin Smith's numbering is slightly different, because she ordered the plays according to their position in the manuscript, while Beadle (*York Plays*) restores them to their proper dramatic order; she also provided different titles, some of which were not accurate. Lancashire's list is concerned with the whole history of the cycle, not just with the surviving text, so his order and numbering are also different from those given here (Lancashire *Dramatic Texts*, 294–6).

6 This play existed, and the opening is known, but it was not registered: see Beadle *York Plays*, 192. On its history and ordering in the cycle, see *ibid.*, 440.

7 This play was not registered: see Beadle *York Plays*, 198 and 441.

24	The Woman Taken in Adultery and The Raising of Lazarus	Cappers
25	The Entry into Jerusalem	Skinners
26	The Conspiracy	Cutlers
27	The Last Supper	Bakers
28	The Agony in the Garden and the Betrayal	Cordwainers
29	Christ before Annas and Caiaphas	Bowers and Fletchers
30	Christ before Pilate 1: The Dream of Pilate's Wife	Tapiters and Couchers
31	Christ before Herod	Litsters
32	The Remorse of Judas	Cooks and Waterleaders
33	Christ before Pilate 2: The Judgement	Tilemakers
34	The Road to Calvary	Shearmen
35	The Crucifixion	Pinners
36	The Death of Christ	Butchers
37	The Harrowing of Hell	Saddlers
38	The Resurrection	Carpenters
39	Christ's Appearance to Mary Magdalene	Winedrawers
40	The Supper at Emmaus	Woolpackers and Woolbrokers
41	The Incredulity of Thomas	Scriveners
42	The Ascension	Tailors
43	Pentecost	Potters
44	The Death of the Virgin	Drapers
44A[8]	The Funeral of the Virgin ('Fergus')	
45	The Assumption of the Virgin	Weavers
46	The Coronation of the Virgin	Hostelers
46A[9]	The Coronation of the Virgin	Hostelers
47	The Last Judgement	Mercers

1.2 Dramatic directions

The dramatic directions of the cycle have been fully discussed by Beadle in his edition, by Beadle and Meredith in their introduction to the facsimile (MDF 7), and by Beadle in an unpublished paper provided at a Medieval English Theatre meeting in Lancaster on 7 January 1984. The discussion that follows relies

---

[8] A play on this subject is known to have existed at various times in the fifteenth and sixteenth centuries (Beadle *York Plays*, 391 and 460), but no text survives.

[9] Play **46A** is a sixteenth-century fragment: see Beadle *York Plays*, 461–3. Toulmin Smith printed it at the end of her text, without number.

heavily on these works.[10]

The main compilation of the York Register is the work of two scribes. Scribe A was responsible for pageants 1–3A, and Scribe B, the main scribe, for almost all of the rest. (The precise divisions are irrelevant for our present purpose.) A number of these plays have dramatic directions in the original hands, and these will be referred to as 'original directions': it may reasonably be assumed, although it cannot be demonstrated, that these appear in the Register because they were present in the guild prompt-copies from which the Register was presumably compiled.[11] Thus the original directions can be regarded as having the authority of the official copies of the guilds concerned. The original directions in the Register are in Latin, written in red in a more formal and ornamental script such as was normally used in service-books.

Most of the original directions are in the space used for the body of the text: but occasionally they are placed to the right or left of the main column, giving rise to the suspicion that they may have been in this marginal position in the guild's own copy. The only surviving guild prompt-copy, that of the Scriveners dating from the first half of the sixteenth century,[12] contains no dramatic directions, as the Register copy of that play (**York 41**) does not. It is sometimes difficult to make a distinction between directions and speech headings or character designations, a problem that the scribes had, too. A single English direction apparently misunderstood by Scribe B (**30/370**) need not be discussed, as it is not a musical one,[13] but of the four exceptionally written in the same ink and script as the text (* in Table 1), one involves music.

It will be seen from Table 1 that of the nineteen original directions no fewer than ten are musical, with an eleventh (**12/240**) probably musical by implication. In addition, it is possible that the missing *Gloria in excelsis* of play **15** included a direction, giving a possible total of twelve musical directions out of twenty. Of the ten non-marginal directions for music, five specify the text, which seems to indicate a substantial interest in the precise pieces to be sung in those plays. There are perhaps two tentative conclusions to be drawn from this:

(i) That music was the largest single reason for directions being added to the plays; and

(ii) That the absence of musical directions in any York play can be taken as possible evidence of the absence of vocal music in that play. (In some cases, of course, text references modify the picture considerably.)

We should also note that only one of the ten or eleven musical directions is in a marginal position, whereas there are three marginal non-musical directions. It is

---

[10] Beadle *York Plays*, 16–19; MDF 7, xxx–xl; Beadle 'Lancaster 1984'. I am grateful to Dr Beadle for permission to use this last work.

[11] Beadle is clear (*York Plays*, 11) that the Register was copied from the guilds' individual texts and neither copied from nor modelled on an earlier register.

[12] See Cawley 'Sykes Manuscript'.

[13] MDF 7, xxxi.

TABLE 1 : ORIGINAL DIRECTIONS IN THE YORK CYCLE

Scribe	Play /line	f.	Mus/ non-mus	Lang	red?	Direction if musical: comments
A	1/24	1r	m/	Lat	r	*Tunc cantant ang[eli] Te deum [laudamus te domi-nu]m confitemur* Partly illegible
	1/40	1v	m/	Lat	r	*Tunc cantant angeli Sanctus sanctus sanctus dominus deus sabaoth*
B	5/79	14v	/n	Lat	*	
	5/82	14v	/n	Lat	*	
	5/105	14v	/n	Lat	*	
	12/240	47v	?/	Lat	r	*Magnificat*
	15/64	60r	m/	Lat	r	*Et tunc cantant*
	15/85	60r	m/	Lat	r	*Et tunc cantant* NB missing leaf (after f. 59) presumably included the angelic *Gloria in excelsis*
	21/154	93v	m/	Lat	r	*Tunc cantabunt duo angeli Veni creator spiritus*
	23/168	104v	/n	Lat	r	Marginal, on right
	30/370	160r	/n	Eng		Copied as part of the text
	33/267	184r	/n	Lat	r	Marginal, on right
	38/186	217r	/n	Lat	r	See Table 2
	43/96	242v	m/	Lat	r	*Angelus tunc cantare*
	44/194	248r	/n	Lat	r	Marginal, on right: see 1.6
			m/	Lat	r	*Et cantant antiphona[m] scilicet Ave regina celorum* In normal text position
	46/80	258r	m/	Lat	r	*Cantando* Marginal, to left. See I, 31
	47/216	264r	m/	Lat	*	*Hic ad sedem iudicij cum cantu angelorum*
	47/380	266v	m/	Lat	r	*Et sic facit finem cum melodia angelorum transiens a loco ad locum* See I, 28–30

TABLE 2 : ADDITIONAL DIRECTIONS IN THE YORK CYCLE

Play/ line	f.	Mus/ non-mus	Lang	Direction if musical: comments
9/266	29r	m/	Lat	*Tunc cantent Noe et filii sui etc.* 16th- century hand, but not Clerke's: direction confirms text reference (**9/260**: see 1.3, below).
12/144	46r	m/	Lat	*tunc cantat Angelus* Clerke
12/152	46r	m/	Lat	*tunc cantat angelus Ne timeas Maria* Clerke
12/240	47v	m/	Lat	*Tunc Cantat* Clerke, added to the original direction. See I, 24 and 27.
16/272	71v	/n	Eng	Clerke
22/91	96r	m/	Lat	*tunc Cantant Angeli veni creator* Clerke (?misplaced: see 1.6)
25/287	118v	m/	Lat	*tunc cant'* Late hand, but not Clerke: for the meaning of the scribal suspension, see 2.6, below.
25/544	121v	m/	Lat	*tunc cant'* Late hand, but not Clerke: for the meaning of the scribal suspension, see 1.6, below.
27/60	132v	/n	Lat	Clerke
29/23	144r	/n	Lat	Clerke
31/42	164v	/n	Lat	Clerke
33/443	187r	/n	Lat	Clerke
37/36	208r	m/	Lat	*Tunc Cant'* Late hand, not Clerke: perhaps Miles Newton (MDF 7, xxxix). See I, 31, and 1.6, below.
37/384	213v	m/	Lat	*tunc cantent* ?Clerke
38/186	217r	m/	Lat	*tunc Ang[e]lus cantat Resurgens* Clerke, additional to original (non-musical) direction *Tunc Jhesu resurgente*[14]
42/176	239r	m/	Lat	*Tunc cant' angel' gloria in excelsys deo* ?Miles Newton. Clerke has deleted the *incipit* and substituted *Ascendo ad patrem meum* above it. See I, 25, and 1.6, below.

---

[14] Not 'Jesus', as in Beadle *York Plays*, 349. This ablative absolute construction, 'Then, Jesus being risen', refers to the speech of the First Mary that follows, warning her not to speak until Christ has risen from the tomb and left the playing area.

43/96	242v	m/	Lat	*venicreator spiritus* (sic)
				Addition by ?Clerke to original direction.

impossible to reach any firm conclusions on the statistics provided by such small numbers, but the figures suggest that music had a rather higher status, and so was generally taken into account rather earlier in the compositional and scribal processes, than other dramatic factors calling for directions.[15] The manuscript also includes many marginal annotations, some of them in the form of directions, apparently made when the Register was in use at the first station during the sixteenth century.[16] The majority of the added directions, as well as much other material, were the work of Miles Newton, Common Clerk of the city c. 1538–50, and of Scribe C, John Clerke, who was Newton's assistant and Common Clerk after Newton's death in 1550 until c. 1567. Beadle notes the evidence that Clerke regarded at least some of his marginal directions as having the status of stage directions proper, and lists those that he thinks could usefully be regarded as such ('Lancaster 1984', 6 and 7). Table 2 is based on Beadle's list.

It will be seen that the sixteenth-century marginal additions provide another seventeen directions, of which three are appended to original directions. No fewer than twelve directions are musical, although these include all three supplementary ones. Five directions give the text *incipit*. These late marginal directions substantially increase the total number of directions in the cycle, and they more than double the musical directions. Again, it would seem that music, in the sixteenth century as in the third quarter of the fifteenth, was the most important of the factors calling for dramatic directions.

The York cycle is the only one to show distinct layers of activity in this way. Clearly, a dramatic direction must have been valid for the time at which it was written down and on such subsequent occasions as we know to have made use of it. Thus the original directions in the York manuscript were presumably valid in the 1460s or 1470s, while the later directions were valid in the middle decades of the sixteenth century. But did the original directions continue to be valid after the 1470s? Were they still in use in mid-sixteenth-century performances? And did the later directions concern new occasions for music, or did they confirm the places where music had been heard in the plays in earlier times?

These questions cannot be answered only in relation to the two periods when the directions were written. It is quite possible, for instance, that the original directions were used after the 1470s but had nevertheless fallen out of use by the time the sixteenth-century directions were added: or that the late directions con-

---

15 Beadle lists these other factors and discusses the relative abundance of musical directions: see Beadle 'Lancaster 1984', 3–4 and 5–6.

16 A full list of marginalia is given by Beadle and Meredith in MDF 7, xxxiii–xli: those in the form of directions are listed in Beadle 'Lancaster 1984', 7.

firmed an earlier usage that nevertheless did not go back as far as the 1470s.[17]

Difficult as the problem is, we are not without useful data. In the first place, the Register had an eminently practical purpose in the sixteenth century, when the Common Clerk of the city, or his assistant, apparently sat at the first station and checked each play as performed against the official version in the Register (Beadle *York Plays*, 12). It is reasonable to suppose that, just as the clerk made a note in the Register of material that he heard in performance – and this is the implication of most of the annotations – so that his record of the text would be complete, so he would cancel any material known to be permanently discarded. John Clerke did in fact cancel play **21** *in toto* when it was superseded. That no musical direction is cancelled by the clerk may therefore show that the original musical directions were in use during the mid-sixteenth century. Indeed, one late addition confirms a text reference to music (**9/266**), while another gives more data for what was already a musical direction (**43/96**). Although this is not conclusive, it suggests that the sixteenth-century additions were partly due to an awareness of a performing tradition that included musical items.

However, it must be admitted that all of the other late directions may be for relatively new musical additions. Even the other two late directions that are additions to original directions could well make a musical moment out of a non-musical one (*Magnificat* at **12/240** and *Tunc Jhesu resurgente* at **38/186**). Nor can it confidently be suggested that the text of the 1460s or 1470s omitted musical directions in places where the sixteenth-century scribes added them. The text reference at **9/260** does not certainly require music at **9/266** or anywhere else (see 2.3, below): and if one does take it as a clear indication of music, then the direction at the end of the speech is largely redundant. Of course, its importance may be that it tells us exactly who the singers are (Noah and his sons), although it seems a little unlikely that this was vital or surprising information. In the case of **43/96** it is quite possible that the purpose of the addition was primarily or wholly to give the *incipit*. When a late direction occurs where there was previously no direction, however, or as an addition to a non-musical direction, it is impossible to posit the transmission of specific information of this sort as a reason for the writing of the direction, rather than the obvious reason – viz., that music was not originally performed at that place, but was required at the time of the sixteenth-century marginalia. As so often, a piece of evidence can be pressed into service in support of two diametrically opposed views.

---

[17] It is of course impossible to be as scrupulous as this in providing music for a production.

1.3 Text references

The York plays have a full range of text references to music, from all the normal metaphorical usages to direct information on performance. Examples of metaphorical use show some grouping in particular plays, suggesting variations in the use of musical metaphors by the original playwrights.

1/104 [LUCIFER] Owte! Ay walaway! I well euen in wo nowe.

1/113 LUCIFER IN INFERNO
        Walaway! Wa es me now, nowe es it war thane it was.

5/174 [ANGELUS] Of sorowe may yhe synge.

6/24–5 ADAM   For vs is wrought, so welaway,
              Doole endurand nyghte and day

6/91–3 [ADAM] Be tyme of none alle lost had wee,
              Sa welawaye.
              Sa welaway, for harde peyne

All of these 'welaway' references are non-musical; that at **5/174** is also a common non-musical usage.

7/52 CAYME   Ya, daunce in þe devil way, dresse þe downe

Beadle glosses the verb 'dance' as 'go, proceed' (*York Plays*, 487): but he also gives the whole phrase as an intensification of 'in the deuel way' (glossed as 'in the devil's name'), with the meaning of 'hence, away, in the devil's name' (*ibid.*, 488). However, he also glosses 'in waye' as 'along the way' (*ibid.*, 529), so that the whole phrase could mean 'go, along the devil's way' – that is, something close to the more recent 'go to the devil'. At any rate, the basic meaning is clear: an irritable and emphasised 'Get out of here'. This metaphor does not seem to refer to the orderliness of dancing, but rather to the wasted expenditure of energy characteristic of the devil's service (see I, 206–8).

8/41   NOE A, lorde, I lowe þe lowde and still

8/145   [NOE] I lowe þi lare both lowde and stille

9/89, 91   [VXOR] ... þe fonnes full faste,
           ...
           ... I am agaste

The first two of these make use of a common metaphor with no particularly musical intention: see I, 47–8. In the last, there is a curious but perhaps accidental verbal likeness to part of the gossips' song, **Chester 3/225–7** (see I, 71–2). The coincidence may be due only to the convenience of the 'faste/agaste' rhyme, but it is still strange that the rhyme appears in the Noah plays of the two cycles. It is entirely possible that the dramatist of one, reading the other cycle's play for experience in writing his own, picked up the rhyme subconsciously.

9/259–64 [NOE] Mare joie in herte never are I hadde,
We mone be saued, now may we synge,
Come hedir my sonnes in hye,
Oure woo away is wente,
I se here certaynely
þe hillis of Hermonye.

Line **260** could indicate an actual vocal performance, although in conjunction with line **265**, 'Lovyd be þat lord ...', a 'praise' ending is possible (here the end of a scene, not a pageant). But the line could also be understood metaphorically, unless 'Hermonye' is a pun. Carter gives a number of spellings for 'harmony', mostly without the H, that could be confused with words for Armenia (*Dictionary*, 14–17), so that the possibility of a pun is there. Beadle gives no punning meaning in his Glossary of Proper Names (*York Plays*, 536), but Gardner sees the parallel line **Towneley 3/466** as a punning reference (*Construction*, 47: see 3.3, below). Gardner's argument is not really supported, however; if the pun has any point it must be in relation to the harmony/discord distinction in that play (see I, 241–3), but that seems unlikely.

It appears, then, that the reference to the hills of Armenia should probably be taken at face value, not as a pun; that the text reference to singing (line **260**) may indicate performance but could alternatively be metaphorical; and that the sixteenth-century marginal direction for singing at **266+md** either makes explicit the implied performance or was designed to make a metaphor an actuality. On the whole I incline to the first interpretation: that is, that line **260** implies performance (lines **261–6** confirming the situation), **266+md** being a later confirmation of production practice.

11/128 [DEUS] His sange ful sone sall be 'allas'.

11/225 REX (PHARAO) Nay, nay, þat daunce is done

Metaphorical use. Beadle glosses 'dance' as 'business, affair' (*York Plays*, 487): thus the phrase means 'that business is finished with' or, more specifically in the present context, 'the situation is altered'. See also **19/96**, below.

11/407–8 [I PUER] *Cantemus domino,*
                    To God a sange synge wee.

This reference does not certainly concern music: the Latin tag is an obvious one that does not presuppose liturgical performance (see 1.4, below). This is the end of the play, however, and an actual performance as part of the final tableau is likely – a 'praise' ending, in fact.

15/60–4, 65, 67, 71 and **82–5.** The shepherds discuss three musical performances: that of the angelic Gloria; their attempt to repeat the angelic music; and their performance of another song to honour the Christ-child while they journey to Bethlehem. The first of these refers to a passage in a leaf now missing (Beadle *York Plays,* 130), where there may have been a stage direction; the second and third do have original SDs (after **64** and **85:** *Et tunc cantant* on both occasions. See Table 1, above).

For the implications of the missing leaf, and for the shepherds' response to the angelic Gloria, see I, 352–3. I conclude that the angelic Gloria was a solo performance (although it could have been accompanied by an organ); that it was florid music, since the Second Shepherd describes their imitation as a 'mery note' (**15/65**); that the shepherds sing in unison to imitate it; and that they are reasonably successful in doing so, since the Third Shepherd describes their performance as a 'noble noyse' (**15/71**).

The Second Shepherd also says that he has so 'crakkid' in his throat that his lips are 'nere drye' (**67–8**). This shows that their performance was an energetic one: for the meaning of the verb 'to crack', see I, 36. Carter (*Dictionary,* 102–3) gives only somewhat noncommittal meanings almost synonymous with 'to sing', although the 'crakkyng of trumpes' cited suggests, in conjunction with the OED's non-musical definitions of breaking into pieces, a percussive style of performance in which there are many small notes. This suggests something nearer to 'knak' (and, therefore, to 'hak' as well: see I, 36–7): at the very least the word denotes an uninhibited performance of florid and decorated music, with many small notes in it.

The shepherds' attempt to repeat the angelic song may not have been an accurate imitation. Differences in vocal style would be enough to distinguish angelic from mortals' music, and it is possible that the angel's performance was instrumentally accompanied.

The shepherds sing again on their way to Bethlehem (**85+sd**). As has already been suggested on the evidence of line 63, it is unlikely that the First Shepherd would be able to join in part music, so that this song, too, is probably sung in unison. It is a song in honour of the Child (**83**), and presumably cheerful, since they 'make myrthe and melody' (**84**), but there are no further clues as to its nature. The stated connection of mirth and music here is one reason why the 'mirthe' of the play's last line may be taken to imply singing at the end of the play:

15/130–1 [III PASTOR] And go we hame agayne
And make mirthe as we gange.

This must be regarded as speculative, however.

16/357   I REX   For solas ser now may we synge

17/103–4 [SYMEON] Nowe certys then shulde my gamme begynne
And I myght se hyme, of hyme to tell

17/318 [PRESBITER] Thowe art our beylde, babb, our gamme and our glee
There is no reason to think that the singing metaphor of **16/357** has a musical meaning here. The use of 'gamme' in **17/103** may have been intended to invoke the word's musical meaning, the scale sung up and down as a vocal exercise with the syllables of the hexachords (Carter *Dictionary*, 160–1). In this case Simeon's meaning would be 'Then should I accomplish the actions for which I was ordained'. Beadle's gloss of 'game', with the meaning of joy, pleasure or sport, is surely correct, however (*York Plays*, 496): 'Then should my joy begin' is a simpler interpretation, and fits better in the context. For **17/318**, 'game and glee' as a phrase does not imply music (Carter *Dictionary*, 169–70).[18]

18/42–4 [JOSEPH] So swete a voyce herde I neuere ayre.
But what arte þou with steuen so shylle
þus in my slepe þat spekis me till?

Such references as this sometimes concern music: 'sweet' is certainly applied to singing more often than to speech (Carter *Dictionary*, 481–3), although it does not preclude speech, any more than 'spekis' precludes singing. 'Steven' is similarly ambiguous, although it does often apply to a musical voice; 'shylle', meaning resonant or sonorous, is in similar case (*ibid.*, 425–6, *sub* 'schil'). In all, one can make out a case either way here. However, there is some doubt about Joseph being treated to angelic singing (see I, 186–8): so although the argument for angelic singing is an attractive one, we should treat it with extreme caution.

19/96   NUNCIUS Nay lorde, þat daunce is done.

'That business is ended': see comment on **11/225**.

---

18 These references are discussed also in I, 48.

20/43   MARIA   Of sorowes sere schal be my sang

21/58   [I ANGELUS]   And thanke hym hartely, both lowde and still.

These metaphorical references do not imply musical performance.

21/69–70   [II ANGELUS]   The fadirs voyce with grete talent
Be herde full riȝt

This reference does not by itself imply music: the angel is saying only that God's voice will be heard at the Baptism of Christ. In fact, it is not heard, at least in the sense that God as a character speaks. Instead, there is an original stage direction for the singing of *Veni creator spiritus* by the two angels (**154+sd**). See I, 177, n. 10.

21/139   [JOHANNES (BAPTISTA)]   Thy subgett lord, both lowde and still

23/47   [JOHANNES]   We love God lowde and stille

Non-musical metaphorical usage in both cases.

23/205–6   JOHANNES   Nay, nay, þat noys noyed vs more
þat here was herde so hydously.

This example is probably not musical. 'Noise' is often a term for musical sound, and is so met elsewhere in the cycles: but Carter (*Dictionary*, 323) cites also under this heading the sound of men blowing horns, which is not a musical sound. In this play there is in fact no indication of any music, even though John and Peter describe the scene fairly thoroughly (**193–8**). This might suggest that 'noise' ought to be understood in its modern meaning. On the other hand, no other type of noise is mentioned either.

There are two possibilities, therefore. First, music would not be unsuitable at the Transfiguration (say, after **60**) or for the appearance of God the Father (at **168+sd**). There is no particular reason for it, however, and no evidence other than this one reference to 'noise'. It is not likely, either, that John would refer to music as sounding 'hideously'. Probably 'noise' carries its modern meaning. It might indicate thunder, perhaps drowning the noise of machinery for the descent of the clouds at **168+sd**, or the noise of the machinery itself.[19] Of these the most likely is perhaps thunder: although English drama shows

---

19 This has been suggested as a reason for loud music during scene-transformations in masques, but it is not a feature one thinks of in mystery plays.

very little of this, English dramatists certainly knew of it (see especially **The Conversion of St Paul 411+sd** and **Mary Magdalen 691+sd** in sections 10.2 and 11.2, below).[20]

24/75–6 [I APOSTOLUS] A, lorde, we loue þe inwardly
And all þi lore, both lowde and still

Non-musical metaphorical usage.

25/217, 252, 260, 262–5, 290, 300, 305, 309–10, 314–16, 319–20, and **488**
In the play of the Entry into Jerusalem, the citizens first describe the occasion as one of praise (line **217**) where 'myrthe and game' are appropriate (**252**); then as a procession (**260**) 'With braunches, floures and vnysoune' (**262**); and finally as an occasion for the singing of their children (**263–5**). For 'game', see I, 48. The OED (*sub* 'unison') regards 'vnysoune' as a scribal error for 'vrysoune' = orison (prayer). Certainly the 'unison' does not necessarily refer to the singing of the children, but there is so much musical reference in this play that it seems unnecessary to posit a scribal error to explain this one. Moreover, Carter (*Dictionary*, 336–7) defines 'oreisun' as 'A liturgical chant or recitation, forming a petition for mercy or forgiveness', which does not seem apposite here (while retaining a musical interpretation). 'Unison', according to the OED, might have meanings other than 'performing the same pitches simultaneously', such as chanting on a monotone and unanimous declamation of an utterance. On the whole, and especially considering the liturgical associations of the branches and flowers (see I, 266–8), music seems very likely here.
A late marginal direction for singing (**287+md**) is clearly correct, since the ensuing scene between the pauper and the blind man shows that the music is indeed melody of 'myrthe' that makes him 'gladde' because of its 'nobill chere' (**288–310** passim, especially **305, 290** and **300**); the pauper also describes the scene as 'þe fayrest processioun/ That euere was sene in þis Jury' (**311–12**). The blind man twice refers to the 'noyse' (**290, 316**), which is clearly the same as the 'melody' (**310**). In suggesting that the blind man call to Jesus the pauper uses musical language: 'Crye faste on hym, ... With voyce right high' (= loud?: **319–20**). The last reference (**488**) is the Janitor's confirmation of the praise to be given to Jesus.
There follow the eight speeches of welcome, with the late MD to singing at the end of the play. The 'Hosanna' is over, so this music, corresponding to the entry to the church in the Palm Sunday procession, must be another piece, not a recurrence of 'Osanna' (see I, section 7.5, and especially 269–70).

---

[20] See I, 206. For continental examples of dramatic thunder, see Meredith and Tailby *Staging*, index *sub* Special Effects: Thunder.

25/477 [JESUS] Thy game, þi gle, al fro þe refte

'Game' is clearly in the non-musical sense: see the comments on play **17**, above, and I, 48.

29/395 [CAYPHAS] Goose onne nowe, and daunce forth in þe deuyll way.

This is the end of the pageant. Carter (*Dictionary*, 113–16) does not give this metaphorical use for 'dance on/forth'. See the comments on **7/52**, above.

30/315, 343–51 These references are the beadle's description of the music sung in play **25**. He says that they sang 'Osanna' to Jesus 'with solempnite' (line **315**), and then that they sang 'Osanna [to] þe sone of Dauid' (**343**). These seem to refer to the same occasion – that is, only one piece is performed, not two. See also 1.4, below.

31/423 REX (HEROD) Daunce on, in þe deuyll way.

See the comments on **29/395**. This is the end of the pageant.

33/422 III MILES 3a, he may synge or he slepe of sorowe and angir

Common non-musical use of the metaphor.

37/101–04 The Second Devil's description of the 'vggely noyse' with which the prophets in Limbo 'musteres grete mirthe' (**101, 104**) apparently refers to the late MD for singing earlier in the play (**36+md**), separating Jesus's prologue from the prophets' discussion of their approaching salvation. 'Noyse' is deliberately ambiguous: it has its musical meaning for the audience, and as so often the music is a means of joy and mirth to God's people. That such music should appear 'ugly' to a devil is not surprising, and the First Devil no doubt uses the word 'noyse' in its more recent sense.[21] Whether the sixteenth-century audience understood the irony of this double meaning is a moot point, but it is likely. On the other hand there is nothing specifically about singing in this reference, and the First Devil's remark that the prophets 'crie on Criste' (**107**) could conceivably refer to their earlier speeches (at **57** and **74**, for example). There is therefore no proof of a musical item at **36+** earlier than the date of the MD there, and we should regard it as entirely possible that at the time of the Register's copying no music was sung at that point.

[21] On the devils' dislike of music, see I, 208.

37/381–4 These four lines of joy, thanksgiving and praise are followed by a late MD for singing. As in the previous instance, the lines might be interpreted as implying music, and indeed were so interpreted in the mid-sixteenth century: but it is quite conceivable that no music was intended at the time of the Register's copying, or even that the singing implied by these lines did not take place until the end of the play (see the next item).

37/407–8 [ADAME] For solas will we syng
  Laus tibi cum gloria etc.

In this case a text reference to music is the sole internal evidence. This is the end of the play: and although the reference could be taken to be metaphorical, it probably indicates performance in a 'praise' ending. 'Gloria' is the last word of Adam's speech, since it rhymes with the 'waa' of line **406**. Thus the 'etc.', indicating that there is more text to follow, is not part of the text but a form of ultra-brief SD requiring the rest of the prophets to join in appropriately. See 1.4, below, for this item, and compare the case of 'Amen' discussed in I, 372.

38/225–8 These lines tell us that a '3onge childe' sits at the tomb 'In white clothyng', thus confirming the singular subject of Clerke's late MD *Tunc Angelus cantat Resurgens* added to **186+sd**.[22] While this is circumstantial evidence concerning the angelic singing of (presumably) *Christus resurgens* at the moment of Resurrection, we must note that neither the (original) SD nor the text in fact implies singing here, so that the MD may be valid only for the mid-sixteenth century.

39/134–5 MARIA (MAGDALENE) Alle for joie me likes to synge,
  Myne herte is gladder þanne þe glee

This is a metaphorical expression of singing for joy in association with the word 'glee'. Beadle glosses 'gladder þanne þe glee' as 'overjoyed' (*York Plays*, 496).

43/131–6 These lines refer to **96+sd**. The Fifth Apostle tells us that angels were singing (**131–2**), and the First Apostle amplifies this with the information that there were two angels and that they sang the text *Veni creator spiritus/ Mentes tuorum visita* (**133–6**). The phrase 'tolde þer talis betwene þem two' (**134**) seems to indicate antiphonal performance, which would be appropriate (see 1.4, below).

---

[22] **38/186+sd** reads *Tunc Jhesu resurgente*. The construction apparently refers to the speech that follows.

44/134, 154–8, 175–8, 194 At the death of the Virgin, Jesus commands the angels to bring Mary to Heaven 'With mirthe and with melody' (**175–8**, especially **178**); at the end of the play (**194**) the Fourth Angel proposes 'A semely song' for the occasion. The SD follows on directly from this line ('Et cantant ...'), prescribing the antiphon *Ave regina celorum*: but a MD 'Cum uno diabolo' is placed in the position of a SH before the SD. Although this MD is in the hand of scribe B, and in red, its marginal position seems to show that it was a marginal note in the guild copy used as an exemplar for the copying of the Register. The MD has been interpreted to imply that a devil joined in the singing (Stevens 'Music in Mediaeval Drama', 85): but this relies on the MD acting as a SH in reference to the SD. There are no other examples of this: that is, SHs always refer to speech. It seems that when Scribe B found this MD in the examplar he did not know how to deal with it. Stevens's second interpretation (*ibid.*, n. 17) is surely correct: that the devil is there because, as Jesus has said (**154–8**) in answer to a plea from Mary (**134**), the Fiend must be present at her death, although she will be surrounded and protected by angels. Thus the 'Cum' of the MD simply signifies the presence of the devil on the scene at Mary's death. (This is not to say that the devil just stands there, of course. There is no doubt a mime of the cosmic battle for Mary's soul, with the angels preventing the devil from approaching her.)

45/123 In this, the only play in the cycle to have notated music in the text, Thomas's description of the scene is almost entirely visual. Only in this one line does he mention the music: his comment that 'þis mirthe and þis melody mengis my mode' is typical in its connecting of mirth with music and its statement of the happy effect of the latter. Thomas has just heard *Veni de Libano* and, before that, *Surge proxima mea*.[23]

46/80 The Sixth Angel's remark to Mary before her coronation, 'Of solas sere þan schall þou synge', is surely metaphorical. The SD *Cantando* that immediately follows must refer to angelic singing: it covers the angels' journey with Mary to Jesus. Although this SD is original (scribe B), it is in marginal position: this, and its curious grammatical character, suggest that it may refer to a SD omitted from the text in error. We may therefore assume that there was a sung item after line **80** at the time that the play was copied, but not that singing was intended there by the original dramatist. (Further on the date of the validity of this MD, we should note the possible hiring of musicians in 1449, 1454 and 1462: see 1.5, below, under this play.)

---

[23] It would be fair to say, however, that the cheering effect of such pieces is always due to the texts, not to any emotional effect of the music *per se*. See I, 198–9.

46/157–8 [JESUS] Myne aungellis bright, a songe ȝe sing
In þe honnoure of my modir dere

This clearly refers to a 'praise' ending with music.

47/65–6 [DEUS] Aungellis, blawes youre bemys belyue,
Ilke a creatoure for to call

This text reference is the sole internal evidence of music here. It seems un-ambiguous about the fact that trumpets are blown, although the placing of the trumpet blasts is problematic (see 1.6).

47/204–6 I APOSTOLUS I loue þe, lord God allmyghty;
Late and herely, lowde and still,
To do thy bidding bayne am I.

47/236 [DEUS] Of sorowe may ilke a synfull synge.

47/378 [DEUS] Of sorowes sere now schall þei syng.

These are all common metaphorical usages.

1.4 Latin and the liturgy

1 *The Fall of the Angels*
1/–1 DEUS Ego sum Alpha et O: vita, via, veritas, primus et nouissimus.

1/24+sd Te deum laudamus, te dominum confitemur.

The opening words of the hymn *Te Deum*: the SD specifies that it is sung. On the extent of the performance, see below.

1/40+sd Sanctus, sanctus, sanctus, dominus deus sabaoth.

Carpenter noted that this is the opening of the Sanctus of the Mass:[24] more importantly, it is a section of text near the beginning of *Te Deum*. It seems clear that after **24+sd** the angels sing from the beginning of *Te Deum* up to a suitable stopping-point before 'Sanctus, sanctus, sanctus' (probably 'terra veneratur'),

---

[24] Carpenter 'English Mystery Plays', 5.

and that at **40+sd** they sing from 'Sanctus, sanctus, sanctus' until, probably, 'gloria tua'. It is also quite possible that the angels continue to sing under God's speech: his 16 lines (**1/25–40**) take about the same time to speak as the opening verses of *Te Deum* ('Te deum laudamus ... incessabili voce proclamant') take to sing – c. 55–60 seconds. The end of God's speech (line **40**) would therefore roughly coincide with the moment at which the angels are about to sing 'Sanctus, sanctus, sanctus'.

2 The Creation

2/1–4   DEUS   In altissimis habito,
               In the heghest heuyn my hame haue I;
               Eterne mentis et ego,
               Withoutyn ende ay-lastandly.

The Latin lines are an integral part of the stanza, and there is no possibility of singing them.

3 The Creation of Adam and Eve

God blesses Adam and Eve at the end of the play (line **96**), but not in any set wording.

4 Adam and Eve in Eden

Again, God blesses Adam and Eve at the end of the play (line **99**), but without using any set wording.

5 The Fall of Man
6 The Expulsion

Nothing relevant.

7 Cain and Abel

7/86–87   ANGELUS   God hais sent the his curse downe,
                  From hevyn to hell, maladictio dei.

The Latin is part of a spoken line, and there is no possibility of singing it.

7/89   [CAYME] Quia non sum custos fratris mei.

A complete line, but rhyming with **87**, above: cf. Genesis 4/9. There is no possibility of singing it, which would in any case be inappropriate for Cain. Note that Cain is capable of speaking in Latin when it suits him.

8 *The Building of the Ark*
Nothing relevant.

9 *The Flood*
9/278 [NOE] Dum dixit Penitet me.

9/283 [NOE] Arcum ponam in nubibus.

These two phrases help to make up the rhymed stanza: cf. Genesis 6/7 and 9/13, respectively.

10 *Abraham and Isaac*
Nothing relevant.

11 *Moses and Pharaoh*
11/173 DEUS I saie þus: ego sum qui sum.

Translated in the following line: cf. Exodus 3/14.

11/406–7 I PUER Cantemus domino,
To God a sange synge wee.

The phrase 'Cantemus domino' does not have to be the *incipit* for a song, since it could simply be a Latin tag ('Let us sing to the Lord') to signal the intention to sing at the end of the play. But the phrase is in fact the start of the Song of Moses (Exodus 15/1–19), and the most likely intention of the line is, therefore, that this text shall be sung. There are four possibilities:

(a) Antiphon (AM, 61):
Cantemus Domino gloriose (in Easter season, 'Alleluia')
Syllabic chant, range f–b♭
Sung with (b), below.

(b) The *Canticum Moysi,* Exodus 15/1–19 (AM, 61–3):
Sung to a psalm-chant.

(c) Responsory (AS, 183–4; WA, 101):
Cantemus domino gloriose enim honorificatus est equ[u]m et ascensorem proiecit in mare. Adiutor et protector factus est michi dominus in salutem.
V. Currus pharaonis et exercitum eius proiecit in mare. Adiu[tor]
Neumatic chant, range e–d', c-clef.

(d) Introit (GR, 864):
   Cantemus Domino gloriose enim magnificatus est. Fortitudo mea et laus
   mea Dominus et factus est mihi in salutem (in Easter season 'Alleluia,
   alleluia')
   Ps. Cantate Domino canticum novum quia mirabilia fecit.
Neumatic chant, range f–e', c-clef.

(e) Tract (Sandon IV, 120):
   Cantemus domino gloriose enim honorificatus est: equum et ascensorem
   proiecit in mare: adiutor et protector factus est michi in salutem.
   V. Hic deus meus et honorificabo eum: deus patris mei, et exaltabo
   eum.
   V. Dominus conterens bella: dominus nomen est illi.
Neumatic chant, range f–e', c-clef.

Of these, (a) is certainly too short to make an effective item. The *Canticum
Moysi* (b) is entirely suitable, and can be performed well by a group of actors
not trained specifically in singing: moreover, such a group could, if the director
so wishes, sing the antiphon (a) before and after it.

Items (c)–(e) are more problematic: they are in neumatic style with occasional melismas, and are really too difficult for amateur singers such as might
have played the Israelites. Should trained singers be available for those roles,
of course, the more difficult pieces become possible here, and any of them
could be very effective. The precise choice would depend on the length of
piece required and whether the verses that do not come from Exodus 15 are
really suitable. On balance, I think that any of (c)–(e) could be used here if
trained singers are available, but (b) should be used – perhaps sung under (a)
as antiphon – if untrained actors are to perform the piece.

12 The Annunciation and the Visitation

This play apparently made a special feature of the Latin lines, for the scribe left
spaces for decorated initials for all Latin lines and the beginnings of a few
English speeches. The Latin lines seem to be 'footnote' authorities that explain
some of the English lines: there is no reason to sing any of them, but it is a moot
point whether they should be spoken or not. The use of 'etc.', even in a context in
which no more text could be spoken (see the commentary on **12/56+lat**, below),
suggests a verbal formula indicating a longer authoritative quotation rather than
a direction that more text should be performed in some way. On the other hand,
the Latin is written in the same script and ink as the English, which may suggest
that it should be heard.

I conclude, taking account also of the evidence presented below, that in this
speech:
   (i) the Latin was not sung by the Doctor, but spoken; and

(ii) the quotation can be extended as necessary when the Latin is extra-stanzaic.

12/16+lat [DOCTOUR]   Deus pater disposuit salutem fieri in medio terre, etc.

Based on Psalm 73/12. The 'etc.', suggesting that more of the quotation may be needed, is confirmed by the explanation that follows (lines **18–22**). The Latin is in fact extra-stanzaic, so the Doctor may be intended to quote as extensively as necessary. As noted above, there is no reason to sing it.

12/32+lat [DOCTOUR]   Quia in semine tuo benedicentur omnes gentes, etc.

Based on Genesis 22/18. Beadle (1982) gives the first word as 'Quoniam'. The Latin is extra-stanzaic, and the 'etc.' could mean that more Latin is required. However, in this case the paraphrase (lines **35–6**) deals only with the one Latin line given, so the 'etc.' should perhaps not be taken at face value.

12/41 [DOCTOUR]   Rorate, celi, desuper

Based on Isaiah 45/8. This quotation is paraphrased and explained in the lines that follow: but it is a part of the stanza, and cannot therefore be extended (nor sung).
   This line is the *incipit* of three liturgical items: an antiphon (AS, 415, j; AM, 213; AR, 238–9), an introit (text in MisE, 6; edition in Sandon II, 20) and a respond (AR, 147*). (See also WA, 16, 18, 23, *17 and *19.)

12/56+lat [DOCTOUR]   Propter hoc dabit dominus ipse vobis signum, etc.

Isaiah 7/14. Extra-stanzaic: but if it is spoken it cannot be extended, because the next words are those of **12/60+lat**.
12/60+lat [DOCTOUR]   Ecce virgo concipiett, et pariet filium, etc.

Isaiah 7/14. Extra-stanzaic, and apparently to be extended.

12/68+lat [DOCTOUR]   Zelus domini faciet hoc, etc.

Based on Isaiah 9/7. Extra-stanzaic, and apparently to be extended.

12/75   [DOCTOUR]   Egredietur virga de Jesse

Based on Isaiah 11/1. This quotation is part of the stanza: it is largely meaningless by itself, and it is notable that there is here no possibility of extending it. Clearly, the audience were expected to recognise it and to know its context. This may mean that in extending the extra-stanzaic quotations we do not need to be too precise about an exact correspondence with the paraphrase or explanation that follows.

12/88+lat [DOCTOUR] Ero quasi ros; et virgo Israell germinabit sicut lilium

Hosea 14/6. Extra-stanzaic. The whole of this stanza (**85–96**) expounds Hosea's prophecy.

12/112+lat, 116+lat. Three extra-stanzaic lines, disposed as two plus one, in the middle of a stanza, the Latin being explained in the lines following in each case:

> [DOCTOUR] Non auferetur septrum de Juda,
> donec ueniat qui mittendus est.
> Et ipse erit expectacio gencium.

Genesis 49/10.

12/124+lat [DOCTOUR] Ecce mitto aungelum meum ante faciem tuam,
qui preparabit viam tuam ante te.

Matthew 11/10, Mark 1/2, Luke 7/27. Extra-stanzaic.

12/128+lat [DOCTOUR] Ego quidem baptizo in aqua vos, autem
baptizabimini spiritu sancto.

Probably based on Mark 1/8, but see also Matthew 3/11, Luke 3/16 and John 1/26. Extra-stanzaic: this text is explained in the lines before and after.

12/144+md No Latin text is given, but the angel almost certainly sings *Ave Maria* here, since he paraphrases it in the four lines of speech that follow. There are many possible items, as a glance at the list in Bryden and Hughes (*Index* I, 55) will show. Rather than discussing all of them here, I propose to limit my selection in two ways: first, to those that appear in the Sarum use; second, to the text translated by the angel, which is only as far as 'in mulieribus'.

(a) Antiphon (AS, 5; also in WA, AR, AM and LU):
   Aue maria gracia plena dominus tecum. Benedicta tu in mulieribus.
   Alleluya.
Syllabic chant, range c–b♭, b♮-clef.

(b) Invitatory (AS, 415):
> Aue maria gracia plena dominus tecum: benedicta tu in mulieribus.
> Neumatic chant, range c–b♭, f-clef.

(c) Alleluia verse (GS, 184; also in GR and LU):
> Aue maria gracia plena dominus tecum: benedicta tu in mulieribus.
> Melismatic chant, range A–g, f-clef.

Of these, (a) is an obvious contender, apart from the 'Alleluia' that does not feature in the angel's speech: but it can be sung without the Alleluia, as it is given in the Solesmes books. The Alleluia verse (c) is perhaps too florid for this dramatic situation, in which (b) would work well.

12/152+sd 'Ne timeas Maria'. The Latin text is paraphrased in English in the lines that follow. The angel sings the Latin text, which is the Magnificat anti-phon for Advent 1, also used at the Annunciation (AS, 16, 419):
> Ne timeas Maria inuenisti graciam apud dominum: ecce concipies et paries filium. Alleluia.

Largely syllabic chant, range d–d', c-clef.

12/240+sd 'Magnificat'. Mary sings 'Magnificat' at the end of the play: the text is not explained in English. It is probably best to sing this to a psalm-chant: indeed, as it is at the end of the play it could be sung under the antiphon 'Ne timeas Maria', which the angel has already sung.

Bryden and Hughes list two antiphons, a tract, a responsory verse, an alle-luia verse, an offertory and a responsory beginning with this *incipit*, but none of them is in AS or GS.

13 *Joseph's Trouble about Mary*
Nothing relevant.

14 *The Nativity*
Nothing relevant.

15 *The Shepherds*
The leaf missing after line **55** presumably contained the angelic 'Gloria in excelsis' and attendant dialogue. There is nothing relevant in the existing text.

16 *Herod and The Magi*
There are no Latin lines or liturgical references of any sort in this play. The kings do however rehearse a number of prophecies, albeit in English: these are some of those already quoted in Latin in play **12** (see above).

17 The Purification

17/37–52 The Priest expounds the law concerning offerings to be made after childbirth. Simeon's first speech contains a number of references to prophecies (**105–31**), including English quotations, but no Latin.

17/47 suggests that there should be a service, as context for 'the preistes prayer': see I, 258–64, and below, under **17/366**.

17/245–69 Joseph discusses the law's requirements, previously expounded to the audience by the Priest. The rich are to offer a lamb and two doves; the poor may offer only the doves. Joseph remarks that as they are poor they can offer only the birds, but because the child is the Lamb of God they can offer him also. Mary offers the Child at **281–9**; Joseph offers the doves at **290–8**, together with the explanation of his poverty.

17/322 [PRESBITER] Welcomme redemptour omnium

The Priest uses a common name for Christ in accepting the Child. The Latin is an integral part of the stanza, and cannot be sung.

17/366 [SYMEON] Haill floscampy and flower vyrgynall

Flos campi is chosen presumably for the scansion.

The liturgical element in this play is slight. **17/47** suggests that there should be a service, as context for 'the preistes prayer'; Joseph mentions the 'tempyll on this hyll' and the waiting 'preest' in adjacent lines (**274–75**), which may mean that the priest is waiting at the doorway – that is, in the church porch; and he says that they should 'knele devowtly' when they make their offering (**278–80**). But there is no indication of a procession, and none that any liturgical texts are heard; and Simeon apparently does not sing the *Nunc dimittis*. It is true that he paraphrases *Nunc dimittis* at **415–24**, but the paraphrase begins and ends in mid-stanza, so that there is no real chance to set it off by Latin lines.

The play seems to follow the biblical events, then, but without adding much to what is there. Certainly any influence of liturgy or even of material such as that of *The Golden Legend* is missing. On the other hand, there are parts of the play in which the pacing is very curious if the text is performed without additions. We should expect that if the priest greets the Holy Family at the church door there would then be a procession to take them to the altar for the offerings to be made: this procession must take place before **17/281**, after which Mary and Joseph make their offerings and these are accepted by the priest. Anna is at or near the altar, where she and the Holy Family will be joined by Simeon. For this procession from the church door to the altar one would expect the liturgical processional piece, the *Nunc dimittis* sung under the antiphon *Lumen ad revelationem*.

Staging any part of the procession before Mass on the Feast of the Purification (for which see PS(P), 134v–140v; PS(H), 139–44) demands a group of professional singers. A second procession may be needed for the priest and singers to leave the church. This might happen before the final dialogue between Mary, Joseph and Simeon (**428–60**) or, perhaps more logically, during the scene between Joseph and the angel (**340–57**). This could include a repeat of *Nunc dimittis*, since Simeon has just paraphrased that text, although this would of course be unliturgical;[25] or the responsory *Responsum accepit Symeon* would be suitable.

18 *The Flight into Egypt*
18/231　　MARIA　Amen as he beste may.

The last line of the play. This is a 'blessing' ending: Mary's 'Amen' may be intended to solicit a spoken response from the audience, but a sung Amen seems unlikely.

19 *The Slaughter of the Innocents*
Nothing relevant.

20 *Christ and the Doctors*
Rather surprisingly, this play contains nothing relevant. The Doctors do discuss the Scriptures, and Christ expounds the Ten Commandments, but all without a single word of Latin. There is no liturgical content.

21 *The Baptism*
21/148–50　[JOHANNES]　Jesus, my lord of myghtis most,
　　　　　　　　　　　　I baptise þe here in þe name
　　　　　　　　　　　　Of þe fadir and of the sone and holy gost.

For the service of baptism at York see I, 283–4.

21/154+sd　　　　　　Veni creator spiritus

The Whitsuntide hymn (Sandon IV, 67; HS, 111–12) is sung by two angels.

22 *The Temptation*
22/91+sd　　　　　　Veni creator

The Whitsuntide hymn (HS, 111–12) is sung by angels.

---

[25] However, the second procession is unliturgical anyway, because in the actual liturgy the priests and singers remain in the church for Mass. It may be best to let the priest and singers process out during the dialogue between Joseph and the angel, perhaps without music.

22a *The Marriage at Cana*
Nothing relevant. Play not registered.

23 *The Transfiguration*
23/27–8 [JESUS] I saide 'Quem dicunt homines
Esse filium hominis?'

From Matthew 16/13, and explained in the two lines following the quotation.

23A *Jesus in the House of Simon the Leper*
Play not registered: John Clerke's note on f. 107r shows that the play included Mary Magdalene's washing of Christ's feet, but there is nothing to show any relationship to the Mandatum.

24 *The Woman Taken in Adultery, and The Raising of Lazarus*
Missing leaves evidently contained (i) the main part of the Jews confrontation of Jesus with the woman taken in adultery and (ii) Christ's arrival in Bethany and his decision to open Lazarus's tomb.

24/184 [JESUS] Lazar, veni foras

John 11/43: a translation follows in the next line. Integral part of the stanza.

25 *The Entry into Jerusalem*
This is a multi-section play, but some of the sections are held together by liturgical action. Christ and his disciples form a procession, with stations at which (1) the blind man is healed, (2) Christ speaks to Zachius, (3) Christ laments over Jerusalem, and (4) the citizens approach Christ. But the citizens themselves constitute a second procession (lines **260**, **311**), with children and singing (lines **211**, **310**), which meets Christ's procession at the city gate. This is so strongly reminiscent of the Palm Sunday procession, with the second procession of the Host meeting the main procession (the one with the choir singing), that we can tentatively identify the music sung at **287+sd** and **544+sd**. We should note, however, that the play is seen mainly from the point of view of what would be liturgically the secondary procession, and that it is this, not the primary procession, that has stations. The liturgical parallel, in other words, is probably not precise. See also play **30**, below.

There are no Latin lines in this play, although a number of prophecies are mentioned and quoted in English.

26 *The Conspiracy*
26/76 [CAYPHAS] Wherfore make ȝe þat appostita, …

A four-syllable word for 'apostate', perhaps chosen for the scansion.

26/89 [I MILES] And þei make domus domini þat deland þare dwellis

Again, the Latin for 'the house of the Lord' is probably chosen for purposes of scansion.

26/127 JUDAS Ingenti pro inuria – hym Jesus, þat Jewe

The Latin is an integral part of the verse.

26/129–33 Judas mentions the anointing of Christ's feet by Mary Magdalene, but gives no details.

27 The Last Supper
27/46–56 Christ washes his disciples' feet here, but no information is given to connect the action with the Mandatum.

27/67 [JESUS] To be buxsome in boure and hall

Like **30/52**, discussed below, this awakes reminiscences of the marriage service (see I, 286): in that Jesus is recommending his disciples to serve one another, this too may be a deliberate use or simply an unconscious reference.

27/89 A missing leaf must have contained the institution of the Eucharist: there is no way of telling whether this showed liturgical connections or not.

27/90–1 [JESUS] Quod facis fac cicius:
          þat þu schall do, do sone.

See John 13/27. These are the last two lines of a stanza otherwise lost: it is unclear precisely why this line had to appear in Latin as well as in translation, but it should not be sung.

27/98–9 JOHANNES Domine, quis est qui tradit te?
          Lord, who schall do þat doulfull dede?

The Latin is an integral part of the stanza: it is again unclear why the Latin is required. It should not be sung.

28 The Agony in the Garden and the Betrayal
After line **42** there is a leaf missing, which presumably contained the episode in

which Christ teaches the disciples the Lord's Prayer. There is no way of knowing if this would have included music, but there is no positive reason to think so.

29 *Christ Before Annas and Caiaphas*
29/373   [III MILES]   Quis te percussit, man? Rede, giffe þou may.

An integral part of the stanza: spoken, not sung.

30 *Christ before Pilate I: the Dream of Pilate's Wife*
30/52   [PILATUS]   In bedde is full buxhome and bayne.

Whether deliberately or not, this line echoes part of the marriage service of York diocese, where the wife promises 'to be buxom in bed and at board': see I, 286–7. But note **33/143**, below, where the implications of this vocabulary are certainly wider.

Lines **343–51** suggest a naturalistic way in which certain liturgical features could arise. 'Osanna [to] þe sone of Dauid' may be the Palm Sunday antiphon *Osanna filio David* (AS, 206), which is a syllabic/neumatic chant, range f–e', written with a c-clef. It is quite possible for untrained actors to perform this antiphon. Interestingly, the Beadle states that this piece was sung (as he has already done in line **315**), and also that 'poure folke ... made myrthe and melody þis man for to mete.' The musical element in this play is unavoidable, therefore.

For the meaning of 'Osanna' see Carter *Dictionary*, 343–4.

A second pointer towards liturgical ceremony is the 'floures of þe frith' that the poor people fetched when they met Jesus (line **345**): this suggests that the flowers would be thrown onto the procession, as happened in the Palm Sunday procession in the late Middle Ages (see I, 269).

31 *Christ before Herod*
31/243, 245   [REX]   Seruicia primet

           ...

           Respicias timet.

These lines are integral to the stanza.

31/261–4   [REX]   Si loqueris tibi laus,
                Pariter quoque prospera dantur;
                Si loqueris tibi fraus,
                Fell fex et bella parantur.

These lines are integral to the stanza.

31/370 [REX] Mi blissing, bewscheris, ȝe bere.

No words of blessing are given, and this is evidently satirical.

32 *The Remorse of Judas*
Nothing relevant.

33 *Christ before Pilate 2: The Judgement*
33/143 [PRECO] If ȝe bid me I am buxhome and bayne.

Note the wording reminiscent of 30/52. Evidently this sort of vocabulary has wider implications for the playwright than just the marriage service as noted above.

33/408 [I MILES] Aue, riall roy and rex judeorum

See Matthew 27/29, Mark 15/18 and John 19/3: 'Hail, King of the Jews' begins an otherwise English stanza of lines beginning 'Hail'.

33/429 II MILES We ar combered his corpus for to cary

There seems no reason for the Latin word to be used, rather than 'body' or (for the sake of alliteration) 'corse': but in any case it is not sung.

33/434 [PILATUS] Sirs, beholde vpon hight and ecce homoo

'Ecce homo' – 'behold the man' – is a comment of Pilate reported in John 19/5, here following its English version in a single line. It should not be sung.

34 *The Road to Calvary*
Nothing relevant. It is difficult to see in this play even the influence of the Stations of the Cross, which might be expected. In fact, the play apparently follows the gospel account without much fleshing-out.

35 *The Crucifixion*
35/273 II MILES Vath, qui destruis templum!

The wording of Matthew 27/40 and Mark 15/29: the line is an intregral part of the stanza.

36 *The Death of Christ*
36/114 PILATUS Quod scripci, scripci.

This line is an integral part of the stanza: the wording follows John 19/22.

36/213, 215 [JESUS] Heloy, heloy!

> ...
>
> Lama zabatanye.

One of the Words from the Cross, following Matthew 27/46 and Mark 15/34. These lines are integral to the stanza.

36/260 [JESUS] Comende I, in manus tuas.

The last of Christ's Words from the Cross: see Luke 23/46. Liturgically these words belong to verses said at the end of the office of Extreme Unction (MS 112). The line is integral with the stanza.

37 *The Harrowing of Hell*

37/121–24 JESUS Attolite portas, principes,

> Oppen vppe, 3e princes of paynes sere,
> Et eleuamini eternales,
> Youre yendles 3atis þat 3e haue here.

Jesus here uses a liturgical formula, taken from Psalm 23 and used in the entry of a bishop to consecrate a church (see I, 278–83). The two Latin lines are integral to the stanza, each followed by its English paraphrase. There is no question of singing these lines, apparently.

The liturgical association of this text is however clear. Lines **121–32** form a dialogue which, although in a different wording from that of the Authorised Version, is clearly recognisable as that of the Psalm. Apart from the distribution of the text between three persons rather than two, however (as the liturgy has it, following the psalm), the text omits 'and the King of Glory shall come in' so as not to pre-empt Satan's derogatory question 'What page is þere ...' (line **125**).

37/181–84 JESUS Principes, portas tollite,

> Vndo youre 3atis, 3e princis of pryde
> Et introibit rex glorie,
> þe kyng of blisse comes in þis tyde.

Line **183**, previously missing (see above), now gives Satan another piece of information. As before, the changed wording and the integration of the Latin in the stanza make singing out of the question, although the debt to the Psalm and to the liturgy is still clear.

37/282–3 and 287–8 Satan quotes the statements of Solomon and Job that those who enter Hell shall never be released. See BS 2/278 and section 15.4, below, under **Castle 3096–7**.

37/373–77 DAUID Als I haue saide, ȝitt saie I soo,
> Ne derelinquas, domine,
> Animam meam in inferno,
> Leffe noght my saule, lorde, aftir þe
> In depe helle where dampned schall goo;

David here quotes Psalm 15/10 (AV 16/10), 'non derelinques animam meam in inferno': the Latin is followed by an English translation (and further explanation, not shown here). The Latin lines are part of the stanza, and there is apparently no question of singing them.

37/408 [ADAME] Laus tibi cum gloria etc.

This line is an integral part of the stanza, 'gloria' providing the rhyme with 'waa' (line **406**). Hence Adam's spoken line surely ends with 'gloria'. The 'etc.' must in that case refer to the singing that Adam has prescribed, so that 'Laus tibi cum gloria' seems to be the *incipit* of the piece, the 'etc.' referring to the rest of the text to be sung.

However, I can find no piece beginning with these words. There are many that start with the word 'Gloria',[26] but I do not believe that we should read the line this way. The line seems to be a statement of praise, to be taken as an indication that the prophets (and perhaps the audience) will sing a liturgical item of praise to end the play. There is no indication of what the item might be.

38 The Resurrection
38/186+md Resurgens

Clerke's MD for the angel's singing (*Tunc Angelus cantat resurgens*) appears in the right margin against line **186**, and therefore comes before the original SD that follows that line. It is clearly intended as an *incipit*. No piece starts 'Resurgens', but it seems possible that Clerke intended 'Jesus resurgens' if he misunderstood the SD that follows (*Tunc Jhesu resurgente*). In fact, this is also incorrect: the only possible incipit is 'Christus resurgens'.

There are four possibilities:

---

26 See Bryden and Hughes *Index* I, 193–6. Some of these are more suitable than others.

(a) Antiphon (AS, 241):
   Christus resurgens ex mortuis iam non moritur: mors illi ultra non dominabitur: quod enim vivit, vivit deo. Alleluia, alleluia.
Neumatic chant, range c–b♭, f-clef.

(b) Responsory (text only, MPE, 171; AR, 166*):
   Christus resurgens ex mortuis jam non moritur, mors illi ultra non dominabitur. Quod enim [AR only: mortuus est peccato, mortuus est semel: quod autem] vivit, vivit Deo. Alleluya, alleluya.
   V. Dicant nunc Judaei, quo modo milites custodientes sepulchrum perdideruntregem; ad lapidis positionem. Quare non servabant Petram justitiae? Aut sepultum reddant, aut resurgentem adorent, nobiscum dicentes: Quod
   [AR only: Gloria Patri, et Filio, et Spiritui Sancto. Quod]
Neumatic chant, range A–b♭, f-clef.
Closely related musically to (a).

(c) Alleluia verse (Sandon V, 39):
   Christus resurgens ... dominabitur. [As above]
Melismatic chant, range g–g′, c-clef. The Solesmes editions include melismas missing from the Sarum chant.

(d) Communion (Sandon V, 18):
   Christus resurgens ex mortuis iam non moritur. alleluya. mors illi ultra non dominabitur. Alleluya, alleluya.
Syllabic/neumatic chant, range e–e′, c-clef.

Of these, (c) is difficult and would demand a professional singer of high quality; (a), (b) and (d) are clearly more easily performed, although (b) is probably too long a piece for performance in the play.

39 Christ's Appearance to Mary Magdalene
40 The Supper at Emmaus
Nothing relevant.

41 The Incredulity of Thomas
41/33   PETRUS On Goddis name, benedicite!

Integral to the stanza, and evidently used for the rhyme.

41/197   [DEUS] And my blissyng I giffe ȝou here

A 'blessing' ending to the play, but not using a liturgical form of wording.

42 The Ascension
42/176+sd   Ascendo ad patrem meum

Liturgical item sung by a single angel. There are two possibilities:[27]

(a) Antiphon (AS, 270; WA, 150; AR, 492–3; AM, 510; LU, 845):
  Ascendo ad patrem meum et patrem vestrum: deum meum et deum
  vestrum. Alleluia.
Syllabic chant, range g–g', c-clef.

(b) Short responsory (AR, 495; LU, 850):
  Ascendo ad Patrem meum et Patrem vestrum. Alleluia, alleluia.
  V. Deum meum et Deum vestrum. Gloria Patri.
Syllabic chant, range d–a, c-clef.

Either of these could be performed by the angel: the antiphon is marginally the
more interesting musically.

43 Pentecost
All Latin lines in this play are written in red.

43/12+lat [PETRUS] Nobis precepit dominus predicare populo, et testificare
              quia prope est iudex viuorum et mortuorum.

See Acts 10/42. These lines are apparently not liturgical: they are extra-
stanzaic, and the text is explained in English in lines 13–16. The lines could be
intended as 'footnote' references, therefore, not to be heard. On the other
hand, all other Latin lines written in the text of this play do need to be heard
(see below), so consistency would suggest that these should be heard, too.
They should be spoken, as there is no reason to sing them.

43/33–6 [JOHANNES] Vs menis he saide vs þus
              When þat he fared vs froo:
              Cum venerit paraclitus
              Docebit vos omnia.

See John 14/26. There are antiphons and an alleluia verse starting with the
first three words, but as they stand these lines are not liturgical: they must be
heard, however, since the speech is incomplete without them, so John must
speak them here. An English version has already been given.

---

[27] The text is also known as an Alleluia verse, but apparently not in the English uses.

43/39 [JACOBUS] Nisi ego abiero

See John 16/7. This text occurs as a responsory verse: but as this line is part of the stanza it must be spoken.

43/43 [JACOBUS] Et cum assumptus fuero

Apparently not liturgical: but it is part of the stanza, and must be spoken.

43/96+sd　　　　　Veni creator spiritus

The Whitsuntide hymn (Sandon IV, 67; HS, 111).
　　The discussion of this performance by the apostles makes it clear that two angels sing the hymn, and that they do so antiphonally (lines **131–6**). It was in fact quite normal for hymns to be sung antiphonally (Harrison *Music in Medieval Britain*, 65), although this was usually between two choirs, not two singers.

43/135–6 The First Apostle quotes the first two lines of the hymn, followed by a brief translation (lines **137–8**). This quotation is an integral part of the stanza, and therefore must be heard: but there is no reason to sing it.

43/147, 149 [III APOSTOLUS] Tristicia impleuit cor vestrum
　　　　　　　　　　　　　...
　　　　　　　　　　　Sed conuertetur in gaudium

Integral to the stanza, providing the a-rhyme in each case: these lines must be spoken, therefore, but could not be sung.

43/192, 192+lat [PETRUS] For þus his wordis wore:
　　　　　　　　　　　Et erit in nouissimis diebus, dicit dominus,
　　　　　　　　　　　effundam de spiritu meo super omnem carnem.

See Acts 2/17 (quoting Joel 2/28): this is not liturgical. These two lines are extra-stanzaic, but they must be spoken by Peter, because his speech is incomplete without them. There is no reason to sing them.

44 *The Death of the Virgin*
44/65 [PETRUS] Benedicite dominus, a clowde now full clere

Peter's exclamation at being brought miraculously to the Virgin's deathbed.

44/194+sd Aue regina celorum

One of the four great Marian antiphons (AS, 529; AR, 66; AM, 175, 179 (simple tone); LU, 274, 278 (simple tone)). Apparently the four angels sing this (see I, 330): it could be a polyphonic setting, therefore (perhaps in two parts: see I, 380), but could also be a plainsong setting. If chant is chosen, then the more complex setting would be appropriate.

Alternatively, if the angels sing polyphony it is likely to be a setting not of the Marian antiphon but of the *Ave regina celorum ... Mater* text, for which see I, 380, and Rastall 'Musical Repertory', especially 172–3. The most famous setting of this text is Walter Frye's, which survives in three voices but can be sung in two; an anonymous setting is in a painting of the Assumption now in Washington, for which see I, 380–3 and plate 8.

45 The Assumption of the Virgin
45/104+music   Surge proxima mea

45/117+music   Veni de Libano

45/208+music   Veni electa mea

45/312+music   B settings of all three texts.

Of these, only *Veni electa mea* is a liturgical text, and neither of these settings uses the chant. For the music of these settings see I, section 3.3, and Rastall *Six Songs*; for the texts, Rastall 'Musical Repertory' and the commentary to Rastall *Six Songs*. There are colour facsimiles in MDF 7 following p. [xlvi].

46 The Coronation of the Virgin
Nothing relevant.

46A The Coronation of the Virgin (fragment)
There are Latin words or phrases in lines **9**, **29**, **40** and **46** of this play. In no instance is the Latin a complete line, and all are integrated entirely into the stanza concerned. While all must be heard, and therefore spoken, none could be sung.

47 The Last Judgement
Nothing relevant.

1.5 Records

It is convenient to divide the discussion of the York records between non-financial and financial documents.

Non-Financial records The York records include many non-financial documents that give information about the plays and their staging. On music, however, they have very little to say directly.

No descriptive banns survive for the York Cycle: but the proclamation found in Burton's *Ordo paginarum* of 1415 and in the second list of the guilds responsible for pageants does give information of the type found in banns (*REED.York*, 16–26, and facsimile in MDF 7, following p. lxi). These lists give brief descriptions of the pageants. In many cases it is possible to calculate the form and extent of revisions made to the plays between 1415 and the copying of the register in 1463–77 (see Robinson 'York Realist').

The *Ordo paginarum* descriptions are full enough to include a reference to music in some cases, but in others the silence on musical matters can hardly be significant. Since the *Ordo* was not written to tempt an audience to witness the plays we cannot assume that the lack of a reference to music is in any way a piece of positive evidence. For instance, the entries for plays **14** and **15** – which both include the annunciation to the shepherds, although that episode does not occur in the Register version of play **14** – do not mention singing, but this does not allow us to think that no singing occurred.

14 *The Nativity* ... angelus loquens pastoribus ...

15 *The Shepherds* ... Angelus nuncians pastoribus gaudium de puero nato

The singing would have been easy enough to mention in both cases: but of course it is the *words* that matter, and Burton is concentrating on those because he is anxious to present the material concisely. Even so, it is a surprise to find that the angelic concert given to Thomas in play **45** is passed over:

45 *The Assumption of the Virgin* Maria ascendens cum turba angelorum ...

The surviving York music had not been written by 1415, at which date, therefore, the play might not have included music.[28]

Only three entries mention music:

---

[28] The style of the music in this play dates from the 1420s or 1430s, but the settings were composed probably not before the 1430s or 1440s: see I, 131–4.

25 *The Entry into Jerusalem*
> ... viij pueri cum ramis palmarum cantantes Benedictus &c. ...

46 *The Coronation of the Virgin*
> Maria, Iesus coronans eam [...]rum cantan[.]

47 *The Last Judgement*   ... iiij^or angeli cum tubis ...

As the last of these shows, Burton was more concerned with a cast list than with the actions of the characters. This attitude is significantly different from that seen in the various sets of banns, and from our point of view it is an unfortunate one.

The second list gives very brief descriptions indeed, and here Burton seems to be giving each play simply a title. The result is that no musical performance is mentioned at all. The Entry into Jerusalem is described as 'Ierusalem cum ciuibus & pueris', the Coronation of the Virgin as 'Coronacio eiusdem [i.e. beate Marie]', and the Last Judgement as 'Iudicium finale'. Thin as this evidence is, Burton's lists are not completely useless to us. For play **25**, we gather that a change happened in the item used between 1415 and the copying of the Register: although the two texts are both scriptural and closely related, the *Benedictus* [*qui venit in nomine domini*] of the *Ordo paginarum* does not presuppose the singing of *Osanna filio David* in addition. In play **46** we have information of a different type. There are not many possibilities for the text of this fragmentary entry, where there is certainly enough lost for some phrase such as 'cum melodia [or 'laudibus', etc.] angelorum cantantium'. Whatever our guesses in this respect, I submit that the meaning is clearly that the singing referred to is that at the time of the Coronation itself: thus the reference is not to **80+md**, but to the text reference at the end (**157–8**) after which the angels presumably sing, at Jesus's request, 'a songe .../ In þe honnoure of my modir dere'.

Further information of the banns type is found in the ordinances of the Minstrels' Fellowship, dating from 1578 (*REED.York*, 389). At this time the Minstrels had taken over the Herod play (play **16**) formerly mounted by the Masons. Disappointingly, no mention is made of any music.

Financial records Financial records are likewise generally unhelpful with respect to music in the plays. Those relevant to this enquiry are the accounts of the Bakers, the City Chamberlains, and the Mercers.

27 *The Last Supper*
The Bakers' accounts begin in 1548. Because of the way *REED.York* is set out it is not always easy to be certain of the precise date and occasion of items, but the payments for minstrels in 1548, 1549 and 1550 appear to be for Corpus Christi Day, while that for 1551 certainly is (*REED.York*, 293, 294, 295, 302). However,

no plays were played in 1550, because of the plague, so the 4d paid to the city waits that year probably related to music at the guild's dinner. The accounts of 1552 (when again the plays were not performed), 1557 and later years show that the Bakers used minstrels, including the waits, for entertainment at dinner (*REED.York*, 306, 325, etc.); and those of 1574 (*ibid.*, 377) show that a pageant-master's 'reckoning' was one of the occasions for such a dinner. In view of the absence of any reference to music in the fairly detailed pageant-accounts of 1553, 1555, 1556 and 1557 (*ibid.*, 309–10, 321–2, 323 and 325), it seems reasonable to conclude that the Bakers did not employ professional musicians in their play.

46 *The Coronation of the Virgin*
This play was the responsibility of the Mayor and Council at the time of the earliest reference,[29] which is in the City Chamberlains' roll of 1433 (*REED.York*, 54). Among expenses for Corpus Christi day is a payment of 20/-d to players in the pageant, immediately followed by

> Et ministrallis eodem die ex consuetudine xx s.

This payment to minstrels 'on the same day' (rather than 'in the same pageant') and 'according to custom' is apparently not for performance during the play. It is probable that the payment is for performance during dinner, although there are other possibilities.

The remaining relevant items in the City Chamberlains' rolls can be considered together (*REED.York*, 75, 86 and 94):

1449	Et Roberto Clerk pro ludo Coronacionis beate marie virginis ex parte Maioris	viij s.

1454	Et Willelmo Dernwater pro lusione ludi Coronacionis beate Marie eodem die [Corpus Christi Day]	x s.

1462	Et sol. Roberto leche pro lusione pagine Coronacionis beate Marie Virginis hoc Anno	ij s.

There is unfortunately little evidence to show the precise role played by these men paid so well for 'playing the play of the Coronation'. However, Dernwater and Leche are both identified as clerks in the Freemen's Roll (Dorrell 'Mayor of York', 38), and 'Robert Leche' could be the same man as 'Robert Clerk'. Beadle has suggested (*York Plays*, 38) that the 'clerks' to whom such payments were

---

[29] For the history of this play see Dorrell 'Mayor of York'.

made were non-guildsmen brought in as experienced dramatic directors.[30] But there is a considerable variation in payment to men who apparently did the same job. These men may have played the part of Jesus, the only extensive role in the play: but even so, the payments of 8/-d and 10/-d seem excessive for what is really a quite short and undemanding part, for which 2/-d would be reasonable enough.

An alternative possibility is that these payments are to the man directing the music. As we shall see (1.6, below, and I, 239–41), there is angelic music at two points in the play, apparently for six angels. If the six singers were all grown men, then 8/-d or 10/-d is not unreasonable as the total sum to be shared out. If the singers were all boys (and especially if not all of the six angels were singers), then 2/-d is a possible payment, although perhaps on the low side. It seems to me that when 'clerks' are paid for involvement in a civic guild-mounted performance the music is the most likely reason for their presence.

Some time between 1463 and 1468 the play of the Coronation of the Virgin became the responsibility of the Hostelers (Dorrell 'Mayor of York', 38; *REED. York*, 101): as their accounts have not survived, we have no more information on the financing of this play. However, we know that the three Marian plays (**York 44–6**) were suppressed in 1548, although they may have been briefly restored at a later date. The sixteenth-century fragment of a new Coronation play (**46A**) has no SDs or references to music.

47 *The Last Judgement*

There is a useful run of accounts of the Mercers' Company concerning their mounting of the final play in the cycle. The following extracts can be found in *REED.York* on the pages shown:

p. 55	1433, 11 June:	[Inventory of goods includes]	
		ij trumpes of White plate and ij redes ...	
p. 78	1449–50:	Item payde for þe Aungels of oure pageand	xx s
p. 82	1451–2:	Item payed of þe comon siluere to Wrangle for plaiyng of our pageants by assent of þe feliship	vj s viij d
p. 91	1461:	Item for makyng of þe bemys	iij d
		...	
		Item for iiij mynstralles	ij s
		...	
(p. 92)		Item for a sopper to ye playeres & ye mynstrelles att euyn	ij s vi d

---

[30] For a discussion of clerks' plays, see Lancashire *Dramatic Texts*, xiv–xviii. It seems that some English and Cornish plays, as well as Latin ones, were played by groups of clerks.

		Item for makyng of ij reees [sic] to ye bemys	iiij d
		...	
		Item payd to ye klarke for playeng	xviij s
p. 95	1462:	In primis paide to þe players for playinge	xviij s ij d
		...	
		Item paide for mendyng of þe tromppez i d	
p. 96	1463:	Item payd for playng	xviij s ij d
p. 97	1464:	[xviij s j d (sic) to 'our players' among costs for the pageant.]	

p. 99	1467:	[partly illegible or damaged accounts include]
		In primis payd to Wyll'm Clark & his players for rehersyng
		x d
		Item to Iohn lytster for goyng with vs ij d
		...
p. 100		Item payd to Wyll'm Clark for a par gloues & half a yerd lynen
		...
		Wyll'm Clark & John lytster & malum vj d
p. 242	1526:	[Properties delivered by the pageant masters include]
		ij trompys

These accounts are hardly extensive enough for firm conclusions to be drawn, but we can reasonably present some tentative ones. In 1433 the play included only two trumpeters: this does not necessarily mean that the text in use was that now surviving in the Register, but it shows that a change had been made since Burton's *Ordo paginarum* of 1415 (see above), which mentions four. 'White plate' presumably means silver plating, in which case these trumpets were of the type used elsewhere in the late Middle Ages for liturgical ceremonies (Rastall 'Minstrelsy, Church and Clergy', 92). The payment for mending these instruments in 1462 suggests only very slight damage, and it is quite possible that the trumpets in the inventory of 1526 are the same instruments.

The 1461 item for the making of 'bemys' could possibly refer to wooden replicas, that being the word used for the trumpets in the text (47/65). This would suggest that the Last Trump was mimed by actors who could not play the instruments, real trumpeters performing behind the scenes. This is of course a perfectly possible way of doing it (see I, 367–8), and has been used in modern performances of the play. On the other hand this item is surrounded by payments for building and carpentering work, and the reference could well be to wooden beams. This is evidently how Johnston and Rogerson understood it, since they gloss 'reees' as 'reeds or rews (burrs for rivets)(?)' (*REED.York*, 923): but their '(?)' is significant, for one does not use rivets in wood. A third possibility is that they are beams of light (cf. **N-Town 12/16** and more especially **11/292+sd,** which must refer to properties of some sort): in this case the 'reees' are *rays* of light scattering from the beams of light. The original orthography, 'reeſ', could be read as either an '-is' or an '-es' ending, and does not help to solve the problem. These remain puzzling items, but on balance I think that they do not refer to trumpets.

Assuming that the two angels do play these silver trumpets, they were clearly professionals who would have to be paid. In addition, there must be other, non-speaking, angels who sing at **216+sd** and **380+sd**. No doubt the 1449–50 payment of 20/-d to 'þe Aungels of oure pageand' covers one or both of these, and the same may be true of the 18/2d paid in 1462 and 1463 and the 18/1d paid in 1464 to 'players' for 'playing'. In fact, I am inclined to regard these payments as being for singing only, partly because the 1461 payment of 18/-d to 'ye klarke for playeng' is comparable. Such a large sum would certainly suggest something as expensive as a body of professional singers, of which a 'clerk' would normally be in charge. As before, Beadle's view that the clerk was the director of the performance (*York Plays*, 38) seems to me doubtful: it is more likely that he directed the music. The 1467 payment for gloves and linen suggests that William Clark was costumed as an angel; there is a payment to him that same year in company with two other players (John Lytster and 'Malum', the latter presumably a Bad Soul); and the 10d given to 'Wyllm Clark & his players for rehersyng' shows that Clark was responsible for an independent group of players that could hardly be anything other than a choir. It is unfortunate that the payments for the performance itself do not survive for this latter year.

The evidence for a band of singers, then, seems to me to be good in these accounts. How many they were, and whether boys or men, we have no means of knowing. These items do not exclude a different interpretation for other payments, of course: the 6/8d given to Wrangle in 1451–2 probably shows that the Mercers imported an outsider to play God that year, and in 1467 John Lytster was presumably borrowed from the Litsters' Company to play a small role, as was another man (known to the scribe only by his role) who played a Bad Soul.

There remains the problem of trumpeters. The four minstrels paid 2/-d in 1461 were certainly involved in the pageant somehow. One would like to think that my assumption about the new text using only two angel-trumpeters at this time was wrong, and that the 'bemys' made in 1461 were two wooden trumpets which, together with the two silver instruments belonging to the Company, formed the properties used by the actors while four professional trumpeters played behind the pageant. The objections to this are two: first, trumpeters were a breed apart, and they would normally be referred to as trumpeters, not as minstrels, in the accounts;[31] second, it is odd that such an important payment should appear only once in the accounts under discussion.

Clearly this is a problem that cannot be resolved by reference only to these

---

[31] There are, however, very rare exceptions to this.

rather inadequate accounts. There are so many unknowns that several possible solutions might be found. My interpretation has only one distinct advantage: namely, that it does at least supply *one* payment for trumpeters in a play that cannot have been performed without them, whereas none appear otherwise.

The arguments regarding trumpeters are not conclusive, then. But if these four minstrels are *not* trumpeters, who were they and what was their function? Almost the only possible solution would be a parallel with some Chester records, in which it seems possible that some minstrels attended the waggon without performing as part of the play.[32] This does at least explain the problematic single payment, just noted, if we assume that the four minstrels were hired on this one occasion only. There is however no evidence in the York records to support this, and it must remain a speculation.

1.6 Music and other aural cues

1 *The Fall of the Angels*

The opening play of the cycle is in regular 8-line stanzas. It has a symmetrical structure, dividing into four sections of 40 lines (five stanzas) each: this division is partly emphasised by the music.[33]

God's opening 40-line speech, which ends with 1_2, is interrupted by 1_1 after line 24 – i.e. after three of the five stanzas. These two parts of the speech concern the creation of the nine orders of angels and the commissioning of Lucifer, respectively. The unity of this first quarter of the play is enhanced by the use of two sections of a single musical item, *Te deum*. 1_2 apparently covers God's recession (probably an exit). The next five stanzas, to line 80, concern the differing views, expressed in God's absence, of the good and bad angels. There is no music at the end of this scene, partly because the next scene (to line 120), in which Lucifer's sin and the fall of the bad angels take place, follows on closely in content. More importantly, both scenes (lines 41–120) concern the lack of harmony in Heaven: and there is a slight negative reference to music in Lucifer's cries of 'Walaway' after the fall (see 1.3), which emphasise his loss.

At the end of this third division, too, there is no music. This is surprising in view of (1) the re-entry of God at this moment, (2) the restoration of order in Heaven by the expulsion of the bad angels, and (3) the continuing work of creation that occurs in the final section of 40 lines, where the last four of the five stanzas are taken up with God's speech about the fallen angels (one stanza), his approbation of the good angels (one stanza), and the continuation of the creation

---

32 See Lumiansky and Mills *Essays*, 132–8, *passim*.
33 For the numerical structuring of this play, see I, 245–6.

up to the division of night and day (two stanzas). At the comparable dramatic point in the Chester cycle, where this play is closely paralleled, there is music (**Chester 1₃**).

Finally, there is no music at the end of this York play, as there is not at the parallel point in Chester, where also God gives his blessing.

One more possible music cue must be discussed: the very first, extra-stanzaic, line of the play:

> DEUS   Ego sum Alpha et O: vita, via, veritas,
>   primus et novissimus.

The antiphon 'Ego sum alpha et oo' omits the words 'vita, via, veritas' (MPE, 181 (text only); GS, 125; PS(P), 94v), so that the line would have to be chanted on a monotone, or to a psalm-tone, if it were sung. There is something to be said for singing it, and thus stating God's characteristic of order even before he begins the act of creation. But music is probably not a good way of starting a pageant, let alone a cycle, when loud speech is really necessary: and I think that we should trust the evidence of modern performances here, which show that the declaimed Latin tends to attract the audience's attention at the start of the play. (**Chester 1** begins with the words of the antiphon, but as part of the stanza-pattern. While this is not admissible evidence for the York play, it is perhaps worth bearing in mind, since singing is there out of the question.)

1₁ 24+sd   Function: (i). The angels sing *Te deum laudamus, te dominum confitemur*: in view of **1₂**, below, they could sing the next verse also, as far as *omnis terra veneratur*. There is also the possibility, suggested in 1.4, above, of singing all the way through to just before 'Sanctus, sanctus, sanctus' under God's speech, because the timing is likely to be about right.

It would be a nice irony if Lucifer were to intone this item: but the irony may not be a medieval one, and probably only the good angels should sing it.

1₂ 40+sd   Function: (h), (i). The angels sing *Sanctus, sanctus, sanctus, dominus deus sabaoth*: they could sing the next verse too, as far as *glorie tue*, but compare **Towneley 1₁**, which ends at 'sabaoth'. This item can be started without solo intonation, even if it does not follow on immediately from **1₁**, and perhaps the bad angels do not sing.

The *Te deum* is a congregational piece. While the singing of it in this play should be of high quality, therefore, it is perhaps not absolutely necessary to use professional singers.

2 *The Creation*
3 *The Creation of Adam and Eve*
4 *Adam and Eve in Eden*
5 *The Fall of Man*
6 *The Expulsion*
No music cues.

7 *Cain and Abel*
No music cues. The surviving text is imperfect, but it is unlikely that any cue for music is lost.

8 *The Building of the Ark*
No music cues.

9 *The Flood*
9₁266+md Function: (h), (i). This is a sixteenth-century MD confirming a text reference at **9/260**: this reference was perhaps metaphorical to begin with, in which case the MD demands the musical realisation of a non-musical moment (see 1.3, above). This is not an obvious place for music, either – it is not associated with a thanksgiving sacrifice, for instance – so that it is perfectly possible that music here was initiated by the MD.[34] As it stands, Noah and his family sing in thanksgiving and praise of God for their delivery from the Flood. In view of Noah's ability to quote Latin (**9/278, 283**) this could be a Latin item, such as a psalm of thanksgiving.

10   *Abraham and Isaac*
No music cues. Heavenly music would seem to be effective after line **300**, when the angel intervenes in Abraham's sacrifice of Isaac, but see 1.2, above: probably there should be no music in this play.

11 *Moses and Pharaoh*
11₁ 408 Function: (g), (i). In thanksgiving for their escape from the Egyptians the Israelites probably sing *Cantemus domino*: it is also possible that the phrase simply implies a song of praise, not an item with that *incipit* (see 1.4). *Cantemus domino* is however the hymn of praise sung by the Israelites in Exodus 15/1–19.[35] As suggested in 1.4, above, the most likely piece for this cue is the *Canticum Moysi*, sung to a psalm chant, with or without the antiphon *Cantemus domino*; or perhaps just the antiphon by itself.

---

34 It is a scene-division, however: for the structure of this play see I, 241–3.
35 As Beadle points out: 'Hosiers' Play', 6.

12 The Annunciation and the Visitation

The play as originally described in the 1415 *Ordo paginarum* consisted of lines **145** to the end of the play as we have it. The addition of the doctor's prologue to that description seems to be in a fifteenth-century hand (MDF 7, A/Y Memorandum Book, 252v). This may simply mean, as Beadle points out, either that the first part of the description was accidentally omitted or, alternatively, that the doctor's speech was added to the play some time between 1415 and the copying of the Register, the description being added to at the time.[36]

Beadle clearly feels that there is insufficient evidence for drawing any conclusion as to the status of the doctor's speech in relation to the rest of the play. But the evidence he presents could certainly point to the doctor's speech being a later addition,[37] and the musical evidence seems to support that view. Of Clerke's three marginal directions, all musical, that at **12₁** divides the doctor's prologue from the Annunciation. Since this and **12₂** both give the Latin texts of the English speeches that follow them, and because the dramatic context is a suitable one for music, we might well expect that line **144** would be the cue-line for an original SD. Given that original SDs are rare in this cycle, we can nevertheless note that if play **12** had originally started at the present line **145** there would in any case have been no music there; and that, this being so, there would be no sung Latin + spoken English pattern set up and therefore no need for music after line **152**. As it is, Clerke's marginal directions are correct for the play as we have it. It may be, then, that the play originally began at the present line **145**; that there was therefore no angelic singing before that line; that no SD for singing was added when the doctor's speech was attached to the beginning of the play; and that in consequence the copying of the complete play as we have it into the Register did not include a SD there, either.

12₁ 144+md Function: (b), (e), (h). The angel sings: **12₂** shows this to be part of a pattern of sung Latin + spoken English, so the item should be *Ave Maria*, of which the subsequent speech is a translation. As noted in 1.4, the antiphon or the invitatory would work well in this play.

12₂ 152+md Function: (i). The angel sings *Ne timeas Maria*, continuing the Latin+ English pattern set up by **12₁**. There are two possible antiphons, for which see 1.4, above.

12₃ 240+sd+md Function: (g), (i). Mary sings *Magnificat*. Although the original SD *Magnificat* does not specify that it is sung, it is hardly likely that the canticle would be declaimed in Latin: an English version would be a possibility, if there were a well-known one in the 1460s. Singing makes the best sense here: the canticle is of course a congregational piece, so that there should be no difficulty in the actor concerned – originally a choirboy or a prepubertal ap-

---

[36] Beadle *York Plays*, 424. On the numerical structure of this play, see I, 244–5.
[37] Beadle *York Plays*, 423–4.

prentice, presumably, but now a young woman – singing it.

13 *Joseph's Trouble about Mary*
No music cues: music might be effective after line **245**, exactly four-fifths of the way through the play, when the angel wakes Joseph: but see 1.2, above.

14 *The Nativity*
No music cues. Joseph sees the light that symbolises and accompanies the nativity after line **77**, but there is no indication that the *Gloria in excelsis deo* is sung here, as in some later nativity plays.[38]

15 *The Shepherds*
15₁ The angelic *Gloria in excelsis deo* is missing in the lost section after line **55**. For a discussion of this music, see 1.3.

15₂ 64+sd Function: none. The shepherds attempt to imitate **15₁**.

15₃ 85+sd Function: (a). The shepherds sing a joyful song as they journey to Bethlehem. The Shrewsbury fragment parallels this play: the cue here, **84–5**, corresponds to **Shrewsbury 1/31–2**, the cue for *Transeamus usque Bethelem* (see I, 91 and 98–9); but this is not evidence for the York shepherds' performance, for which an English song of praise would be more suitable than a Latin piece.

15₄ 131 Function: (g). The shepherds 'make mirthe' on their way home at the end of the play: see 1.3. Although this is not certainly music, a song is extremely likely here: and it is apparently processional, not a tableau.

16 *Herod and The Magi*
No music cues: it is surprising that there are no cues at all, even late ones dating from the Minstrels' responsibility for part of this play.[39] Loud music would seem appropriate for Herod's ranting opening (before line **1**), and soft music after line **368**, when the angel warns the three kings not to return to Herod: but the first of these may well be a modern idea not appropriate in the fifteenth and sixteenth centuries, and there is not the slightest evidence for music in either place.

17 *The Purification*
Apparently no music cues. This is a rather corrupt text, registered by John Clerke in 1567 or soon after.[40] Possible musical allusions are discussed in 2.3 and the liturgical content in 2.4. There is no indication of any angelic music after lines **164** and **339**, when the angel speaks to Simeon; nor is there a suitable place for the singing of *Nunc dimittis*, the spoken English version beginning at line **415** in mid-stanza.

---

38 As noted in I, 236–7, this is exactly half-way through the play.

39 The history of this play is however rather confused: see Beadle *York Plays*, 429–34.

40 Beadle *York Plays*, 434.

The play could be produced with no liturgical content other than what is in the text anyway, and with no music. In my view it would be perfectly acceptable thus, but a second-best. The cues that follow are, therefore, speculative but to be commended when resources allow.

17$_A$ 280 Function: (a). Procession for the Holy Family to be escorted to the altar for the offerings. This is not really the place for *Nunc dimittis* to be sung, since that is strongly associated with Simeon, who is in another location. Of the various pieces set for the procession on the feast of the Purification the antiphon *Ave gratia plena* is the simplest musically, although the responsory *Gaude Maria virgo* would also be suitable.[41]

17$_B$ 339 or 427 Function: (c), (h). A musical item for the recession of the priest and singers would be suitable and convenient. The earliest place at which they could withdraw is probably after line **339**, before Simeon comes to the temple. This is too early to sing *Nunc dimittis*, however, while if the retiring procession does not sing it the canticle will apparently not be sung at all. The alternative is for the priest and singers to withdraw after line **427**, when Simeon has added his welcome to those of the priest and the prophetess Anna, including his English version of *Nunc dimittis*. At this stage the retiring procession could sing *Nunc dimittis*, probably under the antiphon *Lumen ad revelationem*, as in the liturgical procession, leaving the playing area clear for Mary, Joseph and Simeon to hold their final dialogue. It would also be possible to leave the retiring procession until the end of the play, but this seems to me too late.

18 The Flight into Egypt

18$_A$ 36 Function: (b), (e), (h). Joseph's description of the angel's voice suggests that the angel may sing here. However, it is not probable: while singing is not precluded by the word 'spekis' in line **44**, the cue is certainly not demonstrable.

19 The Slaughter of the Innocents
20 Christ and the Doctors

No music cues.

21 The Baptism

The registered version of this play was superseded in John Clerke's time (Beadle *York Plays*, 439). There seems to be no music at the appearance of the angel to John after line **49**, but **21$_1$** occurs immediately after the moment of baptism.

21$_1$ 154+sd Function: (i). Two angels sing *Veni creator spiritus*. This item is not an obvious one, although it is entirely suitable to the occasion: but the SD is origi-

---

[41] The texts of these are given in MPE, 195; the music of the antiphon is also in PS(P), 138v; *Gaude Maria virgo* is in AS, 404.

nal, and in red, so the choice is probably authentic. For the hymn, see HS 111.

22 The Temptation

22₁ 91+md or 180 Function: (a), (h). The angels sing *Veni creator* (for which see **21₁**, above). This marginal direction is by Clerke. Lumiansky and Mills found the use of *Veni creator* here unconvincing (*Chester* II, 311), but did not develop an argument against it. Certainly the piece itself and its position in the play give cause for doubt.

The direction occurs during a speech by the devil, when he turns from his un-successful first temptation towards the second. It is therefore a possible posi-tion for music as regards the content of the text. A reason for this could be that Christ must ascend the pinnacle of the Temple while the devil does not do so, but there are arguments against it. First, as the devil is speaking on either side of the cue music is not needed to cover Christ's ascent unless he takes a consi-derable time (longer than 4 stanzas, or 24 lines) to do it – which is perhaps unlikely in the confined space used by a pageant play at York. Second, if music is required here, why is there apparently none when Christ climbs to the mountain-top between lines **124** and **155**?

Veni creator does have a certain suitability after the first temptation, for it explains the source of Christ's strength to resist: yet in that case it is equally suitable after the second and third temptations, although it is not required by the text. The break is after the first line of a stanza, too, and so seems structurally unsuitable. It is true that the direction is not carefully positioned, so that Clerke may have intended it between the stanzas, after line **90**: but, on the other hand, the sense of the speech carries over into this first line.[42]

On the whole it seems possible that the piece should be performed after **91**, but the rationale for it is thin and, more importantly, there seems no reason to omit music at other places if it is to occur here.

But if this cue is incorrect, where *should* the music be performed? A more obvious dramatically suitable place would be after the third temptation, at the point where 'angels came and ministered unto him' (Matthew 4/11). This is before line **181**, which is the start of a new stanza, a new speech by the First Angel, and the final scene of the play. It is also exactly six-sevenths of the way through the play, although the scenes fall into an inexact and partly asym-metrical pattern of 9+6+6+9+5 stanzas. If **180** is the correct cue-line for the music, therefore, the singing divides the symmetrical part of the play (the devil's opening speech, plus three temptations) from the five-stanza conclu-ding scene between Jesus and the two angels.

It remains to suggest why the MD should have been wrongly positioned by

---

42 In this case the music would come exactly three-sevenths of the way through the play, which could be regarded as supporting evidence. Since placing the cue there contradicts the sense of the speech, however, this position seems impossible.

Clerke. A simple confusion between adjacent recto pages is possible: the MD occurs against the fifth line of f. 96r, which is also the fifth line of a speech by Diabolus that starts at the top of the page; the place I propose as possible, after line **180**, is four lines from the top of f. 97r, these lines also being a speech by Diabolus beginning at the top of the page. A mistake could have occurred if the leaf were turned back in error, although we must note that Clerke then failed to realise his mistake even when he had to repeat the SH 'Diabolus' below the direction (see f. 96r in MDF 7).

In either case, is *Veni creator* likely to be the correct liturgical item? I am a little doubtful about its use so soon after it has been heard in play **21**, especially since it occurs again in the Pentecost play (**43**$_1$, below), where one would expect it. On the other hand the Whitsuntide hymn, as suggested earlier, would clearly indicate the source of Christ's strength in resisting temptation. Moreover, its re-use here could be a deliberate (sixteenth-century?) reference to Christ's 'commissioning' in the previous play. And although one might suggest a number of other suitable liturgical pieces for this occasion, the religious problems of Clerke's time may well have restricted the plainchant repertory available for use in the plays.

That said, one suspects that if music was indeed heard at this point in fifteenth-century performances of the play a different piece would have been chosen. Yet there is no evidence that any other liturgical piece was ever performed. We can only say that Clerke heard *Veni creator* performed on some occasion, or thought that he did: and here a possible mis-identification should be noted. It would be possible to confuse *Veni creator* with something else sung to the same tune, since Clerke certainly might associate the tune primarily with the Pentecost hymn. In the Sarum use, *Salvator mundi domine* was also sung to that tune, and this is a text with much wider associations.[43] Moreover, while *Veni creator spiritus* is specifically in praise of the Holy Spirit, and for that reason is only indirectly relevant to the Temptation, *Salvator mundi* is in praise of the Saviour. One might well think a hymn praising the Saviour's abilities to be appropriate for performance after he has successfully driven off the Devil's attempts to subvert his mission of redemption.

As to its positioning in the play, that too is problematic. There seems no good reason for the angels to sing after line **91** rather than elsewhere, and for various reasons line **180** seems a better cue. In performance I should be strongly tempted to move *Veni creator* to the scene-division position after **180**. My suggestion that Clerke marked the cue on the wrong page seems a little far-fetched, however, and I am unwilling to regard the present positioning as

---

[43] See HS, 10–11 and AS, 46. Bryden and Hughes (*Index* II, 136) list another three hymns (*Hic est dies verus Dei, Mysterium mirabile* and *Nunc sancte nobis spiritus*) with the same *incipit*: but none of these seems to have been sung to the *Veni creator spiritus* tune in the Sarum use, and their texts are no more suitable for the occasion than *Veni creator* itself.

an error in case we have something to learn from it about the staging of the play. Here, perhaps, there is a good case for some experimentally-minded director to try the play both ways.

22A *The Marriage at Cana*
Play not registered.

23 *The Transfiguration*
There should apparently be no music or other sound cue in this play, but see the discussion in 1.3 concerning possible cues after **60** and **168+sd**.

23A *Jesus in the House of Simon the Leper*
Play not registered.

24 *The Woman Taken in Adultery and The Raising of Lazarus*
No music cues.

25 *The Entry into Jerusalem*
This play is rich in references to the performance of 25_1, which covers the procession of Christ and the disciples to the gate of Jerusalem, Christ riding on the ass. This cue also marks the first major structural division of the play: although the stanza-pattern is regular throughout, the first three scenes (up to line **287**) have mid-stanza divisions, emphasising the joining of these scenes by characters common to each pair. The three scenes following **287+sd** are more clearly separated, however, and all begin with a new stanza. Thus the music conveniently separates the two diverse parts of the play, the numerical half-way point coming at line **272**, only two stanzas before the music.

25_1 **287+md** Function: (a), (h). The citizens' children sing a cheerful song of praise in the procession (see 1.3). Eight children 'with palm branches' are specified in the 1415 *Ordo*. This may not refer to the play as we have it, but it does match with the number of citizens. The MD is obviously intended to be read 'Tunc cantant' (or 'cantent').

This same description identifies the song as *Benedictus, etc.*, no doubt the text 'Benedictus qui venit in nomine domini': but the beadle's description in play **30** (see 1.3) identifies it as 'Osanna [?to] þe sone of Dauid', or, presumably, one of the pieces beginning *Hosanna filio David*. The possibilities are discussed in 1.4, above. The 1415 reference is certainly to the equivalent of 25_1 in an earlier version of the play, but so is the beadle's remark at **30/343**, where he has already said (**30/339**) that Christ was riding on an ass. This looks like the Palm Sunday antiphon *Hosanna filio David*, therefore.

25_2 **544+md** Function: (g). The sixteenth-century MD 'Tunc cantant' (or perhaps 'cantent') presumably refers again to the (eight) children. In this second procession, when Christ is entering the city on foot, the text suggests music only by the implications of its general context – indeed, it is likely that the play would end in bathos without a musical performance here. The responsory *Ingrediente domino* (PE 151), which was sung in the York secular use at the Palm Sunday procession's entry into the church, would be very suitable at this point.

26 *The Conspiracy*
27 *The Last Supper*
No music cues.

28 *The Agony in the Garden and the Betrayal*
Apparently no music cues, even at the angel's appearance at line **113**.

29 *Christ before Annas and Caiaphas*
30 *Christ before Pilate 1: the Dream of Pilate's Wife*
31 *Christ before Herod*
32 *The Remorse of Judas*
33 *Christ before Pilate 2: the Judgement*
34 *The Road to Calvary*
35 *The Crucifixion*
36 *The Death of Christ*
No music cues.

37 *The Harrowing of Hell*
37_1 **36+md** Function: (c), (e), (h). The prophets sing in Limbo. Although this is a sixteenth-century marginal direction, its authenticity is attested by the text reference at **101–4** (see 1.3, but also below for the next cue): the MD should be read 'Tunc cantent' (or 'cantant', but see cue 37_2). The text reference also characterises the song as joyful – in fact, a song of hope. It is at this place in **Towneley 25** that the Prophets sing the first verse of *Salvator mundi* (see 3.6).
37_A **96** Functions: (b), (e), (h). Music here makes good sense of the text references at **97–109**, which are then more immediately effective. However, it is not strictly necessary, because those references could be to the music of 37_1. See also the parallel place in **Towneley 25**, section 3.6: if the first verse of *Salvator mundi* is sung at 37_1, the rest could be sung here.
37_2 **384+md** Function: (i). The Prophets give thanks and praise to God before being led out of Limbo. This marginal direction for singing is late, possibly by Clerke. Although music is not mentioned in the text, it is likely that a musical item was always sung here, since the text references to thanksgiving suggest it. It is at a close parallel to this cue in **Towneley 25** that *Te deum* is sung, and perhaps the word 'laude' may suggest that it be sung here, too: or perhaps, following David's lead at **373–80**, the prophets could sing a piece based on Psalm 15. Part of the psalm itself would be suitable, perhaps under the anti-

phon *Ne derelinquas* (LU, 302) or the introit *Ne derelinquas* (Sandon III, 81).

37_3 **408** Function: (g) The text reference of the last two lines of the play seems to name the piece to be sung as *Laus tibi cum gloria*, but this may imply some unspecified song of praise. Further on this matter, see 1.4, above.

38 The Resurrection

38_1 **186+md+sd** Function: (a), (b), (h). The original SD reads *Tunc Jhesu resurgente* and therefore does not refer to any liturgical item: it is an ablative absolute perhaps best translated 'Then, Jesus being risen ...', and merely shows that the Resurrection should take place in mime before the next speech. Music would be highly suitable at the moment of Resurrection, of course, but there is no evidence of musical performance here prior to the sixteenth century, when Clerke added his MD for the angel to sing *Resurgens*. Line **225** states that the angel is 'a 30nge child', who presumably sings with an unbroken voice. The MD, 'Tunc Angelus cantat Resurgens', does not accurately name a liturgical item: but Clerke seems to be correcting the SD, and presumably had *Christus resurgens* in mind. The singularity of the angel is derived from the text later in the play (**225–8** and **239–52**).

39 Christ's Appearance to Mary Magdalene
40 The Supper at Emmaus
41 The Incredulity of Thomas
No music cues.

42 The Ascension

42_1 **176+md** Function: (a) or (c), (h). The sixteenth-century MD 'Tunc cant' angelus Gloria in excelsys deo' is perhaps by Miles Newton. I am not entirely convinced that the MD reads 'angelus' rather than 'angeli', and the verb is suspended, so that it might be either singular or plural. There are two angels present – they speak at **217–32** – and one might expect them both to sing.

The Christmas piece may seem a strange choice here, but it is sung at this point also in the Cornish *Ordinalia* (3_4: see 7.6), and so cannot be dismissed out of hand as a mere mistake. John Clerke apparently thought that it was incorrect, however, for he cancelled 'Gloria ... deo' and substituted 'Ascendo ad patrem meum': but this too is surprising, since we should expect that 'I ascend to my father ...' would be sung by Jesus himself. Did Clerke simply fail to amend 'Tunc cantat angelus', or did he not mind that 'Ascendo ad patrem meum' would be sung by the angel? See I, 25, for a discussion of this problem.

It is quite possible that this MD demonstrates a general unfamiliarity with the repertory of the Latin liturgy in the mid-sixteenth century. But we need not assume this, for it may, on the contrary, show a normal working knowledge of the Latin liturgy: for in the Sarum Use the second lection on the Tuesday after Easter, which concerns the post-Resurrection appearances, also quotes *Gloria in excelsis deo* (see BS 831): this does not occur in the York Use, however, where I cannot find that *Gloria in excelsis* is quoted anywhere in the Easter-to-Ascension period. It seems possible that an earlier, pre-Reformation usage (*Gloria in excelsis deo*, relying on knowledge of the Sarum lectionary) was later altered to a more obviously relevant usage (*Ascendo ad patrem meum*) which had no connection with another season of the Church's year.

42₄ 216 Function: none. The two angels speak after this, with a translation of the *Viri Galilei* text. It seems likely, although there is no evidence, that the two angels sing a setting starting 'Viri Galilei', of which there are several that could be suitable.[44]

43 Pentecost

43₁ 95+sd Function: (i). *Veni creator spiritus* sung by two angels, antiphonally (Sandon IV, 67; HS, 111).

44 The Death of the Virgin

44₁ 194+sd Function: (g). There are four speaking angels, and they presumably sing here: the piece is *Ave regina celorum*. On the basis of contemporary Bruges paintings this could be the *Ave regina ... Mater* text, and could conceivably be in two-part polyphony.[45] Note that the MD 'Cum uno diabolo' does not refer to the singing.

44A The Funeral of the Virgin ('Fergus')

Play not registered, and probably not performed at the time of the Register's compilation.

45 The Assumption of the Virgin

The music cues are those marked by written music in the play text. For information on the notation, music, and performance, see 1.5. As Carolyn Wall noted ('Apocryphal', 172), the play divides into three scenes of 8+8+8 regular stanzas, with music at both divisions. The other music cue, **45₂**, follows the first stanza of the second scene. For the numerical structure of this play see I, 246–8: it is presumably not a coincidence that the notated polyphony occurs in one of the plays that show most interest in numerological structure.

45₁ 104+music Function: (e), (h). Angels – presumably all twelve of them – sing *Surge proxima mea*.

45₂ 117+music Function: (i) The angels sing *Veni de Libano sponsa* as Mary begins her ascent to Heaven.

---

[44] See section 2.4, below, under **N-Town 39**, and my discussion in Lumiansky and Mills *Essays*, 152–3.

[45] See Rastall 'Musical Repertory' and I, 380–3.

45₃ 208+music Function: (e), (h). The angels sing *Veni electa mea*: this covers the rest of Mary's ascent and (presumably) her arrival in Heaven.

46 *The Coronation of the Virgin*

For the difficulties surrounding the positioning of music cues in this play, see I, 239–41.

46₁ 80+md Function: (a), (h). The angels sing as they bring Mary into the presence of Christ. There are six speaking parts for the angels, probably a large enough choir. There is no indication of the item to be sung.

46ₐ 104 Function: (a), (h). See I, 239–41.

46₂ 160 Function: (g). The angels again sing, this time at the express bidding of Christ (**157–8**). This is a 'praise' ending, and the text must be a Marian one.

46A *The Coronation of the Virgin*

No music cues in this late fragment.

47 *The Last Judgement*

47₁ 88 Function: none. The First Angel blows his trumpet. Possibly this cue should be at line **84**: see below.

47₂ 96 Function: (b), (h). The Second Angel blows his trumpet. Possibly this cue should be at line **88**, in which case it apparently has no structural function: see below.

47₃ 216+sd Function: (a), (h). Christ comes to the judgement seat accompanied by the music of angels.

47₄ 380+sd Function: (g). There is angelic music at the end of the play and the cycle.

2

The N-Town Cycle

2.1 Introduction

The N-Town plays form a cosmic play-cycle: the text is preceded by banns, to be spoken by three banner-bearers (*vexillatores*), announcing a performance. The banns and plays were edited by K.S. Block for the Early English Text Society in 1922, under the title *Ludus Coventriae or The Plaie called Corpus Christi*: her edition is now superseded by that of Stephen Spector (*The N-Town Play*). In addition, Peter Meredith has reconstructed two independent plays that were incorporated into the cycle (*Mary Play* and *Passion Play*).

The text is available in a facsimile of the unique manuscript, Medieval Drama Facsimiles (MDF) 4, with an introduction by Peter Meredith and Stanley J. Kahrl. The manuscript and its textual problems are further discussed in various papers by Meredith and by Spector,[1] and in this chapter I shall also cite unpublished papers, given at the N-Town Symposium at the University of Toronto, 3–5 May 1987, by these and other scholars.

The N-Town plays survive in a single copy, MS Cotton Vespasian D VIII at the British Library. At one time thought to be the lost Coventry cycle and mistakenly named *Ludus Coventriae*, the collection has also been known as 'The plaie called Corpus Christi' (following the sixteenth-century heading on f. 1r) and 'The Hegge plays' (after the first-known owner, Robert Hegge: see MDF 4, 24–5). Hardin Craig tried to show that it is a civic cycle from Lincoln,[2] in which he was followed by Kahrl and others: but the language is East Anglian and a Lincoln provenance is hard to sustain.[3] In any case it seems likely that the plays were not collected for performance at any one specific location (Meredith 'Scribes, Texts and Performance', 19–20). They are now known as the 'N-Town' plays,

---

[1] Meredith 'Manuscript, Scribe', 'Reconsideration' and 'Scribes, Texts and Performance'; Spector 'Composition and Development' and in *N-Town Play*.

[2] Craig *English Religious Drama*, although Craig was not the first to suggest this: see Spector *N-Town Play*, xv, especially n. 2.

[3] See Spector *N-Town Play*, II, xxix–xxxviii.

following the location given for the next performance at the end of the banns:

> A sunday next yf þat we may
> At vj of þe belle we gynne oure play
> In .N. town ...

(N-Town proclamation/525–7)

where 'N' presumably stands for *nomen*, the name of the town concerned.

Most scholars now accept that the plays do not strictly constitute a cycle: but for reasons already stated I shall continue to refer to it as such.[4] Similarly, it is convenient to refer to the individual numbered sections of the drama as 'pageants'.[5] The composite nature of this collection of plays affects our consideration of music. This is partly because the plays from which the collection was made up are representative of different types of drama, so that our expectations for musical participation cannot be worked out for the 'cycle' as a whole.

It appears that the plays came mainly from three sources – numbered (i), (ii) and (iv)/(v) below – with other, subsidiary sources also involved (Meredith 'Scribes, Texts and Performance', 19 and 26–9):

(i) The collection was based on a series of discrete pageants. These are described in the banns, although subsequent editorial activity has changed the play-texts so that some of the descriptions are no longer accurate. These pageants may or may not have been a civic cycle put on by trade guilds: they certainly belong to a smaller community – probably a rural one – than the northern cycles (Kathleen Ashley in the N-Town Symposium, 5 May 1987). Nor is there any positive evidence that they were performed processionally: indeed, Meredith thinks that they could originally have been a fixed-stage play (*ibid.*, 3 May 1987). Whatever the case, the material covered was that of a complete Creation-to-Doom cycle. I shall discuss them as a pageant-cycle for convenience, and shall refer to them as the N-Town 'pageant cycle' or 'protocycle'.[6]

(ii) Second, a single play on the early life of the Virgin was imposed on this pageant cycle. This is the play reconstructed by Meredith as *The Mary Play*. The N-Town plays concerned are sometimes known as the 'Contemplacio' group because of that expositor's important role. I shall use Meredith's title for the original play, and 'the Marian group' to refer to the N-Town plays derived from it. Parts of the Mary Play corresponded, not particularly closely, to pageants from the original cycle, which these sections were therefore able to replace. The present play **11** is wholly Mary Play material, while play **10** is basically an original pageant expanded by the insertion of Mary Play material.

---

4   See I, 9, n. 9; also MDF 4, vii, Meredith 'Reconsideration' and Spector 'Composition and Development', *passim*.
5   See especially Meredith 'Manuscript, Scribe', 110–11.
6   More recent thinking suggests that other pageants in this series were originally free-standing plays.

Four sections of the Mary Play treated material that was not present in the pageants: three of these became separate pageants (plays **8**, **9** and **13**), while the fourth, *The Parliament of Heaven*, forms a prologue to the *Annunciation* (play **11**), which displaced the original Annunciation pageant. Finally, one of the pageants (now play **12**) had no corresponding section in the Mary Play and was retained: Meredith has shown convincingly how this original pageant was grafted into the middle of the larger play ('Scribes, Texts', 26–9). The Mary Play shows signs of having been performed in church originally, so that it may have been written for performance under the auspices of a church or of a religious guild. It should not be regarded as a civic play, therefore.

(iii) Third, since the Purification episode was not included in either the pageants or the Mary Play, a separate Purification play (**19**) was inserted at the appropriate place.

(iv), (v) A two-day passion play was imposed later in the original cycle, displacing pageants from the Conspiracy (play **26**) as far as the Burial (play **34**). For convenience, and because the two parts were apparently intended for performance in alternate years, the two days are now usually known as *Passion Play I* (pageants **26–28**) and *Passion Play II* (pageants **29–34**). There is no clear-cut ending to the second day, however, editorial activity having made a seamless join between the passion-play and pageant materials (see MDF 4, xviii). This passion play apparently used a fixed playing-area with scaffolds and therefore, like the Mary Play, was originally given in a non-processional mode: but, unlike the Mary Play, the Passion Play could well have been a civic drama in its original form.

(vi) In addition, a play of the Assumption of the Virgin (**41**) was incorporated physically into the collection. This, too, seems to have been designed for church performance originally.

Meredith has shown that the main scribe was responsible for copying these various plays in the form of a new cycle, replacing as he thought appropriate and editing (with some rewriting) to allow the possibility of playing the various sections as separate plays or of performing at least some of them in their original form. One play, the interpolated *Assumption of the Virgin* (**41**), needed so little editing to make it acceptable to the new collection that the scribe included his exemplar physically in the manuscript without recopying. On the whole, however, it is difficult to see precisely what he did, and perhaps we shall never know for sure what the constituent parts were originally like.

One result of the scribe's work on this collection is that his division of the collection into pageants and his numbering of those divisions cause some problems, with the number 17 missing altogether. Moreover, few of the divisions have titles, although some are headed with a statement in Latin of the play's subject-matter. Block retained the scribal division and numbering, while Meredith and Kahrl suggested revised divisions and numbering as well as English titles for the individual plays (MDF 4, viii–xiii); their titles are slightly amended by Lancashire, who used the same numbering (Lancashire *Dramatic Texts*, 11–12). I follow here Spector's rather different titles and his numbering of the individual plays. He takes the view that play **17** is missing, there being room for it in the blank pages following play **16**, and consequently counts 42 plays in the collection.

The manuscript probably dates from the later fifteenth century. Meredith and Kahrl placed the main scribe's hand in 'the last decade of the fifteenth century at the earliest', leaving open the possibility of a sixteenth-century dating (MDF 4, xxvii, note 4): they regard the date 1468, which appears on f. 100v, as being attached to the particular play (**19**) at the end of which it occurs, and therefore think that it gives 'an indication of the earliest possible date at which the manuscript could have been compiled' (MDF 4, xiii). Spector considers that this may be the date at which the Purification play was incorporated into the main manuscript;[7] it could also be the date of compilation, and is favoured as such by Beadle (*Medieval Drama of East Anglia*). On linguistic grounds Spector dates the composition of the constituent plays at some time after 1450, with the manuscript being copied in the third quarter of the century (N-Town Symposium, 4 May 1987): but he also stated on the same occasion that the Passion Play (which is physically separate although copied by the same scribe) could have been composed as late as 1480. Play **41**, which is a physical interpolation into the collection and presumably 'may be thought of as typical of the material, in its most usable form, from which the main scribe was working' (MDF 4, xiii), was presumably copied earlier than the main part of the manuscript.

The question of the provenance of the N-Town plays is quite as complex as that of dating. The plays seem to belong to south central Norfolk, near the Suffolk border, but the different scribal histories cause different linguistic features to become apparent. Richard Beadle's doctoral thesis, following McIntosh and Samuels, placed the main scribe east-north-east of Thetford, at around East Harling, and the Assumption scribe a few miles north-east of Ely (*Medieval Drama of East Anglia*, 124–5). Later work by McIntosh and Samuels has modified the second of these, and the language of the Assumption play is now thought to belong to the same area as that of the main scribe (see above, n. 3). This is not of course an actual location for the scribes concerned, but only the centre of gravity of the linguistic features discernible in their work: and it is impossible to be sure that these features are wholly those of the scribe rather than the dramatist.[8]

The N-Town plays are rich in dramatic directions and text references, although they contain no notated music. Because the provenance of the plays is unknown, it cannot be shown that any civic or other records relate to the plays or

---

7 Spector *N-Town Play*, I, xxxviii.
8 Spector places both the playwrights and the scribes in East Anglia, but the evidence is more detailed for the scribes: *N-Town Play*, xxix–xxxviii. It may eventually be possible to locate the dramatists by reference to the liturgical content of the plays, but attempts to do this are so far unsuccessful: see I, 294–9 and especially 297–8.

their performance. Of course, close examination of town accounts in East Anglia may yet give information on the performance of plays that could be identifiable as the N-Town collection or constituent parts of it. But the manuscript gives no clear evidence that the collection as we have it was ever performed, although Meredith and Kahrl have demonstrated the probability that performances of the Nativity and Resurrection sequences were at least projected subsequent to the compilation of the collection (MDF 4, xxiv, concerning the work of Reviser B).

The plays of the N-Town cycle are listed below. I give Spector's numbering and titles, with a note on the banns description based on Meredith's work.[9] In the first column the small roman numerals refer to the original pageant-cycle (i), the Marian group (ii), the interpolated Purification pageant (iii), the Passion Play (iv and v), and the separate Assumption play (vi): I use this numbering throughout.

Grp	Play	Title	Banns*
i	1	The Creation of Heaven, and Fall of Lucifer	1
i	2	The Creation of the World, and Fall of Man	2
i	3	Cain and Abel	3
i	4	Noah [and Lamech]	4: no Lamech
i	5	Abraham and Isaac	5
i	6	Moses	6
i	7	Jesse Root	7
ii	8	Joachim and Anna	no entry
ii	9	The Presentation of Mary in the Temple	no entry
i+ii	10	The Marriage of Mary and Joseph	8, 9
ii	11	The Parliament of Heaven; the Salutation and Conception	10: no Parliament
i	12	Joseph's Doubt	11
ii	13	The Visit to Elizabeth	no entry
i	14	The Trial of Mary and Joseph	12: incomplete
i	15	The Nativity	13: incomplete
i	16	The Shepherds	14
	17	*absit*	
i	18	The Magi	15
iii	19	The Purification	no entry
i	20	The Slaughter of the Innocents, and Death of Herod	16, 17
i	21	Christ and the Doctors	18
i	22	The Baptism	19

---

[9] Discussed by him in various conference papers, including that at Toronto, 3 May 1987, and incorporated into 'Manuscript, Scribe', 126–8.

i	23	The Parliament of Hell, and the Temptation	20
i	24	The Woman Taken in Adultery	21
	25	The Raising of Lazarus	22
iv	26	Prologues of Satan and John the Baptist; the Conspiracy, and Entry into Jerusalem	23: brief
iv	27	The Last Supper, and Conspiracy with Judas	24
iv	28	The Betrayal; the Procession of Saints	25
	29	Herod, and the Trial before Annas and Cayphas	26
v	30	The Death of Judas; the Trials before Pilate and Herod	27
		[ ]	28: Judas
v	31	Satan and Pilate's Wife; the Second Trial before Pilate	29
v	32	The Procession to Calvary, and the Crucifixion	30
v	33	The Harrowing of Hell (i)	31: includes Longeus
v	34	The Burial, and Guarding of the Sepulchre	32
i	35	The Harrowing of Hell (ii); Christ's Appearance to Mary; Pilate and the Soldiers	33
i	36	The Announcement to the Three Marys; Peter and John at the Sepulchre	34
i	37	The Appearance to Mary Magdalene	35
i	38	Cleophas and Luke; The Appearance to Thomas	36: no Thomas 37: 4 lines only[10]
i	39	The Ascension; the Selection of Matthias	38
i	40	Pentecost	39
vi	41	The Assumption of Mary	no entry
i	42	Judgement Day	40

* NB The existence of a number in this column shows only that an entry exists for the episode in question: it does not mean that the banns entry is demonstrably for the surviving text. On the relations between plays and banns see 2.3, below. Only major deviations from the text are shown here.

2.2   Dramatic directions

The directions in the N-Town plays have been discussed by Meredith and Kahrl (MDF 4, xviii–xix). With certain exceptions (which they specify) the directions are underlined in red. What Meredith and Kahrl do not say is that – again, with

[10] Appearance to Thomas.

exceptions, noted below – in general the underlining is carefully omitted from the Latin liturgical texts and incipits. In effect, therefore, the prescriptive parts of the directions are underlined, the textual elements being differentiated.

This general situation is useful in suggesting specific information on what is spoken or sung. In **41/455+sd**, for instance, the lack of underlining of the words 'In nomine patris et filii et spiritus sancti' tells us not merely that the blessing was made in the name of the three persons of the Trinity but, more specifically, that these were the actual words used. While this is no surprise, it does exclude certain other wordings that would have been possible.

The exceptions to this general situation, fortunately, occur in directions where the meaning is not in doubt. The complete underlining of **10/115+md** and the total lack of underlining in the associated SD alike make no difference to our understanding that *Veni creator spiritus* is sung at that point. Similarly, the complete underlining of **16/89+md** and **26/453+sd** does not affect our understanding of the music cues there, because the directions are explicit in both cases.

Listing the directions (Table 3) shows that the languages used are related to the types of drama concerned:

(i)   The plays belonging to the original pageant cycle have Latin directions;
(ii)   The Marian group uses Latin for the most part, but a significant number of directions are in English;
(iii) The *Purification* play also uses both languages with Latin dominant;
(iv)   Passion Play I has English directions;
(v)   Passion Play II uses English predominantly, but has some Latin directions; and
(vi)   *The Assumption of the Virgin* uses Latin directions.

Table 3 excludes play-headings, cues for following plays, and *explicit*s at the ends of plays. Since it would be begging the question in this cycle to label directions as 'original', the column for 'position' shows whether a direction is in the main text area (t) or the right margin (m): however, the scribes' intentions in this respect are not always clear.

These data on directions show that the incidence of music in the various source-groups varies considerably.

(i) In the plays belonging to the original pageant series, the numbers of directions (all Latin) are as shown below. Clearly there is no reason to think that the marginal directions in group (i) are more concerned with music than the SDs proper, although the number of examples is too small to ensure statistical significance.

Non-musical directions in text space	53	
Musical directions in text space	8	
Total directions in text space		61
Marginal non-musical directions	8	
Marginal musical directions	1	
Total marginal directions		9
Total musical directions	9	
Total non-musical directions	61	
Total directions		70
Percentage of musical directions in text space	13.1	
Percentage of musical directions in margin	11.1	
All musical directions as percentage of the total	12.9	

(ii) In the Marian Group both marginal position and the language used seem to indicate layers of activity in the writing of directions. The English directions are sometimes long and detailed, in marked contrast to the Latin ones. There are also signs that these divisions correspond to different *types* of direction, with rather different functions.

There are two places where Latin and English come together. The direction at **9/277+sd** falls into three sections, of which the first cannot be deduced from the play or from other sources: 'hic osculet terram'. The rest of the direction is in English. The second section, 'here xal comyn ... Jhesu corona virginum', gives details of the feeding of Mary by angels (here a single angel), a legend well known in the late Middle Ages (see, for instance, the *Golden Legend* under The Nativity of the BVM, 8 September); and many of the audience would know why, in the next speech, Mary does not need the food brought to her by the Minister (**9/260–7**). The music is an addition to this legend. The third section, 'And After ... with a present and seyth', tells us nothing that we cannot deduce from the text following the SD. Thus, leaving aside the question of music for a moment, it seems that the Latin opening could be the original direction, with the English sections added at a later date.

Turning now to **11/340**, we find a Latin direction amplifying the text (**11/339–40**), followed by a cancelled English direction that is nothing more than a speech heading: however, as Meredith has shown, this is a cue to **12/13** (Meredith 'Scribes, Texts', 28–9), **12/13–20** being apparently a linking passage between the present plays 11 and 13. This English part of the direction, 'And þan mary seyth', itself sounds like the result of editorial activity, and again I suggest that it is later than the Latin direction.

Looking at all the Latin directions now, it is noticable that those in marginal position are sometimes not of the same type as those in normal text position. It is, in fact, the difference between SDs proper, with their own grammatical construction, and marginal notes in somewhat abbreviated form. But this generalisation is contradicted several times, and there are evidently other factors involved. For example, at **10/115** the bishop says that they will 'begin' *Veni Creator Spiritus*, and the English SD simply chronologises this, giving the SH for the next speech to be said after *Veni Creator* is finished; it is the Latin marginal direction that tells us that *Veni Creator* is sung rather than spoken. We have, then, two possibilities: either the directions have been subjected to editorial criticism (or omission by oversight), resulting in some late directions being given positional precedence over earlier ones (in this case a late English direction being given precedence over a Latin marginal direction), or the Latin is not necessarily earlier than the English.

Personally, I prefer the former solution. The English directions are so much more detailed than the Latin ones that it is hard to think of them as being contemporary with the latter. To put it a different way: if any Latin directions are contemporary with the English ones, why are the Latin ones so terse? And why is it only the English ones that show the chronological sequence of events? It does seem to me that the languages give a clear indication of the layers of compositional activity where the directions are concerned.

Bearing in mind that the difference between marginal and text-space position may be due to scribal preference or negligence, it will be most useful to consider the directions of these plays in the language/position groupings just suggested. I shall assume that the sequence of layers may be: Latin directions in normal position, Latin directions in marginal position, English directions in normal position, and English directions in marginal position. The incidence of these types is:

Latin, text-space position, non-musical	9*	
musical		0
marginal position, non-musical	8	
musical		4
English, text-space position, non-musical	6	
musical		4
marginal position, non-musical	1**	
musical		0

* Includes the Latin section of **9/259+sd**
** The English part of **11/340+sd**

Some significance attaches to these figures in view of the previously-suggested chronological sequence of events concerning the use of music. The first of our putative layers of activity, the Latin directions in text position, are nine in number and include no musical directions at all. A complete lack of musical directions in the earliest version of this material – the Mary Play itself – would explain some puzzles. The first of these is the notable insistence on the *saying* of *Ave Maria* at **11/223, 226** until the MD after **11/340**: if the MD is later, the text's refusal to

TABLE 3 : DIRECTIONS IN THE N-TOWN CYCLE

Group Play Cue-line	Posn	Lang	Direction if musical: Comments
(i) Pageants from the Original Cycle			
1 *The Creation, and Fall of Lucifer*			
39	t	l	*hic cantent angeli in celo.* Tibi omnes angeli tibi celi et vniuerse potestates . Tibi cherubyn et seraphyn incessabili voce proclamant . Sanctus . Sanctus . Sanctus . Dominus deus sabaoth.
2 *The Creation, and Fall of Man*			
			Two Latin SDs in text position
3 *Cain and Abel* One Latin SD in text position			
4 *Noah, and Lamech*			
141	t	l	
185	t	l	
197	t	l	*Hic recedat lameth et statim intrat noe cum naui cantantes*
245	t	l	
249	t	l	
253	t	l	*Hic decantent hos versus .* Mare vidit et fugit: jordanis conuersus est retrorsum . Non nobis domine non nobis: sed nomine tuo da gloriam . *Et sic recedant cum navi.*
5 *Abraham and Isaac*			No directions
6 *Moses*			One Latin SD in text position
7 *Jesse Root*			No directions
(ii) Plays from the Marian Group			
8 *Joachim and Anna*			
97	t	e	*There they xal synge þis sequens .* Benedicta sit beata trinitas. *And in þat tyme ysakar with his ministeris*

			ensensyth þe autere and þan þei make her offryng . and Isaker seyth
105	m	l	
108	m	l	
109	m	l	*Ministro cantando* Followed by the text to be sung (see 2.3)
116	t	l	
172	t	e	*here þe Aungel descendith . þe hefne syngyng* Exultet celum laudibus . resultet terra gaudijs Archangelorum gloria sacra canunt solemnia.
236	t	e	

9   The Presentation of Mary in the Temple

17	t	e	
41	t	l	
57	t	l	
77	t	l	
101	t	l	See 2.6 for discussion of this direction
217	t	l	*Et recedent cum ministris suis: omnes virgines dicent . Amen* Discussed in I, 372: see also 2.4, below
225	m	l	
226	m	l	
245	t	e	*here þe aungel bryngyth manna in a cowpe of gold lyke to confeccions . þe hefne syngynge . þe aungel seyth*
277	t	l+e	*hic osculet terram . here xal comyn alwey an aungel with dyvers presentis goynge and comyng and in þe tyme þei xal synge in hefne þis hympne . Jhesu corona virginum . and after þer comyth a minister fro þe busschop with a present and seyth* This may suggest an older Latin SD to which an English one was later added.

10   The Marriage of Mary and Joseph
This play is a blend of Marian and pageant plays: see MDF 4, xxii, and Meredith 'Manuscript, Scribe', 115–17.[11]

(i) From pageant material

			One Latin SD in text position

[11] Details of the use of materials from pageants and Mary Play were discussed by Meredith at the N-Town Symposium in Toronto, 3 May 1987.

(ii) From the Mary Play

115	m	l	*Et hic cantent* veni creator
			All underlined
115	t	e	*and whan* Veni creator *is don þe buschop xal* [?kneel] *seyng*
			Nothing underlined. Musical only in conjunction with **115+md**. Spector amends 'seyng' to 'seyn'.
198	m	l	
258	m	l	
301	m	l	et *hic cantent*. Benedicta sit beata trinitas
310	m	l	
313	t	l	

11   The Parliament of Heaven; the Salutation and Conception

188	t	l	
260	t	e	
292	t	e	
340	m	l(+e)	*angeli cantando istam sequenciam*
			Referring to the text *Ave maria gratia plena / dominus tecum . uirgo serena.* None of this is underlined. The direction was originally followed by *And þan mary seyth,* now crossed out (see Meredith 'Manuscript, Scribe', 118–19).

(i) Pageant from the Original Cycle

12   Joseph's Doubt   No directions

(ii) Play from the Marian Group

13   The Visit to Elizabeth

22	m	l	
166	t	e	

(i) Pageants from the Original Cycle

14   The Trial of Mary and Joseph

33	t	l
105	t	l
249	t	l
253	m	l
333	t	l
363	t	l

405	t	l	*explicit cum gaudio amen* is written below the end of the play and set off from the text by flourishes.[12] The phrase 'cum gaudio' may imply music, but this is speculative.

15 *The Nativity* Five Latin SDs in text position

16 *The Shepherds*

–1	t	l	*Angelus ad pastores dicit* Gloria in excelsis deo The *incipit* 'Gloria ... deo' is crossed through, probably by Reviser B (MDF 4, xxiv): see below, 2.6, for a discussion
61	t	l	Gloria in excelsis deo *cantent* The *incipit* is written as text, 'cantent' underlined
89	m	l	*tunc pastores cantabunt . stella celi extirpauit . quo facto ibunt ad querendum christum.* All underlined. The direction's marginal position is connected with the rearrangement (and perhaps re-writing) of material, including the cancellation of the *incipit* at **1–sd**. It is contradicted by text references, however: see 2.6.

[17 *absit*]

18 *The Magi*

110	m	l	In later hand, and partly cut away: in left margin, squeezed above the direction in text position
110	t	l	
215	m	l	In less formal script, but perhaps the same hand, squeezed in near SH
234	t	l	
290	t	l	
314	t	l	

(iii) The Purification Pageant

19 *The Purification*

20	t	e
80	t	l
116	m	l
132	t	l

---

[12] Spector says that it is in 'another hand', but that seems to me questionable.

146	t*	e	*The psalme songyn every vers and per qwyl Symeon pleyth with þe child and qwhan þe psalme is endyd . he seyth*
			Added to the text 'Nunc dimittis servum tuum domine et cetera'
			* The lines are long enough to use up the marginal space as well as the text space
176	m	e	
196	t	e	

(i) Pageants from the Original Cycle

20   The Slaughter of the Innocents, and the Death of Herod

1–	t	l	
88	t	l	
232	t	l	*hic dum buccinant mors interficiat herodem et duos milites subito et diabolus recipiat eos.*

21   Christ and the Doctors

		One Latin SD in text position

22   The Baptism

	Three Latin SDs in text position

23   The Parliament of Hell, and the Temptation

113	t	l	
117	t	l	
156	t	l	
195	t	l	*hic uenient angeli cantantes et ministrantes ei . Gloria tibi domine . dicens*
			Followed by SH 'Jhesus', the subject of 'dicens'[13]

24   The Woman Taken in Adultery

		Four Latin SDs in text position

25   The Raising of Lazarus

100	m	e	In hand of Scribe C.
108	t	l	['et cetera' seems to involve known stage actions]
			And six more Latin SDs in text position

---

13 Spector's edition is misleading here, as his punctuation implies that 'Gloria tibi domine' is the text spoken by Jesus. In fact, the hook-plus-underlining on the word 'dicens' separates it from the incipit and by implication relates it to the SH just below it. This is clear in the manuscript (see MDF 4, f. 119r). The incipit is that of the text sung by the angels, as one would expect (see 2.4 under this play).

(iv) Passion play I

26 *Prologues of Satan and John the Baptist; The Conspiracy, and the Entry into Jerusalem*

164	t	e	Multiple direction, which is a feature of both parts of the Passion Play. Directions in other plays often include two or three elements, but only rarely more (**7/72, 9/259**, e.g.): here 'multiple' indicates at least four elements, and sometimes six or more
208	t	e	Multiple
244	t	e	Multiple
256	t	e	
272	t	e	
280	t	e	
288	t	e	Multiple
342	t	e	Cancelled, together with six lines of speech
359	t	e	
385	t	e	Multiple
441	t	e	
449	t	e	Multiple
453	t	e	*here cryst passyth forth . per metyth with hym a serteyn of chylderyn with flowris and cast beforn hym and They synggyn* Gloria laus *and beforn on seyt* All underlined.
481	t	e	

27 *The Last Supper, and the Conspiracy with Judas*
No directions for music. 25 English directions, of which two are marginal: some multiple directions

28 *The Betrayal*
No directions for music: 14 English directions, none marginal, some multiple

(v) Passion play II

29 *The Preliminary Examination: Annas and Caiaphas*
No directions for music. There are nine SDs, all in English, some multiple: also four MDs, all in Latin. Of the latter, two are the direction *et cantabit gallus* (**28/198** and **212**), which is not musical: the verb 'cantare' was used in several ways in the Middle Ages, of which this is a common non-musical way.[14]

---

[14] See *Revised Medieval Latin Word-List* under 'gallus'. What Spector prints as a multiple SD here is in fact the MD followed by a tripartite SD in the text-space.

30 The Death of Judas, and the Trials before Pilate and Herod
No directions for music. There are nine English SDs, some multiple, and a single Latin MD

31 Satan and Pilate's Wife, and the Second Trial before Pilate
No directions for music. There are eleven English SDs, some multiple; one Latin SD; four Latin MDs; and one English MD

32 The Procession to Calvary, and the Crucifixion
No directions for music. Counting the last sentence of the SD between plays 31 and 32 as belonging to this play, there are fourteen English SDs, some multiple; two Latin SDs; and one English MD.

The only direction of musical interest is that at **32/76+sd**: *here xule þei leve of and dawncyn abowte þe cros shortly.* See I, 212–15, and 2.6, below.

33 The Harrowing of Hell (1)

24		t		e		The sowle goth to helle gatys and seyth . V. Attollite portas principes vestras et eleuamini porte eternales et introibit rex glorie
24		m		l		

34 The Burial, and the Guarding of the Sepulchre
No directions for music. There are ten English SDs (two of them multiple), one English MD, and one Latin SD

(i) Pageants from the Original Cycle

35 The Harrowing of Hell (2), and Christ's Appearance to Mary; Pilate and the Soldiers

1–		t		l		Link between plays: presumably not part of the original pageant. And three more Latin SDs in text position

36 The Announcement to the Three Marys; Peter and John at the Sepulchre

1–		t		l		Link between plays, presumably not part of the original pageant; and seven more Latin directions, the last of which is marginal

37 The Appearance to Mary Magdalene

1–		t		e		Link between plays, and presumably not part of the original pageant

16	t	l	
37	m	l	

38 Cleophas and Luke; the Appearance to Thomas

One Latin SD in text position

Meredith and Kahrl (MDF 4, xxv) think that the various marginal notes *worlych, vade worlych* and *nota worlych* are directions; Spector regards them as referring to an actor (*N-Town Play* I, xxiv).

39 The Ascension, and the Selection of Matthias

47	t	l	*hic ascendit ab oculis eorum et in celo cantent et cetera*
82	t	l	This non-musical direction also ends with 'et cetera', although there seems no real purpose in it
90	t	l	This non-musical direction also ends with 'et cetera', although there seems no real purpose in it

40 Pentecost

One Latin SD in text position

(vi) The Assumption Play

41 The Assumption of Mary

All directions in Latin, none demonstrably marginal

93	
116	*hic discendet angelus ludent' cithar' et dicet marie* [SH *primus Angelus*]
	Directions at lines 165, 187, 195, 233, 302 and 311
313	*hic cantabunt organa*
329	
347	*hic cantabit omnis celestis curia*
355	
368	
370	*hic angeli dulciter cantabunt in celo . Alleluia*
409	
422	
448	
452	*hic ponent corpus in sepulcrum insensantes et cantantes* The text is given in **41/453–4**: see 2.4
455	*hic vnanimiter benedicent corpus .* In nomine patris et filij et spiritus sancti
	Directions at lines 463, 469, 495 and 508
521	*Et hic assendent in celum cantantibus organis.* Assumpta es maria in celum

(i) Pageant from the Original Cycle		
42 *Judgement Day*		
26	t	1
30	m	1
35	m	1

mention singing makes better sense (see 2.3, below). Second, a general non-use of music seems a better context for the rather unusual saying of *Magnificat* after **13/81**, in which Mary and Elizabeth seem to speak the Latin and its translation antiphonally (see the discussion in 2.3, below, of **13/127–30**). This is in line with the less ceremonial spoken liturgy suggested also in the performance of the gradual psalms after **9/101** and part of Psalm 82 at **11/187–8**. Even *Veni Creator* is apparently said (**10/115**) in the original version, in contrast to the singing specified for *Alma chorus domini* (**10/332–4**: see 2.3, below).

This last is a reminder that the lack of musical SDs does not imply a total lack of music, and indeed there is a second text reference to music at the end of play 13 (see 2.3, below). But this ending to play 13 may not be the original: and so it seems likely that the Mary Play originally included two items of music at most.

Our putative second layer is the twelve marginal directions in Latin, which more than double the directions already there. Of these, four (one third) are musical. Three of them require the singing of a liturgical piece that had previously been said (after **8/109**, **10/115** and **11/340**); the other (after **10/301**) adds a piece that is not required by the text (*Benedicta sit beata trinitas*).

There are ten English directions in text position, of which four are musical. In none of the four cases is music demanded by the text. Although 4:10 is a higher proportion of musical occurrence than in the Latin directions, we should remember that this is a misleading figure: for the English SDs proper are multiple, only one of several elements being for music. However, these four are all SDs specifying considerable movement of actors around the playing-space, so that music is dramatically very useful as well as representationally suitable. In three of the four cases the liturgical piece is specified. All four are important 'set-piece' moments of great effectiveness: it is quite possible that the stage movement was elaborated in the course of time, music being a necessity only at a certain stage in the development of the performances.

Finally, there is one marginal direction in English, which is not musical and is really a SH only (**11/340**): as already noted, it seems to be a link direction that was deleted when play **12** was grafted into the space between the present plays **11** and **13**.

To summarise, then, there is evidence to suggest that the Mary Play had little or no music, and that in the course of time two things happened: first, that liturgical items originally said began to be sung, with Latin MDs added as a reminder; second, that the elaboration of staging later required musical set pieces that were specified in detailed English SDs.

(iii) In the Purification play, too, it seems likely that the Latin directions are older than the English ones. The English SD after **19/146** is clearly added to specify musical performance for a text (the canticle *Nunc dimittis*) that was originally said. Although this play is not part of the Marian group, therefore, it may be said to have this characteristic in common with the plays of that group, as noted under (ii), above.

(iv) There is obviously very little music in Passion Play I, which uses English directions throughout. Even around the one direction for music (**26/453+sd**), where *Gloria laus* is specified, the text itself notably omits any reference to singing ('late us þan welcome hym with flowrys and brawnchis of þe tre': line **448**). However, **26/450–51** and **454–7** are English paraphrases of Latin items (see below, 2.3).

   Again, it is possible that an earlier version of the play used no music at all, the SD in question being a later addition.

(v) Passion Play II contains no directions for music: as elsewhere, some of the English directions are multiple. The figures for the various categories are:

	Latin	English	Total
Directions in text space	4	54	58
Marginal directions	10	3	13
Total directions	14	57	71

(vi) Of the 24 directions in the Assumption play, only six demand music, with a seventh doing so when a text reference is taken into account. The occurrence of music in a quarter (25%) of the directions is an incidence almost twice as high as that of music in the pageant plays (12.9%) although less than in the Marian group (33%). The directions in play **41** are especially interesting for three reasons. First, they specify angelic instrumental music, naming instruments in three cases; second, **41/370+sd** specifies a performance style, 'dulciter'; third, although two items are named (**41/370+sd** and **521+sd**), the dramatist seems less interested than most in the actual liturgical pieces to be heard: the other two occasions of vocal music (**41/347+sd** and **452+sd**) are fairly specific occasions on which we could have expected the item to be determined in the script.

2.3   Text references

Consideration of text references in this cycle shows that the various constituent dramas display quite different attitudes to music. This is not merely a matter of the concentration of musical performances, which largely depends on the episode being dramatised: most obviously it is seen in the metaphorical references – that is, in the dramatist's use of musical imagery independently of a need or inclination for the actual performance of music in a play. It will be convenient to summarize these attitudes before discussing the cycle play by play.

(i) The Original Cycle

The metaphorical uses of musical reference are rather fewer here than in the York cycle, for instance. 'Lowde and still' does not occur at all, but a single non-musical use of 'lowd and lowe' (**28/142**) may be the East Anglian equivalent. The metaphorical singing in sorrow appears rarely: the Second Soldier promises it for the mothers of the Innocents in a passage that also includes an unusual metaphor concerning a harp (see **20/65–8**, below).

Two 'welaway' references are musical (see **20/244–5** and **42/29**), but most are not. The one from Eve (**2/296**), two from Cain (**3/178** and **193**), two from Joseph in his trouble about Mary (**12/57** and **78**), one from the midwife Salomee when her hand is withered for her disbelief (**15/254**) and one from Martha at the death of Lazarus (**25/113**) are not discussed below. A related reference is Den's comment on Mary's pregnancy (see **14/197**).

Metaphorical references to dancing are absent in these plays.

These plays are not over-generous in their use of metaphorical references to music, then. This attitude is echoed in the banns, which mention music in only two plays (plays **1** and **16**), and in the play texts themselves, where mention of music is largely confined to its connection with mirth.

(ii) The Marian Group

Metaphorical references to music are entirely absent in these plays: this is in line with the fact, noted above (2.2), that they seem to have included little or no music in their original version. Indeed, this lack of metaphorical reference suggests that the smaller over-all concentration of musically-oriented material is due not only to the lack of actual performance in the plays, but to a whole conceptual context in which music plays little or no part.

(iii) The Purification Play

This play contains no relevant metaphorical references. It should however be noted that a reference to Simeon's 'mirth' at the Christ-child's arrival (**19/62**) apparently does not imply music.

(iv) Passion Play I

Considering the general non-use of music in the Passion sequence, the two metaphorical usages (at **26/8** and **27/204**) perhaps show a more musical dramatic mind at work than might have been expected.

(v) Passion Play II

This part of the cycle contains no metaphorical references to music.

(vi) The Assumption Play

Despite all the music required by this play in performance – and its evidence makes it musically one of the most exciting plays in the repertory – the dramatist may fairly be described as interested in liturgy rather than music. Nevertheless, two factors may demonstrate his positive attitude towards music: the angels' references to the music and its performers; and, more specifically, the use made of such references by mortals to construct a narrative misunderstanding which is of dramatic and formal importance (see the comments on **41/371–87**, below).

There follows a play-by-play discussion of musical references in the cycle.

(i) Pageants from the Original Cycle

1 *The Creation of Heaven, and the Fall of Lucifer*

Banns/18–19 The banns for this play correspond closely to the text, and mention the singing of the newly-created angels:

> Than angell with songe, þis is no nay,
> Xal worchep God as it is ryth.

The descriptions of Heaven as a joyful place in play 1 are closely related to the sound of music there: we find that Heaven and the stars were created to exist 'In myrth and joy' (**1/30–1**), and that the angels were created to worship God 'with merth and melody' (**1/32–4**) and 'With myrth and song' (**1/36–8**). The last of these results in music at **1/39+sd**.

When God deprives Lucifer of the 'merth and joye' in Heaven (**1/71**), therefore, the audience is aware that this is a deprivation of music, too, even though Lucifer has clearly taken no part in the angels' song (**1/40**). As discussed in I, 205–6, he now cracks a fart (**1/81**) instead of musical notes. (The cracking of a fart is not yet a parody of the angelic music, merely a substitution. A similar allusion is probably intended by Satan's letting of 'a crakke' at **23/195**).

The definition of Heaven as being full of mirth, joy and music is repeated at the Last Judgement (**42/55–6**), and mirth is associated with music elsewhere throughout the pageant plays.

2 *The Creation of the World, and the Fall of Man*
3 *Cain and Abel*
No references to music.

4 *Noah*
4/198–9 Noah makes 'grett mornyng' for the flood and the loss of life occasioned
by it. These lines immediately follow the SD in which Noah and his family
enter singing. The singing is a surprise to the extent that Noah's first lines are
of great sadness. The music to be sung is presumably sorrowful – a rare
enough phenomenon in the plays – which also suits the end of the previous
scene, in which Caym and Adolescens are both killed by Lameth, while
Lameth knows himself to be a cursed outcast.

4/240–3 [VXOR JAPHET] Hym for to wurchipe in euery stede and place
             We beth gretly bownde with myght and with mayn.
        NOE xl^ti days and nyghtys hath lasted þis rayn,
             And xl^ti days þis grett flood begynnyth to slake.

Although there is neither text reference nor SD for music here, the speech of
Japhet's wife might put the need for a musical item into the producer's mind,
since music is perhaps the best way in the plays of showing 'worship': and
this would certainly be in line with the use of music elsewhere to cover the
passage of time.

4/253   [NOE] Oure lord god to worchep: a songe lete vs synge.

A 'praise' ending to the play. The text (Psalm 113/a3, b1) is given in the SD
following.

5 *Abraham and Isaac*
6 *Moses*
No references to music.

7 *Jesse Root*
7/15–16 Isaiah's statement that angels will make 'joy' at Christ's birth: he does
not specify music, however.

(ii) Plays from the Marian Group

8 *Joachim and Anna*
8/97 [YSAKAR]   Than devowtly we wyl begynne servyse.

This is followed by the SD for singing *Benedicta sit beata trinitas*: the piece is therefore to be sung 'devoutly'. It may be that the SD is not as old as the text: that is, the service may originally have been said, with the music being added at some stage.

8/174 [JOACHYM] It is as lyth abowt me as al þe werd were fere!

Joachim mentions the light, but not the angelic singing of *Exultet celum* required by the SD after **8/172**. Here, too, the SD may not be as old as the text.

8/211–12 1us PASTOR We xal make us so mery . now þis is bestad
þat a myle on ȝour wey . ȝe xal here us synge.

Note the connection of merriment with song: the shepherds can sing loudly, apparently. The song must happen immediately, covering the scene-change after **8/212**.

9 *The Presentation of Mary in the Temple*
9/100–1 [EPISCOPUS] Every man þat thynk his lyf to amende,
þe fyftene psalmys . in memorye of þis mayde say.

This is not a musical reference as it stands: it is discussed in 2.4, below.

10 *The Marriage of Mary and Joseph*
10/114–15 [EPISCOPUS] Mekely eche man falle down on kne
And we xal begynne . Veni creator spiritus.

The directions for singing *Veni creator* follow: evidently it is to be sung 'meekly', while kneeling.

10/301 [EPISCOPUS] Now ȝelde we all preysyng to þe Trenyte.

Although this is not a musical reference, it is the cue for the singing of *Benedicta sit beata trinitas*, shown by a Latin MD: 'praising' suggests joy.

10/332–4 [EPISCOPUS] þe hyȝ names of oure lord we wole now syng hy.
We all wole þis solempn dede record
Devowtly: Alma chorus domini nunc pangat nomina summi.

The bishop evidently speaks line **334**, because it is needed for the rhyme. This reference shows that the piece is sung, that it is performed chorally, and that it is sung 'devoutly'.

11   *The Parliament of Heaven and the Annunciation*

11/339–40 [GABRIEL]   And as I began I ende . with an Ave new
Enjouyd hefne and erth . with þat I ascende.

Not a reference to music, but made so by the MD following. See under **13/69**.

(i) Pageant from the Original Cycle

12   *Joseph's Trouble about Mary*
No references to music.

(ii) Play from the Marian Group

13   *The Visitation*
13/69   [MARIA]   Gabryel come and seyde to me Ave.

Refers to **11/216+**, Gabriel's salutation of the Virgin: note the 'seyde', and cf. the commentary on **11/339–40**, above.

13/127–30   MARIA   This psalme of prophesye seyd betwen vs tweyn,
In hefne it is wretyn with aungellys hond,
Evyr to be songe . and also to be seyn
Euery day amonge us at oure evesong.

This shows that Mary and Elizabeth have just said the *Magnificat*, not sung it. Indeed, Mary seems to be making the distinction between the angelic singing of the canticle in Heaven and its spoken performance on earth.

13/137–8 [ELIZABETH]   All hefne and herthe wurchepp ȝow mow,
þat are trone and tabernakyl of þe hyȝ trinite.

Note the language of the Marian liturgy found in the musical items of **York 45** and **N-Town 41**.

13/152–3A   [CONTEMPLACIO]   þe aungel seyd . Ave gratia plena dominus
tecum,
Benedicta tu in mulieribus.

Refers to **11/216+**, Gabriel's salutation to the Virgin: note the 'seyd'.

13/154–5   [CONTEMPLACIO]   Elyzabeth seyd . et benedictus
Fructus uentris tui ...

Elizabeth did not say this, but the translation (**13/59**). Although the translation occurs at the beginning of a stanza, there is no evidence that the Latin should be sung (or spoken) first: the Latin here may simply point to the connection between the seen drama and the previously-known Latin text.

13/184–5A   [CONTEMPLACIO] With Aue we begunne . and Aue is oure
conclusyon

            Ave regina celorum . to our lady we synge.

A 'praise' ending to the play: presumably the whole cast sings *Ave regina* here.

(i) Pageants from the Original Cycle

14 *The Trial of Mary and Joseph*
14/197   [DEN]   Fayr chylde lullay sone must she syng.

Den's comment on Mary's pregnancy, in addition to being a clear metaphorical use, is also no doubt to be taken literally.

15 *The Nativity*
No references to music.

16 *The Shepherds*
Banns/191–6   In þe xvj pagent Cryst xal be born.
                     Of þat joy aungelys xul synge
                     And telle þe sheperdys in þat morn
                     The blysseful byrth of þat kyng.
                     The shepherdys xal come hym befforn
                     With reuerens and with worchepyng,

16/7 [ANGELUS]   Therfore I synge a joyful stevene.

'Synge' apparently contradicts the 'dicit' of **16/1-sh** and the cancellation of *Gloria in excelsis deo* in the same place, which we should expect to be sung. The performance of the Gloria before **16/1** is also suggested by the fact that the angel's speech begins (**16/1–2**) with a paraphrase of the Gloria text. A sung performance here would create an anomaly (albeit one that occurs elsewhere) in that the Gloria was originally delivered by the heavenly host, not by the solo angel. On the other hand, the angel need not sing the Gloria at all, although he appears to say that he has (**16/7**): the SD's statement that he says the *Gloria in excelsis deo* could refer to the English version – see the similar case at **13/154–5**, above.

    A more basic anomaly is that in the speeches that follow (**16/14–61**) the shepherds do not mention the angel's words but discuss instead the bright light and various prophecies that it brings to mind. This would suggest that the singing of the Gloria at **16/61+sd** should indeed follow the shepherds' discussion of the prophecies in **16/14–61**, and that the Angel's first speech, lines **1–13**, originally came later still, perhaps immediately after that SD.

This opening speech seems to result from an unsuccessful scribal reordering, then. It does not entirely make sense as it stands, and some directorial intervention is needed. For our present purpose, it will be much more useful to propose an original order in which the Gloria is given a proper context.

The direction for the singing of *Gloria in excelsis deo* by the heavenly host at **16/61+sd** gives the clue: this not only follows the biblical narrative but is also consonant with the description of the play in the proclamation (see **Banns/ 191–6**, above, where it is clear that several angels should sing the Gloria). The cancelled *incipit* at the beginning of the play seems to be an aborted attempt to relocate the SD when its associated speech was relocated. Strictly, the biblical narrative requires lines **3–4** to be spoken before the heavenly host sings the Gloria, so the play's first stanza may have been recast quite radically.

If this is broadly correct, the play originally started with the current line **14**, which begins a discussion of the light in the skies and the prophecies that it brings to mind (see I, 257). This section ends at line 61. The angels then sang *Gloria in excelsis deo*, still correctly cued at **16/61+sd**, and then the angel spoke the English paraphrase, now lines **1–13**.[15] The cancelled 'Gloria in excelsis deo [cantent]' before the present line **1** is thus the correct cue for that speech, removed during the incomplete editorial process. At the end of the angel's speech the shepherds discussed the music, the text, and the angel's words, starting at line **62**. This discussion is copied in misplaced sections labelled by the scribe A, B and C, indicative of the unsuccessful editorial reordering of the material.

16/30   TERCIUS PASTOR   Thow I make lyty[l] noyse

Not a reference to music: 'although I am a quiet man'.

16/62–73   The shepherds' discussion of the Gloria sung by several angels at **61+sd**. Each of them uses the word 'song' as a noun or verb in speaking of the Gloria. According to the First Shepherd it was a 'wondyr note' and they sang 'gle glo glory' (**16/62, 65**); the Second Shepherd says that it was 'gle glo glas glum' (**16/69**), which is surely a parody on declining a Latin noun; the Third Shepherd settles the question with 'glory' (**16/70**).

---

[15] This speech does not follow the order of the biblical narrative, but its order is confirmed by the Third Shepherd at **16/70–73**.

16/82–9   SECUNDUS PASTOR   Lete us folwe with all oure myght.
With songe and myrth we xul us dyght,
And wurchep with joye þat wurthy wyght
þat lord is of mankynne.
Lete us go forthe fast on hye
And honowre þat babe wurthylye,
With merthe, songe and melodye.
Haue do! þis songe begynne.

The Second Shepherd's suggestion that they travel to Bethlehem to see the Christ-child associates first song, mirth, worship and joy (**16/83–4**), and then mirth, song and melody (**16/88**). The song obviously takes place at the end of this speech (**16/89+**), where there is in fact a MD for it. While the text expresses an intention to walk singing to Bethlehem, however, the MD requires them to sing *in situ* and only then to go in search of the Child. See below, also, under **16/152–4**.

16/152–4   In the last speech of the play Mary refers to the shepherds' homage and to their singing. This may mean that they sang as they walked to Bethlehem (contrary to **16/89+md**) and were still singing when they arrived; or that they sang another song while they were at the stable; or that we are to suppose that Mary heard their singing from a distance. There is no evidence for the second of these; and as there is really nothing to choose between the first and last, the question must be resolved according to the director's staging of the episode.

17[absit]

18 The Magi
18/19–20   [HERODES REX]   3e mynstrell, of myrth blowe up a good blast
Whyll I go to chawmere and chaunge myn array.

Very little music is required by text references without dramatic directions being given as well, although in some cases the directions are later additions. This is the first of three text references to music at Herod's court, the others being **20/153–4** and **20/231–2**. Only the last has a SD.

(iii) The Purification Pageant

19 The Purification
No references to music, despite Simeon's comment that it is a 'mery tyme' and Anna's reference to the 'myrth' that Simeon is making (**19/59–60 , 62**).

(i) Pageants from the Original Cycle

20 *The Slaughter of the Innocents*
20/65–8 SECUNDUS MILES   For swerdys sharpe
                            As an harpe
                            Quenys xul karpe
                            And of sorwe synge!

It is not clear to me in what sense this simile would be understood c. 1500: see I, 49–50.

20/153–4 [SENESCALLUS] Now blowe up, mynstrall, with all ȝoure myght!
                           þe servyse comyth in sone.

20/231–2 [HERODES REX] þerfore, menstrell, rownd abowte,
                            Blowe up a mery fytt!

For these two passages see above, under **18/19–20**.

20/244–5 [DIABOLUS] Of oure myrthis now xal ȝe se
                           And evyr synge Welawey!

Note the nature of the perversion of heavenly mirth: it results not in the joyful singing of the mirthful person but in someone else metaphorically singing sadly.

21 *Christ and the Doctors*
21/11 'Swete musyke' is among the accomplishments of the two doctors in the Temple. This is part of a list that includes the whole of the liberal arts as well as other, less important, subjects, so that Music would be conspicuous by its absence: but we should surely take this as an indication that the doctors have their hearts in the right place.

22 *The Baptism*
No references to music: in the context of play **1** and elsewhere, however, John the Baptist's description of Heaven as a place of 'merthe, joye and glee' with the angels would almost certainly bring music to mind (**22/18–22**).

23 *The Parliament of Hell; the Temptation*
23/195 [SATAN]   For sorwe I lete a crakke

An allusion to the cracking of a fart, occasioned by Satan's failure to tempt Christ: see I, 206, and above, under play **1**.

24 **The Woman Taken in Adultery**
25 **The Raising of Lazarus**
No references to music.

(iv) Passion play I

26 *Prologues of Satan and John the Baptist; the Conspiracy, and the Entry into Jerusalem*
26/8 [DEMON] þat he xal syng wellaway . ever in peynes felle.

26/450–1 PRIMUS CIVES Now blyssyd he be þat in oure lordys name
To us in any wyse wole resorte.

A translation of 'Benedictus qui venit in nomine domini'. The citizens have prepared to greet Christ on his entry into Jerusalem: this is the opening of a four-line speech before the SD for the singing of *Gloria laus*. Although no singing is mentioned in **450–3**, that of the SD following is clearly in line with the context.

27 *The Last Supper; the Conspiracy with Judas*
27/204 [JHESUS] Off mercy is here mornyng songe.

Metaphorical usage.
28 *The Betrayal*
28/1034 [JHESU] And herd me preche bothe lowd and lowe

Metaphorical usage.

(v) Passion play II

29 *Herod: the Trial before Annas and Cayphas*
No references to music.

30 *The Death of Judas; the Trials before Pilate and Herod*
30/419–20 [REX HEROWDE] Spare not, but telle me now . on hey
How þu canst þiself . excuse.

'On hey' [high] presumably has the meaning 'out loud' here, but it has no musical connotations.

31   *Satan and Pilate's Wife; the Second Trial before Pilate*
32   *The Procession to Calvary; the Crucifixion*
33   *The Harrowing of Hell (1)*
34   *The Burial; the Guarding of the Sepulchre*
No references to music.

(i) Pageants from the Original Cycle

35   *The Harrowing of Hell (2), and Christ's Appearance to Mary; Pilate and the Soldiers*
35/72+sd   Music is notably absent at the Resurrection here, but it may have been considered unnecessary to specify something that was an established convention. However, the references to the Resurrection in the next play (36/106–7 and 36/118) do specifically mention the angel's speech but not his singing. The omission of music from the text of this scene seems to reflect the true state of affairs, therefore.

36   *The Announcement to the Three Marys; Peter and John at the Sepulchre*
See above, under play 35.

37   *The Appearance to Mary Magdalene*
38   *Cleophas and Luke; the Appearance to Thomas*
No references to music.

39   *The Ascension, and the Selection of Matthias*
39/46–7   [JHESUS]   With myrthe and melody and aungell songe
                              Now I stey streyte from 3ow to hevyn.
Spector places a stop after 'songe', so that line 46 belongs with the previous clause. Associating that line with the following one shows that the song covers the Ascension, a matter that is confirmed by the SD following.

40   *Pentecost*
No references to music.

(vi) The Assumption Play

41   *The Assumption of Mary*
41/116   ANGELUS ij   For qwyche message injoyeth the hefnely consorcyte.

Although 'consorcyte' need not imply a consort in the musical sense, this group of angels is presumably responsible for the 'playing of harps' as the first angel descends to Mary in 116+sd.

41/316–17 [DOMINUS]   ... I wyl ben here redy,
                          Wyth the hefnely quer yowre dirige to rede

This line is followed by the Latin versicles of lines **318–29**. The word 'rede' does not necessarily exclude singing here.

41/368 [PAULUS]   Seyng oure observaunce . wyth devouth sound.

This is followed by the opening of Psalm 103 (lines **369–270**. 'Seyng' seems to exclude singing, but see below.

41/371–2 EPISCOPUS   ... what noyse is all this?
                     The erthe and the eyer . is ful of melodye!
                     I herde neuyr er . swyche a noyse now, iwys.

Probably 'noyse' is intended here in the non-musical sense, the bishop and princes being opposed to the apostles: but the audience may well have been aware of the pun occasioned by the musical meaning, brought home by the conversion of two of the princes later in the play.

41/376 PRIMUS PRINCEPS   ... hougely they crye!

41/381 [SECUNDUS PRINCEPS]   But sweche another noyse . herd I neuyr er.

41/387 [TERCIUS PRINCEPS]   And makyn alle this merthe ...

Although 'mirth' is here a metaphor for music, it refers to actual sounds.

41/411 [SECUNDUS PRINCEPS]   I here here noyse . ...

41/455 [JOHANNES]   Now god blysse this body . and we oure synge make.

Immediately following the Latin lines at **453–4**: the SD that follows gives information about the blessing. The 'synge' is the sign of the Cross, made in blessing the body.

41/488–9 SECUNDUS DEMON   Go we now, helle houndis, ye crye:
                      Sere Sathan may heryn oure son!

Not a musical reference, apparently: the implication is that the demons make a dreadful noise (in the modern sense).

41/495 ANGELI   Ya, for yowre hye mercy, lord . al hefne makyth melode.

The SD that follows makes no mention of music, but it is clear from this reference that there is angelic singing.

41/510–11   [DOMINUS] Arys now, my dowe . my nehebour and my swete
frende,
               Tabernacle of joye . vessel of lyf . hefnely temple to reyn.

This is a translation of *Surge propera mea* as it appears in **York 45**:
    Surge propera mea, columba mea, tabernaculum glorie, vasculum vite,
    templum celeste.
It is possible, then, that a setting of the Latin text was sung after the soul's return to Mary's body at **508+sd**.

41/528   MICHAEL For this holy assumpcyon alle hefne makyth melody.

The last line of the play, and a clear indication of a musical tableau to end. The Latin *incipit* that follows, 'Deo gracias', which is in a different hand, may identify the work to be sung but is more likely an expression of thanksgiving for the end of the play.

(i) Pageant from the Original Cycle

42 *Judgement Day*

42/1–2   See 2.4: the Last Trump has already sounded at the very start of the pageant.

42/29   [OMNES RESURGENTES]   Now may oure songe be weleaway

42/55–6   [PETRUS] Com on and sytt on goddys ryght syde
                     Where myrthe and melody nevyr may mys.

42/65   [DEUS]   To myrth and joye welcum ȝe be.

This last is not a musical reference as it stands, but it strengthens the connection between mirth and music (see also the comments on play **1**, above).

2.4   Latin and the liturgy

Before discussing the plays one by one, it will again be useful to say something about two of the constituent dramas from which the cycle is constructed.

In the pageants from the protocycle, the amount of Latin accords well with the assumption that they were originally part of a civic cycle. The scribe has generally copied Latin lines, whether references or liturgical texts, in the same script as the rest of the text. Most examples, being integral with the rest of the spoken text and written in the same script, were apparently meant to be spoken; it is certainly hard to imagine them being sung, and there is no reason to think that they were. Generally, these Latin tags are not such as to tax the audience: even those who knew no Latin at all would not be offended at such short quotations, which would be known to anyone hearing scriptural readings regularly; and in any case explanatory translations are provided for most of them.[16] Such declamations, with explanation afterwards, are consonant with the rather outgoing spectacular effect of much civic drama.

The line that begins the plays (1/1–) raises the opposite question: are these Latin lines to be heard at all? Here the answer is surely 'yes'; but in play 6 the question is more difficult, and it is possible that, like many such lines in the Chester cycle (Lumiansky and Mills *Essays*, 101–2), there are the alternative possibilities of speaking the lines or retaining them simply as literary references. Of the Latin in play 6, the first line (6/48+lat) seems unsuitable for speech.[17] The rest, being the Ten Commandments themselves, and short, might well be spoken: but, on the other hand, the presence of numerals instead of paragraph marks, and the fact that the texts are underlined, suggests that they were intended as references.

It is tempting to invoke a parallel with the gradual psalms in play 9, but we must reject the assumptions that lie behind such a procedure. It is also tempting to see a parallel with the litany-like repetitions of the Latin line ending the stanzas of Thomas's last speech in play 37: and although the parallel here is obviously tenuous, the idea of a Latin line emphasising the structure of a major speech is clearly relevant. In this respect, plays 6 and 37 stand out among the pageant-plays of this collection.

The fact that the Ten Commandments in play 6 are underlined as if SDs or SHs does not necessarily invalidate the possibility of their being spoken. Several of the plays end with an 'Amen' which is similarly underlined. In all such cases the Amen is necessary as a response to the final speech of the play – indeed, it is suitable to elicit the response from the audience, too – and should obviously be spoken.[18] The difference is that the 'Amen' is spoken by other people, whereas

---

[16] In this respect it is notable that the Banns use no Latin at all. Their purpose was to advertise and to persuade people to come, and they would repel members of the potential audience if any part were less than completely comprehensible.

[17] This includes the reference itself, something that we now expect only at the start of a sermon. However, see my comments on **Chester 22** in I, 81 and n. 189.

[18] See I, 371–3. In no case is there any indication that the Amen should be sung, however.

the Latin lines at issue here are apparently to be spoken by the character named in the previous SH.

In the Marian Group, as already noted, the liturgical items seem not to have been sung originally, but spoken. The evidence is however a little ambiguous and seems likely to have become so through changes made in favour of music. In this section more of this evidence will be presented.

In the play-by-play examination that follows some consideration is given to the liturgical use of the various items of liturgical material. The immediate reason for this is purely practical. It is readily apparent that the different source-groups of the cycle do not always show the same liturgical face – that is, that the liturgy used by the dramatist is not always the same one. That being so, some identification is necessary before we can be certain that the correct piece is being sung (see especially the comments on plays **8** and **10**, below). Secondly, the liturgical use apparent in any play should tell us something about the education of the dramatist, and therefore, by implication, about the possible provenance of the relevant source-group.

(i) Pageants from the Original Cycle

1 *The Creation of Heaven, and the Fall of Lucifer*
1/1–   DEUS   Ego sum alpha et oo . principium et finis

This, the very first line of the cycle, is written in the normal script of the text. It is not the antiphon noted in 1.6 under **York 1**, which uses the wording 'primus et novissimus, initium et finis', and in any case there is no reason to think that the line should be sung.

1/39+sd   Tibi omnes angeli ... Dominus deus Sabaoth

Three text–phrases of the prose hymn *Te deum*.

2 *The Creation of the World, and the Fall of Man*
No Latin or liturgical content, other than notes on the earliest generations, from Adam to Noah, at the bottom of ff. 16v–18r.

3 *Cain and Abel*
3/62–91 and **122–6** Abel does not seem to use any standard form of words for his sacrifice, and Cain certainly does not.

4 *Noah*
A genealogy from Noah to Lot is written at the bottom of ff. 21r–22v.

4/105–6   [DEUS] Fecisse hominem nunc penitet me:
þat I made man sore doth me rewe.

Integral part of the stanza, which must be spoken.

4/253+sd   Mare vidit et fugit . jordanis conuersus est retrorsum.
Non nobis domine non nobis . sed nomini tuo da gloriam.

The second of these verses exists as an Alleluia verse in the Beneventan Gradual, but otherwise I can find neither as a liturgical item. They are, respectively, Psalm 113a/3 and Psalm 113b/1 (AV 114/3, 115/1).

5 Abraham and Isaac
5/177–84   Abraham's final preparations for the sacrifice of Isaac include no verbal formula of sacrifice.

5/193–200   Abraham's thanksgiving appears to use no liturgical forms.

6 Moses
6/48+lat   Custodi precepta domini dei tui . deuteronomini vj^{to}

The next line, 'The comaundment of þi lord god, man, loke þu kepe' (**6/49**), translates this line (Deuteronomy 6/17a), which appears between stanzas, an integral part of neither although written in the normal text script. It is possible that the dramatist intended a fuller declaimed or sung quotation, of which this is the *incipit*. But the evidence is for this being a reference, not a text to be heard by the audience: the naming of the sixth chapter of Deuteronomy; the absence of a paragraph mark (this is not conclusive, but certainly suggestive: cf. the examples in play **4**, above, for instance); and the fact that the entire line is underlined in red, the scribe's usual treatment of the prescriptive (non-textual) parts of a direction.

6/66, 82, 98, 114, 130, 138, 146, 154, 162, 170   The Ten Commandments in Latin follow these cue lines, and are themselves followed by spoken glosses. The Latin lines are written in the same script as the text, although none of them is part of a stanza. All are underlined in the manner of SDs, and each is prefaced by a marginal numeral in place of a paragraph mark, followed by the phrase 'Primum [Secundum, etc.] mandatum'.

The wording of these *incipits* is sometimes the same as that of the Vulgate version of Exodus 20, and sometimes quite different. If the dramatist was quoting the Vulgate he was doing so from memory. The Second Commandment (graven images) is missing altogether, while the Tenth is divided into two. In some cases the incipit given is incomplete, providing only the merest mnemonic for the whole text. Only in the Tenth Commandment does the phrase 'et cetera' appear at the end of the incipit, and this is in fact the one commandment where the end is given.[19]

7 *Jesse Root*

7/9–10 [YSAIAS]   Wherefore I sey quod virgo concipiet
                   Et pariet filium, nomen Emanuel

Isaiah 7/14b: 'Ecce virgo concipiet, et pariet filium, et vocabitur nomen ejus Emmanuel'. The text appears as a liturgical item in several places,[20] but not with the 'quod ...' wording. The play text is a somewhat modified version, presumably for the sake of the scansion and rhymes. These lines are an integral part of the stanza that they begin, and must certainly be heard: but they are presumably spoken, not sung. The following lines do not give a translation.

7/17–18   RADIX JESSE Egredietur virga de radice Jesse,
                   Et flos de radice eius ascendet.

Isaiah 11/1: 'Et egredietur ... ascendet'. The text as found in the play – i.e. without the initial 'Et' – occurs in the Sarum use as an antiphon in the Advent season.[21] In the play this text is an integral part of the stanza, and must be spoken, not sung: but it seems likely that it was the liturgical version that the dramatist remembered.

(ii) Plays from the Marian Group

8 *Joachim and Anna*

The liturgical content of this play is not immediately recognisable as a Christian office or sacrament. One reason for this is that the offerings at the centre of the play's ceremonial – the sacrifice of two turtle-doves in the case of Joachim and Anne – have no precise parallel in Christian worship, although there are plenty of analogues.

8/25   [CONTEMPLACIO]   Amen for Charyte

---

[19] In **Towneley 18** the same happens to the ninth and tenth commandments, and the first two are those quoted by Christ. A.C. Cawley ('Medieval Drama and Didacticism', 9–10) suggested that the presentation of the Ten Commandments in the northern plays of Christ and the Doctors may derive from the apocryphal *Gospel of Thomas*, and obviously the same may be true of **N-Town 6**.

[20] In the Sarum use it occurs as an antiphon, as a responsory and as a communion: see Bryden and Hughes *Index*, 149; AS, plates 13, c and E; and GS, 6, 12 and 184.

[21] Bryden and Hughes *Index*, 155; AS, 33 and k, wrongly listed as 'Egredietur virgo' in the index to AS. The text appears as a gradual and responsory in the Roman rite, and the responsory also in the monastic use of Lucca.

Integral with the stanza, and must be spoken.

8/26–9   YSAKAR The prestys of god offre sote ensens
                     Vnto here god, and þerfore they be holy.
                     We þat mynistere here in goddys presens,
                     In vs xuld be fownd no maner of foly.

This is a free translation of the Offertory for Corpus Christi:[22]

> Sacerdotes Domini incensum et panes offerunt Deo:
> et ideo sancti erunt Deo suo, et non polluent nomen ejus, alleluia.

It is therefore possible, especially in view of the offerings made later in the play, that the entrance of Ysakar and his priests is a processional one with the singing of *Sacerdotes Domini*.

8/34–7   [YSAKAR] This we clepe festum Encenniorum,
                  þe newe fest . of which iij . in þe ȝere we exercyse.
                  Now all þe kyndredys to Jerusalem must cum
                  Into þe temple of god . here to do sacryfyse.

This seems to refer to the feast of the dedication of the Temple.[23]

8/40   [YSAKAR] We be regal sacerdocium ...

That is, the royal priesthood, of the order of Melchizedek (1 Peter 2/9, after Psalm 110/4 and elsewhere). There is no particular significance, for performance purposes, in the use of Latin.

8/97+sd The sequence *Benedicta sit beata trinitas* is found in the Sarum Use as the sequence for Trinity Sunday, but it also appears in the octave of the Feast of Pentecost and for a Nuptial Mass.[24] This play is not concerned with a marriage but with the Immaculate Conception, so a reference to the Holy Spirit was perhaps intended.

---

[22] Sandon VI, 9.

[23] Attwater *Catholic Encyclopaedic Dictionary*, under 'Encaenia'; also Psalm 29 (AV 30) and John 10/22.

[24] Trinity Sunday: Sandon VI, 2, and in a fifteenth-century missal of Norwich diocese, Lbl Add. MS 25588. Octave of Pentecost: thirteenth-century Crowland gradual, Lbl MS Egerton 3759. Nuptial Mass: BS II, 503, the Westminster Missal (see *Missale ad usum ecclesie Westmonasteriensis* iii: Henry Bradshaw Society 12 (1897), col. 1239); MPE, 30; and a fifteenth-century Lincoln pontifical, Cambridge University Library MS Mm.iii.21.

The censing of the altar, the offerings of the priests, and the invitation to the people to make their offerings do not follow events in the Mass, although the parallels would presumably be clear to the audience. They are, in any case, prepared for by the English version of *Sacerdotes Domini* (if not by the singing of the Latin piece) and by Isakar's explanation of the 'newe fest' (lines **34–7**, above).

8/110–16	[MINISTER][25]	Adjutorium nostrum in nomine domini
	CHORUS	Qui fecit celum et terram.
	MINISTER	Sit nomen domini benedictum
	CHORUS	Ex hoc nunc et usque in seculum.
	EPISCOPUS	Benedicat vos diuina majestas et vna deitas,
		+ Pater + et filius + et spiritus sanctus.
	CHORUS	Amen.

The responsorial performance of *Adjutorium nostrum* and the episcopal blessing *Benedicat vos divina* are found in the Sarum Manual after the nuptial mass (MPE, 25*, but not in MS, 59), although they do not seem to have been invariable. **109+md** turns it into a sung performance. The signs of the Cross in this blessing are written in red in the play text, as they would be in a liturgical source.[26]

| **8/172+sd** | Exultet celum laudibus . resultet terra gaudijs |
| | Archangelorum gloria sacra canunt solemnia |

This hymn appears in the Sarum Antiphoner,[27] as elsewhere, with 'Apostolorum' in the second line for N-Town's 'Archangelorum'. It is possible that N-Town (f. 40v) gives the whole of the first verse in order to specify a known variant version: but it seems more likely that 'Archangelorum' is stated precisely because it is a deviation from any normal text.

9 *The Presentation of Mary in the Temple*

9/69–73	[MARIA]	Now good fadyr . with þat fadyr ȝe me blysse.
	JOACHYM	In nomine patris et filij et spiritus sancti.
	MARIA	Amen . Now ȝe, good modyr.
	ANNE	In nomine patris et filij et spiritus sancti.
	MARIA	Amen.

25 The character of the Minister, apparently an assistant to the bishop, is specified in the SH for line **112** but has already appeared in **109+md**.

26 On f. 39v: see MDF 4, xviii. Perhaps this blessing implies that the actor playing the part of Isakar was a priest.

27 The hymn is in AS, 66, 67 and Q; see also LH, 270 and Wieland *Canterbury Hymnal*, 114.

Joachim and Anne use a common form of words for a blessing, presumably laying their hands on Mary's head as they say it. There is no reason to consider sung performance for these Latin lines, which are written in the normal text script.

9/105+, 109+, 113+, 117+, 121+, 125+, 129+, 133+, 137+, 141+, 145+, 149+, 153+, 157+

The Latin incipits of the 15 gradual psalms, Psalms 119–33 (AV 120–34) inclusive, written in a larger and more formal script: each has a large red initial. The pattern here is the reverse of the usual one: that is, the English comes first, with the Latin following. In each case the English takes the form of a 4-line introductory commentary on the psalm that follows, while the Latin is a single verse, not integrated with the rhyme-scheme.

Each Latin incipit corresponds to the first verse of the psalm as it would be recited or sung. (The division into verses is different in modern editions of the Vulgate Bible, but the N-Town divisions can be seen in Gutenberg's 42-line Bible).

It is curious that in the speech immediately following this passage Isakar remarks on the ability of a three-year-old child to ascend the steps to the Temple, calling it a 'mervelyous thynge' and an 'hey meracle' (9/162, 166), but does not mention her remarkable ability to recite the opening of each psalm in turn: in these circumstances, his omission of any comment on her *singing* of the psalms cannot be taken positively. On the other hand, in encouraging Mary to climb the steps Isakar has previously called on all present to say the relevant psalms (9/100–1):

> Every man þat thynk his lyf to amende,
> Þe fiftene psalmys . in memorye of þis mayde say.

It is not clear whether he requires the congregation to say the psalms at the time, or later in their private devotions. The direction at 101+ is not clear enough as to precisely what happens:

> Maria . et sic deinceps usque ad fine[m] xv^cim psalmorum.

The word 'deinceps' normally means 'successively', and so requires each psalm to be treated the same way as the one before. As the text simply gives Mary's four English lines followed by the one Latin line for each psalm, this is not helpful to us. The best suggestion I can make is that Mary declaim her lines in each case, after which all present say (or sing, to a normal psalm-chant) the first verse of each in Latin, as given.

9/216–17(+sd) The bishop's blessing, in standard wording. For the staging of this, see I, 371–2.

9/259+sd   Jhesu corona virginum

This hymn is set for the common of a virgin and martyr in the Sarum use.[28]

(i) and (ii) Composite Play

10   The Marriage of Mary and Joseph
This play, as noted before, is an amalgam of elements from an original pageant and sections of the Mary Play. Quotations in this section are designated (i) or (ii), accordingly. Parts of the marriage service are found in both pageant and Mary Play elements.

(ii) 10/94 [EPISCOPUS] Vovete et reddite . in scripture haue we

Psalm 75/12 (AV 76/11). The line is in normal text script and integral to the verse: it should be spoken.

(ii) 10/114–5(+md) [EPISCOPUS] Mekely eche man falle down on kne
                                                    And we xal begynne . Veni creator Spiritus.

This is followed by the MD for the singing of *Veni creator spiritus*, the hymn for Pentecost: the hymn is sung by all, kneeling. This performance of *Veni creator* is additional to the marriage service, and comes well before it in the play: its function is that of a prayer for guidance.

(ii) 10/175 JOSEPH   Benedicite ...

Integral part of the line, to be spoken.

(ii) 10/301 [EPISCOPUS] Now ȝelde we all preysyng to þe trenyte.

Followed by the MD for the singing of *Benedicta sit beata trinitas*. As noted under play **8**, this is a sequence, although it is not described as such here.

The next section of the play, lines **302–30**, is the marriage ceremony itself. The passage is discussed in I, 286–9. The Sarum and York versions can be found in the published manuals of those uses (MS, 47–9; MPE, 19*; MPE, 26–7). At the end of the service there is a rather informal declaration of the marriage:

---

[28] See BS II, 448; also Wieland *Canterbury Hymnal*, 131, and LH, 310–11.

(ii) **10/331** [EPISCOPUS] Here is þe holyest matremony þat evyr was in þis
werd!

It will be seen that the original pageant material consists only of the giving of the
ring, while the Mary Play element is the marriage vows. The play's changes to the
structure of the marriage service no doubt accommodated the dramatist's intention without making the service unrecognisable to the audience. The N-Town text,
although modified in accordance with the demands of metre and rhyme, retains
much of the actual wording of the English versions of the service.

(ii) **10/332–4** [EPISCOPUS] Þe hy3 names of oure lord we wole now syng hy
we all wole þis solempn dede record
devowtly . Alma chorus domini . nunc pangat nomina summi

Alma chorus domini is the sequence for a Nuptial Mass in the Sarum Use (MS,
52; MPE, 22*), and is given as such in a missal of Norwich Diocese, Cambridge University Library MS Ff.ii.31, which is dated 1397.

The nuptial mass is not included in British Library MS Egerton 3759 (a
Crowland gradual), and it is unfortunately lost from the thirteenth-century Ely
missal, Cambridge University Library MS Ii.iv.20. In a fifteenth-century
Norwich Diocese missal, British Library Add. MS 25588, however, *Alma
chorus domini* is set for the Mass of the Trinity on the day of a marriage. The
emphasis on the Trinity here is perhaps because of the dedication of Norwich
Cathedral: but in the context of play **10**, and specifically in view of the
'preysyng to þe trenyte' after line **301**, it may have been chosen for the specific
purpose here.

(ii) **10/342–3** EPISCOPUS He blysse 30w þat hath non hendyng
In nomine patris et filij et spiritus sancti.

A blessing using a standard wording.

(i) **10/383–95** Joachim and Anne do not use any set form of words for their
parental blessing.

(ii) **10/455** [MARIA] Benedixisti, domine, terram tuam

In normal text script, and an integral part of the verse: it must be spoken. The
line is the opening of Psalm 84 (AV 85), and identifies the particular part of
the psalter that Mary has reached in her reading. This psalm foretells the
Incarnation, and is here appropriate for that reason: but it also looks forward
to the use of the psalm in play **11** (see below).

The liturgical content of this play is primarily concerned with the marriage of Joseph and Mary: in particular, there are elements of both the marriage ceremony itself (mainly from the Mary Play, but partly also from the protocycle pageant) and the nuptial mass.

In respect of the latter, the question arises whether the two items are precisely appropriate and, if so, in the right position. *Benedicta sit beata trinitas* is, as noted under play 8, the sequence at a nuptial mass in the York Use. **301+md**, which pre-scribes the sequence, can hardly be intended to show a realistic position in the liturgy, since this would place the marriage itself after the sequence: whereas the normal order of events then as now was to have the Mass following the marriage. A further problem is that *Alma chorus domini*, sung in the play after the marriage – and therefore in the right position for the Mass – is set as the sequence for a nuptial mass in the Sarum Use (MS, 52; MPE, 22*).

In solving the problem of the mass items it does not help to postulate an error for the introit *Benedicta sit sancta trinitas*, since this, too, is part of the Mass, although earlier in the service. Because *Benedicta sit beata trinitas* is prescribed only marginally, while *Alma chorus domini* is given as part of the text, we should give precedence to the latter. It is fair to suppose that the liturgical use known to the dramatist set *Alma chorus domini* as the sequence for the nuptial mass, and there-fore that *Benedicta sit beata trinitas* appears in the play on account of a general appropriateness, not for its precise placing in the liturgy. It would also appear that **301+md** was added by someone other than the dramatist – someone, in fact, whose 'native' liturgical use was not that of the dramatist, and to whom *Benedicta sit beata trinitas* might come to mind as an appropriate liturgical item.

(ii) Play from the Marian Group

11   *The Parliament of Heaven; the Salutation and Conception*
11/48+   PATER   Propter miseriam inopum
                        Et gemitum pauperum
                        nunc exurgam.

Psalm 11/6a (AV 12), not a liturgical *incipit*: these lines are not integral to the text, and are written in the larger, more formal script. On the other hand they follow the SH 'Pater' and the lines immediately following are an English trans-lation. Thus they seem to be more than merely a reading reference and should probably be spoken.

11/85 [MISERICORDIA] Thu seyst . Veritas mea et Misericordia mea cum ipso

Psalm 88/25 (AV 89): in text script, integral to the verse, and evidently to be spoken.

11/187–8 [MISERICORDIA] Misericordia et Veritas obviauerunt sibi,
Justitia et Pax . osculate sunt.

Psalm 84/11 (AV 85): this psalm gave rise to the concept of the Daughters of God (and see above, under **10/455**). These lines are in normal text script, are integral to the text, and must certainly be spoken.

11/216+   Ave, gratia plena, Dominus tecum

Not integral to the text, and written in a larger, more formal script, with a red initial. The word 'Maria' occurs after 'Ave', but is cancelled. Block (*Ludus Coventriae*, 104, n. 2) suggested that this was to make the Latin conform to line **217**. It is however more likely to be the correction of a recognised error: the line as it now stands is the gospel version (Luke 1/28), and is also the incipit of an offertory (LU, 1379, but not in GS), the text of which – including as it does 'Benedicta tu in mulieribus' – corresponds to lines **217–18**. See also **13/150A– 153A**, below.

This offertory would be very suitable for a greeting sung by an archangel, who would have to be played by a professional singer. The lack of any indication of singing would however suggest that the line was spoken in the Mary Play, whatever might have been the case later.

11/340+   Aue Maria, gratia plena,
Dominus tecum . uirgo serena.

In normal text script. According to the SD associated with it, this text is that of a sequence. Dutka *Music*, 21, quotes the complete text of the sequence from BS II, 517.

(i) Pageant from the Original Cycle

12 Joseph's Trouble about Mary
12/160   JOSEPH   A, lord God, benedicite

12/215   [MARIA]   And gret me fayr, and seyd 'Aue'

These are in the normal text script, integral to the line, and to be spoken.

(ii) Play from the Marian Group

13 The Visit to Elizabeth
13/21   JOSEPH   Amen, amen, ...

No musical or liturgical significance.

13/26   [CONTEMPLACIO]   þei wer clepyd summi sacerdotes ...

13/69   [MARIA]   Gabryel come and seyde to me 'Ave'

These two quotations are in normal text script and integral to the verse: they have no musical significance.

13/81–126   The *Magnificat* and doxology are said in pairs of lines antiphonally, the Latin by Mary and its translation by Elizabeth: the whole Latin text is in larger, more formal script, while the translation is in the normal text script. The SHs make it clear that the Latin is heard, and Mary also states her intention to 'begynne' the 'holy psalme' (line **81**). Although 'begin' in this context, as a translation of *incipiat*, might imply singing, it evidently does not do so here, for in line **127** Mary states that the psalm has been *said* between them.

13/127–30   MARIA   This psalme of prophesye seyd betwen vs tweyn,
　　　　　　　In hefne it is wretyn with aungellys hond,
　　　　　　　Evyr to be songe . and also to be seyn
　　　　　　　Euery day amonge us at oure evesong.

Note the stated distinction between heavenly singing and earthly recitation. 'Evensong' was the English name for Vespers.[29]

13/150A–153A   CONTEMPLACIO   Lystenyth, sovereynys, here is a conclusyon.
　　　　　　　How þe Aue was mad . here is lernyd vs:
　　　　　　　þe aungel seyd . 'Ave, gratia plena. Dominus tecum,
　　　　　　　Benedicta tu in mulieribus'.

Note the 'seyd'. This text corresponds to the corrected version of **11/216+lat** (see above), and therefore to the translation in the two lines following it. The Latin words are in the larger, more formal script.

13/154A–155A   [CONTEMPLACIO]   Elizabeth seyd . 'et benedictus
　　　　　　　Fructus uentris tui' . Thus þe chirch addyd 'Maria' and 'Jhesus' her.

This refers to **13/59**, where Elizabeth speaks the English translation of this phrase: she nowhere speaks the Latin. The Latin words are again in the larger, more formal script, as are the names 'Maria' and 'Jhesus'. Line **155A** refers to the liturgical text which adds the two names – 'Ave Maria gratia plena, domi-

---

[29] Attwater *Catholic Encyclopaedic Dictionary*, under 'Evensong'.

nus tecum, benedicta tu in mulieribus: et benedictus fructus ventris tui Jesus', which is the first half of an antiphon (LU, 1861) that I have not found in the Sarum use. A shorter antiphon using the same chant does not include the word 'Jesus'.

13/171A–172A [CONTEMPLACIO] They mad 'Benedictus' . them beforn.
And so 'Magnificat' . and . 'Benedictus'

The Latin titles are all in the larger, more formal hand, but they are obviously to be spoken as part of the verse.

13/184A–185A [CONTEMPLACIO] With 'Aue' we begunne and 'Aue' is oure
conclusyon:
'Ave regina celorum' to our Lady we synge.

The Latin incipit – but not the Aves in line **184A** – is in the larger, more formal script. *Ave regina celorum* is one of the vespers antiphons for the Virgin: see AS, 529 and LU, 274 (which shows some differences); also 1.4, above, under **York 44/194+sd**.

(i) Pageants from the Original Cycle

14 *The Trial of Mary and Joseph*
At the bottom of the first page of this play (f. 74v) is a note of two calendar entries: of 14 kal. aprilis (19 March) for the Translation of St Mary Magdalene and for St Joseph, spouse of the Blessed Virgin; and of 10 kal. aprilis (23 March) for the creation of Adam (*Adam creatus est*). The hand is apparently the formal script of the main scribe.

It is hard to say what significance should be attached to these notes: nor is it possible to say whether the main scribe copied them from his exemplar or, if so, whether from the exemplar of the Mary Play or that of the protocycle.

14/405+   explicit cum gaudio, amen

In darker ink, but possibly in the hand of the main scribe (although Spector says not). This is at the end of the play, and is apparently a pious thanksgiving by the dramatist or a previous scribe: it does not suggest participation by the audience and cast.

15 *The Nativity*
15/321 [JOSEPH] God þat best may, grawnt ȝow his grace. Amen.

The Amen is extra-stanzaic. This is a 'blessing' ending to the play, in which the cast and audience could be expected to respond with the Amen.

16 The Shepherds
16/1–[sd], 61+sd   Gloria in excelsis deo

The relationship between the two SDs, and between these and the text, is discussed in 2.3, above. This is clearly the usual item, the verse of the first responsory at Christmas matins.

16/89+md   Stella celi extirpauit

This was one of several Mary-antiphons in use in the late fifteenth and early sixteenth centuries: but it never held a regular place in the service-books, and no single tune was exclusively associated with it (Bent 'Fragments', 145–7). Indeed, the main documentation on it refers to collegiate performance, specifically in Oxford (Harrison *Music in Medieval Britain*, 85, 88). The sources and tunes of *Stella celi extirpavit* are discussed by Bent ('Fragments', 147), as is an incomplete polyphonic setting of c. 1450 in Oxford, Christ Church, MS Okes 253 (*ibid.*, 144, 149, and Plate III). The text is printed by Dutka (*Music*, 37–8). There is no indication in this play that the shepherds would sing polyphony, and we should assume a plainsong performance.

The text is in fact a prayer for protection against plague. Granted that such a prayer was always necessary at the time, it is not at all clear why it should be considered appropriate in a shepherds' play.

16/154+lat   Amen

This is an appropriate response to what is very nearly a 'blessing' ending, and is presumably to be said by all the cast.

17   [absit]

18 The Magi
No relevant material.

(iii) The Purification Pageant

19 The Purification
19/18   [SYMEON JUSTUS]   To sancta sanctorum . wyl I go

There seems no strong reason for Simeon to say this rather than 'holy of holies', except that the extra, unwanted, syllable 'the' would spoil the verse: but the Latin may help to establish his status as a priest.

19/115–16   [JOSEPH]   Whereffore we xal take us betwene
Dowys and turtelys for sacrefyce.

For the relationship between this play and the ceremony of Purification, see I,
section 7.4.

19/136+   Suscepimus deus misericordiam tuam

In the larger and more formal script, with a red initial. The text is Psalm
47/10 (AV 48/9), 'We wait for thy loving-kindness, O God' (Psalter version).
Lines **137–44** are a paraphrase of verse 10 and all but the last part of verse
11:
Suscepimus, Deus, misericordiam tuam in medio templi
tui: secundum nomen tuum, Deus, ita et laus tua in fines
terrae.
Lines **145–6** do not obviously paraphrase the remainder of v. 11.
   In the Latin liturgy the words of **136+lat** are the *incipit* of the following
pieces:

(a) Antiphon for matins at the Nativity (LU, 378; WA, 27 and 53):
Suscepimus, Deus, misericordiam tuam in medio templi tui.
Syllabic chant, range f–c′, c-clef.

(b) Introit, Feast of the Purification (Sandon VI, 35, and GS, 149 and j):
Suscepimus, Deus, misericordiam tuam in medio templi tui: secundum
nomen tuum, Deus, ita et laus tua in fines terrae: justicia plena est
dextera tua.
Syllabic/neumatic chant, range c–e′, c-clef.

(c) Gradual, Feast of the Purification (GS, j; LU, 1362; GR, 433):
Suscepimus, Deus, misericordiam tuam in medio templi tui: secundum
nomen tuum, Domine, ita et laus tua in fines terrae.
[The Roman use has 'Deus' for 'Domine']
Neumatic chant, range c–f′, c-clef.

Of these, (a) is too short, and (b) fits only if lines **145–6** are regarded as a
very loose paraphrase of 'justicia ... tua'; otherwise, (c) is the piece intended,
with lines **145–6** making a more general reference to the Incarnation. Note that
(b) and (c) are both set for the Purification.
   The Latin line may be only an unheard reference, but in view of the following paraphrase this seems unlikely. I favour the singing of a liturgical item
– probably the gradual, as noted above – by the play's singers of the temple.

19/146+sd   Nunc dimittis seruum tuum domine . et cetera

The direction makes it clear that *Nunc dimittis* is sung complete, but not (as in other Purification plays) by Simeon. The fact that the whole 'psalm' is sung precludes the possibility of the responsory, antiphon or antiphon verse being intended here. On the other hand there is no mention of the canticle being sung under an antiphon, nor is the lesser doxology included in the rather loose English paraphrase that occurs immediately afterwards (lines **147–54**). Thus the canticle seems to be performed in the manner of a tract.

The text is sung as a tract on the Feast of the Purification,[30] and this seems the most likely solution for the performance of the canticle here. It is however worth noting that in two late missals of Norwich Diocese (Cambridge, University Library MS Ff.ii.31, dated 1397, and London, British Library Add. MS 25588, fifteenth century) *Nunc dimittis* is prescribed to be said *privatim*. Furthermore, the thirteenth- or fourteenth-century Crowland gradual London, British Library MS Egerton 3759 prescribes the tract *Gaude Maria* for the Feast of the Purification and that use can positively be rejected. This may also cast doubt on other Benedictine houses as possible homes of this part of the cycle: and we see also that not every church in Norwich diocese could be its home.

For the relationship between play **19** and the liturgy, see I, section 7.4.

(i) Pageants from the Original Cycle

20 *The Slaughter of the Innocents, and the Death of Herod*
No relevant material.

21 *Christ and the Doctors*
In this play the Latin is integrated with the verse, often with a following translation, paraphrase or gloss. Latin is written in the same script as the English text.

21/1–4   PRIMUS DOCTOR   Scripture sacre esse dinoscimur doctos,
                           We to . bere þe belle of all manere clergyse.
             ijus DOCTOR   Velud rosa omnium florum flos,
                           Lyke onto us was nevyr clerke so wyse.

The Latin helps to characterise the doctors immediately.

21/33–4   JHESUS Omnis sciencia a domino deo est:
                           Al wytt and wysdam, of god it is lent.
21/181–2   [JHESUS] Ysaye seyd þus . Ecce virgo,
                           A mayd xal conceyve in clennes a chylde

---

[30] LU, 1363; GR, 434; GS, k gives a non-Sarum example.

The prophecy of Isaiah 7/14.

21/288+   The 'Amen' at the end of the play is extra-stanzaic: the First Doctor's speech is a prayer for salvation for those present, and the response should be said by all.

22 *The Baptism*
22/1   [JOHANNES]   Ecce vox clamantes in deserto

With translation, and integrated in the speech. This is part of the Gospel narrative of John the Baptist, in the same script as the rest of the (interpolated) leaf.

22/14–15, 17, 19, 21   These quotations follow the pattern of **22/1**.

22/40   [JOHANNES]   Ecce Agnus dei qui tollit peccata mundi

This follows the horizontal line separating **39+sd** from John's speech and is in the same script as the English text. It therefore looks like the first line of the stanza, and is given a rhyme-bracket. However, it is not part of the stanza. In view of the other examples in this play I feel that it should be spoken, but the matter is not clear.

23 *The Parliament of Hell, and the Temptation*
23/195+sd   Gloria tibi domine

This is the opening of a common hymn-doxology (the second line varies according to the occasion). The version sung on the Feast of the Transfiguration is given in AM, 997:

> Gloria tibi Domine
> Qui apparuisti hodie
> Cum Patre et Sancto Spiritu
> In sempiterne secula.

This is not suitable, however, for Christ would hardly address himself in this way. Dutka refers to the doxology (BS 1/cccxix, lxxii; 2/331, 234, 235), but her first choice is the response to the announcement of the Gospel (MS, 38).[31] This is more credible, and adds to the staging implied by **23/195+sd**: while the singing angels 'minister to him', Christ responds 'Gloria tibi, Domine' to their ministrations, as appropriate. Christ's following speech, starting at line **196**,

---

31 Dutka *Music*, 30.

does not seem to paraphrase any relevant text.

23/221 The final 'Amen' is extra-stanzaic and should presumably be said by all present as a response to the 'blessing' ending.

24 *The Woman Taken in Adultery*

24/1 The quotation 'Nolo mortem peccatoris' is probably derived ultimately from Ezechiel 33/11: it is found in the antiphon *Vivo ego, dicit Dominus* (AS, 158) and the responsory *Tribularer si nescirem* (AS, 154). A related text appears in the verse *Non vult Dominus* of the responsory *Derelinquat impius*, apparently not in the Sarum use.[32]

The text is written on the same line as the play heading, but is integral to the verse – the line is needed for the rhyme-scheme – and must be spoken by Jesus, as Spector sets it out.

24/296 The 'Amen' which ends the play is extra-stanzaic: it should be spoken by all present as a response to the last speech.

25 *The Raising of Lazarus*
No relevant material.

(iv) Passion Play I

26 *Prologues of Satan and John the Baptist; the Conspiracy, and the Entry into Jerusalem*
26/48 [DEMON] Quia in inferno nulla est redemptio

As elsewhere, a demon can quote Latin when it is to his advantage to do so. For the text, see BS 2/278 and 15.4, below, under **Castle 3096–7**. Integral with the verse, and to be spoken.

26/450–1 i^us CIUES Now blyssyd he be þat in oure lordys name
To us in any wyse wole resorte.

We should perhaps expect the singing of *Benedictus qui venit* here, but apparently the citizens only say this rather free English version. This may be because it refers to the Gospel of Palm Sunday, which is recited. See I, 268–9, and Sandon IV, 10: in the Palm Sunday procession the subsidiary procession (i.e. Christ and his disciples) approaches the main procession at the words 'Benedictus qui venit in nomine Domini' at the end of the Gospel reading.

---

[32] For help with this text I am grateful to Ike de Loos and others, and especially to David Hiley, who provided more information than I have been able to include here.

26/453+sd *Gloria laus* is sung by the children. This is the hymn *Gloria laus et honor* sung during the Palm Sunday procession.[33] In this, perhaps the most liturgical of the Entry plays, the singing of *Gloria laus et honor* while the children throw flowers down is the central liturgical event. The liturgical content is considerably telescoped at this point of the play, however: in the Sarum use the genuflexion of **26/453+sd** occurs during the singing of *Salve quem Jesum*, and *Gloria laus* is sung at the next station (Sandon IV, 9–10 and 14).

27   *The Last Supper; the Conspiracy with Judas*
27/392   [JHESU] Seyng . 'Ecce agnus dey'.

Integral to the verse: Christ is quoting the words of John the Baptist heard at **22/40** (see above).

27/449–50   [JHESU] This is my body, flesch and blode,
                             Þat for þe xal dey upon þe rode.

27/490–1   [JHESU] Þis is my blood þat for mannys synne
                            Outh of myn herte it xal renne.

The words of distribution at Mass, taken from the Gospel narratives: both paraphrases are in normal text script.

27/511+sd, 515+sd, 527+sd The three directions for the washing of the apostles' feet. Note the word 'roberych' (rubric) in the second, referring to the first.
       On the liturgical content of this play, see I, section 7.5.

28   *The Betrayal*
28/61–2   [ANGELUS] Þis chalys ys þi blood, þis bred is þi body,
                              For mannys synne evyr offeryd xal be.

The angel in effect administers Communion to Jesus.

The Procession of Saints
28p/5   2 DOCTOR   A fily altissimi . clepyd by eternalyte

'Son of the Most High'. Part of Gabriel's salutation at the Annunciation, 'Hic erit magnus, et Filius Altissimi vocabitur': Luke 1/32. Apparently not part of a liturgical item: integral with the verse, and to be spoken.

---

[33] See I, 269 ff, and the edition in Sandon IV, 14; also GS, 83 and PS(P), 46r–v.

28p/7   [2 DOCTOR] And we prey þe . spiritus paraclyte

Integral to the verse, and to be spoken.

(v) Passion Play II

29 Herod; the Trial before Annas and Cayphas
30 The Death of Judas; the Trials before Pilate and Herod
No relevant material.

31 Satan and Pilate's Wife; the Second Trial before Pilate
31/110–13   ijus DOCTOR   Jesus xal on þe cros be don!
                           Crucifigatur, we crye echon!
                   PYLAT   Serys, what hath Jesus don amys?
                   POPULUS CLAMABIT   Crucifigatur . we sey atonys.

The cry of the crowd would be well known from the Passion readings of Holy Week. This wording is from Matthew 27/23: the other three evangelists all give 'crucifige eum'.

32 The Procession to Calvary, and the Crucifixion
32/129   JHESUS   Amen, amen . þu art ful wyse.

Integral with the verse, and to be spoken: 'Truly, truly'.[34]

32/183   [JHESUS]   Heloy . Heloy . lamazabathany?

Integral with the verse, and to be spoken. Again, this Aramaic speech would be well known from the Passion readings: the phrase is transmitted by Matthew and Mark only.[35]
   The script is that of the main text, but very slightly larger. Lines **184–5** are a paraphrase, with the former line giving the rhyme with 'lamazabathany': 'My fadyr in hevyn on hy, / Why dost þu me forsake?'.

32/214   JHESUS   In manus tuas, domine

Incomplete quotation: integral with the verse, evidently to be spoken, and with a following paraphrase.[36]

---

[34] This is however scriptural: the Gospels are full of Christ's words 'Amen, amen, dico vobis' – 'Truly, truly, I say unto you'.
[35] Further on this and the next item, see section 1.4 under **York 36**.
[36] See section 1.4, above, under **York 36/260**.

32/221   [JHESUS]   Nunc consummatum est

Only John (19/30) transmits this phrase, but without 'Nunc'. This is not a liturgical wording, as far as I know. The line is integral with the verse, and must be spoken.

33   The Harrowing of Hell (1)

33/24+sd   [ANIMA CHRISTI]   Attollite portas ... introibit rex glorie

Spector treats this text as part of the SD, but in fact it is set out as a prose text, in normal text script and with a *versus* mark in front of it. While Spector's SD might suggest that the Soul of Christ speaks only the paraphrase of the Latin text, therefore (lines **25–8**), the original shows clearly that the Latin text must be spoken first. Set out in verses, it is as follows:

> V. Attollite portas principes vestras
> et eleuamini porte eternales
> et introibit rex glorie

The liturgical significance of this text is noted in I, 278–83. No more of the liturgical dialogue is given, however, and Christ appears to have no assistants in this very short scene: we should probably take the SD's 'seyth' at face value, therefore, and assume that no singing is intended. The Soul might nevertheless use the butt of his staff to break down hell-gate at around line **45**.

34 The Burial, and the Guarding of the Sepulchre

34/4   [CENTURIO]   Quod vere filius dei erat iste.

The words of the centurion as reported by Matthew 27/54 (but without 'quod'): Mark and Luke use quite different wordings, while John does not transmit this episode. The use of Latin here is presumably to characterise the Centurion as a God-fearing man.

Christ is placed in the grave at **137+sd**, and wrapped and anointed in the next four lines. There is no liturgical content in the text, so that this scene could be played as the very brief – even perfunctory – event that it appears in a reading. Probably it was played like this, with no additional liturgical content. There is no doubt, on the other hand, that it would be perfectly possible to sing appropriate liturgical items during the potentially lengthy process of winding and anointing the body.

(i) Pageants from the Original Cycle

35 *The Harrowing of Hell (2); Christ's Appearance to Mary; Pilate and the Soldiers*

35/89 [JHESUS] Salue, sancta parens, ...

With paraphrase, integral to the verse, and in the same script as the main text, this phrase must be spoken.

The introit *Salve sancta parens* is set in the Sarum use for the vigil of the Assumption of the Blessed Virgin.[37] Harrison notes that the period between the Purification and Advent, when *Salve sancta parens* was widely sung as the introit at Lady-Mass, was the longest such period of the year, and that the Mass in this period was often called the Salve Sancta Parens Mass, or simply *Missa Salve*. The *incipit* used in this speech would probably have been recognised by many of the audience, therefore. There was also a sequence beginning with these words.[38]

36 *The Announcement to the Three Marys; Peter and John at the Sepulchre*

No relevant material.

37 *The Appearance to Mary Magdalene*

37/101+ The play ends with an extra-stanzaic 'Amen'. The last speech, by Peter, is a prayer: the Amen seems the proper response, presumably from everyone present. Unusually, 'Amen' is written three times in the margin, although two of these are not quite in the expected place: none of them is underlined.

38 *Cleophas and Luke; the Appearance to Thomas*

38/360, 368, 376, 384 [THOMAS] Quod mortuus et sepultus nunc resurrexit.

An integral part of the verse, but without translation: the line acts as a refrain at the end of each stanza, and should be spoken. It is in the same script as the rest of the text.

38/392 [THOMAS] That mortuus et sepultus iterum resurrexit. Amen

As above. The 'Amen' is extra-stanzaic and marginal, following what is very nearly a 'blessing' ending: it would be appropriate for everyone present to respond.

---

[37] GS, q; see also LU, 1263.

[38] Harrison *Music in Medieval Britain*, 79 and 392.

39 *The Ascension; the Selection of Matthias*
39/1 JHESUS Pax vobis: Amonge 3ow pes

There is a large red initial P for the Latin, which is in a larger and slightly more formal script, although an integral part of the verse. The phrase must be spoken.

39/48–56 Probably the angel's speech relates to the unspecified music sung at **47+sd**, by amplifying it. The angel advises the apostles to return to Jerusalem, and states that Jesus, whom they have just seen departing from them in a cloud, will doubtless come again to judge all men.

There are several liturgical pieces of which this could be a paraphrase. They are as follows:

(a) Offertory (Sandon V, 61; GS, 133):
>   Viri galilei quid admiramini aspicientes in celum: hic ihesus qui
>   assumptus est a vobis in celum in sic veniet quemadmodum
>   vidistis eum ascendentem in celum. Alleluia.
>   Melismatic/neumatic chant, range A–c', F-clef.

(b) Respond (WA, 149):
>   Viri galilei quid admiramini aspicientes in celum: Alleluia.
>   Quemadmodum vidistis eum ascendentem in celum ita veniet:
>   Alleluia, alleluia, alleluia.
>   Neumatic/melismatic chant, range f–f', c-clef.

(c) Introit (Sandon V, 63; GS, 135):
>   Text as for (b)
>   Neumatic chant, range f–f', c-clef.

(d) Antiphon (WA, 149; AM, 508; AR, 491; LU, 850):
>   Viri galilei quid aspicitis in celum: hic iesus qui assumptus est a vobis
>   in celum sic veniet: Alleluia.
>   Syllabic chant, range g–e', c-clef.

Of these, (d) is missing an element of the speech ('vidistis eum'), and can be excluded: but any of the others would be possible, despite the lack of an Alleluia in the paraphrase. All are easily within the capabilities of competent professional singers.

40 *Pentecost*
40/13 SYMON Sey we all togedyr, Amen . Amen.

The second 'Amen' is extra-stanzaic, and evidently should be spoken by all the apostles, as a response, no doubt with the audience joining in.

40/39+   Amen.

Extra-stanzaic and underlined. The play has a 'praise' ending, and the 'Amen' is a suitable response to be said by all present.

(vi) The Assumption Play

41 *The Assumption of Mary*
This play seems to have a large concentration of liturgical material. Not only are there many liturgical texts, but the *versus* sign appears in three areas, clearly demonstrating a liturgical origin for the texts concerned (**41/318–29, 343–7** and **369–70+sd**). However, the texts cannot all be identified as liturgical, so that the situation is not as straightforward as it appears.

41/13   [DOCTOR] Legenda Sanctorum autorysyth this trewely.

The doctor cites the 'legends of the saints' – that is, the *Golden Legenda* – as authority for the facts here dramatised. See below.

41/318–29 [DOMINUS] V. Veni tu, electa mea, et ponam in te thronum meum,
                                  Quia concupiuit rex speciem tuam.
               MARIA   V. Paratum cor meum, deus, paratum cor meum,
                                  Cantabo et psalmum dicam domino.
               APOSTOLI V. Hec est que nesciuit thorum in delictis,
                                  Habebit requiem in respectu animarum sanctarum.
               MARIA   V. Beatam me dicent omnes generaciones,
                                  Quia fecit michi magna qui potens est, et sanctum
                                                                          nomen eius.
               DOMINUS V. Veni de Libano, sponsa mea, veni, coronaberis.
               [MARIA]   Ecce, venio quia in capite libri scriptum est de me,
                                  Vt facerem voluntatem tuam, deus meus,
                                  Quia exultauit spiritus meus in deo salutari meo.

Mary dies at **329+sd**. These versicles are in the same script and ink as the main text, the versicle-signs being in red.

   This section is described by Jesus as Mary's 'dirige' (**317**). 'Dirige' comes from the opening of the first antiphon of Matins for the dead, 'Dirige, Dominus Deus meus'.[39] Jesus and his assistants do not literally recite or sing the text of this antiphon, however, and Jesus's statement may be intended only in a general sense.

The texts of **41/318–29** are taken from the *Golden Legend* account of Mary's death, burial and assumption, although with two differences. First, Mary's line 'cantabo et psalmum dicam domino' (**321**) does not appear in the *Legend*; second, lines **322–3** are here assigned to the Apostles, whereas the *Legend* assigns them to Christ's heavenly attendants. The *Golden Legend* also confirms that Spector was right to assign lines **327–9** to Mary, as the sense suggests: the SH has been omitted by the copyist.

The *Legend* and the play are agreed on Mary's death occurring immediately after this speech (GL, 451). The *Legend* also confirms that the play text should be sung at this point, a matter that is not stated in the play.

While it would be possible for this section to be spoken throughout, therefore, with the angelic singing at **313+sd** being the 'dirige', the *Golden Legend* account and the versicle signs suggest that the dramatist intended this section to be sung throughout. That being so, we should look at the available settings of these verses to see if a coherent musical performance is possible.

'Veni tu electa' may derive partly from Psalm 43/12, but it is otherwise unidentifiable as a scriptural text. *Veni electa mea* is identified by Dutka as an alleluia and a respond in both the Sarum and York uses, and as an antiphon in the York use only. The Sarum items are as follows:

(a) Alleluia verse (GS, 227):
   Veni, electa mea, et ponam in te thronum meum; quia concupiuit rex speciem tuam.
Largely melismatic chant, range c–d', c-clef. Mode 1.

(b) Respond (WA, 355; not in AS, but text in BS II, 446):
   Veni, electa mea, et ponam in te thronum meum. Quia concupiuit rex speciem tuam.
Neumatic chant, range c–a, c-clef. Mode 2.

(c) Antiphon (LU, 1211, 1233; text in BE II, 77, but perhaps not Sarum):
   Veni, electa mea, et ponam in te thronum meum. Alleluia.
Largely syllabic chant, range c–a, c-clef. Mode 1.

Of these, (c) does not have enough text, while either (a) or (b) would be textually suitable.

'Paratum cor meum ...' is a psalm verse (Vulgate 57/2, Psalter 56/10, AV

---

[39] AS, 580; AR, [154–5]; for the full office see MPE, 68* ff.

57/7): the Psalter version is closest to the *Golden Legend* and play text, omitting the word 'Domino' but otherwise the same. Dutka identifies the text as given in the play as a respond (BS I, ccccxxvii) but there are other possibilities:

(a) Respond (AS, 117):
> Paratum cor meum, deus, paratum cor meum. Cantabo et
> psalmum dicam domino.

Neumatic chant, range f–f', c-clef. Mode 5.

(b) Alleluia verse (GS, 158):
> Paratum cor meum, deus, paratum cor meum. Cantabo et
> psallam tibi in gloria mea.

Melismatic chant, range e–g', c-clef. Mode 1.

There is also an Introit verse (see GR, 106**), but it is not in GS and I do not know of a Sarum version. Item (b) is the only Sarum piece with the right text.

'Hec est que nescivit ...' is identified by Dutka as an antiphon (BS II, 445), and that does seem to be the only liturgical item with this text:

(a) Antiphon (AS, 666; LU, 1211):
> Hec est que nesciuit thorum in delicto. Habebit fructum in
> refectione animarum sanctarum.

Syllabic/neumatic chant, range c–c', c-clef. Mode 3

Although there are small differences in the text, this could be the piece intended by the dramatist.

'Beatam me dicent omnes generationes' is part of the *Magnificat*, and so could be sung to a psalm-tone. Dutka identifies it as a respond, but without a reference, and according to Bryden and Hughes it is also the opening of other liturgical pieces. I can find only the following, however:

(a) Antiphon (LU, 1313):
> Beatam me dicent omnes generationes, quia fecit mihi
> magna qui potens est. Alleluia.

Syllabic/neumatic chant, range f–d', c-clef. Mode 8.

(b) Respond (AS, 498):
> Beatam me dicent omnes generaciones. Quia fecit michi
> dominus magna quia potens est. Et sanctum nomen eius.

Neumatic/melismatic chant, range d–d', c-clef. Mode 8.

Text (a) omits the final clause of the verse in the play, while the differences between (b) and the play are small and easily explained: 'Dominus' is not part of the canticle – i.e. not scriptural – and 'qui' is an obvious slip of the memory (or of the pen) for 'quia'. Item (b) is likely to have been intended, therefore: and as Mary would have to be played by an experienced boy actor, it is not surprising to find that this piece requires a very experienced singer.

Veni de Libano is not identified by Dutka as a liturgical piece, and it does not appear in the Sarum use. Bryden and Hughes list a responsory verse (*Liber Responsorialis*, 263), an introit (LU, 1668) and an antiphon (*Processionale Monasticum*, 234). The introit has a text that cannot be made to match the play text:

> Veni de Libano, sponsa mea, veni de Libano, veni: vulnerasti cor meum, soror mea sponsa, vulnerasti cor meum.

Neumatic chant, range e–d', c-clef. Mode 3.

'Ecce, venio ...' is not identified by Dutka as a liturgical piece, and it is not listed by Bryden and Hughes. Line **329** is however derived from the *Magnificat*.

It is notable that the last versus-sign comes at the beginning of line **326**. This may mean that the last four lines of this section should be a single text: or, ac-cepting that line **326** must be delivered by an different person from lines **327–9**, either the scribe omitted a versus-sign needed at the start of line **327** or the last three lines of the section are not liturgical. This last possibility, how-ever, would seem to make it impossible to sing the last three lines of the section, unless perhaps a psalm-chant – as for the *Magnificat*? – were used.

This problem and the lack of a setting for *Veni de Libano* apart, the pos-sibility of a series of musical settings that will fit together seems good. While it is not easy to find and decide on settings for the whole section, therefore, and spoken dialogue may seem an attractive solution, a sung section is certainly not out of the question.

41/343–7 CHORUS MARTYRUM
> V. Que est ista que assendit de deserto
> Deliciis affluens, innixa super dilectum suum?

ORDO ANGELORUM
> V. Ista est speciosa inter filias Jerusalem sicut vidistis
> > eam,
> Plenam caritate et dilectione; sicque in celum gaudens
> > suscipitur,
> Et a dextris filii in trono glorie collocatur.

As before, the versicle-signs are red but the text is in the same script and ink as the rest of the play.

117

The text at **343–7** is that quoted in the *Golden Legend* (GL, 452), but rather longer. It is similar to various liturgical texts used at the Assumption (AS, 494–5 and 499), but not precisely the same. No text is given to correspond to **347+sd**, the singing of 'the whole heavenly court', so it is possible that another verse belongs to these two.

In the *Golden Legend* these two given verses are sung by those who have remained in Heaven and those who went to fetch Mary from earth: here the verses are given, respectively, to the Chorus of Martyrs and the Order of Angels, suggesting that the former remain in the Heaven and the latter attend Jesus in visiting his mother. The Order of Angels, then, is either part of or synonymous with the 'heavenly court' of **311+sd**.

Dutka does not identify 'Que est ista' as a liturgical piece. There is a fourth-mode antiphon with that incipit (WA, 356), which has a different text after 'affluens'; a first-mode antiphon (WA, 358), which has a different text after 'assendit'; and a fourth-mode respond (WA, 355), also with a different text after 'assendit'. While none of these is apparently the piece intended, any of them could be a version of the dramatist's chosen item.

'Ista est speciosa', similarly, is not identified by Dutka. Settings with this incipit are:

(a) Antiphon (LU, 1211):
>   Ista est speciosa inter filias Jerusalem.
> Neumatic chant, range e–c', c-clef. Mode 3.

(b) Antiphon (LU, 1233):
>   Ista est speciosa inter filias Jerusalem.
> Syllabic/neumatic chant, range f–d', c-clef. Mode 8.

(c) Antiphon (WA, 365):
>   Ista est speciosa electa a domino ...
> Neumatic chant, range d–c', c-clef. Mode 8.

(d) Respond (AS, 494; WA, 356):
>   Ista est speciosa inter filias ierusalem sicut uidistis eam plenam caritate et dilectione. In cubilibus et in ortis aro-matum.
> Neumatic/melismatic chant, range c–c', c-clef. Mode 2.

(e) Responsory verse (WA, 433):
>   Text as (a) and (b)
> Neumatic chant, range f–g', c-clef. Mode 7.

None of these has the text of **41/343–7**, and we should perhaps assume that any musical setting used in staging the play was composed for the purpose.

41/369–70 PETRUS V. Exiit Israel de Egipto . domus Jacob de populo barbaro.
Alleluia.

APOSTOLI V. Facta est Judea sanctificacio eius, Israel potestas eius.
Alleluia.

This takes place during the procession with Mary's body for burial: it is followed by the SD *hic angeli dulciter cantabunt in celo 'Alleluia'.*[40] Again, the versicle-signs are red and the text in the same script and ink as the rest of the play. The *Golden Legend* tells how the angels joined in the singing of this psalm (GL, 453).

Lines **369–70** are not quite the usual version of the opening of Psalm 113 (AV 114), 'In exitu Israel de Egypto', but in the wording used also in the *Golden Legend* (GL, 453), starting 'Exiit Israel'. The Sarum rite used 'In exitu Israel' both during the commendation of the recently-departed soul (MS, 119) and during the procession to burial (MS, 124 and 154–5).

In the Easter season the psalm was normally sung under the antiphon *Alleluia, alleluia, alleluia* (LU, 254–6; a longer version of this antiphon, with four Alleluias, is in AS, 234, 238 and 249), and the Sarum Antiphoner has a slightly different setting, with an antiphon giving a single Alleluia (AS, 239). The difficulty here is that singing the psalm under an antiphon requires the antiphon to be sung first, and the play text does not provide an initial 'Alleluia'. The psalm is however sung with an Alleluia after each verse at processions in Easter-time (see PS(P), 89v ff.), and this is the setting perhaps intended by the dramatist.

A possible performance is discussed in I, 290. It seems most likely that after Peter has sung the first verse and its Alleluia and the apostles have sung the second verse the angels take up the Alleluia and continue to sing the Alleluia after each verse. The implication of this is that they continue this to the end of the psalm. Another possibility is that the angels simply repeat each Alleluia after the Apostles have sung it. There is nothing to indicate whether they sing the Alleluias in the chant or in a polyphonic version: this might depend on the singers being used.

41/453–5+sd JOHANNES De terra plasmasti me et carne induisti me;
Redemptor meus, domine, resuscita me in novissimo die.
Now God blysse this body . and we oure synge make.

Hic vnanimiter benedicent corpus . In nomine patris et filii et spiritus sancti.

---

40 The relationship of this play to the burial service is discussed in I, 290–1.

This passage is in the same script and ink as the rest of the play.

This is a sung Latin text followed by English speech and a blessing when Mary's body is placed in the sepulchre. **453–4** is a text sung at a burial, an antiphon that appears in the burial service in the Sarum use (MS, 158) and in the York use (ME, 99 and 10–11) with the Psalm *Domine probasti me*. In both uses it is sung complete only after the psalm. In both uses, too, this psalm is sung immediately after the body is placed in the grave and earth put on it in the shape of a cross. Apparently John intones the antiphon, which is presumably taken up, with the psalm, by the other apostles.

In neither use is this followed by a blessing of the body. The blessing in N-Town is, of course, a very common form of wording: 'synge' is for 'sign' – i.e. the sign of the cross made in blessing the body.

41/510–14

> [DOMINUS] Arys now, my dowe . my nehebour and my swete frend,
> Tabernacle of joye . vessel of lyf . hefnely temple, to reyn.
> Ye schal haue the blysse wyth me, moder . that hath non ende.
> For as ye were clene in erthe . of alle synnys greyn,
> So schul ye reyne in hefne clennest in mend.

This is almost a translation of 'Surge proxima mea', the text of **York 45/ 104+music**, but using the variant 'Surge propera, amica mea' (Canticum Canticorum 2/10: see Rastall *Six Songs*, 7). It is possible, therefore, that the angels sing a setting of this text during the action of **41/508+sd** (which should properly come after line **509**):

> Surge propera, amica mea, columba mea, tabernaculum
> glorie, vasculum vite, templum celeste.

As noted before, this is not a liturgical text.

41/521+sd   Assumpta es, Maria, in celum

The incipit 'Assumpta est Maria in celum' is well known, but I know of no version of the text addressed to the Virgin and therefore using the word 'es'. Probably this incipit indicates that an Assumption text was modified for the dramatic purpose of having the angels address Mary directly.[41]

Possible liturgical items are as follows:

[41] This hardly seems necessary, but it may indicate very specific staging circum-stances.

(a) Antiphon (AS, 499; LU, 1606):
> Assumpta est Maria in celum. Gaudent angeli, laudantes benedicunt Dominum.

Syllabic chant, range g–e′, c-clef.

(b) Short responsory (LU, 1605)
> Assumpta est Maria in celum. Gaudent angeli.
> V. Laudantes benedicunt Dominum. Gloria Patri.

Syllabic chant, range f–b♭, c-clef.

(c) Alleluia verse (GS, 195):
> Assumpta est Maria in celum. Gaudent angeli et collaudantes benedicunt dominum.

Neumatic/melismatic chant, range A–b♭, f-clef.

(d) Alleluia verse (LU, 1603):
> Assumpta est Maria in celum. Gaudet exercitus angelorum.

Melismatic chant, range c–c′, c-clef.

(e) Offertory (LU, 1604):
> Assumpta est Maria in celum. Gaudent angeli collaudantes benedicunt Dominum. Alleluia.

Melismatic chant, range c–e′, c-clef.

There is a range of difficulty here, from the simplest syllabic chant with a very narrow vocal range (b) to a complex chant demanding considerable vocal skill (e). Any of these might be performed in the play, depending on the skill of the singers, with the word 'es' substituted for 'est'.

41/501 Deo Gracias

This line occurs at the very end of the play, following the Archangel Michael's final speech, which is a 'praise' ending. It is in the same script and ink as the rest of the text, but placed rather to the right of centre, so that it may be a pious colophon by the scribe. On the other hand it has a red paragraph–mark, which makes it look like part of the speech. In this case it should probably be regarded as a response for all the cast to make. It is also possible that it is the text of the heavenly 'melody' about to be performed.

As will be obvious from the discussion of the liturgical material in this play, both here and in I, 290–1, there is reason to think that the use known to the dramatist was not that of Salisbury. The offices concerning death and burial are among the occasional offices found in the manuals, but they also find their way into breviaries, antiphoners and pontificals. The Peterborough antiphoner and the Ely breviary cited above contain nothing of these services. The fifteenth-century Lincoln pontifical follows the normal Sarum sequence of events in having the antiphon *De terra plasmasti me* preceded by the censing of the corpse and followed by a commendation ending 'In nomine patris et filii et spiritus sancti', as in the play; but this manuscript, like the Ely pontifical and the fourteenth-century breviary from Bury St Edmunds (London, British Library, MS Harley 5334), has *In exitu Israel* sung in procession to the graveside, rather than N-Town's *Exiit Israel*. This latter wording must be searched for further.

The material in these books allows a positive rejection of the Bury St Edmunds use, for the wording of the antiphon *De terra plasmasti me* differs significantly from that of the N-Town text. While the Sarum text, also used by N-Town, has as its second line 'redemptor meus domine resuscita me in novissimo die', the Bury version is 'Memento mei domine dum veneris in novissimo die'. I confess that this is so obviously a version of the more usual text that I may have failed to note it elsewhere: and if it turns out to be a common Benedictine version, that will narrow the field of possibilities for the provenance of play **41**.

(i) Pageant from the Original Cycle

42 The Last Judgement

42/1–2   MICHAEL   Svrgite! All men aryse!
                              Venite ad judicium!

The Latin is integral to the text: there is a large red initial S. 'Surgite' is in slightly larger script, but this is otherwise in normal text script.

It is clear from this speech that the Last Trumpet has already sounded, at the very beginning of the play.

42/40–1   DEUS   Venite, benedicti, my bretheryn all,
                              Patris mei ʒe childeryn dere!

Integral to the text, and in the same script as the rest of the text. There is no question of singing this text, as there is in **Chester 24** (see 6.4, below): indeed, it should probably be argued that the selective quotation of the Latin text makes it unnecessary for the complete text of *Venite benedicti* to be heard.

A review of the liturgical content of the cycle in connection with East Anglian uses shows a few probabilities, although there are no data for the pageant series. For the Marian group the relevant liturgical use will probably have the sequence *Benedicta sit beata trinitas* in the Pentecost–Trinity area, with *Alma chorus domini* as the sequence for a nuptial mass.

As regards the separate Purification play (play **18**), I have given reasons for rejecting Crowland as the place of liturgical origin: and although this is not important in itself, this conclusion may reflect on other Benedictine houses. The situation in regard to the Passion Play is highly unsatisfactory: but on the basis of the 'Tollite portas' wording we are probably justified in rejecting Ely, Lincoln and Peterborough, although none of these is a likely home for the Passion Play in any case. Finally, for the separate Assumption play we can reject Bury St Edmunds, and perhaps also Ely and Lincoln.

2.5 Records

No records survive that can be associated with the N-Town plays.

2.6 Music and other aural cues

(i) Pageants from the Original Cycle

1 The Creation, and Fall of Lucifer
1_1 **39+sd** Function: (i), (h), ?(c). The angels sing part of the *Te Deum*:

> Tibi omnes angeli tibi celi et universe potestas . Tibi cherubyn et seraphyn incessabili voce proclamant . Sanctus . Sanctus . Sanctus . Dominus deus sabaoth.

This section of the *Te Deum* is clearly appropriate textually, and it makes good musical sense when sung to the normal chant (cf. **York 1_2**). As in the York cycle (see 1.6 under **York 1**), there is the possibility that Lucifer and the bad angels do not sing this item.

Lucifer's fart at **1/81** is discussed in I, 205–6.

2 The Creation of the World, and the Fall of Man
3 Cain and Abel
No music cues.

4 Noah
4_1 **197+sd** Function: (b), (c), (h). Between the end of the Lamech scene and the start of Noah's

> With doolful hert, syenge sad and sore,
> Grett mornyng I make for this dredful flood!
> (4/198–9)

the song here can hardly be a cheerful one. 'Intrat Noe cum naui' really means 'enter Noah's pageant', for otherwise 'cantantes' is incorrect: with this interpretation, however, it can be assumed that the other characters enter at the same time, and that they all sing. Since the Flood is already happening, something like Psalm 68 (69) would be appropriate: 'Salvum me fac, Deus, quoniam intraverunt aque usque ad animam meam' (see the discussion of **Chester 3**). Although the song could be in English, note that Noah and his family sing a psalm in Latin at the end of the play (cue 4_2).

4_A **241** Function (d). There is no evidence for music here, which would mark the 40 days of the Flood (cf. **Chester 3**, although it cannot be used as evidence). We can however note that the two lines immediately before (**240–1**) seem designed to allow for such an occurrence if it were desired:

> [VXOR JAPHET] Hym for to wurchipe in euery stede and place
> We beth gretly bownde with myght and with mayn.

Such an item could be in either English or Latin.

4_2 **253+sd** Function: (g), ?(i)/(c). Noah and his family sing verse 3 of Psalm 113 (114), and then the first verse of the second part of that psalm (115/1 in the AV), as set out in the SD. The cast's withdrawal at the end of the play may take place only after the singing is concluded: but the wording of the SD 'et sic recedant cum navi', which follows the text to be sung, suggests a singing procession.

5 Abraham and Isaac
No music cues.

6 Moses
See section 2.4: the Latin lines are probably references, and it is unlikely that they were intended to be heard. In any case there is no reason to think that they should be sung, and these texts are not part of any normal liturgical item.

7 Jesse Root
No music cues.

(ii) Pageants from the Mary Play

8 Joachim and Anna
8_1 **97+sd** Function: (a). The singing of the sequence *Benedicta sit beata trinitas*

serves to characterise the service that is taking place, and also covers the sensing of the altar and perhaps some or most of the offerings. The singing is probably to be performed by a musical staff in the Temple, the actors being professional church-singers.

8₂ **109+md**   Function: none. The singing of the versicles and responses, with the blessing, marks the end of the service and prepares for the end of the scene, only four lines of speech following it before the change of focus to Joachim and the shepherds. See 2.4, above.

8₃ **172+sd**   Function: (a). The text of *Exultet celum laudibus* given in this SD is close to that of the hymn for (among other occasions) the common of apostles: but it is made more immediately appropriate to the drama by the substitution of 'archangelorum' for the 'apostolorum' of the hymn. There is no reason to think that more than the one verse is sung. Several tunes are available for this hymn.

8ᴀ **200**   Function: (a). Perhaps music in Heaven while the angels returns there (cf. 8₃).

8₄ **212**   Function: (a), (c), (h). While the reference at **212** shows that the shepherds do sing here, there is no indication of the type of song or even of the language used.

Although the angel descends to Anne after **216**, and returns to Heaven at **236+sd**, there is no indication of further angelic music. It is however possible that Anna, like Joachim, was treated to a heavenly concert that covered the angel's movement about the playing-place.

9   *The Presentation of Mary in the Temple*

9₁ **105+lat**, and the fourteen subsequent Latin incipits. Function: none. This matter is discussed in 2.4. In view of the English, which in each case is an introduction to – not a translation of – the Latin line, I feel that the Latin must be heard: that is, we should reject the possibility that Isakar is suggesting in lines **100–1** that the bystanders say the psalms later as part of their own devotions. In this case the 15 psalms could be dealt with as follows:

1)   the bystanders say the Latin lines given in the text;
2)   they sing these same lines;
3)   they say the whole of each psalm; or
4)   they sing the whole of each psalm.

For each psalm there is the possibility that Mary initiates the Latin version: however, this seems to me to be unnecessary, since her English lines introduce the psalms one by one in any case. Thus I suggest that Mary introduce each psalm (in English) and the bystanders, recognising it, then take it up in its

Latin text.[42]

Although none of these psalms is long – Psalm 131, with 18 verses, stands out in this respect – a performance of all 15 complete would demand the recitation of 101 verses plus 15 doxologies. The time taken for this would depend partly on the size of the participating cast, but it is likely to add 16–20 minutes to the playing-time. The modern aversion to taking very long over anything is out of place here: the 'active contemplation' that arises out of liturgy would be appropriate, and is indeed a good reason for taking seriously the possibility that all fifteen psalms are to be heard all the way through. To a congregation used to Latin psalms and to the ceremonial of liturgy the effect of reciting all 15 in this play would be both moving and – in the proper meaning of the term – entertaining. There is no inherent reason why the psalms should not have been performed in full originally, therefore, although a modern producer may be averse to making so great a demand on a cast and audience who have not been brought up in the same tradition.

While time in itself should not be a deciding issue in matters of staging, full performance of the gradual psalms here would almost double the length of the play and the performance-mode chosen is, therefore, important for the overall effect. Recitation of the first verse only of each psalm would keep the scene of Mary's climbing the steps to about 10 minutes, which is half of the play. In this case the cast should recite the first verse of each psalm in a normal speaking voice, because it would not make good sense to sing just the first verse of each following Mary's spoken introduction. Recitation of each psalm complete, with its doxology, would increase the length of this scene to some 25–30 minutes, so that the whole balance of the play is redistributed towards the recitation of the Gradual Psalms. This would make the play, in effect, a major event of psalmody with a relatively short dramatic introduction (lines **1–101**). This being so, singing the psalms would have a more appropriate effect than speaking them.

There is no reason otherwise to think that these psalms are sung, although singing would be admissible on grounds of liturgical convention: Isakar's use of the word 'say' in line **101** seems to preclude it. Perhaps, too, we should take account of the stated view in play **13** (also part of *The Mary Play*) that there is a distinction to be made between angels singing and mortals speaking (see 2.3). But the ambiguity in this pageant may be deliberate. Perhaps here, as in other pageants derived from *The Mary Play*, an originally spoken item is open to sung performance in a more opulent production.

To summarise: Mary's English introduction to each psalm should be followed by the cast speaking or singing the Latin. The cast may have recited the complete text of each psalm, with a doxology, in which case a sung

---

[42] This pattern, of an English text introducing a Latin one, is rare in the plays but is found in several other places, such as the *Lay Folk's Mass Book*.

performance is appropriate to the major piece of psalmody that this scene then becomes. The normal psalm-chants should be used. For a modern audience it may be appropriate to say the first verse only of each psalm, as a reminder of which is the psalm concerned. It will however be necessary to attempt complete performance with a modern audience at some time, since it would be wrong to assume that a modern cast and audience cannot cope with so much psalmody.[43]

9_2 **245+sd** Function: (a), (h). There is no indication of the piece sung by the angelic choir here. An obvious possibility would be the communion 'Panem de celo' (Sandon VI, 55; GS, 156; LU, 1035); the *varium* 'Panis angelicus' (AR, 95*, 96* and 110*) seems not to appear in the Sarum use, although that or other items for the Holy Sacrament would also be suitable.

9_3 **277+sd** Function: (a), (h). The hymn *Jesu corona virginum*, for the Common of Virgins, has five four-line verses: there is a choice of musical settings (see 2.4).

(i) and (ii) Pageant derived from the Original Cycle and the Mary Play

10 *The Marriage of Mary and Joseph*

10_1 **115+sd** Function: (h). Presumably the bishop, or perhaps the minister, intones *Veni creator spiritus*, which is then sung by all present. Note that the citing of the hymn in line **115** must be spoken, since it is needed to complete the rhyme-scheme. *Veni creator spiritus*, the hymn for Whitsuntide, has seven four-line verses.

10_2 **301+md** Function: (h). *Benedicta sit beata trinitas* serves to separate Joseph's agreement to his marriage with Mary from the marriage-service itself. As with 8_1, the singing of a liturgical item here characterises the service that is about to happen, setting the scene simply and unambiguously. Although the main evidence for singing here is only a MD, line **301**, 'now ȝelde we all preysyng to þe trenyte', would probably imply music in any case.

10_3 **334** Function: (h). As in the case of 8_2, this item concludes the service – in this case, the marriage-service of Joseph and Mary. Again, the citing of the piece in line **334** requires the incipit to be spoken there: presumably the bishop (or the minister) intones it afterwards.

(ii) Pageant from the Mary Play

11 *The Parliament of Heaven; the Salutation and Conception*

The psalm-verse at **48+lat** should probably be spoken by God before his translation in lines **49–51**: there seems no reason for him to sing them.

---

43 As in other cases in which the audience is no longer trained to appreciate something that the original audience could probably take in its collective stride, considerable help will be needed: translations of the psalms, perhaps with Mary's introduction to each (in modern English), would seem necessary, for instance.

11₁ 216+lat Function: (h). The offertory *Ave gratia plena* (LU, 1379) gives the correct text, corresponding to the translation of lines **217–19**, although the piece is not in GS.

11ₐ 292+sd Function: (a). This movement and heavenly activity would suggest the use of heavenly music, but there is no evidence for it.

11₂ 340+lat+sd Function: (a), (g); but in the original form of the play, when this item led straight on to Joseph's entrance, **12/13**, the functions were evidently (b), (c) and (h). The Latin lines are the sung text: there is no point in Gabriel speaking the text before he sings it, especially in view of his statement, in line **339**, that he will end with an 'Ave' as he began. Clearly Gabriel sings this sequence himself:[44] it is probably a piece of virtuoso singing, for the sequence is not an easy piece.

(i) Pageant from the Original Cycle

12 *Joseph's Doubt*
No music cues.

(ii) Pageant from the Mary Play

13 *The Visit to Elizabeth*
13₁ 185A Function: (g). The play, and indeed the Marian sequence of plays, concludes with the singing of *Ave regina celorum*. Contemplacio's announcement of the piece suggests that he expects the audience to join in this piece, one of the Compline antiphons to Our Lady. The chant is not easy, however, and some trained singers would be needed for an adequate performance.

(i) Pageants from the Original Cycle

14 *The Trial of Mary and Joseph*
14₁ 405 Function: (g). The 'Explicit cum gaudio amen' at the end of the play is a later addition, and is therefore unlikely to be a pious scribal 'signing-off'. It may indicate a musical performance at the end of the play, therefore. 'Amen' may be the text of the piece, although this is not certain.

15 *The Nativity*
No music cues, even for the angel's appearance after line **277**. the 'Amen' at the end of the play, after line **321**, should be said by all.

---

[44] The 'Angeli' of the SD is clearly an error, and was presumably intended to be singular.

16 *The Shepherds*

16₁ 1–sd Function: (f). The later cancellation of the Latin line *Gloria in excelsis deo* suggests a change in production from the Latin+English sung-spoken pattern to an opening in which no singing occurs. That singing did originally occur is shown by line 7: 'Therfore I synge A joyful stevene'.

This play is one of the two shepherds' plays (the Coventry one is the second) that has the *Gloria* sung twice: this evidently stems from the gospel account (Luke 2), which shows that an angel spoke to the shepherds, after which the heavenly host appeared 'praising God'. 'Gloria in excelsis, etc' is of course the text of the song sung by the host: the words of the single angel were different, and not sung, so that it is dramatic licence to have the angel singing *Gloria in excelsis* solo before speaking to the shepherds. Again, it is clear that this really *is* what happens in the play, since the first two lines of the play are a translation of the Latin 'Gloria' text.

It seems that editorial activity in this text has moved the angel's opening speech from elsewhere in the play: the shepherds give no indication that they have heard the angel's singing, or his speech, but discuss prophecies of the Virgin Birth. When the shepherds discuss the *second* angelic 'Gloria', however, the third shepherd mentions (lines 71–2) the words spoken by the angel after the *first* 'Gloria': so it seems that a single discussion of a single performance of the 'Gloria', with its associated speech by the angel, has been split into two discussions of two performances, but without the necessary rewriting being done.

It is tempting to say that this cue should not be performed: but that does not solve the problem, because the angel's opening speech (**1–13**) is equally out of place. Unless the play can be reconstructed in its original order, it may be best to let 'Gloria in excelsis' be heard here – it is an effective opening to the play – and let the shepherds apparently come at the text crabwise, through the prophecies. This is not particularly convincing, but it may be better than the alternatives.

16₂ 61+sd Function: perhaps (h), but the second angelic singing of *Gloria in excelsis deo* does not really mark the transition to a new scene: the separate subject-matter occurs only gradually. At first the shepherds are concerned, as before, with prophecies and the message that has been given to them. Only afterwards, at line **73**, does the subject move on, when the third shepherd suggests that they go to Bethlehem to find the child.

16₃ 77+md Function: (i), (h). The shepherds sing *Stella celi extirpavit* before walking to Bethlehem. It is interesting that they sing in Latin and, given that, very curious that they sing a rare antiphon rather than the biblical text *Transeamus usque Bethlehem* at this point: concerning this text, see 2.4, above.

The direction makes it clear ('quo facto, ibunt ...') that the shepherds sing this piece as a musical tableau before they set out to Bethlehem. Whether they then walk silently, with some improvised conversation, or with another piece of music, is a moot point. It is however important to note that Mary thanks them for their singing (see line **152**), so they have certainly sung something that was audible to her. While the audience might understand this to be their performance of *Stella celi extirpavit*, it is much more likely that they have sung during or soon after their arrival at the stable.

Moreover, as she thanks them for their homage and their singing together, it seems especially likely that it was the textual content of their song that was important to her, perhaps because it was a song of praise to her Son. This could perhaps be started during the walk to Bethlehem, but should still be happening by the time they arrive at the stable.

This cue, then, is probably for two performances: *Stella celi extirpavit*, sung before they leave for Bethlehem, and a song of praise to the Christ-child, perhaps started during the journey but certainly to be heard as they arrive at the stable. Considering the iconography of the shepherds' at the Nativity, their unison singing could well be accompanied by an instrument: see I, section 8.4 and especially p. 349.

The 'Amen' following line **154** at the end of the play should be spoken by all. Music would seem appropriate after that, but there is no evidence for it.

17 [absit]

18   The Magi

18₁ 20 Function: (h). Minstrelsy at the end of the scene. Since the minstrels are required to blow up 'a good blast' they may have been shawms and a trumpet, playing ceremonial loud music, or perhaps a group of trumpets (see **20₂**).

There is no evidence for soft music at the angel's appearance at **290+sd**, and it is probably unnecessary: see I, 188 for angelic music in appearances to mortals.

(iii) The Purification Pageant

19   The Purification

19₁ 136+lat Function: none. I think that *Suscepimus deus misericordiam tuam* should be sung: see 2.4. It could be sung by Simeon himself: but, as **19₂** shows, there must be singers in the Temple, and they are the more likely performers.

19₂ 146+sd+lat Function: none. The SD shows clearly that Simeon does not sing *Nunc dimittis*: therefore there are singers in the Temple – professionals forming a choir for the purpose. *Nunc dimittis* is sung complete, probably without the doxology (see 2.4).

(i) Pageants from the Original Cycle

20 *The Slaughter of the Innocents; the Death of Herod*
Apparently there is no music after line **72**, when the angel appears to Joseph: see
I, 188.
20₁ 154 Function: (a). The minstrels are told to 'blowe up' (line **153**), so that
loud ceremonial music of shawms and trumpet, or perhaps a group of trumpets, is probable (see **20₂**). While the music is heard, the food is served and
Herod washes his hands and sits at table.
20₂ 232+sd Function: (a) The minstrels again 'blowe up a mery fytt' (line **232**),
during which Herod and the knights are killed and their souls delivered to the
Devil. The 'buccinant' of the SD suggests trumpets rather than shawms (for
which 'biccinant' might be expected), but it is not certain that the terms were
used so precisely.

21 *Christ and the Doctors*
Apparently no music cues. Probably all present should say the 'Amen' at the
end, after line **288**.

22 *The Baptism*
Apparently no music cues even after line **91**, when the Holy Spirit descends to
Jesus.

23 *The Parliament of Hell; the Temptation*
The Devil cracks a fart after **195** ('Ffor sorwe I lete a crakke'), perhaps with
fireworks: see I, 206.
23₁ 195+sd Function: (a), (h), (c). This item marks the end of the Temptations,
only Jesus's final summing-up speech following: the Devil presumably exits at
this point, having farted. *Gloria tibi domine* is the end of the Epiphany hymn
'Hostis Herodes'. Note that this is not a tableau in Heaven: the singers are the
angels who come to Jesus, not those (if any) who remain in the heaven.

24 *The Woman Taken in Adultery*
No music cues.

25 *The Raising of Lazarus*
No music cues.

(iv) Passion Play I

26 *Prologues of Satan and John the Baptist; the Conspiracy, and the Entry into Jerusalem*
26₁ 453+sd Function: perhaps (a), but more likely (i). The SD requires a number

of children to sing *Gloria laus*. In the Sarum use this piece was sung during the Palm Sunday procession by seven boys, who also threw down flowers from their elevated position (Tyrer *Holy Week*, 59):

> The main feature of this [second] Station was the singing, by seven boys from a higher position (probably a platform or gallery over the [south] door), of the first four verses of the hymn *Gloria laus et honor* .... At the end of each verse the boys threw down cakes and flowers ..., while the choir responded by repeating the first verse.

Other English uses varied this ceremony in small ways, and it is clear that N-Town 26 does not follow the Sarum use: see I, 269–71. The singers are certainly choirboys, however, and seven of them would make a suitable choir, although another number would be possible.

27 *The Last Supper; the Conspiracy with Judas*
27$_A$ 527+sd Function: (a). Psalms and antiphons are needed for the Mandatum: see I, 274–5.

28 *The Betrayal*
No relevant cues.

(v) Passion Play II

29 *Herod; the Trial before Annas and Cayphas*
29$_1$ 198+sd Function: none. The first cock-crow.
29$_2$ 212+sd Function: none. The second cock-crow.

30 *The Death of Judas; the Trials before Pilate and Herod*
31 *Satan and Pilate's Wife; the Second Trial before Pilate*
No relevant cues.

32 *The Procession to Calvary; the Crucifixion*
32$_1$ 76+sd Function: (h). The Jews' dancing about the cross separates the scene of the nailing from that with the raised cross leading to Christ's death. It seems that the four executioners must dance around the cross after they have raised it – that is, their work is done and they celebrate in this way before taking their ease in mocking Christ. There is little evidence for the kind of dance performed, and none for the kind of music (if any) that accompanies it: perhaps they sing for their own dance.

The subject of dancing at the crucifixion was first discussed by Dutka, and my examination of her arguments suggested the following conclusions (I, 212–15):

1   The SD for dancing should be taken at face value;
2   The dancing is not a social event, but may be most easily thought of as a capering that has the humiliation and mockery of Christ as its sole or main purpose;
3   It should continue any 'game' element included in the torturers' previous treatment of Christ;[45] and
4   The torturers should move anticlockwise about the cross, rather than clockwise.

33   The Harrowing of Hell (1)

33₁ 24+sd+lat Function: (h). The *versus* sign before the Latin text suggests a liturgical item, and perhaps, therefore, singing: but only the opening of the dialogue is given,[46] and in any case speech, implied by the SD's 'seyth', would be more effective here.[47] The Latin is followed by a rather free translation (lines 25–8).

34   The Burial; the Guarding of the Sepulchre

No relevant cues.

(i) Pageants from the Original Cycle

35   The Harrowing of Hell (2); Christ's Appearance to Mary; Pilate and the Soldiers
36   The Announcement to the Three Marys; Peter and John at the Sepulchre
37   The Appearance to Mary Magdalene
38   Cleophas and Luke; the Appearance to Thomas

No relevant cues.

39   The Ascension, and the Selection of Matthias

39₁ 47+sd Function: (a) or (c). The angels sing in Heaven at Christ's Ascension. The angel's speech that follows has some references to the Ascension introit *Viri Galilei*, which is perhaps a contender for the piece to be sung here: but the angel does not translate the opening of it, and other Ascensiontide pieces would be suitable.

40   Pentecost

No relevant cues.

---

45 See Meredith *Passion Play*, 208–9 and 197. It is worth repeating here (as stated in I, 213, n. 96) that this dance could be treated as part of a ritual, children's games being played according to strict procedures.
46 For a discussion of the full text and its performance, see I, 278–83.
47 Or, rather, declamation, for Christ will surely shout this text.

(vi) The Assumption Play

41 The Assumption of Mary

41₁ 116+sd Function: (a), (e). Music while the angel descends to tell Mary that she is to die in three days' time. Although the angel's greeting, lines **117–20**, is reminiscent of well-known Marian texts, I cannot find that the speech is a translation of any of them.

The abbreviated form *ludent' cithar'*, expanded by both Block and Spector to *ludentibus citharis*, is ambiguous. The singular form, *ludente cithara* (to the playing of a harp) is possible, but it is hardly worth abbreviating: the plural seems much more likely,[48] and in any case the Second Angel has mentioned 'the hefnely consorcyte', which must mean a group of musicians.

The Elche Assumption play demonstrates the effect of a whole group of angels singing and playing while they descend. Probably no outdoor performance (whether on a pageant or not) could match the machinery possible in a large late-medieval church and still to be seen at Elche. But **N-Town 41** as we have it is an indoor play. In any case, there is evidence that the musical angels remain in Heaven while their fellow descends to talk to the Virgin: for at **311+ sd** Christ descends 'with the whole heavenly court', which shows that wholesale descent is possible and that it has not previously happened in this play.

This wholesale descent suggests that communication between Heaven and earth is not, as in Elche, by means of a suspended *mangrana*,[49] but by some means that allows freer movement of a larger number of actors.

41₂ 285+sd Function: (a). The SD 'Hic cantabunt organa' is ambiguous. With 'organa' as the subject, 'cantabunt' should mean 'play' rather than 'sing' (cf. 'cantabit gallus' for the cock-crow in play **29**): but 'organa' could mean 'organ' in the modern sense of 'the instrument that we call the organ' (the word is plural in earlier centuries), or the meaning from which this is derived, 'instruments'. However, the SD is actually written *hic cantabunt org'*, so that the expansion 'organis' is perfectly possible. This gives us another alternative meaning, 'here they sing with instruments' (or 'with the organ'). On balance, I feel that the last of these is the most likely. What the instrumental accompaniment should be is a difficult question. We know that harps, or at any rate

---

[48] In both cases the abbreviation is that used mainly for -re/-er, obviously used here as a general sign of suspension. 'Cithara' can mean other stringed instruments, but it was most often used for the harp.

[49] For a description of the Elche Assumption play, see King and Salvador-Rabaza 'La Festa d'Elxe'.
  The parallel with the N-Town Assumption is clearly not exact, since movement of Christ and all the heavenly court from Heaven to earth requires a walkway or other wide space for the transition. I also here assume that the staging of **N-Town 40**, as shown in its SDs, etc., is that of its original, indoor, production, and that this may well not match up with the (apparently outdoor) performance conditions for which the N-Town cycle was compiled.

stringed instruments, were available in Heaven (see **41₁**), but a small organ in Heaven was not unusual (see I, 365, where I have treated an organ as the likely solution in **N-Town 41**): the presence or otherwise of an organ would depend on the financial situation for the production.

There is no way of deciding what piece should be sung: Mary speaks immediately afterwards, so that there is no chance of a translation. There are several suitable texts in praise of the Virgin.

40₃ 318–29 As previously explained, although these lines could be sung I think that they should be spoken.

40₄ 343–7 Function: (i). The first two lines are a short responsory: I have not identified the next three. Assuming that they all come from the same liturgical piece, perhaps there is additional text in which all can join in. There is in any case more reason here to think that the Latin might be sung, but perhaps we should look for a liturgical form that makes sense of the SD of **40₅**.

40₅ 347+sd Function: (h). Follows on from **40₄**. Unless the text of **40₄** can be identified, and it can be shown that this SD refers to the same text, we have little chance of deciding what piece should be sung here. Again, a text in praise of the Virgin would be suitable.

40₆ 370+sd Function: none. Here, too, I do not think that the mortals sing the Latin lines: indeed, the whole point seems to be that the mortals are saying their texts and the angels join in by singing the 'Alleluia', thus confusing the Jews, who think that the apostles are singing. The 'Alleluia' could presumably be the setting proper to the psalm being used, but it need not be.

40₇ 452+sd Function: (a). The apostles sing while the Virgin's body is sensed and placed in the sepulchre. As the text is set out, it seems that John speaks the text *De terra plasmasti me* and then continues to the blessing: but the Latin text has no rhyme-brackets, which suggests that *De terra plasmasti me* is the text of the apostles' singing, while John begins speaking only at line **455** (see MDF 4 221r–v). The too-early SH for John may however indicate that he intones the piece, which is certainly likely.

40₈ 455+sd Function: none. This blessing is apparently spoken.

40₉ 495+sd Function: (a) Here the SD does not imply music, but line **495** does. There is no indication of a possible piece, but the text is evidently in praise of God's mercy.

40ₐ 508+sd Function: (a). There is no evidence for heavenly music here, while Mary's soul returns to her body, but it would certainly be appropriate.

40₁₀ 521+sd Function: (a). *Assumpta est Maria in celum* is both an antiphon and a short responsory: note the reading 'es' for 'est'. The performance by the heavenly chorus is again *cantantibus organis* (which is here unambiguous), and this does imply vocal music, since the text is given.

40₁₁ 528 Function: (g). 'Alle hefne' makes music in honour of the Assumption at the end of the play. I do not think that 'Deo gracias' must be considered the whole text, or indeed the text at all, although it could be.

(i) Pageant from the Original Cycle

41 *Judgement Day*

This play is incomplete, the end being missing. There was presumably a musical set piece at the end.

41_1 1– Function: (f). The trumpet must certainly sound before Michael begins to speak at the start of the play.

3

The Towneley Cycle

3.1 Introduction

The Towneley plays survive in a single manuscript, now MS HM 1 in the Huntington Library at San Marino, California. A facsimile was published in 1976 as Medieval Drama Facsimiles 2, with an introduction by A.C. Cawley and Martin Stevens.

A complete text of the cycle was first published by the Surtees Society in 1836. This edition was superseded in 1897 by that of England and Pollard. The six plays revised by the dramatist known as The Wakefield Master – plays 2, 3, 12, 13, 16 and 22[1] – were edited separately by Cawley in 1958 (*Wakefield Pageants*): Cawley's introduction and appendices remained the standard work on the cycle in general, and on these six plays in particular, until the edition by Stevens and Cawley was published (*Towneley Plays*). This last, which modernises the orthography of the text, is the one cited here. A modern-spelling edition by Peter Meredith (*Towneley Cycle*) has also been consulted.

The cycle consists of thirty-two plays, of which the last two, 'Lazarus' and 'Suspencio Jude', are misordered in the manuscript: they were copied after the Last Judgement play, but should follow the plays of John the Baptist and the Buffetting ('Coliphizacio'), respectively.[2] Cawley and Stephens noted that play 7 ('Processus Prophetarum') is also out of sequence and should follow play 8, 'Pharao' (MDF 2, viii). Like previous editors, they leave these plays in their manu-script positions, but Meredith restores them to narrative order. It is impossible to know why these plays were misordered. Those at the end of the manuscript may have been unavailable when the scribe reached the appropriate point in the manuscript, but it may have been a simple mistake: 'Lazarus' was copied by the scribe responsible for most of the manuscript, although 'Suspencio

---

1 For the numbering of the plays, see below.
2 Meredith regards the first of these as 'certainly' the correct position, and the second as only 'probably' the intended one. The latter could indeed be wrong by one play in either direction, but Meredith's positioning seems much the best fit.

Jude' is in 'a different, though probably not much later, hand' (Meredith *Towneley Cycle* II, ii).

Like other English cycles, this one starts with the Creation and ends with Doomsday. There are however some unexpected omissions: 'Lazarus' is the only Ministry play, and there is nothing else between 'John the Baptist' and 'The Conspiracy', so that the Entry into Jerusalem is not covered; we should also expect the cycle to include a Pentecost play. Three or four plays have presumably been lost with the twelve leaves now missing after play **29**: some of these would be Marian plays removed in Elizabethan times,[3] but this is also where a Pentecost play may have been lost. Twelve leaves are missing after play **1**, 'The Creation', and these presumably contained 'The Fall'. Other missing leaves are responsible for the incomplete state of several plays.

Among these losses is the whole of the first quire, which presumably contained the banns for the cycle (MDF 2, viii). No copy of the banns, or any other contemporary list of the plays, is known to have survived.

The activity of a single main scribe has imposed a certain amount of unity on the cycle, although his editorial work was principally (as far as one can see) a matter of visual presentation. There is also a unity of style due to the revising and compositional activity of the Wakefield Master, an assured dramatist apparently responsible for the six plays originally identified by Cawley (see above) and for revisions in several other plays (Stevens and Cawley *Towneley Plays*, xxviii–xxxi). Stevens and Cawley, in fact, regarded the Wakefield Master as the redactor and compiler of the cycle (*ibid.*, xxxi). The cycle is clearly a more unified collection than the N-Town plays because of this compositional and editorial consistency, and there is also a stylistic unity (discussed in Cawley *Wakefield Pageants*, xvii–xx) that is not wholly dependent upon the reviser's activity. In all, we can regard the Towneley cycle as unified in the way that the York and Chester cycles are but the N-Town collection is not. In the case of Towneley there is an additional factor contributing to its unity: the relationship of some of the plays to those of the York cycle.

Scholars generally agree that the text transmitted in the Towneley manuscript is closely related to that of the York cycle. At least five of the Towneley pageants were derived from York plays: Pharao (play **8**), *Pagina Doctorum* (play **18**), *Extraccio Animarum* (play **25**), *Resurreccio Domini* (play **26**) and *Judicium* (play **30**).[4] A sixth pageant, *Processus Talentorum* (play **24**), 'may well have been based on a York pageant now lost',[5] while many of the remaining pageants show

---

3   M. Stevens 'Missing Parts', 258–9. For a discussion of the losses in the context of religious iconoclasm of the time, see Davidson 'Devil's Guts', 121–2. Stevens considers the missing plays to be those of the Death, Assumption and Coronation of the Virgin.

4   Reasons for thinking that Towneley borrowed from York are given in Stevens and Cawley *Towneley Plays*, xxvii–xxviii.

5   Stevens and Cawley *Towneley Plays*, xxviii.

similarities of wording with the relevant York plays that can hardly be coincidence. Stevens and Cawley considered that some of the York plays date from around 1430, even though the York cycle was not compiled until some time in the 1460s:[6] this means that York exemplars could have been known in the Wakefield area by the mid-fifteenth century

In the process of adaptation of, and addition to, the pageants borrowed from York and elsewhere, the Wakefield Master shows himself as a major figure in late medieval English drama. He was certainly responsible for revising, recasting or adapting six plays: *Mactatio Abel* (play **2**), *Processus Noe cum filiis* (play **3**), *Prima pagina pastorum* (play **12**), *Secunda [pagina] pastorum* (play **13**), *Magnus Herodes* (play **16**) and *Coliphizacio* (play **21**). John W. Robinson doubted that *Mactatio Abel* contained more than one stanza by this author, but added another eight pageants that he thought had the Wakefield Master's work in them.[7] Stevens and Cawley, as already noted, concluded that the Wakefield Master 'had a hand as either author or redactor in half the cycle as it survives' and that 'he was a major redactor of the full cycle, if not the compiler himself'.[8]

Despite the fact that some of the Towneley texts apparently represent older versions of plays revised in the mid-fifteenth century for the York cycle, the Towneley manuscript seems to be a good deal later than the York register. Estimates vary, but no-one disagrees substantially with Cawley and Stevens's dating of 'c. 1500'.[9] This history, which makes the two cycles related in a potentially complex way, expains why the evidence of texts and stage directions is sometimes quite different in the two cycles. In particular, even the similarities in closely-related plays do not guarantee similar musical cues or even the same use of music. While a comparison makes fascinating reading, therefore, I have treated the two versions – where a play survives in both Towneley and York – as independent plays for the purposes of this book.

The plays derive their name from the Towneley family of Towneley Hall, Burnley, who possessed the manuscript (with a single short break) from the early seventeenth century until its sale to the collector Bernard Quaritch in 1883.

The provenance of the cycle is unknown. Cawley long believed the plays to be those of Wakefield and the manuscript to have been used as the civic register of that town.[10] Certainly the scribe produced a visually consistent copy, with decorative work suggesting an intended use as an important reference copy of

---

6 Stevens and Cawley *Towneley Plays*, xxviii.

7 Robinson *Studies*, 17.

8 Stevens and Cawley *Towneley Plays*, xxxi. Of course, this leaves open the possibility that the Wakefield Master was also the main scribe of the cycle, although this is not a necessary conclusion.

9 Stevens and Cawley *Towneley Plays*, xxii.

10 Cawley *Wakefield Pageants*, xii–xiii, refers to the evidence that the manuscript was a register; Stevens and Cawley *Towneley Plays*, xxii–xxv, are careful to say that it was *used* as a register but apparently not *copied* as one.

both functional and intrinsic value to a powerful body such as a corporation. The evi-dence for Wakefield was never strong, however, except for local place-names that appear in plays **2** and **13**: and although one would wish to be able to match up the surviving records from Wakefield with the text that we have, it is not possible to do so.[11] The name 'Wakefeld' attached to plays **1** and **3** may or may not be the name of the town: if it were a personal name, for instance, it still would not demonstrate more than a likely connection with the area,[12] which is demonstated anyway by linguistic features of the text. Stevens and Cawley retained the connection with Wakefield as a strong probability, stating that the plays 'were almost certainly presented [there]' and assuming that, as the book was used as the civic register, the manuscript was kept in Wakefield until at least 1576.[13] On the evidence currently available, the provenance of the Towneley cycle must remain a matter of doubt, with Wakefield the only credible contender so far put forward.

The derivation of Towneley plays from the York cycle before the latter's mid-century revision raises the possibility that those pageants were originally processional plays to be performed on waggons. The title of play **3**, *Processus Noe cum filiis Wakefeld*, suggests this, as does the word *pagina* in the titles of plays **12**, **13** and **18** and the use of *incipit* as the first word of the title for most plays. There is a strong body of opinion, however, that the cycle as we have it was designed for place-and-scaffold performance with a single cast.[14]

The pageants of the Towneley cycle are listed here in manuscript order, as retained by Stevens and Cawley, and with their titles:

1	The Creation	Heading: *The Barkers: Wakefeld*
2	The Murder of Abel	Heading: *The Glovers*
3	Noah and his Sons	Heading: *Wakefeld*
4	Abraham	incomplete at end
5	Isaac	incomplete at start
6	Jacob	
7	The Play of the Prophets	incomplete: should probably follow play 8

[11] The evidence is briefly reviewed by Meredith *Towneley Cycle*, ii–iii, and at length by Stevens and Cawley *Towneley Plays*, xix–xxii. The case was much weakened when the record evidence, which was always circumstantial, was shown to include forgeries: see Palmer '"Towneley Plays" ... Revisited'.

[12] Meredith *Towneley Cycle*, ii, although Meredith uses the evidence positively to demonstrate the connection.

[13] Stevens and Cawley *Towneley Plays*, xv–xvi, and Cawley's discussion of the Wakefield records in *Revels* I, 50–8. There is of course only circumstantial internal evidence that this manuscript was used as a register unless one accepts that it is the book mentioned in the Wakefield records.

[14] Stevens 'Missing Parts'. See also Cawley's section on the staging of the cycle in *Revels* I, 58–66.

8	Pharaoh	= **York 11**. Heading: *The Litsters or Dyers*
9	Caesar Augustus	
10	The Annunciation	
11	Mary's Salutation of Elizabeth	
12	The First Shepherds' Play	
13	The Second Shepherds' Play	
14	The Offering of the Magi	
15	The Flight into Egypt	
16	Herod	
17	The Purification of Mary	incomplete at end
18	Christ and the Doctors	= **York 20**. Incomplete at start
19	John the Baptist	
20	The Conspiracy and Capture	
21	The Buffeting	
22	The Scourging	
23	The Crucifixion	
24	The Play of the Dice	
25	The Harrowing of Hell	= **York 37**
26	The Resurrection	= **York 38**
27	The Pilgrims	Heading: *The Fishers*
28	Thomas of India	
29	The Ascencion	incomplete
30	The Judgment	= **York 47**
31	Lazarus	belongs between 19 and 20
32	The Hanging of Judas	belongs probably between 21 and 22

3.2 Dramatic directions

The physical aspects of the Towneley cycle's dramatic directions were described by Cawley and Stevens (MDF 2, x, section J). The functions of the directions were analysed by Philip Butterworth at a Medieval English Theatre conference in 1981: the results of his analysis are here discussed on the basis of a document handed out at that meeting.

Cawley and Stevens noted that directions occur in all but twelve plays; that all original directions are in Latin, except for three (all in play **14**) in English; and that a single English direction occurring marginally in play **12** is added by a late hand. By 'original', they presumably meant 'by the main scribe'; by 'a late hand' they apparently meant a sixteenth-century one. In fifteen plays the directions are in black ink and placed to the right of the text. Usually these are marked with red underlining and a red oblique stroke. Some black directions occur in the text itself: most of these are distinguished with red underlining or some other attention-drawing red mark. In two plays the directions are in red: one of these, the direction for the singing of *Christus resurgens* in play **26**, has the title of the piece in black – a sort of reversed rubrication (c.f. the special treatment given to text-incipits in the Chester banns and in the N-Town manuscript – the latter not in red, however). In a further three plays there are directions in both red and black.

Apart from the case of the one truly marginal direction, it is doubtful if any useful purpose will be served by attempting to distinguish between real directions and marginal ones. Those placed to the right of the text inevitably use the right margin if the text-line is a long one or if the direction itself is long. The scribe must have left room for the red directions when he was writing the text, and this argues a certain amount of planning and forethought, even if he was not consistent. In the matter of red directions, Cawley and Stevens noted that none appears before play **8**, and they also cited Frampton's comment that at least three of the five plays with red directions were among those shared with the York cycle. As we have seen (1.2), the original directions in the York manuscript are normally in red. Cawley and Stevens played down this factor, pointing out that 'the Towneley plays in question were not copied from the extant York register' (MDF 2, xviii, n. 25).

The directions in the Towneley plays are summarised in Table 4. As is often the case, the boundary between directions and speech headings is a difficult one, and it would be possible to arrive at a list of directions slightly different from that offered here. A direction such as 'Tunc dicet malis' (**30/647**) fails to be a SH proper only because it comes in the middle of a speech and its import can therefore be seen to be gestural. Moreover, a direction of this sort may include more information, as that at **30/607** does: 'Tunc vertens se ad bonos dicit illis', where the SH import is obviously minimal. From here it is only a step to the omission of the SH element: 'Tunc expandit manus suas et ostendit eis Wlnera sua' (**30/575**), which becomes completely directive by default. Thus these lines seem to show an interest in the directive element at the expense of the SH element, and they are all included in the table. Only one such line is omitted from the table, on the ground that the potentially directive element is both static (i.e. adjectival) and subsidiary to the SH element: 'primus angelus cum gladio' (**30/115**), which occurs at the beginning of the angel's speech.

This accepted, the table lists a total of 67 directions, one of which is a late MD in English (and is in fact illegible in the reproduction, MDF 2, 37r). Of the 66 true directions, 8 are musical: however, one of these 8 is for the ringing of the bells, and might arguably be thought of as being in a related but separate category. The late MD is also musical ('sing'), but as it confirms a text reference it is probably the result of a more precise placing needed in rehearsal. The most reasonable calculation of the incidence of musical directions would, I think, be 7 in a total of 66 directions, therefore, or 10.6%: but however we calculate it, we

TABLE 4 : DIRECTIONS IN THE TOWNELEY CYCLE

p/line	f	mus/ non-m	lang	red/ blk	posn	direction if musical: comment
1/76	1r	/n	lat	/b		
1/131	2r	/n	lat	/b	in text	includes SH
1/167	2r	/n	lat	/b		
1/197	2r	/n	lat	/b	in text	includes SH
2						no directions
3/273	9v	/n	lat	/b		
4/107	14r	/n	lat	/b		
4/278	15v	/n	lat	/b		
5/18	16r	/n	lat	/b		
5/66	16v	/n	lat	/b		
6/34	16v	/n	lat	/b		
6/58	17r	/n	lat	/b		
6/84	17r	/n	lat	/b		
6/114	17r	/n	lat	/b		
6/122	17v	/n	lat	/b		very much squashed in
6/130	17v	/n	lat	/b		
7						no directions
8/88	22r	/n	lat	r/	in text	
8/109	22r	/n	lat	r/	in text	
8/390	25r	/n	lat	/b		no red marking
8/413	25r	/n	lat	/b		
9						no directions
10						no directions
11						no directions
12/617	37r	m/	eng	/b	margl	*sing* In a 'later hand' (Stevens and Cawley *Towneley Plays*, 123)

13/273	40r	/n	lat	/b	in text	
13/290	40v	/n	lat	/b		
13/386	41r	/n	lat	/b		
13/919	45r	m/	lat	/b	in text	*Angelus cantat gloria in exelsis: postea dicat* includes SH
14/84	47v	/n	lat	/b	in text	includes SH
14/504	51v	/n	eng	/b	in text	
14/510	51v	/n	eng	/b	in text	
14/522	51v	/n	eng	/b		
15						no directions
16						no directions
17/102	61v	m/	lat	/b		*tunc pulsabant*
17/132	61v	m/	lat	/b		*Angeli cantant simeon justus et timoratus*
18/48	62r	/n	lat	/b		
18/196	63v	/n	lat	r/	in text	includes SH
19/212	66v	/n	lat	/b		
20/197	68v	/n	lat	r/		
20/337	69v	/n	lat	r/		
20/357	69v	/n	lat	r/	in text	
20/369	69v	/n	lat	r/	in text	
20/375	69v	/n	lat	?r/	in text	
20/407	70r	/n	lat	r/		
20/409	70r	/n	lat	r/	in text	
20/523	71r	/n	lat	r/		
20/527	71r	/n	lat	r/		
20/535	71r	/n	lat	r/		
20/539	71r	/n	lat	r/		
20/543	71r	/n	lat	r/		
21						no directions
22/435	82v	/n	lat	/b		
23						no directions

24						no directions
25/44	97v	m/	lat	/b		*Et cantent omnes salvator mundi primum versum*
26/44	101v	/n	lat	r/		
26/229	103v	m/	lat	r/	in text	*Tunc cantabunt angeli christus resurgens et postea dicet ihesus* includes SH: the incipit is written in black ink
27/103	108v	/n	lat	r/		
27/290	110v	/n	lat	/b		
27/296	110v	/n	lat	/b	in text	includes SH: multiple direction, covering a line and a half and spreading into the R margin
28/104	112v	m/	lat	/b	in text	*Tunc venit ihesus et cantat pax vobis et non tardabit hec est dies quam fecit dominus*
28/120	112v	m/	lat	/b	in text	*Iterum venit ihesus et cantat pax vobis et non tardabit*
28/176	113r	/n	lat	/b		
28/234	113v	/n	lat	/b		
28/240	113v	/n	lat	/b		
28/296	114r	/n	lat	/b		
29/52	117v	/n	lat	/b		
29/189	118v	/n	lat	/b		
29/281	120r	/n	lat	/b		
29/289	120r	m/	lat	/b		*Et sic ascendit cantantibus angelis Ascendo ad patrem meum*
30/575	126r	/n	lat	/b	in text	no red marking
30/607	126v	/n	lat	/b	in text	no red marking
30/647	127r	/n	lat	/b		SH
30/697	127v	/n	lat	/b		SH
30/701	127v	/n	lat	/b		SH

31/88	130r	/n	lat	/b		includes SH
32						no directions

arrive at a result very different from that obtained for York, where musical directions accounted for more than 50% of the total (see 1.2).

This result notwithstanding, we should note that music is involved in those directions that occur in Towneley but not in York among the plays common to the two cycles: so it will be useful to discuss the occurrence of these directions in the two versions of the plays concerned. These plays give us a possible tool for increasing our understanding of the directions, although it is unlikely that we can offer anything more definite than suggestions on the basis of such investigation.

It will be best to set out first the relevant Towneley directions play by play, with commentaries. Most of this material is not concerned with music.

Play 8: Pharaoh
This is broadly parallel to **York 11**. Towneley is marginally longer and has a slightly more complex distribution of speeches among the characters.
8/88 *Tunc intrat moyses cum virga in manu etc.*

Yk 11/84   No SD

8/109 *hic properat ad rubum et dicit ei deus, etc.*

Yk 11/104   No SD

These two directions, not in York, appear in red and in text position in Towneley. the first gives descriptive information not obvious from the text (*cum virga in manu*). More importantly, for us, it uses the word 'intrat' in a context where waggon staging would not find an 'entrance' pertinent. The direction may, therefore, reflect the change from processional presentation to that of the place and scaffold.[15]

The second direction also prescribes movement, making it clear that the movement occurs before the speech following is started. The apparent SH is tautologous, since there is an actual SH before the next line.

In both of these, the 'etc.' is something of a puzzle.
8/390   *hic pertransient mare*

Yk 11/382   No SD

8/413   *Tunc merget eos mare*

Yk 11/404   No SD

Both of these, in black and at the end of text lines, have no equivalent in the York play. In both cases the direction gives only information that is already obvious from the text: and it may be the precise placing of the information that is

---

[15] Note that both of these SDs are written in red.

important. These directions are clearly not of the same order as the first two, however.

Play 18: Christ and the Doctors
18/48 *Tunc venit ihesus*
> **Yk 20/72** No SD

The first scenes are different, and this direction starts the second scene, where the two plays come together. The Towneley direction is black, and is at the end of the text line. Since the next speech is assigned to Jesus, who speaks here for the first time in both plays, the direction is quite unnecessary. As at **8/88**, however, it may indicate an entrance in place-and-scaffold presentation.

18/196 *Tunc venient Josephus et Maria et dicet Maria*
> **Yk 20/204** No SD

As above, the importance of this direction may well be that it indicates an entrance in a place-and-scaffold presentation:[16] the appearance of Mary and Joseph is otherwise obvious (they then speak), and the last three words are made unnecessary by a normal SH on the line following.

This direction is in red, and in text position.

Play 25: The Harrowing of Hell
25/44 *Et cantent omnes salvator mundi primum versum*
> **Yk 37/48** No SD

In the York version, Isaiah's speech begins on the next line, **49**; but in the Towneley play Isaiah has already delivered 8 lines that do not appear in York, so that this direction occurs in the middle of his speech. The singing of 'Salvator mundi' is relevant to these extra lines, but would not fit into the York play at this point.

The direction is in black, and in line-end position.

25/392 Towneley has no music here, lacking a number of lines that follow **York 37/380** (= **Towneley 25/392**). **York 37/384** has a late MD *tunc cantent* in the speech missing from Towneley: the singing is hinted at by the York text, but no more than that, and is not vital to the drama (see **York 37₃**).

25/400 = **Yk 37/408** At the end, Towneley has a text reference to *Te deum laudamus*, while York seems to require *Laus tibi cum gloria* (but see **York 37₃**).

Play 26: The Resurrection
The openings of **Towneley 26** and **York 38** differ, but the first direction occurs after they have started to run in parallel.

26/44 *Tunc veniet centurio velut miles equitans*
> **Yk 38/36** No SD

This SD is in red, in line-end position. The next speech is assigned to the

---

[16] Note that this is a red SD.

centurion, with a SH, so that the appearance of this character is not in doubt. The 'veniet' may again indicate an 'entry' appropriate to non-processional performance, which in any case is on horseback. The latter part of the direction, too, may indicate that the character was not mounted in the original (processional) version of the play.

26/229 *Tunc cantabunt angeli Christus resurgens et postea dicet ihesus*

In red (but the *incipit* in black) and in text position. The latter part of this is strictly unnecessary, since there is a SH for Christ's long monologue that follows. (This speech, one of those rivetting sermons that are a feature of some Towneley plays, does not occur in York.) The main part of the direction tells us (a) that the angels sing, which is important symbolically; (b) what piece they sing, which is important practically; and (c) that Christ should not try to speak over the music, but should wait until it has finished. The dumbshow covered by this music is of course the focal point of the whole cycle.

The SD at the parallel place, **Yk 38/186**, reads *Tunc Jesu resurgente*. As noted in 1.2, Table 2, this suggests that the Resurrection takes place before anything else happens (the next line is the beginning of the scene with the guard, after Christ has disappeared).

The York direction does however have a sixteenth-century MD added to it: *Resurgens*. This is not unambiguous but, as noted in 1.4, it is likely to be Clerke's abbreviated note for the performance of *Christus resurgens*, an obvious choice for music here.

Play 30: The Judgment

The opening of the Towneley play is lost, but in any case the two plays do not run in parallel to begin with. The first York direction is in a short scene that does not occur in Towneley:

Yk 47/216 *Hic ad sedem judicii cum cantu angelorum*

(Note that this, too, is grammatically incomplete.)

In the part of the plays that does run in parallel, Towneley has five directions (see Table 4), none of which has a parallel in York:

30/575 (= **Yk 47/244**) *Tunc expandit manus suas et ostendit eis Wlnera sua*

Although this is in black ink, like all directions in this play, it is in text-position. The following part of the speech makes clear that Christ is showing his wounds, but the detail of extending his hands is not mentioned. (One might easily guess at it, however, and he does refer to his hands in listing the parts of his body wounded for Man's sake.)

30/607 (= **Yk 47/276**) *Tunc vertens se ad bonos dicit illis*

In text position. Although it is clear to whom Christ now speaks (and this is true of the directions that follow), the purpose seems to be to make sure that the gesture of turning is made: and perhaps, once dealt with, it is assumed that this turning should happen each time in the following directions.

30/647 (= **Yk 47/316**) *Tunc dicet malis*
30/697 (= **Yk 47/364**) *Tunc dicet bonis*
30/701 (= **Yk 47/368**) *Tunc dicet malis*

All of these three seem to depend on that after line **607**: there is no doubt about those to whom Christ is speaking. These are also in line-end position, however, and this seems to indicate that they were regarded as of lesser importance.

The endings of the two versions of this play are rather different, but no directions are concerned until the very end. There, the York play has a direction, discussed at length in I, 28–31:

Yk 47/380+sd *Et sic facet finem cum melodia angelorum transiens a loco ad locum*

The equivalent place (it is not a parallel) in Towneley, **30/830**, gives a text reference to the singing of *Te Deum laudamus*.

An attempt to make sense of this information is necessarily speculative. We cannot know how dramatists, revisers and scribes viewed the relative importances of text-position as opposed to line-end-position directions, of black ink as opposed to red, or of the various types of information transmitted by the directions; nor can we be sure that our own prejudices on these matters have been eliminated. In exploring the possibilities, too, we must bear in mind that these plays did not exist in sources where such views were unified. We cannot assume, therefore, that the dramatist and reviser of Play A took the same view of these matters as the dramatist and reviser of Play B, while this in itself obscures the fact that we do not know the part played by revisers and scribes (nor how many of them there were) in the production of the exemplars used when the Towneley manuscript was copied.

It will be best to start with that event that must be seen as central to a cycle, the moment of Resurrection itself (**26/229+sd**). Play **26** uses red directions, and this one is in text position. Turning to play **8**, where there seems to be a distinction between red directions in text position and black ones in line-end position, we see that, whereas the latter (**8/390, 413**) merely confirm facts that are obvious from the text, the former deal with more important matters – **8/88+sd** apparently with an entrance and facts that would not otherwise be known, and **8/109+sd** with movement. Even so, the first of these is surely much more important than the second. This suggests, first, that the four directions in this play represent layers of activity; and, second, that the red directions in text position belong to a layer of SDs proper, while the black ones in line-end position are a later accretion to the text (but not necessarily to the red directions: see below).

Play **18** is another in which both black and red directions are found. Here, however, the possibility of layers of activity is only faint. It is true that the red direction in text position is slightly more informative than the black one in line-end position, but there is very little in it: both are basically entry directions that might have resulted from the change of production-method, but they are also confirmatory in that the next speech in each case tells us that those characters have appeared. It is of course possible that the black direction arose from an error of omission when a scribe (the Towneley one? an earlier one?), coming upon a red text-position direction in his exemplar, failed to leave a blank line for it, adding it in line-end position later with the black pen that he had already been using.[17] While this is not unlikely, it is too speculative to support my suggestion – which I make, after all, on the evidence of only two directions (one black, one red) – that this is really an 'all-red-directions' play.

A similar speculation could work for play 25. Here, however, we have the fact of the addition of lines not in **York 37** and to which the singing is relevant. If we accept that at some stage those lines have been added to an existing play, we must also accept that the direction for singing was added then or later, but in any case not earlier. The direction, then, did not appear in the text before the new lines were added, and in this sense it need not be regarded as 'original'. However, there are no other directions in this play, so that the scribe copying from a guild text would have no precedent for his treatment of this direction: placing it on the right of the page may have seemed the best way of distinguishing it from the text.

The first direction in play **26** combines the kind of information given by **18/196+sd**, including the mood and tense, and the descriptive element noted in **8/88+sd**. Although it is in red ink, like the other direction in this play, it occurs in line-end position. This, too, may be explicable in terms of an error of omission: or – more likely, I think – its marginal position may show that it was added to the complete text, perhaps to make clear the changes necessitated by the new method of staging.[18]

Finally, play **30** again shows directions of two different levels of importance. Colour plays no part, since at some stage – perhaps from the beginning – directions were made to be in black. The first two directions (**30/575, 607**) clearly give more information than, and in the case of the second act as a full model for, the brief directions following **30/647, 697** and **701**. Whether these last three are in line-end position because they were in fact added later than the other two, it is impossible to tell. They may well be later additions, corresponding to marginal additions in other cycles. Of course, the suggested layers of activity cannot be extended from one play to another. For instance, those directions that could perhaps reflect a change from processional to non-processional performance are un-

---

[17] I assume here that the scribe copied the material in black, leaving suitable spaces for material that was to be red, and then changed pens and ink in order to fill in the red material. Finding that the required space was not there, he then copied the material in the next most suitable place. Why he should do this in black ink is another matter.

[18] It is also possible that, in the situation suggested in note 17, above, the scribe used the pen that he had just taken up and filled in the expectation of copying a red direction in text-position.

likely to be the oldest directions in this group of plays: in fact, they could conceivably be among the most recent, their importance for the new staging methods ensuring them red ink and a place in the text where the relative unimportance of existing MDs was responsible for the lack of any change in their status. It is quite impossible to suggest a firm chronology for the various layers that this implies through just this group of plays: but this line of thought could become useful if more information on the play-texts were to be found.

3.3 Text references

1 *The Creation*
No references.

2 *The Murder of Abel*
2/300   CAIM   We! who was that that piped so smal?

Metaphorical: Cain is referring slightingly to God.

3 *Noah and his Sons*
3/383   [NOE]   This is a sory note

This is not a musical metaphor: Stevens and Cawley offer 'affair, business' for 'no(y)te' in their glossary.

3/674   The Ark has come to rest on what Noah calls 'the hyllys of armonye'. It seems clear from this that 'Armony' or something like it was a normal spelling for Armenia. See also the discussion of **York 9** in 1.3, above.

3/765   [NOE] With gle and with gam

Not a musical use of 'gam': see I, 48.

3/806   [NOE]   Amen, for charite.

This, the last line of the play, is apparently designed to elicit an 'Amen' response from the audience. See I, section 8.6, and especially pp. 372–3.

4 *Abraham*
5 *Isaac*
6 *Jacob*
No references

7 *The Play of the Prophets*

7/104–5   [DAVID]   Shall I now syng you a fytt
                         With my mynstrelsy.

7/109–11   Myrth I make till all men
                         With my harp and fyngers ten,
                         And warn theym that thay glad.

7/118   For that I harp and myrth make

7/157   Now haue I songen you a fytt.

David is the speaker throughout the speech occurring at **7/90+lat–162**. The singing of a 'fytt' is what one expects of a minstrel, a 'fit' being a section of a romance or ballad: hence the reference to minstrelsy at **105**. The first of these quotations states David's intention of singing, and the last confirms that he has done so. The second and third items associate David's minstrelsy with mirth and gladness, mention his harp, and indicate that he uses all ten fingers in playing the instrument: but they do not help with the limits of the sung 'fit'.

Looking at the complete text of David's speech, there is no clear beginning to his singing. At the very least he must sing the Latin lines following **150** and their 6-line commentary (followed immediately by line **157**, quoted above). But this hardly fits with the 'now' of line **104**, and in any case the verse at lines **151–6** is not readily separable from the verses preceding the Latin. Working backwards we find no seam in his argument until the beginning of the prophecy, line **109**. It therefore looks as if the greater part of David's speech, lines **109–56**, should be sung, the first and fourth of my quotations, above, being immediately before and after the sung section. In this case the second and third quotations are both in the sung part of the speech.

7/199-201

[SIBILLA PROPHETA]   At hys commyng shall bemys blaw,
                     That men may his commyng knaw;
                     Full sorrowfull shall be that blast.

The Sibyl foretells the call to the Judgement, This remark tells us nothing new, but it confirms two points noted under play **30**, below: that men recognise the Last Trumpet for what it is, and that it heralds sorrow, at least for some.

8 *Pharaoh*

8/141   [DEUS]   Ful soyn hys song shall be alas

Metaphorical use.

8/237   PHARAO   Fy on hym! nay, nay, that dawnce is done

Metaphorical: 'that business is finished'.

8/429   The 'Amen' is not placed with the rest of the text, but out to the right, almost in line with the SHs. The final stanza is complete without this word. The 'Amen' is not part of Moses's final speech, then, and should be spoken by the cast and audience. See I, 372.

9   Caesar Augustus
10   The Annunciation
11   Mary's Salutation of Elizabeth
No references.

12 The First Shepherds' Play
12/48, 51   [PRIMUS PASTOR]   I may syng

      ...

      ...

Wo is me this dystres.

12/383–9   [2 PASTOR]   Who so can best syng
                Shall have the begynnyng.
PRIMUS PASTOR   Now prays at the partyng;
                I shall sett you on warke.
                We have done oure parte
                And songyn right weyll;
                I drynk for my parte.

The Second Shepherd proposes a singing competition, with the first pull on a new bottle of ale as the prize: for the circumstances and the result of this, see I, 353–4.

12/439–42, 447–8

PRIMUS PASTOR   A, godys dere dominus!
                What was that sang?
                It was wonder curiose
                With small noytys emang.

                ...

                ...

                Me thoght
                Oone scremyd on lowde.

12/471–4   [3 PASTOR] It was a mery gle:
                    Sich hard I neuer none,
                    I recorde,
                    As he sayde in a skreme

12/588–92 [2 PASTOR] I wold that we knew
                    Of this song so fre
                    Of the angell;
                    I hard by hys steuen
                    He was send downe fro heuen.

12/596–8 [2 PASTOR] It was a mery song.
                    I dar say that he broght
                    Foure and twenty to a long.

12/602–5 PRIMUS PASTOR So many [notes] he throng
                    On a heppe;
                    Thay were gentyll and small,
                    And well tonyd withall.

These passages are taken from the shepherds' long discussion of the angel's song to them, which takes place after line **425**. The angel's speech, lines **426–38**, corresponds very loosely to the biblical account and, unless we assume that this speech is itself sung, we must suppose a Latin item with roughly the biblical text ('Nolite timere'). Carpenter ('Music in the *Secunda Pastorum*', 217) assumed that the heavenly host sings *Gloria in excelsis* at this point, which is also a possibility.[19]

Although the bulk of the shepherds' discussion of this song concerns the text, some of it, quoted here, is about the music and the performance. We learn first that the song was 'wonder curiose', with 'small noytys emang' (**442**): clearly, it was a virtuoso performance, a fact that is confirmed when we hear that the angel is thought to have 'broght foure and twenty to a long' (**598**). The meaning of this is, primarily, that the song was very florid, and therefore difficult to sing, with many small notes in it: for the technical details, see I, 37–41. The virtuoso element is allied, as so often, to the idea of mirth, the song being described as 'a mery gle' (**471**) and 'a mery song' (**596**). The song was also pleasant to hear, however, since the Third Shepherd describes it as 'well tonyd withall' (**605**), which I take to mean 'well-tuned' in the modern sense (see I, 42–4).

12/620–2   [3 PASTOR]   Take at my sangre.
          PRIMUS PASTOR   Now an ende have we doyn

---

[19] The Gloria would not otherwise occur in this play, which would certainly be strange.

Of oure song this tyde.

The shepherds evidently sing a song after line **620**, having first discussed the matter (**606–20**).[20] The Third Shepherd wants to repeat the angel's song (**599–600**), and boasts that he can remember it and will immeditely sing it (**606–7**). After encouragement from the First Shepherd (**608–9**: 'Brek outt youre voce / Let se as ye yelp', with a possible pun on the musical meaning of 'break'), he decides that he cannot do it without help (**610–11**): on the reason for this, see I, 355.

12/718–24 PRIMUS PASTOR Amen to that worde!

> Syng we therto
> On hight;
> To ioy all sam
> With myrth and gam,
> To the lawde of this lam
> Syng we in syght.

The final lines of the play show that the shepherds sing in honour of the Christ-child after taking their leave of the Holy Family. The phrase 'in sight' has been taken to imply an example of three-part improvised polyphony:[21] but it probably means only 'in the sight of this company', and so the song could be sung in unison, which is more likely. See I, 355–6.

13 *The Second Shepherds' Play*
13/150–2

> [SECUNDUS PASTOR]   Had she oones wett hyr whystyll,
> She couth syng full clere
> Hyr Pater noster.

This is taken from the Second Shepherd's unflattering portrait of his wife. On its possible interpretations, see I, 197.

13/162–4   [1 PASTOR]   Yee, on a ley land
> Hard I hym blawe.
> He commys here at hand

This is not strictly a musical reference, but it was treated as such by England and Pollard, who regarded the Third Shepherd as having blown his pipe. The

---

20 See the explanation by Cawley in *Wakefield Pageants*, 104.
21 N.C. Carpenter 'Music in the *Secunda Pastorum*', 217; J. Stevens 'Music in Mediaeval Drama', 90.

proper instrument is however a horn (see I, 360–1), which he has presumably blown at an earlier stage. Since the Second Shepherd asks (line **161**) 'Sagh thou awre of Daw?' only two lines after his meeting with the First Shepherd, the latter's reply 'Yee, on a ley land / Hard I hym blawe' must refer to a time before their meeting. Apparently the First Shepherd, but not the Second, hears the blowing of a horn shortly before their meeting after line **156**, when the Second Shepherd is speaking his monologue: for that matter, the horn could be heard even during the First Shepherd's monologue, before the Second Shepherd enters. As long as it is clear (a) that it is not the Second Shepherd sounding the horn and (b) that the horn is not far away (and even getting closer), the exact placing of the horn-calls is a matter for the producer and actors to work out, with appropriate reaction by the First Shepherd.

13/265–73 [PRIMUS PASTOR] Yit I wold, or we yode,
          Oone gaf vs a song.
SECUNDUS PASTOR So I thoght, as I stode,
          To myrth us emong.
TERCIUS PASTOR I grauntt.
PRIMUS PASTOR Lett me syng the tenory.
SECUNDUS PASTOR And I the tryble so hye.
TERCIUS PASTOR Then the meyne fallys to me.
          Lett se how ye chauntt.

The SD following line **273** concerns the entrance of Mak, who does not immediately make contact with the three shepherds. There is no reason to doubt that the shepherds sing here, which in view of the text just quoted would not require a direction.

'Treble', 'Mean' and 'Tenor' are the names of the voices in three-part music, defining the highest, middle and lowest ranges, respectively, of the musical texture. What sort of music this might be, and the nature of the song, is discussed in 3.6.

13/636–9, 643 [UXOR] Com and make redy all,
          And syng by thyn oone;
          Syng lullay thou shall,
          For I must grone,
          ...
          Syng lullay on fast

13/686–9 TERCIUS PASTOR Will ye here how thay hak?
          Oure syre lyst croyne.
PRIMUS PASTOR Hard I neuer none crak
          So clere out of toyne.

The shepherds evidently arrive at Mak's house after line **685**, which is Mak's cue for starting the lullaby. He sings this alone (line **637**), while Gyll groans as if in the aftermath of childbirth. The Third Shepherd's first remark, however, seems to include the noise made by both of them (**686**): Mak's singing is so bad that the Third Shepherd cannot distinguish it (or so he pretends) from Gyll's groaning, and assumes that Gyll is singing, too.

On 'crak' and 'hak', see I, 36–7 and 357; on Mak's poor tuning, I, 42–4.

13/933–4 PRIMUS PASTOR This was a qwant stevyn
That ever yit I hard.

13/946–51 SECUNDUS PASTOR Say, what was his song?
Hard ye not how he crakyd it,
Thre brefes to a long?
TERCIUS PASTOR Yee, Mary, he hakt it:
Was no crochett wrong,
Nor no thyng that lakt it.

On this discussion of the angel's singing of 'Gloria in excelsis' see I, 39 and 357. Note that the angel's voice was distinctively different from a human one – a 'qwant stevyn'.

It is possible that the Second and Third Shepherds are showing off and do not really have the expertise to make an accurate technical description of the music. But the writer of this play was clearly musical, so the technical details are probably correct. Further on this matter, see I, 36–41.

13/952–8 PRIMUS PASTOR For to syng us emong,
Right as he knakt it,
I can.
SECUNDUS PASTOR Let se how ye croyne!
Can ye bark at the mone?
TERCIUS PASTOR Hold youre tonges! Have done!
PRIMUS PASTOR Hark after, than.

The shepherds must sing immediately after this, attempting to imitate the angelic 'Gloria in excelsis' (**919+sd**) that they have just been discussing (**946–51**). The First Shepherd says that he knows how to sing the angel's song, and implies ('us emong', line **952**) that the others could join in. The Second Shepherd is scornful of his ability: Cawley (*Wakefield Pageants*, 113) identifies 'to bark at the moon' as a popular saying, meaning in this case that the First Shepherd is wasting his time in attempting to repeat the song. 'Hark after, than' (**958**) shows that the First Shepherd does start off. Perhaps he sings the Gloria once through before the others join in, or perhaps they do not need to hear it all the way through before they start to sing themselves: this, too, is a matter for the producer and actors, but the effect is of the First Shepherd being confident enough to start and the others joining in.

13/1087–8   TERCIUS PASTOR To syng ar we bun –
                                 Let take on loft!

The shepherds' willingness to evangelize explains their feeling of obligation to sing, since singing is the best way to praise the Saviour. They therefore begin the song loudly, for all to hear (**1088**). Further on this, see I, 358.

14 *The Offering of the Magi*
No references.

15 *The Flight into Egypt*
15/13   Joseph's description of the angel's message as 'so swete of toyn' at the beginning of *The Flight into Egypt* probably does not indicate a singing voice. There is no evidence otherwise for the angel's singing, and Joseph does not hear angelic singing in other cycles unless he is accompanied by the Blessed Virgin (see I, 184, 186 and 188). This reference is therefore evidence for the sweetness of the angel's *speaking* voice.

16 *Herod*
No references.

17 *The Purification of Mary*
17/103–4 [SYMEON] A, dere God, what may this be?
                              Oure bellys ryng so solemply

17/113–4 [SYMEON] For sich noyse hard I never ere –
                              Oure bellys ryng by thare oone!

These quotations refer to the ringing of bells required by **102+sd** *Tunc pulsabunt*. 'Solemply' does not mean quite what it would mean now: solemn ringing in the modern sense would not elicit the remark of line **113**, which indicates something special. The word implies that the sound of bells is appropriate to a ceremonial occasion, perhaps (as is here the case) a joyful one. It may be helpful to think in terms of the sound required for a wedding rather than for a funeral, therefore.[22]

---

[22] In the Middle Ages bells were rung for many more occasions – and many more joyful and ceremonial occasions – than is now the case.

18 Christ and the Doctors
18/126 [PRIMUS MAGISTER] Erly and late, both lowde and styll.

Metaphorical.

19 John the Baptist
19/8, 101 [IOHANNES] ... both lowd and styll.

[IOHANNES] ... lowd and styll

Metaphorical: 'in all circumstances'.

20 The Conspiracy and Capture
No references.

21 The Buffeting
21/188 [CAYPHAS] Of care may thou syng!

Spoken to Christ: metaphorical.

21/231 CAYPHAS As euer syng I mes

This is an oath: see I, 208.

21/443–5 Cayphas curses the man

That fyrst made me clerk
And taght me my lare
On bookys for to barke

This must also refer, slightingly, to his own singing of the service: see I, 208.

21/513–14 [PRIMUS TORTOR] We must hop and dawnse
As cokys in a croft.

Metaphorical.

21/543 [FROWARD] I may syng ylla hayl!

Metaphorical. There are many more cries of 'illa hayl' in this play, but not with reference to singing.

22 *The Scourging*

22/58 [PRIMUS TORTOR] Of care may he syng

Metaphorical: spoken of Christ.

22/92–3 TERCIUS TORTOR I shall lede the a dawnse
                          Vnto Syr Pilate hall

Metaphorical.

22/482–4

[SECUNDUS TORTOR] Walk on, and lefe thi vayn carping!
                         It shall not saue the fro thy dede,
                         Wheder thise women cry or syng

Metaphorical: spoken to Christ.

23 *The Crucifixion*

23/435   MARIA   Alas may ever be my sang/ ...

23/470   MARIA   Sore syghyng is my sang

Both of these are metaphorical.

24 *The Play of the Dice*

24/86 Pilate's request for silence during his rest includes a warning that no servant annoy him with 'cryyng nor with cronyng'. The glossary of Cawley and Stevens's edition gives 'crooning, singing' for this last word, and we see the musical meaning at **13/955**: but in the present context neither seems entirely apposite. Any musical meaning would imply that Pilate's servants sang at their work, and that this would annoy him, much as it annoys the demons (**25/92, 101**: 'sich a dyn'; 'ugly noyse'): but it does not seem likely that the dramatist intended Pilate's servants to be those doing God's will. Although the 'croyning' at first sight seems to be an alternative to 'cryyng', therefore, it is more probable that 'cryyng and croyning' refers to only one type of activity, to be understood as 'moaning' or perhaps 'complaining'. Certainly it is more in keeping with Pilate's character as it is presented here that his servants might be expected to give way to 'crying and complaining' while he tries to sleep.

24/353 PILATUS What whistyll ye in the wenyande?

Metaphorical. Stevens and Cawley's glossary gives 'time of the waning moon, considered an unlucky time' for 'wenyand(e)'. The Third Torturer thinks that he has won Christ's robe, but Pilate implies that he has not: Stevens and Cawley offer 'whistle in the wind' as the modern equivalent.

25 *The Harrowing of Hell*

25/91–2 [RYBALD] Sich sorow neuer ere I had,
Nor hard I sich a dyn.

25/98 [RYBALD] Sich harow was neuer hard in hell.

25/101–04 RYBALD Whi, herys thou not this vgly noyse?
Thyse lurdans that in lymbo dwell,
Thay make menyng of many ioyse,
And muster myrthes theym emell.

These comments all refer to the singing of the first verse of *Salvator mundi* at 25/44+sd. The demons' reaction to the singing is quite clear: it is very painful to them, an 'ugly noise', a 'din' that brings cries for help ('haro') from those afflicted by it. The beginning of Rybald's speech (89) shows that the distress has been going on for some time in hell, and its continuation brings the demons out to see what is going on. See I, 208.

25/413–16 YSAIAS Therfor now let vs syng
To loue oure Lord Ihesus;
Vnto his blys he will vs bryng,
Te deum laudamus.

Evidently *Te Deum laudamus* is sung after this speech, which is the end of the play: all the souls should sing. Liturgically, *Te Deum* was intoned by the senior responsible person present: the dean, abbot or prior in a major establishment. In the present case, where there are no priests among the patriarchs, Adam is the senior, and should probably therefore sing the intonation.

26 *The Resurrection*

26/537–40 [SECUNDUS MILES] We hard neuer on euyn ne morne,
Nor yit oure faders vs beforne,
Sich melody, mydday ne morne,
As was maide thore.

This is a rather different reaction to the music of the Kingdom, signalling the difference between fallible human beings – the soldiers set to guard the tomb – and the demons of play 25. The soldiers recognise the angelic singing of *Christus resurgens* (229+sd) as something special and beautiful, so presumably it was a virtuoso performance.

27 *The Pilgrims*
28 *Thomas of India*
No references.

29 *The Ascension*
29/362–5 BARTHOLOMEUS A more meruell men neuer saw
                       Then now is sene vs here emang;
                       From erthe till heuen a man be draw
                       With myrth of angell sang.

This speech refers to the angelic singing of *Ascendo ad patrem meum* at **289+sd**. The association of mirth with angelic song is normal, but the speech also confirms that the music covers the actual ascension, with Christ being taken to Heaven from the main playing area.

30 *The Judgment*
30/5–6 [SECUNDUS MALUS] Alas, I harde that horne
                         That callys vs to the dome!

30/51–3 QUARTUS MALUS Alas, I am forlorne!
                       A spytus blast here blawes,
                       I harde well bi yonde horne

30/131–5 PRIMUS DEMON Oute, haro, out, out!
                       Harkyn to this horne,
                       ...
                       ...
                       So sturdy a showte

30/144–6 SECUNDUS DEMON I shoterd and shoke,
                       I herd sich a rerd;
                       When I harde it, I qwoke

30/157–8 PRIMUS DEMON It was like to a trumpe;
                       It had sich a sownde

30/252–3 [SECUNDUS DEMON] Thai haue blowen long syne;
                       Thai will not abide vs.
30/364 [TUTIVILLUS] My horne is blawen.

The beginning of this play is missing, and the Last Trumpet has already sounded when the surviving text begins. It is however likely that it sounds again at intervals during the first part of the play: lines **51–2** and **131–2** may fall a little flat unless the trumpet-blast has been repeated. Lines **131–2** follow a speech by Jesus in which he signals his intention to go to earth and deal out judgement, and it would be entirely appropriate to have the trumpet sound again as Jesus goes to the judgement-seat. (I assume that the movement to the judgement-seat takes place here, although Jesus does not speak again until **560**, after a long scene given to the demons.)

It will be seen, however, that the angel who speaks at **115–22** cannot be the trumpeter, since he holds a sword: the SH reads 'primus angelus cum gladio'. On the other hand the surviving part of the play has no other angel, and 'primus angelus' assumes at least one more in the missing opening of the play. Presumably we have lost a scene in which God proposes the Judgement and orders the Last Trumpet to be sounded, with at least a second angel involved. If the trumpet is indeed sounded at intervals throughout the first part of the play, as I have suggested, then it is blown by this second angel, or by a pair of them.

That the Last Trumpet is an impressive affair is demonstrated by what the souls and demons say about it. It is clearly the herald of the Doom (lines **5–6**), a 'spytus blast' that is 'like to a trumpe': no-one is in doubt as to its significance.

30/827–30 [PRIMUS BONUS]   Therfor full boldly may we syng,
On oure way os we trus;
Make we all myrth and louyng
With te deum laudamus.

This is the end of the play, and clearly *Te Deum* is sung by all the saved souls. As before (play **25**, above) there arises the question as to who shall sing the intonation: again there is no clear answer, unless characters from earlier plays (such as Adam, who would again be the obvious choice) are presented at the Judgement. Perhaps a nameless soul should do it, or the senior angel (Primus Angelus?).

31 *Lazarus*
31/177   Lazarus refers to the singing of Mass for the dead, in the long monologue after his raising, remarking that when one is dead one cannot expect the living to help by paying for 'mes syngyng' for one's soul.

32 *the Hanging of Judas*
No references.

3.4 Latin and the liturgy

1 *The Creation*
1/1   [DEUS]   Ego sum alpha et o

This first line of the cycle is immediately followed by its translation. It is a part of the rhyme-scheme, an integral part of the stanza, and must be spoken.

3 *Noah and his Sons*
3/235   NOE   A, benedicite!

A pious exclamation.

3/363–4   [NOE] In nomine patris, & filij,
                         Et spiritus sancti. Amen.

These lines are not only necessary to the rhyme-pattern but also carry on the sense of the previous (English) lines. There is no reason to sing them.

7 *The Play of the Prophets*
In this play each of the four prophets introduces himself or herself with a Latin quotation that is subsequently expanded and explained in English. These Latin lines are extra-stanzaic and could, therefore, be sung if appropriate: and as they all follow the relevant SH there seems no doubt that each should be spoken or sung by the prophet concerned.

Singing may not be a sensible option unless the quotations are liturgical pieces, which none of these appears to be. I conclude, therefore, that they are most likely to be declaimed. However, there is in addition a two-line text quoted by David towards the end of his speech (7/150+lat) which not only is a liturgical item but occurs during a section of the text that is certainly sung by David (see 2.3, above). It seems safe to assume that this Latin text should be sung.

7/1–lat   MOYSES   Prophetam excitabit deus de fratribus vestris;
                         Omnis anima que non audierit prophetam illum
                         Exterminabitur de populo suo;
                         Nemo propheta sine honore nisi in patria sua.

The last line is derived from Matthew 13/57, Mark 6/4 and Luke 4/24. None of this appears to be a liturgical text.

7/90+lat   DAVID   Omnes reges adorabunt eum;
                         Omnes gentes seruiunt ei.

This is apparently not a liturgical text.

7/150+lat [DAVID] Ostende nobis domine misericordiam tuam,
              Et salutare tuum da nobis.

David has been singing before this, and does not stop doing so until **156**: see
3.3, above. These Latin lines thus occur in the middle of his singing, and
should properly be sung as well. The text is Psalm 85/7, which could be sung
to a psalm-tone. However, it is a liturgical text:

(a) Gradual (Sandon II, 25; GS, 7):
        Ostende nobis domine misericordiam tuam: et salutare
        tuum da nobis. V. Benedixisti.
   Neumatic/melismatic chant, range c–f', c-clef.

(b) Alleluia verse (GS, 1; LU, 320):
        Ostende nobis domine misericordiam tuam: et salutare
        tuum da nobis.
   Melismatic chant, range f–e', c-clef.

(c) Gradual (GS, 7):
        Ostende nobis domine misericordiam tuam: et salutare
        tuum da nobis. V. Benedixisti.
   Neumatic/melismatic chant, range c–e', c-clef.

Any of these pieces would have demanded a professional singer in the role,
and in modern performance, too, a singer of professional quality is required. It
is impossible to say that any of these three items is more suitable than the
others. Singing the 'fit' of lines **109–56** also requires a professional singer, however. While one might expect a minstrel type rather than a church singer in the
latter case, it seems that we may be dealing with a singer who can be both – a
trained church singer who can also perform in a quasi-improvisatory secular
way.

7/162+lat SIBILLA PROPHETA Iudicii signum: tellus sudore madescit;
              E celo rex adueniet per secla futurus,
              Scilicet in carne presens ut iudicet orbem.

David has reverted to speech, so that these first lines of the Sibyl would
sound perfectly natural if spoken: there is no reason to sing them. The Sibyl
explains these lines afterwards.

7/216+lat DANIEL Cum venerit sanctus sanctorum cessabit vncio vestra.

Daniel's first words, presumably spoken.

10   *The Annunciation*

There is no Latin in this play, but the text follows the biblical account closely and in ways that allow the audience to follow the direct speech of the biblical text through paraphrase. There are also moments in which the text would remind an audience of a biblical text that is, as happens, liturgical. Gabriel's greeting of Mary at line 77, 'Hayll, Mary, gracyouse!', is reminiscent of the text *Ave Maria gratia plena*, just as lines 83–4, 'Hayll, Mary, and well thou be! / My Lord of heuen is wyth the', would remind them of the next biblical and liturgical phrase, 'Dominus tecum'. For the possible liturgical items, see 1.4, above, under **12/144+ md**. There is however no indication that Gabriel sings this text before he begins to speak at line 77.

11   *Mary's Salutation of Elizabeth*

11/48+lat MARIA Magnificat anima mea dominum

> This, the first line of the canticle *Magnificat*, is extra-stanzaic, but it is in normal text script and follows the SH 'Maria'. It therefore appears to be spoken by Mary, although it is just possible that it should be understood as a 'footnote' reference to what follows.
>
> The line is followed by a complete translation of the canticle (lines **49–78**), so another possibility is that the whole canticle should be said or sung, in Latin, with the translation following. A liturgical performance, whether said or sung, would normally include the doxology, however, and that is missing from the translation. The indications are, therefore, that a normal performance of the canticle as psalmody is not intended here.[23] Unsatisfactory as it seems in some ways, I suspect that the play text should be taken at face value, Mary first speaking the one Latin line and then continuing to the translation of the whole canticle, exactly as written.

12   *The First Shepherds' Play*

12/419 [TERCIUS PASTOR] Cryst-crosse, benedyght

---

[23] Performed as a tract, the canticle would have been sung without the doxology. The tract that appears in the *Graduale Sacrosanctae Romanae Ecclesiae* published by H. Dessain at Mechlin in 1909, p. (182), does not have the full text, but ends at '... omnes generationes.' Moreover, I am not aware that any of the English uses included this tract. It therefore seems most improbable that the canticle was sung complete in Latin at this point in the play.

12/422–5 [TERCIUS PASTOR] Iesus onazorus
                Crucyefixus,
                Morcus, Andreus,
                God be oure spede!

This passage is discussed by Stevens and Cawley (*Towneley Plays* II, 489–90), who identify the prayers from which the Latin is taken. 'Benedyght' seems to be an Anglicisation of 'benedictus', and is needed for the rhyme.

Stevens and Cawley discuss the beginning of this passage as a night-spell. 'Christ's cross be my speed' is however also a formula for starting the recitation of the alphabet or the singing of the gam by crossing oneself.[24]

12/502–03 [TERCIUS PASTOR] Exiet virga
                De radice Iesse.

This is an integral part of the stanza-pattern, so it must be heard. The Latin is apparently derived from Isaiah 11/1, 'Et egredietur virga de radice Jesse'.

12/559+lat [PRIMUS PASTOR] Iam noua progenies celo demittitur alto;
                Iam rediet virgo, redeunt Saturnia regna.

Stevens and Cawley (*Towneley Plays* II, 491) quote the correct version of Virgil's prophecy of Christ's birth (Fourth Eclogue, lines 6–7). The First Shepherd's quotation is extra-stanzaic, although it appears in mid-stanza. It has to be spoken.

13 *The Second Shepherds' Play*
13/384–5   [MAK] Manus tuas commendo
              Poncio Pilato.

Mak's 'prayer' before he lies down to sleep is mixed up and poorly remembered: see I, 202.

13/386   [MAK] Cryst crosse me spede!

See above, under 12/419, 422–5.

13/504–06 PRIMUS PASTOR Resurrex a mortruus!
                Have hold my hand.
                Iudas carnas dominus!

---

[24] See, respectively, Morley *Plain and Easy Introduction*, 63; and London, British Library, Add. MS 38599, f. 133r.

Stevens and Cawley identify the texts from which these phrases come (*Towneley Plays* I, 503).

16 *Herod*
16/309–10 [PRIMUS CONSULTUS]   Virgo concipiet,
                          Natumque pariet

The first councillor quotes Isaiah's prophecy (Isaiah 7/14) of the birth of Christ. These lines are an integral part of the verse and must be spoken.

17 *The Purification of Mary*
17/132+sd   Simeon iustus et timoratus

There are two possibilities for the piece sung by the angels:

(a) Antiphon for the Feast of the Purification (AS, 403):
         Symeon iustus et tymoratus expectabat redemptionem
         israel et spiritus sanctus erat in eo.
Largely syllabic chant, range e–c′, c-clef.

(b) Responsory for the Feast of the Purification (AS, 400):
         Symeon iustus et timoratus expectabat redempcionem
         israel. Et spiritus sanctus erat in eo.
         V. Responsum accepit symeon a spiritu sancto non
         uisurum se mortem nisi uideret christum domini. Et
         spiritus.
Melismatic chant, range f–f′, c-clef.

18 *Christ and the Doctors*
18/90+lat
     PRIMUS MAGISTER   Ex ore infancium & lactencium perfecisti laudem.

Psalm 8/3 and Matthew 21/16. The line is extra-stanzaic and written in the margin, but the sense requires it to be spoken.

19 *John the Baptist*
19/187, 189 [JOHANNES]   In nomine patris & filii,
                       ...
                  Et spiritus altissimi

John's formula for the Baptism of Christ is the usual one. 'Altissimi' is presumably used for poetic purposes; the liturgical formula uses 'sancti'. Line **188** is (spoken) English, and the Latin lines are integral to the stanza: they should apparently be spoken.

21 *The Buffeting*

21/207–08 [CAYPHAS] Et omnis qui tacet
Hic consentire videtur.

These lines are an integral part of the stanza, and must be spoken. Caiaphas is quoting a tag, 'Qui tacet consentire videtur': he who is silent is seen to consent, or silence indicates consent. See Stevens and Cawley *Towneley Plays* II, 558.

21/310–11 [ANNA] Et hoc nos volumus,
Quod de iure possumus.

Like the previous item, this is an integral part of the stanza, and is clearly a spoken tag. Annas's twisting of the proverb is explained by Stevens and Cawley (*Towneley Plays* II, 559).

21/389–90 ANNA Sed nobis non licet
Interficere quemquam.

See Stevens and Cawley *Towneley Plays* II, 560, and John 18/31: 'Nobis non licet interficere quenquam' (It is not lawful for us to put any man to death). As with the last two items, this is clearly a spoken quotation, in this case a biblical one.

23 *The Crucifixion*

23/611 [PILATUS] Quod scriptum scripsi

An inaccurate quotation of John 19/22: it is an integral part of the stanza, and must be spoken.

24 *The Play of the Dice*

24/1–65 Pilate's opening speech, a block-busting affair, begins by using a great deal of Latin. None of it is extra-stanzaic, and none of it is liturgical.

25 *The Harrowing of Hell*

25/44+sd Saluator mundi, primum versum

The 'first verse' identifies this incipit as belonging to the hymn 'Salvator mundi Domine' (AS, 46; HS, 10), which is sung to the same tune as 'Veni creator spiritus'.

169

25/120+lat   IHESUS   Attollite portas, principes, vestras & eleuamini porte
eternales, & introibit rex glorie.

Psalm 24/7: 'Lift up your heads, O ye gates, and be ye lift up, ye everlasting
doors, and the King of Glory shall come in'. On the liturgical versions of this
text and its transfer to drama, see I, 279–82. It would be possible for Christ to
sing this text: but there is no indication that he should, and declamation
would be more effective dramatically.

25/188+lat IHESUS   Attollite portas, principes, vestras, &c.

As above.

25/299–302 Satan quotes the statements of Solomon and Job that those who
enter Hell shall never be released. See BS 2/278 and section 15.4, below, under
Castle 3096–7.

25/401–5   [DAVID]   As I saide ere, yit say I so,
               Ne derelinquas, Domine,
               Animam meam in inferno:
               Leyfe neuer my saull, Lord, after the
               In depe hell wheder dampned shall go.

David quotes Psalm 16/10 and translates the verse. The Latin is an integral
part of the stanza, and should be spoken.

25/416   [YSAIAS]   Te deum laudamus.

The last line of the play. Isaiah announces the singing of *Te Deum*, but it is not
clear that he also intones it.

26 The Resurrection
26/229+sd Christus resurgens

For this piece, see section 1.4 under **York 38**. It is here sung by two angels.

28 Thomas of India
28/104+sd   Pax vobis et non tardabit; hec est dies quam fecit Dominus.

The Third Apostle immediately translates the second part of this text, sung by
Jesus: 'This is the day that God maide' (**28/105**). Stevens and Cawley discuss
at length the problem that this text presents (*Towneley Plays* II, 620): as presented here, the text is neither biblical nor liturgical, but seems to be an

amalgam of phrases from various biblical texts. There is no obvious way for Jesus to sing these lines, therefore: they could be sung to a psalm-tone, or perhaps to a newly-composed tune.

28/120+sd   Pax vobis et non tardabit.

Again sung by Jesus, who later translates the first words: 'Peasse emangys you euerichon!' (**28/129**). This presents the same problem as **104+sd**, noted above, and the same solutions are possible. it is not clear, however, whether Jesus is intended to sing the rest of the text on this occasion.

29   *The Ascension*
29/289+sd   Ascendo ad patrem meum.

This text is sung by the two angels. For the possible liturgical pieces, see section 1.4, above, under **York 42**.

30   *The Judgment*
30/364+lat   [TUTIVILLUS]   Fragmina verborum,
                         Tutiuillus colligit horum;
                         Belzabub algorum,
                         Belial belium doliorum.

These lines are extra-stanzaic. There is no reason to sing them, although doing so as a parody of liturgy would not be inappropriate.

30/415–6   [TUTIVILLUS]   Diabolus est mendax
                         Et pater eius.

Tutivillus quotes John 8/44, speaking of the devil: '... quia mendax est, et pater ejus' (for [the devil] is a liar, and the father of [lying]). The quotation is here an integral part of the verse: there is no reason to sing it.

30/428   [TUTIVILLUS]   Cum suis adinuencionibus

An integral part of the verse: there is no reason to sing it.

30/441–2   [TUTIVILLUS]   Et eam fecistys
                         Speluncam latronum.

As above.

30/558–9 PRIMUS DEMON   Qui vero mala,
                          In ignem eternum.

An integral part of the verse, and obviously to be spoken. Stevens and Cawley
identify Matthew 25/41 as a source (*Towneley Plays* II, 643).

3.5 Records

Wakefield has very few surviving records concerning its Corpus Christi play.
Such as there are date from the sixteenth century: they offer neither information
on the plays and their performance nor any identification of the Wakefield play
with the Towneley cycle. The surviving records are described and printed in
Cawley *Wakefield Pageants*, 124–6, in Forrester *Wakefield Mystery Plays*, and in
Forrester and Cawley 'Corpus Christi Play'. The most recent discussion of the
evidence is in Stevens and Cawley *Towneley Plays*, xix–xxii.

The identification of the Towneley cycle as the Wakefield Corpus Christi play
was demonstrated by Cawley on the basis of local allusions in the text of the
plays (Cawley *Wakefield Pageants*, xiv–xvii). Cawley himself pointed out that, if
the manuscript is indeed the Wakefield register, then some confirmatory evidence
is missing that one would expect to be present. One of the surviving documents
concerning the Wakefield play records the contents of a letter from the Ecclesiastical Commissioners to the Wakefield authorities, dated 27 May 1576, giving instructions for the revision of the plays so that they shall conform to Protestant
theological views. As Cawley stated, H.C. Gardiner (*Mysteries' End*, 78) believed
that the various emendations in the Towneley manuscript were the result of these
instructions: but Cawley demonstrated that, although the changes made were
probably for this broad purpose, in detail they are so far from the terms of the
instructions that the Commissioners would not have been satisfied (Cawley
Wakefield Pageants, 126). Cawley was too wedded to the idea of the Towneley
manuscript as the Wakefield register to draw conclusions from this, but several
could in fact follow:

1 that the required emendations were not made;
2 that the manuscript is not in fact the register but a related copy of the cycle;
   or
3 that the Towneley cycle does not come from Wakefield.[25]

The lack of records of payments to actors and others, and of even a list of plays
for Wakefield, means that the surviving documentation tells us nothing useful for

---

[25] It must come from somewhere close by, however: and even if the cycle as we have it
does not come from Wakefield, some constituent pageants may do so. For a discussion
of the Wakefield problem, see Palmer '"Towneley Plays"'.

present purposes. Possibly further research will either confirm the cycle's Wakefield provenance or show that it comes from elsewhere.[26] With the current work going on in the REED project, however, it seems likely that if any other place had records matching the Towneley text we should already know about it. On the whole it seems now that we shall not be able to prove the provenance of the cycle – whether it be Wakefield or not – and that in consequence we shall not in the future have documentary evidence for its performance.

3.6 Music and other aural cues

1 *The Creation*
Apparently there is no music in this play, even at the creation (**1/76+sd** would be a suitable place for a heavenly concert).

2 *The Murder of Abel*
3 *Noah and his Sons*
No cues for music.

4 *Abraham*
Apparently no music. The play is incomplete at the end, but the missing section is unlikely to have included a music cue.

5 *Isaac*
No cues for music. The play is incomplete at the beginning, but we should expect no music in the missing portion.

6 *Jacob*
No cues for music.

7 *The Play of the Prophets*
7_1 David sings his speech, from **109** until **156**. **7/150+lat** is an alleluia verse, and so has its own music, which David could sing: the actor playing David must be a very competent singer. For the piece in question, see 3.4, above.

For the rest, discussion of his music must be speculative. Liturgy has ways of intoning a text with different types of cadence corresponding to punctuation marks: see Sandon II, vi, for an explanation of this in lessons, Gospels,

---

[26] This view is restated in Stevens and Cawley *Towneley Plays* I, xix–xxii, where the editors state that 'The burden of proof rests with those who would ascribe the cycle to a place other than Wakefield' (I, xx).

and so on. David's description of his song as a 'fit', however, suggests the techniques of a minstrel performing a *geste*, romance or ballad. This would use the same tune for each of the eight stanzas concerned, or for each half-stanza: the tune can be quite simple, with a chordal accompaniment on the harp. A competent singer will find that the music reaches a certain level of musical interest once the piece has been performed a number of times.

8   Pharaoh
9   Caesar Augustus
10   The Annunciation
11   Mary's Salutation of Elizabeth
No cues for music.

12 The First Shepherds' Play

12₁ 386 Function: none. The competition song (see 3.3), started by the First Shepherd. There is no reason to think it part-music: it is presumably a cheerful vernacular piece in popular style, and could be sung in unison.

12₂ 425 (or **438**: see below) Function: (b), (h). The angel sings, solo. It is tempting to think that this is a Latin version of the angel's speech, **426–38**, which corresponds to the biblical narrative of Luke 2/10–12. But there is no obvious liturgical item for this, and in the same playwright's play **13** a similar speech is preceded by a SD for the solo singing of *Gloria in excelsis*. The same may be the case here.[27]

This reverses the biblical order of events, however, in which the Gloria follows the angel's message. This order would be restored if the Gloria were sung after line **438**: and this would also bring the song nearer to the shepherds' discussion of it (starting at **439**).

The Angel gives a virtuoso performance, with many small-value notes, and he has a fine voice (see 3.3). Further on this song, see I, 36–43.

12₃ 620+md Function: (h). This song does not coincide with the shepherds' journey to Bethlehem (function (a)), but it does signal the end of a scene: the shepherds have discussed the angel's song and its relation to the prophecies, and after their own attempt at it they turn their thoughts towards Bethlehem. It is, then, a scene-change by content and action rather than by locale.

For the Third Shepherd's eagerness and subsequent inability to start the singing, see I, 355.[28] He does in fact start it, with what success does not

---

[27] See I, 346, and Rastall 'Musical Repertory', 166–7. This is an exception to the general rule that sung Latin is followed by its English translation, but the rule is not invariable: see I, 81–4. Singing the Gloria after **437** would be consonant with the order of the biblical narrative.

[28] Carpenter's explanation that the Third Shepherd needs help because he wants to sing in 'discant in three parts, the only type of music he knows' ('Music in the *Secunda Pastorum*', p. 217) will not do. This is not what the text says. The shepherds

appear.

We may therefore suppose that the Third Shepherd begins, rather tentatively, and the others join in, singing in unison with him. Between them, they must remember at least most of the text, even if the music defeats them in its details.

The First Shepherd's next remark (**621–2**) does not show him to be dissatisfied with the result; and we must suppose that the first evangelists do in fact get the basic message right. Thus what comes out of this performance is, no doubt, a (?slightly comically) simplified version of the angel's song, in which the gist of the verbal message is intact.

12₄ 724 Function: (g). Carpenter was so wedded to the idea of three-part descant in this play (due to her erroneous conflation of material from this play and play **13**) that she proposed 'sing we in sight' (**724**) as another piece of evidence for this sort of musical texture. As suggested in 3.3, 'in the sight of this assembled company' is a more probable interpretation.[29] To repeat, there is no evidence of part-singing in this play. This final song of the shepherds, which ends the play, is likely to be a song of praise, sung in unison. As with **12₁**, we can probably assume an English text.

13   *The Second Shepherds' Play*

13₁ Before **156** Function: (a), (h). The Third Shepherd's horn must be heard by **156** at the latest, and perhaps at intervals in all or most of this first part of the play: see 3.3.

13₂ 273 Function: (h). The shepherds sing in three parts: a texture consisting of treble, mean and tenor parts could be anything from quasi-unison singing in parallel organum to complex three-part polyphony. ('Tenor' is simply the main tune, often a pre-existent one: it is frequently the bottom or middle voice of three.) Carpenter has suggested that the shepherds make use of one of the techniques available to church singers, by which sometimes complex polyphony was improvised over a plainsong melody. These methods are discussed in I, 94–6. The technique used here was probably not too demanding and is unlikely to have made use of notation.[30] A form of strict organum, with all three voices singing the tune at intervals of a fifth and a fourth above the bass-

are discussing the vocal line of a single angelic singer, so that there is no question of part-music in imitating him: that is why the First Shepherd encourages the Third Shepherd to sing it alone. The Third Shepherd's problem is not that he can only sing in parts, which is preposterous (if that were so he would hardly be incapable of singing a solo line), but, on the contrary, that he feels unable to bear a line by himself. Thus, although he thinks that he knows the tune, he cannot sing it unless he is supported *in unison* by other voices. Any choir-trainer working with amateurs will know this phenomenon.

[29] See I, 355–6: and compare **N-Town 9/163**, '... we se here all in syght'.

[30] The shepherds in **Coventry 1** must have been played by professional singers, but even so there is no reason to think that they performed the polyphonic songs in that play from written notation. See I, 62–71, *passim*, and 137–52.

line, would be suitable. When this technique is used deliberately and with comparable volume for each voice, the effect is a strong one as long as the singers are in tune. We need nothing more than this for the shepherds to make an impressive and even exciting effect in their singing.

13₃ 685 Function: (h). Mak's singing of a lullaby, accompanied by Gyll's moaning, comes at the division of scenes after the setting-up for the mock-nativity in Mak's cottage. It does not much matter which lullaby Mak sings, for it is so out of tune that it would probably be unrecognisable in any case. The precise placing of Mak's awareness that the three shepherds are on their way, and his consequent starting of the lullaby, is a matter for the producer and actors: it depends on the timing of the shepherds' arrival at the cottage, how far they have to travel, and so on. The lullaby must however be well established by the time the Third Shepherd starts line **686**.

13₄ 919+sd Function: (b), (d), (h). The angel's singing of *Gloria in excelsis* is followed by the text, in English, of the angelic song that occurs first in the biblical narrative. The Gloria is a virtuoso piece of singing: the metrical structure of it is discussed in I, 39–42. Probably the song consists of the plainsong tune subjected to divisions (embellishments), a technique in which a really competent church singer would be adequately trained.

13₅ 958 Function: none. The shepherds attempt to imitate the angel's song, the First Shepherd starting (see 3.3).

As with the similar circumstances in play **12**, the shepherds presumably have some success with the words, even if only in a limited way with the music (see **12₃**). Here it may be that their relative lack of musical success leads to at least one of the shepherds continuing the attempt while the Second Shepherd is speaking (line **973**).

13₆ 1088 Function: (g), and either (c) or (i). The shepherds sing a cheerful song of praise to the Christ-child: it is presumably a setting of an English text, and sung in unison (or parallel organum).

14 *The Offering of the Magi*
15 *The Flight into Egypt*
16 *Herod*
No cues for music.

17 *The Purification of Mary*
17₁ 102+sd Function (h). The temple bells ring. As suggested in 3.3, this should be a joyful sound: Simeon says that 'This noyse lyghtyns ful well myn hart!' (**109**). If this play was ever performed processionally the ringing was presumably managed with a set of chime-bells hidden behind the 'temple' (see Rastall 'Minstrelsy, Church and Clergy', 94–5): but Cynthia Tyson has

suggested that the phrase 'oure bellys' is evidence for staging in a fixed location, the bells being those of the community – i.e. the bells of the parish church (now the cathedral) of Wakefield.[31]

17_2 **132+sd** Function: (b), (h). *Simeon justus et timoratus* is both an antiphon and a responsory for the Feast of the Purification, the texts being based on Luke 2/25. The choice of item must depend on the ability of the singers, the responsory being more difficult than the antiphon.

The play is incomplete at the end, breaking off some time before the Holy Family reaches the temple. Consequently the liturgical element is missing, together with the music that we should expect in the latter part of this play.

18 **Christ and the Doctors**
19 **John the Baptist**
20 **The Conspiracy and Capture**
21 **The Buffeting**
22 **The Scourging**
23 **The Crucifixion**
24 **The Play of the Dice**
No cues for music.

25 **The Harrowing of Hell**
25_1 **44+sd** Function: none. The souls in Limbo sing the first verse of the hymn *Salvator mundi*.
25_A **88** Function: (h). It is possible that 25_1 should be repeated here, or the next verse of *Salvator mundi* sung by the souls in Limbo.
25_2 **416** Function: (g). *Te Deum* is sung by all the souls, perhaps with the audience taking part: as suggested in 3.3, Adam is the obvious character to intone this piece.

26 **The Resurrection**
26_1 **229+sd** Function: (a), (b), (h). The two angels sing *Christus resurgens*. This covers the action of Christ rising from the tomb: but it may also cover the angels' descent from heaven, since they need to be at the tomb when the three Marys arrive (line **351**). The piece is however a florid one, not ideal for processional performance. It must certainly be a very impressive piece of professional singing (see lines **537–40**, discussed in 3.3).

27 **The Pilgrims**
No cues for music.

---

[31] Tyson 'Property requirements', 187–8.

28 Thomas of India

28₁ 104+sd Function: (b), (h). Jesus sings *Pax vobis*, etc. See section 3.4.

28₂ 120+sd Function: (b). The same. (However, the first time Jesus appears he disappears again; on the second occasion he stays.)

29 The Ascension of the Lord

29₁ 289+sd Function: (a), (c). During the angelic singing of *Ascendo ad patrem meum* Jesus ascends out of sight, while two angels presumably descend, or appear, to speak to the apostles. Whether these two angels are the ones that sing, and whether – if so – they are the *only* ones that sing, cannot be determined. Quite possibly these details were left open in the original performances. Here, as very often, the angelic singing is associated with 'myrth' (line **365**).

This play is incomplete at the end, but it is unlikely that any music cue has been lost.

30 The Judgement

30₁ 1– Function: ?(h). See 3.3 for a discussion of the Last Trumpet: the trumpet has obviously sounded before the first surviving line of this play, and it could well be sounded again at intervals up to line **130**: lines 50, **114** and **130** are obvious possible cue-lines.

30₂ 830 Function: (g). See 3.4. The singing of *Te Deum* here should include the audience: it could be intoned by the first angel.

31 Lazarus
32 The Hanging of Judas

No music cues.

4

The Coventry Plays

4.1 Introduction

The Coventry cycle is now mainly lost, only two plays surviving. There is some useful material available about the cycle, mainly in the form of guild accounts, but it is a measure of the fragmentary nature of this evidence that we cannot be sure what plays were presented and by what guilds. Although a picture of the cycle's history is emerging, there is still much to be learned. The texts and music of the songs in these two plays are discussed in I, 62–71 and 137–52. For editions of the music, see I, 138.

In the early nineteenth century, when crucial research was undertaken by Thomas Sharp, these two plays survived in the prompt copies of the guilds concerned: the Shearmen and Tailors' play of the Nativity and Slaughter of the Innocents, and the Weavers' play of the Purification and Doctors in the Temple. The former was edited by Sharp in 1817, but published in a print-run of only 12 copies: a second publication, in his *Dissertation on the Pageants ... of Coventry* in 1825, differs very little from the 1817 print but – unlike the earlier version – includes the music of the songs. The text is printed as a quasi-facsimile which purports to show the orthography and layout of the original, and the music, which is engraved, also seems to be made to look as much like the original as possible. The manuscript was a revision made by Robert Croo, and is dated 14 March 1534. It was destroyed in a fire at the Birmingham Free Library in 1879, so that Sharp's edition is now our only source.

The manuscript of the Weavers' play was lost at the time that Sharp was working on the *Dissertation*, but it was rediscovered in 1832[1] and Sharp published an edition of it in 1836. This manuscript, too, is a revision by Robert Croo, in this case dated 2 March 1534, twelve days before the revision of the Shearmen and Tailors' play. In the course of working towards his edition of the

---

[1] Sharp *Presentation*, 3.

Coventry plays, Hardin Craig found two related leaves with the Weavers' manuscript, containing fragments of an earlier version of the play in a fifteenth-century hand. These may have belonged to the version of the play that Croo used as the basis of his revision.

Hardin Craig's edition of the two plays (*Two Coventry ... Plays*, 1902) was reissued in a slightly revised version in 1957. The edition of King and Davidson (*Coventry Corpus Christi Plays*, 2000) supersedes earlier editions, and is referred to here: it includes a re-presentation of Dutka's edition of the music for the Shearmen and Tailors' pageant, originally in Dutka *Music*.

A facsimile reprint of Sharp's *Dissertation* was published in 1973; there is no facsimile of the Weavers' play, but there are now plans to publish it electronically.

As stated in I, 62–7, it is difficult to date the musical settings of the song-texts in the Shearmen and Tailors' play. I believe that the inscriptions of Thomas Mawdycke's name on the song-texts, with the date of 13 May 1591, point towards an attempt by Mawdycke to collect the materials necessary to mount the play in the summer of that year, although the civic authorities did not, in the end, allow the cycle to be revived. Mawdycke's name appears also on the song-texts at the end of the Weavers' play. It seems to me just possible, too, that the second song in the Weavers' play, 'Behold now hit ys come to pas', was composed for the Cappers' play in 1563. The evidence for this is however very fragmentary and entirely circumstantial: it is rehearsed in I, 64–5.

In late 1996, in a lecture given to the Society of Antiquaries, I reviewed the evidence of the song-texts and settings and raised the question of Thomas Mawdycke's identity, my preliminary researches having failed to find him. Two Fellows present that evening subsequently made independent searches that uncovered several families of Mawdyckes in and around Coventry.[2] While it will be necessary to follow up several of the Mawdyckes found, there is perhaps one Thomas Mawdycke who presents as a prime contender for our man: a tailor living in St Michael's parish, Coventry. His will, dated 12 September 1590, was witnessed by his 'lovinge neighbours and frendes' Richard Styffe, innholder, Thomas Owen, dyer, Thomas Ambrose, baker, and Frannces Pynnynge (who wrote out the document). The will was proved on 23 September 1591.[3]

Richard Stiff the wait is not known (as far as I know) as an innholder, but it

---

2   I am very grateful to Dr Arnold Taylor CBE FSA and Dr N.W. Alcock FSA for their generosity in taking the time to search for Mawdycke.
3   Lichfield Joint Record Office: probate records, referenced by year and name. The information given here is from Dr Alcock. This Thomas Mawdycke was presumably ill throughout the year September 1590 to September 1591, since wills were normally written on the deathbed. This Thomas also had a son Thomas, however, and the latter is presumably also a possible candidate for the name on the song-texts of the two plays.

may be the same man;[4] Francis Pyninge, a member of the Cappers' guild, was paid for copying or composing a play in 1568, and also copied the Cappers' accounts early in the seventeenth century (*REED.Coventry*, 247 and 576). His will is dated 22 July 1606 (*REED.Coventry*, 576). There was a strong but currently indefinable connection of some kind between the Pyninge family and the Weavers' guild (*REED.Coventry*, 319, 352 and 371).

The fire that destroyed the manuscript of the Shearmen and Tailors' play also caused the loss of much documentary evidence about the Coventry guilds and their plays. It is a measure of this loss that we cannot be sure precisely how many plays the Coventry cycle contained and what episodes were enacted. Nevertheless, there is much material. Sharp, Halliwell-Phillipps and others collected and published evidence from manuscripts that were later destroyed. Craig included the work of these two in the appendices to his edition, and in compiling *REED.Coventry* (1981) Reginald Ingram widened the field to scholars not specifically interested in drama, so that *REED.Coventry* presents material relating to a broad picture of dramatic and ceremonial activity, including information about the texts and performance of Coventry plays that have not survived.

After examination of the surviving guild accounts Craig came to certain conclusions about the Coventry cycle which he set down in his edition (*Two Coventry Plays*, xi–xvii): that the cycle consisted of ten pageants; that episodes tended to be grouped together into a single pageant; and that only New Testament subjects were treated, with a putative Procession of Prophets being split up and distributed in the form of prophecies in various pageants. His list of subjects and crafts appeared in tabular form (*ibid.*, xv).

On further reflection, Craig described in 1955 a slightly different cycle (*English Religious Drama*, 287–91). He added the episode of the meal at the house of Simon the Leper to the play starting with the Baptism, but removed the Entry into Jerusalem from the end of this pageant to the beginning of the Smiths'. At the other end of the Smiths' pageant he considered it possible that the Smiths had played the Burial. In the Cappers' pageant, by implication, he reversed the positions of the Harrowing of Hell and the Setting of the Watch, so that the Harrowing came second; and he suggested that the Appearance to the Disciples might have belonged to the Cappers' play rather than to the next one.

More radically, Craig retreated from his argument that only New Testament subjects had been included, and proposed three Old Testament pageants (a minimum needed to maintain narrative and theological consistency) to have been mounted by the remaining three guilds known to have produced pageants. These were a Creation play, a Noah play, and a pageant of Abraham and Isaac.

This discussion, with the author retreating from a clear and well-defined position to a much less confident one, showed Craig's ideas in a state of flux. He

---

4 For Stiff, see *REED.Coventry, passim*, and I, 65. It is currently unclear from the records whether there were two men called Richard Stiff or only one.

did not present his new list of plays and guilds in tabular form as before: had he done so, he would no doubt have realised that he had failed to account for a pageant that had appeared in his earlier list, and from which he had in fact removed an episode to the Cappers' play. This pageant, still including the episodes of Doubting Thomas, the Ascension, and Pentecost, if Appearance to the Disciples, can hardly be omitted from a cycle that intends to be narratively and theologically complete.

Craig thus finished in an impossible position. With only ten pageants available (a condition of which he remained certain), and assuming that both a Ministry pageant and a pageant including Ascension and Pentecost are necessary, only two guilds remain to take on the three Old Testament plays that form the basic minimum Old Testament content. Perhaps two of these could be amalgamated, but it does seem unlikely that this solution is entirely correct.

Two years later, in the second edition of *Two Coventry Plays*, Craig added a section in which he reiterated this later argument in a more consistent form (*Two Coventry Plays*, xl–xli). The problem remains, however: Craig still thought that only ten pageants were played, and in suggesting that 'two or even three of the pageants may have been devoted to Old Testament subjects' he was forced to admit 'that the absence of plays dealing with Christ's ministry and with the conspiracy, trial and capture is most unlikely' (*Two Coventry Plays*, xli). His tentative solution to this problem was that the Ascension and Pentecost might have been amalgamated with the Assumption, the whole pageant being played by the Mercers, so that all three suggested Old Testament plays could be produced.

In the tabular form first used by Craig, the cycle would consist of the following pageants:

1   Creation
     (Fall of Lucifer)
     Fall of Man
     (Cain and Abel)

2   Noah

3   Abraham and Isaac

     (Procession of Prophets, broken up and distributed among other plays)

4 Shearmen and Tailors: surviving Play 1
     Annunciation
     Visit to Elizabeth
     Joseph's trouble
     Journey to Bethlehem
     Nativity

Shepherds
Magi
Flight into Egypt
Slaughter of the Innocents

5 Weavers: surviving Play **2**
Purification
Doctors

6 [One guild]
Baptism of Christ
Temptation
Jesus at the house of Simon the Leper
The raising of Lazarus

7 Smiths
The Entry into Jerusalem[5]
Conspiracy
Last Supper
Agony in the Garden
Betrayal and capture
Appearances before
High Priest and Pilate
Pilate's wife
Appearance before Herod
Second appearance before Pilate
Despair and Hanging of Judas
The way to Calvary
Parting of garments
Crucifixion
Death of Christ
(?Burial)

8 Cappers
Setting the watch[6]
Harrowing of Hell
Resurrection
Amazement of soldiers

---

[5] The first three episodes in this play were perhaps presented by another guild.
[6] King and Davidson state (*Coventry Plays*, 34) that in 1531 the Cappers' play began with the Harrowing of Hell. Since the setting of the watch is needed, it seems likely that that should take its normal place after the Harrowing episode.

Peter and John at the tomb[7]
Appearance to Mary Magdalene (*hortulanus* scene)
Travellers to Emmaus
(?Appearance to disciples)
9 Perhaps played by the Mercers[8]
Doubting Thomas
Ascension
Pentecost
Death, Assumption and Coronation of Mary
Appearance of Mary to Thomas

10 Drapers
Doomsday

4.2 Dramatic directions

The Shearmen and Tailors' Play

According to Sharp's edition, the directions for this play are all in English and, with a single exception, written in red ink. It is impossible to be sure of the original placing of SDs in relation to the text. Sharp more or less centres each line of an SD in the text-space, but this seems likely to be a typographical nicety of the edition rather than a detail of manuscript layout. There is thus no indication of marginal status in any SD, but the possibility must remain that originally marginal directions have lost their marginal status in the process of publication.

Sharp's edition gives no line-numbers. In Table 5, therefore, line-numbers refer to the edition of King and Davidson, while the second column gives the page-reference in Sharp 1825.[9] The table shows that out of 14 directions, five (36%) are musical. This is not a high proportion compared with that of the York cycle (see 1.2), but it is significant. Moreover, the significance of the musical directions increases when the nature of the SDs in this play is taken into account. No fewer than six of the non-musical directions concern exits and entrances at the major scene-divisions: and it is doubtful if an earlier play would have included most of

---

7 King and Davidson (*Coventry Plays*, 40) note that Christ's appearance to Mary apparently preceded this episode, at least until its suppression in 1548.
8 King and Davidson (*Coventry Plays*, 43) consider that the evidence – which is only circumstantial in any case – shows only that the Mercers played the Death, Assumption and Coronation of the Virgin (which must include the episode with Thomas, although Craig did not say so).
9 Sharp gives the folio-numbers throughout the edition, but I do not include those in Table 5.

these, since there is little doubt as to the characters 'on stage' at any point. Two of the musical directions (**1/312+sd** and **775+sd**) are mainly of this type, with the musical information subsidiary to the rest. As so often, too, an SD frequently includes a direction for the next speaker, so making the following SH redundant: seven of the directions do this, including the musical directions at **1/263+sd** and **312+sd**.

At least some of the purpose of the SDs concerning exits and entrances at the scene-divisions may be to distinguish between exits that leave the players in the sight of the audience and those that do not. **1/93+sd** (*Here the angell departyth* ...), **1/489+sd** (*Here erod goth awey* ...) and **633+sd** (*There Erode goth his weyis* ...) seem to suggest that the actors do not go far, whereas **1/312+sd** (requiring the shepherds to go 'forthe of þe place' and **424+sd** (*There the profettis gothe furthe* ...) seem to imply a final exit in which the players disappear from the audience's view. In the case of the shepherds this is an important point to which we shall return (see 4.6).

Craig prescribed Sharp's 'Song I' for **1/263+sd** and 'Song III' at **1/312+sd** (*Two Coventry Plays*, 10, n.3; 12, n.2). As noted in I, 67, the first of these seems right, since the *incipit* is given in the SD; but the second cannot be correct, because the Prophets' description of this singing does not match the song 'Down from Heaven' (see 4.3, below). Sharp directed his reader to the music at the end of the play for 'As I out rode', without specifically naming his 'Song I': and, like Craig after him, he did not mention that 'Down from Heaven' has the same music as 'As I out rode' nor offer an explanation for its separate numbering and its physical separation from Song I by the lullaby. Further on this problem, see I, 138. Sharp did not give a second footnote drawing attention to the composed music for **1/312+sd**, however. This may have been an oversight, but perhaps Sharp realised that this song was not extant. Once it is understood that **1/312+ sd** does not require 'Song III', that song is free to take its rightful place as the second verse of 'Song I' and to be sung on the same occasion, at **263+sd** (see 4.6).

The Weavers' Play

In this play, too, the dramatic directions are amongst the material in red ink (Craig *Two Coventry Plays*, xi): there are 21 in all, listed in Table 6. All are in English, except for four single-word directions in Latin. All of these last are marginal and written in a more hasty hand: only the first is marked off from the text by horizontal lines, as most of the SDs proper are. Despite the use of Latin, which may be thought to indicate an earlier date (but see 6.2), these four directions are certainly later additions. I am unable to say that they are in a different hand from the rest of the text, which is presumably in Croo's writing.

King and Davidson, like Craig, reverse the positions of **364+sd** and **364+md**: the marginal direction is clearly added at the end of the SD proper, not after line 364. See 4.3 and 4.6, below.

Another marginal direction could be expected at **290+sd**, except that the text-reference to singing here is a clear one (see 4.3).

TABLE 5 : DIRECTIONS IN COVENTRY PLAY 1

pl/l	page in Sharp	mus/ non-m	red/ black	Direction if musical: comments
Nativity				
1/93	86	/n	r/	
1/228	90	/n	r/	
1/249	91	m/	r/	*There the angelis syng glorea in exselsis deo*
1/263	92	m/	r/	*There the scheppardis syngis ASE I OWT RODDE & Josoff seyth*
1/277	92	m/	r/	*There the angellis syng gloria in exsellsis ageyne*
1/312	93	m/	r/	*There the scheppardis syngith ageyne and goth forthe of þe place and the ij profettis cumyth in and seyth thus*
Prophets				
1/424	97	/n	r/	
1/489	99	/n	r/	
1/548	101	/n	/b	
1/633	104	/n	r/	
1/643	104	/n	r/	
1/728	107	/n	r/	
1/746	108	/n	r/	
1/775	109	m/	r/	*Here the wemen cum in wythe there chyldur syngyng them and mare & Josoff goth awey cleyne*
Massacre of the Innocents				No SDs in this scene

TABLE 6 : DIRECTIONS IN COVENTRY PLAY 2

pl/l	f.	mus/ non-m	lang	direction if musical : comments
Prophets				
2/151	2v	/n	Lat	Marginal
2/175	3r	/n	Eng	
Purification				
2/216	3v	/n	Eng	
2/290	4v	/n	Eng	
2/320	5r	/n	Eng	
2/364	5v	/n	Eng	This and the next item reversed in editions
2/364	5v	m/	Lat	*Cantant* Marginal
2/404	6r	/n	Eng	
2/502	7v	/n	Eng	
2/589	8v	m/	Lat	*Cantant* Marginal
2/634	9r	m/	Lat	*Cantant* Marginal
2/634	9r	/n	Eng	
2/691	9v	m/	Lat	*Cantant* Marginal
2/691	9v	/n	Eng	
2/701	11r	/n	Eng	
2/718	11r	/n	Eng	
Doctors in the Temple				
2/799	12r	m/	Eng	*There the all goo vp to the awter & Ihesus before. þe syng an antem*
2/807	12r	/n	Eng	
2/849	13r	/n	Eng	
2/906	13v	/n	Eng	
2/1005	14v	/n	Eng	

Of the seventeen SDs proper, all original and in English, only one is musical (see below). This is a disappointingly low proportion: but taking account of the marginal directions (and the lack of one at **290+sd**) suggests that, as elsewhere, a musical tradition was assumed until some time in the sixteenth century when the marginal directions were added. The paleographical evidence suggests that the MDs were added during rehearsals, probably by Robert Croo and perhaps quite soon after he copied the play. This situation is clearly different from that found in play **1**, where there is an apparent absence of Latin directions or indeed any brief directions that may have been marginal in the manuscript.[10]

The musical directions in the Weavers' play are not quite as straightforward as they seem. **2/364+md** cannot refer to the singing of Simeon and his clerk, since lines **361–4** show that their singing is reserved until **633+md** (a matter that is confirmed by **2/630–3**). **2/364+md** is probably not an error, however: considering also its placing after **2/364+sd**, it must refer to an otherwise unnoticed sung item that begins the next scene. This can only be celestial music, sung by two or more angels in the heaven to accompany Gabriel's movement to visit Mary. Craig's suggestion that this is Song I is therefore incorrect,[11] for the text of Song I is inappropriate there. The angels presumably sing an 'Ave Maria' item, since Gabriel's speech begins 'Hayle, Mare, ...'.[12]

The English direction at **2/799+md** is discussed elsewhere.[13] The two parts seem not to have originated together, since 'the[y]' refers to the Holy Family and others in the first sentence but a group of liturgical singers in the second. While both sentences appear to be production-notes, it is not clear whether the various actions occur simultaneously or consecutively – that is, whether the singers perform their anthem (antiphon) during the procession or after it: see 4.4.

The Early Fragment of Play 2

There are no directions in this fragment.

---

10 Some editors might omit marginal directions as obvious later additions that lacked the authority of the SDs proper, but I cannot see Sharp doing so.

11 Craig *Two Coventry Plays*, 45, n. 1. Song I is probably intended for **633+md**: it is hard to see where else it might be performed.

12 For possible items, see 1.4, above, under **York 12/144+md**.

13 See I, 27 and 224; also Rastall 'Female Roles', 40.

4.3 Text references

The Shearmen and Tailors' Play
Nativity

1/250–63 Following the angelic Gloria at **249+sd**, the shepherds discuss the angels' song and its performance. The 3rd shepherd remarks that [the angels] 'syng abowe in the clowdis clere', so that they are evidently in a high place above the shepherds (**250**). The word 'clere' is open to two interpretations. The first is to regard 'clere' as an adjective qualifying 'clowdis': it means that the clouds are brightly illuminated (OED under 'Clear'), presumably by the heavenly light surrounding the angelic host. A second possibility is that 'clere' is an adverb qualifying 'syng', but forced to the end of the line for poetic reasons. In this case the line means 'They sing brilliantly/incisively/excitingly above us in the clouds' (Carter *Dictionary*, 84–5). Although a choice must be made – not least because the 3rd shepherd must decide how to speak the line – in a sense it does not matter which interpretation a producer prefers. Both are relevant, and a producer would be wise to follow both in performance, with the angels brightly lit and singing in a highly-skilled virtuoso style.[14]

There is other evidence to support the second interpretation. The third shepherd also says that he never heard 'soo myrre a quere' (**251**), and this is confirmed by the first shepherd, who realises that 'myrth and solas' have come to them (**254**). As usual, we can almost certainly assume that mirth and virtuoso performance go together in this angelic music. This music is described as 'armony' (**253**), and is evidently going on while the shepherds speak, since the third shepherd suggests that they 'draw nere' to listen to it (**252**). The first shepherd recognises by its 'swettnes' that the song heralds God's son (**255–7**). Quite what these terms mean as descriptions of the music is not clear. 'Sweetness', which was regularly used in opposition to 'harshness', as now,[15] really implies a trained voice which is a pleasure to hear. 'Armony' at this time did not necessarily mean harmony in the modern sense, but could also be used of agreeable sounds heard successively (Carter *Dictionary*, 14–16): the simultaneous sounding of notes was a more technical meaning of the word (*ibid.*, 16). The question whether monody or polyphony was heard depends partly on the shepherds' musicality and technical knowledge of music, therefore. It is also true, however, that if this wording dates only from Croo's revision, the case for considering polyphony here is stronger. In any case, we should regard the angelic singing as an obviously accomplished professional performance of its time. Although **249+sd** gives only the *incipit* 'Gloria in excelsis deo', **263** shows that the angels sang at least as far as *Et in terra pax ho-*

---

[14] For possible forms of lighting, see Butterworth *Theatre of Fire*, chapter 4.

[15] See I, 35–6. In addition to A.E. Davidson's 'Performance Practice', see Ramm 'Style' and Uberti 'Vocal Techniques'.

minibus: we can assume that they sang through to 'bonae voluntatis'. Although the first shepherd suggests that they will want to sing 'Et in terra pax' in the Christ-child's presence, there is no evidence that they do so on their arrival. *As I out rodde* is the song that immediately follows (**263+sd**): and although this does not cover the whole of their journey (they do not arrive in the stable until after line **290**), there is no evidence that they sing again after the angels speak to them (**287–90**).

1/264–7 At the beginning of the nativity scene Joseph refers to the 'noise' that he has heard. This is evidently not the shepherds' song (**263+sd**) but the angelic Gloria (**249+sd**), since he refers to the 'grett solemnete' of the song and the fact that the song has made him happier ('Gretly amendid hath my chere'). Such is the effect of the music that Joseph expects it to presage important news ('I trust hy nevis schortly wol be'): the music is clearly identifiable to him as a supernatural or divine utterance.[16] The second angelic singing of the Gloria follows immediately (**267+sd**): it covers the birth of the baby, and Joseph does not again mention the angelic music. The angels have apparently been in the audience's sight at least since the first Gloria (**249+sd**).

The first shepherd has nothing to give the Child except his pipe. He tells the Child to take it in his hand (**294**), so it is presumably a small instrument – a recorder or whistle rather than a bagpipe, which would be too large for the baby to hold. He also tells the baby that he hopes the pipe will 'make the(e) myrthe' (**297**).

1/311–12 Not a musical reference, but perhaps one to be noted, as it forms the cue for the shepherds' song that ends the Nativity section of the play. Mary gives a 'blessing' ending, to which the shepherds' singing seems the appropriate response. This will be the place, if anywhere, for the shepherds to sing 'Et in terra pax hominibus', as they intended (lines **262–3**).

Prophets
1/399–401 The prophets mention music only at the end of their discussion of the Nativity. After detailing the story of the star's appearance to the shepherds, the first prophet says that the shepherds sang as loudly as they could in praise of the King of Israel. This seems at first sight to refer to **263+sd**, which does not fit the description: but the speeches following (**414–24**) show that the song after the adoration-scene is meant (**312+sd**). This cannot be 'Down from Heaven', the second verse of 'As I out rode', therefore, which contains only a description of the angelic Gloria and no element of praise.

---

16 But see King and Davidson (*Coventry Plays*, 228), who take the opposite view, that Joseph hears the shepherds' singing as they approach. The fact that Joseph does not mention the angels' second performance of *Gloria in excelsis deo* is perhaps supporting evidence for this view.

We are to understand, then, that the song at **312+sd** was a song of praise to the Redeemer. This is the only possible place for the shepherds to fulfill their stated intention to sing 'Et in terra pax hominibus', so perhaps they repeat the 'Gloria ... bonae voluntatis' text here. See below.

1/416–24 On being asked where the shepherds went after their experience, the first prophet says that they went away singing:

> With myrthe and solas the made good chere
> For joie of that new tything.
>   **(416–17)**

This fits as a further description of a song of praise. In the last five lines of the section (**420–4**) the first prophet seems to step outside time. Earlier he said that the time for the Nativity had come (**380–2**), and described the events of the Nativity as happening 'This othur nyght soo cold' (**385**): now, he refers to the shepherds' joyous entry into Heaven after death, as if looking back over a longer period. He also says that 'there songe hit ys "Neowell"' (**424**). This is not connected to the song sung at **312+sd**, but 'Nowell' ('news') might very well have formed part of their song of praise at that time. A practical solution when music is chosen for a performance might be to let the shepherds sing the whole responsory rather than just the verse, for this is written in the liturgical present ('Today ...') and could therefore be regarded as the 'news' – the Gospel – that the shepherds must disseminate (AS, 47):

> Hodie nobis celorum rex de virgine nasci dignatus est, ut hominem
> perditum ad regna celestia revocaret: gaudet excercitus angelorum.
> Quia salus eterna humano generi apparuit.
> V. Gloria in excelsis deo, et in terra pax hominibus bone voluntatis.
> Quia.

This leaves a residual problem: do the shepherds go to Heaven in the sight of the audience, as the Prophet suggests? The shepherds' singing of the 'news' through the audience at **312+sd** could certainly suggest their evangelising through life, and entering the heaven at the end of that performance would show them still singing the news and praising God after death. A producer who followed this solution would be justified, I think, in having the angelic choir join in the singing as the shepherds enter the heaven. An alternative solution would be to let the shepherds evangelise by singing 'Gloria ... bone voluntatis' and then to sing an English carol starting 'Nowell' for their entry into Heaven. This solution allows a direct link to the First Prophet's opening words (**313**), 'Novellis, novellis of wondrfull marvellys'.

The Magi

1/487–9 In the opening scene of the Magi section of the play Herod goes to rest with the demand that 'Trompettis, viallis, and othur armone' shall play to him. 'Harmony' could certainly mean polyphony here, whether composed or improvised, although it need only refer to an agreeable melodic style (see above, with reference to line **253** of this play). The reference to trumpets and viols together presents a performance-problem at first sight, since the loud instruments would certainly spoil the effect of the *bas* instruments if they were played together in concert. In fact, the playwright is probably only making the point that Herod has the full range of minstrelsy available to him – trumpets for ceremonial music befitting his status as a king, viols to provide domestic music – on the assumption that the groups of instruments would perform separately. This may be regarded as a purely academic question here, since there is no indication that the minstrels actually performed at this point in the play. But to have silence here after such an obvious reference to instruments would probably seem strange, and minstrelsy here would serve a useful function in providing a scene-division.

The song texts at the end of the play are discussed in I, 66–71.

The Weavers' Play
The Presentation in the Temple

2/298–9 Simeon is woken by the First Angel, who speaks in lines **291–7**. There is no mention of music at **290+sd**, but Simeon's reference to the 'solam noyse' that woke him (**398–9**, and again at **590**) strongly suggests it. The angel's speech might be regarded as noise in the modern sense, although this would suggest that the sound was not pleasant; or, if the angel had a pleasant and well-modulated voice, the reference might be a metaphorical one, with the normal musical associations indicating this type of vocal quality. But the meaning is probably the normal one of a musical sound or combination of sounds (Carter *Dictionary*, 322–3), or even the rather later meaning of a group of musicians. It is likely, then, that angelic music should be heard at **290+sd**. Simeon strengthens this supposition in line **300** with a clear connection between the 'noise' and the rejoicing of his spirit.

2/361–4 SEMEON   And when he aprochis nere this place,
                Syng then with me thatt conyng hasse,
                And the othur the meyne space,
                For joie rynge ye the bellis.

Simeon and his two clerks have been preparing the temple (see 4.2). These lines record the commissions given to them by Simeon:[17]

1 That the one who knows how to sing is to do so with Simeon when the Child arrives; and

2 That the other clerk is meanwhile to ring the bells.

'Meanwhile' ('the meyne space') is open to two interpretations. It could mean 'in the meantime starting now', in which case **364+md** should be for ringing the bells, not for singing; or it could mean, with reference to the previous line, 'while we are singing on the occasion of the Christ-child's arrival'. The second of these is more likely, since at **620–1** Simeon repeats his order for the bells to be rung, after the announcement of the Child's arrival; it must be noted, however, that Simeon and the other clerk do not sing until the bells have stopped ringing (see below).

This does not explain the marginal direction at **364**, which, as already noted, is probably an addition to the original SD. Craig was no doubt right to assign Song I to this position, for it can go nowhere else.[18] Thus, while one might expect here an angelic concert to accompany Gabriel's journey to visit Mary (**364+sd**) it seems that Simeon and his clerk do in fact accompany themselves vocally while they process to the temple. We can note here that the song text not only comments on what the angel has just told Simeon but also encourages the preparation of the temple.[19]

2/590–4 As before, Simeon is woken by an angel: a substantial scene between Mary and Joseph has intervened. Once more Simeon refers to the 'solam noyse' (**590**), but this time it is 'From the Maker of heyvin and hell' (**591**). Although this might refer to the angel's speech, heavenly music is more likely to elicit such a comment. Again, the reference to 'myrthe' (**593**) supports a musical interpretation.

2/620–1, 630 Simeon bids the clerks 'cum forthe' with him to greet the Child and 'myrrele the bellis ryng'. The bells certainly are rung at this stage, since the clerk responsible completes his task in the next eight lines of text, stating in **630** 'Mastur, now ar the bellis rong'.

It is only now, despite the earlier indication that singing and bell-ringing should be simultaneous (**361–4**), that Simeon starts the singing (**632–3**):

---

[17] Although the text includes a single speaking part for a clerk, **320+sd** and **364+sd** show that there is more than one. More precisely, there are two of them: for 'hasse' (**362**) and 'the othur' (**363**) are both singular. Note that my comment in I, 264, that the number of clerks is unspecified, is erroneous.

[18] Cawley, in *Revels* I, 47–8, expressed the opinion that **363+sd+md** was an error, that Song 1 should be sung at **636+md**, and that Song 2 should occur at **691+md**.

[19] Specifically, the song exhorts all of us to put 'Owr temple' in order: this, it seems to me, is both a reference to the narrative of the play text and a reference to the need for each Christian individually to confess and receive absolution, the body being 'the temple of the soul'.

> SEMEON   Then lett me see with hart and tonge
> How myrrely thatt ye can syng.

As usual, music and joy are overtly connected. This temporal division of bells and singing makes good sense (despite **363**), and helps us to understand what is sung at **634+sd+md**. The ringing of bells at the approach of the Holy Family indicates joy at their arrival. The ceremony of Purification starts when the mother presents herself with her baby at the church door, so that the singing at **633+md** is actually the procession that brings the clergy to that place from the sanctuary: **636+md+sd** reads *Here the cum downe with pressession to mete them.* Further on this, see I, section 7.4. The music here should be liturgical, therefore,[20] and cannot be Song II, as Cawley suggests.[21]

Christ and the Doctors in the Temple

2/801–3   After the service in the temple Joseph praises the singing, saying that the service was 'song full sollamle'. This presumably refers mainly to the 'antem' sung at **799+sd** (see 4.2), which was evidently a fine piece of professional singing. For the possible use of the organ in accompanying singers for this item, see I, 27.

2/840   MARE Off sorro now schal be my songe

Metaphorical usage, not implying actual performance.

At the end of the play-text are the texts of two songs (King and Davidson *Coventry Plays*, 149). The first bears Thomas Mawdyke's name at the top, which, if the case is parallel to that of Song I in the Shearmen and Tailors' play, suggests that this text was copied c. 1591. But, as Ingram noted, Mawdyke's name is in a later hand than the text of the song, the main hand being that responsible for marginalia on ff. 5v and 11r of the main play-text (*REED.Coventry*, 566). According to Ingram, the author-ascription 'Rychard' which appears at the bottom of Song I is also in the hand that wrote the song: that is probably true. On Richard's identity, see I, 62–5. Song II, with its author-ascription 'James Hewyt' at the end, is in yet another hand. Hewitt figures largely in the Coventry records between 1554 and 1583 (*REED.Coventry*, passim): see I, 64–5. His long career as a wait and singing-man in Coventry suggests that he could have been responsible for the music of this song as well as the text (if indeed his name here is an author-attribution). There is presumably a very slim chance that Song II is in Hewitt's own hand. No payments to Hewitt for copying or composing songs are

---

20 In contrast to the music that accompanies the procession of Simeon and the clerks to the temple at **364+sd+md**, which need not be liturgical.
21 *Revels* I, 48.

known, however, while Thomas Nicholas did receive such a payment from the Drapers in 1566, a year when Hewitt was also concerned in their pageant (*REED.Coventry*, 237). For our present purpose this is not useful evidence either way, of course. But we need to learn as much as we can about the activities of musicians in all of these pageants (see 4.5).

One reason for this is that Song II certainly does not belong to the Weavers' play, contrary to suggestions that it should be performed at **691+md** (Craig *Two Coventry Plays*, 54, n.4; Cawley in *Revels* I, 48). The text deals with Judas's betrayal of Christ (v. 1) and with the Crucifixion (vv. 2 and 3). Thus it belongs to a Crucifixion pageant or to one of the plays dealing with the immediately post-Crucifixion period.

The Early Fragment of Play 2
No references to music occur in this fragment.

4.4 Latin and the liturgy

The Shearmen and Tailors' Play

1/22–3 [ISAYE]Yett 'Ecce virgo consepeet',
Loo, where a reymede schall ryse.

This line is integral to the verse. Craig correctly identifies the line as coming from Isaiah 7/14 (with the spelling 'concipiet'): several liturgical pieces have this incipit.

An English paraphrase follows the line, which is there as an authority written by the prophet who is speaking.

1/42 [ISAYE] ... in secula seculorum amen.

Integral to the verse: it follows its own paraphrase, in the fashion of a 'blessing' ending to the first scene of the play. It is the last line of the lesser doxology (*Gloria patri*), but is not the *incipit* for any liturgical piece. There is no question of singing it here.

1/249+sd The direction for *Glorea in exselsis Deo* (sic). The opening of the verse to the first respond of Christmas mattins: see I, 157–9 and 256–8, for discussions of this and the other liturgical possibilities. This is certainly sung, as required by the SD.

1/258, 263 The shepherds quote parts of the Gloria text. The lines are integral to the text, and are not sung.

1/267+sd   As for **249+sd**, above. The spelling 'exsellsis' presumably reflects the pronunciation.

1/436   ERODE Qui statis in Jude et Rex Iseraell

The Messenger has just made a proclamation, much of it in French: Herod speaks in English, except for these, his first words. They are integral to the text, and there is no apparent case for singing. On the other hand these two words are written in red, and it is possible that they refer to a liturgical text. *Qui statis in domo domini* is the *incipit* of an offertory-verse: so the use of the words *Qui statis* here may be an indication of Herod's opinion of his own importance, and to the audience a clear statement about his relationship to God.

The Weavers' Play
2/25 [I PROFETA] Seying Orietur stella ex Jacobo et exorgit homo de Israell.

The Prophet quotes Balaam, with a paraphrase in the following line. Craig identifies the quotation as Numbers 24/17, which reads *Orietur stella ex Jacob et consurget virga de Israel*. The responsory *Orietur stella ex Jacob* is found in the Sarum antiphoner (AS, plate j): it has the text 'Orietur stella ex Jacob et exurget homo de Israel ...', so the dramatist (?Croo) seems to be remembering the liturgical version. The Latin is integral to the text, however, and is not sung.

2/30   [I PROFETA] Et ipse dominabitur omni generacioni.

This may be Psalm 144/13, '... et dominatio tua in omni generatione et generationem'. It does not appear to be a liturgical text.
This quotation, too, is integral to the text and should not be sung.

2/41 [I PROFETA]   Ecce virgo concipiet apariet filium.

2/45 [I PROFETA]   Et vocabitur nomen eius Emanvel.

The Prophet now quotes Isaiah 7/14, the second half of which reads 'Ecce virgo concipiet, et pariet filium, et vocabitur nomen eius Emmanuel'. In the Roman rite this text occurs as an introit and as a communion in Advent (LU, 1683 and 356): the latter is found also in the Sarum rite (GS, 6). Both lines are integral to the verse, however, and there is no reason to sing them.

2/105 [I PROFETA] Seyinge Natus est nobis oddie rex Iudeorum et sethere.

This is an integral part of the verse. Luke 2/11 reads 'quia natus est vobis hodie Salvator, qui est Christus Dominus, in civitate David'. An antiphon based on this text comes a little closer but does not approach the 'Rex Judeorum': 'Natus est nobis hodie salvator qui est Christus dominus in civitate David' (AS, 56). A Christmas trope known in England starts 'Hodie natus est nobis rex regum ...' (Planchart *Repertory of Tropes*, I, 128–9 and 303–4). The quoted text seems to have started as the antiphon but to have been changed, perhaps by contamination from the text of Matthew 2/2: 'Ubi est qui natus est rex Judeorum?' In any case there is no question of singing it.

2/1765 [II PROFETA] In secula seculorum, amen.

The end of the prophets' scene. The text is the end of the *Gloria patri*: cf. the note to **1/42**, above. It forms an integral part of the verse, and the sense carries over from the previous lines. There is apparently no question of singing it.

2/239–40 [SEMEON] In facie populorum, thes did he sey,
   Cum venerit sanctus san[c]torum cessabit vnctio vestra.

The text attributes this quotation to Isaiah, but I cannot find it. Craig identified it as Daniel 9/24, but the Vulgate wording is quite different. It is a quotation for authority, integral to the verse, and the question of singing does not arise.

2/513 [JOSOFF] Lorde, benedissete, whatt make I here

Merely an exclamation. *Benedicite* is liturgically too common to need identifying in any specific text.

2/617 [CLARECUS] Sey all you, Deo gracias.

Integral to the verse. The phrase would be well known as the response to the *Ite missa est*, and needs no further explanation.

2/718 [ANE] In secula seculorum. Amen.

End of the scene. The text is the end of the *Gloria patri*, but it is presumably not sung, although all the cast present (and the audience?) might respond 'Amen'. A sung procession would be very suitable for the withdrawal of Simeon and the clerks at **718+sd**: this single line would however be inadequate.

2/789 [JOSOFF] Lord God, benedicete

As **513**, above.

2/925 [III DOCTOR] Ex ore infanciam et lactancium perfesisti laudem.

The Third Doctor quotes Psalm 8/3 (8/2 in the AV): the Vulgate has 'infantium' and 'lactentium', but otherwise the wording is the same. There is a short respond with this text in the Worcester Antiphoner (WA, 47), but the line is an integral part of the verse and there is no reason to sing it.

The Early Fragment of Play 2
2f/25–6 [I PROFETA] Orre Etur stella Ex Jacob
et Exvrge homo de yseraell

= **2/25**.

2f/31 [I PROFETA] et ipse dominabetur omni gen[eracione].

= **2/30**.

2f/42 [I PROFETA] Ecce virgo concepith aperet fillium

= **2/41**: Croo apparently corrected this rather corrupt version.

2f/46 [I PROFETA] et vocatur nomen eius Emanevell

= **2/45**.

4.5 Records

Sharp, and Hardin Craig after him, printed a large enough selection of Coventry records to show that some very useful information was available. It was not clear quite what percentage of the records these publications represented, however, and in Sharp's case it was not always apparent that material had been omitted. The transcriptions made by Dutka for her PhD thesis (*The Use of Music*) improved this situation.

The full range of surviving evidence became generally available only with the publication of Ingram's *REED.Coventry* volume in 1981. Ingram's volume supersedes all previous work, and I refer to it throughout this section, but it does not provide the answers to all the questions that have to be asked. As will become apparent, there are frustrating gaps both in the ranks of the surviving documents and in the information that individual documents offer.

Play 1 *The Nativity, and the Massacre of the Innocents* (Shearmen & Tailors)
The Tailors' pageant house is mentioned in a document of 1434 (*REED.Coventry*, 10), but the period of the company's dramatic activity is almost completely devoid of information on their play. Most references in the surviving records are very late, long after the last performance of the cycle in 1579 (328–31). Financial accounts of the guild give information on music and ceremonial in 1621 (413–14) and 1624 (420), but nothing of relevance to the present enquiry.

The Walkers contributed to this pageant until 1447, but none of their accounts survives from this period.

Play 2 *The Purification, and Christ with the Doctors* (Weavers)
Various records of the Weavers' Company survive, including a book of accounts running from 1523 to 1634. The Weavers had a pageant as early as 1424 (*REED.Coventry*, 9), and information on their pageant house runs from 1434 (10). Craig says that the Skinners and Walkers contributed (*Two Coventry Plays*, xv), but no relevant accounts survive.

The first year of the extant Weavers' accounts, 1523, gives only a summary of expenses (121), but those for the next year include (122)

> 1524   Item for Wyne & bred to syng withall   xx d

This payment is presumably for subsistence for the singers performing on some occasion for the Weavers. It is impossible to tell whether the occasion was that of a play or some other event.

The accounts for 1525 include, in the 'exspencys on corpus christi day' (124), 2/4d to Simeon, 14d to Joseph, 10d each to Mary, Anna and Simeon's clerk, 8d to the angels (between them), and 16d to the singers. For some reason that is not known to us the Doctors and Prophets do not appear in this list. Simeon's is clearly the most important role, and his payment is commensurate also with his function as a singer.[22] The payments to Anna, Simeon's clerk and the two angels seem to go with the number of lines that they speak in the existing text – 33 each for Anna and the clerk, 15 each for the angels: but Mary, with 174 lines in the existing text, seems underpaid. Perhaps Croo's revision gave Mary a much larger part than the original.

On this evidence the speaking clerk is the one who does not sing (and is therefore the one who rings the bells), while the singing but non-speaking clerk must be one of those described as 'þe synggers'. It is hard to know how many singers are implied by the 16d payment. *Prima facie* there should be two or four of them: but presumably the second clerk, who sings with Simeon alone, has more to

---

[22] Compare the payments to Robert White at Chester, discussed in 6.4, below.

perform than those singing only the liturgical music, so that the money might have been divided as 8d+4d+4d. It is important to note, I think, that there were not enough singers to provide an angelic choir as well as the Temple choir.

The accounts for 1526 (126) give only a summary. Those for 1527 (126) record a payment of 3/-d to 'the mynstrell for the yere', which is certainly not specifically for performing during the play. This payment is repeated in subsequent years, those for 1535 showing that the minstrel's name was Wyllyam Blakbowrn (142). The accounts for 1536 record a payment of only 2/-d to the minstrel 'for Corpuscrysty day & mydssomer ny3ght' (143).

A fuller list of expenses on Corpus Christi day is found in the accounts for 1541 (156–7), the first detailed figures for the revised play. Payments to the players are substantially increased, which may show that Croo expanded the play, but they remain roughly in proportion as before. Simeon is now paid 3/4d and Joseph 2/4d; Jesus still receives 20p, but Mary, Anna and Simeon's clerk have increased payment at 20d each; the two angels remain at 8d between them and the singers at 16d. This, and the similar wording to that of the 1524 records, suggests that the play was not so different from the earlier version, at least in its narrative, characters and production details.

These sums are repeated in 1542, except that the singers' payment is raised to 18d (161). The sum is correct, however, so this is probably not a mistake despite the fact that the payment reverts to 16d in 1543 (165), the other payments remaining the same as before. The accounts for 1544 are notable for the first mention of Richard the capper, 'borsleys man that playth ane' (see I, 320) and the connection of Borsley himself with the pageant (*REED.Coventry*, 168–9): they also include, among payments to players much as before, the information that the singers were 'yn ye paggant'.

Payments to players remain as before in 1545 (172), but are missing in 1546 (173): in the latter year, however, the payment 'to the mynstrell of corpus christi day And Mydsomer ny3th xiiij d' confirms the suggestion of earlier accounts that the company's minstrel did have some regular and well-defined role in the events of Corpus Christi. It is of course not possible to show that this role was in the play. The accounts for 1548, however, where the payments to players are as before, divides the minstrel's payment into one of 4d for Corpus Christi Day and one of 8d for Midsummer Night. It is clear from the Midsummer payments that the Weavers' pageant was used on that occasion (180).

The accounts of 1549 (183–4) include a payment of 4d to a new actor, the 'lettell chyld', who presumably played Jesus at the Purification.[23] There are also two items of special interest for musical matters. First, the payment of 8d to the minstrel on Corpus Christi Day is in the middle of payments for the play (he received 9d on Midsummer Night, so he had been given an increase), which implies strongly that his performance was part of the dramatic presentation.

---

[23] In some later years this becomes 'to the womon for hyr chyld'.

This being so, his obvious role would be that of a *bas* accompaniment to the Angel's appearances to Simeon.

Second, the singers are described as 'the clarkes' and the payment of 16d made 'for syngyng yn ye pagant'. This may mean that the singers were dressed as clerks (i.e. in minor orders) of the Temple, or that they actually were singing-men in real life. Both were probably the case, although I think that the scribe intended the latter.

Payments in 1550 are as before, although the singers are again merely 'ye syngars yn ye paggane' (186), as they are also in 1551 (189). The accounts for 1552 contain no relevant details (192).

Payments are as before in 1553 (196), but in 1554 two possibly significant changes are found (199). First, there is no separate payment to a minstrel at Corpus Christi, and the 16d given to the minstrels for Midsummer Night is unlikely to include it.[24] Second, the Corpus Christi payments include:

1554   payd to Iames hewet for hys Reyggalles   viij d

This is the first time that Hewitt appears in the Coventry guild accounts.

The use of regals might fulfill any one of three purposes:
(i)   as a substitute for the minstrel's *bas* music during the Angel's appearances to Simeon;
(ii) to support the singers in the Temple during the Purification service; or
(iii) to provide solo organ music for that service, either by playing *alternatim* in vocal pieces or by adding purely instrumental movements.

Hewitt does not appear in the accounts for 1555 (203–4), when the minstrel received 12d for Corpus Christi, suggesting that the minstrel had been unable to perform in 1554 and Hewitt took his place. As Hewitt had received only 8d in 1554, the minstrel's payment in previous years, it is likely that the minstrel negotiated a higher payment this year: and perhaps the company was happy to pay more to their usual minstrel than to a stranger.

The very full accounts for 1556 support interpretations (ii) and (iii), however, for they include (206):

1556   Item payd to the syngeres   xvj d

    Item payd to Iames hewet for playing of
      hys Rygoles in the paygent   viij d

    Item payd to ye mynstrell   xij d

---

24 The Weavers had paid 16d to 'the ij mynstrells' for Midsummer Night 1552 (*REED.Coventry*, 192).

(These three items are not adjacent.) These interpretations are confirmed also by a payment in the accounts of 1557 (208), a year in which the minstrel received 12d as usual (209):

> 1557　Item payd to ye syngers & to Iames hewyt
> 　　　　for playinge of Rygols　　　　ij s

This sum is presumably made up of the usual 16d to the singers and 8d as before to Hewitt.

1558 was a cheaper year for music in the play, for no payment was made to Hewitt and the minstrel received only 8d (210). This may have been due to circumstances beyond the Weavers' control, for the payments in 1559 included only 6d 'for the Rygoles' and no mention of the minstrel (211–12); the following year the regular payment to the singers is missing, there is no mention of Hewitt or the regals, and the minstrel again received 12d (213–14). This suggests that there were problems with the availability of the singers, Hewitt and the usual minstrel in these years.

In 1561 the minstrel was again not paid for Corpus Christi, and the payment for vocal music is not worded as usual (216):

> 1561　Item payd Iames huytt for hys Rygoles & synggyn　　　ij s iiij d

Hewitt was a singer, so this may mean what it appears to mean – that Hewitt both provided (and played) the regals and sang in the pageant. But 2/4d is larger than the 2/-d paid for this in 1556 and 1557. The sum may suggest a larger body of singers, and certainly it seems likely that Hewitt provided and trained the singers, as well as playing the regals. As we shall see, however, the singers' group probably remained the same size, so perhaps Hewitt was being paid the extra 4d for extra work. This implies, in view of the missing minstrel, that Hewitt and the singers were now supplying both the liturgical music and the angelic music formerly played by the minstrel.

The following year the company spent 3/-d on the music (219), made up of 20d 'to Iames hewet for hys rygoles' and 16d (the adjacent item) 'for syngyng'. The minstrel has now disappeared from the Corpus Christi expenses; and as all the Midsummer Night payments have gone, as well, the minstrel does not figure at all in the Weavers' accounts. Perhaps the previous years had seen his illness and death, with the Weavers making *ad hoc* arrangements as necessary.

The 1563 accounts are worded the same way and record the same payments (222). The accounts for 1564 give no details of the players in the Weavers' pageant (226), but those for 1565 again repeat the wording and payments of 1562 (228). From 1566 (235) the payment to Simeon's clerk is increased to 2/-d, and the payments for this year are repeated in 1567 (239), 1568 (244),[25] 1569 (248), 1570 (252), 1571 (255), and 1572 (258). Perhaps Simeon's clerk was now required to undertake something extra, such as singing in the liturgical items.[26]

In the accounts for 1573 (262) the payment to 'Iames hewet for playng on the rygoles' is only 4d, although that 'for syngyng' is still 16d; and this seems not to be a mistake, since the same sums were paid in 1574 (268):

| 1574 | Item paid for singinge in the pagand | xvj d |
| | Item paid for playing on the rigoldes | iiij d |

The 1575 accounts are not full ones (272), but the same sums were paid again in 1576 (279). In this year the Rentgatherers' Book records 16d to the minstrels, again for unspecified duties (280).

The accounts for 1577 show these same payments (284) – except that nothing is recorded to the minstrels in the Rentgatherers' Book (285) – as do those for 1578 (288) and 1579 (292). This last year saw the final performance of the cycle, but the Weavers continued to make payments to minstrels and singers, presumably on other types of occasion. Most of these need not concern us here, except that the Weavers again brought out their pageant in 1584. No music figures in the accounts, but the payment of 12d to singers in the Rentgatherers' Book for that year may relate to that occasion (306–7).

One more payment may be important before the Weavers' pageant was sold in 1587 (318): in 1586 the Weavers paid 16d 'to mr goldston for mendinge our Instrumentes' (315). Goldston was a trumpeter: he took James Hewitt's place in the waits, and was leader of the waits by 1590 at the latest (588). This payment suggests that the Weavers possessed musical instruments. Minstrels normally had to effect running repairs on instruments, and some of them no doubt became very skilled at it. It is not surprising, then, that a minstrel should be paid for repairing instruments: but it is surprising that the Weavers owned musical instruments to be repaired.

It is not easy to summarise the probabilities of performance as shown in these accounts. In the pre-1535 period, when the old text was being played, there were clearly at least two singers, and probably three, who took the roles of the singing-men in the Temple; and there was a minstrel who may have accompanied the Angel's appearances to Simeon. The same musical resources seem to have been used for Croo's revised version at first, but the appearance of the regals from

---

25 In this year, 1568, the Weavers' Rentgatherers' Book has an unspecified payment of 8d to 'the mynstreles', but this is probably not for Corpus Christi (*REED.Coventry*, 245).

26 I have assumed earlier that Simeon's distinction between the clerk 'thatt conyng hasse' in singing and the other (see 4.3 under **2/361–4**) would preclude singing by the speaking clerk: but in difficult circumstances perhaps this would be overlooked.

1553 onwards adds another dimension to the pageant's music. The player (and probably owner) of the regals, James Hewitt, seems not to have substituted for the minstrel at first, but to have been involved in the vocal music of the Temple. Whether he supported the singers, played *alternatim* with them or played solos, or some combination of these three, it is impossible to determine. Eventually he may have been involved in the angelic music as well, playing instrumental music or perhaps accompanying singers.

Play A *The Passion* (Smiths)[27]

The play mounted by the Smiths, and the evidence for it, is discussed by King and Davidson (*Coventry Plays*, 29–33). They consider that the Smiths played the Passion sequence from the Agony in the Garden as far as the Death of Christ: this sequence includes the episode of Pilate's wife and the Hanging of Judas. It is possible that the Smiths also played the Burial of Christ.[28]

The extensive accounts of the Smiths' company begin in 1450 (*REED.Coventry*, 19–20). In that year 2d was 'spend on ye mynstrell at ye first cumyng', which may be a payment for a rehearsal. Later items record 20d spent on the minstrel's dinner and supper on Corpus Christi Day and a payment of 7/-d for 'ys hyyr'. This last is a very considerable sum, and may perhaps be mainly for music during the procession. If the minstrel also performed during the play, he was presumably a loud minstrel playing fanfares, and so on, for Herod.

The expenses for Midsummer Night include 9d to 'ye harper', and those for St Peter's night 7d to 'ye mynstrell'. The first is evidently for entertainment at the banquet, as the second may be: both contrast sharply with the relatively huge sum earned by a minstrel on Corpus Christi Day.

The accounts for 1451 (23–4) are slightly confused by the fact that Corpus Christi fell on Midsummer Day. Sharp records payments of 8/-d to 'þe mynstrells for þer hyr', 2/6d 'spend on þer bord on Corpus Christi evyn & daye', and, for the Midsummer and St Peter's watches, 11d to 'ij harpers'. A possible reason for the high Corpus Christi payment presents itself here, in that two occasions – the eve and the day itself – are involved. Even so, the high payment suggests considerable duties in the Corpus Christi celebrations.

These payments are sorted out a little in the 1452 accounts (25). In the Corpus Christi section the minstrels receive 8/-d and the sum of 20d is expended on their dinner and supper; on Midsummer Night the harper received 12d; and the minstrel was paid 6d for St Peter's Watch.

While later accounts retain this broad picture, it is not possible to calculate how many minstrels were involved on these various occasions. For 1453 the

---

27 Craig (*Two Coventry Plays*, xv) says that the Cooks, Fishers, Bakers, Millers, Chandlers and Wire-Drawers contributed to this pageant, but no relevant accounts survive.

28 Craig believed that the Smiths played the Entry into Jerusalem: *Two Coventry Plays*, xv; *English Religious Drama*, 287–91.

Corpus Christi records have only a payment of 12d to 'þe mynstrell on corpus christi even & day' (28); there are no items concerning music for the Midsummer and St Peter's watches; and at the dinner on St Loy's Day the company paid 8d to a luter and 12d to the Waits of the city. The following year the Smiths made the same payment for Corpus Christi (28), but Sharp transcribed no other musical items, if indeed they existed.

No accounts of the Smiths' company survive for 1455; those for 1456 contain only a brief account of expenses for the queen's visit the following year (35); there are none for 1457–60. Those for 1461 relate only to the visit of the prince, in which a harper appears (40): the pageant produced was apparently not the Smiths' cycle-play. The accounts for 1462 do not help with music (42).

For some years after this the accounts are available only in selections, principally Sharp's. The only relevant item for 1463 is a payment of 9/-d to 'the iiij mynstrells' at Corpus Christi (43). Mention of a specific band of four minstrels usually means a shawm-and-trumpet band, the city waits being the most likely. There is no relevant item in the selections made for 1464–6, but the accounts for 1467 mention the waits, 8/8d being expended on 'ther hyr & ther bord' for Corpus Christi and St Loy's day (45). This seems to confirm that the waits as a group had already started the association with the Smiths' company that was to be regularised in 1481 (see below).

The surviving records for 1468 include nothing immediately relevant, and there are no payments for music in 1469 or 1470.

The accounts for Corpus Christi 1471 include 6/-d to the waits for their minstrelsy (50). No payments for music are recorded in 1472 or 1473; the accounts for 1474 include 3/4d to two minstrels 'for melody' at the Midsummer Watch, although this was the year of Prince Edward's visit to Coventry, and the Smiths must have made payments for music not recorded by Sharp. No Smiths' accounts for music survive from 1475 or 1476.

There is a fuller surviving list of the Smiths' dramatic accounts for 1477, including a cast-list with payments. From this it is clear that Herod was the most important role, paid 3/8d, with Pilate a close second at 3/4d. These roles give a reason for the hiring of a band of *haut* minstrels, and the waits were paid 5/-d that year 'for pypyng' at Corpus Christi. The accounts for 1478 show no music, and no musicians are mentioned in the accounts for 1479 (62), which are concerned with rehearsals; the same is true of those for 1480 (63).

The Smiths' records for 1481 include the well-known account for the company's agreement with the waits, who are named as Thomas West, Adam West, John Blewet and Brese (64). Each of these four paid a fine of 2d, on which he and his wife became a brother and sister of the company. The condition of their membership was that the four waits would 'serve the crafte' on Corpus Christi day for 8/-d and their dinner. Of the 2/-d due to each wait, 12d were to be given to him and 12d retained as part-payment of his fine until all the fine was paid.

There are then no music payments in the Smiths' accounts until 1490, when there is a very full record of expenses at rehearsals and payments to the players, together with an inventory of the costumes (72–4). Immediately under the payments to players on Corpus Christi day, apparently added as an afterthought, is a record of 14d paid to 'þe Mynstrell'. It is impossible to be sure that this is singular: 14d would be a large payment to one minstrel for the performance, although perhaps not unreasonable if it included payment for one or more rehearsals; on the other hand it cannot be for the waits, who are listed later in the accounts as receiving 5/8d, apparently (though not certainly) for Corpus Christi day. But this is itself a strange sum for a performance: it divides awkwardly into four (1/5d each), and cannot be divided between three; and it does not obviously follow from the 1481 agreement.

No relevant records occur under 1491–4. In 1495 the accounts show that the Smiths paid 5/-d to the waits (85). There are again no relevant items surviving for 1496–8.

The Smiths' records for 1499 are full, including the list of payments to the players (92–4). They are made up from a number of selections, however, and payments for music with the pageant at Corpus Christi are almost certainly missing. The accounts for 1500, likewise, are constructed from several sources and include no items for music (95). No relevant items are then found until 1549, when the Waits were paid 2/8d 'for the pagent' (184); then again none until 1555, when 'the mynstrells' were paid 2/6d 'for prosesyon and pageants' at Corpus Christi (205).

The next relevant entry is in the records for 1561 (218), when the minstrels were paid 2/-d in a list of expenses for the pageant. This is in fact the last item from the Smiths' records that is relevant to music in their play. Sharp states that in 1577 the Smiths had a new play (285), although the subject apparently remained the same: but no mention of music appears in the records.

In 1584 the Smiths took their part in *The Destruction of Jerusalem*, and their accounts for it survive (307–9). See section 9.9, below.

Play B *The Harrowing of Hell, Resurrection, and Appearances to the Marys, to the Virgin, and to Mary Magdalene* (Cappers: Cardmakers until 1531)[29]
The Cappers' pageant, which they took over from the Cardmakers in 1531, is discussed by King and Davidson (*Coventry Plays*, 33–41). Sharp used an account book of the Cappers that showed them to have contributed to the Girdlers' pageant: they were associated with the Cardmakers from 1531, and brought out that pageant for the first time in 1534 (Craig *English Religious Drama*, 286).

The Cappers' accounts survive from c. 1485, but the problems of dating are such that Ingram put many of the earlier ones in an appendix as undatable

---

[29] Craig (*Two Coventry Plays*, xv) says that the Painters and Masons, Walkers, Skinners, Joiners and Cardmakers were contributory, but no relevant accounts survive.

(*REED.Coventry*, xliii and 449–54).[30] The first datable account, that for 1520, is notable as recording Robert Crow's election to membership of the company, but there are no Corpus Christi payments. The company had its own minstrel, who was paid retainers of 12d and 13d that year (116). These payments to the minstrel varied considerably: in 1521 he was paid 14d and 4d (117); in 1522 and 1523 there is a single payment of 2d (119, 120), with some confusion caused by a reference to 'minstrelles' (the plural being an abbreviation) in the latter year; and in 1524 the single payment of 4d is to 'amynstrell' (sic: 121). If this change from 'the minstrel' to 'a minstrel' signifies any loosening of a bond, that is confirmed in the accounts for 1525, where no minstrel appears: these accounts are however the fullest yet, with payments for the festivities at Candlemass including one of 20d to 'the syngers' (123).

The Cappers' accounts for 1526 contain nothing relevant (126), and *REED. Coventry* prints no accounts for the period 1527–32 inclusive. Those for 1533 include payments of 8d to 'the mynstrell' and 3/-d to 'the mynstrelles' (136, 137): although the plural is again an abbreviation, the size of the payment does suggest more than one minstrel.

The accounts for the Resurrection play begin with those of 1534, which include a payment of 4/-d to two minstrels at a riding. From now on I shall not notice such payments unless they provide information necessary to the understanding of the play-accounts. Those taking part in the play include 'the Syngers' (paid 16d) and 'the mynstrell' (8d), and the cast-list (139–40) also includes 'two awngelles' (paid 8d). The latter presumably guarded the tomb after the Resurrection, and the singers must have performed angelic music at the Resurrection itself. The sum paid suggests that there were two singers. The minstrel might have supplied *bas* music for the various appearances, but I think it more likely that they provided loud minstrelsy for Pilate, who was paid 3/8d (the largest payment in the list) and who therefore took a major role in the play.

The accounts for 1535, 1536 and 1538 (*REED.Coventry* prints nothing for 1537) give only a summary of expenses for the pageant, but for 1539 the accounts again give a cast-list with payments (150). The minstrel received 6d, 'the Sengyng men' 16d, and 'the menstyrlles on corpos christi day' 6d. This last payment, which is adjacent to that for the singers, apparently refers to minstrels performing in the play. The first, which immediately follows the heading 'The expensses and paymentes for the pagant', is itself followed by payments relating to the preparation of the pageant and for food and drink. Thus it is quite likely to relate to minstrelsy at rehearsals, a probability supported by the fact that only one minstrel is involved as opposed to those paid for work 'on corpos christi day' rather than at another time. Probably 'the minstrels' here, as elsewhere, are the city's waits. The waits were certainly busy on Corpus Christi day (xxi), and

---

[30] Those for the Cappers (450–4) are all from before 1534: they contain no relevant items.

6d is perhaps a reasonable payment for a brief appearance. On the other hand, a single brief appearance does not fit with the need for music for the important role of Pilate.

The accounts for 1540 are again considerable (152–4). Under the heading 'The Costes of the pagant' are 16d to the singers with, adjacent to this, 8d to 'the mensterell'. Under the 'Costes of corposchristi day and myssymor nyght' come first two items that can be quoted in full:

> 1540 Item paid to the mensterlles of corposchristi day <and myssymor nyght and sent peteres nyght>   xij d
> (The words in < > are interlined)

> Item paid to ij menstrelles of myssymor ewen   ij s viij d

It is clear from these, first, that the single minstrel, paid 8d, performed in the play. Almost certainly this was not loud music for Pilate, then, but *bas* music concerned with one or more of Christ's appearances. Second, the waits (if indeed it is they) were paid for minstrelsy at the banquet (or, just possibly, for the procession), although the main work on Midsummer Night was done by two other minstrels.

This interpretation cannot be used for the 1539 accounts quite so simply, however. In the first place, there are separate payments to a single minstrel for Midsummer night and St Peter's night; in the second, the payment to the minstrels on Corpus Christi day follows that to the singing men, and is in any case in the middle of expenses for the pageant. I conclude that 'the minstrels' (?waits) at least played between stations, if not for the play itself.

Returning to the 1540 accounts, it is interesting to see that 6d was paid for the mending of 'ij Senssares' (153): presumably these were used by the two angels.

Only summary accounts survive for 1541, but those for 1542 are again detailed (159–60): they include 16d to the singers and, adjacently, 8d to the minstrel. The accounts for 1543 include extensive payments for maintenance and repairs, and also some usefully explicit payments for music (164):

> 1543 paid to ye syngares in ye pageant   xvj d
> paid to ye mynstrell in ye pageant   viij d

---

31 It may be relevant that the Corpus Christi Guild accounts for 1539 show that the characters – apparently in the play of Pentecost or the Death of Mary – made offerings at the altar during the procession. Perhaps a *bas* minstrel performed then: see Rastall 'Minstrelsy, Church and Clergy' for minstrels performing during the making of offerings. The Corpus Christi Guild made no payment to minstrels, however, on this occasion.

Near the bottom of the list is a payment of 2/8d to 'ye mynstrell for Corpus christi day & mydsomer nyght'. This allays any suspicion that the singers performed at the banquet rather than in the play, and also makes the vital distinction between the (single) minstrel performing in the play and the (usually plural) minstrels performing for 'Corpus Christi day and Midsummer night'. Where possible I shall concentrate from now onwards on the singers and minstrel in the play.

In 1544 the singers' payment was increased to 20d, that to the minstrel remaining at 8d (167). There are no recorded payments for the pageant in 1545, nor for 1546. For 1547 there is again a list of payments to the players (175–6), reverting to 16d for the singers, the minstrel receiving 8d as before. These payments are repeated in 1548 (178). In 1549 the minstrel's payment is the same, but the singers are for some reason omitted. The following year they are reinstated, at 16d, but now some several lines below the minstrel, who received 8d as usual (185). There are no relevant payments in 1551, but payments to the singers and the minstrel, once more adjacent, in that order, and of the usual sums of 16d and ·8d, occur in the accounts for 1552 (191) and for 1553 (in reverse order), the section now being headed 'paymentes to ye plears'. In 1554, under the same heading, the singers appear but not the minstrel. That this was an oversight or due to unusual circumstances is shown by the accounts for the following year: both payments were made, but the singers come second, several lines behind the minstrel.

There are no relevant accounts for the years 1556–61. Those for 1562 were abstracted by Halliwell-Phillipps, who recorded the usual 8d to the minstrel but nothing for singers (220). Those for 1563, again copied by Halliwell-Phillipps, show the two payments in their most frequent positions, but with an important addition concerning the singers (223):

| 1563 | Item, payd to the syngers & makynge the songe | ij s iiij d |
| | Item, payd to the mynstrell | viij d |

Whatever 'makynge the songe' entailed, it was worth 12d: no doubt it was a piece of composition. At this date we should probably assume that it was to an English text, but whether it replaced an older English-text setting or – very belatedly – superseded Latin plainsong, it is impossible to tell.

There is a possibility that the second song-text preserved with the Weavers' play, and there ascribed to James Hewitt, is the one concerned. Hewitt was a

---

[32] The word 'minstrel' in Middle English is often to be understood as plural: here, however, apart from some rather loose usage on the part of the accounting scribes, it seems that the plural normally requires an 's' or, more usually, an '-es'/'-is' abbreviation.

[33] See I, 65. Thomas Nicholas received 12d on several occasions for setting a song or for copying more than one song.

singing-man as well as a wait and organist, but he does not appear in any accounts as a composer. That such a man would be unable to compose is almost unthinkable: but if he were not noted for it he might very well do it in collaboration with a colleague. In this case, two conclusions more or less follow:

1) Hewitt and a colleague are the 'clarkes' singing in the Cappers' play, perhaps for some years prior to 1563; and
2) The ascription to Hewitt in the Weavers' second song-text shows him to be the part-composer: but it almost certainly makes him the poet, too.

This song-text is however unsuitable unless for an early part of the Cappers' play, for it deals only with Christ's work of redemption on Calvary. An even more suitable place for it would be the end of the Smiths' play, but, as we have seen, the Smiths' accounts do not include payments to singers. Let us assume, then, that this song, written by Hewitt, and set to music by Hewitt and a colleague, was sung by them at the beginning of the Cappers' play. It could be sung after the Harrowing of Hell, in the position occupied by **York 37$_2$** and **Towneley 25$_2$**. If this is correct, then Hewitt and his companion singer were playing the parts of two of the patriarchs in Limbo, or of angels, appearing again in the Resurrection sequence. Unfortunately the accounts do not record any payments to the Souls in Limbo, although King and Davidson identify Adam, Eve and one other prophet as those appearing (*Coventry Plays*, 34–5).

REED.Coventry prints no records for 1564. Those for 1565 are transmitted by Sharp, and include both the usual 8d to the minstrel and the 16d to the singers (228–9). 1566 was exceptional, in that the pageant was played during a visit of the queen. The payments to the minstrel and the singers are as usual, and adjacent in the selection made (236). There is also a payment of 16d 'for prikynge the songes', which means that there were at least two items of vocal polyphony. Moreover at this stage, only three years after the 'setting' of a song, it seems unlikely that that particular song would need recopying, although it is possible: so either a new song had been written (but it does not say so) or there were at least two songs in addition to the one that was new in 1563.

Although an inventory of properties survives for 1567, the only known expenses for that year are those abstracted by Halliwell-Phillipps: they include 8d to the minstrel but nothing to singers. Those for 1568 are from the same source. They include nothing to musicians: but there certainly was vocal music, since there is a payment of 12d for 'prikynge the songes' (245). Again, it seems strange that two or more songs should need to be recopied only two years after the last 'pricking'. In fact, this problem arises again in relation to the following year's accounts. Although the extracts do not include payments to musicians, there is a payment of 12d to 'Thomas Nyclys for prikinge þe songes' (249).

---

34 See I, 63–4.

35 See later, for 1566, when it appears that there could be three or more polyphonic songs in the play.

Ingram's index makes no distinction between Thomas Nichols and Thomas Nicholas, although it is unlikely that the first, who was one of the city waits in 1570, was identical to the second, a draper who was mayor in 1570–1. Thomas Nicholas the wait was also a clerk at Holy Trinity church (491), and Ingram is surely right to identify him with the man responsible for setting a song for the Drapers in 1566 and pricking songs for the Cappers in 1569 (573).

REED.Coventry prints no accounts for 1570; Halliwell-Phillipps's extracts for 1571 include no musicians; and the surviving accounts for 1572 give a summary only (257).

A full set of accounts for 1573 gives the usual payments of 8d to the minstrel and 16d to the singers (261); in those for 1574 the minstrel again receives 8d but the singers, further down the list, receive 20d (267). It is hard to account for the occasional fluctuation of this sort. The accounts for 1575 do not include a cast-list, and no musicians are mentioned; those for 1576 are complete, and we find that the singers' fee has risen to 2/-d and the minstrel's to 10d (278: these payments are adjacent); in 1577 the singers stayed at 2/-d but the minstrel's fee reverted to 8d (283: again adjacent); these fees were repeated in 1578 (288: adjacent), and again in 1579 (291: adjacent).

1579 was the last year in which the play was performed, and subsequent accounts are generally irrelevant for our present purpose. I shall return to those for 1584, however, in section 9.9.

Play C *The Death and Assumption of Mary, the Appearance of Mary to Thomas* (Mercers)

There is considerable doubt about the material treated in the Mercers' play. King and Davidson present circumstantial evidence that the Mercers played the Death, Assumption and Coronation of the Virgin (*Coventry Plays*, 41–4): but Craig had been unable to say what company played Doubting Thomas, the Ascension and Pentecost (*Two Coventry Plays*, xv), a problem that he ignored in his later discussion (*English Religious Drama*, 287–91). Assuming that these episodes were played – and it is difficult to see how the Ascension and Pentecost could be omitted – it is possible that they were included in the Mercers' pageant.

The surviving accounts of the Mercers' company start in 1579, the year of the last performance of the cycle, although there are memoranda dating from before

---

36 The sixteenth-century orthography is not as clear as these two names would suggest: the wait is normally known as Thomas Nicholas, and I have continued to use that name.

37 Perhaps two singers at 8d each were joined by another, less experienced, colleague at 4d; or perhaps four singers at 4d each were the norm, with a fifth joining them in this year.

38 Craig believed that the Cappers contributed (*Two Coventry Plays*, xv); but he later stated (*English Religious Drama*, 286) that there were no contributary crafts for this play, and assigned the Cappers to the Girdlers' play.

then (*REED.Coventry*, 188, 196 and 279). Unfortunately, the account for 1579 is only a summary (292). This is a disappointingly small survival that explains why there is so much doubt over the extent of the play's subject-matter. Later accounts have nothing of relevance in them, except for that relating to *The Destruction of Jerusalem* in 1584: see 9.9, below.

Play D *Doomsday* (Drapers)

The Drapers' accounts survive only in a nineteenth-century transcript made by Daffern (*REED.Coventry*, xlvii and 455–7). There is considerable doubt about the dating of much of this material. The first firmly datable account is that for 1561 (216), but the accounts certainly go back to 1534 and probably to 1524 and 1525. The earlier records present such huge problems that Ingram placed them at the end of his volume, as Appendix 2 (455–81). For our present purposes it is necessary only to accept Ingram's tentative datings.

As in other guild accounts from Coventry, the Drapers' records do not always make a clear distinction between payments made on different occasions. The accounts for ?1524, however, do not mention music (463): and the pattern of payments is retained in those for ?1525 (461), undated accounts of the 1520s or 1530s (462–3), and those for ?1534 or 1535 (461), and ?1537 (463–4).

With another set of accounts for 1535 we find a payment of 3d 'for beryng forth of the organs' (471). Ingram explains, with reference to later payments, that the organs used in the play were borrowed from the Nethermill family, who were well-known drapers living some six miles from Coventry (599–600). This payment is unfortunately not repeated in accounts for 1536 and 1536 (471). In the accounts for ?1538 there is a fairly extensive list of repairs to costumes and properties, including the sum of 6/8d 'for mendyng of our Lady orgaynes' (465). What 'our Lady' means here is open to conjecture: it can hardly refer to the BVM in the play unless the Coventry Doomsday included material not known elsewhere; it is possible, but unlikely, that the organs were borrowed from a Lady chapel, a church dedicated to the BVM, or a church where the organ was used in the performance of the Marian antiphons; perhaps one of the Mrs Nethermills was regarded in that light by the company; or perhaps the organ was decorated with a painting of the Annunciation, Assumption or other Marian event. What is sure is that the sum of 6/8d represents extensive repairs to the instrument, so that the Drapers either felt responsible for serious deterioration or damage, or else they considered that their use of it justified the expenditure.

In the accounts for 1539 the organ does not appear. There is however a payment of 7d for mending 'the Trumpetts' (466). These were presumably the

---

39 This company included the Linen-drapers, Haberdashers, Grocers and Salters (Craig *English Religious Drama*, 286), but there were apparently no contributory companies for this play.

40 King and Davidson *Coventry Plays*, plate 4, show the tomb of Julian Nethermyl, dating from ?1539: and see *ibid.*, 44–51, for their discussion of the Drapers' play.

trumpets with which the angels blew the Last Trump: 7d is not a large sum for mending such instruments, and the fact that they were mended together suggests that the company decided to deal with some fairly minor problems such as dents – repairs not of a serious nature but nevertheless requiring the services of a professional smith.

Ingram prints accounts for every year from 1540 to 1546 inclusive (467–71), but they contain nothing relevant to music. In most years it is clear that the expenses of the play are included in a global sum, so that individual payments are not recorded. The accounts for 1550 and 1551 seem to be incomplete, and nothing relevant is recorded (471–2).

It is with the accounts for 1558 (477–80) that a more extensive list of payments is found. Under the heading 'paymentes for pagane' are many items identifiable as relating to the Doomsday play, several relating to music (478):

1558	payd to the trvmpyter	iijs iiijd
	payd to Jhon to synge the base	iiijd

These are adjacent. Near the end, after the payment to four angels, who are the last characters on the cast-list, comes

1558 payd to the clarkes for syngyng & playng ij s vj d

The payment to John – presumably a member of the company – is strange, since it implies that he sang the bass line to the professional singing of the clerks. Whether this was an experiment (not repeated thereafter, apparently) or simply that John stepped into the breach when one of the clerks was unable to perform, we shall probably never know. Nor can we tell how much of the 2/6d paid to the clerks was for their singing and how much for their playing. Playing might refer to performance on the organ, either as accompaniment to the singing or in a solo instrumental item: but it probably means 'acting', as one would expect, since we know that they were costumed (see below).

The accounts for 1560 have a similar list of expenses for the pageant (478–9). The trumpeter again received 3/4d, but the clerks had only 2/-d 'for syngyns' (479): there is no mention of an organ or the playing of it.

The trumpeter presumably blew the Last Trump. This could be done by a single trumpeter if, as may have happened elsewhere, the two angels blew separately, miming the actions to the sound of a real trumpeter behind the pageant. In this case the (two) trumpets mended in 1539 need not have been in

---

[41] There is little evidence to support this suggestion, although it is an approach that has proved itself in modern performance. It would allow the company to use two of its own members as costumed actors, and to pay for only one professional trumpeter; the alternative is to import (and pay appropriately) two professionals, who must be costumed and rehearsed on stage for roles that others could undertake.

playing order – indeed, they may even have been dummies.

A second set of accounts listed under 1560 again records 3/4d to 'the trumpetter' and 2/-d to 'the syngers' (480): but there is also a payment of 12d 'for playnge of the Rygells'. Here we see the probability that the singing of the clerks was worth 2/-d, the payment for playing the organ being additional to that; and that the 'organs' of the accounts may well have been a regals in this play as elsewhere. James Hewitt had been playing the regals in the Weavers' play since 1554, so it is also possible that at this stage the Drapers found it convenient to make use of a regals rather than transport the organ kept by the Nethermill family: and Hewitt himself is named as the player in the Drapers' accounts for 1563 (see below).

The next few years of Drapers' accounts are positively dated and appear in Ingram's main sequence. In those for 1561 (216–17) the expenditure listed under 'The Charges of the pageant' (217) includes 3/4d to the trumpeter; 2/-d to the singing-men below the angels as before; and, at the end of the section, a composite sum of 5/-d for the players' supper and 'for playng of the Rygalls'. This fits with the previous year's payment (481), where 4/-d for the players' supper is immediately followed, as the last item in the list, by 12d for the playing of the regals. Evidently, we may assign 12d of this composite sum with some certainty to the playing of the regals: what is not so clear is whether the regals appear here because the player was paid at a late stage or because his payment was actually for playing at the supper, not in the pageant. The latter is certainly a possibility, for the expenses of any meal on such occasions normally included payment to a minstrel – this is clear from the accounts of all the guilds.

The accounts for 1562 help a little in this problem (220–1). The trumpeter received 4/-d that year, but the singers the usual 2/-d, following the payment to the four angels, as before. Immediately after the singers come the last three items in the section concerning expenses of the play itself (the items following these are all for preparations, repairs, and costumes): they are 4/-d for the players' supper, 16d for the playing of the regals (a significant increase), and 18d to the three patriarchs. The inclusion of the patriarchs in this position of the list makes it more possible that the payment for the regals also concerns the play itself. There is another possibility, too: for the 4/-d paid for the players' supper is commensurate only with the 2/-d paid to the players 'for their drynkyng at the fyrste stage' (220). Evidently the players had to take refreshment during the performance period, and had drinks at the first station. The 4/-d for their supper suggests that this was not a full meal but only light refreshments 'on the hoof', perhaps at the last station. In this case, there is no reason to think that the payment for regals was not concerned with the play performance.

The trumpeter's fee reverted to 3/4d in 1563 (224), and one wonders why it had been raised in the previous year. Following the four angels, the payments continue:

1562	Itm payde to the iij patryarkes	xviij d
	Itm payde to the Syngyng men	ij s
	Itm payde to James huyt for the Regalls	xij d
	Itm payde to the players for there Sowper	iiij s

Here the Drapers' accounts name James Hewitt for the first time.

We have already noted the possibility that Hewitt, who had first played the regals for the Weavers in 1554, had been involved with the Drapers' play as early as 1560. We also see that the positioning of these items in the accounts for 1561 suggests that the regals were indeed played in the pageant rather than on some other occasion.

The Drapers' accounts for 1564 are uninformative (226), but in those for 1565 there is again a list of expenses for the play (229–30). The trumpeter was paid 5/-d, James Hewitt 12d 'for the Rygalls', and the singing men 2/-d.

The Drapers set out the items in their accounts slightly differently in 1566, where the usual three payments for music come as a group (237):

1566	Itm pd to Jamys hewyt for Rigalls	xij d
	Itm pd to the Trompeter	ij s
	Itm pd to the Syngyng men	ij s

A little further down is another item for music:

| 1566 | Itm pd to Thomas nycles for settyng a songe | xij d |

'Thomas Nicolas' appeared second to James Hewitt in the list of waits this year (231: the others were Richard Stiff and Richard Sadeler), and it is probable that he was one of the singing men performing in the play. Here there seems no doubt that Nicholas was the composer of the song: 'setting' is quite distinct from 'pricking'.

The relevant items in the 1567 accounts are (242):

1567	Itm pd to the plears for Syngyng	ij s
	Itm pd to hewyt for hys Rygalls	xij d
	(one item intervening)	
	Itm pd to the trompeter	ij s

The first two of these are adjacent. The payment to the players for singing must surely be a mistake, unless it arises from the fact (and it must be a fact, I think) that the singing men appeared costumed as angels in the play.

In 1568 the trumpeter received only 18d (246); but the other payments were,

---

[42] Hewitt's career is discussed in I, 64–5: see also above, under play 2.

as before, 2/-d 'pd for Synggyng' and, adjacent to this, 12d 'to hewytt for hys Rygalls'. The accounts for 1569 show 2/-d to 'the Synging mene' (249), a rather surprising 2/-d 'ffor the Rygals', and an even more surprising 2/6d to 'the trumppeter' (250). The first two of these sums were repeated in 1570 (254), but for some reason the trumpeter does not appear in that list of payments. He reappears, however, in the accounts for 1571, in the sum of 20d (256), where the other musical items are listed as a single payment of 4/-d 'for Rygalls and Synging'. Judging by previous accounts, this is 2/-d for the regals and 2/-d for the singing. This is confirmed for 1572 (259), when 2/-d was paid for each of the musical items (singing, the regals, and the trumpeter), as it is also in the accounts for 1573 (264). The accounts for 1574 are unfortunately only a summary (269), as are those for 1575 (272), 1576 (280), and 1577 (285); those for 1578 are also largely a summary, although they include a separate payment of 2/-d to the singers (289). Those for the last performance, in 1579, are a summary.

No later records of the Drapers' company are relevant for our present purpose. The undated accounts that Ingram assigns to 1565 and 1566 provide no relevant information (472–3). Those for 1567, however, are valuable in giving new information. A payment of 4d for 'beryng the orgyns from master nethurmylls' (474) is apparently not for use in the play, as it comes in a different section: and, on the contrary, the 'chargys for the pagande' include 6d 'payd to Raffe Aman for playng on the ryggellys' as well as 2/-d 'payd to ij clarkys for Syngyng' and 3/4d to 'the trompyttar' (475). Apart from confirming our conjecture that two clerks were the singers, these entries are useful in naming the regalsplayer. Rauff a Man, organplayer, is found first in the Council Book for 1558, where he is recorded as receiving 40/-d of White's alms money (209), and again in the list for 1564, where he is described as 'the weit' (225). Although he appears in the Holy Trinity churchwardens' accounts for 1560 and 1561, the entry of 1564 is the latest datable mention of his name (570).

Ingram does in fact mention the entry for playing the regals in the Drapers' play as being 'in the 1550s' (570), so there is some confusion about the dating of the entries discussed here under 1567. Indeed, the payments just quoted contradict the payments quoted earlier for 1567, so we cannot be sure that – as the payments to Hewitt and Aman must show if they are for the same occasion – Hewitt was not the organist in these accounts but merely owned the instrument played by Aman. It seems more likely that these accounts are misdated, and that Aman performed on some occasion when Hewitt could not.

The accounts for ?1568 include among the 'paymenttes for the pagges' (476):

?1568	payd for facheng of a pere of hovrgens at hamton & the carrege of them whovme	ij s
	payd to the truppetur	iij s iiij d
	payd for the berreng of the orgens	vj d
	payd to the clarkes for sengyng	ij s

Leaving aside the payments to the trumpeter and the singer – but noting the higher payment to the trumpeter – it is the items concerning the organ that are most interesting. It seems that the same organ is concerned in both entries, so that one payment is for the removal of the instrument between Coventry and the Nethermills' house at Hampton, while the second is for carrying it through Coventry with the play. This second payment is small compared with the usual fee for playing the regals, yet there is no such fee elsewhere in the list. Evidently someone played it without fee. This entry does at least confirm that the Nethermills' organ is not the same as the regals belonging to James Hewitt. Perhaps Hewitt's regals were hired to another play in ?1568, one with which a doubling of resources was impossible.

Plays of unidentified subjects and guilds

Although Craig was unable to identify the subjects of the remaining four plays, or to associate them with specific guilds, our discussion here would be incomplete without a review of such evidence as there is. According to Craig, the companies involved were (*English Religious Drama*, 286–7):

The Girdlers, for whom no records survive. The Cappers (until 1530), the Fullers and the Painters contributed to this play, but of these only the Cappers provide surviving accounts. As we have seen, the Cappers' accounts give no useful information prior to the date of taking over play **B**. This may have been a play of the Creation.

The Pinners, Needlers, Tilers and Wrights. No accounts survive. The Carpenters and the Coopers were contributory. Accounts exist for the Carpenters' company from 1446 to 1652, showing a regular annual contribution of 10/d to the Tilers' pageant. There are many payments for minstrelsy on Corpus Christi day, and it is possible that the minstrels performed in the play rather than at the dinner afterwards: however, this is perhaps unlikely in view of the monetary contribution, and in some years – 1511, for instance (107) – this payment is associated with similar payments for minstrelsy on St John's night and St Peter's night. No accounts survive for the other companies. This may have been a play of Noah and the Flood.

The Tanners (Barkers). The Shoemakers contributed to this play. No accounts survive for either company. This may have been a play of Abraham and Isaac.

The Whittawers (including the Glovers, the Fellmongers and the Parchment-makers). No accounts survive. The Butchers and the Needlers contributed to this play: there is a book of the Butchers' accounts in a nineteenth-century transcription, but no useful itemised expenses are included (216, 220). This may have been a play of Christ's ministry.

---

[43] On the doubling of James Hewitt and/or his regals between plays, see I, 341–3. (Note that in Table 20, the timing for play 10 at station 1 should read '9.19–10.19'.)

4 *The Coventry Plays*

Further on the other guilds, see King and Davidson *Coventry Plays*, 51–2.

4.6 Music and other aural cues

1 *The Nativity, and the Massacre of the Innocents* (The Shearmen and Tailors)

1_1 **249+sd** Function: ?(h). The angels sing *Gloria in excelsis* in a high place. Line 253 may show that they sing a polyphonic setting.

1_2 **263+sd** Function: (a), (e), (h). The shepherds sing one or both verses of *As I out rode* at the start of their journey to Bethlehem (see below, 1_A). However, the second performance of the angelic Gloria occurs before they finish the song, so this cue can cover only up to line **267** – or line **264** if Joseph is deemed to have heard the angels singing, not the shepherds. The latter do not arrive at the stable until after **290**.

For this song, see I, 140–5.

1_3 **267+sd** Function: (e), (h). The angels repeat their performance of *Gloria in excelsis*.

1_A **290** Function: (a), (e), (h). After the angels speak to them again, the shepherds sing as they approach the stable. The second verse of *As I out rode* would be suitable here, although it does not quite conform to the First Shepherd's stated intention to sing 'Et in terra pax hominibus' to the Child (**1/260–3**). There is no other suitable occasion for *Down from Heaven, from Heaven so high*, which must have been performed at cue 1_2 if the shepherds imitate the angelic Gloria here.

My own instinct is to sing *Down from Heaven* here, regarding the First Shepherd's intention as metaphorical. This solution does at least give a reason for the separation of the two verses of this song in Sharp's edition.

1_4 **312+sd** Function: (b), (c), (e) and originally, perhaps, (g). A song of praise to the Christ-child, probably with a 'Nowell' refrain. This could presumably be a polyphonic piece. Craig's identification of this song as Song III, *Down from Heaven, from Heaven so high* (*Two Coventry Plays*, 12 n.2), is clearly incorrect. It is possible that the song performed here should be used to show not only the evangelising of the shepherds (through the audience) but also their entry into Heaven, as described in **1/416–24**.

1_B **424+sd** and/or **435+sd** Function: (b), (e), (h) and orginally, perhaps (f). Loud music for Herod's entrance. There is no evidence for this, but in view of cue 1_5 it seems likely.

1_5 **489+sd** Function: (c), (e), (h). Minstrelsy: either loud music for Herod's exit or soft minstrelsy of 'viols and other harmony'. The former would be more immediately effective.

1₆ 775+sd Function: (b), (e), (h). The three women, the mothers of the Innocents, sing the lullaby, Song II. For the song and the three singers (an alto, a tenor and a bass), see I, 145–52.

2 *The Purification, and Christ with the Doctors in the Temple* (The Weavers)

2_A 290+sd Function: (a) or ?(b).[44] There is no certainty about this cue, but it is probable that the appearance of the angel is accompanied by angelic music. The records of the Weavers' company suggest that a solo *bas* minstrel was used here.

2₁ 364+sd+md Function: (a) or ?(b), (h). Simeon and his two singing clerks process to the Temple, singing the song given as the first song text at the end of the play. This is a late addition to the musical cues (see 4.2), and should not be interpreted as the result of any text references to music. The setting of this song text is not extant.

2_B 581 Function: (a) or ?(b), (e), (h). Heavenly minstrelsy as in **2_A**.

2₂ 621 Function: none. Clarecus, the speaking but non-singing clerk, rings the bells: he must be finished before **630**, when he reports to Simeon that his task is completed.

2₃ 633+md+sd Function: (a), (h). Simeon and the clerks process to meet the Holy Family at the Temple door: one of the psalms that start the medieval office of Purification could be used here.[45] As noted earlier, the singers are apparently Simeon and two singing clerks.

2₄ 691+md+sd Function: (a). The whole cast processes to the altar. The music sung by Simeon and his singing clerks could be the appropriate processional item for the Purification service, *Ingredere in templum*.[46]

Certainly it is not the second of the song texts at the end of the play that should be sung (see I, 264). It is a pity that a leaf of the manuscript is missing here, so that the Purification service, including Simeon's singing of *Nunc dimittis*, is now lost.

2_C 718+sd Function: (c), (h). There is no evidence for music when Simeon and his clerks leave the Temple, but a processional psalm or antiphon would be very suitable.

2₅ 799+sd Function: (a). The procession to the altar is no doubt accompanied by other indications of a service going on, but this would be difficult to reproduce precisely because the Christian Church has no real equivalent of the Passover. It is therefore hard to know what anthem/antiphon should be sung here, and whether it should be plainsong or polyphony. Evidently the Temple staff do

---

[44] Here, as elsewhere, it is impossible to know whether the entrance of an angel implies movement from the heaven to some other part of the acting area, with the angel in the audience's sight throughout, or an entrance from some place hidden from view.

[45] MS, 43–4 names *Levavi oculos meos* (Psalm 120) and *Beati omnes* (Psalm 127), with the doxology.

[46] MS, 44. See I, 260, for the text.

sing a set piece here, and it is quite possible that the procession is a musical one, too.

There is a question as to who sings this antiphon. Simeon's clerks left with him at **718+sd**: and as the accounts suggest only a very small group of singers it seems clear that no singers remain in the Temple at that stage. Either there are more singers than seem likely, therefore, and they remain in the Temple after **718+sd**, or they return in time to sing here. I suspect that having them return is the simpler and more satisfactory solution.

Play 2F *Fragment of an earlier version of the Weavers' Play*
This fragment, which corresponds to lines **1–58** and **181–234** (approximately) of Croo's revised version of play **2**, includes no cues for music.

Play A *The Trials and Crucifixion* (The Smiths)
No text survives: so although we can come to some tentative conclusions about the use of music in this play (see 4.5), no specific cues can be listed.

Play B *The Harrowing of Hell, Resurrection, and Appearances* (The Cappers)
This play probably included soft minstrelsy for one or more of Christ's post-Resurrection appearances, and angelic vocal music for the Resurrection itself; it is possible, but not likely, that there was loud music for Herod or Pilate. On these matters, and on the possibility of the second song text of the Weavers' play belonging to this play, see I, 62–4. As no text survives a cue list is impossible.

Play C *The Death, Assumption and Coronation of Mary* (The Mercers)
No text survives, and the records are not helpful (see 4.5), so no cue list is possible.

Play D *Doomsday* (the Drapers)
The company paid a trumpeter, apparently for blowing the Last Trump. A payment for repairing trumpets suggests that the two angels blew on separate occasions, as elsewhere (see **York 47$_1$** and **47$_2$**, **Towneley 30$_1$**), miming to the playing of one real trumpeter behind the pageant. This play also included singing men, who were apparently accompanied by a regals from 1560 onwards. Existing Doomsday plays have angelic singing at various places, and for this a polyphonic setting would be suitable (see 4.5 under 1566). It is also possible that the angels led the singing of the Saved Souls (as in **Towneley 30$_2$**), which would presumably be plainsong. Although no text survives, so that a cue list is impossible, we can see that the cues for this play would probably have demonstrated a close parallel with those of other Doomsday plays.

Unidentified Plays (The Girdlers; Pinners, Needlers, Tilers and Wrights; Tanners; Whittawers)

Neither texts nor helpful records survive. It is therefore impossible to say anything about the use of music in these plays, much less to speculate as to the probable main features of their cue lists.

The Destruction of Jerusalem
See section 9.9.

5

The Norwich Grocers' Play

5.1 Introduction

A biblical cycle is known to have been played at Norwich in the period c.
1530–65. Its earlier history is an almost total blank: it may have been played on
Corpus Christi day originally, but if so it was later transferred to Whit Monday.[1]
It is possible that the transfer occurred as early as the middle of the fifteenth
century or as late as 1524.[2]

A list of pageants survives from c. 1530, with 63 guilds named as responsible.[3] It is not clear that these are plays rather than tableaux for the Corpus
Christi procession, however: if it represents a list of dramatic episodes, then the
coverage is markedly different from that of other play-cycles. The problem is
discussed by Nelson (*Medieval English Stage*, 131–2), who believes that the list
relates only to the Corpus Christi procession and not to the plays. But we cannot
assume that all cycles ran from Creation to Doomsday, as Lawrence M. Clopper
has pointed out.[4]

Only one play from Norwich, the Grocers' play of the Expulsion from Eden, is
extant. It survives in two versions, however, although neither is transmitted in the
original manuscript. The story of the sources and editions of the Grocers' play
and the company's records of its dramatic activity is a complex one, and for our

---

1 This matter is discussed in Nelson *Medieval English Stage*: see especially 131 and
132–3. Nelson concluded that the plays were suppressed after 1547 and briefly
revived in the 1560s, being finally suppressed after the performance of 1565. He
admitted that the evidence is too sparse for firm conclusions, however, and his
views have not gained general acceptance.
2 Dutka 'Mystery Plays at Norwich', 116.
3 Lancashire *Dramatic Texts*, 237–8; also Dutka 'Mystery Plays at Norwich', *passim*.
4 Clopper 'Lay and Clerical Impact', 124–5. The continental pattern is quite different,
and so is the Cornish cycle: and the survival of English cycles is hardly enough to
demonstrate an invariable pattern.

present purpose only a brief summary is necessary.[5] The Grocers' Book, the volume belonging to the Grocers' company and containing the play texts and financial records, was apparently still in existence in the eighteenth century, when at least one antiquarian copied the play texts and extracts from the records concerning the play. It had disappeared, however, by 1856, when Robert Fitch published his edition based on what he identified as an early eighteenth-century transcript. J.M. Manly's edition (1897) was based on Fitch's, and Osborn Waterhouse collated these with an eighteenth-century transcript that he thought dated from late in that century. When Norman Davis made his edition for the Early English Text Society he had to be content with Fitch's edition as his oldest source, no eighteenth-century copy then being known.

Two years later, F.I. Dunn announced the discovery of a transcript made by the Norfolk antiquarian John Kirkpatrick (1687–1728), presumably in the 1720s:[6] this text was later published in facsimile by JoAnna Dutka ('Fall'). Comparisons of the various versions of the text, and of their editor's descriptions of the sources, shows that Waterhouse almost certainly did not use the same transcript as Fitch, and that neither of these editors used Kirkpatrick's copy. The precise relationship between the three eighteenth-century transcripts is now probably impossible to determine. This may not matter, however: Kirkpatrick's transcript appears to have been copied direct from the Grocers' Book, and the nature of the variants suggests that the transcripts used by Fitch and Waterhouse were more distantly related to the original – perhaps even dependent upon Kirkpatrick's copy.

No notated music is known for the Grocers' play, although some music probably did once exist. The song-texts do however survive as part of the plays. For a discussion of these texts and what we can guess about the music, see I, 74–6.

Records from 1540 onwards are edited in *REED.Norwich*; earlier records will be in a forthcoming REED volume.

In Norwich, unlike other places, the question of iconographical evidence arises. M.D. Anderson (*Drama and Imagery*, chapter 7) suggested that the series of roof-bosses in Norwich Cathedral, dating from the late fifteenth and early sixteenth centuries, illustrate the city's Corpus Christi plays (*ibid.*, plates 10–13). These bosses do indeed offer a very full iconographic record of certain biblical episodes dramatised in the religious plays, and it is hard to believe that the bosses and the Norwich plays might have followed different traditions. While Anderson's attempt to demonstrate a specific link between the bosses and the cycle was unsuccessful, the Norwich roof-bosses can offer possible solutions to problems of staging and costuming.

---

5   The history as he knew it is presented by Norman Davis in his introduction to the Norwich texts in NCPF, xxii–xxvi; Dunn 'Norwich Grocers' Play' offers a revision following the discovery of the Kirkpatrick transcript. The present situation is most fully discussed in Dutka 'Lost Cycle', 1–2.

6   Dunn 'Norwich Grocers' Play'.

Rose and Hedgecoe have recently presented a study of the roof-bosses, opening up a more detailed examination of the iconography in relation to the details of costuming, etc., that the dramatic records of Norwich provide.[7] Although no direct connection can be proved, the bosses, in their visual clarity and brilliance, are themselves a compelling witness to the possibility of parallel iconographies. The study by Rose and Hedgecoe is, in any case, well worth reading for its exposition of the issues.

5.2 Dramatic directions

All dramatic directions are in English. They are more or less in a centralised position in the text, as speech headings are: indeed, many of them in play **B** include, or consist solely of, SH information.

The play's directions are listed in Table 7, where I have given the orthography and line-ends of Kirkpatrick's transcript. **A/80+sd** is equivalent to **B/103+sd**, but it is notable that the latter does not include a direction for music. Text **B** represents a substantial re-thinking of the play: even the last, musical, SDs in the two are not equivalent, for the song at **A/88+sd** is a sorrowful song, whereas that at **B/153+sd** is joyful, occasioned by the comfort of the Holy Ghost given in a scene not present in text **A**. **A/90+sd** is discussed in I, 74–5.

The two texts display quite different attitudes towards directions and the importance of music. Text **A** has four directions – I count that at **A/80+sd** as two – and three of them are for music. Text **B** has six directions (I exclude those having only SH function), only one of them being for music.

Of these four directions concerning music, perhaps only that at **A/88+sd** is a true direction. The other three read much more like production notes of the type that we see elsewhere in the form of marginal notes. The simplest is that at **A/80+sd**, which gives the bare notice that music is to be heard there; that at **B/153+sd** gives in addition a minimal description of the type of music; and that at **A/90+sd** gives a fuller description apparently designed to alert someone – the play's director, perhaps – to the repetitions of the text given.

We now know that Manly and Davis were wrong in thinking that **A/90+sd** and **B/153+sd** were added by Fitch, but the knowledge raises a problem of the status of these directions: for, since they appear in Kirkpatrick's transcript, either they formed part of the text that came to him in the Grocers' Book, or else Kirkpatrick added them. The implications of these two situations need to be examined.

---

7 Rose and Hedgecoe *Stories in Stone.*

1 If these notes were in the Grocers' manuscript and were faithfully copied by Kirkpatrick, the scribe probably knew the musical settings, or perhaps had them in front of him when he wrote the descriptions. But it is not at all necessary: the descriptions could be the result of information given verbally, perhaps by the director of music for a performance or by one of the singers. This suggests that the musical manuscripts were kept separately from the play texts at the time that the latter were entered in the Grocers' Book.

TABLE 7 : DIRECTIONS IN THE NORWICH GROCERS' PLAY

Play/ cue-line	Text if musical : comments
A/80	*Musick.*
A/80+sd	*aftyr that Adam & Eve be drevyn owt of Paradyse / they schall speke this foloyng.*
A/88	*And so yᵉⁱ xall syng walkyng to gether abowt the place wryngyng ther handes.* Text given as lines **89–90** (see 5.4 and I, 74).
A/90	*NB. these last 2 lines set to musick twice over / and again for a Chorus of 4 Parts* Not strictly a SD. 'Manly notes that this note is apparently added by Fitch' (NCPF, 11, n.2), but we now know that the note was in Kirkpatrick's transcript.
Bp1/	No directions: notes about the use of alternative prologues at beginning and end.
Bp2/	No directions.
B/23	= SH
B/24	= SH
B/35	= SH
B/58	non-musical, includes SH
B/64	non-musical, includes SH
B/103	non-musical, includes SH
B/110	non-musical, includes SH
B/122	non-musical, includes SH
B/153	*Old Musick Triplex Tenor Medius Bass* Davis notes this direction as 'evidently added by Fitch' (NCPF, 18, n.l), but it appears in Kirkpatrick's transcript. Lines **154–61** are the text of the song (see I, 74).

2 If Kirkpatrick added these directions, he was giving his reader information additional to that transmitted by the Grocers' Book itself, which implies that he had the musical settings in front of him. (It also means that the eighteenth-century transcripts used by Fitch and Waterhouse were derived from Kirkpatrick's.) In this case the musical settings were presumably kept with the Grocers' Book and were no doubt lost with it. It is a pity that Kirkpatrick apparently did not have enough interest to say something more about the setting: JoAnna Dutka believes that the notes originated with Kirkpatrick, apparently a non-musician whose interest in the verbal text did not extend to music.[8]

It is not easy to decide precisely what information **A/90+sd** was intended to convey. 'Set to musick twice over and again' must mean three times: Kirkpatrick gives no punctuation, and we should surely read it as 'twice over, and again for a Chorus of 4 parts', rather than with the comma after 'again', as Davis has it. Kirkpatrick's line ends with 'over', and the line-end may take the place of punctuation. The text is set twice for solo voices, then – that is, either a duet for Adam and Eve or a solo each – with a final refrain set à 4.

This seems to me the most likely solution, but there is another possibility. If 'again' means 'at the repeat', then 'twice over and again for a Chorus ...' requires the piece to be performed twice only in all, the repeat being for Chorus.

The final four-part refrain matches the 'old music' for triplex, tenor, medius and bass of **B/153+sd**. These songs are however to different texts, and the only point of comparison that we can make is that both versions of the play end with four-part music. At first sight 'Old Musick' suggests the perception of an identifiable style, but 'old' may refer to something quite recent as long as it is recognisably old-fashioned. It may simply mean that the manuscript itself seemed old, but this is unlikely.

There is one more explanation that must be considered for the music at **B/153+sd** – namely, that it was never in existence, or at least that the Grocers never possessed a copy. Granted that this SD seems at first sight to describe existing music, it may nevertheless be wholly prescriptive of music still to be found or composed.

5.3 Text references

Text A
A/88   [EVA]   therfor owr handes we may wryng with most dullfull song.

---

[8] In a private communication.

Although this would seem to be a metaphorical usage, with a sorrowful speech to come, it is in fact literal, as the SD shows immediately afterwards. The text of the song is given as **A/89–90**, discussed in I, 74:

> Wythe dolorous sorowe we maye wayle & wepe
> both nyght & day in very sythys full depe

The line-division in Kirkpatrick's transcript comes after 'both', but this is clearly a rhyming couplet (as here), and Davis prints it as such (NCPF, 11).

The two stanzas, one each for Adam and Eve, that form lines **81–88** are spoken, according to **A/80+sd2**, but there is an interesting feature: namely, that line **81** runs

ADAM   O with dolorows sorowe we maye wayle & weepe

which suggests that these two stanzas are (or were, once) part of the song. This would however require a considerable corruption of dramatic practice, if not of the text, and the 'speke' of **80+sd2** would be incorrect. It is possible, I think, that the whole of lines **81–90** were at some stage set to music; that for practical or other reasons the amount of singing was cut down; and that the sung part – only two lines – was then so short that the setting was sung three times (or twice?) in all to make an adequate ending to the play. This is however entirely conjectural: and while it offers an alternative and more music-filled ending for a modern production, Dutka is probably right in her comment that the text of the musical setting, lines **89–90**, provides a verbal link with the preceding speeches – a perfectly acceptable gambit, both theatrically and from a purely literary point of view.

Text B
Prologue 1 No references to music.
Prologue 2 No references to music.

Play B
B/152–3   [ADAM]   together lett us synge, & lett our hartes reioyse
                                & gloryfye owr god wyth mynde, powre & voyse
                                             Amen.

This is a 'praise' ending, for which music is highly appropriate. The text of the song is discussed in I, 75–6. The poem is otherwise unknown. It does have the feel of a psalm-paraphrase, however, and indeed presents the main ideas and some of the vocabulary of Psalm 144 (AV 145), verses 1–7.

5.4 Latin and the liturgy

Latin words and phrases are underlined in Kirkpatrick's transcript, and I have therefore presented them in italics here. It is impossible to know if underlining was the method by which Latin words were distinguished in Kirkpatrick's exemplar.

Text A

A/1   PATER   *Ego principium Alpha & oo in altissimis habito*

An integral part of the verse, rhyming with line 3 (see below). *Ego principium* is the incipit of an antiphon (SA, 167; LU, 1085). The whole line echoes **N-Town 1/1–**, 'Ego sum alpha & oo principium et finis', **York 1/1–** and **Towneley 1/1**, 'Ego sum alpha et o', and **York 2/1**, 'in altissimis habito'. There is no question of singing.

The remaining Latin in this play is in single words or phrases: they are spoken by all the characters – God, Adam, Eve, and the Serpent – so they are not a matter of characterisation. Nor can they be regarded as giving authority to the drama, since they are fragments of the Vulgate wording rather than complete statements. In every case they are integral to the verse, and there is no question of singing them.

A/3   [PATER]   ... *sine adjutorio*

'Adjutorium' is the word used for Adam's helpmeet in Genesis 2/18: much of lines 3–4 is a direct translation of this verse.

A/19–20   [ADAM]   This creature to me is *nunc ex ossibus meis*
                   And *virago* I call hyr ...

Genesis 2/23 reads: 'Dixitque Adam: Hoc nunc os ex ossibus meis, ...; haec vocabitur Virago ...'

A/33   [PATER]   *morte moriemini* ...

A/59   EVA   *Ne forte* we shuld dye, ...

A/61   SERPENS   *Nequaquam*, ye shall not dye

These are clearly references to the Vulgate version of the story. Genesis 3/3 reads (Eve speaking) 'ne forte moriamur'; and 3/4, the serpent's reply to Eve, 'Nequaquam morte moriemini', is surely one of the most quotably dramatic sentences in the Scriptures. The entire story, God's speech to Adam and Eve excepted, is in the lections and responsories for the week of Septuagesima.[9]

This dramatist's habit of sprinkling odd bits of Latin around his play is reminiscent of the way P.G. Wodehouse dropped phrases from the Psalms through his novels, and it has one of the same results: namely, that if the audience/reader does not know the quotations, nothing is lost; but if they know their Genesis/ Psalms well enough, the quotations provide an enjoyable and – especially in the case of the Norwich play – wholly relevant intellectual challenge. Wodehouse expected that many of his readers would know the Psalms; and, more importantly for our purpose, these Latin quotations surely imply that the dramatist was writing at least partly for an audience that knew its lectionary, if not its Vulgate – a cleric or religious scattering in-jokes which his colleagues would be among the first to appreciate.

Text B
Prologue 1   No Latin.
Prologue 2   No Latin.

Play B
B/1   GOD THE FATHER   I am *alpha et homega.* my *Apocalyps* doth testyfye

The Latin quotation is shortened, and the authority given: Revelation (i.e. Apocalypse) 1/8 reads 'Ego sum Alpha et Omega ...'

The two texts of the Grocers' play diverge significantly in their use of Latin. It would not be too much to say that they exemplify particular pre- and post-Reformation attitudes. In the first, biblical quotation is the accepted norm. It implies a working knowledge of biblical texts, not only in the dramatist but to some extent in his audience. (It must be remembered that most laypeople picked up such texts aurally, not through the written word.) In the second play, where the revision is stated to be 'accordynge unto ye Skripture',[10] there is probably no more direct scriptural content, but it is treated quite differently. The first prologue tells its audience where the story can be found; the opening Latin quotation has its source stated; and the Holy Spirit names St Paul as the author of the passage on the Armour of God which he uses to comfort Adam.[11] If the audience knew the Bible at all, it was by now the English Bible, not the Vulgate.

---

[9] See BS, ccccxciv and diii–div.
[10] Dutka 'Fall', 5.
[11] NCPF, 17.

5.5 Records

Surprisingly few guild records survive at Norwich. Of the craft guilds, only the Grocers have records known, and that only in the form of the selections made from the Grocers' Book in the eighteenth century: as will become apparent, these are very limited in scope, giving apparently full accounts for only one year's presentation of the play. Davis printed a version of the Waterhouse/Fitch collation of accounts in NCPF, xxxii–xxxv; REED.Norwich, 339–45, prints a new transcription from the Kirkpatrick papers, and Dutka 'Mystery Plays at Norwich', 112–16, provides a useful commentary on them. Of the non-craft guilds, St George's Guild has various records surviving, all now kept in the Norfolk Record Office. There are also extensive records of civic and ecclesiastical administration. The extant records from 1540 onwards are listed in REED. Norwich, xliv–lxxi.[12]

The earliest Grocers' records are the accounts presented in 1534: they concern the performance of 1533 (REED.Norwich, 339–40). Three items, spaced out in the ac-counts, give hard information about the music: 12d paid to Sir Stephen Prowet 'for makyng of a newe ballet'; 4d given as a present 'for ye borowyng of ye Organs'; and 6d to John Bakyn for 'playeng at ye organs'. This evidence is briefly reviewed in I, 74–5.

Little is known of the two men named in this account. Davis drew together the information about Prowett (his name is variously spelt) given by Blomefield, Fitch, and Waterhouse (NCPF, xxxii, n.l), and Dutka added to this, with some corrections (*Use of Music*, 21–2, n.14; 'Fall', 9, n. 27). I give here a chronological digest of the information, with Dutka's references (Davis's are readily available):

1526 The churchwardens of St Mary's, Bungay (Suffolk), made a payment to 'Ser Prewett prest of Norwic'. It is not clear that this was in connection with the copying of their game-book (Bolingbroke 'Pre-Elizabethan Plays', 338).

1534 Payment for work done in 1533 in making a 'newe ballet' (*REED.Norwich*, 340).

1536 Seventh prebend of the College of St Mary in the Fields (Fitch 'Norwich Pageants', 24).

1544 Rector of St Margaret, Westwich (Blomefield *Essay* IV, 258).

1547 Stipendiary priest of St Peter Mancroft (Blomefield *Essay* IV, 186).

1556 Rector of St Peter Mancroft for life, at the presentation of Barbara Catlyn, widow (Blomefield *Essay* IV, 187).

1559 Will of Stephen Prowet, clerk, proved (Norwich Consistory Court, ref. Goldingham, 1559–60, ff. 314r–318v).

---

12 Fire destroyed much of the Central Library at Norwich on 1 August 1994, however, and this caused considerable smoke and water damage to holdings in the Norfolk Record Office: see Dutka 'News from Norwich'.

Much of this has not been confirmed by reference to original documents, and some of it no doubt cannot be. Bowers ('Prowett', 318) identifies Prowett with the Dom Stephen Prowett known as the composer of two five-part Latin antiphons in part books dating from c. 1530 (Cambridge, University Library MSS Dd.xiii.27 and Jesus College K31). He points out that St Peter Mancroft and the collegiate church of St Mary both maintained choirs, and that Prowett's will shows that he owned 'a payer of Clavycords'.[13] Prowett's style 'Dom' in the musical sources suggests that he was a religious, although it may refer only to his association with a collegiate church.

John Bakyn is more briefly dealt with.[14] Dutka (*Use of Music*, 22) notes that he was a grocer, made a freeman in 1550-1 (Second Register of Freemen, Norfolk Record Office, case 17, shelf c, f. 19r); and that he was an executor of Prowett's will (Norwich Consistory Court, ref. Goldingham, 1559-60, f. 317v).

Bakyn was apparently younger than Prowett, perhaps by ten years or more. Prowett must have been born around the turn of the century: Bowers says 'c. 1495'.[15] Bakyn, who was in the Grocers' pageant as organist in 1533 but did not obtain his freedom until 1550-1, could have been born as late as 1515 or so, although an earlier date is probable. Nothing more is known of him.

There are no items relevant to music in the remaining Grocers' accounts, except for payments to the waits at Corpus Christi. Kirkpatrick copied incomplete selections for the years following 1534, and none at all for the period 1547-55 inclusive. The plays were performed rather irregularly throughout the period of the accounts (Dutka 'Mystery Plays at Norwich', 112-16), and there is doubt as to the date of the last performance. Dutka gives this as 1565 (*ibid.*, 116): there was an order to all the crafts that year to perform, and consequently the Grocers made an inventory of their goods (*REED.Norwich*, 344-5) and had their play rewritten (Text **B**). There is however no evidence that the cycle, or any individual play, was played that year (and indeed the same is true for the performance ordered in 1563). The Grocers' waggon was dismantled in 1570 (*REED.Norwich*, 53 and 345), by which time it had been out in the street at Blackfriars bridge for two years and was deteriorating badly.

There is no evidence, then, that Text **B** was ever performed, and in this connection it is interesting to note two things. First, the provision of alternative prologues suggests uncertainty about the extent of the total production: this would not be surprising if difficulties encountered in mounting the cycle in 1565 were such that the performance was eventually abandoned. Second, the note on the music at the end of Text **B** is not really descriptive of existing music: rather, it is prescriptive of music still to be provided (see 5.2). Thus, while it is clear that

---

[13] Bowers says that the will was proved in March 1560. Perhaps the confusion is due to the use of an old-style date on the document.

[14] *REED.Norwich*, 340, calls him 'Bakyr', but earlier commentators read the final letter as 'n'.

[15] Bowers 'Prowett' says 'c. 1495'.

the song at the end of Text **A** had existed and had been performed at some time, it is not at all certain that the song at the end of Text **B** had been performed or even that a copy of it had been obtained.

5.6   Music and other aural cues

Text A (performance of 1533)

A₁ 80+sd   Function: (a), (h). The direction for 'Musick' at the Expulsion at first sight seems strange: but, as John Stevens pointed out in connection with **Chester 2₄** (see I, 183), it is the restoration of Divine Order in the Garden of Eden that calls for music. More specifically, 'Musick' suggests instrumental music, although this is not invariable. Certainly the organ borrowed by the Grocers and played by John Bakyn that year must have been involved in this cue. It is possible that singing was also involved, but there is no payment to singers in the accounts. This is at any rate angelic music, requiring professional vocal and/or instrumental performance.

On the evidence, this 'Musick' was an organ solo.

A₂ 88+sd   Function: (a), (g). The SD has Adam and Eve singing, while the sd note after **90** shows that the music set the two-line text three times (perhaps twice), the last being for 4-part chorus (see 5.3, 5.4). The use of the organ is doubtful, even at so late a date, because of its 'divine' connotations in this sort of drama. On the face of it, Adam and Eve sing a duet, with a 4-part refrain following. It is possible that they sang an unaccompanied verse each.[16]

This is presumably the 'newe ballet' made by Stephen Prowett. It is hard to know whether he was responsible for the words, the music, or both: the wording of the accounts suggests that he wrote at least the music, and it does not preclude his composition of the text.

Text B (1565: ?not performed)

There are no cues for music in the prologues.

B₁ 153   The 'Amen' should be said by all present, including the audience, as this is a 'praise' ending to the play.

B₂ 153+sd   Function: (g). The music is apparently a four-part setting of lines **154–61**. Adam makes it clear that he and Eve are the singers (**B/152**), but there is nothing to say who takes the other parts. The possibilities are:

---

[16] I thus marginally reject Dutka's proposal ('Fall', 9, n. 27) of two solo verses, with organ accompaniment, followed by a chorus, the whole performance taking the form of a miniature verse anthem. I do suggest the solo-plus-organ format for **Chester 7₄** (see 6.6), but that is angelic music.

I feel happier about an organ accompaniment to mortals' singing in the case of a hymn of praise in the 1565 text: see the comments on cue **B₁**.

(i) two other singers joining Adam and Eve;

(ii) two instruments taking the other parts, as in (i);

(iii) instruments playing the whole texture, with two of them doubling the lines sung by Adam and Eve; and

(iv) instruments and voices performing with the two soloists in the manner of a verse anthem.

It is impossible to know how far this performance might have adhered to tradition or, alternatively, how up-to-date it might have been. Solution (i) requires two other singers relevant to the play: two angels would be the obvious roles, bringing the song into the realm of songs of praise shared by angels and humans. Perhaps in this case the performers need not be trained singers: or perhaps Adam and Eve *were* both trained singers, and the Grocers would have hired two more to play the angels. Solutions (ii) and (iii) are equally possible on that basis.[17] Solution (iv) would be a thoroughly up-to-date, in fact *avant-garde*, way of performing. Galloway mentions (*REED.Norwich*, xli) that the distinguished composer Osbert Parsley was well established in Norwich at that time: Parsley's surviving work does not include verse anthems, however, and the verse-anthem principle may not have arrived in Norwich by 1565. There is one other solution, suggested by the 1533 accounts and standard practice of the time: namely, that an organ was used to accompany Adam, Eve and the other two singers.

This question of performance-method is relevant even if the play was never performed: the Grocers must have had some knowledge of how they *intended* to perform it, and the question must be answered if twentieth-century performance is contemplated. One helpful approach, perhaps, is to take account of the deliberately post-Reformation nature of this late play (see 5.4) and regard it in the light of Bale's protestant biblical plays rather than as part of a late medieval tradition.[18] In this case we can first admit that any of the solutions just listed is perfectly possible; and second, we can point to Bale's precedent in using the organ to accompany 'divine' singing (although this is of course a remnant of medieval practice in the plays). Thus, while my own preference would be for unaccompanied vocal presentation, as in (i), it may be that modern performances should test all of the various possibilities for their dramatic effect.

---

[17] Note that solution (iii) does not depend on instrumental doubling being needed by singers who could not be trusted to hold their lines.

[18] John Bale had used an organ, perhaps in this way, for his Kilkenny performance of *God's Promises* on 20 August 1553, and we have seen the possibility in the Coventry plays: see Peter Happé, ed., *The Complete Plays of John Bale* (Cambridge: D.S. Brewer, 1985–6) I, 7; and 4.5, above. It may be relevant that Bale was educated at the Carmelite house in Norwich and was later (1551–3) vicar of Swaffham, Norfolk, on the pilgrim route to Walsingham.

6

The Chester Cycle

6.1 Introduction

A Corpus Christi play existed in Chester at least as early as 1422. This play took one day to perform, but as it consisted of constituent pageants, it was probably a version of the cycle that we know. From 1521 onwards the play – soon referred to as 'plays' – took place at Whitsuntide. Later, perhaps by 1531, the plays became a three-day cycle spread over the Monday, Tuesday and Wednesday in Whitsun week. The last performance of the cycle was in 1575, held at Midsummer instead of Whitsuntide. Efforts were made to revive it subsequently, but the cycle was not played again until modern times.[1]

There is a greater wealth of surviving material for the Chester cycle than for any other, and in consequence the cycle has always attracted scholarly attention. The text is extant in no fewer than five manuscripts (in contrast to the unique copies of all other cycles), with three additional manuscripts of single plays. Lumiansky and Mills have shown that the cyclic manuscripts depend upon a lost register copy – the Exemplar – dating from the mid-sixteenth century (*Essays*, 48). These cyclic texts are all late, and the element of antiquarian interest is very strong. For the same antiquarian reasons, two sets of banns have survived, the later one in four copies.

Chester has also been lucky in the survival of its civic and guild records, which are especially rich in their documentation of dramatic activity. In this respect they are more helpful than the records of York which, just as extensive, are disappointingly uninformative about the York cycle. The Chester records are edited by Lawrence M. Clopper in *REED.Chester* (1979); selected records appear in Lumiansky and Mills *Essays*.

The city of Chester, like York, has retained its medieval ground-plan to a large

---

[1] The cycle was performed regularly, but in a much-abbreviated version, from 1951 onwards. The first complete modern performance was Jane Oakshott's Leeds production on waggons in May 1983. In June that year, as noted below, eight of those pageants played in Chester.

extent, so that one can walk the pageant-route with some sense of the spaces and acoustics of a sixteenth-century performance.[2] The processional performance of eight of the Chester pageants at the High Cross on 26 June 1983 was the first occasion in modern times on which a substantial proportion of a cycle had been performed at one of the original stations. The occasion provided general information on the acoustics of the area and the effect of music and speech there, but not the kind of detailed evidence that would be relevant to this chapter.

Three of the cyclic manuscripts have been produced in facsimile: MDF 1 (Bodley 175) and 6 (Huntington HM 2) have introductions by Lumiansky and Mills; MDF 8 (Harley 2124) is introduced by Mills alone.

The cycle was edited by Thomas Wright in 1842–7, and then by Deimling and Matthews for the Early English Text Society (1892 and 1916). The standard edition now is that by Lumiansky and Mills (*Chester*) of 1974 and 1986, an Early English Text Society publication replacing that of Deimling and Matthews. Volume 1 is the text, volume 2 the textual commentary. References in this chapter are to volume 1 unless otherwise specified. Lumiansky and Mills also published essays on the texts and the development and history of the cycle, together with supporting documentation, in *The Chester Mystery Cycle: Essays and Documents* (1983: *Essays*). My own essay dealing with the material concerning music in the cycle is on pp. 111–64 of that volume; more practical aspects of music for the cycle are discussed in a second essay (Rastall 'Some Myrth'); and the notated music is discussed in I, 152–9.

The nature of the surviving texts of the Chester cycle demands consideration of the individual manuscripts. In listing them I use the abbreviations of Lumiansky and Mills (*Chester*, ix–xxvii):

Hm San Marino, California: Henry E. Huntington Library, MS 2. Facsimile in MDF 6. The main scribe is Edward Gregorie, who dated the manuscript 1591. Lumiansky and Mills used Hm as their base text.

A London: British Library, Additional MS 10305. The main scribe is George Bellin, scribe to the Coopers' guild at Chester (*Chester*, xv). He dated the manuscript 1592. Wright used A as the base text for his edition.

R London: British Library, Harley MS 2013. This manuscript includes the Proclamation and the Banns. The main scribe is George Bellin, who wrote everything except for the Proclamation. He dated his work 1600.

B Oxford: Bodleian Library, MS Bodley 175. This manuscript includes much of the Banns. Facsimile in MDF 1. The scribe is William Bedford, clerk to the Brewers' guild from 1606: he dated it 1604.

These four manuscripts, which transmit largely synoptic versions of the cycle, are known as 'the Group'. The latest of the cyclic manuscripts stands apart from the

---

2 See Marshall 'Manner', *passim*.

Group in many ways (*Essays*, 71–6):

H   London: British Library, Harley MS 2124. Facsimile in MDF 8. Of the three scribes, the last and principal is James Miller, rector of St Michael's, Chester, 1605–18. Miller also revised the work of the other two scribes, completing the text on 6 August 1607 (*Chester*, xxv). Deimling and Matthews used H as the base text for their edition.

In additon to the cyclic manuscripts there are three manuscripts of single plays surviving:

M   Manchester: Central Library, MS 822.11C2. A single vellum leaf containing part of play **18**. It is apparently not from a guild reference copy, nor from an acting text (*Chester*, x). Suggested datings vary widely, but Lumiansky and Mills favour the earlier end of the range, placing it as perhaps late fifteenth-century.

P   Aberystwyth: National Library of Wales, Peniarth MS 399. A parchment manuscript of play **23**, probably dating from c. 1500.

C   Chester: Coopers' Company. Written by George Bellin on 22 August 1599, apparently as an archive copy. It contains play **16**.

The cycle consists of twenty-five plays (Lancashire *Dramatic Texts*, 109–10), but Lumiansky and Mills numbered them 1–24, with the Passion play as no. **16A**, in recognition that MS H transmits **16** and **16A** as a single play. This matter is discussed by Lumiansky and Mills in *Chester* II, 223. Their numbering is inconvenient for production purposes, but I retain it here (rather than Lancashire's) because it is used in the edition and in all the facsimiles.

The Chester cycle consists of the following plays:

1	The Fall of Lucifer	Tanners
2	Adam and Eve; Cain and Abel	Drapers
3	Noah's Flood	Waterleaders and Drawers of Dee
4	Abraham, Lot and Melchysedeck; Abraham and Isaac	Barbers
5	Moses and the Law; Balack and Balaam	Cappers
6	The Annunciation and the Nativity	Wrights
7	The Shepherds	Painters
8	The Three Kings	Vintners
9	The Offerings of the Three Kings	Mercers
10	The Slaughter of the Innocents	Goldsmiths
11	The Purification; Christ and the Doctors	Blacksmiths

12	The Temptation; The Woman Taken in Adultery	Butchers
13	The Blind Chelidonian; The Raising of Lazarus	Glovers
14	Christ at the House of Simon the Leper; Christ and the Money-lenders; Judas's Plot	Corvisers (i.e. Shoemakers)
15	The Last Supper; the Betrayal	Bakers
16	The Trial and Flagellation	Fletchers, Bowyers, Coopers, Stringers
16A	The Passion	Ironmongers
17	The Harrowing of Hell	Cooks
18	The Resurrection	Skinners
19	Christ on the Road to Emmaus; Doubting Thomas	Saddlers
20	The Ascension	Tailors
21	Pentecost	Fishmongers
22	The Prophets of Antichrist	Clothworkers
23	Antichrist	Dyers
24	The Last Judgement	Websters

Two sets of banns exist for the Chester cycle. The sources are fully discussed and an edition of the texts presented by Lumiansky and Mills in *Essays*, 272–310: Clopper also edited the banns (*REED.Chester*, 31–9 and 240–7).

The Early Banns were probably composed in their present form by 1540. Lumiansky and Mills suggest that they were originally written when the plays were moved from Corpus Christi Day to Whitsunday, which had happened by 1521 (*Essays*, 166–7). They postulate later emendations to account for the change from performance on a single day to the three-day presentation (by 1531) and some erasures following the suppression of the feast of Corpus Christi in 1548 (*Essays*, 190). Clopper expresses similar views, with initial composition in the period 1505–21 and the final (but uncut) version in the mayoral year 1539–40.[3]

Lumiansky and Mills considered that the fundamental purpose of the Early Banns was 'to create high expectations for the coming performance' by enumerating 'selling points' to the potential audience (*Essays*, 179). Among the matters discussed in the Banns is the spectacle concerned, the visual impact of the plays. One might think that music would be mentioned if it were associated with spectacle, as it so often was. But the Early Banns make no mention whatever of music or musicians: and although we should not expect that music would be mentioned for its own sake, its total absence may be significant. It is possible that music played a smaller part in the cycle before 1540 than it did in the second half of

---

3 Clopper 'History and Development', *passim*.

the century. However, the usual *caveat* obtains for the Early Banns, that omissions cannot safely be regarded as positive evidence: for the Early Banns are antedated by the Painters' charter (see 6.5), which mentions 'the angells hyme' in the Shepherds' play.

The Late Banns were apparently written as a Protestant replacement for the Early Banns. Lumiansky and Mills do not hazard a guess at a date of composition (*Essays*, 190), but they note that there was increasing Protestant opposition to the plays from about 1560 onwards, and that the tone of the Late Banns is defensive. Clopper has suggested that the Late Banns were part of the attempt to persuade the City Council to allow a performance in 1572 ('Development', *passim*), while Keane has put forward the view that they were part of an official application for permission to perform the plays ('Kingship', *passim*).

Whatever the truth of this, considering the amount of music apparently performed in the cycle (see 6.6) the Late Banns are surprisingly silent about it. Music is mentioned in the banns only for plays **7** (The Shepherds), **11** (The Purification), and **24** (The Last Judgement). See 6.3, below.

Because of the differences between the various manuscripts, throughout this chapter I shall adopt the system used by Lumiansky and Mills for noting textual differences between them. Thus 'omitted ARH' means that the quoted reading appears only in manuscripts Hm and B; 'Songe A only; Gossip H' identifies variant readings to be found in those two manuscripts. Manuscripts M, P and C contain no material relevant to music and therefore play no part in these commentaries.

In general I shall not treat separately the variant versions of plays or scenes presented by Lumiansky and Mills in the appendices to their edition. Where music is concerned – which, as it happens, is very rarely – the variants make no difference to the cues assembled from the edition's principal text: only in Play **3** is a major variant taken into account, and then its importance is a structural one.[4]

6.2 Dramatic directions

In discussing the non-textual information transmitted by the play texts, Mills has identified two distinct types of dramatic direction ('Directions', 46). Although the way of treating them differs from scribe to scribe, these types appear to stem from the Exemplar. First, there are directions that begin at the left-hand margin and run across the page, often set off from the text itself by ruling above and

---

4 See 6.6, below, concerning the Raven and Dove scene: the musical consequences of these alternative texts are discussed in I, 227–8.

below, and by rubrication. The scribes seem to have recognised this material as part of the 'official' text, and to have treated it as it was presented in the Exemplar. Only Miller (Manuscript H) apparently felt free to transfer this material to the margins or to alter it significantly. Second, there is marginal material, usually in the left-hand margin. Miller, who used the left margin for speech headings, tended to transfer such directions to the right of the text. In general, material of the first type is in Latin, that of the second in English: but Miller habitually translated the English directions into Latin (Mills 'Stage Directions', 46–7).

Lumiansky and Mills consider that these marginal, English, directions were situated in the margins of the Exemplar and that they were production notes made by and/or for the producer concerned (*Essays*, 28–32). The SDs proper generally further the dramatic action in some way, being integral to the drama and concerning matters that we should expect to be prescribed by the dramatist. In general they are purely factual, although there are interesting exceptions in play **4**. Marginal directions, on the other hand, may amplify a SD (by providing the title of a piece unspecified in the SD, for instance, as happens at **7/447+ sd+md**) or, if there is no SD present, may refer to music or other 'business' prescribed by the dramatist in the text (as with the music at **1/85+md**, mentioned in that line) or even to such business not prescribed (for instance the minstrelsy in play **2**). Marginal directions often give the impression of mnemonics, and are presumably the producer's reminder to himself or to others of what has been decided shall happen at a particular moment in the play. As a mere reminder, such an MD need not be complete, as long as it serves to identify the music, gesture, etc., for the producer's purpose.

The example after **1/85** shows that the prescription of music occurs in definable stages: first, the dramatist calls for (suitable) music, either in the text or in a SD, but does not demand a specific piece, the choice being left until the occasion of a production; second, the producer notes the piece chosen (perhaps his own choice, but much more likely that of the professional musician acting as his director of music). It is not necessary for the expression of this choice to be accurate, since it is only a mnemonic for immediate purposes: but probably the information will be enough for a professional singer to remember, for a later production, what the piece was, or for a new director of music to work it out.

In the case of Chester there is also a third stage, which concerns the scribes and the way they transmitted information. The direction for music at **1/85+md** must have been *Then a songe. Dignus es domine Dei*, or something like it, in the Exemplar: but none of the manuscripts gives all of this (see Table 8, below). 'Dei' should of course be 'Deus': Lumiansky and Mills reasonably suggest that 'Dei' may be the incorrect extension of an abbreviation – presumably 'Dne' for 'Domine' – in the pre-Exemplar (*Chester* II, 10). It may be that the incorrect Latin of the Exemplar contributed to the confusion of some scribes and to the decisions of the scribes of B and H to shorten the direction as they did. This is, then, a very clear indication that the process of post-register editorial activity has itself caused significant changes to certain readings.

The problem of the MDs and their treatment by the various scribes is very fully dealt with by Lumiansky and Mills (*Essays*, 28–32). Although their discussion is too complex to repeat here even in abbreviated form, the list of dramatic directions that follows refers to that discussion when necessary.

Its implications for the use of music are important. First, if an MD is added to a SD proper, we cannot assume that it follows any dramatic tradition: rather, it may reflect a purely personal choice made by a producer (or musician) for a particular performance. The direction *Here singe troly loly loly loo*, written to the left of **7/448–50** in Hm, certainly amplifies the SD *Tunc cantabunt et postea dicat Tertius Pastor*, but its authority is limited in time, perhaps even to a single performance. Even if the MD dates from the early sixteenth century and was followed in all subsequent performances, we do not know what music was sung during the fifteenth century, nor what relation *Troly loly loly loo* bore to that earlier music.

Second, when there is only a marginal note calling for music, and no SD proper, it cannot be assumed that the use of music there follows any tradition at all. So while we can see that music at a place such as **2/424+sd** is appropriate for various reasons, we cannot be certain that the dramatist had intended music there. In play **2** the inconsistency among the manuscripts suggests a confused situation in the Exemplar reflecting the fact that even the precise number of places at which minstrelsy was heard might vary from one production to another.

Third, the existence of MDs cannot be taken as exclusive evidence. Manuscript H notes no music in play **2**, only B has music at the start of that play, and no music is noted after **2/616** in either A or B. Thus the loss of Hm would have increased the incompleteness, and if H had survived alone play **2** would include no musical directions at all. Our knowledge of minstrelsy in play **2**, then, is due to an accident of transmission, since some scribes took a decision to omit some or all of the evidence. The question must arise how many more musical directions were suppressed by the scribes. Music would certainly have been suitable in other places as well: and indeed in play **11**, where we could fairly have hoped for evidence of music in the text, the surviving accounts of the Smiths' guild do give us reason for adding to the musical cues (see in 6.5).

Table 8 shows the dramatic directions of the cycle. The second column shows the language of the direction: I here ignore the tendency of H to translate into Latin (all liturgical incipits are of course given in Latin anyway, but this does not affect the language of the direction). The third column (Position) shows whether the direction is placed centrally or marginally. In view of the differences in scribal treatment of the Exemplar's directions, this column takes account of the discussion of Lumiansky and Mills already mentioned: thus the positioning shown here is often not that of the direction in any particular manuscript. Indeed, Lumiansky and Mills commented, in relation specifically to play **4** (*Essays*, 29), that '... paradoxically, ... it is not a necessary feature of a MD that it should appear in the margin of an extant manuscript ....'.

TABLE 8 : DIRECTIONS FOR MUSIC IN THE CHESTER CYCLE

Line	Lang	Posn	Direction if musical, and comments

1 The Fall of Lucifer
(NB This play was missing in Hm, and was supplied in the nineteenth century from the copy in R.)

Line	Lang	Posn	Direction if musical, and comments
85	e	m	*A songe: dignus es Dei* A
			Dignus Dei R
			Then a songe: dignus es domine B
			Tunc cantabunt H (placed centrally)
			The Exemplar direction was evidently *Then a songe Dignus es domine Dei* (recte *Deus*), or something close to that
125	(l)	(c)	*Tunc cantant et recedet Deus* H only
213	?	m	*Gloria tibi Trinitas*
			Omitted H (where it coincides with a page-turn and was perhaps overlooked)

Non-musical directions occur at lines 212, 215 and 229, all marginal

2 The Creation and Fall of Man

Line	Lang	Posn	Direction if musical, and comments
-1	e	m	*Minstrels play* B only
112	e	m	*minstrelles playe (playinge)*
			Omitted H
280	e	m	*minstrelles playe (playinge)*
384	e	m	*minstrelles playe (playinge)*
			Omitted H
424	e	m	*minstrelles playe (playinge)*
			Omitted H
616	e	m	*minstrelles playe*
			Omitted ARH

There are more than twenty non-musical directions in addition, many of them marginal.

3 Noah's Flood

Line	Lang	Posn	Direction if musical, and comments
252	e	?C	*Then the singe and Noe shall speake agayne* HmRB
			Omitted H
			For this direction and the next, see my comments in *Essays*, 121, and I, 227–8.
260	e	c	Non-musical in HmARB
			Tunc Noe claudet fenestram Archae et per modicum spatium

> *infra tectum cantent psalmum (Save mee o God) et aperiens*
> *fenestram et respiciens* H
> In H this direction is followed by the Raven and Dove
> scene (*Chester*, Appendix IA), which does not appear in
> the Group manuscripts. The scene has three (Latin)
> directions, none of them musical.

4 Abraham

This play presents a particularly interesting situation in respect of directions
and their original positioning (*Essays*, 28–32 passim, and especially 29): but in
more than thirty directions there is not one for music.

5 Moses

Manuscript H transmits a text so different from that of the Group that
Lumiansky and Mills print it separately (*Chester*, Appendix IB). No directions
for music are included in that version, nor in the Group's (which has more than
twenty directions in all). One direction that has been interpreted as musical in
the past – a flourish of trumpets – is given below.

111	e	m	*Florish*
			Not a direction for music: for the history of the interpreta-
			tion of this item, see *Essays*, 117[5]

6 The Annunciation

64	1	c	*Maria gaudiens incipiet canticum magnificat etc*
			Not a direction for music as it stands, but see 6.6
72	(1)	c	*Et exultavit spiritus meus in Deo etc*
			Not really a direction: it is justified on the left with the text
			(unlike the SDs) in Hm, although it looks more like a SD in
			BH. For the musical interpretation, see 6.6
666	1	c	*Tunc angelus cantabit haec est ara dei caeli / fiat notam*
			secundum arbitrium agentis etc

These are the only three musical directions in a total of sixteen (i.e. including
72+sd/sh). Of the thirteen non-musical directions, eight are probably marginal
in origin.

7 The Shepherds

There are twenty directions in this play, of which seven are probably marginal
in origin. The five musical directions (I include **48+sd** in this) present some
interesting material and a few problems:

---

5 For interpretations see Dutka 'Mysteries', 122, and Meredith 'Scribes, Texts', 26.

48	l	c	*hic flabit primus pastor* HmARB
			Tunc flat cum Cornu et reddit Aho. io. o ... H
164	l	m	*Tunc cantabit et dicat Garcius (Trowle)*
			Tunc cantant et venit Gartius H (marginal, against line 162)
			It is clear that *cantabit* refers to Garcius, and that the reading *cantant* in H is mistaken: but it is not possible to reconstruct the process by which a direction using both the future and present tenses (*cantabit, dicat*) came into being (*Essays*, 127). I therefore reject H's version
357	l	c	*Tunc cantet Angelus / Gloria in excelsis deo et in terra pax hominibus bonae voluntatis*
			With written music H: see I, 152–9, 384–5 and Plate 7)
447	l	c	*Tunc cantabunt et postea dicat tertius pastor* HmAR
			Tunc cantabit et postea dicat tertius pastor B
			Tunc omnes pastores cum aliis adiuvantibus cantabunt hilare carmen H
			On the interpretation of these variants, see 6.3.
447	e	m	*here singe troly loly loly loo*
			Omitted H

8 The Three Kings

| 144 | e | m | *minstrells here must playe* Hm |
| | | | On this direction see *Essays*, 30. |

This play has a total of 25 directions, most of which are or were marginal.

9 The Gifts of the Magi
One direction only, not for music.

10 The Slaughter of the Innocents
This play has eight directions, of which two seem to be marginal.

288	l	c	*Tunc ibunt et Angelus cantabit, Ecce dominus ascendet super nubem levem, et ingrediatur Egiptum, et movebuntur simulachra Egipti a facie domini exercituum Et si fueri poterit caldet aliqua statue sive Imago* Hm
			Omitted A
			Misplaced after 264 R

11 The Purification, and Christ and the Doctors
Of eight directions, one apparently marginal, only the last is for music:

166	1	c	*Tunc cantabit Nunc dimittis servum tuum domine etc* B adds *in pace* instead of *etc*

12 The Temptation, and the Woman Taken in Adultery
This play has thirteen directions, of which rather more than half are probably marginal in origin. None of them is for music.

13 The Blind Chelidonian, and the Raising of Lazarus
This play has fourteen directions, of which probably five or so are marginal in origin. None of them is for music.

14 Christ at the House of Simon the Leper, and the Entry into Jerusalem
This play has twelve directions, of which four seem to be marginal. Only one direction is for music:

208	1	c	*Tunc ibunt pueri versus Jerusalem cantantes hosanna cum ramis palmarum in manibus et cives prosternent vestimenta sua in via: hosanna filio david benedictus qui venit in nomine domini hosanna in excelsis* HmARB *Tunc ibunt pueri versus Jerusalem cum Ramis palmarum in manibus: et cives prosternent vestimenta sua in via et cantabunt Hosanna filio David Benedictus qui venit in nomine Domini Hosanna in excelsis* H

15 The Last Supper
This play has 19 directions, of which four are probably marginal in origin. There are none for music.

16 The Trial and Flagellation
There are 19 directions in this play (including the SD material in the play heading), of which nine or so seem to be marginal. None is for music.

16A The Passion
There are 21 directions in this play. Many of them are found only in manuscript H, which has a different version of the Deposition scene at the end: this does not however affect the total number of directions in the play. Around half of the directions seem to be marginal, but there are none for music.

17 The Harrowing of Hell
This play has eleven directions, if we include the SD material in the play heading and count that after line 276 as two directions, shown by the form adopted in manuscript H. Of these directions, three may be marginal. Those for music (or sound) are:

152	l	c	*Tunc venit Jesus et fiat clamor vel sonitus magnus / materialis: et dicat Jesus: / Attollite portas principes vestras et elevamini / portas aeternales et introibit rex gloriae*
276	l	c	*Tunc eant omnes et incipiat Michaell: Te deum laudamus*
			H gives a different SD, with a marginal note above it, against line 276:
	l	m	*Te Deum laudamus te dominum confitemur*
	l	c	*Et sic Ibunt glorificantes Deum cantantes Te Deum*

18 The Resurrection

153	l	c	*Tunc cantabunt duo angeli. Christus resurgens a mortuis etc. et Christus tunc resurget, ac postea cantu finito dicat ut sequitur*
	l	m	*Jesus resurgens et pede eos milites quatiat*
			Omitted H

The play includes another eleven directions, of which perhaps four are marginal. In addition, manuscripts R and H contain an extra section at the end (*Chester*, Appendix ID): this has five directions, all in Latin, none of which seems to be marginal. None is for music.

19 Christ on the Road to Emmaus, and Doubting Thomas
This play has ten directions, none of them for music: five of them seem to be marginal.

20 The Ascension
This play contains 14 directions, if we count the English after line **104** separately and regard the multiple direction after line **152** as two: several are really SHs, however, as noted. Only one of the directions is obviously marginal, although others may be, too. Those concerned with music are:

104	l	c	*Tunc Jesus ascendet et in ascendendo cantet*
104	e	m	*God singeth alonne*
/+b	l	c	*Cum autem Impleverit Jesus canticum stet in medio quasi supra nubes. et dicat major angelus minori angelo*
			Omitted R
/+b+	l	c	*primus angelus cantat*
			SH
/+c+	l	c	*minor angelus respondens cantat*
/+d+	l	c	*Jesus cantat solus*
			SH
/+e+	l	c	*Chorus cantat*
			SH

/+f+	1	c	*Jesus cantat solus* SH
/+g+	1	c	*primus angelus dicat in materna lingua* SH
152	1	c	*Tunc ascendet et in ascendendo cantent angeli canticum subscriptum*
	1	c	*Cantent* HmB only
	1	c	*Exaltaremus domine in virtute tua cantabimus et psallemus virtutes tuas* [H adds *Alleluya*]
	1	c	*Tunc descendent anaeli et cantent viri Gallilei quid aspicitis in caelum* HmBH only

In H the direction at **104+e+** reads *An[g]elus Tertius*: in this version there are three solo singing angels, then, rather than two solo singers plus one or more other angels joining them to make a chorus.

21 Pentecost

Of twelve directions in this play, three seem to be marginal, one of those three being a translation of a Latin direction. Only two directions are for music:

120	1	c	*Tunc omnes apostoli genuflectentes cantent / Veni creator spiritus. postea dicat* H omits the last two words and adds the rest of the verse: *mentes tuorum visita/ imple superna gratia/ que tu creasti pectora*
238	1	c	*Tunc deus emittet spiritum sanctum in spetie ignis / et in mittendo cantent duo angeli antiphonam accipite spiritum sanctum Quorum remiseritis peccata / remittentur eis etc. et cantando projecient / ignem super apostolos finitoque Angelus in caelo dicat* R gives an English direction, with no singing
310	1	c	SH for starting of Credo: 'incipiat' may demand singing. See 6.4

22 The Prophets of Antichrist
No directions

23 *Antichrist*
This play has a total of 16 directions: at least the first three are marginal, and others may be. Only the last of the play's directions is for music:

| 722 | 1 | c | *Tunc abducens eos ad coelos / cantabit Angelus* [H adds *Michael*]: / *Gaudete iusti in domino etc.* |
| | | | In Hm the e of 'etc' is changed from an h |

24 *The Last Judgement*
Of six directions in this play, at least one is marginal. Two directions are for music:

40	1	c	*Tunc angeli tubas accipiunt et flabunt et omnes mortui de sepulchris surgent, quorum dicat primus papa salvatus*
508	1	c	*Tunc angeli ibunt ac cantabunt euntes ac venientes / letamini in domino vel salvator mundi domine ac omnes salvati eos / sequentur postea veniunt demones quorum dicat primus*
			Only H provides the word *vel*, which is obviously correct.

Quotation of the musical directions follows the readings of Lumiansky and Mills (*Chester*) using Hm as base text, but with the orthography and punctuation of the manuscript. I have shown line-ends by / if I consider that in a particular direction this may be relevant in lieu of punctuation.

Variants in the directions are quoted only if they are clearly significant. Most minor variants noted by Lumiansky and Mills are errors, and I ignore these. It is not possible, of course, to reconstruct the original readings of the Exemplar, and I have not generally tried to do so: I have made the occasional speculation, however.

One more matter, not strictly a musical one, requires some explanation. Four directions are involved, shown in Table 9. The phrase '[cum] alta voce' does not here mean 'in a high voice' but 'in a loud voice': the meaning is the same as when 'alta' is used as a technical term for loud musical instruments. Applied to the voice, 'alta' is used in the rubrics of liturgical books in opposition to the speaking of text in secret: that is, 'alta voce' signifies that text is to be spoken out loud, so that the congregation can hear it. The relationship between liturgical rubrics and dramatic directions has yet to be investigated in detail, but it does seem – not surprisingly: see 6.1 – that religious dramatists drew on their experience of liturgical 'stage directions' when writing the directions for plays.

In the present cases the distinction is apparently between speaking normally and speaking deliberately in what the audience will hear as a loud voice.

TABLE 9 : 'ALTA VOCE' DIRECTIONS IN THE CHESTER CYCLE

Pl/line	Direction and comments
2/281	... *et venit Deus clamans cum alta voce* This SD corresponds to the main direction following line **280** in other sources.
5/303	*Tunc Balaak rex ... dicat alta voce*
6/372	*Tunc orat Sibilla, et dicat Preco alta voce*
15/288	*Tunc iterum ad orationem, et alta voce loquitur*

6.3   Text references

1 *The Fall of Lucifer*
1/84–5   [ARCKEANGELIS]   him for to thanke with some solace,
  a songe now let us singe here.

This refers to **85+md**.

1/20   [DOMINACIONES]   this daunce will tome to teene and traye.

Metaphorical use. Lumiansky and Mills (*Chester* II, 13) cite a meaning for 'dance' given by the MED, 'a situation or predicament': but more simply it means here 'business' or 'affair'.

1/249   [PRIMUS DEMON]   till the day of Dome that beames shall blowe.

Reference only, looking forward to play **24**.

2 *The Creation and Fall of Man*
No musical references.

3 *Noah's Flood*
There are no references to music in this play. **3/80+sd** (MS H only), **3/96+sd** (MS H only) and **3/112+sd** refer to 'Instruements' ('instrumentes' in Latin), which are tools for building the Ark. Noah uses the phrase 'lowde and still' once (line **41**), with its usual meaning of 'in all circumstances': Lumiansky and Mills offer 'at all times' (*Chester* II, 443, citing the OED, in which see under 'loud' as an adverb).

3/225–36 There is a considerable problem over the song sung by Mrs Noah's gossip(s). It seems that the text was written specially for this play, and that there can therefore have been no pre-existent musical setting; that stanzas 29–30 were originally intended as a solo song, with stanza 31 as a chorus; and that the various SHs stem from an attempt to allow the lines to be spoken if necessary. See I, 71–3.

4 Abraham

4/350 [ABRAHAM] My songe maye be 'Wele-Awaye'.

Metaphorical usage.

5 Moses, Balaak and Balaam

No text references to music.

6 The Annunciation and the Nativity

6/65-72   MARIA Elizabeth, therefore will I
                   thanke the lord, kinge of mercye,
                   with joyfull myrth and melody
                   and laud to his likinge.
                   'Magnificat', while I have toome,
                   'anima mea dominum'
                   to Christe that in my kind is come,
                   devoutly I will singe.

This is the first part of the speech, ending at line **112**, in which Mary paraphrases the Magnificat: these lines follow **64+sd**. The paraphrase here is a very loose one, but that does not affect the importance of the words 'melody' (line **67**) and 'sing' (**72**). These must mean that Mary sings Magnificat, since this reference cannot be to anything but this moment in the play. See 6.6.

6/564–643 The Expositor's speech recounts a miracle that happened at Christ's birth. He describes a temple in Rome containing for each province an image with a bell round its neck (**582–3**), which bell rang of its own accord if an enemy threatened Rome in that province (**598–9, 604–5**). This story is not unique to the play – Lumiansky and Mills discuss the sources, *Chester* II, 94–6 – and has no effect on the provision of music for its performance. But it is interesting as showing a parallel for the temple bell ringing by itself in **Towneley 17** (see 3.3): if the parallel holds good, we may see Christ's approach to the temple as an assault on the authority of the Old Law.

6/667–70   [OCTAVYAN] A, Sybbell, heres not thow this songe?
My members all yt goeth amonge.
Joy and blys makes my harte stronge
to heare this melody.

This speech immediately follows **666+sd** and clearly refers to the angel's singing of *Haec est ara Dei caeli*.

6/707–12   The Expositor gives as a reason for the naming of the church of Ara Caeli, otherwise St Mary, the emperor's need to retain a memory of two things: the angel's song and the sight that he saw, in that order.

7 *The Shepherds*

Late Banns 96–102   The appearinge angell and starr upon Cristes birthe,
the sheapeardes poore of base and lowe degree,
you Paynters and Glaseers decke out with all myrth
and see that *Gloria in Excelsus* be songe merelye.
Fewe wordes in the pagiante make merthe trulye,
for all that the author had to stande uppon
was 'glorye to God on highe and peace on earthe to man'.

This whole stanza makes much of the angel's appearance to the shepherds and his message to them. Despite the shepherds' discussion of the song (**7/361–435**, probably two alternative discussions, for which see below), the emphasis on it here is perhaps surprising, for it seems from the text only a small part of the play. But the Painters' charter also emphasises the song, referring to it as 'the sheppherds wach with the angells hyme' (see 6.5). Moreover, R's copy of the Late Banns has the title *Gloria in Excelsis* written in red, an indication that it was considered of importance in the cycle as a whole. To some extent this is explained in lines **101–2** of the Late Banns, which identify the Gloria as the text on which the whole play is based, but that also supports the view that the angel's song was a dramatic event of prime importance. This is further supported by the emphasis on mirth in three adjacent lines (**98–100**), which indicates musical style and resources calculated to make a considerable impression on an audience.

7/47–8   [PRIMUS PASTOR] Thow maye not here excepte I blowe,
as ever have I heale.

The First Shepherd realises that he cannot attract Harvey's attention with his voice alone, and must therefore blow his horn. He does so at **48+sd**.

7/151   [PRIMUS PASTOR] Blowe thy horne and call after Trowle

7/155–6 [SECUNDUS PASTOR]   My home to lille I wyll not lesse
       tyll that lad have some of our leekes.

7/159–64 [TERTIUS PASTOR] Blowe a note for that meetinge
       whyle that horne in thy hand ys.
PRIMUS PASTOR   With this home I shall make a 'Hooe'
       that hee and all heaven shall here.
       Yonder lad that sittes on a lowe
       the lowd of this horne shall here.

There is some confusion here as to which of the shepherds is to blow the horn: see I, 361. The First Shepherd tells one of the others to do it (**151**), and the Second Shepherd says that he will (**155**). But although the Third Shepherd seems to be encouraging the latter to blow his horn while it is in his hand, it is the First Shepherd who answers (**161–4**). The SH is apparently correct, since it appears in all manuscripts. The Third Shepherd was certainly not addressing the First Shepherd, however: the First Shepherd does not have his horn still in his hand from blowing it at **48+sd**, for he has taken off his cloak and emptied food from his satchel since then, and in any case would hardly have told one of the others to blow (at **151**) if he himself had been holding his horn in his hand. Probably the First and Third Shepherds both intend the Second Shepherd to blow: but either the First Shepherd becomes impatient with the Second Shepherd's inaction, or else there is an element of competition in the First Shepherd's decision to do it himself.

This passage is followed by **164+sd**. As explained above, 6.2, that SD surely refers to Garcius throughout, so that it does not tell us when the horn is blown. For practical reasons the horn–blowing must not distract attention from Garcius's singing, so perhaps the shepherds go on discussing or arguing for a few lines yet: this would support my second suggestion above, that the First Shepherd is in competition with the Second. Perhaps some comic business has gone on for some time before Garcius hears the First Shepherd's horn and declines to join them (**195–7**). Among the reasons he gives is that they are 'sittinge withowt any songes' (**205**). Further on this, see 6.6.

7/358–435 The shepherds' long discussion of the angelic Gloria heard at **357+sd** contains a number of separate strands, not all of which are very important for our present purposes. They are much concerned with the text: for it is clearly important to the shepherds to be able to repeat the angel's words, and they piece it together from their memories, apparently not understanding the Latin text or even recognising it. Much of the point of all this is humorous: but for some reason there is a pre-echo of all the 'glorus glarus glorius' verbal juggling (**382, 384, 388, 391–2, 400–1**) even before the discussion starts or the Gloria is heard (**332–3**).

Lumiansky and Mills note that the passage from the angelic Gloria to the shepherds' arrival at the stable seems to contain certain duplications: the shepherds discuss the Gloria text twice as far as 'excelsis', and they also seem to arrive at the stable twice. The solution is, no doubt, that the sources give, but do not distinguish between, alternative texts (*Chester* II, 118, under notes for **448–51**). Lumiansky and Mills suggest two ways of proceeding from **357+sd** to line **496** (where the two versions converge). These are shown in I, 348 (Table 21).

(1) Lines **358–75** and then **464–95**. The first section consists of a discussion of the Gloria text only as far as 'excelsis', while the second adds nothing to that particular discussion;

(2) Lines **376–463**. Although this probably is a single section, as Lumiansky and Mills suggest, there are divisions additional to those that they propose. First, the shepherds discuss the words 'Gloria' and 'excelsis' in lines **376–89** and then return to 'Gloria' in line **390**, continuing the discussion through 'excelsis', 'terra', 'pax', 'hominibus' and 'bonae voluntatis' by **427**. But then they start again, discussing 'Deo', 'terra' and 'pax' before the discussion ends at line **435**.

If these are indeed the correct alternative sections of the text, (1) is very brief, with a discussion of the text only as far as 'excelsis', in comparison with (2), where the whole text is discussed.

More important, musically speaking, are the hints given about the style and effect of the singing, which the First Shepherd refers to as 'mutinge on highe' (**360**). 'Muting' does not appear in Carter's *Dictionary*, but I suspect a technical meaning for it nevertheless. It is found again at **420**, where the Second Shepherd says that the angel 'muted' upon the word 'hominibus'. The OED offers an intransitive verb apparently meaning 'to murmur' (related to the more obvious meaning of reducing the sound?), but this does not really make sense in either context. In the field of technical terms there is the possibility of a connection with mutation, i.e. the art of moving from one hexachord to another, which in this context would suggest a wide-ranging and therefore presumably ornate and melismatic line. In this case Garcius's comment that the angel 'tamed' the word 'terra' (**432**), although probably important for the alliteration rather than anything else, presumably means that the singer was able to control something that was very difficult, i.e. to sing accurately a very intricate piece of music. There are, in any case, more clues about the angel's singing. Garcius's comment that 'that note went over the howse' (**385**) suggests florid or high-pitched music or both; the Third Shepherd's description of the angel as 'wounder defte' in his singing supports the idea of dexterity and vocal skill (see *Chester* II, 116 for a discussion of word-play here), while the use of 'whewted' (i.e. 'whistled', **422**) also suggests high pitch. (See also 15.3, below, under **Castle 1938**, for the use of this word in *The Castle of Perseverance*.) The First Shepherd's 'When hee sange I might not be sorye' (**402**) is apparently contradicted by the Second Shepherd's comment that on the word 'celsis' 'sadly hee sett him', but this probably only means that the song was emotionally varied. At any rate there is a general admiration for the singing and for its spiritual effect: for the Second Shepherd says unequivocally (**406–7**) that

> He had a mych better voyce then I have,
> as in heaven all other have soe,

while Garcius states that the singing of 'Deo' healed his heart (**431**). It is not always easy to see how seriously their remarks should be taken, however: the First Shepherd's 'up as a pye hee pyped' is not, on the face of it, particularly flattering to the angel unless magpies sounded better then than now. But perhaps he is only commenting on the angel's vocal agility or self-confidence: and here again the alliteration is an important factor.

If Lumiansky and Mills are correct in their supposition about alternative passages, not all of these references should be heard in any performance. Alternative (1), lines **358–75** and **464–95**, contains only two pieces of information: **360** describes the singing as 'mutinge on highe', and **368** suggests the effect of the music on the hearer. The more informative passage (2), **376–463**, offers the same types of information – including the use of the word 'muted' in **420** and a clear indication of the effect on the hearer in **402** – but in addition tells us something about the angel's voice and his performance. It seems fairly clear that the musical information is intended to be similar in the two passages, although the quantity is very different.

7/410–11 [TERTIUS PASTOR] nayther singes 'sar' nor soe well 'cis',
      ney 'pax merye Mawd when shee had mett him'.

This may be a line of a popular song, but it is so far unidentified. See *Chester* II, 117.

7/436–49 In these fourteen lines the Shepherds state their views on the suggestion that they should sing. All approve of it: but the First Shepherd sees it as a means to pray for grace (**436–9**), while the Second regards a 'merry song' as a means to personal solace (**442–3**); the Third, after the event, is anxious that the singing shall not take their minds off the real business in hand, which is their journey to Bethlehem. Only Garcius, at this stage, gives no reason for wanting to sing. His speech is however an important one from the production point of view (**444–7**):

> GARCIUS   Singe we nowe; lett see,
>   some songe will I assaye.

All men nowe singes after mee,
for musicke of mee learne yee maye.

This is followed by **447+sd**, which, as already noted, varies among the manuscripts. HmAR read 'cantabunt', which presumably means that all three Shepherds and Garcius sing here: H also reads 'cantabunt', but is more specific in describing the song as an 'hilare carmen' – the 'merry song' of line 443 – and the singers as 'omnes pastores cum aliis adiuvantibus', which apparently means not only Garcius but also the Shepherds' Boys who appear in H's version of the play. Only B reads 'cantabit'. Lumiansky and Mills point out that 'cantabunt' confirms 'sing we' of line **444**, while the singular form confirms Garcius's 'some songe will I assaye' of line **445** (*Chester* II, 118).

These versions are not incompatible. Since Garcius clearly intends to teach a song, the others repeating it after him (**446–7**), the singular verb can reasonably be used to indicate Garcius's lead while the plural form recognises that the others join in after him. Both versions of the SD, in other words, reflect the dramatic action of Garcius starting a song and the others picking it up.

But there is more to it than this. There is no possible dramatic reason for having Garcius teach the others a song unless it be the song that the angel provided and which they have to sing to others: but that is not the case here, since Garcius has made the choice of song (**445**). Even as a comedy moment, it would be dramatically meaningless. Moreover, Garcius specifically demands more than this: he requires 'all men' to sing after him, since they can learn music from him. This is not the case of hyperbole that it seems at first sight, then, but a 'pantomime' act in which Garcius will get the whole audience singing with him. This matter is discussed in I, 376–7.

7/476–9 [GARCIUS] And singe we all, I read,
                some myrth to his majestee,
                for certayne now see wee it indeede:
                the kinge Sone of heavon is hee.

No SD follows this speech: but as the Shepherds come in sight of the stable in the very next line, they must sing the song immediately after **479**. The song may thus cover their journey to Bethlehem: but if they are to sing it to the Christ-child in person, rather than simply in his honour, they must arrive at the stable before the song is finished.

Lumiansky and Mills point out that the Shepherds make two decisions to go to Bethlehem, of which this is the second: as with the episode noted above, they suggest that alternative passages have been incorporated into the text (*Chester* II, 118 and, more fully, *Essays*, 18–19). It is not possible to disentangle these alternatives entirely, but we can see that the two versions affect the character of Garcius. I have elsewhere suggested ('Some Myrth', 83 and 86) that the scene in which Garcius wrestles with his three masters, and throws them in turn, allows us to consider him as spiritually more powerful than they; that his superior musicality, and his understanding that music should be used for praise of God rather than for personal solace, help to define this power more precisely; and that, putting these two factors together, we may reasonably regard him as a sort of early example of Muscular Christianity. This interpretation is based on that developed by Kolve (*Play Called Corpus Christi*, 156 f) and Woolf (*English Mystery Plays*, 187 f). Some would certainly regard this as going too far, but I would still support it as a viable reading that can be justified by the text. The situation is clearly more complex than that, however, if we are to see **464–79** as an alternative to **436–63**. In the former case – which I would imagine to be the earlier version – Garcius's recommendation that they sing 'some mirth to his majesty' is not offered in opposition to less pious suggestions from the others; with the latter version – which I should expect to be a late alternative, with secular 'business' over-riding an older tradition of symbolic convention – Garcius's musicality is seen as a talent for its own sake, and nothing to do with his closeness to the Divine Will. It is in this second case, of course, that HmARB prescribe 'Troly loly loly loo' as the Shepherds' song – not a text likely to be particularly close to the Divine Will, one imagines, whatever song this *incipit* was intended to recall.

This problem cannot be solved, unfortunately, since there are insufficient data. But a producer must certainly try to come to a practical solution, bearing in mind the musicality shown by the Shepherds later in the play. My own view is that what follows here supports a traditional convention for music as a reflection of the Divine Will, and casts doubt on the original validity of the secular 'pantomime' version presented by **436–63**.

7/559 [PRIMUS PASTOR] Loe, I bringe thee a bell

What sort of bell would this be? Presumably a small one, such as might be tied around the neck of a sheep.[6]

7/625–32 THE THYRD BOYE O noble child of thy Father on hye,
                    alas, what have I for to give thee?
                    Save only my pype that soundeth so royallye,
                    elles truely have I nothinge at all.
                    Were I in the rocke or in the valey alowe,
                    I could make this pipe sound, I trowe,
                    that all the world should ringe
                    and quaver as yt would fall.

6 See I, 353 and plate 10.

This is an impressive instrument. Even allowing for some exaggeration on the part of the boy, his claim that whatever the acoustics ('up on the rocky hills or in the valley low down') he could make the earth tremble with it suggests a formidable noise. I have elsewhere explored the possibilities and concluded that the boy must have presented a bagpipe ('Some Myrth', 86–9). Bagpipes are commonly included in late medieval representations of shepherds (so are recorders, but their soft sound does not match the boy's description); the instrumental sound is loud; and the symbolic association with pilgrimage – the shepherds are, after all, the first Christian pilgrims as they journey to Bethlehem – is a strong one. (There is another, less suitable, association, with gluttony and lechery: but the two obviously co-existed, and were presumably understood according to the context in which the bagpipe was found.)

7/651–6 SECUNDUS PASTOR Brethren, lett us all three
                     singinge walke homwardlye.
                     Unkynd will I never in noe case bee,
                     but preach all that I can and knowe,
                     as Gabryell taught by his grace mee.
                     Singinge awaye hethen will I.

This is the first speech of the final, post-adoration, scene of the play. A song is obviously required by this, but it is not easy to see where it should go. If the shepherds sing immediately, the music covers their journey back from the stable. This does not quite fit the text, however, for the Second Shepherd's speech is itself the opening of the final scene, so that a song after it might be dramatically disruptive. If they do not sing after **656** there is no place for a song until the end of the play, where it would be useful in covering their exits. This is forty lines on, but the reference will not have been forgotten: in play **17** (see below) the dramatist clearly expects the audience to connect references sixty lines apart. But in fact the shepherds disperse at the end of play **7** (having all in one way or another renounced the world in their final speeches), which would cause practical problems in singing and in any case would lessen the dramatic effect of the song. This problem perhaps has no ideal solution: formerly I have preferred the song to come at the end of the play (*Essays*, 126), but on maturer reflection I now think that it is better incorporated into the final scene, after **656**.

7/691 [TERTIUS PASTOR] Amen, all singe you

Metaphorical: this is simply a 'Hear, hear' in answer to the Third Shepherd's own pious hope that God will bring his fellows to bliss (**689–90**). There is no reason to think that the shepherds actually do sing 'Amen', although it would be reasonable for them to say it while the Third Shepherd is still speaking.

8 The Three Kings
8/51   [PRIMUS REX] thou give us grace, both lowd and styll

Metaphorical: 'both great and small' (i.e. important and unimportant), or perhaps 'in all circumstances'.

9 The Offerings of the Three Kings
No references to music.

10 The Slaughter of the Innocents
10/287–8 [ANGELUS] at your comminge downe shall fall
                 when I beginne to synge.

This is followed by **288+sd**, to which it clearly refers.

10/494–8 [ANGELUS] And I will make a melodie,
                 and singe here in your companye
                 a worde was sayd in prophecye
                 a thousande yeares agoe:
       Ex Egipto vocavi Filium meum, ut salvum faciet populum meum.

This is the end of the play: evidently the angel does sing here. The problem is to decide the status of this last line: should it be spoken, with the same text sung afterwards, or is this presentation of the text just the record of what the angel sings? In Hm (f. 65r) there is a clear full stop (in the form ./) at the end of line **97**, and the Latin text is written beneath with completely different layout, size, and type of script; the same layout occurs in B (f. 78v), although the punctuation is missing and the same script is used as for the rest of the play. In H the same punctuation as in Hm is seen, and again the script is larger and slightly more formal for the Latin, which is also separated from the previous text by a horizontal rule such as occurs every two or three lines of the text anyway. (The Latin is also in red, but this is the case for all Latin lines, spoken or unspoken: MDF 8, ix.)

It seems clear from these three sources that the Latin was not to be considered merely a part of the spoken text but that, on the contrary, the spoken text came to an end with the punctuation in line **97**. It seems most likely, then, that the Latin text was not to be spoken by the angel, line **97** being the introduction to the singing of the text given on the following line.

11 The Purification and Christ and the Doctors
Late Banns 115–18   Yow Smythes, honeste men, yea and of honeste arte,
               how Criste amonge the Doctors in the temple did dispute,
               to sett out your playe comlye hit shalbe youre parte;

gett mynstrelles to that shewe, pype, tabrett and flute.

The only direction for music in the Blacksmiths' play is for Simeon's singing of *Nunc dimittis* (**11/166+sd**). Instrumental accompaniment would be inappropriate for this, since in the context of the plays instruments would imply Heaven (if *bas*) or royalty (if *haut*). There are places where heavenly minstrelsy would be appropriate in this play, however, and it is therefore possible that the three minstrels played *bas* music. At **11/40+sd**, and again at **11/71+sd**, the angel actively intervenes by reversing Simeon's 'correction' of a biblical text; after **11/103** the angel again intervenes, but only to give Simeon information; and the angel returns after **11/326** to speak to the audience. From the point of view of representing Heaven, the first two of these seem very likely places for music, the third much less so, and the last most unlikely. At the first two places, too, music would cover the angel's actions. In all, music at **11/40+sd** and at **71+sd** is a distinct possibility, but perhaps not elsewhere. In this case we should expect the 'pype' to be a recorder and the tabor to be a small and relatively quiet instrument such as was used for marking the beat during dancing indoors.

A flute is a *bas* instrument in any case. The type of minstrelsy is therefore not altered by B's substitution of 'harpe' for 'flute', but a harp makes better sense as solo minstrelsy. As 'flute' is present but cancelled in B, it is quite possible that the cancellation and replacement were in the Exemplar, reflecting a production change. Both pipe and tabor could be *haut* music: 'pipe' can refer to a shawm or to a bagpipe, and it is also possible that pipe and tabor were to be played by one man, which would again be loud dance music. As we shall see (6.5), the accounts of the Smiths' Guild suggest very strongly that minstrels were employed to accompany the waggon, which would certainly be loud music. We need not be too concerned, perhaps, that this would not strictly be a part of the play: probably the Banns would 'plug' any audience-attractor that presented itself in the performance as a whole. If 'pype' and 'tabrett' are loud music, however, this still leaves flute/harp, which must be *bas* music. There is a possibility, then, of either *bas* music only or both *bas* music in the play and *haut* music accompanying the waggon.

11/163–6 [SIMEON] Therefor a songe, as I have tyght
and laudes to thee with hart right
I will shewe here in thy sight;
of mee, lord, thou have mynde.

This is followed by **166+sd**, to which it evidently refers.

12 *The Temptation, and The Woman Taken in Adultery*
No references to music.

13 The Blind Chelidonian, and The Raising of Lazarus
No references to music. In **13/300** Lumiansky and Mills prefer AR 'taberte' (coat) to HmBH 'tabret': see *Chester* II, 192.

14 Christ at the House of Simon the Leper, Christ and the Money-Lenders, and Judas's Plot
14/189–92 QUARTUS CIVIS Branches of the palme tree
                eycheon in hand take wee,
                and welcome him to this cittie
                with fayre processionn.

14/205–8 SECUNDUS PUER Make wee myrth all that we maye
                pleasant to that lordes paye.
                'Hosanna' I read, by my faye,
                to synge that we founde.

These two speeches, together with intervening lines dealing with the spreading of clothes in the way, give more information about the musical scene of **208+sd**. The Second Boy's speech (especially **208**) does not match the SD as transmitted by manuscript H: see **6.6**.

15 The Last Supper, and The Betrayal
16 The Trial and Flagellation
16A The Passion
No references to music.

17 The Harrowing of Hell
17/126 [TERTIUS DEMON] he shall synge a sorye songe

Metaphorical usage.

17/211–12 [JESUS] Mychaell, lead these men singinge
             to blys that lasteth ever.

17/273–6 ADAM Nowe goe wee to blys, ould and yonge,
             and worshippe God all willinglye;
             and thiderward I read we singe
             with great solempnitie.

These two references go together: the second is followed by **276+sd**, which requires Michael to intone *Te Deum laudamus*, which is then sung by all the Souls. Between **212** and **272** are a speech by Michael, one by Satan, and a dialogue between Adam, Enoch, Elias and the Good Thief, a total of sixty lines. There is, then, a gap of 64 lines between Jesus's command to Michael and the singing exit of the Souls. There is no question of alternative scenes here, and we must take this as an indication that the audience might be expected to remember the required consequences of a speech over this period of time (perhaps 4 or 5 minutes).

17/299   [MULIER] Sorrowfull maye I syke and singe

Metaphorical usage.

18 The Resurrection
No references to music. It is interesting that, despite the music at **153+sd**, the soldiers mention only the light and brightness that accompanied the Resurrection, not the sound (**187, 195, 210**).

19 Christ on the Road to Emmaus, and Doubting Thomas
20 The Ascension
21 Pentecost
No references to music.

22 The Prophets of Antichrist
There are no references to music. Three lines do seem to contain verbal references to a carol, however:

22/125–6 DANYELL I, Daniell, as I laye on a night,
methought I sawe a wondrous sight.

22/174 [JOHANNES EVANGELISTA] as I laye in greate longinge

Several carols use this idea, with much of the same vocabulary, but the closest is perhaps a late fourteenth-century carol the first verse of which is:

> Als I lay upon a nith
> Alone in my longging
> Me thouthe I sau a wonder sith
> A maiden child rokking.

Greene gives versions of this from manuscripts in Edinburgh, Cambridge (2), and London.[7] The Chester lines are not necessarily a deliberate incorporation

---

[7] See Greene *Early English Carols*, 92–4, and Stevens *Mediaeval Carols*, 110; for a facsimile, Rastall *A Fifteenth-Century Song Book*, f. 169r, and Rastall *Two Fifteenth-Century Song Books* [Cambridge, University Library, Add. MS 5943], f. 169r.

of carol material for a specific purpose: both Chester speeches relate dream sequences for which the language of a well-known lullaby carol might well come to mind. The earliest of the four carol sources is probably of the second half of the fourteenth century, while the latest is of the late fifteenth.

23 Antichrist
23/694 [SECUNDUS DEMON] A sorrowful songe, in fayth, shall hee singe.

Metaphorical usage.

24 The Last Judgement
Late Banns 179–85   The commynge of Christe to geve eternall judgmente
yow Weavers laste of all your parte is to playe.
Domesdaye we call it, when the Omnipotente
shall make ende of this worlde by sentence, I saye.
On his righte hande to stande, God grante us that daye,
and to have that sweete worde in melodye:
'Come hither, come hither, *Venite benedicti*'.

'Venite benedicti' is the reading in RB: other manuscripts (listed in *Essays*, 272) give the incorrect title *Venite benedicitie*. *Venite benedicti* occurs several times in the Sarum and English monastic uses: possible items are discussed in 6.4, below. There is no hint of a performance in the play text: but the play includes a paraphrase of the *Venite benedicti* texts in 24/453–6, so the usual pattern of sung Latin plus spoken English could be followed. See I, 81–3.

24/33–4 SECUNDUS ANGELUS   Take wee our beames and fast blowe.
All mankynd shall them knowe.

This speech is followed by **40+sd**, when the two angels do blow their trumpets. There is an almost immediate reaction to this sound:

24/45–6 [PAPA SALVATUS] Nowe through thy might and thy postye
thy beames blast hath raysed mee

24/66 [PAPA SALVATUS] ..., both lowde and styll

Metaphorical: 'in all circumstances'.

24/240 [REX DAMNATUS] Of sorrowe nowe may I synge.

Metaphorical usage.

6.4 Latin and the liturgy

The Chester cycle is notable for its many Latin quotations in the text, a feature discussed at some length by Lumiansky and Mills in their section on the evocation of authority in the cycle (*Essays*, 99–110). Such evocation indicates the need to defend material that is potentially or actually under attack, by stating its biblical or other authority. Lumiansky and Mills apparently believe at least many of the Latin quotations to have started life as MDs, later incorporated into the Exemplar (*Essays*, 101). By implication, such MDs are likely to date from the middle of the sixteenth century. Lumiansky and Mills list 27 biblical quotations in Latin (with a further seven in manuscript H's version of play 5, only one of which corresponds to a quotation given by the Group in that play), with others not readily identifiable as biblical (*Essays*, 100–1).

There are examples where it is clear from the dialogue or a SD that the Latin quotation is to be sung; occasionally the same type of evidence shows that it is to be declaimed; and a certain amount of Latin text is incorporated into the stanza form and must therefore be spoken with the rest of the text. Often the biblical source is stated, even when it seems that the quotation itself is declaimed. There may be a choice here as to whether the reference is to be spoken or not.

The element of choice in the texts is of considerable importance. When we ask for each individual Latin quotation 'Should this text be heard? – and, if so, Should it be sung or declaimed?', we should be wrong to look for one, and only one, correct answer. As we shall see, the various manuscripts of the cycle suggest that occasionally more than one possibility was offered by the Exemplar, a situation that we have already seen over the singing or non-singing of the Gossip's song (see the discussion of **3/225–36)** and the musicality of Garcius in play **7** (see 6.3, above).

The element of choice is aided by a feature frequently met with in the biblical plays: namely, that a Latin quotation is usually followed by a translation, paraphrase or explanation (it is often impossible to say which of these terms is most apposite) in the vernacular text (*Essays*, 102). There are several consequences of this: first, that the audience's understanding of the Latin can be anywhere between complete comprehension and total incomprehension of the Latin without any loss of the sense of the play; second, that the inclusion of Latin must have brought into being a set of related performance-conventions, any one of which might be chosen by the producer; and third, that the existence of such conventions may occasionally be responsible for the omission from the text of information that is necessary to us but was less necessary at the time. An important example of this occurs in play **24** (see 6.3 and below, under **24/452+[lat]**).

When Latin phrases are incorporated into the main vernacular text as part of the stanza-form, no translation, paraphrase or explanation usually occurs. These phrases are noticed here, but there is no question of singing them: they are spoken as a normal part of the text.

In listing liturgical items for the Chester cycle we are confronted by a major problem. Assuming the kind of connection between the Abbey of St Werburgh and the plays that is suggested by traditions of the origin of the plays, or even assuming that before the Reformation, as later, the guilds tended to recruit their directors of music from the Abbey's music staff, liturgical items should be sought in the Benedictine liturgy of the Abbey. The survival rate of the Abbey's service books is disappointingly small, however: and we can do no better, unfortunately, than to trust to other Benedictine books. Of these, the most easily accessible is the Worcester Antiphoner, which is accordingly used as a primary source here.

The indications that liturgical items were taken from the Abbey's Benedictine use are, however, far short of proof (see under play 5, below). We must therefore take account of the possibility that the plays' directors of music (if indeed we can generalise on this matter) provided liturgical items from the secular use of the diocese of Lichfield. Here again, survival rates are not good, however, and I have relied on the Sarum books for information.

For the post-Reformation period we can see from the guild accounts that the music was generally provided by clerks from the Cathedral, formerly the Abbey. Did they have access to the old Benedictine books? The poor survival rate would suggest that they did not.

For our present purpose, therefore, I can do no better than offer liturgical items in the Worcester and Sarum sources. It should be noted that, even where a liturgical item has the same text and basically the same music in the Sarum and monastic uses, and when it occupies the same position in the liturgy, the music often shows minor or even considerable melodic variation between the two uses.

In the rest of this section account is taken of the lists of Latin quotations made by Lumiansky and Mills (*Essays*, 100–2).

1 *The Fall of Lucifer*

1/1–2	DEUS	Ego sum alpha et oo, primus et novissimus.
1/12	[DEUS]	and Patris sapiencia.
1/16	[DEUS]	cum Dei potentia

God's first speech incorporates Latin in the stanza-form: all this is spoken. For the text of **1/1–2**, see under **2/-1**, below.

1/85+md	Dignus es domine Deus

See 6.2 for the reconstruction of this *incipit*. There are three possibilities:

(a) Respond, first Sunday after the Octave of Easter (WA, 139);
  Respond, first Sunday after Easter (AS, 251):
    Dignus es domine accipere librum et aperire signacula eius
    quondam occisus es et redemisti nos deo. In sanguine tuo.
    Alleluia.
  Neumatic/melismatic chant, range f–f', c-clef.

(b) Magnificat antiphon, first Sunday after the Octave of Easter (WA,
  139); Magnificat antiphon, second Sunday after Easter (AS, 256):
    Dignus es domine deus noster accipere gloriam et honorem et
    virtutem quia tu creasti omnia et propter voluntatem tuam erant
    et create sunt salus deo nostro qui sedes super thronum et agno.
    Alleluia.
  Largely syllabic chant, range c–c', c-clef.

(c) Antiphon for the sixth Sunday in Lent (Palm Sunday) (GS, 82; PS(P), 45r):
    Dignus es domine deus accipere gloriam et honorem.
  Largely syllabic chant, range c–g, f-clef.

Of these three we can dismiss (a): first, because its text is less suitable to the
occasion (the newly-created angels praising the Creator); and second, because
its omission of 'deus' as the fourth word makes it less likely than (b) or (c) to
give rise to the readings of Manuscripts A and R. Of (b) and (c) the former is
more appropriate, since it refers specifically to the creation: (c) is however
clearly possible if a shorter piece is required.

1/213+md   Gloria tibi Trinitas

Rhymed antiphon for Trinity Sunday (WA, 158; AS, 286). Syllabic/neumatic
chant, range c–d', c-clef. Note that there is a reference to the Trinity in **1/200**.

2 *The Creation and Fall of Man*
2/1–   DEUS   Ego sum alpha et omega, primus et novissimus.

(I follow the suggestion of Lumiansky and Mills (*Chester* II, 18) that the I/of
after 'omega' is due to scribal error.)
  This text opens the antiphon at processions on Sundays after Easter (WA,
136–7 and 225; PS(P), 94v; GS, 125): this first line is musically able to stand
alone. Although the MD for minstrels represents a musical opening to the
play, the instrumental music is clearly not an alternative to God singing this
line. It seems unlikely that God would sing rather than speak the line, for
reasons given elsewhere (see *Essays*, 115), and it could also be said that since
there is no possibility of this text being sung at **1/1–** (see above) there would

be no rationale in singing it here.

There is also a stronger reason, however. All the liturgical versions noted here provide a single-syllable 'ω' ('oo' in the printed version of PS(P), 94v) in place of the Vulgate's 'omega': the single-syllable setting is musically inescapable. **1/1** follows this, 'oo' being rhymed with 'soe' (line **3**). Thus **1/1–2** uses the liturgical version, although it cannot be sung, while **2/1–** uses the Vulgate version.

2/208+lat supremus volucris, penna serpens, pede forma, forma puella

This line seems to provide the authority for the Demon's description of the serpent in the previous speech, and there is surely no reason to speak it. It is not a liturgical text, as far as I know, and would not be sung.

3 Noah's Flood
4 Abraham
No Latin text.

5 Moses
5/131+lat Surgite dei patriae et opitulamini nobis et in
      necessitate nos defendite.

Lumiansky and Mills identify this text as coming from Deuteronomy 32/37–8, and point out that there is no textual indication that it should be spoken. Declamation by Balaak is a possibility, of course: this appears not to be a liturgical text, and the question of singing it does not arise.

5/319+sd Orietur stella ex Jacobb et exurget homo de Israell et
      consurget omnes duces alienigenarum et erit omnis
      terra possessio eius.

The speech following gives a paraphrase of this text, so this SD need not necessarily be taken to mean that Balaam actually speaks the Latin. There is however no point to the SD if the Latin is not spoken (and AR omit the SD, presumably for that reason).

Lumiansky and Mills note that this text is not close to the biblical source, Numbers 24/17 (*Chester* II, 72). This is in fact the liturgical version, used for an 8th-mode responsory in Advent (AS, plate j). The monastic version has 'confringet' for 'consurget': see **IB/288+sd**, below. It does not seem likely that Balaam sings this text, but this leaves us with a question to answer: In what circumstances would the dramatist (or a later producer) introduce the liturgical version of this prophecy rather than the Vulgate version? A possible reason, suggested by Lumiansky and Mills, is that this version is more suitable in

the context of the play. Another reason may be that the dramatist (or producer) was for some reason better acquainted with a non-Vulgate version with
this wording. A third would be specifically that the non-Vulgate version with
which he was best acquainted was in fact the liturgical version. I have already
suggested this last possibility in general terms (6.1, above), and the question is
further discussed below, under Manuscript H's version of the text.

5/435+lat Stetit Phinees et placavit et cessavit quassatio et
      reputatum est ei ad justitiam in generatione sue etc.

The Doctor's discussion in the lines before this requires the text to be heard by
the audience. It should presumably be spoken: certainly there is no reason to
sing it. Lumiansky and Mills identify it as Psalm 105/30–1, with some
variation. I have not found it as a liturgical text.

Appendix IB Moses (Manuscript H)
The version of play 5 transmitted by manuscript H, as stated above, contains
seven Latin quotations. All but one appear under the SH for the speech following
in which a translation/paraphrase is found, and the one exception is ascribed to
the writings of the prophet concerned. It would appear, then, that each prophet
should speak the Latin quotation before the vernacular speech dealing with it:
and as only the first is apparently a liturgical text, it seems that the dramatist
did not intend them to be sung. **IB/288+sd+lat** is the equivalent of **5/319+sd**, but
with 'confringet' for 'consurget'. As noted above for the Group version of the
play, this is the monastic reading of the text (WA, 5). How are we to explain the
two versions? It seems most likely, I think, that the original dramatist took his
text (as we should expect) from the monastic liturgy that he knew best; that the
text was 'corrected' according to the Sarum version after the dissolution of St
Werburgh's Abbey; that the Group scribes copied the 'corrected' version; but that
Miller, the most learned and thoughtful of the Chester play copyists (*Essays*, 75–
6), decided to reinstate the cancelled monastic reading. *Inter alia* this means that
the Exemplar was in existence before the dissolution of the Abbey (1539–40) but
was also in use afterwards.

IB/312+lat, IB/328+lat, IB/344+lat, IB/360+lat, and **IB/376+lat** Lumiansky and
  Mills discuss these texts, their references, and their relation to the Vulgate
  versions (*Chester* II, 387–8). They are apparently not liturgical texts, and there
  is no question of singing them.

IB/392+lat Lumiansky and Mills discuss this quotation (*Chester* II, 389). The 3rd-
  mode antiphon (for the Benedictus in the 3rd week of Advent) on this text has
  'non eris' for 'nequaquam' (WA, 17; AS, plate h): this quotation is apparently
  not a liturgical version, therefore, and there is no question of singing it.

6 *The Annunciation*
6/64+sd Magnificat etc.

6/72+lat Et exultavit spiritus meus in Deo etc.

The word 'canticum' in **64+sd** (see 6.2) probably indicates the Vespers canticle rather than any of the various other liturgical pieces that use the text. Of these latter, two are found in the Worcester use: an antiphon (WA, 64–5: largely syllabic chant, range f–c') does not set enough text, but a responsory verse (WA, 356: neumatic/melismatic chant, range f–d') sets the text 'Magnificat anima mea dominum et exultavit spiritus meus in deo salutare meo' and so could in theory be used. Further on the choice of piece here, see 6.6.

6/666+sd   Haec est ara Dei caeli

This is apparently not a liturgical piece: but there are several parallel texts, on which this could have been modelled, in the services for the consecration of a church. The first verse of *Salve festa dies* on that occasion begins 'Hec est aula dei pacis', for instance (PS(P), 129r: syllabic chant, range c–c'). Assuming that the text of which this SD gives the incipit has the same number of syllables as the hymn-verse, therefore, the same tune could be used: but we do not have any more text than is given in the SD, and in any case the SD requires the actor to provide a tune, which suggests that none exists for it.

7 *The Shepherds*
7/357+sd Gloria in excelsis Deo et in terra pax hominibus bonae voluntatis.

This text is from Luke 2/14, except that 'excelsis' is substituted for the Vulgate 'altissimis': this reading shows the text to be the liturgical version.

This is not the Gloria of the Mass: as the SD and the shepherds' discussion both show, it is the incipit Gloria with text up to 'voluntatis'. The text appears twice in the services of Christmas Day:

(a) Verse of the first responsory at Matins, *Hodie nobis celorum rex* (WA, 27–8; AS, 47).
Syllabic/neumatic chant, range f–d', c-clef.

(b) Benedictus antiphon at Lauds (WA, 32; AS, 53).
The text has two alleluias added.
Largely syllabic chant, range d–c', c-clef.

Both versions are known in liturgical dramas, but the lack of alleluias in this

SD points towards (a) rather than (b) in the present case. In England, too, there was a tradition of special performance of the responsory verse, which has a bearing on its dramatic possibilities. In the Sarum use the verse was sung by five boys in a high place above the choir altar, holding lighted candles (Harrison *Music in Medieval Britain*, 107, and see the rubric on AS, 47): here the visual and aural reference to the angelic hymn, including the effect of light, is obvious even if it remains within the orbit of liturgy. This treatment suggests that the responsory verse rather than the antiphon would come to the dramatist's mind as a dramatic item.

The identification of the Gloria as the responsory verse is supported also by the incidence of polyphonic settings of the verse, rather than of the antiphon, in England. Further on this, see I, 256–8.

The shepherds' discussion of various parts of the Gloria text is noticed above, 6.3.

7/691 [TERTIUS PASTOR]   Amen ...

This line is discussed in 6.3, above.

8 *The Three Kings*
8/212+lat   Vidimus stellam eius in oriente et venimus cum muneribus adorare eum

As Lumiansky and Mills note, the Vulgate text of Matthew 2/2 reads:
    vidimus enim stellam ejus in oriente et venimus adorare eum.
This differs considerably from the Chester version. The liturgical text is however closer:
    Vidimus stellam eius in oriente et venimus cum muneribus adorare dominum.
There are three possible sources for this liturgical text:

(a) Alleluia verse for Epiphany (GS, 19).
    Neumatic/melismatic chant, range A–a, f-clef.

(b) Communion for Epiphany (GS, 19).
    Syllabic/neumatic chant, range d–c', c-clef.

(c) Antiphon (given as Benedictus antiphon, fourth day of the Octave of the Epiphany, in AM, 299).
    Syllabic chant, range c–a, f-clef.

Although the text 'Vidimus stellam' is not indexed in WA and no piece with this text is given there, the verbal incipit does appear (WA, 58). It therefore seems that the liturgical text was known in the monastic liturgy. Since the liturgical items all give 'dominum' for the SD's 'eum', the SD does not seem to present a liturgical text, even though the quotation is much closer to the liturgical version than to the Vulgate. The quotation appears under the SH, so the First King apparently speaks it: but there is no reason to think that he should sing it.[8]

8/268+lat   Non auferetur sceptrum de Juda et dux de foemore
             eius, donec veniet qui mittendus est et erit ipse
             expectatio gentium

This quotation is correctly ascribed to Genesis 49/10 (*Chester* II, 132). The Vulgate has 'femore' for 'foemore', 'veniat' for the Chester 'veniet' and 'ipse erit' for 'erit ipse'.

The two liturgical items using this text both follow the Vulgate wording exactly:

(a) Magnificat antiphon (WA, 13).
    Syllabic/neumatic chant, range c–a, c-clef.

(b) Respond (WA, 23; AS, 37).
    Neumatic/melismatic chant, range c–b♭, d-clef.

A different antiphon (AS, plate B) does not set all of the text.

Only Manuscript B shows this quotation below the SH, where the Doctor would speak it. There seems no reason to sing it in any case.

8/289+lat   Cum venerit sancta sanctorum cessabit unctio vestra.

Lumiansky and Mills discuss this text (*Chester* II, 132–3), pointing out that it is not a scriptural text as it stands. Nor can I find it in the liturgy, and there is apparently no question of singing it.

8/310+lat   Et tu Bethlem quidem terra Juda nequaquam minima es in
             principibus Judae. Ex te enim exiet dux qui reget populum
             meum Israell

The Benedictus antiphon 'Tu Bethleem' is too far removed from this for there to be any question of the liturgical item being sung: see above, under **IB/392+ lat** for play 5.

---

[8] Perhaps 'eum' was a misreading for dn̄m (i.e. dominum); or the change could have been made for dramatic purposes.

8/317+lat Ambulabunt gentes in lumine tuo et reges in splendore ortus tui.

Lumiansky and Mills identify this as part of the third lection at Matins on the Feast of the Epiphany in the Sarum use, which comes from Isaiah 60/3.[9] Apart from the initial 'Et' that occurs in both the Vulgate and the lection, this quotation is precise. The text also occurs as the verse to the responsory 'Illuminare illuminare ierusalem' (WA, 53; AS, 85):

> Et ambulabunt gentes in lumine tuo et reges in splendore ortus
> tui.

Syllabic/neumatic chant, range f–d', c-clef.

8/324+lat Effundam super parvulum istum furorem meum et super consilium juvenum, disperdam parvulos de fores, et juvenes in plateis morientur gladio meo

Lumiansky and Mills discuss this text (*Chester* II, 134). It is apparently not a liturgical item.

8/338+lat Reges Tharsis et Insule munera offerent. Reges Arabum et Saba dona adducent.

As the text goes on to say, this is Psalm 71/10 (AV 72): it is precisely quoted. The text occurs in the liturgy as follows:

(a) Antiphon for the Epiphany (WA, 53; AS, 85):

> Reges tharsis et insule munera offerent regi domino.

Syllabic chant, range d–b♭, c-clef.

(b) Respond for the Epiphany (WA, 55; AS, 85; PS(P), 18v):

> Reges tharsis et insule munera offerent reges arabum et saba
> dona domino deo adducent.

Neumatic/melismatic chant, range A–g, c-clef.

(c) Responsory verse (WA, 53; AS, 85):

> Reges tharsis et insule munera offerent reges arabum et saba
> dona adducent.

Neumatic chant, range b–f', c-clef.

---

9   *Chester* II, 134; and see BS, cccxxii.

(d) Short responsory (WA, 58):
>Reges tharsis et insule munera offerent.
>V.   Reges arabum et saba dona adducent.
>Syllabic chant, range c–g, c-clef.

(e) Offertory, Feast of the Epiphany (GS, 19):
>Text as (c), with considerable addition.

The obvious probabilities are (c) and (d), since these give the Chester text exactly. The short responsory is musically easy, the responsory verse considerably more difficult.

9 *The Offering of the Three Kings*
No Latin text or incipits.

10 *The Slaughter of the Innocents*
10/288+sd   Ecce dominus ascendet super nubem levem, et ingrediatur
>Egiptum, et movebuntur simulachra Egipti a facie domini
>exercituum

This is the text sung by the angel, Isaiah 19/1. In the Roman rite it is the first reading at Matins on the Thursday in Advent II; but I cannot find it in the Sarum use, as a reading or as a sung liturgical text, nor in WA.

It is obviously related to the Advent text 'Ecce dominus veniet', however, and it is possible that the Chester words were intended to be fitted to one of the tunes for that piece. The liturgical text was probably inspired by Zechariah 14, although it is not a quotation of any of it, and that chapter also provides almost all of the vocabulary and ideas contained in the Chester text. The liturgical texts starting with 'Ecce dominus veniet' are:

(a) Antiphon for First Sunday in Advent (WA, 6–7):
>Ecce dominus veniet et omnes sancti eius cum eo: et erit in die illa
>lux magna. Alleluia.
>Syllabic chant, range f–d', c-clef.

(b) Responsory in Advent (WA, 10):
>Ecce dominus veniet et omnes sancti eius cum eo: et erit in die illa
>lux magna et exibunt de ierusalem sicut aqua munda et regnabit
>dominus in eternum super omnes gentes.
>V.   Ecce cum virtute ...
>Melismatic chant, range f–e', b♭-clef.

(c) Communion in Advent (GS, 7):
  Text as for (a), without the Alleluia.
  Syllabic/neumatic chant, range g–g′, c-clef.

Of these, (b) is perhaps too long, especially in view of its melismatic character, while the Alleluia of (a) is unnecessary. It would be possible to adapt the Chester words to the chant of (c). This solution is not convincing, however, as a piece of word-setting, and the search should continue for a setting of the Chester words.

10/497+sd   Ex Egipto vocavi Filium meum ut salvum faciet populum meum

The Advent antiphon 'Ex Egypto' is found in the Worcester Antiphoner (WA, 16), where it is set for St Lucia's day, and also in the Sarum use (SA, 20 and 21):
  Ex egipto vocavi filium meum veniet ut salves populum suum
The Sarum version is a syllabic chant: the Worcester tune is syllabic/neumatic, recognisably the same but with some decoration, and with a range f–e′.

In view of the singing, and the fact that (as Lumiansky and Mills note, *Chester* II, 159) the Chester text is an amalgamation of two Vulgate texts, it would seem that the liturgical version was intended. Whether the text-variants were intended or not is another matter: 'salvum faciet' comes from Matthew 1/21, and it may simply be the result of the dramatist quoting the liturgical text from memory and confusing it with the Vulgate reading.

11 *The Purification, and Christ and the Doctors*
11/24+sd   Ecce virgo concipiet et pariet filium etc.

This comes from Isaiah 7/14. The 'etc.' implies the rest of the verse, which adds 'et vocabitur nomen eius Emmanuel'. The whole sentence is used as a liturgical text for a communion in the Sarum use (GS, 6). A related text, which owes its second half to Isaiah 9/6, appears as a responsory at Worcester (WA, 5):
  Ecce virgo concipiet et pariet filium dicit dominus et vocabitur
  nomen eius admirabilis deus fortis

The SD carries two clear implications. The first is that Simeon reads the Bible, so that the text is a single one and therefore Isaiah 7/14, the first of those given above. In any case, **11/29**, part of the English paraphrase, gives 'a sonne called Emanuell', which excludes the responsory text. Second, there is no reason for Simeon to sing the text, although he must apparently read it out loud.

11/166+sd   Nunc dimittis servum tuum, domine

The text is biblical, from Luke 2/29. The SD requires it to be sung, so a liturgical setting of the words is likely. The text appears as follows:

(a) Compline canticle (= Luke 2/29–32). In this guise, *Nunc dimittis* is chanted as a psalm. In some cases (e.g. in the Purification procession, PS(P), 138r) it is sung under an antiphon.

(b) Tract, feast of the Purification (GS, plate k):
Complete canticle.
Neumatic/melismatic chant, range c–d', c-clef.

(c) Verse to the antiphon *Lumen ad revelationem*, feast of the Purification (GS, 180). The whole psalm (i.e. canticle) is required to be sung, so this is equivalent to PS(P), 138r, listed as (a), above.

(d) Antiphon, feast of the Purification (WA, 272; AS, 404):
Nunc dimittis domine servum tuum in pace: quia viderunt
oculi mei salutare tuum
Mainly syllabic chant, range g–e', c-clef.

The word order is different from that of the Chester SD: on the other hand this antiphon, like manuscript B, omits 'secundum verbum tuum' (see below).

The SD is followed, **11/167–74**, by Simeon's English paraphrase of the whole *Nunc dimittis* text, which is evidence that the whole canticle should be sung here, as in (a) or (b), above. The choice may depend on the singing ability of the actor playing Simeon, and on the dramatic effect required. Singing the text as a psalm would certainly be more direct: singing it as a tract would be more decorative and, with a good singer, more impressive musically. If the former method is chosen, then the text should not be sung under an antiphon.

Manuscript B's reading 'in pace' for 'etc' leaves out 'secundum verbum tuum', so it is not a plain re-substitution of omitted text but an indication of how far the text goes. The most likely reason for B's reading is that the words 'in pace' were added to the Exemplar at some stage, perhaps marginally, to indicate a shorter version of the *Nunc dimittis* in which Simeon should sing only as far as those words – that is, to the end of the first verse of the canticle. In the case of either (a) or (b), above, this verse would be musically self-contained. It is also possible that 'in pace', by its omission of 'secundum verbum tuum', indicates the (complete) antiphon, (d) above, as the piece to be sung.

It is impossible to know when this shorter performance was proposed.

12 *The Temptation, and The Woman Taken in Adultery*
No Latin text or incipits.

13 *The Blind Chelidonian, and The Raising of Lazarus*
13/1–   Ego sum lux mundi. Qui sequitur me non ambulat in tenebris
              sed habebit lumen vitae

This is an exact quotation of Christ's words in John 8/12. The text appears as
an antiphon in the fourth week in Lent:

(a) Monastic use (WA, 105):
      Ego sum lux mundi qui sequitur me non ambulabit in tenebris sed
      habebit lumen vite dicit dominus
   Neumatic chant, range c–a, c-clef.

(b) Secular use (AS, 189):
      Ego sum lux mundi qui sequitur me non ambulat in tenebris sed
      habebit lumen vite dicit dominus
   Largely syllabic chant, range d–c', c-clef.

'Dicit dominus ' would be inappropriate in the Chester context, because the
play text gives this line to Christ in all manuscripts. It is tempting to see A's
reading 'ambulabat' as reflecting the monastic antiphon text, but A is not
trustworthy here (see the notes to *Chester* 230). There seems no reason to think
that this should be sung, although no doubt Christ proclaims it: a paraphrase
follows in lines **1–3**.

13/8   [JESUS]   Ego et Pater unum sumus: my Father and I are all on

Latin and its translation in a single line. There is clearly no question of this
Latin being sung.

13/21   [JESUS]   bonus pastor ponit animam suam pro ovibus suis

This line is an integral part of the stanza, rhyming with 'wytnes' in the
previous line. The text is a well known one (John 10/11), the Vulgate reading
'animam suam dat' for Chester's 'ponit animam suam': but the text does not
seem to occur in the liturgy, and in any case there is no reason to think that it
should be sung here. The paraphrase has already occurred, at **18–19**.

13/35+Lat   Si vos manseritis in sermone meo, veri discipuli mei eritis, et
              cognoscetis veritatem, et veritas liberabit vos

This text is the words of Christ in John 8/31–2, quoted exactly: the para-phrase has already occurred, at lines **31–5**. As with the Latin preceding the first line of the play, there seems little reason to think that it should be sung rather than spoken. The text does appear, as above, set as an antiphon (WA, 90; SA, 160).

13/356+lat [JESUS] Oportet me operari opera eius qui misit me donec dies est; venit nox quando nemo potest operari. Quamdiu sum in mundo, lux sum mundi

Christ's words in John 9/4–5 begin 'Me oportet operari opera eius', but are otherwise quoted exactly in Chester. This text is not paraphrased, but the speech before it, lines **337–56**, is explanatory.

I can find no liturgical setting of this text. As in previous instances in this play, there seems no reason why the text should be sung: but in this case I feel less convinced than in the others that the text needs even to be spoken.

14 Christ at the House of Simon the Leper; Christ and the Money-Lenders; and Judas's Plot

The episode of Mary Magdalene in the house of Simon the Leper is important for its liturgical associations, although no Latin text is involved. At **14/56+sd** Mary opens her box of ointment, makes 'an indication of anointing', wets the feet of Jesus with her tears, and wipes them dry with her hair.[10] This is not quite what happens according to the later speeches of Jesus, however, where it appears that the order of events has been:
1 she washed his feet with her tears (line **103**);
2 she wiped them with her hair (**104**);
3 she kissed each of his feet (**107**); and
4 she anointed his feet with oil (**110**).

Clearly this is a more sensible order in which events happen, and it follows one of the gospel narrations (see I, 273). Lumiansky and Mills rehearse the dif-ferences between the various Gospel accounts of this episode (*Chester* II, 200, notes to **104**, **110**), but note that the play is based on St Luke's Gospel at this point. In fact, Luke 7/38 mentions the four events just listed, in the order just given (which is the order of the play). **56+sd**, then, is inadequate: the full infor-mation, based on Luke's account, is contained in Jesus's words in lines **103–4** and **107–10**.

It is perhaps most important to see that in this play the episode is raised to the level of a Mandatum. We are accustomed to think of the Mandatum as being

---

[10] I am indebted to Mills *Chester Modernised*, p. 240, for the translation of this SD; and before that to his translation made for the 1983 performance of the cycle at Leeds.

based on Christ's own actions at the Last Supper, and indeed the antiphon texts for the Mandatum ceremony (like the name Mandatum itself) are taken from the Gospel accounts of that event. But Luke 7/38 has all the constituents of a Mandatum, including the kissing of the feet which is so important a part of the liturgical ceremony but does not appear in the narratives of the Last Supper (see I, 272–6). In **14/101–10**, however, Jesus makes a point of spelling out the events just detailed and of emphasising their significance. It would seem, therefore, that in expanding the bare narrative of Luke 7/38, the dramatist has drawn on his experience of the Mandatum ceremony.

14/207 and **208+sd** Hosanna

> Hosanna filio David. Benedictus qui venit in nomine domini.
> Hosanna in excelsis

The text is from Matthew 21/9, accurately quoted, except that the Vulgate has 'altissimis' for 'excelsis'. John 12/13 gives a similar text, but omitting 'filio David' and 'hosanna in altissimis' and adding 'rex Israel' after 'domini'.

The Chester text reference, line **207**, goes with the SD. In all manuscripts but H the boys sing 'Hosanna' and the citizens sing the whole text: this may mean that the boys sing the intonation, but if so the citizens repeat it. Manuscript H does not require the boys to sing, but makes it explicit that the citizens do. We may assume, I think, that only one text is involved.

The only liturgical setting is the antiphon for Palm Sunday (AS, 206; WA, 112 and 209):

> Osanna filio david: benedictus qui venit in nomine domini rex
> israel. Osanna in excelsis

This is a largely syllabic chant, range f–e'. It is the only liturgical piece that begins 'Osanna filio David': it is close to Matthew's text, but borrows the 'rex Israel' from John's.

The antiphon *Pueri hebreorum vestimenta* uses Matthew's version in a musically complete section, but it does not include the final 'Hosanna in excelsis' of the Chester SD (WA, 113 and 207; AS, 206–7; PS(P), 40r; GS, 78). It seems probable that the antiphon *Hosanna filio David* was intended, despite the omission of 'rex Israel' from the SD.

15 *The Last Supper, and The Betrayal*
No Latin text or incipits.

16 *The Trial and Flagellation*
16/134–5 PILATUS   Per vous, syr Cayphas; dye vos, syr Annas
                    et sum desepte Judas; vel atres in fuit.

There are problems connected with this French/Latin text, discussed by Lumiansky and Mills (*Chester* II, 230–1). There is no question of singing it, however.

16/275 PILATE Ergo, a kinge thou art, or was.

There is no question of singing.

16A: The Passion
16A/359+lat Consummatum est

The last Word from the Cross, reported in John 19/30: omitted in H.

This is not a liturgical incipit: and, although it is not actually paraphrased in the preceding speech, it does not really need even to be spoken, although it could be. Certainly there is no question of singing.

17 The Harrowing of Hell
17/32+lat Populus qui ambulabat in tenebris vidit lucem magnam

This is spoken by Isaiah, as the previous lines show, although it is not an integral part of the stanza: it is paraphrased in the three lines following. It is accurately quoted from Isaiah 9/2.

This text is apparently not a liturgical incipit: in any case there is no reason to think that Isaiah sings it rather than speaking it.

17/48+lat Nunc dimittis servum tuum, domine, secundum verbum tuum, in pace

An accurate quotation, by Simeon, of Luke 2/29 (see under **11/166+sd**, above). As with **32+lat**, the text must be heard but there is no reason to think that it should be sung rather than spoken.

17/64+lat Penitentiam agite! Appropinquat enim regnum caelorum

Matthew 3/2 reads 'appropinquavit' for Chester's 'appropinquat'. This is probably a misreading or misremembering on the part of the scribe who wrote the line in the Exemplar. This is apparently not a liturgical text, and, as before in this play, there seems no reason for it to be sung rather than spoken (by John the Baptist).

17/72+lat Ecce agnus Dei, ecce qui tollit peccata mundi

Again spoken, rather than sung, by John the Baptist. It is a quotation from

John 1/29: but the gospel reads 'peccatum' for Chester's 'peccata', which is presumably by contamination from liturgical texts.

The most obvious candidate for causing contamination is the Agnus Dei of the Mass Ordinary:

> Agnus dei qui tollis peccata mundi, miserere nobis.
> Agnus dei qui tollis peccata mundi, miserere nobis.
> Agnus dei qui tollis peccata mundi, dona nobis pacem.

This is clearly not the text quoted in Chester, however, for which there are other possibilities:

(a) Responsory for the Circumcision (AS, 77):
Melismatic/neumatic chant, range f–f'.
The text concerned is only the first part of this responsory, although it is musically self-contained.

(b) Verse to the Responsory *Rex noster* (WA, 12; AS, 26 and plate f):
Neumatic/melismatic chant, range d–a.

It does not seem likely that the text is sung, rather than spoken, in the play: but the scribe's knowledge of any of these liturgical items might have caused him to write 'peccata' instead of 'peccatum' when writing this text into the Exemplar.

17/108+lat   Tristis est anima mea usque ad mortem (BH only)

Part of Christ's words in Matthew 26/38 and Mark 14/34. This text is the opening, musically self-contained, of a responsory (WA, 118; AS, 216). Since the text is associated in Chester with Satan's report of Christ's words, it is doubtful if it needs to be heard at all: its omission from all but BH perhaps reflects this. Certainly Satan is unlikely to sing it.

17/152+sd   Attollite portas, principes, vestras, et elevamini portae aeternales, et introibit rex gloriae

For the liturgical use of this psalm-text, see I, 278–83, and especially 279. There is no reason to think that Christ sings this text, although he must presumably declaim it: it is paraphrased in the four lines that follow it.

17/192+lat Confiteantur domino misericordiae eius et mirabilia eius, filius hominis contrivit portas aereas et vectes ferreas confregit

A not wholly accurate quotation of Psalm 106/15–16. The text is used, up to 'filiis hominum' (which is the correct reading) as a gradual verse in the Sarum use (GS, 21–2 and 182): this piece's exclusion of the text from 'contrivit' onwards confirms the impression given by the Chester text, that David should speak the Latin, not sing it, if indeed it needs to be heard at all (it is omitted in H).

17/276+sd   Te Deum laudamus

Sung, according to the SD, and intoned by Michael. This can only be the Matins hymn. Michael requires it to be sung 'with great solempnitie' (line **276**) – that is, in a dignified, ceremonial, but joyful manner – so the setting should be the solemn tone used for acts of thanksgiving. The Sarum version is printed in Wolfgang Hopyl's Sarum Antiphoner (*Pars aestivalis*, 1520); the monastic version is in WA, 5 and AM, 1250–3.

18 *The Resurrection*
18/1–8 A mixed French/Latin speech by Pilate, with French dominant. As was the case in **16/134–5**, there is no question of singing here.

18/153+sd   Christus resurgens a mortuis etc.

This text appears in the liturgy for Easter Day as follows:

(a) Alleluia verse (Sandon V, 39):
     Christus resurgens ex mortuis iam non moritur mors illi ultra non
     dominabitur
  Melismatic/neumatic chant, range g–g'.

(b) Responsory (WA, 223):
     To the text of (a) is added 'quod enim vivit vivit deo alleluia alleluia'.
     Neumatic/melismatic chant, range e–a'.

(c) Communion (Sandon V, 18):
     Text as (a), with an 'alleluia ' following 'moritur ' and two more at the end.
     Neumatic/syllabic chant, range e–e'.

(d) Antiphon (WA, 133; AS, 241; PS(P), 83v–84r):
     Text as (b).
     Neumatic/melismatic chant, 1st mode, range c–b flat.

There is little to choose between these four possibilities, either in difficulty or in textual and musical suitability.

There are no more Latin lines or incipits in this play, either in the main text or in the final scene as transmitted by HR (*Chester*, Appendix ID).

19 The Road to Emmaus, and Doubting Thomas

19/95+lat Quemadmodum mater consolatur filios suos, ita et ego consolabor vos; et in Jerusalem consolabimini. Esaias, capitulo sexagesino sexto

This is not an accurate quotation of Isaiah 66/13, which begins 'Quomodo si cui mater blandiatur, ...'. The text does not seem to be used for a liturgical item.

Probably Jesus should speak these Latin lines, since they give the original of what he has just quoted in English. There is no reason to think that he should sing them.

20 The Ascension

20/1– Pax vobis; ego sum; nolite timere

This is the start of Jesus's speech: they are his words in Luke 24/36. In lines **1–4** he translates them.

The Latin should certainly be spoken, but I see no reason to sing it. The text seems not to occur in the English liturgical uses.

20/16+lat Spiritus quidem carnem et ossa non habet sic me videtis habere

This text, an inaccurate quotation of part of Luke 24/39, has been translated in lines **14–16**: but lines **9–12** have already translated verse 38 and the earlier part of 39, so that this Latin text is only a part of what has been said.

I cannot find the antiphon *Spiritus carnem et ossa* in the Sarum and monastic books: but in any case there is no reason to sing this text, although speaking it would be dramatically sensible.

20/96+sd Data est mihi omnis potestas in caelo et in terra

Jesus speaks this line, which is an accurate quotation of his words in Matthew 28/18. The line occurs as a Magnificat antiphon, with 'alleluia' added (WA, 135), and as a communion, with 'alleluia', the next gospel verse, and two final alleluias (Sandon V, 26; GS, 123). There is no reason to think that the quotation should be sung, however.

20/104+sd+lat The musical scene at the Ascension consists of six versets. Lumiansky and Mills number the Latin sections from [a] to [h], but [b] and [h] are SDs. Sections [c]–[g] inclusive all consist of SH plus text.

[a] Ascendo ad Patrem meum et Patrem vestrum, Deum meum et Deum vestrum. Alleluya

This is part of John 20/17, accurately quoted. The 'alleluia' is not scriptural, but is added when this text occurs as the Benedictus antiphon on Ascension Day (WA, 150; AS, 270): this has a syllabic chant, 7th mode, range g–g'.

The remaining sections draw their texts from Isaiah 63/1–3. In the Roman use they form part of the Old Testament reading at Mass on Wednesday in Holy Week, and as such they could be sung to a reading tone.[11] If the Chester speeches were performed in this way there was of course no musical problem in singing them after [a].

The Chester speeches omit the first half of Isaiah 63/2, however, and although this may be an unintended omission in the Exemplar it suggests that these lines should be sought in a different liturgical context. In fact, the verses appear also as the Vespers antiphons for the Feast of the Blood of Jesus (1 July) in the Roman use (LU, 1536–7), but I have not found them in the medieval monastic or Sarum uses. Like the Chester version, the antiphons use only the first half of Isaiah 63/3: but they also omit part of verse 1, and they add Revelation 19/13. The distribution of text in the Chester version and in the antiphons is shown in Table 10.

Although the antiphons do not precisely correspond to the Chester text, it is possible that some other use includes antiphons based on the same passage from Isaiah but with the text distributed as it is in the Chester text. The Roman antiphons are musically compatible with the Sarum *Ascendo ad Patrem meum*, a matter that is discussed below, and this gives at least some hope that the Chester text was based on a musical source.

An additional matter that must be discussed here is the appearance of three of the Chester speeches in the Fleury *Peregrinus* play, with different music.[12] The distribution of the Fleury text is also shown in Table 10. It may be, therefore, that French uses also included antiphons based on this Isaiah text, and that the Chester text was based on a French source.

The musical characteristics of the antiphons and the relevant sections of the Fleury settings are:

---

[11] See *Essays*, 150.

[12] See Dutka *Music in the English Mystery Plays*, 69; the music is in Coussemaker *Drames liturgiques*, 198–9.

Antiphon 1	Syllabic chant, 7th mode, range g–e′.
Fleury 1	Syllabic/neumatic, 4th mode, range e–c′.
Fleury 2	Neumatic/syllabic, 4th mode, range e–c′.
Antiphon 2	Syllabic chant, 8th mode, range f–d′.
	Not in Fleury.
Antiphon 3	Text from Revelation 13/19, not in Chester.
Antiphon 4	Syllabic chant, 8th mode, range e–d′.
	Not in Fleury.
Antiphon 5	Syllabic chant, 2nd mode, range c–a.
Fleury 3	Syllabic/neumatic chant, 4th mode, range c–a.
	In Fleury this text appears as the second half of a speech, with the changed word-order 'Solus calcavi torcular': the first part of the speech begins 'Quid turbati estis' (Luke 24/38).

The readings from the Fleury play are perhaps slightly closer to the Chester version than are the Roman antiphons. The sections from Isaiah 63 are not contiguous in the Fleury manuscript, however, and more information is needed about the immediate source of the Fleury version before any conclusion can be reached about the Chester dramatist's source for this scene.

The antiphon *Ascendo ad Patrem meum*, which is in the 7th mode, is musically compatible with the Roman antiphons, which are in modes 7, 8, and 2. The whole scene therefore works well musically if the antiphons are used. The Fleury settings, on the other hand, are all in mode 4, which would not follow well from the 7th-mode chant of *Ascendo*. Although it would be possible to put the Sarum *Ascendo* with the Fleury pieces, therefore, that is not an ideal solution.

In all, the problem raised by this scene is as yet insoluble. The best practical solution, probably, would be to perform *Ascendo ad Patrem meum* in the Sarum setting, followed by the rest of the text sung to a reading tone. But I do not think that this was what the Chester dramatist intended, and expect that the dramatist was using some setting that I have not found.

The Latin text is partly, and only loosely, translated in lines **105–28**.

20/152+sd1   Exaltare domine in virtute tua: cantabimus et psallemus virtutes tuas

This is an exact quotation of Psalm 20/14, and so could be sung as a single psalm-verse to a psalm-tone. But H adds 'Alleluya' at the end, and this sug-

TABLE 10 : DISTRIBUTION OF TEXT OF CHESTER VERSETS

Chester versets	Text	Isaiah 63	Anti-phons	Fleury
[b]	SD			
[c]	Quis est iste, qui venit de Edom, tinctis vestibus de Bosra?	1(i)	1a	1
[d]	iste formosus in stola sua, gradiens in multitudine fortitudinis suae	1(ii) 1(iii)	1b	2
[e]	Ego qui loquor justitiam, et propugnator sum ad salvandum	1(iv)		2
	[Revelation 13/19] Vestitus erat veste aspersa sanguine, et vocatur nomen ejus Verbum Dei			3
	Quare ergo rubrum est indumentum tuum	2(i)		4a
[f]	et vestimenta tua sicut calcantium in torculari?	2(ii)		4b
	Much intervening material			
[g]	Torcular calcavi solus, et de gentibus non est vir mecum	3(i)	5	3
	NB changed word order			
[h]	SD			

gests one of the liturgical items with this text, of which there are two:

(a) Antiphon 6, Ascension (WA, 147; AS, 271):
  Exaltare domine in virtute tua: cantabimus et psallemus. Alleluya.
Syllabic chant, transposed 4th mode, range f–e'.

(b) Responsory, Ascension:

This responsory occurs in both the monastic and the secular uses, with the same music in the respond: but the verses are different. The monastic version (WA, 147) is:

Exaltare domine, Alleluia: in virtute tua, Alleluia.

V. Cantabimus et psallemus virtutes tuas domine.

R. In vir[tute tua, Alleluia].

Neumatic/melismatic chant, 7th mode, range e–g'.

The secular version is (AS, 274):

Exaltare domine, Alleluia: in virtute tua, Alleluia.

V. Cantabimus et psallemus.

R. In virtute [tua, Alleluia].

Neumatic/melismatic chant, 7th mode, range f–f'.

The surviving texts show that the Exemplar transmitted a corrupt version of this incipit. It is not easy to decide between the various liturgical texts: 'virtutes tuas' suggests the monastic version of the responsory, but is not conclusive. Either piece would lead well into *Viri Galilei*, which follows immediately.

20/152+sd2 Viri Gallilei, quid aspicitis in caelum?

Acts 1/11 reads 'statis aspicientes' for 'aspicitis': so Chester's version is liturgical, the antiphon for Ascension Day (WA, 149; AS, 269):

Viri galilei quid aspicitis in celum: hic iesus qui assumptus est a vobis in celum sic veniet. Alleluia.

Syllabic chant, 7th mode, range f–e'.

The first line, up to 'celum' is not self-sufficient musically, although it ends on the final. It may therefore be assumed that the whole antiphon was sung.

The Ascension Day responsory (WA, 149; AS, 269; PS(P), 113r–v), introit (GS, 135) and offertory (GS, 133; PS(P), 107r–v) all begin 'Viri galilei quid admiramini aspicientes', and therefore need not be considered.

The text of the antiphon is translated in lines **153–60**, although without the Alleluia.

21 Pentecost

21/32+lat   Fiat habitatio eius deserta et non sit qui habitet in eo. Episcopatum eius accipiat alter.

Spoken by Peter, but not integral to the stanza. The Latin is not translated, and is necessary for the sense of Peter's speech. It must therefore be heard, but there is no reason to think that it should be sung.

Lumiansky and Mills identify and discuss the scriptural sources for this quotation, which is inaccurate (*Chester* II, 308). There is apparently no liturgical version of it.

21/96+lat   Tunc Johannes quidem baptizavit aqua: vos autem baptizabimini Spiritu Sancto non post multos hos dies.

Acts 1/5. This is the authority for the preceding eight lines, which are its paraphrase. The Latin does not need to be heard: indeed, since its paraphrase is divided between Bartholomew and Mathias it may even sound a little strange if spoken. There is no reason to think that it should be sung. The text does not seem to be a liturgical incipit, but it appears as the chapter at none on Whitsunday (AS, 277).

Lumiansky and Mills discuss Chester's corruptions of the biblical text (*Chester* II, 310).

21/104+lat   Non est vestrum nosse tempora vel momenta quae Pater posuit in sua potestate.

Acts 1/7. This is paraphrased in the previous three lines, spoken by Thaddeus. There is a better case here for speaking the lines, but still none for singing them. This text does not seem to be a liturgical incipit.

21/112+lat   Accipietis virtutem supervenientes Spiritus Sancti in vos, et eritis mihi testes in Jerusalem et in Judea, Samaria et usque ad ultimum terrae.

Acts 1/8: the Chester transmission of the biblical text is discussed by Lumiansky and Mills (*Chester* II, 311).

This text probably needs to be spoken, for although it is referred to in the preceding eight lines the speech is not a direct translation. The text seems not to be a liturgical incipit, and in any case there is no reason to think that it should be sung.

21/120+sd   Veni creator spiritus

The Pentecost hymn, sung by all the apostles. The incipit is in WA, 153, and the hymn appears also in the Sarum use (HS, 111).

The complete text of the first verse is given in H: as the next seven stanzas (lines 121–48) paraphrase the seven stanzas of the hymn (of which the last is a doxology), however, it seems most likely that the whole hymn is sung.

21/238+sd   Accipite spiritum sanctum: quorum remiseritis
peccata, remittentur eis etc.

This text is from John 20/22–3. The SD is for two angels to sing the antiphon with these words. The antiphon is not in WA, but occurs as the Benedictus antiphon for Pentecost in SA, 280. The text is as above, with the 'etc.' displacing a single Alleluia. This antiphon has a neumatic chant, range c'–c" (which is a 4th higher than the Roman version in LU, 877).

21/310+sd, 314+lat, 318+lat, 322+lat, 326+lat, 330+lat, 334+lat, 338+lat, 342+lat, 346+lat, 350+lat, 354+lat

The Apostles' Creed is divided amongst the Twelve, each reciting a four-line English stanza corresponding to the Latin line allotted to him. Such a division is traditional, and this particular division the most commonly found.[13]

In all of the Chester manuscripts the Latin verse precedes its paraphrase. The version transmitted in A places the SH after the Latin line in each case, thus apparently showing that the Latin line is an unspoken reference: but the other manuscripts place the SH before the Latin. It therefore appears that the Latin was intended to be heard in all versions except A's.

The only evidence for singing is the use of 'incipiat' in **310+sd**. This is not conclusive here, however, since the play's first SD uses it (**21/1–sd**) in a situation where speech, not singing, is clearly intended. On the other hand the word there has its more prosaic meaning, since the play itself is being started. That is not the case in **310+sd**, which brings us back to the singing option. Certainly it would be more normal to sing the Apostles' Creed than to speak it, and the singing option is apparently open.

In manuscript A, then, the Latin lines of the Creed may be intended as an unspoken reference; in the other versions the producer no doubt exercised a choice in any case, choosing speech or singing according to the ability of his players to chant convincingly. Probably the different versions reflect the fact that all of these options were incorporated in the Exemplar.

There is no plainsong tune for the Apostles' Creed, which is chanted on a monotone.

22 *The Prophets of Antichrist*

22/1–lat, 48+lat, 124+lat, 164+lat, 172+lat, 260+lat There is no reason to think that any of these six Latin quotations in the play should be sung, and not one of them can be identified as a liturgical piece.

The question arises whether they should be spoken or regarded merely as written references. Lumiansky and Mills cite four of them as quotations for which 'there is no indication in the stanzaic text that the Latin is to be uttered'

---

13 Mezey 'Creed' shows that the Chester distribution of text is the usual one. The same division is used in Wilkinson's 13-part round on the Apostles' Creed: see Harrison *Eton Choirbook*, no. 50 and commentary, and Harrison *Music in Medieval Britain*, 414 (where Simon's name is omitted, however).

(*Chester* II, 101–2). In **1–lat**, however, the reference 'Hec in Ezechielis 37' rather than merely 'Ezechielis 37' suggests to me that the prophet is speaking aloud to the audience; and in **124+lat** the opening words 'Ego Daniell' added to the biblical text suggest the same. In **48+lat** and **172+lat** the different scribal treatments of SHs and ascriptions may show the kind of production choice in this matter that we have seen before in the cycle. On balance, I believe that the producer was given the option of letting the Latin be spoken in these four places.

In **164+lat** and **260+lat** the Expositor produces the Latin texts supporting his contentions. **164+lat** is the authority for the three lines just heard, and could certainly be spoken. Lumiansky and Mills are more doubtful about **260+lat**, which is not a biblical text (*Chester* II, 326).

23 *Antichrist*

23/1–8 Antichrist's opening stanza is all in Latin. Lumiansky and Mills cite L.H. Martin's opinion that this stanza might be sung (*Chester* II, 331), but I can see no reason for that: indeed, there are positive reasons why it should not be sung (see under **23/196+sd**, below). The stanza seems to bear no relation to an actual composition, so that there is no question of parody. The nearest analogue to this stanza is perhaps Pilate's ranting in **Towneley 24/1–46**.

23/24+lat, 40+lat These two prophecies seem to be spoken by Antichrist, since they begin with the formula 'De me dicitur ...'. Lumiansky and Mills take this view of **24+lat**, and point out that this Latin may be misplaced (*Chester* II, 333: the correct place would be after **32**). There is certainly no reason to think that these texts should be sung. Neither of them is a liturgical item. The alleluia verse 'Adorabo ad templum' (Sandon VI, 111; GS, 175) is taken from Psalm 137/2, and is not the text of **40+lat**, which is from Psalm 5/8.

23/56+lat Probably this text, too, should be spoken by Antichrist, although there is no indication of it. It is apparently not a liturgical text.

23/120+lat This is certainly spoken by Antichrist, who says in advance (**117–20**) that he will 'rehearse' the prophecy. It is apparently not a liturgical text.

23/196+sd Dabo vobis cor novum et spirtum novom in medio vestri

This is an interesting case, because it provides a parallel with **21/238+sd**, where the Holy Spirit is given to the Twelve. There are really two theoretical solutions for the dramaturgy here:
1 Antichrist sings, as a detailed reference to and parody of Pentecost. In this case we must assume that, like Mak in **Towneley 13** (see I, 202), it is an unmusical performance that shows him up as not doing God's Will; or

2 He does not sing, thus clearly demonstrating the non-divine nature of his actions.

If the text were to be found as a liturgical item the choice between these two might exist. But it is apparently not liturgical, which greatly reduces the possibility of its sung performance in this context – indeed, the possibility virtually disappears. I therefore think that Antichrist does not try to sing this text, which should consequently be spoken.

23/573–5   [HELIAS] In nomine Patris that all hath wrought
                          et Filii virginis that deare us bought
                          et Spiritus Sancti ys all my thought

The Latin follows the normal form of a blessing, *In nomine Patris et Filii et Spiritus Sancti*. It is integral to the stanza, and apparently should not be sung.

23/722+sd   Gaudete justi in domino etc.

Lumiansky and Mills identify the text as Psalm 32/1 (*Chester* II, 349), but the Vulgate wording is slightly different: 'Exultate justi in Domino: rectos decet collaudatio'. The SD quotes the liturgical incipit, for which there are two possibilities:

(a) Responsory in Easter time (AS, plate K):
        Gaudete iusti in domino. Alleluia alleluia.
        V.   rectos decet laudatio.
        R.   Alleluia alleluia.
    Syllabic chant, range d–a.

(b) Communion, Common of Martyrs (GS, 218):
        Gaudete iusti in domino Alleluia: rectos decet collaudatio
        Alleluia
    Neumatic/melismatic chant, range c–c'.

Justification could be found for using either of these, but the dramatic context is too important for such an easy and relatively uninteresting piece as (a) to be used. Since Michael is singing this piece and it is the end of the play, the more exuberant (b) is suitable; and (b) is from the Common of Martyrs, which is appropriate for leading the martyred Elias and Enoch to glory. A producer should perhaps not consider using (a) unless in an emergency – for instance, if circumstances dictated an actor playing Michael who was too weak a singer for (b) but who could cope with the undemanding simpler setting.

24 *The Last Judgement*

24/1–lat Ego sum alpha et omega, primus et novissimus

See the note to **2/1–lat**, above. As there, this is the Vulgate version, and even were it the liturgical version there would be no reason to think that God should sing it.

24/452+[lat]   Venite benedicti

There are several possibilities, as follows:

(a) Benedictus Antiphon, Lent (AS, 158):
      Venite benedicti patris mei percipite regnum quod vobis paratum est
      ab origine mundi
   Syllabic/neumatic chant, range g–e'.

(b) Benedictus Antiphon, Lent (WA, 89):
      Text as above.
   Neumatic chant, range g–e'. This is a decorated version of (a).

(c) Verse to the Responsory *Sancti mei* (WA, 429):
      Venite benedicti patris mei
   Neumatic chant, range g–d'.

(d) Introit, Wednesday after Easter (Sandon V, 15; GS, 120):
      Venite benedicti patris mei percipite regnum Alleluya. quod vobis
      paratum est ab origine mundi Alleluya alleluya alleluya
   Neumatic chant, range f–f'.

The text is from Matthew 25/34, part of Christ's own description of the Last Judgement: the Vulgate reads

   Venite benedicti patris mei, possidete paratum vobis regnum a
   constitutione mundi.

The most appropriate person to sing this in the play, then, would be Christ himself, although angelic singing was perhaps acceptable. The pattern of sung Latin plus spoken English normally has the same character delivering both, however, which argues that Christ should sing this text immediately before **24/453–6**, where the liturgical text is paraphrased:

            Come hither to mee, my dearlynges deare,
            that blessed in world alwayse weare.
            Take my realme, all in feare,
            that for you ordayned ys.

If confirmation were needed, it would be supplied by the opening of this passage, the 'Come hither' cited in the **Late Banns** (line **185**: see 6.3, above, under play **24**).

From this it will be seen that the responsory verse, (c) in the list above, is the least suitable of the liturgical pieces for performance here because it has so little of the text. Of the others, (d) is perhaps less likely to be used because of the Alleluias, not included in the translation. This leaves the Benedictus antiphon (a) and (b) as the most likely: but any one of these could be used. Probably the matter would be decided by the musical ability of the actor playing Christ. The introit (d) needs a good professional singer; (b) is less demanding; and (a) even less so.

24/508+sd   Letamini in domino vel salvator mundi domine

These two items are cited as alternatives to be heard at this point: only H includes the 'vel', but the SD makes poor sense without it.

(1) *Letamini in domino.*
    This is Psalm 31/11. The liturgical settings are:

(a) Antiphon (WA, 395):
    Letamini in domino et exultate iusti et gloriamini omnes recti corde.
    Syllabic/neumatic chant, range e–d'.

(b) Antiphon (WA, 421):
    Text as for (a).
    Neumatic/syllabic chant, range f–e'.

(c) Verse to the Responsory *Letabitur justus in domino* (WA, 304):
    Letamini in domino et exultate iusti et gloriamini omnes.
    Neumatic chant, range f–d'.

(d) Verset (WA, 385 and 395):
    Letamini in domino
    Inflected monotone.

(e) Responsory, Innocents (AS, 71):
    Letamini in domino et exultate iusti Alleluia alleluia.
    V. Et gloriamini omnes recti corde
    R. [? Alleluia alleluia]
    Syllabic chant, range d–a.

(f) Responsory, Common of Martyrs (AS, 649):
   Letamini in domino et exultate iusti
   V. Et gloriamini omnes recti corde.
   R. [? Et exultate]
   Syllabic chant, 6th mode, range e–a.

(g) Offertory, Common of Martyrs (GS, 218):
   Text as for (a).
   Melismatic chant, range c–d'.

The verset (d) is too short and simple to fulfil the necessary function here. Of the rest, no real choice can be made *in vacuo*: production choice would depend on the ability of the singers. All the remaining pieces require some concentrated training if professional singers are not used.

(2) *Salvator mundi domine*
   The 'domine' (omitted in AR) distinguishes the verse hymn (AS, 46) from two antiphons beginning 'Salvator mundi salve nos'. AS gives the hymn five verses: the music is an easy congregational tune (also used for *Veni creator spiritus*) which would have been known to all the actors.
   The choice between the two texts to be sung probably depended on the singing abilities of the actors playing the angels.

24/540+lat 'Qui non credit, jam judicatus est': identified by Lumiansky and Mills as John 3/18 (*Chester* II, 371). Perhaps spoken by the First Devil, or possibly only a reference (it is not particularly well placed in relation to the speech): certainly not sung, and it is not a liturgical incipit.

24/564+lat 'Filius hominis venturus est ... opus suum': identified by Lumiansky and Mills as Matthew 16/27 (*Chester* II, 372). Certainly spoken by the Second Devil, who says in **563–4** that he is going to speak Latin. It is apparently not a liturgical text. As above, there is no question of it being sung.

24/580+lat 'Sic erit in consummatione ... et stridor dentium': identified by Lumiansky and Mills as Matthew 13/49–50 (*Chester* II, 372). Spoken by the First Devil, who says in **579–80** that he will 'rehearse' the text. It is apparently not a liturgical text. As above, there is no question of it being sung.

6.5 Records

Chester records relevant to drama and minstrelsy are edited by Lawrence M. Clopper in *REED.Chester*. A number of documents edited by Clopper, and some that are not, are to be found also in *Essays*, pp. 203–310, translated from the original Latin or, if originally in English, edited afresh. Lumiansky and Mills confined themselves to the records of performances and therefore excluded much material that is found in *REED.Chester*. John Marshall has considered the problems of dating some of the Smiths' accounts, and his work, too, is taken into consideration here ('Chester Plays Dating'). Peter Meredith provides a concise assessment of relevant records in 'Staging Chester', together with much detailed discussion and some very useful summary tables of expenditure.

Payments concerning music in the plays are to be found in the accounts of four guilds: the Painters (play **7**), the (Black)Smiths (play **11**), the Shoemakers (play **14**), and the Coopers (play **16**). In additon, the charter of the Painters' and Glaziers' company gives information on the content of play **7**.

7 *The Shepherds*

The charter of the Painters, Glaziers, Embroiderers and Stationers dates from 1534–5, and therefore antedates the Early Banns. The relevant part of it is edited by Clopper (*REED.Chester*, 29 f). The charter is the official recognition of the long-standing co-operation of the Painters, Glaziers, Embroiderers and Stationers in, among other things, the presentation of 'þe plae of þe shepperds Wach with þe Angells hyme'. This description is interesting as showing the importance of the angelic Gloria before the Early Banns were written, since those banns do not mention music at all in the Painters' play.

The surviving accounts of the Painters' Guild are for the performances of 1568, 1572, and 1575 (*REED.Chester*, 81–4, 91–3, 106–8; *Essays*, 246–53). In each year both singers and minstrels were hired.

In 1568 the guild spoke to 'master Chaunter for Shepertes Boyes'. The cantor can be identified as Sir John Genson, precentor of the cathedral (Dutka 'Use', 4: Dutka calls him Jonson). This payment does not necessarily mean that the shepherds' boys sang, for trained choristers would in any case make suitable child-actors, and it is not certain that the shepherds' boys are the 'helpers' who sang with the shepherds at **7/447+sd** (H only). On the other hand, the wages paid to the boys in various years – 2/8d to four of them in 1568, 4/-d in 1572, and 3/-d to three of them in 1575 – are too generous unless the boys were hired for a specialist skill such as singing. Moreover, we know that more than one singer was hired, for the guild spent 2d on 'the iiij syngares' at an audition or rehearsal in 1572, and ld 'for synges' and 6d 'for pouder [?] for the sengers' in 1575. The first of these payments may be an exact parallel to the payment of 2d spent 'upon the shepertes Boyes' during rehearsal in 1568. It seems reasonable to conclude that the choristers playing the shepherds' boys were required to sing, and therefore that they are indeed the 'helpers' who sing with the shepherds at **7/447+sd**.

The vocal music in the play presents a problem, in that the text and the surviving accounts do not seem to agree in one important respect. As has already been noted, the angelic Gloria was an important part of the play, the high quality of the singing being emphasised by the Second Shepherd's remark that the angel had a fine voice (**7/406**: see 6.3). The play seems to demand a trained singer for this part. It is therefore a surprise to find that in all three years the angel's wage was a mere 6d, the usual wage for an actor with a very small part. This was the wage given also in 1572 and 1575 to Mary. She, like the angel, has only a single eight-line speech in the play: and her wage of 8d in 1568 perhaps reflected the longer time that she spends on stage. It is inconceivable that the Gloria did not merit extra payment in these years, and the only possible explanation is that it received a professional performance, either behind the waggon, the angel acting his part but not singing, or from a costumed second angel supernumary to the cast requirements of the text. A group of choristers could not sing here, for the shepherds' discussion of the Gloria (**7/361–435**: see 6.3) shows that it was a solo. Probably, therefore, the Gloria was performed by a professional singing-man whose name perhaps appears, as yet unrecognised, in the accounts.

The payments to minstrels do not form a discernible pattern. In 1568 minstrels were paid 3/4d on the day of the play and 6d for their performance on Midsummer Eve, and the guild also paid for bread and ale provided for them by Richard Halewood's wife. In 1572 minstrels cost the guild 2/-d (although they were probably given food and drink as well, recorded in an item of general expenditure), and in 1575 minstrels received 12d (*REED.Chester*, 106). In this last year, a payment of 2/-d to 'the mynstrell to the plase' (107) presumably refers to a minstrel entertaining the audience at one of the stations and does not imply minstrelsy during the play.

The only place for minstrelsy in play 7 is at the angelic Gloria (**7/357+sd**), which could be accompanied by *bas* instruments. The lack of consistency in the payments to minstrels argues against such a specific use of minstrelsy, however. Rather, it suggests that minstrels were hired, to no regular plan, for a much less precisely defined purpose. The most likely purpose is the provision of loud music in the procession from one station to another (excepting the 'minstrel to the place' of 1575, who would presumably be stationary). This purpose is hinted at in the proximity of payments to minstrels and those to the 'putters' of the waggon. The minstrels' payment in the 1568 accounts immediately follows payments for beer and wages to the 'viij putters of the caryage' (82); and in that year also there is a single payment for bread and ale for the putters and the minstrels (83). (The accounts for 1572 are less specific: payment for the breakfast of the players and putters is a single item, while bread and beer were also given to the players. There is no payment for the minstrels' food and drink.) The implication is, at least in 1568, that the minstrels were part of the team responsible for moving the waggon. This use of minstrels is seen also in the accounts of the Smiths' Guild.

A final problem in these accounts concerns payment for 'whysteles'. In 1568 the guild spent ld on them; in 1572, 2d on 'ij wystyles for trowe'; and in 1575 2d again for an unspecified number. It seems clear that Trowle (Garcius) used whistles for some sort of extra-textual 'business': the implications of this are discussed in I, 351–2. Whistles can be made out of various materials, but the money paid at Chester suggests something fairly robust – perhaps wood. It seems, anyway, that the Painters bought two whistles, such as a shepherd might use, for each year's performance. Possibly they were of different pitches, necessary to whatever stage business they were intended for. Presumably wooden whistles would survive the year's performances but would not be worth keeping for a subsequent occasion.

11 *The Purification*

Records survive for the Smiths' performances of 1546, 1561, 1567, 1568, 1572 and 1575 (*REED.Chester*, 53, 65–7, 77–8, 84–6, 90–1 and 105–6; *Essays* 236–46). The first of these is dated 1554 by Clopper, as it is by Lumiansky and Mills, but Marshall's examination of the Smiths' accounts convincingly assigns that account to the performance of 1546 ('Chester Plays Dating', 56) The records appear to be for play **11** as we have it, but there are some unexpected references to singers.

The Smiths' accounts show the various stages at which payments were made to singers. The guild went first to someone who could procure singers: in 1561 this was Sir Randle Barnes, a minor canon of the cathedral, and in 1567 Sir John Genson, the precentor. There are then payments concerning singers at auditions and rehearsal. Finally, payments were made direct to the performers, one sum to the singers and another apparently to the musical director.

For reasons that will become apparent, these payments have to be discussed in the context of payments to the actors. The relevant figures for the various accounts are set out by Meredith ('Staging Chester', 71).

The interpretation of these accounts is made difficult by the various omissions of named roles from the payments to players. The accounts also show a number of changes that took place, and these, too, make our task harder. Payments to all the characters vary over the years, and those to Joseph and Mary do so to an extent that may well reflect alterations to the scope and/or nature of their roles. The angel's role also changed, but in a different way: for there were two angels in 1572 and 1575, and certainly more than one in 1546.

There is also a problem over the role of Simeon. In 1546 and 1561 the actor playing the part of Simeon was paid 3/4d, a sum that reflects not only the size of the role but also the fact that Simeon must sing. No doubt part of the musical director's work each year was to coach this player in his performance of *Nunc dimittis*. Simeon's name is missing, however, from the accounts for 1567 and 1568. Simeon's part is crucial in any discussion of the musicians performing in the Smiths' play, and it therefore figures largely in what follows.

I have suggested in the past that White probably played Simeon in 1567 and

1568 (*Essays*, 135), but Meredith has cast doubt on this interpretation ('Staging Chester', 59). Meredith sees White's participation as connected with 'a special development of the liturgical music of the temple in the play', pointing out that White was paid for singing and not for playing. This is not an easy distinction to make, for White would still be costumed as a temple singer: but perhaps 'playing' would relate to roles specified in the play text – those listed as 'the players' in the accounts – rather than to 'extras' such as temple singers. Meredith further considered that the omission of Simeon from the accounts for 1567 and 1568 is not significant ('Staging Chester', 57 f), and had earlier noted that the 3/4d paid to Randle Barnes in 1568 was not really evidence for Barnes playing the part of Simeon (in Dutka *REED Proceedings*, 36).

The argument for White playing Simeon is certainly not strong. On the other hand, as a year-by-year examination of the Smiths' accounts shows, the alternative demands that we reconsider Meredith's opinion that Barnes need not have done so in 1568:

1546 The accounts for this year include a full cast-list. 'Barnes and the syngers' were paid 3/4d for performing. Marshall suggests that this was Thomas Barnes, a singing man and then (1551–c.1558) organist of the cathedral, who may have been Randle Barnes's father ('Chester Plays Dating', 53: Marshall uses the lack of a style and christian name as evidence that this account dates from before Thomas's appointment as organist). It seems probable that Barnes acted as director of music, and – in view of the accounts for 1561 – likely that the singers were a group of boys.

This is our first evidence of music not mentioned in the play text itself, which indicates only the singing of *Nunc dimittis*. It might of course be argued that the choir sang *Nunc dimittis* instead of Simeon: but this is unlikely because Simeon was paid 3/4d this year, the sum paid on subsequent occasions.

1561 Singers were procured through the agency of Sir Randle Barnes, the guild spending 3d in the process. The accounts for this year show a payment of 12d to Sir John Genson 'for songes' and, on the same line, 2/6d 'to the 5 boyes for singing': that is, 3/6d in all. The inference is that Barnes, having given advice, took no further part in the proceedings, Genson being brought in as director of music. The designation 'for songes' as a description of Genson's work is however problematic: clearly, it may refer to the performance itself – Genson directing music actually heard – although a modern interpretation would think of him first as a composer or procurer of written copies. Consideration of the 1572 accounts suggests the former meaning. However that may be, these accounts shed some light on the payments for 1546: it seems clear that at the earlier performance the sum of 3/4d to 'Barnes and the syngers' probably consisted of 2/4d to the singers and 12d to Barnes as director (or perhaps 2/6d+ 10d). This seems to leave Genson and the five boys doing the same job as Barnes and the singers in 1546, and at much the same cost to the guild – 3/6d in 1561, as opposed to 3/4d in 1546. The similarity of the sums concerned also suggests that the singers in 1546 were boys.

The cast-list is not complete in this year, for Mary and Joseph are both missing. Meredith argues convincingly that Thomas Ellam and William Loker played those roles, although it is impossible to know which actor played which role (in Dutka *REED Proceedings*, 34 f).

1567 This is the first of the years in which Simeon is missing from the accounts: so, too, is Mary. In this year no boys were paid for singing, but there are payments of 12d to 'mr chanter' (Genson) and 4/-d to 'mr white'. Genson and White are presumably the '2 clarkes of the menster' who were paid 8d during the casting/rehearsal period. White is now generally accepted to be the composer Robert White (c. 1538–74), who could have been at Chester from 1566 or 1567 until 1570, between appointments at Ely and Westminster. The accounts of the Dean and Chapter of Chester for 1567 refer to White as *magister choristarum* (Dutka *Use of Music*, 231–2).

The objection to White taking Simeon's role is that there were then no singers to do whatever the boys had done in previous years. Meredith's conclusion, already cited, is probably a good one, therefore, even if not really demonstrable: that is, that White took the place of the choir, and that Simeon is omitted from the accounts for reasons unconnected with White. In this case Genson's 12d is evidently for his work as director of music, as before.

In this year there is also a payment of 2d 'for Carringe of the Regalls'. We may expect this instrument to have been used to accompany White's singing, or perhaps to provide solo instrumental music in place of vocal music: presumably Genson was the organist, for he and White appear in the accounts immediately after the players.

White's 4/-d could of course have been for distribution among a group of boys as well as for himself: but the accounts for 1568 show this to be unlikely.

1568 Again Simeon is missing from the payments to actors, and so are the three doctors, Anna, and the angel(s). In the preparation period the guild first spent 5d 'on the chanter & clarke of the mynster' and 7d 'vpon mr wite & Sir Rondle barnes': in the event, Barnes was paid 3/4d for his work on the play, and White received 4/-d 'for singinge'. Since White's payment was the same as in the previous year, we can assume that he did the same work. As suggested under 1567, it is possible that White's 4/-d was for a group of boys: but 'for singinge' seems to parallel the 'for plleyinge' of William Loker in 1561, and therefore to refer to White personally. Besides, we know that Genson supplied boys to the Painters in 1568, and it is unlikely that a second group could have been made available.

This leaves the problem of the 3/4d given to Barnes. Why was his wage so large, and did it subsume the 12d that would be given to a director of music? If White did indeed receive the same payment as in 1567 for the same work, then he was not director of music. In fact, if White was simply repeating the previous year's performance, the director's only task was in coaching Simeon. We might expect that Barnes would be paid 12d for this, then, but not so large a sum as 3/4d. It is at this stage that we must reconsider Meredith's opinion that Barnes did not play the part of Simeon. It is not just that the 3/4d does not make sense, or that the director's 12d is missing. Immediately before the item for money 'Spent at Gilb flowers vpon mr wite & Sir Rondle barnes' is one for expenses 'at the ... consell of Simion'. This suggests that there was difficulty in filling this role. Is the proximity one of cause and effect? Were White and Barnes canvassed for the role? In the account for 1567 White and Genson appear immediately after 'the Players', which suggests the kind of part they took in the performance.

These items, then, may indicate that the Smiths were unable to find a suitable actor and that the musicians were involved in solving the problem. An experienced professional singing-man from the cathedral would certainly be a good stand-in: and as White was apparently repeating a former performance, the task would automatically fall to Barnes. True, the evidence is circumstantial: but it is at least very possible that Randle Barnes played Simeon in 1568.

1572 The accounts for this year include all the names of the characters, but only half of the payments are actually entered. However, the payments to singers do not seem to be relevant to acting: there is merely a single payment of 4/2d 'for the clergy for the songes', with no indication as to how the money was to be distributed. As before, this could mean composition, arrangement, provision of copies, or the direction of the music. As there is no payment to 'singers', however, it is likely that 'the clergy' performed: so 'for the songes' means 'for the performance of the music'. Although this payment is not the same as in previous years, it is roughly commensurate with earlier payments and may well indicate the same kind of events during the play.

1575 The accounts for the final performance include a full set of payments to the players, but the musical payments are disappointing: 14d to '3 of the synngares' and 16d to one of the singers 'for his panes & gloffes'. Judging by their positions in the records, either or both of these may be for the riding of the banns rather than for the play itself. What we can learn from them is probably applicable to the play, however: that there were at least three singers, and that one of them (at least) was costumed. In fact, we should surely expect the singers to be costumed in this play, whatever the occasion of their singing.

There are two possible types of occasion for singing in this play. The first, mentioned by Meredith in connection with White's singing, is a liturgical one. The offering made by Mary and Joseph would be preceded by a procession from the temple door to the altar,[14] and this would involve the singing of a psalm. It has to be said, I think, that this particular play text does not obviously require such a procession, and that the introduction of a musical procession is not conducive to

---

[14] See I, 261.

smooth-running drama in this play. Indeed, if there is to be a procession, it could well be during Simeon's singing of *Nunc dimittis*: that is, it becomes a medieval Candlemas procession rather than a part of the office of Purification. This happens in other Purification plays.

As noted before (6.3), **11/40+sd** and **11/71+sd** are suitable places for 'heavenly' music. On balance, it seems to me likely that these were the occasions for singing. The use of boys points in that direction, boys being more obviously suitable as angels than as temple singers; and the accompaniment of White by a regals points in that direction, too, accompaniment of angelic music being very suitable and liturgical processions being of necessity unaccompanied. Moreover, singing at those points covers the 'business' of the angel's correction of the text altered by Simeon, which is otherwise a long silence. (There is no objection to long silences, of course, but they do tend to break up the dramatic impetus of the play.) In modern performances a producer might be tempted to provide music in both types of situation: but it is important to note that the musical resources shown in the accounts would not be sufficient for both types – a choice must be made.

The minstrels are no easier to deal with than the singers, but a certain pattern can be seen. In general, the minstrels who performed 'with our pagan' appear in connection with those who pushed the waggon as much as with the players:

1546 'To the mynstrells in mane ijs' is immediately followed by payment 'to the porters of the caryegs'.

1561 'To the minstrells iijs vjd Payd for drinke for ther breckfast before they play and after they had done when the were unbowninge them iijs' is followed by a payment of 18d to 'the porters of the carriage'.

1567 Payment of 2/-d to the minstrels is several items later than payment to the porters of the carriage and immediately before those to the players.

1568 Payment of 2/-d to the minstrels is several items later than that to the porters of the carriage and among those to the players.

1572 The main payment of 3/4d 'To the minstrells for our pagent' is among miscellaneous expenses: but the last item in the list records a payment of 4d 'For bringinge of the cariag home and spent on minstrells and porters'.

1575 The main payment of 5/-d 'To the minstreles at our generall rehers and Midsamer and with our pagan' is followed by the payments to players, with the porters of the carriage several items later still.

Certainly this evidence is not conclusive: but the item for 1561 reads as if the minstrels had performed independently of the players, while the second item for 1572 seems to cite both minstrels and porters as those responsible for 'bringinge the carriag home'. As I have already suggested (6.3), it seems most likely that these were *haut* minstrels sent out with the waggon to play in the procession between stations. This would certainly be the minstrels' function at Midsummer, and the item for 1575 therefore supports the suggestion.

There are also payments that indicate a different use of minstrelsy:

1546 'To Randle Crane in mane ijs'. This item follows immediately after that to Barnes and the singers. Crane was a minstrel: both the use of his full name and the sum paid indicate that he was a respected and skilful performer.

1561 William Lutter, a minstrel, was paid 42d at the general rehearsal. He should be distinguished from William Loker, paid 'for plleyinge' in an item immediately following the payment to the five choristers. William Loker or Luker was a respected member of the Smiths' Guild who may have died in 1567 (*REED.Chester*, 521).

William Lutter's name also appears in guild records as 'luter' or 'leuter' (*REED.Chester*, 52, 60 and 69), so he was probably a *bas* minstrel, the player of a lute. Randle Crane, too, was surely a *bas* minstrel, for a lone minstrel given the responsibility indicated by a fee of 2/-d was rarely a loud minstrel.[15] It is significant that the main payments to Crane and Luter follow those to the singers: the overwhelming probability is that they were hired to play 'heavenly' music, either as virtuoso solos or as an accompaniment to the choristers, or perhaps both. Crane and Luter do not appear in any surviving accounts later than those discussed here. Probably Crane had died by 1561, or was working for another guild; and perhaps Luter, brought in to replace him, was himself replaced by 1567, the year in which regals were used by the Smiths. It is possible that the *bas* minstrel was permanently supplanted by an organist from the cathedral, although this is highly speculative.

14 Christ at the House of Simon the Leper; Christ and the Money-Lenders; and Judas's Plot

The surviving Shoemakers' accounts, probably for the performance of 1550, are not for play **14** as we have it. The differences do not affect consideration of the music, but it cannot be assumed that the musical resources shown in the accounts are applicable to the play text in the form in which it has survived.

The only music shown in the text is the singing of *Hosanna filio David* (**14/208+sd**). Since this is entrusted to citizens and boys we might expect to find a group of choristers in the accounts, but there are none. Moreover, the 'vj chelder of Esaraell' who were paid 3/-d between them accord better with the six *cives* of the text than with the boys, of whom there are only two.

The accounts are no more informative on the subject of minstrelsy. The single payment of 2/4d for the minstrels' wages suggests that there were two of them. There are two possible uses for minstrelsy: it might be *haut* minstrelsy played at and/or between stations, or *bas* minstrelsy played at supper in the house of Simon the Leper, for which the cue would be **14/40+sd**. Of these, the *haut* minstrels playing in procession seem more likely.

---

[15] Such a fee might suggest a trumpeter, but there is no reason to think that a trumpeter was needed for this play.

16 *The Trial and Flagellation*

The accounts of the Coopers' guild for 1571–1611 make no mention of either singers or minstrels. Dutka noted that Hugh Gillam, who was paid 3/4d in 1572, was a morris dancer, and she suggested that Gillam danced in the role of one of the executioners (*Use of Music*, 6: for Gillam's dancing, see *REED.Chester*, 70 and 74). The point is an interesting one, but at present the evidence – which is discussed in I, 212–14 – is so far from demonstrating the possibility of Gillam dancing in the play that it can hardly be considered. In fact, it is likely that Hugh Gillam did not play a torturer at all, but the role of Herod (Meredith 'Staging Chester', 61 and 71).

6.6   Music and other aural cues

1 *The Fall of Lucifer*

1_1 **1/85+md** Function: (h). The angels sing *Dignus es domine deus*, probably the Magnificat antiphon (WA, 139; AS, 256).

1_2 **1/125+sd** Function: (c), (h). H only. The angels sing in praise of God. It would be suitable for Lucifer and his followers not to sing here if it is clear that they are already disaffected: but this is a production decision – there is no contemporary evidence.

No incipit is given, and I suspect that this cue is really the original, with 1_1 being a later alternative. Any suitable song of praise will work here: the angels might repeat *Dignus es domine deus* (although I do not think that repeating a song was ever the medieval strategy) or another such piece could be chosen.

1_3 **1/213+md** Function: (h), (b). The angels sing the antiphon for Trinity Sunday, *Gloria tibi Trinitas* (WA, 158; AS, 286): clearly Lucifer and his followers do not join in. Omitted H.

2 *Adam and Eve; Cain and Abel*

2_1 **2/1-** Function: (f). Angelic minstrelsy opens the play (B only).

2_2 **2/112+md** Function: (a), (h). Angelic minstrelsy. Omitted H.

2_3 **2/280+md** Function: (a), (h). Angelic minstrelsy. Omitted H.

2_4 **2/384+md** Function: (a), (h). Angelic minstrelsy. Omitted H.

2_5 **2/424+md** Function: (a), (d), (h), (e). Angelic minstrelsy. Omitted H.

2_6 **2/616+md** Function: (b), (h). Angelic minstrelsy. Omitted AR.

3 *Noah's Flood*

3_1 **3/224+sh** Function: (a). Lines **225–36** are discussed in I, 71–3. This song covers the sons' movement from the ark to their mother, as well as any 'business' for Mrs Noah and the gossips. It should be sung by a single gossip, with the other gossips perhaps joining in for the last four lines.

There may be a verbal connection between this song and the next item.

3₂ 3/252+sd Function: (d). Omitted H.

  or 3/260+sd Function: (d). H only.

These two are alternatives: see I, 227–8. If the Raven and Dove scene is played, as transmitted by H, then there is no singing at **252+sd** and Noah and his family sing 'Save me O God' inside the closed ark at **260+sd**. If the version of HmARB is used, in which the Raven and Dove scene is omitted, then they sing at **252+sd** instead: there is no indication of what is sung here, but of course the simplest practical solution would be to perform 'Save me O God'. Nor in fact does either SD indicate who sings, although it would be surprising if the whole family were not involved.

As noted in I, 73, the metrical version of Psalm 68 (AV 69) to the tune used by Sternhold and Hopkins is the most likely solution to the identity of 'Save me O God'. The piece is edited, with the first two verses of text, in *Essays* 159–60.

4 *Abraham, Lot and Melchysedeck; Abraham and Isaac*
5 *Moses and the Law; Balaak and Balaam*

There is no evidence for music in these plays. The various Latin lines in play **5** should probably be spoken, but certainly not sung.

6 *The Annunciation and the Nativity*

This play is surprisingly lacking in music cues: no music is demanded for the appearances of the angel or the star, nor for the entrance of Octavian.

6₁ 6/64+sd Function: none. Mary sings the first verse of *Magnificat*. For the type of performance, see **6₂**.

6₂ 6/72+sd Function: none. Mary sings at least the second verse of *Magnificat*. As she then translates the whole canticle from verse 2 onwards, including the doxology, it would be most logical for her to sing the Latin of all those verses first.

Almost certainly the whole canticle was used here, then (except for verse 1, already sung at **6₁**), sung as such and including the doxology. It would have been sung to one of the psalm-tones normally used for it. Presumably the Alleluias sung in Easter time would not be performed, as they do not appear in the translation. I assume also that the canticle should not be sung under an antiphon, although it is possible that lines **81–6** translate a Magnificat antiphon. If so, I have not been able to identify it.

6₃ 6/666+sd Function: (a). The angel sings *Haec est ara dei caeli*, discussed in 6.4, above: the music covers Octavian's offering of the incense. There is no indication of any further text, and according to the SD music has to be provided for it.

7 *The Shepherds*

7_1 **7/48+sd** Function: (b), and (e) in so far as it helps the audience to focus on the Second Shepherd as he is brought into the action. This is a hornblowing, not a musical event.

7_2 **7/164+sd** Function: (e) or (b). Garcius sings. On the problems raised by this SD, see 6.2.

7_3 **7/165+** Function: (e). Again a horn-blowing, not a musical event. As noted above, 6.3, there must be some stage business between the three shepherds while Garcius speaks his soliloquy, **165–94**: this business includes the First Shepherd's blowing of his horn, although Garcius notices it (or pretends to notice it for the first time) only at line **195**. One thing that the three shepherds are not doing is singing, as Garcius's comment at lines **202–5** makes clear ('Fye on your ... sittinge withowt any songes!').

7_4 **7/357+sd** Function: (h). The angel sings *Gloria in excelsis*, the text of the verse of the first responsory at Christmas Matins (WA, 278; AS, 47). This is apparently a florid and intricate performance (see 6.3), which would suggest melismatic chant or a very ornate polyphonic setting. In performances of the fifteenth century or the first half of the sixteenth, I should expect that plainsong was used, and this of course raises no insuperable questions of performance–practice. The chant for the responsory verse is however neither florid nor ornate, which may point towards a polyphonic setting being used.

The surviving line of music in MS H can hardly be described as florid and intricate, either (see I, 153–5). It seems to be a late piece – certainly mid-sixteenth-century, and perhaps Elizabethan. But I believe it to be the incipit of a polyphonic setting, and in that guise it perhaps fitted the description better. The main problem is that any polyphonic setting will contradict the SD, which requires the angel to sing the *Gloria in excelsis* as a solo. The solution most in line with known practice is to sing the given line as a solo for baritone voice with the accompaniment of an organ. This gives a musically sensible solution which is apparently to be seen also in the Smiths' accounts (6.5, above, under play **11**, where a regals is used) and in some only slightly later verse anthems. My four-part reconstruction, which includes a short score to be used in performance by voice and regals, is in I, 384–5. (This reconstruction cannot be used by itself in a performance of the play, however, because the second section is missing, for the words 'Et in terra ... bone voluntatis'.)

7_5 **7/447+sd** Function: none. Garcius leads a 'merry song'. As suggested in I, 376–7, this is apparently a 'pantomime' performance, with Garcius teaching the song not only to the other shepherds but to the audience too.[16] There being no dynamic function at this point – although the song does separate the musi-

---

16 In I, 376–7, I noted that the process of 'lining out' would require two or three others to support the audience while they were learning the piece. This may be the function of the 'helpers' (see 6.5 under this play), assisting all the shepherds in this way.

cal discussion from the journey to Bethlehem – it was probably unnecessary to specify the piece to be sung: any cheerful song would serve the purpose as long as it was not positively unsuitable. An MD gives the title 'troly loly loly loo' in Hm, the spelling being rather garbled in ARB. This title may be relevant to only a single performance, of course, and we need not worry too much about the song's identity. The refrain 'Trolly lolly lo' was not uncommon in the sixteenth century, but, as noted in I, 58–9, a song by William Cornish, dating from c. 1515, is a possible contender.[17]

7_6 7/479 Function: (a), (e). As noted in 6.3, above, there are two alternative passages in which the shepherds walk to Bethlehem. This cue occurs in the second, and is therefore an alternative to 7_5, which occurs in the first. It is however not certain that the 'Troly loly loly loo' song can simply be transferred to this position: for while 7_5 is a 'merry song' to 'solace' the shepherds (line 443), 7_6 is 'some myrth to his majestee' (line 477). This may mean only that the shepherds sing a happy song that the Christ-Child will enjoy (in which case 'Troly loly loly lo' may indeed fit the bill), but Garcius's words really seem to mean that he intends a song directed specifically at the Child (lines 476–9):

> [GARCIUS] And singe we all, I read,
> some myrth to his majestee,
> for certayne now see wee it indeede:
> the kinge Sone of heavon is hee.

If Garcius did not intend a song of praise specifically in the Child's honour, the insistence on the Child's status is surely irrelevant here.

Whatever they sing, there is no question of audience participation, apparently: and in this respect, too, 7_6 is not simply a replacement for 7_5.

7_7 7/656 Function: see below. The Second Shepherd's speech (651–6) demands a song. The problem over its position is discussed in 6.3, above: no clear solution seems possible, but my own preference is for the song to be placed after 656. Whether the song is sung after 656 or at the end of the play (or both, a solution that may follow the spirit of the text but is not justified by the letter), it is apparently a song in praise of Christ, or at least of Christmas rejoicing.

If the song is sung at the end of the play, as 656 seems to imply, this item fulfills dynamic functions (c) and (g); if after 656, it has the function of removing the shepherds from the stable to another location (a), where they discuss their futures.

7_A 7/696 Function: (g), (c). Although the shepherds have agreed to go their separate ways, Garcius's final speech, in which he addresses the audience,

---

[17] Examples are discussed in Stevens *Music and Poetry*, 243 and 401.

makes it clear that they leave the playing place as a group. A song would be a suitable way of doing this.

8 *The Three Kings from the East*
8₁ 8/144+md Function: (a), (b), (e) and (h). The MD for minstrels covers the Messenger's move from the Kings to Herod, with Herod's entry or discovery. The music should be loud minstrelsy, therefore, suitable for the entrance of a king to his audience chamber.

9 *The Gifts of the Three Kings*
No relevant cues.

10 *The Slaughter of the Innocents*
10₁ 10/288+sd Function: (a), (h). The Angel sings *Ecce dominus ascendet*. See above, 6.4, for a possible solution to the problem presented by this piece.

10₂ 10/497+lat Function: (g). The Angel sings the antiphon *Ex Egipto vocavi*: as Joseph and Mary are now starting on their way home, the end of the play can be a procession out of the playing place.

11 *The Purification of the Blessed Virgin*
11₁ 11/166+sd Function: none. Simeon should sing the whole of the *Nunc dimittis*, probably in the tract version (see 6.4).

11ₐ 11/206 Function: (d), (h). The text gives no hint of any liturgical ceremony here. Mary and Joseph have made the required offerings (lines **135–46**); Mary comes for purification (**136–8**), but Simeon seems tacitly to take Joseph's view (**127–8**) that purification is unnecessary. There is something to be said dramatically for a musical item here, however. Simeon and Anna have prophesied about the Child, and the (largely *ad hoc*) ceremony ends at line **206**. A final procession would conveniently mark the end of this liturgical section of the play, and would also allow Simeon and Anna to leave the playing-area and Christ to join the doctors. At this moment there is a chronological gap of twelve years. Some suitable piece from the Candlemas procession, such as the verse *Hodie Beata Virgo* (PS(P), f. 139v), might be used processionally. We have no means of knowing what a sixteenth-century producer might have done, of course, whether a musical item was used or not.

12 *The Temptation*
13 *The Blind Chelidonian, and the Raising of Lazarus*
No cues for music.
14 *Christ in the House of Simon the Leper, and the Entry into Jerusalem*
14₁ 14/208+sd Function: (a) The citizens and boys sing, probably the antiphon *Hosanna filio David* (but see the alternatives in 6.4, above), to welcome Christ to Jerusalem.

15 The Last Supper

15_A 15/160+sd Function: none. Jesus washes the disciples' feet. See the next cue.

15_B 15/168+sd Function: (a), and perhaps (h). This cue and **15_A** are both at a foot-washing. There is no evidence for music here, but the lack of text suggests reference to the Mandatum ceremony, with some of its music: the thinking behind this is detailed in I, section 7.6. The psalms and their antiphons used for the Mandatum ceremony are listed in I, 275.

16 The Trial
16A The Crucifixion

No cues for music.

17 The Harrowing of Hell

17_A 17/152+sd Function: (h). The 'cry, or a great physical din' of the SD apparently comes from the demons, who do not want Christ to come to Hell. The cries may be partly of fear, but the 'great physical din' (*sonitus magnus materialis*) suggests that they try to frighten him off.[18] This play was performed by the Cooks, who could supply the kind of hardware – flesh-hooks, and the like – that one sees in scenes of Hell by Bosch and other artists: such ironmongery can be made to produce a great deal of noise.

17₁ 17/276+sd Function: (h), but in MS H, and perhaps originally, (g). The archangel Michael intones *Te deum*, which is then sung by all – that is, by all the prophets, but presumably not by the demons. When this formed the end of the play, perhaps the audience joined in as well: certainly Adam's invitation to sing, **273–6**, is pointless if addressed only to the cast.

When the singing is at the end of the play it could be a set-piece performance; but when the alewife scene follows, *Te deum* should presumably be a procession out of the playing area.[19]

18 The Resurrection

18₁ 18/153+sd Function: (a). Two angels sing *Christus resurgens*. There are four possibilities for this piece: see 6.4 under this play.

19 The Road to Emmeus, and Doubting Thomas

No music cues.

20 The Ascension of Christ

20₁ 20/104+sd Function: (a). Jesus sings *Ascendo ad patrem meum* (the text is given as **104+sd+lat[a]**. Benedictus antiphon on Ascension Day (AS, 270;

---

[18] These translations are from Mills *Chester Modernised*.

[19] A processional performance is less likely to be joined by the audience: so perhaps the addition of the ale-wife scene coincided with an acceptance of less audience participation here. Further on the character of the ale-wife, see Ryan 'Item paid'.

WA, 150).

This is followed by five versets, sung by the angels and Jesus. There is no ideal solution to the problem of choosing a musical setting for these: the possibilities are discussed in 6.4, above.

20_2 **20/152+sd1** Function: (a). The three angels sing *Exaltare domine*: this could be either the antiphon (AS 271, WA 147) or the responsory (AS, 274; WA, 147).

20_3 **20/152+sd2** Function: (a). After singing *Exaltare domine* the angels descend and address the apostles in *Viri Gallilei*: this seems to be the antiphon (AS, 269; WA, 149).

21 Pentecost

21_1 **21/120+sd** Function: none. All the apostles sing the hymn *Veni creator spiritus* (HS, 111), kneeling: apparently all the verses should be sung.

21_2 **21/238+sd** Function: (a), (h). Two angels sing the antiphon *Accipite spiritum sanctum* (AS, 280).

21_A **21/310+sd**, and eleven more Latin lines before **355**. Function: none. These verses of the Apostles' Creed should if possible be sung, each apostle in turn singing a Latin line and speaking the following stanza in English. The Creed is chanted on a monotone.

There is no direct evidence for singing here, however, and if the cast prefer not to sing the Latin lines, speech is acceptable (and was perhaps usual).

22 The Prophets of Antichrist

No cues for music. On the question of speaking the Latin lines, see 6.4, above.

23 The Coming of Antichrist

23_1 **23/722+sd** Function: (g). The archangel Michael sings the communion *Gaudete justi in domino* (GS, 218) as he leads Elias and Enoch to glory.

24 The Last Judgement

24_1 **24/40+sd** Function: (b), or (a). The two angels blow their trumpets.

24_2 **24/452** Function: none. Jesus (or one or more angels?) sings *Venite benedicti*. For the possible settings, see 6.4, above.

24_3 **24/508+sd** Function: (a). The angels sing either *Letamini in domino* or the hymn *Salvator mundi domine* (AS, 46): for the sources and settings of *Letamini in domino*, see section 6.4, above. The piece is sung while the angels are separating the blessed from the damned.

24_A **24/708** Function: (g), (i). There is no cue for music at the end of the play, but it seems strange that the end of the cycle, and the final restoration of Divine Order, should not be so marked.

7

The Cornish Cycle

7.1 Introduction

The Cornish plays or *Ordinalia* form a three-day cycle written in Cornish with Latin speech headings and directions.[1] They survive in a single fifteenth-century source, now MS Bodley 791 at the Bodleian Library, Oxford.[2] It can be shown that this manuscript is not the original (Bakere *Cornish Ordinalia*, 1), and there is general agreement that the cycle itself dates from the late fourteenth century. No facsimile has been published.

The standard edition and translation of the cycle is that of Edwin Norris, *The Ancient Cornish Drama* (1859), which is in two volumes. It is generally accurate, according to Bakere,[3] and as it gives the Cornish text in parallel with the translation I have preferred it for reference in this chapter. The other translation easily available is that of Markham Harris, *The Cornish Ordinalia* (1969). This is a more readable (and probably more actable) translation than Norris's: but it is freer as a translation, it is set out as prose, without the original line-numbers, and it does not have the Cornish in parallel. It is therefore not convenient to cite. Phyllis Pier Harris's edition of the first day, *Origo Mundi*, is available only as a PhD thesis (1964).

Cornish drama has been slow to stimulate critical work. The work of Nance,

---

[1] For the name *Ordinalia*, see Longsworth *Cornish Ordinalia*, 104–6. It is unclear to me whether the name relates to the authority of the manuscript as the text that sets out the way the drama should be played, or to its status as the book used by the regulator of a performance, the ordinary, who prompted the actors. See Butterworth 'Prompting' for a review of the evidence concerning prompting in full view of the audience.

[2] Bodley 791 is described in *REED.Cornwall*, 541–3. While there is a consensus that the manuscript dates from the fifteenth century, no closer dating has been agreed. Two eighteenth-century copies of this manuscript have no independent authority.

[3] Alan Kent has also checked the quotations used in this chapter: he, too, reports a high level of accuracy in Norris's translations. Where Norris seems inaccurate or questionable I have noted the fact.

Longsworth and Bakere forms a core of older scholarship in Ordinalia studies, together with Neville Denny's essay 'Arena Staging' (1973): but more recently Evelyn Newlyn, Gloria Betcher and others have opened up aspects of Cornish drama, while Brian Murdoch has given this work a context in Cornish literature as a whole.[4] This scholarship has been brought together in the REED volume on Dorset and Cornwall (1999), in which the editors for Cornwall, Joyce and Newlyn, have also published the extant records of early dramatic activity in the county.[5]

Early Cornish drama has not received many performances, for various reasons, although the situation is improving. In a sense this slow start is a surprise, for Neville Denny's complete performance of the Ordinalia in Piran Round (1969) was the first full-scale revival of a play cycle in modern times, ante-dating Jane Oakshott's processional waggon performance of the York Cycle by six years. The language problem – and more specifically the problem of devising a suitable translation – is one reason why Cornish drama has not been among the most often performed. As one would expect, the revival of interest in Cornish drama and literature has developed simultaneously with a revival of the language itself.

Most scholars have considered the place-names in the Ordinalia to show that the cycle originated in the area of Penryn. The College of Glasney, just south of that town, seemed the only place in the area that could have produced a playwright for the cycle (Longsworth *Cornish Ordinalia*, 6; Bakere *Cornish Ordinalia*, 31). There is still much to be said for this view, although Betcher has recently put forward a case for Bodmin as the Ordinalia's place of origin.[6]

No banns or other proclamation survives for the Ordinalia. The cast-list that appears at the end of the text for each day shows the length of each role (in stanzas), but there is no information on the actors or on the auspices under which the play was performed.

Each of the three parts of the drama includes a staging diagram.[7] These seem to show that the cycle was performed in a *plen-an-gwary,* or circular playing-place with *sedes* around the sides for the major characters and locations. Interest in these diagrams has centred on their similarity to that for *The Castle of Perseverance* and on their relationship to the two surviving Cornish playing-places, Piran Round and St Just Round. The *REED.Cornwall* editors have made considerable additions to Bakere's list of playing-places, however, and these two rounds are now of less direct importance than they were as evidence for the staging of the Ordinalia.

There is no notated music in the manuscript of the Ordinalia. As noted in

---

4 For works additional to those cited here, see Higgins *Bibliography*.

5 See *sub* Hays in the Bibliography, below. In regard to the Ordinalia, however, *REED.Cornwall* adds nothing substantial to the material presented by Bakere in her second chapter. ('*REED.Cornwall*' refers to the second section of the REED volume devoted to Dorset and Cornwall.)

6 Betcher 'Place names'.

7 These diagrams are reproduced in Norris *Ancient Cornish Drama* I, 219 and 479, and II, 201; Davidson *Illustrations*, 43–4; and *REED.Cornwall*, 551–3.

section 7.3, below, the refrain at **3/733–4, 3/753–4** and **3/779–80** may be pre-existent, and a pre-existent musical setting is therefore possible.

The cycle consists of a three-day drama, but that was not necessarily its original form. Bakere noted that the place-names appearing in the second day, *Passio Domini* (hereafter PD) are from West Penwith, whereas those in the other days are from the Penryn area: and this was a factor in her belief that PD is probably older than the first day, *Origo Mundi* (OM), and the third, *Resurrexio Domini* (RD).[8] It has been noted that the Cornish cycle owes more to continental dramas than to the English cycles, since there is no Nativity sequence, very little of the Ministry, and no Last Judgement in the cycle as it survives. This is however a little misleading, for an alternative ending to OM shows that on some occasion, at least, the first day was followed by a Nativity.[9] While the content of the Ordinalia is unusual for English drama, therefore, in its lack of episodes around the Nativity and Ministry and after the Ascension, and in its inclusion of the Maximilla episode and the Death of Pilate, we cannot say that all of these were characteristic features of the drama. The Ordinalia as we have them may be only a part of a larger collection of biblical plays in Cornish, a possibility that is confirmed both by the extant records of drama in Cornwall and by *The Creacion of the World* (see 7.6 and chapter 8, below).

The Cornish cycle contains the following episodes:

1 Ordinale de Origine Mundi
The Creation, and Fall of Man
Cain and Abel
Seth, and the Death of Adam
Noah, and the Flood
Abraham and Isaac
Moses and the Burning Bush; Pharaoh; the Plagues
The Exodus, and the Crossing of the Red Sea
The Children of Israel in the Wilderness
King David, and the Rods of Grace
David and Bathsheba
Solomon and the Building of the Temple
Maximilla

---

8 Later scholars do not seem to have followed up Neville Denny's suggestion ('Arena staging', 125) that PD and the first part of RD constitute a pre-existent passion play that was incorporated into the Ordinalia.
9 See *REED.Cornwall*, 542. Alan Kent has now written a nativity play, *Nativitas Domini*, which is being translated into Cornish by Tim Saunders.

2 *Passio Domini Nostri Jhesu Christi*
The Temptation of Christ
The Entry into Jerusalem
The Expulsion of the Traders from the Temple
The Healing of the Blind and the Crippled
Jesus at the House of Simon the Leper
The Conspiracy
The Last Supper
The Agony in the Garden, and the Betrayal
Christ before Caiaphas; Peter's Denial, and the Buffetting
The Remorse and Death of Judas
Christ before Pilate
Christ before Herod
The Dream of Pilate's Wife
The Scourging, and the Crown of Thorns
The Condemnation
The *Via Crucis*
The Forging of the Nails
The Crucifixion
The Two Thieves
The Last Words, and the Death of Jesus
Longius
The Deposition, Anointing, and Burial

3 *Ordinale de Resurrexione Domini Nostri Jhesu Christi*
The Resurrection
    The Imprisonment of Joseph and Nicodemus
    The Harrowing of Hell
    The Freeing of Joseph and Nicodemus
    The Setting of the Watch
    The Resurrection, and Christ's Meeting with the Virgin
    The Soldiers with Pilate
    The Maries at the Tomb
    Magdalene and the Gardener
    Doubting Thomas, and Christ's Appearance to the Apostles
    The Journey to Emmaus
    Christ's Appearance to Thomas and the Other Apostles
The Death of Pilate
The Ascension of Christ

7.2 Dramatic directions

Dramatic directions in the Ordinalia are in Latin. Bakere distinguished two types (*Cornish Ordinalia*, 1–2). Directions of the first type are in the hands of the two main scribes, in a rather more formal script than the text: they run across the page in the main text-area, but are not bracketted on the right side as the text lines are. These are clearly original directions, at least in the sense that they were in the exemplar used by the main scribes. Directions of the second type, which Bakere thought might relate to actual performance, are obviously not original in any sense: they are inserted in the margin in a different hand, a cursive script that is often small and difficult to read. Bakere dated them to the late fifteenth century.

The Ordinalia manuscript thus shows the distinction, seen in other plays, between original and marginal directions. The closest parallel as regards the origin of the two types is perhaps with the York cycle (see section 1.2), where, too, a more formal script was used for original directions: the scribes of the Ordinalia, however, did not use red ink for these.

The text of the Ordinalia includes a total of 388 places at which directions are found, but only ten of these need be considered here. It is therefore convenient to give basic statistics about the directions in tabular form (see Table 11). It must be emphasised that these are the numbers of places in which directions occur. The actual number of directions is of course much greater because of the multiple directions: 388+53 = 441.

TABLE 11 : NUMBERS OF DIRECTIONS IN THE ORDINALIA

Type of direction	Numbers			
(o = original, m = marginal)	OM	PD	RD	Total
o	47	63	20	130
o+o	0	0	1	1
o+m	10	25	5	40
o+o+m	0	0	1	1
o+m+m	0	1	1	2
m	65	106	38	209
m+m	2	2	0	4
m+m+m	0	1	0	1
TOTALS	124	198	66	388

TABLE 12 : MUSICAL AND OTHER AURAL DIRECTIONS IN THE
    ORDINALIA

Play/line	type	Direction and comments
Origo Mundi		
1/1708	o	*Et veniet moyses et aaron et facit eis hallelujah et dicet moyses*
1/2254	o	*Et tunc sub arbore sancta incipit psalterium scilicet Beatus Vir.* For this reading, see section 7.4 under **1/2254+sd.**
Passio Domini		
2/3066	m	*flat cornu*
Resurrectio Domini		
3/422	o+m+m	(1) *hic dormiunt milites*
		(2) *tunc surrexit Ihesus a mortuis et iet ubicunque voluerit et cantant angeli cristus resurgens*
		(3) *et postea dicit maria*
3/732	o	*cantant*
3/874	o	*mulier noli me tangere*
3/1260	o	*tu peregrinus es*
3/1320	o	*nonne cor nostrum ardens erat nobis in uia*
3/2360	o+o	(1) *et sic finitur mors pilati*
		(2) *et incipit ascencio Xti in celum et dicit petrus*
		Direction (1) follows a text passage in which the demons agree to sing a partsong at Pilate's passage to Hell: the 'et sic' therefore seems to refer to the manner of the demons' exit with Pilate's body, singing.
3/2528	o	*tunc cantent omnes angeli Gloria in excelsis deo*

The figures in Table 11 may remind us of the probability that the Ordinalia were performed at some time – indeed, more than once, as the alternative endings to OM suggest. Original directions (SDs) are found in 174 places, while marginal directions (MDs) occur in 257; and these 257 include no fewer than 214 places that are additional to the locations of SDs. The directions that seem to stem from producers' notes for performances, then, far outnumber those that were presumably written in by the playwright.

Table 12 quotes the musical and potentially musical directions. Many of the original directions incorporate a SH, and this is so common that I have not noted it in the Comments column. We might expect, with the York and Chester cycles in mind, especially, that the specific directions for music would be in the MDs rather than the SDs proper, but this is not the case: **2/3066+md** and **3/422+md1** are definite cues for aural events (including singing), but so are **3/732+sd** and **3/2528+sd**; and **3/2360+sd1** is also musical, although only by implication. The conclusion to be drawn is not, perhaps, that the producers showed little interest in music, but that aural effects did not play a large part in any of the thinking behind this cycle.

7.3 Text references

1 *Origo Mundi*
1/207–8

| [EUA] dyson hep whethe the gorn | [EVE] Quietly without blowing thy |
| dysempys gvra y thybry | Eat it immediately.   [horn, |

This is metaphorical: 'without drawing attention to yourself'.

1/214–16

[EUA] clewys a'n nyl tenewen	[EVE] I heard on one side[10]
vn el ov talleth cane	An angel beginning to sing
a vghaf war an wethen	Above me on the tree.

Line **215** seems to mean 'sing' literally, as if the Devil had sung to Eve at **148+ sd**. That SD says that 'the Devil, like a serpent, speaks to Eve in the tree of knowledge, and he says wickedly to Eve' (... *diabolus tanquam serpens loquitur ad euam in arbore scientie et dicit male ad euam.*): but in his speech with Eve the Devil suggests that he can both bring 'joy and mirth' to her and help her to achieve Heaven (lines **151–6**). Moreover, he later states that he has come from Heaven in order to help her: *A'n nef my a theth yn nans / eua wek gvella the cher* ('From heaven I come now / Sweet Eve, to better thy condition': **165–6**). This is consonant with the Devil's use of song to deceive Eve into thinking that he is an angel: see below and, for a fuller discussion of the Devil's strategy, I, 200–1.

1/223–4

| [ADAM] rag ef o tebel ethen | [ADAM] For he was an evil bird |
| neb a glewsys ov cane | Whom thou didst hear singing, |

Line **224** seems to carry the same literal meaning as **215**.

---

10 Alan Kent suggests 'beside me' for 'on one side' in line **214**.

1/309–10

> [DEMON] the behe may fe ellas [DEVIL] ... so that 'alas' may be
> aga han kepar ha my Their song like as mine.

Metaphorical usage.

1/545–6

> [LUCIFER] may hallo cane ellas [LUCIFER] That he may sing 'alas'
> nefre yn tewolgow tew Ever in black darkness.[11]

Metaphorical usage.

1/561–2

> [SATANAS] my a gan an conternot [SATAN] I will sing the counter note,
> ha ty dyscant ym-kener And thou shalt sing descant
> with me.

Satan is addressing Beelzebub, and seems to mean that the latter will sing the descant (top line of the musical texture) and he will supply the counter-melody. Alternatively, since Satan is suggesting to Beelzebub that the two of them return (with the soul of Abel) to Lucifer, it may be that he expects Lucifer to sing the tune, himself the counter-melody (i.e. contratenor) and Beelzebub a third line at the top.[12] But Norris has doubts about his translation, and in a note (*Ancient Cornish Drama*, 42) suggests that 'ym-kener' must be a reciprocal passive, implying that they will sing to each other. 'And thou ... to me' might be a better translation, therefore. Markham Harris interprets the passage to imply two-voiced counterpoint, although for technical reasons the translation cannot be right: 'I'll stick to the plainsong while you improvise the descant above it' places the main tune precisely where it cannot be – at the *conternot* or counter-melody.[13]

If two or more of the demons do sing on this occasion, it is surely most likely that Satan and Beelzebub use music between lines **562** and **563** as part of a hellish triumphal procession to Lucifer's seat. But this reference may well be a metaphorical one: Satan is speaking of their pleasure at capturing the soul of Abel, and is also suggesting that he and Beelzebub act together as partners in bringing Abel to their master. (If this is so, however, Beelzebub apparently

[11] Alan Kent suggests 'dense' as a better translation than 'black'.
[12] These possibilities depend on whether a pre-existent tune appears as the upper or lower voice of a two-part texture: if the former, then the counter-melody is the lower voice ('tenor'); if the latter, then the counter-melody is the upper voice (discantus). In either case a third voice (contratenor) is likely to be in a range near, or overlapping, that of the lower voice.
[13] Harris *Cornish Ordinalia*, 17, and note 4 on p. 250.

reneges on the agreement, since he hails Lucifer with the news that 'I have fetched home ... the son of Adam': lines **563–6**.)

1/770

    [SETH] menestrouthy ha can whek   [SETH] Minstrels and sweet song

This line is part of Seth's description of Paradise, and must presumably be taken literally. Seth accepts the angel's invitation to look into Paradise in lines **749–52**, and the music is clearly part of a vision with set-piece music. ('Menestrouthy' should no doubt be translated 'minstrelsy'.) The SD following those lines is the best time (and certainly the latest) for music to begin. From **763** onwards all is in the past tense, so the music has stopped by then.

1/1556–8   [I NUNCIUS]   [FIRST MESSENGER]

              yma ov cul sacryfys   He is making a sacrifice,

              ha'y pobel ef kekeffrys   And his people also,

              the'n keth dev-na gans mur tros   To that same God, with a

                                                    loud noise.[14]

'He' is Moses, and the 'loud noise' seems not to be in the musical sense. Nance and Smith translate 'tros' as 'noise' (1934, 76), with no musical connotation. We should probably infer that the sacrifice is carried out with acclamations from the people.

1/1815   [MOYSES]   [MOSES]

          a son a'n debel bobel   At the noise of the wicked people

There is no need to take this as a musical usage of 'noise', which in this case translates the Cornish 'son'.

1/1995–2000

       REX DD   KING DAVID

       whethoug menstrels ha tabours   Blow minstrels and tabours;

       trey-hans harpes ha trompours   Three hundred harps and trumpets;

       cythol crowd fylh ha savtry   Dulcimer, fiddle, viol and psaltery;

       psalmus gyttrens ha nakrys   Shawms, lutes, and kettle drums;

       organs in weth cymbalys   Organs, also cymbals,

       recordys ha symphony   Recorders, and symphony.

For a commentary on this passage and its relationship to Psalm 150, see I, 60–1.

---

[14] Alan Kent suggests 'with much noise' as a more accurate translation.

The 300 harps would be impossible to stage, and we can think of the enumeration as a rhetorical device: but the passage does seem to call for minstrelsy, with most or all of those instruments represented, after **1/2000**. With so many varieties of instrument, loud and still, a single consort is impossible: there must be at least one loud consort (trumpets, nakers, and perhaps bells) and at least one still consort (everything else), so that the performance is more protracted than it might appear at first sight. This is in fact a 'set-piece' performance.

1/2255–6	REX DD		KING DAVID
	ov conselar whek y'th pesaf		My sweet adviser, I pray thee,
	dysk thy'mmo vn ankenek		Teach me a penitential hymn
	rag ov fehas pan-dra wraf		For my sins; what shall I do,
	may te sorre a tas whek		That I have angered thee, O sweet Father?

The Counsellor answers only the second part of the question, advising David to build a new temple to the glory of God to atone for his sins. But 'penitential hymn' is a free paraphrase, as Norris explains (*Ancient Cornish Drama*, 170–1, note). David has just sung Psalm 1: this is not one of the Seven Penitential Psalms, and its composition is clearly not what David means. The phrase is no doubt meant metaphorically: 'Teach me how to say that I am sorry'.

1/2583	[IIS CARPENT]		[SECOND CARPENTER]
	gurys yv the temple hep son		The temple is done without noise;

Metaphorical: 'without a fuss'.

1/2603–4	[REX SAL]		[KING SOLOMON]
	servys the dev the gane		To sing the service to God,
	y sacra scon my a wra		Consecrate him forthwith I will.

Solomon lists the duties of the bishop who is to serve in the new temple, and in the following lines consecrates and invests his counsellor as bishop. The bishop states his intention of saying the service, at **2621–2** and again at **2623–4**, which would not necessarily contradict either 'sing' or Harris's translation of 'the gane' as 'intone': but **2628+sd** shows that the prayers are spoken (*murmurabunt quasi dicendo orationes*: they shall ... speak low, as if saying prayers).[15]

---

[15] Harris *Cornish Ordinalia*, 71–2. Harris translated this part of the SD in the same way as Norris.

1/2638–40

MAXIMILLA	MAXIMILLA
del vyth gans the gorf prennys	As by thy body redeemed was
adam hag eva kefrys	Adam, and likewise Eve,
ha gorrys the nef gans can	And placed in heaven with song.

'Song' translates 'can', as usual. Although the release of the Souls from Limbo is a normal place for song in the English cycles, it is not clear that that is what happens in the Ordinalia: see below, in relation to **3/288**.

1/2845–6 [REX SAL]   [KING SOLOMON]

a barth a'n tas · menstrels a ras	In the name of the Father; minstrels,
pebough whare	Pipe immediately. [I pray,

This is a cue for actual music at the end of the first day: see I, 375–6.

2 *Passio Domini*

2/150

[SATHANAS] may canaf trew   [SATAN] That I may sing 'alas!'

Metaphorical usage.

2/247–8 [IVˢ PUER]   [FOURTH BOY]

peb ol war pen y dev glyn	Every one upon his knees
a gan yn gorthyans dotho	Will sing in worship to him.

2/252–4 [Vˢ PUER]   [FIFTH BOY]

hagh a gan th'agan sylwyas	And will sing to our Saviour,
bynyges yv map a ras	'Blessed is the Son of grace,
yn hanow dev devethys	Who is come in the name of God.'

The seven boys spread olive branches, palm, bay and box, flowers, and their own clothes before Jesus. The singing must happen at **2/264+sd**, although this is a non-musical direction: Jesus rides on the ass to the temple. (The SD does not mention the actual entry into the city, and nor does the text: apparently this play did not stage the city gate.)

2/274–6 [Iˢ PUER]   [FIRST BOY]

bynyges yv neb a thue	Blessed is he who comes
yn hanow dev thy-lawe	In the name of God, be he praised,
myghtern israel arluth cref	King of Israel, mighty Lord.

The First Boy has already addressed Jesus as 'Son of David' (**2/271**), and these three lines continue (and nearly complete) the text of the antiphon *Hosanna filio David* (AS, 206): 'Osanna filio David: benedictus qui venit in nomine domini, rex Israel: Osanna in excelsis'. This is presumably what the boys have sung.

Harris notes at line **271** (*Cornish Ordinalia*, 88 and 258, n. 1) Jenner's identification of lines **271 ff** as a free paraphrase in Cornish of *Gloria, laus et honor*. As he mentions the change of metre in the speeches of the Fourth, Fifth and Sixth Boys (i.e. **289–300**), Jenner evidently refers to the whole of the boys' speeches, **271–306**. While this passage does present ideas present in *Gloria, laus et honor* it does not particularly follow either the vocabulary or the order of ideas of the piece.[16]

The different metre at lines **289–300**, the speeches of the Fourth, Fifth and Sixth Boys, might suggest a pre-existent Cornish lyric in praise of Christ, but this is very unlikely: the new metre has already been heard at **235–8** and **261–4**. These are single stanzas that do not stand out as passages to be performed differently from those around them, and lines **289–300** are part of a larger passage in which all seven boys praise Jesus. There is no question of these stanzas being sung, therefore.

2/431–2 PILATUS	PILATE
ihesu pendra leuerta	Jesus, what sayest thou
a'n fleghys vs ow cane	Of the children who are singing?

The First, Second and Third Boys have each spoken to Jesus, addressing him once more as 'Son of David' and 'King of Israel' (lines **419–30**). This reminder of the text of the antiphon *Hosanna filio David* may mean that they have sung the piece again, presumably after **2/418**, immediately after the healing of the blind man and the lame man. Alternatively, they may sing after **430**, following the Boys' speeches and before Pilate addresses Jesus.

2/1358–9 [CAYPHAS]	[CAIAPHAS]
hep whethe corn na gul son	Without blow of horn, or making a
kerugh ihesu thy'nny ny	Bring Jesus to us. [noise,

Metaphorical usage: 'without a fuss'. It is just possible that it is meant literally, and that the whole operation of Jesus's capture has been organised as a hunt, or hue and cry: but this does not really make sense, as Annas was involved in the capture and Caiaphas has already examined Jesus at some length – in which case there seems little point in asking for *this* movement of Christ to be a silent one.

---

16 For *Gloria, laus et honor* see I, 269; also PS(H), 52 and PS(P), 46r–v.

2/1810 [HERODES] [HEROD]

ow tyweth na ganno tru That he may not sing sad at last.

Metaphorical usage.

2/3055–7 LUCIFER LUCIFER

belsebuc whek wheyth the corn Sweet Beelzebub, blow thy horn,
ha galwy dre a pup sorn And call through every corner
an thewolow The devils;

2/3061–3

BELSEBUC BEELZEBUB

me a whyth gans mur a grys I will blow with much force,
kynyuer dyaul vs yn beys Every devil that is in the world,
certan yn ta may clewfo Certainly, that he may hear well;

The horn is used to summon demons to withstand the approaching Harrowing
of Hell. Beelzebub blows his horn at **2/3066+md**.

3 *Resurrectio Domini*

3/83–4 [PILATUS] [PILATE]

pan fons fast ro thy'm hep son When they are fast, give me, without
the alwethow Thy keys. [noise,

'Noise' in the sense of unordered sound, not in the musical sense: perhaps
'without a sound'.

3/88–9 [CARCERATOR] [JAILER]

syr iustis kymmer hep son Sir magistrate, take, without noise,
naw alwyth agas pryson Nine keys of your prison,

Clearly meant in the non-musical sense.

3/129–30 [LUCIFER] [LUCIFER]

dylleugh luhes ha taran Send forth lightnings and thunder,
quyt a'n losco That it burn him quite.

Beelzebub immediately says (line **131**) that nothing the demons can do will be
any good, so apparently the lightnings and thunder are not sent out against the
Soul of Christ: this is confirmed in the demons' later discussion, **289–97**. Line
130 is not a cue for thunder, therefore.

3/185–6   [SPIRITUS]   [SPIRIT]
    myhal yn scon gorr'y th'y   Michael, put them forthwith there,
    yn tekter hag yn mur ioy   In pleasure and in much joy,

Michael does not take the Saved Souls to Paradise at **190+sd**, because Adam then has a conversation with various prophets and others. This scene ends at **288**: in the ensuing discussion between Tulfric, Beelzebub and Satan it is clear by line **304** that the Souls have gone. Thus it seems that Michael leads the Saved Souls to Paradise after **288**. To be consistent with **1/2638–40** (see above), the 'pleasure' and 'much joy' should include music at this point, as in other cycles, although there is no specific evidence for it here.

3/733–4
    [MARIA SALOME]   [MARY SALOME]
    ellas mornyngh y syngh   Alas! mourning I sing,
           mornyngh y cal   mourning I call,
    our lord ys deyd that bogthe   Our Lord is dead that bought
           ovs al   us all.

This looks like a metaphorical reference, and can certainly be performed that way. In that case the same text is spoken by Mary Salome again at **753–4** and **779–80**, and these lines can be regarded as a spoken refrain imposing a ritual structure on the speeches of the three Marys.

But this ignores the SD *cantant* after **732**. By itself, this SD suggests that the three Marys sing at that point, after which Mary Salome declaims the final two lines of her speech. Those two lines appear twice more, however, clearly as a refrain, as just noted, but without the SD on either occasion. Why should the singing occur only the first time? Common sense suggests that **732+sd** simply sets up a pattern that is to be repeated, in which case another question arises: Why should Mary Salome speak a refrain for a text in which all three Marys are involved? Answering this brings another factor forward for consideration. *Cantant* may be not only a SD but a SH as well: and perhaps the two lines in question are not spoken by Mary Salome but sung by all three Marys. This makes much better sense of a two-line refrain to speeches by three characters.

3/866   [MAR. MAG.]   [MARY MAGDALENE]
    kueth a portha · ny gansen tru   I feel sorrow; · I would not sing 'alas!'

Metaphorical usage.

3/1010   [THOMAS]   [THOMAS]
    sav ef ny vew gas the son   But he is not alive, leave off thy
                  noise

'Noise' in the non-musical sense.

3/1899–900

[IIIˢ TORTOR]	[THIRD EXECUTIONER]
neffre ny gan ef yn cur gans	He shall never sing in his court
y ganow	With his mouth.

Metaphorical: 'He'll never open his mouth in the (?) court again'. The Third Executioner is referring to the imminent death of Pilate. The word for 'court' is normally 'lys': 'cur' is rare or unknown apart from this. Nance suggests 'choir' rather than 'court', which makes good sense.[17]

3/2296–7

[IVˢ TORTOR]	[FOURTH EXECUTIONER]
me a glew vn hager noyes	I hear an ugly noise
yn carn yn mor er y byn	On a rock in the sea meeting him.

The Fourth Executioner later says (**2299–2300**) that many devils took the body of Pilate, which was pushed out to sea in a boat. The First Executioner says that devils, crying loudly, took Pilate (**2302–4**). The 'ugly noise', then, is a hellish sound, not a musical one, and it includes the vocal sound of demons.

This scene gives way to a scene between Lucifer and several demons starting at line **2307**, so the hellish noise should carry over from the executioners' scene into the next one.

3/2313–14 [LUCIFER] [LUCIFER]

ha'y gan a vyth ogh goef	And his song shall be 'Oh! miserable
the'n bys-ma pan fue genys	That I was born to this world!' [me,

Metaphorical: Lucifer is foretelling Pilate's lament in Hell.

3/2350

[SATHANAS]	[SATAN]
the cane a vyth goef	Thy song shall be 'Wo is me!'

Metaphorical: Satan is addressing Pilate.

3/2353–4

[BELSEBUK]	[BEELZEBUB]
ha ty tulfryk pen pusorn	And thou Tulfric, the end of a
dalleth thy'nny ny cane	Begin to sing to us. [song

---

[17] I am grateful to Alan Kent for advice on this matter.

This seems to refer to an actual performance – see the next item – but its meaning is far from clear. Alan Kent suggests that 'the end of a song' must be a mistranslation for 'the head of a song', i.e. the beginning: and 'head' is in fact what Norris gives for 'pen' in his glossary (*Ancient Cornish Drama* II, 411). While it would be tempting to suggest that the demons sing a song backwards, therefore, this probably means that Tulfric leads the song by singing the first line.

3/2358–60 [TULFRYK] [TULFRIC]

belsebuk ha sattanas — Beelzebub and Satan,
kenough why faborden bras — You sing a great bass,
ha me a can trebyl fyn — And I will sing a fine treble.

The demons are dragging Pilate to hell in the boat: this is presumably a funeral piece, or a parody of one. These are the last lines of the Death of Pilate section of the play, so a musical (or 'musical') exit for the demons is in order, before the next scene begins.

There are three singers apparently involved, as it is not suggested that Lucifer sing. Perhaps, as the senior, he takes the parodic role of the 'priest'. Tulfric clearly sings the top voice of the three, the treble, but the Cornish does not give the 'bass' to Beelzebub and Satan: 'faborden' really means a counter-melody to the tune. This might suggest that one of those two actually sings the plainsong or other pre-existent tune. For methods of improvising around a chant, see I, 94–7. However, this need not mean that the three demons improvise polyphony in the way that the best church singers could: they may simply have sung in parallel 4ths and 5ths.

Another interpretation of this passage is to take Tulfric's information at face value: in this case the tune is in Tulfric's treble line and the other two do sing together, perhaps a fifth lower, being less accomplished singers than Tulfric. (On the matter of a lead singer, see I, 376–7, although there is no question of 'lining-out' in this case.) If Beelzebub and Satan sing the same line, that might explain why Tulfric describes their faburden as 'bras' – that is, coarse or fat (see Norris's glossary entry, *Ancient Cornish Drama* II, 330). On the whole, this interpretation fits the text better and also makes no professional demand on the actors' musical ability.

There remains the question of the type of parody involved. As noted elsewhere (I, 199, 208–9) the text itself is an obvious pointer to the perversion of musical use, and we should assume that an inversion of liturgical ideas will be incorporated in the text. It is quite likely that the parody will be of some well-known funeral piece, so that the audience is aware of the perversion: and other plays use both Latin and English perversions of the liturgy to make the point. At the same time, the performance will not be a high-quality one musically.[18]

18 On these questions of musicality and parody, see especially I, 202–3.

3/2526–8

[VS ANGELUS]	[FIFTH ANGEL]
ioy del yl ov dythane	As joy may gladden me,
ny ny tywyn ow cane	Let us not be silent, singing
Gloria in excelsis deo	Glory to God in the highest!

The translation of these lines should perhaps have left the Latin in its original form: *Gloria in excelsis deo* is the title of the piece to be performed, as **2528+sd** shows.

3/2645–6

[IMPERATOR]	[EMPEROR]
now menstrels pybygh bysy	Now minstrels, pipe diligently,
may hyllyn mos the thonssye	That we may go to dance.

The last lines of the Ordinalia: the two previous lines (**2643–4**) show this to be a 'blessing' ending. Further on the dance at the end, see I, 198, and especially 374–6.

7.4   Latin and the liturgy

It is tempting to regard Latin as the second language of the Ordinalia, since that is the language of the directions. But in the body of the text Latin probably comes only fourth. The Middle Cornish is larded with English loan-words, sometimes making whole phrases in English, while some characters use passages of French: compared with these, the Latin content is not considerable. However, Bakere concludes that, although English and French are not consistently used for purposes of characterisation, Latin is very specifically used to 'give the events the dignity of liturgical association' (*Cornish Ordinalia*, 9).

Bakere's third chapter, entitled 'Biblical and Liturgical Sources', discusses the relevant sources for both the Cornish text and the Latin lines and incipits.

1 Origo Mundi
1/462

[EUA]	amen, yn della re bo	[EVE]	Amen, so be it.

The end of Adam and Eve's blessing of Abel.

1/666 ADAM	ADAM
in nomine dei patris	In the name of God the Father

The opening of Adam's submission to God's will. The line is integral to the verse, and could hardly be sung. See **1/2020–2**, below.

1/860   [ADAM]   [ADAM]
      Amen pysys pup pryueth   Amen, I pray, all quiet.

Adam's last words.

1/1708+sd   *Et veniet moyses et aaron et facit eis hallelujah et dicet moyses*
            And Moses and Aaron shall come, and sing hallelujah; and Moses shall
            say:

This immediately follows the drowning of the Egyptians in the Red Sea. There are two problems:

1 The Latin seems defective.

 (i) 'Veniet' should presumably be plural (*venient*), so perhaps an abbreviation-sign is omitted over the second 'e': or perhaps 'et aaron' should be 'cum aaron';

 (ii) 'facit' perhaps has 'moyses' as its subject (as 'dicet' does); and

 (iii) 'eis' must refer to the Israelites, although nothing but dramatic context suggests it. The direction may mean, then, 'And Moses and Aaron shall come (or 'And Moses shall come, with Aaron'), and [Moses] shall sing "Alleluia" to [the Israelites], and Moses shall say': or perhaps '... and [Moses] shall intone "Alleluia" for [the Israelites to sing]'. With this interpretation, however, one would expect 'moyses' to be with 'facit' rather than with 'dicet': so it might mean '... and one [i.e. a cantor] shall sing "Alleluia" to [Moses and Aaron; or perhaps to the Israelites?], and Moses shall say'.

2 It is not clear that the making of 'Alleluia' should be musical, nor that it should be taken literally rather than metaphorically: but if it is metaphorical, one would expect a more specific direction; and if literal, shouts of 'Alleluia' – to the present century reminiscent of a revivalist prayer-meeting – may be dramatically weak. Singing an Alleluia or some other song of praise with an Alleluia refrain may be the best way of effecting the scene-change here following a particularly exciting episode.

1/1898   [MOYSES]   [MOSES]
      in manus tuuas dumine   In manus tuas Domine.

The last words of Moses before his death. This phrase stems from Christ's last words on the cross, 'Pater, in manus tuas commendo spiritum meum' (Luke 23/46); more precisely, *In manus tuas Domine* is the *incipit* of a responsory used in the Sarum rite on the fifth Sunday in Lent (SA 190). The phrase is integral to the verse, but Moses might intone the responsory, as this line is the last of the scene. However, this does not seem necessary, and the point of the quotation is adequately made if Moses speaks the line, especially as we think of Christ *speaking* it from the cross.

1/1953

REX DD   bene dicite dominus   KING DAVID   Lord, you say well;

David's first words on being woken by Gabriel with the mission to recover the rods that will eventually form Christ's cross. The canticle *Benedicite* (Daniel 3/57–90) is a possible origin of the phrase, as is the 'Benedicamus Domino' used at the end of Mass and various offices. 'Dominus' is in any case wrong unless 'Benedicit dominus' (the Lord blesses [me]) is intended, a possibility to which we shall return. Norris's translation, in any case, assumes that 'Benedicite' is a mistake for 'benedicis' and 'dominus' for 'domine'.

Various permutations are possible, but three factors incline me to accept 'Benedicit dominus' as the most likely. First, 'dominus' is required for the rhyme with **1/1954** and ought to be retained if at all possible; second, this reading requires the very smallest of orthographic changes, the omission of a single letter; and third, it makes most sense in the circumstances, for David refers to the angel in the third person and, considering the message relayed to him, could reasonably be expected to acknowledge God's blessing similarly.

1/1975–8

[REX DD] In nomine dei patris   [KING DAVID] In the name of God the
    a nef mennaf yskynne   Of heaven, I will mount,   [Father
    ejus atque spiritus   And his Spirit
    re worro wyth am ene   Set a guard over my soul.

These are David's words of dedication as he begins his appointed task. Bakere identified **1975** as part of a blessing that would have been familiar to most people (*Cornish Ordinalia*, 9), and **1977** is related to such a blessing (see **2020–2**, below).

1/2020–2

[REX DD] in nomine patris et filii   [KING DAVID]   In the name of the
    atque spiritus sancti   And Holy Ghost,   [Father, and Son,
    salui modo eritis   You shall now be cured.

The words with which David cures the blind man: these are the lines referred to by Bakere as the 'familiar ecclesiastical words of blessing' (*Cornish Ordinalia*, 9). They form the second half of a stanza, so there is no question of singing them.

1/2252–4 [REX DD]   [KING DAVID]

deus mei miserere	O God, have mercy upon me,
herweth the grath ha'th pyte	According to thy grace and thy pity,
na'm byma peyn yn gorfen	Let not my punishment be to the end.

After Gabriel has shown him his sin with Bathsheba, David confesses his fault in the opening words of Psalm 50, the psalm traditionally associated with this occasion (although in the Bible it is Nathan, not Gabriel, who comes to him). Only this first line is in Latin, however: the Vulgate and psalter versions read 'Miserere mei deus', the transposition being for purposes of the rhyme. The line is integral to the verse, and can hardly be sung.

1/2254+sd   *Et tunc sub arbore sancta incipit psalterium scilicet Beatus vir*
                  And then, under the holy tree, he begins the Psalter, namely, Beatus vir

David recites Psalm 1, clearly a set piece, a special event. Singing it would be an effective and proper way of presenting the psalm (especially for David, traditionally a singer), but it is of course possible that he declaims it.

Norris had some problems with the Latin: he queried what he read – correctly, in my view – as 'scã' (the abbreviation for 'sancta'), and he read 'v[idelicet]' for what is clearly 's[cilicet]'. I therefore give my own reading of the line here, confirming 'sancta' and reading 'scilicet'; and in the translation 'holy' replaces Norris's ellipsis and 'namely' his 'viz.'[19]

2 Passio Domini

2/254–64 As noticed in 7.3, the seven boys spread olive branches, palms, flowers and their own clothes before Jesus: the flowers alert us to the liturgical origin of the details of this scene, as does the specified number of boys.[20] For reasons discussed in 7.3, above, it is likely that the boys sang the antiphon *Hosanna filio David* (AS, 206).

2/405–7 [IHC]   [JESUS]

in nomine patris et filii	In the name of the Father, and Son,
et spiritus sancti amen	And Holy Ghost, amen,
transite a me sani	Go from me healed!

Jesus cures the lame man and the blind man with the invocation used in

---

[19] Norris *Ancient Cornish Drama* I, p. 170, presents a facsimile of the line 'scilicet Beatus vir' instead of a transcription.

[20] Longsworth *Cornish Ordinalia*, 109, notes Bishop Grandisson's directions for seven boys to sing *Gloria in excelsis* at Christmas; he also notes that *Gloria in excelsis* is sung at **3/2528**; and that this cue no doubt used a similar group of singers. He may be right, although the conclusion does not follow as a matter of course.

1/2020–1. This is an integral part of the verse, and cannot be sung. I do not know the origin of **2/407**.

2/2475–6 [IIˢ DOCTOR]	[SECOND DOCTOR]
ha warbarth ol sur crye	And all together surely cry,
crucifige	'Crucify'.

These lines are followed by the SD *et dicunt omnes iudei crucifige*; **2482+sd** reads *crucifige eum* and **2488+sd** *et dicunt omnes crucifige eum*. In Matthew 27/23 the Jews shout 'Crucifigatur'; in Mark 15/13 and 14, 'Crucifige eum'; in Luke 23/21 and John 19/6 and 15, 'Crucifige, crucifige eum'. These SDs therefore give the majority Latin reading.

Since two of these SDs, and the third by implication, are effectively SHs and text, we can probably assume that 'Crucifige' and 'Crucifige eum' are what the crowd in the play actually shout.[21]

3 *Resurrexio Domini*

3/97–124 This passage, together with the SDs before and after it, uses the *Attollite portas* dialogue in a much-shortened form (see I, 278–83). Although the dialogue is entirely in Cornish, it is clear that the author has constructed the scene to make Christ demand entrance three times, with speeches from Lucifer between. It is only after the third demand that Christ enters Limbo: hence the MD after 124, *franguntur portae inferni*, and the original SD, *et sic tercio. tunc intrabit in infernum* ....

There is nothing to indicate a procession here, nor that Christ has supporters with him, but the ritual aspect of this dialogue would be made more effective by these means. In place-and-scaffold performance Christ cannot process around Limbo, which is on the perimeter of the playing-place,[22] but a procession in the playing-place would have the required effect.

3/422+sd *Christus resurgens*, here sung by the angels, exists as an alleluia verse, a responsory, an antiphon and a communion (GS, 126; WA, 22; WA, 133; and GS, 121, respectively). These vary in length and difficulty, but none of them is short or easy to sing. The singers playing the angels must have been professionals, but even the least difficult setting of *Christus resurgens* is very testing for a boy, and the Alleluia verse surely demands an experienced mature singer.[23]

---

[21] Cornish presumably had no word for crucifixion, so that a loan-word – either Latin or English – was needed. The former seems to be the author's choice; modern performance in English translation might be better served by the English phrase.

[22] Limbo is presumably located with *Infernum* (Hell), since **3/124+sd** says that Christ will enter *Infernum*.

[23] See I, section 8.3. *Christus resurgens* was apparently sung at **York 38/186+sd+md** by a boy ('зonge childe': see I, 330): a gifted and experienced boy might indeed sing the

3/455

IHC   o salve sancta parens   JESUS   O hail, holy parent,

Christ addresses his mother after the Resurrection. *Salve sancta parens* is the introit at lady-masses from the Purification to Advent and on the vigil of the Assumption (GS, lxi and plate q; Harrison *Music in Medieval Britain*, 79), and there is a sequence that starts with that *incipit* (Harrison *op. cit.*, 392). The continuation of Christ's speech bears little relation to the introit text, however (**456–62**).

The initial 'O' is extra to the liturgical *incipit*, and was presumably added for metrical reasons: there is no question of singing the liturgical piece. Probably this *incipit*, which gave the name 'Missa Salve' to the lady-masses that it began, was familiar enough for the reference to be understood by some of the audience.

3/648   [PILATUS]   [PILATE]

        ty a fyth drok oremus   Thou shalt have an evil oremus.

The meaning is, presumably, that the servant (whom Pilate holds responsible for the loss of his prisoners Joseph of Arimathea and Nicodemus) will be punished unpleasantly, despite his pleas. The word 'oremus', as a frequent invitation to prayer in various services, would be well known.

3/816

    [MAR. MAGD.]   amen amen   [MARY MAGDALENE] Amen, Amen.

Integral to the verse, and a necessary rhyme: the two previous lines constitute a prayer to Christ. This could not be sung. It is possible that the first 'Amen' would act as a cue to the audience to say the second: but see the next item.

3/829

    MARIA SALOME amen amen ...   MARY SALOME   Amen, amen, ...

Mary Salome's response to the prayer of Mary Magdalene in the previous three lines. Here at the beginning of a speech it seems most unlikely that the audience would be involved, which must cast doubt on the possibility of an audience response at **3/816**.

3/874+sd The SD *mulier noli me tangere* probably refers to John 20/17, 'Noli me tangere': it is not a liturgical item, as far as I know. The use of a biblical quotation may be for the purpose of authentication, giving the scriptural source from which the next speech is derived.

antiphon or the communion.

3/1260+sd The SD *tu peregrinus es* may refer to Luke 24/18, which reads 'Tu solus peregrinus in Jerusalem ...'. The purpose is presumably authentication, as in **3/874+sd**, above.

3/1320+sd The SD *nonne cor nostrum ardens erat nobis in uia* should be co-sidered in conjunction with the text at **1321–5**, which follows Luke 24/32. That verse reads 'Et dixerunt ad invicem: Nonne cor nostrum ardens erat in nobis, dum loqueretur in via, et aperiret nobis Scripturas?' (And they said one to another, Did not our heart burn within us, while he talked with us by the way, and while he opened to us the scriptures?) As so often, **3/1320+sd** is a version both shortened and rather modified, and may have been written down from memory. The possible liturgical items with that *incipit* are an antiphon in the Worcester Antiphoner (WA, *63) and an alleluia verse in the Sarum Gradual (GS, 118): the text of the latter is 'Nonne cor nostrum ardens erat in nobis de ihesu dum loqueretur nobis in via'.

3/1321–5 The Cornish translates 'Nonne ... in nobis' and 'et ... Scripturas', but also adds 'When he did break the bread', which is not in the Vulgate. The 'de Ihesu' of the alleluia verse text noted above is an addition to the biblical account, presumably so that the liturgical text shall be self-explanatory. It may explain **3/1323**, 'a ihesu map maria' (O Jesus, Son of Mary), where 'maria' is the rhyme with 'via' in **1326**. It is possible that the two disciples – or perhaps an angel or two – sing after **1320**, but I am inclined to see this SD as authentication of the ensuing verse, as in the two previous examples.

3/1326

[CLEOPHAS]   literas nobis in via   [CLEOPHAS]   Literas nobis in via.

The last line of the stanza, and of the speech. This is part of the paraphrase noted above under **1321–5**: the Latin is needed as a rhyme for 'Maria' at line **1323**, but 'literas' is not in the Vulgate.

3/2487–516 These speeches by the five angels are loosely based on the text of Isaiah 63/1–3 ('Quis est iste, qui venit de Edom, ...') or its various liturgical derivatives (for which see *Essays* 150–2 and section 6.4, above). There is however no question of a musical performance here.

3/2525 [Vͨ ANGELUS]   [FIFTH ANGEL]
      honor sit deo meo   Be honour to my God!

Integral to the verse, rhyming with **2528** (see below). This is apparently not a liturgical *incipit*, and I do not know of it in any other context. The meaning is a commonplace one, however, as is the wording: and it would be a fairly obvious Latin tag, given **2523–4** (of which this is a summary) and the need to provide a rhyme for **2528**.

3/2528 [V^S ANGELUS]	[FIFTH ANGEL]
Gloria in excelsis deo	Glory to God in the highest!

The SD follows for the singing of *Gloria in excelsis deo*, so that this line is clearly a cue for music.

7.5   Records

The evidence of place-names in the Ordinalia led Bakere to conclude that the plays were 'clearly written for an audience in the neighbourhood of Penryn', and that the kind of person with the right qualifications to write the plays would be found in that area only among the canons of Glasney College (*Cornish Ordinalia*, 48). She further noted that the topographical references to the West Penwith area in *Passio Domini*, with the subsequent proposal that that play may be a little earlier than the other two, need not invalidate the proposition that the three plays were the work of a single playwright (*Cornish Ordinalia*, 47–8). Bakere supported Phyllis Pier Harris's suggestion that the playwright may have been Reginald of St Austell, Rector of St Just in Penwith with a prebend at Glasney from 1358: and she noted that there is a round at St Just (*Cornish Ordinalia*, 48). Performance under the auspices of the College was not proposed, however, since the Ordinalia were apparently written for staging in a *plen-an-gwary* and no such site was known in the vicinity of Penryn (*Cornish Ordinalia*, 23 and 29).

The records presented by Bakere did nothing to solve this problem, so common in drama of this period, of non-association of different types of evidence. No records of drama appeared to survive from any place in the vicinity of Penryn, although there were references to biblical dramas in the fifteenth and sixteenth centuries, and to Robin Hood plays. Bakere assembled and discussed items from the borough accounts of St Ives in the 1570s and 1580s, as well as records from Stratton, St Columb Major, and St Breock.[24]

The publication of *REED.Cornwall* has added much to our knowledge of Cornish drama, but not specifically about the cycle. The six-day play at St Ives, tentatively dated 1575 by Bakere, is dated 1571–2 by the REED editors. The REED volume also includes an item of payment (the sum is unfortunately missing) to 'the pypers for there wages'. This may be a record of the minstrels playing at the end of the drama, as in the Ordinalia and other plays; or it may be to coopers,

---

[24] Bakere's discussion of the records is in *Cornish Ordinalia*, 15–23.

since it appears in a section that is much concerned with drink.[25] A drama taking six days to play could well be a longer version of the Ordinalia or of the cycle of which *The Creacion of the World* was apparently the first day: a payment to 'the carpenters yat made hevin' suggests at least that the 1571–2 performance was of a biblical play. But there is no evidence that actually connects the St Ives performance with any of the extant texts.

Bakere discussed also the record from St Breock for 1557–8 that seems to show a Susanna play being performed there. Unfortunately no detail is given: but again, the story of Susanna is not included in the biblical plays of Cornwall, and is very rare elsewhere in England.[26]

Bakere also studied the records of Bodmin, which *REED.Cornwall* shows to provide evidence of dramatic activity between 1470 and 1566.[27] Inventories from St Petroc's Church include costume items for Jesus and four tormentors in 1539, and additionally for devils in 1566. This certainly looks like costumes for a biblical play: but Bakere noted that it might be a drama played in the church, not in a *plen-an-gwary*.[28] Besides, Bodmin had a Corpus Christi 'show', and this could have included biblical characters.

REED.Cornwall also extends the list of possible playing-places well beyond the two extant examples and twelve other locations in which place-name or other evidence suggested a playing-place to Nance.[29] The current list includes the two extant sites and another 37 likely or possible sites, not all of which can be located with any precision. While there is no evidence that any of these sites was used for drama, the existence of such sites in west Cornwall helps to support the concept of outdoor drama in the county.

7.6 Music and other aural cues

1 *Origo Mundi*

1_1 **1/148+sd** Function (a), (b), (h). The Serpent sings to Eve (cf. 8.6 at 3_1): although the SD does not mention singing, text references at **1/214–6** and **1/223–4** show that this is what happens. No information is given about Satan's voice such as is found in the *Creacion of the World* (see 8.3), nor about the song performed.

1_2 **1/752+sd** Function: (i), and perhaps (a). At the sub-scene level, Seth's visions of Paradise articulate his scene with the angel. The SD does not mention music, but the text at **1/770** shows that Seth sees and hears 'minstrels and sweet song'

---

25 *REED.Cornwall*, 513–14.

26 *REED.Cornwall*, 506.

27 *REED.Cornwall*, 469–75.

28 Bakere *Cornish Ordinalia*, 22–3.

29 The list given in Bakere *Cornish Ordinalia*, 26 is taken from Nance 'Plen an gwary'.

when he looks into Paradise: still minstrelsy and a Latin song of praise would be appropriate, although an English text would also be possible. This must be a complete musical unit, and perhaps a complete piece: to that extent it is a tableau, a set-piece performance. It may also cover Seth's movement away from the gate and back to the angel.

1A 1/794+sd Function: (a), (i). Seth looks into Paradise again, and presumably hears and sees the same as at cue **1₂**. It is not clear how far he has to travel when he 'goes [from the angel], looks and returns', but presumably the music is already in progress when he arrives at the gate, and continues until after he leaves. The music therefore covers the whole of the action between speeches on all three occasions (see the previous cue and the next one).

1B 1/802+sd Function: (a), (i). As noted in 7.3, under **1/770**, the discussion of Paradise is mainly in the past tense from **1/763** onwards. This makes the situation over **1A** and **1B** a little uncertain, but it may give us useful information about these three cues. There are three possibilities:

(i) Cues **1A** and **1B** do not occur. In this case there is music when Seth first looks into Paradise (starting not later than **1/752+sd** and ending before **1/763**), but not when he looks in subsequently;

(ii) Music is continuous from not later than **1/752+sd** until some time after **1/802+sd**, despite Seth's use of the past tense from **1/763** onwards. In this case the dialogue must be spoken over the top of the music; and

(iii) The music is tied strictly to the vision – in fact, it is a part of the vision. In this case the music takes place in the three 'bursts' indicated by **1₂**, **1A** and **1B**, which are therefore set-piece performances. The corollary to this is that the vision itself is not in sight between these events – that is, that except when Seth looks into Paradise at the angel's invitation, Paradise is cut off from his (and our) sight, perhaps by a curtain, the music ceasing also. Clearly, in practical terms the music must be a piece of the right length to be performed in these circumstances.

Of these possibilities, I reject (i) because of its iconographic and/or aural inconsistency. I also reject the twentieth-century time-saving voice-over technique of (ii), which ignores the use of the past tense. This option reduces the place of the music to a strictly incidental role, in which the music's significance is weakened by the overlaying of the dialogue (and, I imagine, the speech is weakened by the musical background). This is especially important if the music is vocal, as it apparently is: the voice-over technique then allows two texts – one narrative and the other contemplative – to interfere with one another.

My preferred solution is (iii). This demands a set-piece performance at each of the cues **1₂**, **1A** and **1B**, during which the audience, like Seth, could contemplate the wonders of Paradise as revealed visually and aurally in the 'vision' (an inadequate word in the circumstances). The music is that of voices and instruments together. Probably three different but related pieces are performed, as in the notated music of **York 45**; or perhaps they are three musically-discrete sections of a single longer work (cf. the sections of *Te Deum* performed in **York 1**). Finally, Seth's vision is stage-managed for the audience by means of a curtain or other device which reveals the vision and hides it again at appropriate times.

1c 1/1558   It is possible that singing or loud music accompanies the sacrifice made by the Children of Israel, but it seems unlikely: there is no structural articulation where this could happen. As noted in 7.3, above, the Israelites probably praise God with loud shouts of acclamation.

1_3 1/1708+sd   Function: (h). The possibilities for this cue are discussed in 7.4, above. In view of the problems with the Latin, I suggest that either Moses or a cantor (i.e. a professional singer) intone an Alleluia or some suitable piece with an Alleluia refrain, which is then sung by either a choir or the Israelites. These choices are partly interdependent, of course.

1_4 1/2000   Function: (h). The music of loud and soft consorts for King David. It is unlikely that the minstrels could represent all the instruments mentioned in lines **1995–2000**, but there is clearly a wide range of minstrelsy.

1_5 1/2254+sd   Function: (a) or (c) (Gabriel), (h). Reciting Psalm 1 here is the less satisfactory solution: David probably ought to sing it. There seems not to be a tract on this psalm, which would be the only normal way of singing it complete, to its own musical setting, without an antiphon. Perhaps he should chant it to a psalm-tone, without accompaniment or with his own accompaniment on a harp (cf. Section 3.6, cue 7_1, for a similar performance in the Towneley cycle).

1_6 1/2846   Function: (g). Minstrels pipe for the end of the first day. This does not seem to be music for the audience to dance to, but is presumably loud playing-out music, perhaps on shawms and trumpet.

2 *Passio Domini*

2_1 2/264+sd   Function: (a), (h). The SD does not mention singing, but see 7.3 for lines **247–76**. The boys apparently sing the antiphon *Hosanna filio David*: note that they also throw down flowers after **2/254**, for which see I, section 7.5. Seven boys is the right number for the singing of *Gloria laus et honor* in the Sarum rite, which the Exeter rite followed closely.[30]

2_2 2/418 or 2/430   Function: ?(h). See 7.3, above, under lines **2/431–2**. It is fairly clear from the text that the boys repeat their performance of *Hosanna filio David*, but it is not clear where. One possibility is after line **418**, immediately following the healing of the blind man and the lame man: this allows three of the boys then to paraphrase parts of the text that they have just sung (lines **419–30**). On the other hand, while this is not incompatible with Pilate's question (**431–4**) about the singing children, a performance after line **430** fits better with it. My

---

[30] Cornwall was part of the Exeter diocese until the Truro diocese was created in 1877.

preference is for the performance after **430**, even though this puts the spoken text first and the more important structural articulation is after line **418**. Of course, it would also be possible for the boys to sing in both places, making three performances in all.

2_3 **2/3066+sd** Function: none. Beelzebub blows his horn to summon the demons to the defence of Hell. On the use of the horn for signalling in this way, see I, 349 and 360–1.[31]

2_A **2/3210+sd** Function: ?none. The 'worship' here could include a sung dirge after Christ's burial.

There is neither music nor dancing, apparently, at the end of the second day: neither would be appropriate.

3 *Resurrexio Domini*

3_1 **3/288** Function: (a), (h). The text reference at **1/2638–40** suggests that the Souls are led to Heaven with song (see 7.3): music is therefore demanded here if a production of the Ordinalia as a whole is to be consistent. This is the only instance in the biblical plays where the sole evidence for music comes from another play. The reference admits of an alternative use of music, however: namely, that angelic music greeted the Souls on their arrival in Heaven. Either interpretation is possible. The apparent parallel in **Chester 17/276+sd** is for a different type of staging and is therefore of limited help.

3_2 **3/422+sd2** Function: (a), (h). The Angels sing *Christus resurgens* at the Resurrection. See under 7.4, above, for the possible liturgical items.

3_3 **3/732+sd** Function: possibly (h) at the sub-scene level. The Marys sing: the song is unknown, unless the following lines, **733–4**, are the text or at least the refrain. On this question, see 7.3: using these two lines as the sung text is surely the best solution, with the piece repeated at 3_A and 3_B.

3_A **3/753–4** should be sung, as above.

3_B **3/779–80** should be sung, as above.

3_C **3/1320+sd** Function: none. The disciples, or one or two angels, might sing the alleluia verse *Nonne cor nostrum* but, as explained in 7.4, above, under lines **3/1321–5**, it seems more likely that this text is not heard.

3_D **3/2360+sd1** Function: (c), (h). If the demons do sing here it should be an obviously parodic performance: vocal noise is in order in any case.

3_E **3/2486+md** Function: (a), (h). There should surely be angelic singing if Jesus ascends here, as lines **2487–9** indicate. A chant or polyphonic setting of *Ascendo ad patrem meum* would be suitable.

[31] Further to I, 349, it should be noted that, although the natural animal horn must have been most often used, ceramic horns were surprisingly common: see Le Patourel 'Ceramic Horns'.

3₄ 3/2528+sd Function: (i). The angels celebrate Christ's entry into Heaven by singing *Gloria in excelsis deo*.

3₅ 3/2646 Function: (g). Pipers play for dancing at the end of the day (which is also the end of the Ordinalia). It is a 'blessing' ending (see **3/2643**). As in **1₆**, the minstrels were probably a shawm-and-trumpet band.

8

The Creacion of the World

8.1 Introduction

The Creacion of the World is found in a manuscript copied by William Jordan, who dated the end of his work 12 August 1611. It is a fair copy, apparently of a prompt-script. The manuscript is now Oxford, Bodleian Library, Bodley MS 219.[1]

No facsimile is available. The play has been edited and translated several times, most recently by Paula Neuss (*The Creacion of the World*, 1983). Neuss presented the Cornish text and her translation on facing pages. References in this chapter are to her edition: all quotations are from the same work.

The play is written in Cornish with English directions. From her study of the language and content of the drama, Neuss concluded that the play itself dates from after 1500 in the form in which it survives, and perhaps from c. 1550 or even later (*Creacion*, lxxii and lxxiv). Further, Neuss believed that this text could have been performed as late as 1602. There is however no known record of its performance, and the provenance of the text is unknown.

The Creacion of the World is subtitled 'The First Daie of Playe'. If it was indeed the first day of a multi-day drama the complete cycle may have been considerably longer than the Ordinalia. In its 2549 lines the *Creacion* reaches only to the end of the Flood sequence, covering 'less than half the biblical history contained in O[rigo] M[undi]' (*Creacion*, 207). Neuss remarked that the whole cycle might have been on the scale of the six-day play mentioned in the St Ives borough accounts for 1575 (*Creacion*, 207: see 8.5). We know nothing about subsequent days of the drama, however: and apart from the subtitle of the *Creacion* our evidence for their former existence consists of Noah's final speech, in which he tells the audience to return the following day to see 'very great matters, / and redemption granted' (lines **2543–4**). This implies that the second day takes the story at least as far as the Parliament in Heaven, and probably into the New Testament, so

---

[1] For a fuller description of the play and its manuscript, see *REED.Cornwall*, 544–6.

that the complete drama may not have been as long as Neuss suggested. Nevertheless, it is a spacious drama constructed on a scale very different from that of the English plays of the Old Testament.

There are no banns or other proclamation for *The Creacion of the World*. No surviving records can be said to refer to this play, since the text and its performances cannot be assigned to a specific location.

The action of the play can be divided into several main sections:[2]

> The Creation of the Angels and of the world to the fifth day (lines 1–112)
> The Fall of Lucifer (113–335)
> The Creation and Fall of Man (336–1053)
> Cain and Abel (1054–428)
> Lamech (1429–725)
> Seth and the Oil of Mercy (1726–2094)
> Enoch (2095–211)
> Noah and the Flood (2212–549)

8.2 Dramatic directions

Dramatic directions are in English. Neuss distinguished two types of direction, corresponding to what in earlier chapters we have called 'stage directions proper' and 'marginal directions' (*Creacion*, lxxv–lxxvi):

1 Directions to the actors, and on the sets, copied in the original prompt-book at the same time as the text; and
2 Notes about the actors' movements, and about properties, written in during rehearsals. These usually occur some lines earlier than the need for them arises in the text.

Whoever wrote these, they cannot now be distinguished through variations in hand, ink-colour and so on, because the extant script is a copy of this prompt-book. Neuss found it easy to decide which was which, however, and printed type 2 in parentheses. In the summary list, Table 13, directions are stated to be of type 1 or type 2 according to Neuss's classification. It should however be noted that, contrary to Neuss's distinction, directions of type 1 sometimes occur several lines early (see 8.3).

---

2 These are not quite the same as those given in Neuss *Creacion*, xx.

TABLE 13 : SUMMARY LIST OF DRAMATIC DIRECTIONS IN
THE CREACION OF THE WORLD

line	type	direction (if relevant) and comments
The Creation of the Angels and the Fall of Lucifer		
		Directions of type 1: 13 (3 of them multiple)
		Directions of type 2: 5
No directions relevant to music		
The Creation and Fall of Man		
		Directions of type 1: 21
		Directions of type 2: 7
		Directions of type 1+2: 1
538	1	*The Serpent singeth in the Tree*
916	1+2	(1) contains multiple directions. The last section is: *And lett hem* [Lucyfer] *crepe on his belly to Hell with great noyse*
Cain and Abel		Directions of type 1: 9
		Directions of type 2: 10
No directions relevant to music		
Seth		Directions of type 1: 1
		Directions of type 2: 1
No directions relevant to music		
Lamech and Cain		Directions of type 1: 10
		Directions of type 2: 1
1720	1	*The devills careth them* [Cain and the servant] *with great noyes to Hell*
Seth's Journey to Paradise, and the Death of Adam		
		Directions of type 1: 11
		Directions of type 2: 1
		Directions of type 1+2: 1
2064	1	*They* [the devils] *go to Hell with great noyse*
2078	1	*Lett Adam be buried in a fayre tombe with som churche songys at hys buryall*

Enoch		Directions of type 1: 5
		Directions of type 2: 1
No directions relevant to music		
Noah and the Flood		
		Directions of type 1: 11 (one of them multiple)
		Directions of type 2: 1
2491	1	*Some good church songys to be songe at the alter*

From Table 13 we can extract the numbers of directions of the different types for the whole play:

Total directions of type 1:	81 (of which 4 are multiple)
Total directions of type 2:	27
Total directions of type 1+2:	2

The total of three directions for music and three directions for other aural events is disappointing, but not surprising when we consider those in Creation, Fall, and Noah plays elsewhere: **Chester 2**, with a single MD for heavenly music, is the only Cain and Abel episode to have a direction for music, and the episodes of Seth, the Oil of Mercy, and Enoch are not dramatised in the English cycles. This can be seen more clearly in a tabulation of the figures, Table 14: in this table, an SD proper in the English cycles is equivalent to type 1 in *Creacion*; MD is equivalent to type 2.

TABLE 14 : DIRECTION TYPES IN CREATION, FALL AND FLOOD
EPISODES

Cycle Plays	Yk 1–9	NT 1–4	Ty 1–3	Ch 1–3	*Creacion*
original SDs	5	10	5	26	83
musical SDs	2	3	0	3	3
added MDs	1	1	0	7	29
musical MDs	1	0	0	7	0

This table shows that not even the relevant Chester plays approach the number of directions contained in the *Creacion*, although they have more than three times as many directions for music: *Creacion* has three musical directions out of a total of 112; Chester has ten out of 33. Although the situation is altered somewhat by the text references in *Creacion*, this is in fact a good indication of the place of music in the Cornish play.

Quite apart from the statistics of the *Creacion* directions, they are unusual in the context of the English plays. That at **538+sd** has the Serpent singing, presumably as a part of Lucifer's deceit, so that Eve will think the Serpent to be an angel. The 'churche songys' at Adam's burial and at Noah's service of Thanksgiving are not specified (**2078+sd**, **2491+sd**), and the question arises whether they were intended to be in the vernacular rather than in Latin.

I have also noted the three directions referring to 'great noise' in connection with entries into Hell (**916+sd**, **1720+sd**, **2064+sd**). This is not a musical noise, of course, but it does create parallels with musical occasions – notably with the Entry into Jerusalem – and should certainly be treated as 'anti-music' (see I, 207, concerning the shouting of demons).

8.3 Text references

25–6 [THE FATHER]
Hag yny y fythe gorrys
Neb an gorth gans joye ha cane.

[THE FATHER]
And in it shall be put
those who will worship me with
joyful song.

'Joye he cane' literally means 'joy and song' (*Creacion*, 208), but this makes little difference to the significance of the lines, which place worship, joy and song together. God again mentions worship of himself in lines **42** and **49**, and eternal praise and honour at lines **58–9**.

67–8 [THE FATHER]
Hag y wrewgh ow aradowe
Gans joy bras ha cane pub
preyse.

[THE FATHER]
and do my commands
with great joy and song always.

Evidently there is heavenly music in this episode: see 8.6.

531–2 [LUCYFER]
Ow voice oll yta changys
A vel mayteth in tevery.

[LUCIFER]
see, my voice is all changed,
just like a maiden.

536–8 [LUCYFER]   [LUCIFER]

    Hag a vyn mos, heb gwill   And I will go without making a
             gycke,   sound
    In wethan pur smoth, heb   smoothly into the tree, without
             mycke,   noise,
    A vell eall wheak afynes.   dressed up like a sweet angel.

These two passages relate to **538+sd**, where the Serpent sings: the music cue is discussed in I, 201.

549–50

EVA   Pew ostashe es in wethan   EVE   Who are you in the tree,
    A wartha gans troes ha cane?   with noisy song above?

'Troes ha cane' literally means 'noise and song' (*Creacion*, 218). 'Noise' is apparently in the modern sense (unless Lucifer brought minstrels with him): is Eve teasing him, or is his singing really not as good as he thinks it is? Later Eve says that she has no fear of the Serpent because her face is lovely (**563–4**), leaving the singing out of it. Later still (**1018–19**) Eve says that it was the Serpent's 'many fair words' that made her think she was an angel. But in recounting the story to Adam afterwards she implicitly links the Serpent's singing with her supposed nature:

759–61

[EVA]   Me a glowas a wartha   [EVE]   I heard above
    War an weathan udn eal   on the tree a sweet angel
    Sure ow cana.   [wheake   surely singing.

On the whole, it may be wise to regard 'noise' as a mild piece of banter and assume that Lucifer's borrowed voice was quite attractive.

918 [LUCYFER]   [LUCIFER]
    May hallaf kyny ellas.   I may well bewail it.

The literal meaning is 'That I may sing "alas"' (*Creacion*, 211): metaphorical usage.

1710–11 [LAMEC]   [LAMECH]
    Ny amownt gwythell duwhan   It's no use making a song and
    Lemyn ragtha.   about him now.   [dance

Metaphorical usage.

2082–3 [SEYTHE] [SETH]

    Gorryn an corf in gwyrras   let us set the body in the ground
    Gans solempnyty ha cane.   with ceremonial song.

The literal meaning of **2083** is 'with ceremony and song'. These lines relate to **2078+sd**, the SD being rather earlier than expected: according to the text, the singing should probably not occur before **2086**. 'Ceremony and song' suggests liturgy in these circumstances.

2487–8 [NOY] [NOAH]

    Me a vidn gwythyll canow,   I will have songs,
    Ha sacryfice ...   and sacrifice ...

2492–3 [NOY] [NOAH]

    Ha rag hedna gwren ny cana   And therefore let us sing
    In gwerthyans ȝen Tase omma.   here in honour of the Father.

Noah, good man that he is, is able to return to the music/praise connection that was stated after the creation of the angels. These lines refer to **2491+sd**, which is therefore a little early.

2547–9 [NOY] [NOAH]

    Mynstrells, grewgh theny peba,   Pipe up for us, minstrels,
    May hallan warbarthe downssya   that we may dance together,
    Del ew an vaner han geys.   as is the manner and the custom.

This is quite explicit about three things:
1 There are minstrels present;
2 The cast and the audience dance together at the end; and
3 This dancing is a custom.[3]

8.4 Latin and the liturgy

1 THE FATHER IN HEAVEN Ego sum Alpha et Omega:

This, the only Latin line in the play, is part of the quotation from Revelation 1/8 seen in most of the English creation plays. It is integral to the verse, and there is no question of singing it.

---

[3] For dancing at the end of the Cornish dramas, see I, 274–6, and especially 275 for this cue.

Two evil characters use the term *Tety valy*: Cain at **1303** and Jabel at **2379**. Neuss suggests comparison with 'tilly-vally' ('fiddlesticks!)' first used by Skelton, and says that it may come from the devil Titivillus (*Creacion*, 226).

Both the text (**2079–94**) and the opening direction (**2078+sd**) suggest that the burial of Adam makes reference to a recognisable burial service, but the author was unspecific about what 'ceremony' and 'songs' should be performed. On this passage in particular, and burials in the plays generally, see I, 289–93.

At the very end of *The Creacion of the World* Noah makes a sacrifice to God in thanksgiving for the safety of himself and his family (**2485–93**). This appears to follow Old Testament practice in sacrificing beasts and birds on an altar, and incense is used (**2493+sd**). In addition, there are 'Some good church songys' sung in God's honour (**2491+sd**, **2492–3**). The SD for singing seems to be misplaced, however: the singing should apparently take place after **2493**, not after **2491**.

8.5 Records

As noted in 7.5, the borough accounts of St Ives include receipts for six days of drama in the accounting year 1571–2. The first item in this list concerns 'the first daye of the playe', and money was received 'for drincke monye after the playe':[4] so it seems clear that this was a single six-day drama. There is also a payment of 4d to 'the carpenters yᵗ made hevin'.[5] This does not suggest a very extensive structure, but the payment may be for incidental expenses: certainly a play such as this seems to have been could be expected to demand a substantial Heaven – as, indeed, the frequent mention of Heaven in the SDs of *The Creacion* suggest.

The St Ives accounts for 1571–2 also include payments for lambskins:

> for halfe a dosin of white lambes skyns   ijd
>
> ...
>
> payd ... for ij dosin of lams skynes ...   iiijs

This amount of skin could conceivably be required in *The Creacion* for the costumes of Adam and Eve, whose initial nakedness is simulated by their apparelling in whi.e leather (**343+sd**). Leather was also required for making dummy demons that fall into Hell during the battle between the nine orders of angels and the angels of Lucifer (**326+sd**).

As noted in 7.6, too, a payment to 'the pypers for there wages' may be for musicians, although it could be to coopers. It is unfortunate that the sum is missing, as it might have furnished a clue as to the number of people concerned.

---

4   *REED.Cornwall*, 513.
5   *REED.Cornwall*, 514.

It is certainly impossible to say, on the basis of these accounts, that *The Creacion of the World* was performed at St Ives in 1572, although it seems that the town probably mounted a cycle play like that of which *The Creacion* is the surviving first day. Neuss offered only two pieces of information that might be relevant to the play's provenance, and they do not constitute direct evidence. First, it is thought that William Jordan, the scribe, 'may have come from the parish of Wendron, in the borough of Helston'.[6] Neuss showed throughout her study, however, that Jordan was ignorant of important aspects of the play, and we can probably regard him as someone with antiquarian interests who had no direct connection (including a geographical connection) with *The Creacion*. Second, Neuss demonstrated that the compiler or playwright of *The Creacion* had probably played God in a performance of *Origo Mundi*. Again, this does not in itself help to locate the play.

No other Cornish records come as close as those of St Ives to showing that a cycle play of the type represented by *The Creacion* was mounted. As Bakere noted, the inventories of St Petroc's church in Bodmin for 1539 and 1566 include costumes for a Passion sequence:[7] but these could not be connected with *The Creacion*, and may not have been for a vernacular spoken drama at all.

8.6   Music and other aural cues

1   *The Creation to the Fifth day*

1_1 **50, 58, 68, 73, 78** Function: (h) and, in effect, (d). At lines **25–6** God states his intention of creating beings who will always praise him 'with joy and song': they are described as nine orders of angels in lines **27–8**. It is therefore appropriate that the angels worship God in music when they have been created. The problem is to know where this should be, and on how many occasions.

The scene of the angels' creation ends at line **78**, when God descends to earth to undertake the second day's creation. This is a possible place for angelic music, and it is a convenient one because of God's movement from Heaven to earth: but it is not an obvious place for the angels to praise God. More obvious places are at the end of each burst of creation: **37–50**, the creation of cherubin, seraphin and thrones, with Lucifer at their head; **51–5**, principalities, powers and dominations;[8] and **59–68**, the creation of archangels, virtues and angels. God's reiteration that each of these groups will honour and praise him suggests that there will be music after each of these

---

6   *Creacion*, lxiv.

7   Bakere *Cornish Ordinalia*, 22; *REED.Cornwall*, 473.

8   The line-numbering is wrong here in Neuss's translation, although it is correct in the Cornish: line 54 is numbered 55.

acts of creation, after lines **50**, **55** and **68**. Alternatively – but this is less likely for narrative reasons – the angels might sing just once, after line **73**, when God blesses all the newly-created angels; or (as noted above) after line **78**, when he leaves the angelic host and descends to earth for the second day of creation.

There is a possibility, then, of a single musical event or – as seems more likely – of at least three musical events during the creation of the angels. If the three or more events are chosen, they could still be taken from a single long work, such as *Te Deum*.

It is worth noting here that at **154** the Angel of Lucifer presumably does *not* sing in the course of praising Lucifer 'above the Trinity': this would be un-characteristic of a follower of the Devil.

2 *The Fall of Lucifer*
No relevant cues.

3 *The Creation and Fall of Man*
3_1 **538+sd** Function: (a). Lucifer, in the form of the Serpent, sings to Eve: on this cue, see 1, 201. The voice is that of a girl; the execution is apparently good enough for Eve to think that the Serpent is an angel. But the song should pro-bably be a give-away for the audience, perhaps a vernacular song in praise of Eve's beauty: Lucifer states his love for Eve at **670** and **700**, and at **1015–16** Eve says that she was nonplussed by the Serpent because she 'received so many fair words'.

The placing of the SD after **538** is a little misleading. Eve appears at **535+sd** and starts speaking at **539**, but the Serpent does not address her until **544**, and she does not mention his singing until **550**. While the Serpent might start singing at **538+sd**, therefore, he could well sing also after **540** and/or at **548+sd** – *Then Eva wondreth of the Serpent when she speaketh*. Again, there is no clear indication whether this is a single performance or more than one musical event, and it must be a producer's decision.

3_2 **916+sd** Function: (a), and perhaps (c). Hellish noise, presumably vocal, for Lucifer's return to Hell: the noise apparently starts at **916+sd** and continues (?intermittently) until Lucifer enters Hell after **934**. The second part of this SD, *And let him creep on his belly to Hell with great noise*, suggests that it is Lucifer himself making the noise, and it is possible that it simply means that Lucifer shouts his lines and adds wails; but it is possible that the demons in Hell express sorrow at his punishment.

4 *Cain and Abel*
5 *Lamech*
No relevant cues.

6 *Seth and the Oil of Mercy*

6₁ 2064+sd Function: (a). Lucifer and three demons return to Hell 'with great noyes', which presumably begins at **2064+sd** and continues (?intermittently) until after **2070**. As in **3₂**, this is likely to mean that they shout their lines and wail loudly.

6₂ 2083 Function: (a). **2081** is the cue for taking Adam's body to the place of burial, and **2082–3** are the cue for placing it in the sepulchre. For the music to be sung at this stage of a burial, see I, 290: the need for a procession from the place of death to the place of burial will depend on the individual production.

Lines **2084–6**, following this event, are an expanded paraphrase of part of the commendation that starts 'Commendo animam tuam' (see I, 291): *terram terre* (earth to earth). The placing of the three pips in Adam's mouth and nostrils follows easily from this, so there should be no music after **2086**, which seems at first sight to be a possible cue for the singing.

2078+sd, the direction for the singing, is clearly too early. Like many of the SDs in this play, it functions more like a section-heading than a direction: but, as elsewhere, its presence as a heading makes a SD unnecessary at the actual moment of action.

Who are the singers at this burial? Although there are no other speaking roles, Seth obviously has helpers for this ceremony, if only because others are needed to carry the body and to place it in the tomb. Seth's 'Let us ...' (**2081**, **2082**) also shows that others are involved. These must include singers, so that the whole event does make some reference to the medieval office.

6ₐ 2094 Function: (h), and perhaps (c). At the end of this scene Seth gives thanks to God. There is no mention of music, but some response is certainly required. An 'Amen' spoken by all the helpers would suffice, but a musical procession out of the playing area (although Seth does not make an exit) is quite possible.

7 *Enoch*

No relevant cues.

8 *Noah and the Flood*

8₁ 2493 Function: (a). 'Some good church songys' cover Noah's sacrifice of thanksgiving. The direction for music is at **2491+sd**, but clearly this is too early: the SD here is again an advance warning. Songs 'in honour of the Father' (**2493**) would suggest liturgical items of praise to God the Father.

8₂ 2549 Function: (g). Minstrelsy for dancing at the end of the play.

9

Miscellaneous Biblical Plays

9.1 Introduction

In this chapter several biblical plays are discussed. The designation 'miscellaneous' is not intended as a value judgement, but implies that there is some problem in categorising them. Some are plays apparently not part of a civic cycle; others are fragmentary; and some have left evidence behind although the play text itself does not survive.

For all of these plays the range of evidence is far from comprehensive. Only one has notated music, and that not demonstrably belonging to the play; none has a set of banns attached; and the provenance is known for only a very few, so that records are of limited help. The plays to be discussed therefore range from some fine dramatic texts that can be performed effectively to plays that are now lost.

The Shrewsbury and Pepys fragments do not appear here. They are discussed in Volume I because of their musical content: the Shrewsbury Fragments in I, 88–107 (which includes a cue-list), and the Pepys Fragment in I, 107–21.

9.2 The Beverley cycle

The case of the Beverley cycle is the most frustrating that we have to consider. No text or banns survive; but there is an important body of civic records relating to the cycle. These documents have been edited and translated by Diana Wyatt.[1] Many of them have appeared in print, the main publications being those of Dennett, Leach and Poulson.[2] The publication of Wyatt's work as a REED

---

[1] *Performance and Ceremonial in Beverley* (1983).

[2] Dennett *Beverley Borough Records, 1575–1821*; Leach *Beverley Town Documents*; Leach *Report on the Manuscripts of the Corporation of Beverley*; Poulson *Beverlac*.

volume will eventually make available a comprehensive collection together with a full scholarly introduction, but meanwhile I shall cite her dissertation here.

Beverley lies north of Hull in the East Riding of Yorkshire, some 30 miles from York by road and 50 from Wakefield. It was a prosperous town, and geographical considerations alone suggest that its Corpus Christi cycle might have been substantially related to the York cycle and its Towneley sibling. The surviving documentation does not allow conclusions to be drawn on this score, however.

The earliest mention of a Corpus Christi pageant is in the Tailors' ordinance of 1377, and in 1390 the town's Governors ordered thirty-nine crafts to perform on Corpus Christi Day according to custom (Wyatt *Performance and Ceremonial*, xxxvi f). There was also a Corpus Christi procession, and a Governors' ordinance of 1431 lists eight religious guilds and twenty crafts in the procession. Records of the procession continue until 1503. Wyatt thinks, on the evidence of a Governors' ordinance of 1498, that by then the procession was delayed until the day after Corpus Christi if the play was performed, the play taking precedence on Corpus Christi Day itself (*ibid.*, xxxvii–xxxix). The pageant route can be worked out for 1449 and 1450, with seven stations on a relatively straight, flat route along the main streets from North Bar to the Beck (*ibid.*, xlii).

Wyatt reports that 36 pageants are 'the maximum recorded at any stage in the cycle's existence', and considers that these could have been performed on a single day (*ibid.*, xlii). The main sources of information about the pageants are the various guild ordinances. From these it is possible to reconstruct a list of the pageants. It was evidently a full cycle, starting with the Fall of Lucifer and ending with Doomsday.[3] Plays 1–9 are the Old Testament section, which includes a play of Seth – the only one in an English-language cycle. Plays 10–20 concern the Nativity and Ministry. Plays 21–32 start with the Entry into Jerusalem and end with the Resurrection. The last group, 33–6, comprises the Castle of Emmaus, the Ascension, the Coronation of the Virgin, and Doomsday. There was apparently no Whitsun play and, unless it was included in the Coronation of Our Lady, no Assumption play.

There is a little hard evidence for the history of the cycle. The accounts for 1423–4 show that Thomas Bynham, a Dominican friar, was paid for composing the banns, and that the proclamation was accompanied by the waits. Wyatt makes the reasonable guess that Bynham may have been responsible for some dramatic material, too, but there is no firm evidence for this (*Performance and Ceremonial*, l–li and 336).[4] In 1519–20 a poet named William Pyers was paid for

---

3   The list for c. 1520 is in Lancashire *Dramatic Texts and Records*, 82–3; the reasoning behind the listings is in Wyatt *Performance and Ceremonial*, xliv–xlix.
4   Bynham was paid 6/8d 'for making and composing' (*pro factura et composicione*) the banns. The banns were proclaimed on 4 May, and the waits were paid 20d for riding with the proclamation. Lancashire dates this 1423, which must be correct: Corpus Christi was on 4 June that year, which gives a little over four weeks between proclamation and play. In 1424 the space between 4 May and Corpus Christi was

coming to Beverley and making revisions to the cycle. Wyatt identifies him with the William Peers who was secretary to the fifth Earl of Northumberland: his work includes a verse chronicle and the famous musical proverbs from the New Lodge at Leckingfield (*ibid.*, li–liv).[5]

The performance of 1520 presumably incorporated Peers's revisions, but nothing is known of the cycle thereafter. Unfortunately, the records of the 1520s are too sparse to answer any questions about the fate of the Beverley cycle.

As neither banns nor individual guild records survive we have no evidence of music in the Beverley cycle. We may however be fairly certain that music played a considerable part in the performances. This would be a reasonable assumption on the grounds of the comprehensive nature of the cycle's contents, of the prosperity of the town, and of the geographical proximity of two other cycles (York and Towneley) with considerable musical content.

More specific reasons can be brought forward. The carvings of minstrels in Beverley Minster, the institution of the Beverley waits in the first decade of the fifteenth century, the building of a pillar in St Mary's Church by the minstrels in 1524, and the clear indication in the 1555 ordinances of the Minstrels' Fellowship that Beverley was the administrative centre of minstrelsy in the north-east – all these show the importance of minstrelsy in Beverley and its surroundings, even if many vital questions concerning this evidence cannot be answered.[6] Moreover, the use of the waits at the riding of the banns in 1423–4 suggests a working relationship between music and the plays: and as far as the final stage of the cycle's history is concerned, we must remember that Peers himself, the reviser of the text, was interested enough in music to have composed the 32 Leckingfield proverbs that are an important source of information about the theory, practice and instruments of music c. 1520.[7]

In all, the Beverley evidence is tantalising in its omissions. We can, I think, be fairly sure that the Beverley text, banns and guild records, had they survived, would have offered a substantial addition to our knowledge of music in the English cycles.

more than seven weeks.

5 See the article on Peers in the *Dictionary of National Biography*.

6 On the carvings of minstrels in Beverley Minster, see Montagu 'Beverley Minster Reconsidered'; on the ordinances of the Beverley minstrels' fraternity, see Wyatt *Performance and Ceremonial*, lxxxiii, and Rastall 'Minstrel Court', especially 101; on the minstrels' pillar, see Rastall *Secular Musicians* I, 23.

7 The proverbs are in British Library, MS Royal 18 D ii: they were edited as Wilson *Musicall Prouerbis*. For a useful discussion of them, see Cooper 'Leckingfield Proverbs'. A little more work on the Northumberland household at this date may prove useful, for the Earl's almoner (who was one of his chaplains) could have been the 'maker of Interludys' c. 1512: see Rastall 'Minstrels and minstrelsy in household account books', especially 13 f.

9.3   The Hull *Noah*

The Noah play at Kingston upon Hull was not part of a Corpus Christi cycle but a separate play performed on Plough Monday.[8] No text survives. The accounts of the Trinity Guild at Hull give considerable information about the staging of the play between 1461 and some time early in the 1530s, however, and although the accounts have not been published there are discussions of them by Anna J. Mill and Robert W. Johnson.[9] From these accounts it is clear that Mrs Noah had a major role in the play, as in some of the cycles.

Singers were paid in many years. Johnson notes that six children of the parish clerk – presumably children trained by him – were sometimes rewarded for singing, but that by the 1520s all payments for singing were to priests and clerks ('Noah at Hull', 106). Johnson also says that the parish clerk and the children sang inside the ship (which was a real sea-going vessel modified for the purpose). They presumably sang during the Flood itself, therefore, as at Chester; and this may have been in addition to a hymn of praise at the end of the play.

9.4   The Newcastle cycle

The Corpus Christi play of Newcastle was a processional cycle, using wheel-less pageant-cars carried by porters. There were 25 or more pageants, but subject-matter can be assigned to particular guilds in only a few cases. The cycle was apparently well established by 1426: the last mention of it is in a document of 1581 (*REED.Newcastle*, 71–2), although it is not known if the cycle was actually played that year.

No manuscripts of the cycle survive, and the only text now extant is the Ship-wrights' play of Noah's Ark, printed by Henry Bourne in 1736.[10] It is not clear that the manuscript used by Bourne was contemporary with performances (as the company's prompt copy would be) rather than a later one. Bourne's work is not easily available: but Anderson and Cawley published a facsimile of pp. 139–41, which contain the play, in 1977.[11] Bourne had some difficulty in reading the manuscript, and produced a text that Anderson and Cawley characterise as 'obviously unsatisfactory ..., corrupted and modernised' ('Newcastle Play', 11). Because of the problems created by this, Davis printed the play twice: first as a transcription of Bourne's text (NCPF, 19–25), and then in an edited version that distinguishes his emendations by means of italics (NCPF, 25–31). Line-numbers

---

[8]   The Monday following the Feast of the Epiphany, 6 January.

[9]   Mill 'Hull Noah Play'; Johnson 'Noah at Hull'.

[10] Bourne *History of Newcastle upon Tyne*.

[11] Anderson and Cawley 'Newcastle Play'.

used here are those of Davis's edited text.

Davis provides an informative introduction to the play, including the history of scholarly work on it (NCPF, xl–xlvii). There is a more recent critical assessment of the text by Cawley ('Noah's Ark'), and Anderson discusses drama and music in *REED.Newcastle* (1982), where the relevant records can be found.

No banns survive for the Newcastle cycle. The Chamberlains' accounts for 1510 and 1511 refer to banns, however, as do those of 1568. As Anderson points out (*REED.Newcastle*, xiv), this last entry shows that crying the banns was itself a considerable performance, as we know it to have been elsewhere. The total ex-pense was £4/3/4d, which included dinner and wine for 60 men and the provision of 35 horses for the players. 8d was paid for a drum, and the waits received 2/-d for 'playinge befor the playeres' (*REED.Newcastle*, 56), presumably at the head of the procession.

There is no surviving list of participating guilds, although it is possible to derive a list of plays and the guilds responsible for them from some of the records. The records are so scattered in date, however, that the list can be given only with the *caveat* that specific dates are involved: in Newcastle, as elsewhere, it was possible for a guild to shift its responsibility from one play to another, as the Bricklayers did. The list below is taken from information given by Davis (NCPF, xlii–xliii) and Anderson (*REED.Newcastle*, xii–xiii).

A	The Creation of Adam	Bricklayers and Plasterers (1454)
1	Noah's Ark	Shipwrights
B	The Offering of Isaac by Abraham	Slaters and Bricklayers (1579)
C	The Deliverance of the Children of Israel out of the Thraldom, Bondage and Servitude of King Pharaoh	Millers (1578)
D	The Three Kings of Cologne	Goldsmiths and others (1536)
E	The Flying of Our Lady into Egypt	Bricklayers and Plasterers (1454)
F	The Baptising of Christ	Barbers (1442)
G	The Last Supper	Fullers and Dyers (1561)
H	The Bearing of the Cross	Weavers (1525)
I	The Burial of Christ	Housecarpenters and Joiners (1579)
J	The Burial of Our Lady St Mary the Virgin	Masons (1581)

A further eight companies or groups of crafts are known to have mounted plays; the Walkers may have done so; and no fewer than five plays were the responsibility of the Merchant Adventurers. It is also possible that some of the eight, or the Walkers, mounted more than one play. The cycle therefore totalled 25 pageants at least. On the pattern of other cycles it is not difficult to find another 15 or more subjects that might have been dramatised at Newcastle, but the evidence to support specific speculation does not exist.

Play 1 contains no SDs. SHs are in Latin, the format being 'Uxor dicat'. On two occasions this form is made more specific: 'Noah respondit'. Only one SH, 'Deabolus intrat' (**1/94+sh**), provides material proper to a direction; the first in the play ('Deus incipitur': **1/1–sh**), may perhaps be regarded in the same light. No music is suggested by these.

There are no text references to music in this play, nor any notated music.

Play 1 contains no Latin lines in the text (see above for the SHs). In connection with the 'Amen' endings of many of the biblical plays (see I, 371–3), it is interesting to note that the 'Amen' of **1/207** is inappropriate as a response from the audience or the named cast. The Devil has just given a curse, so that this is the opposite of a 'blessing' ending. It may be that other, non-speaking, devils appeared in the play, and that they spoke this 'Amen': but there is certainly no evidence for them. The 'Amen' is probably a pious signing-off by the scribe or the dramatist, not to be spoken.

The records of dramatic activity at Newcastle collected in *REED.Newcastle* include extracts from a very fine set of Chamberlains' accounts, a number of civic enrolment books (which contain the ordinaries of some guilds), some records of incorporated companies, and miscellaneous antiquarian material. No account books of the Shipwrights' company survive, but of the other companies to which specific plays can be assigned, the following have accounts still extant: the Goldsmiths, Plumbers, Pewterers, Glaziers and Painters; the Barber Surgeons and Chandlers; and the Housecarpenters.

Records relevant to the Corpus Christi drama at Newcastle are listed here under the individual pageants.

A *The Creation of Adam* (Bricklayers and Plasterers)
A summary of this company's ordinary shows them to have been responsible for this play and play E in 1454 (*REED.Newcastle*, 6). No accounts survive.

1 *Noah's Ark* (Shipwrights)
No records survive.

B *The Offering of Isaac by Abraham* (Slaters and Bricklayers)
The Slaters' accounts for 1568 give a rather uninformative list of expenses for their play, including 8d 'for the Pyper' (*REED.Newcastle*, 57). It is not known for what play the company was then responsible: the payment for a piper does not make the play of Abraham and Isaac very likely, although the minstrel may have been employed to play in procession between stations.

The Slaters and Bricklayers' ordinary dated 1579 names this play but gives no other relevant information (*REED.Newcastle*,63).

C *The Deliverance of the Children of Israel* (Millers)
The Millers' ordinary of 1578 names their play (*REED.Newcastle*, 62).

D *The Three Kings of Cologne* (Goldsmiths, etc.)
The ordinary of the Goldsmiths, Plumbers, Pewterers, Glaziers and Painters' company, dated 1536, names their play (*REED.Newcastle*, 20–1).

The company book has an inventory of properties among the entries for 1599 (132): it includes nothing relevant to music. The entry for 1613 has nothing relevant (*REED.Newcastle*,148).

E *The Flying of Our Lady into Egypt* (Bricklayers and Plasterers)
See under play **A**, above.

F *The Baptising of Christ* (Barbers)
The Barbers' ordinary of 1442 names their play (*REED.Newcastle*, 5–6). Later records of the Barber Surgeons and Chandlers' company date from 1622 onwards and contain no-thing relevant.

G *The Last Supper* (Fullers and Dyers)
The accounts for 1561 show that the Fullers and Dyers were responsible for this play (*REED.Newcastle*, 29). The expenses for the play included 3d to a minstrel who apparently entertained the company after the rehearsal; and a more substantial payment of 12d to the minstrel – the changed article may or may not be relevant – amongst the costs of the performance. It is hard to see how a minstrel would be used in a Last Supper play. He could conceivably perform at the supper itself, but no other Last Supper play is known to include this; he might have played ceremonial entrance-music for Herod or Pilate; or he might have entertained the audience before the play started and/or after the performance.

A payment at the end, of 2/-d 'to the Clerk this yere because of the Play', could conceivably be a fee to a singing-man for performing in the play. There is no obvious place in the Last Supper story for a professional singer, unless a cantor were employed to act the part of one of the apostles and lead the singing in the Mandatum part of the play. This payment comes after the total for the expenditure on the play: thus it would seem to have been made for a wider purpose, not merely for the company's performance. On balance, it seems more likely to be a payment to the company's clerk, who would be responsible for writing out the actors' parts and undertaking other scribal duties.

H *The Bearing of the Cross* (Weavers)
The Weavers' ordinary names their play (*REED.Newcastle*, 17).

I *The Burial of Christ* (Housecarpenters and Joiners)
The company's ordinary of 1579 names their play (*REED.Newcastle*, 63). The House-carpenters' records, starting in 1605, contain nothing relevant.

J *The Burial of Our Lady St Mary the Virgin* (Masons)
The Masons' ordinary of 1581 names their play.

The records give evidence about only one other play:
1568 The Chamberlains' accounts record expenditure on the Hostmen's play
(*REED.Newcastle*, 55): a sum was paid to the players for playing, but none to
singers or minstrels. Anderson says that the Hostmen probably played either the
Harrowing of Hell or Doomsday, since their performance involved fire and
gunpowder. Although the negative evidence is not conclusive, a lack of professional musicians would suggest the former rather than the latter, since at the
very least a Doomsday play would require a professional trumpeter.

There is no evidence for music cues in the only extant play of the Newcastle
cycle, the Shipwrights' play of *Noah's Ark;* and there are only two pieces of evidence concerning identifiable plays:

Play G As already noted, the Fullers and Dyers paid a minstrel for their play of
The Last Supper in 1561. 12d is a substantial sum for this, suggesting an important part in the performance. As noted above, he may have been a *bas* minstrel
performing during the Supper itself (as at a banquet), or a loud minstrel playing
ceremonial music for a role in the play or for the entertainment of the audience.
The latter seems more likely.

Play ?B The Slaters paid a piper in 1568, which may mean that they did not
then play *Abraham and Isaac*.

Finally, as noted above, the lack of a payment for professional music in the
Hostmen's play in 1568 suggests that, of the two plays proposed for this
company, the Harrowing of Hell is more likely than Doomsday.

9.5   The Northampton and Brome *Abraham* plays

The Northampton play is found in Dublin, Trinity College, D.4.18, catalogue no.
432, ff. 74v–81r: there is a facsimile (with introduction) in MDF 5, 33–45. The
standard edition is Davis's in NCPF, 32–42, with extensive introductory notes,
xlvii–lviii.

Davis dated the copying of the play to 'the latter half of 1461', but pointed
out that this is not the author's copy (NCPF, li). He accepted a Northampton
provenance for the play, regarding its survival in Dublin as accidental. His study
of its verse and language led him to conclude that its composition could be dated
'in the first half of the fifteenth century' but not more precisely (NCPF, lviii).

There is no evidence that this play is one of a cycle.

The play contains six directions, all in Latin: but none of them is for music. There are no text references to music, text-lines in Latin, liturgical incipits or notated music in the play. There are no banns associated with it.

There is a record of pageants being stored in St George's Hall, Northampton, c. 1530 or later,[12] but no details relating to the play or its music.

On this evidence no music cues can be listed.

The Brome play of *Abraham and Isaac* is found in a fifteenth-century common-place book probably from Brome Hall, Suffolk: this is now New Haven, Yale University Library, Beinecke Rare Book and Manuscript Library, MS 365: the play is on ff. 15r–22v. There is a facsimile (with introduction by Norman Davis) in MDF 5, 49–65. The standard edition is Davis's in NCPF, 43–57, with extensive introductory notes, lviii–lxx: this is the text referred to here. It has also been edited by Happé (in *English Mystery Plays*) and Bevington (in *Medieval Drama*).

Davis dated the play's composition early in the fifteenth century for linguistic reasons (NCPF, lxx), although the surviving copy is obviously much later: he wrote that its language seems to belong to 'the third rather than the fourth quarter of the century' (NCPF, lxii). The Brome play is textually related to **Chester 4**, Brome lines **105–315** being close to **Chester 4/229–420** (NCPF, lxiii).

The play's three directions are all in English and descriptive: none is for music.

There is a single musical text reference in the play, clearly intended to be understood metaphorically:

234   ABRAHAM   So welawey may be my songe

There are no Latin lines in the text, no liturgical incipits, and no notated music in the play: and there are no banns or records that can be associated with it.

On this evidence no music cues can be listed.

9.6   The Killing of the Children

The full title of this play is *Candelmes Day and the Kyllyng of þe Children of Israelle*, but it is usually known by the shorter title. It is one of the plays in Oxford, Bodleian Library, MS Digby 133, this one appearing on ff. 146r–157v. There is a facsimile (with introduction by Donald C. Baker and J.L. Murphy) in MDF 3. The standard edition is that of Baker, Murphy and Hall in LMRP, lii–lxiii and 96–115. The other plays in the manuscript are *The Conversion of St Paul*, *Mary Mag-*

---

12 Markham and Cox *Records of Northampton* ii, 181–4.

dalen and *Wisdom*, but there is little bibliographical unity in what is really a collection of separate manuscripts: however, the editors believe that the principal scribe of *The Killing of the Children* also copied the Digby *Wisdom* (LMRP, liv).

The date 1512 appears three times in the manuscript of *The Killing of the Children*, and the authors of the introduction to MDF 3 think that the play is not much older than that (MDF 3, xiii). Like other material in Digby 133, this play is East Anglian, perhaps from Bury St Edmunds (LMRP, xiii–xiv).

The prologue spoken by the Poet shows that in the previous year the play of the Shepherds and the Magi had been performed, while at the end he promises that Christ and the Doctors in the Temple will be shown the following year. Thus *The Killing of the Children* was originally one of a group of plays, although the others have apparently not survived. The editors suggest that these dramas formed a cycle played one part at a time annually on St Anne's day (26 July), the occasion stated in the prologue, but reject the theory that this play belonged to an earlier version of the N-Town cycle (LMRP, lx–lxi).

The editors also reject the idea of this play as the text of a travelling company, since the text demands a company of at least seventeen actors. They conclude that the evidence gives some support to Craig's view that the plays belonged to a local annual religious drama. Whether the plays were civic or produced under the auspices of the Church is another matter.

The main directions are in English, but the shorter ones – most of which are marginal – are in Latin. The play's directions are listed in Table 15.

A number of text references are relevant to music and related events:

53–5   [POETA]   And ye menstrallis, doth youre diligens!
                              And ye virgynes, shewe summe sport and plesure,
                              These people to solas, ...

This reference is amplified by **56+sd**.

60   [HERODES]   Fortune, I fynde that she is not my foo!

This may refer to the ballad *Fortune my foe*, definite references to which are known only from the late sixteenth century.[13]

477–9   SYMEON   Ye virgynes alle, with feythfulle intent
                              Dispose youresilf a song for to synge,
                              To worshippe this childe ...

---

[13] See Simpson *British Broadside Ballad*, 225 ff.

TABLE 15 : DIRECTIONS IN *THE KILLING OF THE CHILDREN*

line	marginal?	Eng/ /Lat	Direction if relevant : comments
1 The Massacre of the Innocents			
56	*no	l	*Et tripident*: *this comes at the bottom of a page (f. 146v), or it would no doubt have been marginal.
133	no	e	
216	yes	l	
232	no	e	
276	yes	l	
280	no	e	multiple direction
314	yes	l	
349	no	e	multiple direction
385	no	e	
2 The Purification			
412	no	e	
428	no	e	
436	no	e	
444	yes	e	*Here declare Nunc dimittis*
460	no	e	
464	no	e	
484	no	e	*Here shal Symeon bere Jhesu in his armys, goyng a procession rounde aboute þe tempille, and al þis wyle þe virgynis synge Nunc dimittis and whan þat is don, Symeon seyth:*
516	no	e	
524	no	e	
550	no	e	*Anna Prophetissa et [virgynes] tripident*

483–4 [SYMEON] Now, ye virgynis, to this Lordes preysyng
Syngyth 'Nunc dimittis' of whiche I spak afforn.

These two references are followed by 484+sd.

549–50 [ANNA PROPHETISSA] And shewe ye summe plesure as ye can,
In the worshippe of Jhesu, Oure Lady, and Seynt Anne!

This reference is followed by **550+sd.**

563–6   [POETA]   Wherfor now, ye virgynes, er we go hens,
With alle your cumpany, you goodly avaunce!
Also, ye menstralles, doth your diligens;
Afore oure departyng, geve vs a daunce!

The last lines of the play. This and other references, together with some of the directions, show that a group of 'virgins' both sang and danced. In the list of players at the end of the play text the entry for 'v virgyn' is altered to 'a virgyn', and it is on this basis that a total of 17 players is needed. The play text nevertheless requires a group of virgins throughout, so that the change seems to have been a reduction of forces for a particular performance. Five singers and dancers seem to have been the original requirement, therefore, with a total of 21 players.

Although lines 563–6 are addressed to specific groups, this final dance seems likely to be for the audience to join in, as in the Cornish plays.[14] That being the case, loud minstrelsy would be appropriate.

Apart from the Latin directions the only Latin in the play is the incipit *Nunc dimittis*: this is found in the text at **484**, and in directions at **436+sd**, **444+md**, and **484+sd**. There is no notated music in the play, and neither banns nor records that can be associated with it.

The cues for music and related events in this play are therefore as follows:

1 Prologue, and Massacre of the Innocents
1_1 **56+sd** Function: (h), (e) and probably (b). The (five) virgins dance to the music of minstrels, for the pleasure of the audience.
2 The Purification, and Epilogue
2_1 **484+sd** Function (a). The virgins sing *Nunc dimittis* during the procession round the Temple. Symeon has already 'expounded' the meaning of *Nunc dimittis* (lines **437–44**: see **436+sd**) and then 'declared' (i.e. paraphrased) it (lines **445–60**: see **444+md**).

All of this is a preparation for a Latin performance here. As explained in I, 261–2, this play contains the elements of a Candlemas procession, so that *Nunc dimittis* ought properly to be sung under the antiphon *Lumen ad revelationem*. For other settings of the *Nunc dimittis* text, see I, 263.

2_2 **550+sd** Function (e), (h). Anna and the virgins dance in honour of the Child.
2_3 **566** Function (g). The virgins dance to the music of minstrels. It is likely that the rest of the cast join in this dance, and perhaps the audience too.

---

[14] See I, 374–6.

9.7 The *Burial* and *Resurrection*

These two plays are found in Oxford, Bodleian Library, MS e Museo 160, ff. 140r–172r. There is a facsimile (with introduction by Donald C. Baker and J.L. Murphy) in MDF 3. The standard edition is that of Baker, Murphy, and Hall, LMRP, lxxiv–xcix and 141–93.

The Buryalle of Criste and Mowrnyng perat and *His Resurrection on Pashe Daye at Morn* were regarded by their author as two halves of a single play, the first to be performed on Good Friday and the second on Easter Day (note after **1/55+sd**). They are very nearly self-contained plays, however, and can be performed as such, so that for our present purpose it is convenient to treat them separately. In fact, full dramatic performance was not the author's first thought, for he started to write up his material as a 'treyte [treatise] or meditation' (heading to play 1) and decided to cast it in dramatic form only at a later stage: it is from **1/434+sd** that the writer seems decided on writing a play (LMRP, lxxxv–lxxxvi and 154).

The plays were apparently written by the scribe of this, the unique copy. Other material written by the same scribe is clearly Carthusian in origin, and the dialect is a north-eastern one that points to south Yorkshire. The editors conclude from their study of the manuscript that the author was a Carthusian, writing around 1520 in a Yorkshire priory, perhaps Mount Grace or Axeholme, but most likely Kingston-on-Hull (LMRP, lxxiv–lxxxiii, *passim*).

These plays do not belong, then, to the category of civic drama in which the majority of vernacular biblical plays fall. Their origin as a meditation (and they could still be read, aloud or to oneself, in that form) sets them apart from most civic drama, but any careful reading of the plays – and, even more, any performance – will show that the author's approach and the whole feeling of the drama is very different from that of the civic plays. The editors conclude that these plays 'could easily have been played in a priory', although there is no evidence that they were designed to be played liturgically (LMRP, lxxxviii–lxxxix). My feeling is that, while the intended meditation might have been read to the monks assembled in the refectory or chapter-house, the singing by the whole community at cue 2_2 suggests a performance in the church.

In **1**, the *Burial*, all dramatic directions and speech headings are in red ink. To begin with they are added in the margins: but from **1/434+sd** onwards, when the author had decided to cast his material in dramatic form, they are centred in the text area. Speech headings and directions in **2**, the *Resurrection*, are mainly in black ink: the exceptions are the directions following **2/691**.

Because of the special compositional and scribal circumstances of these plays, the normal distinction between stage directions proper and marginal directions is hardly valid. The directions are listed in Table 16.

TABLE 16 : DIRECTIONS IN THE BODLEY *BURIAL* AND
RESURRECTION

Play/line	lat/ /eng	black/ /red	direction if relevant : comments
The Burial			
1/55	e	?bl	not a direction so much as a section heading
1/56-	e	r	
1/391	l	r	
1/434	e	r	
1/449	e	r	
1/455	e	r	
1/507	l	r	
1/832	l	r	
1/833	l	r	
The Resurrection			
2/-1	e	bl	SH
2/60	e	bl	SH
2/105	e	bl	SH
2/133	e	bl	SH
2/134	e	bl	SH
2/266	l	bl	
2/398	l	bl	
2/557	l	bl	
2/569	l	bl	
2/601	l	bl	
2/618	l	bl	Directions are reported speech
2/628	l	bl	
2/637	l	bl	
2/665	l	bl	
2/691	l	bl/r	[Roman type indicates words in red ink; < > surrounds interlined words; except for interlined words, the first sentence is underlined] *Tunc hee tres cantant idem i.e.Victime pascha[li]* *<totum usque ad Di[c nobis]> in cantifracto vel saltum in pallinodio. Tunc occurent eis apostoli scilicet Petrus Andreas et Johann[es] cantantes hoc scilicet Dic nobis Maria quid vidisti in vi[a.]* Respondent mulieres cantantes *Sepulcrum Christi viuen[tis]* et cetera usque ad *Credendum est.* Apostoli respondentes cantant *Credendum est*

2/691+sd	1	r	*magis soli Marie veraci quam Judeor[um] turbe fallaci.* Mulieres iterum cantant *Scim[us] Christum surrexisse vere.* Apostoli et mulieres s[imul] cantant quasi concredentes *Tu nobis Christe rex mise[rere] Amen.* Post cantum dicit Petrus. *Sufficit si cantetur eisdem notis <et cant[ibus]> vt habetur in sequentia predicta.* The first SD, above, ends the page (f. 170r) by encroaching into the bottom margin, evidently in order to keep the whole direction together on the page. This second direction is added at the foot of the page, in what remains of the bottom margin.
2/691 +sd2	1	r	*Petrus dicit post cantum.* At the top of the next page.
2/721	1	bl	Includes SH
2/755	1	r	*Tunc cantant omnes simul Scimus Christum vell aliam sequentiam aut ympnum de resurrectione. Post cantum dicit Joh[an]nes finem faciens.*

Relevant references in the text are as follows:

1/1–3 [PROLOGUE] A soule that list to singe of loue
Of Crist that com tille vs so lawe,
Rede this treyte ...

An interesting metaphorical use, characterising as musical the soul that will gain from reading what follows.

1/719–21 [MARIE VIRGYN] I sange lullay to bringe you on slepe.
Now is my songe Alese ales my child;
Now may I wayle wringe my hands and wepe.

Line **719** is no doubt to be taken literally, in the sense that 'lullay' (originally 'lully', and the a added) is a lullaby; **720** neatly turns this into a metaphorical usage, since the Virgin is not now literally singing.

2/632 [MAWDLEYN] Now may thou entone a mery songe

Metaphorical: Mary Magdalene is addressing her heart, following her meeting with the risen Christ. 'Entone' means 'sing' or 'chant'; but it has a subsidiary meaning of 'intone',[15] and so may carry the metaphorical meaning 'begin'.

2/689–91 [MAWDLEN] A songe of comforte lete vs expresse
With notes of armonye
Victime paschali laudes immolant Christiani.

These lines are followed by the detailed instructions of **691+sd**. The editors note that the scribe brackets line **691** with the rest of the stanza and give that as their reason for including the line in the numbering. But there is no doubt that the line should be spoken by Mary Magdalene, since it is in any case an integral part of the verse: in fact, it is two lines, 'laudes' and 'Christiani' being rhymes with *ioyfullnese/expresse* and *glorioslye/armonye*. What 'armonye' means here is not certain. The word could refer to the agreeable sound of notes sounded consecutively (Carter *Dictionary*, 14), although one might expect it to be used rather in the sense of an agreeable mixture of simultaneous sounds by 1520. Further on this, see the entry for cue 2_1 below.

2/753–5 [JOHANNES EVANGELISTA] There, brethere, with ioyfulle harte,
And, devowt sisters, on your parte,
Enton sum ermonye!

The same problem arises here as in the previous text reference. Here, however, since both men and women are enjoined to sing, there is harmony in their singing in any case, the men singing in a lower octave than the women in a 'unison' performance. These lines may suggest the presence of a trained choir of nuns, therefore: but at none of the Carthusian houses suggested as possible homes for these plays – Kingston-on-Hull, Mount Grace and Axeholme – was there a nearby house of nuns or canonesses that might have taken part in the dramas.

It seems probable, therefore, that these lines are addressed to the three Marys in role, and therefore that 'St John' is likewise addressing his brothers in role. Presumably the Marys were played by novices or young monks: it may not be safe to assume that they had unbroken voices.

The editors are much concerned with the textual relations between the plays, the Vulgate, and certain medieval critical works and commentaries. They do not think that the author's use of Latin is on the whole informed by liturgy (LMRP, lxxxix). Their notes on the various Latin quotations are in LMRP, 222–30, where they discuss far more material than the Latin quotations presented here.

1/434   *Nemo ascendit in celum nisi qui descendit de celo*

---

[15] See Carter *Dictionary*, under 'entunen'.

This is an exact quotation of John 3/13, except that the initial 'Et' is here omitted. It is apparently not a liturgical item, and there is no reason to sing it.

1/645   *Speciosus forma*, the prophet told.

The editors identify this as a phrase from Psalm 45/2 (44/3 in the Vulgate). Part of this verse, also starting with *Speciosus forma*, is a gradual for various occasions (Sandon II, 76; GS, 177). As it is only a part of a line, however, the question of singing it does not arise.

2/140   *Mulier, quid ploras?* ...

This is John 20/13, although the words were in fact spoken by Christ, not by an angel as here. There is an antiphon with this incipit, but apparently not in the English uses. Again, as this is only part of a line, it must be spoken.

2/352–4   Dauid did say in prophecye,
                Homo pacis mee, in quo speraui,
                Supplantauit me.

The editors justifiably identify this as a 'somewhat garbled version' of Psalm 40/10 (AV 41/9). I have not found it as a liturgical text otherwise. The quotation is integral to the verse, and I see no reason to think that it might have been sung.

2/431–2   ... *Omnes vos scandalum patiemini* –
                'Alle ye shalle suffer sclaunder for me' –

The editors identify this as part of Matthew 26/31: the quotation is not grammatically complete, but the English version gives a little more. The quotation is not a liturgical incipit, as far as I know.

2/458   *Quodcumque ligaueris*, he said ...

Identified as Matthew 16/19. Again, the quotation is grammatically incomplete. Bryden and Hughes (*Index*) list a number of liturgical items beginning with this incipit, but the phrase can hardly be sung in the midst of speech.

2/566–7   *Ostende faciem tuam et salui erimus!*
                Schewe thy powere, gud Lord, and to vs appere!

The editors offer part of Canticum Canticorum 2/14 as the source of this quotation, but the only parallel is 'Ostende mihi faciem tuam'. This is a liturgical

363

incipit, but there is no question of singing it here: and in any case the quotation is an exact one of the refrain of Psalm 79 (see verses 4, 8, and 20).

2/569   *Super nos ...*

Not identified.

2/579–80 *Quem diligit anima mea, quesiui;*
            Quesiui illum, et non inueni!

Identified as Canticum Canticorum 3/1, 2. This is not a liturgical incipit, as far as I know: and as these lines are integral to the verse, there is no case for singing them.

2/594–6   *Filie Jerusalem*, wheros ye goo,
            Nunciate dilecto meo
            Quia amore langueo!

The lines following give a close English paraphrase. The editors identify this as being based on Canticum Canticorum 5/8. It is not a liturgical incipit, and as it is integral to the verse there is no question of singing it.

2/602   *Mulier, ploras? Quem queris?*

Followed by the translation. The editors identify the quotation as John 20/15: the Vulgate is *Mulier, quid ploras?*, which is correctly translated in **2/603**. It is a liturgical *incipit*, but apparently not in the English uses.

2/618++ *Jhesus dicit:* 'Maria!'
            Mawdleyn awnswers: 'Raboni!'

These lines seem to be remnants of the author's original intention, although that intention is seen to be changed – hence the two languages side by side. This continues the narrative of John 20 (verse 16), as does the next quotation. The editors consider that the author's original intention was for 'Maria' and 'Raboni' to rhyme, being the first two lines of a stanza.

2/619   *Noli me tangere!*

The next speech of Jesus, John 20/17. The editors consider that the author meant 'tangere' to rhyme with 'praye' and 'awaye' (**615**, **618**), so that this line is an integral part of the verse.

2/638   *Soror, nuncia nobis!*

This line is not a part of the rhyme-scheme of the verse, although – as the editors point out – the scribe has bracketted it with other lines. The line is not part of the Vulgate version of John 20, and although it parallels lines in liturgical dramas I have not found this wording. The line does not seem to be a liturgical *incipit*.

2/666   *Auete! ...*

Identified as Matthew 28/9. This is only part of a line, and there is no question of singing it.

2/691   *Victime paschali laudes immolant Christiani!*

This is the *incipit* of a sequence for the Easter season:[16] the SD following gives instructions for the performance of the whole sequence (see above and below).

2/755+sd The direction names *Scimus Christum* 'or another sequence or hymn of the Resurrection' as the piece to be sung. *Scimus Christum* is the last section of *Victime paschali laudes*, which the Marys and apostles have recently sung.

Although the fragments of Latin follow liturgical drama as well as the story of the Resurrection as told in St John's Gospel, the actual words chosen are not the *incipits* that could be expected in a sung Latin drama: in fact, there is no obvious rationale behind the use of Latin phrases in this play. The editors are surely right in their judicious conclusion that, although an analogy with Latin drama may have been in the author's mind in play **2**, there is no evidence that the play was designed as a part of the liturgy (LMRP, lxxxviii–lxxxix).

As the editors report (LMRP, lxxxiii), unidentified hands have written on f. 172r, after the end of play **2**, including a line of plainsong on a four-line staff drawn freehand: see Example 1. The notation is in void breves, some of them in ligature, with a C-clef on the third line up. The tune begins rather like those of the 8th-mode antiphons *Bene fundata est* and *Hoc est praeceptum meum* (AS, plates w and Q), but it is neither of these. Immediately above the notation, following the *Explicit* of the play, is a copy of lines **737–8** and the beginning of **739**. These could be a cue for music, in view of the last of these lines, 'Youre name euer blessit bee!', and if so the following lines might be an English paraphrase of the Latin text: these are Andrew's three-line speech beginning 'This resurrection to

---

16 The text in modern Roman service-books reads 'immolent', but English books give 'immolant', as here (Sandon V, 24; ME i, 129).

alle þe warld is consolation'.

This does not seem to paraphrase any liturgical text, however. Moreover, the lines following the *Explicit* are in an unidentified hand, not that of the main scribe; the last line is incomplete; the whole has been cancelled by smudging; and line **739**, in mid-stanza, is not a suitable place for music. On the whole it seems unlikely that the notation has any direct connection with the play.

On the back of this leaf, f. 172v, the last page of the manuscript, are a number of rough writings, the meanings of which are not clear. They include, at the top, an unused five-line staff with what may be an F-clef on the third line up.

EXAMPLE 1 : NOTATION AT THE END OF THE BODLEY
RESURRECTION

There are no surviving banns that can be associated with these plays; and no records are known that might refer to them.

There are no cues for music or other aural events in play **1**. Those for play **2**, *Christ's Resurrection*, are as follows:

2₁ 691+sd Function (a), (b), (h). The three Marys sing *Victimae paschali laudes* as far as 'regnat vivus'. The method of performance is specified: the whole section is to be sung 'in cantifracto vel saltum in pallinodio': that is, according to Stevens, polyphonically or at least antiphonally.[17] It is hard to see how the three Marys could, strictly speaking, sing this section antiphonally. Presumably Magdalene, as the instigator, would intone the sequence and sing verses alternately with the other two women.

Then Peter, Andrew and John run to them, singing the next couplet, 'Dic nobis ... in via'; the Marys reply with 'Sepulchrum Christi ... in Galileam'; the apostles sing 'Credendum est ... fallaci'; the women sing 'Scimus Christum surrexisse a mortuis vere' (the words 'a mortuis' are omitted from the SD, probably because the scribe was put off by making a mistake, which he corrected, with the word 'surrexisse'); then all together sing 'Tu nobis Christe

---

[17] Stevens 'Music in Mediaeval Drama', 90; neither word is in Carter *Dictionary*. The *Revised Medieval Latin Word List* offers only 'pricksong' for 'cantifractus', which strictly means measured music, and which could be monody rather than polyphony; and 'recantation' for 'palinodia'. I am not sure what 'recantation' might mean, but if 'antiphony' is correct, then even monodic measured music might be regarded as technically more demanding.

rex miserere. Amen'.

How the second and subsequent sections are to be performed is not specified, so it is hard to know if the polyphony or antiphonal singing is to continue past the first section. Of course, the piece as set out in detail here *is* an antiphonal performance, although not what might be expected and not strictly what the SD says.

The second SD seems to offer a third – and to the author least attractive – alternative, perhaps to be used only if nothing better can be achieved. It seems to mean: It will suffice if this is sung using the notation and tunes found in the aforesaid sequence. That is, sing it 'straight', if you have to, as set out in the book – unadorned chant.

2_2 **755+sd** Function (h). *Scimus Christum* is sung, presumably right to the end with the 'Amen'. The Marys are perhaps intended to sing the intonation. The wording of this direction, 'Tunc cantant omnes simul', presumably means two things: that everyone sings – not just the Marys and the apostles, but the whole congregation – and that they are all to sing throughout, not antiphonally as in 2_1.

With both of these cues we have the problem of the word 'armonye' in the relevant text reference. It seems to me that in 2_1 a polyphonic setting is envisaged if possible, with antiphonal or even 'straight' plainsong performance as an alternative. The polyphony may, of course, be improvised polyphony of the usual type, although this raises some interesting speculations as to its exact nature. (Further on this, see I, 95–6.) In the case of 2_2, however, simple chant performance is apparently intended, whether the congregation is involved or not. 'Armonye', then, implies a pleasing melodic style of performance.

9.8   The Rickinghall and Ashmole fragments

Two shorter fragments, of widely differing dates, present the speeches of a single character each. These fragments are of considerable interest historically but of little value to the study of music in the plays. They are edited by Norman Davis in NCPF, and are available in facsimile in MDF 5.

The Rickinghall fragment, now London, British Library, Add. Roll 63481 B, is an early fourteenth-century parchment membrane, reproduced in MDF 5, 15–17. The back contains some Latin accounts from the manor of Rickinghall, Suffolk, for the year 1370. The fragment presents a French and parallel English text (NCPF, 116–17), the language of the latter being from the East Midlands (NCPF, cxiv). Since Rickinghall Manor belonged to the abbey of Bury St Edmunds, the manuscript is sometimes known as the Bury St Edmunds fragment.

The French text is a 'pomping' opening by a king, perhaps Herod, who speaks to his messenger in the last three lines of the 15-line text. There is a single dramatic direction, in Latin, for the king's speech to the messenger. There is no indication of music. The English text, which has no direction, is a shorter and probably imperfect version of the French.

There are no text references, Latin lines, or other indications of music: nor are there any banns or records that could be associated with the fragment. There are therefore no cues for music in this text.

The Ashmole fragment, dating from the late fifteenth century, is in Oxford, Bodleian Library, MS Ashmole 750, f. 168r: there is a facsimile in MDF 5, 83, with a brief introduction by Norman Davis on p. 81. The standard edition is Davis's (NCPF, cxviii–cxx and 120): the rather later introduction to MDF makes some corrections to that in NCPF.

This fragment preserves the text of a single role – the Second Soldier – with its cues. The text is hastily written by someone making use of some blank paper in an existing manuscript. The language is English, except for the Latin SH SECUNDUS MILES.

The text seems to be part of a play of Caesar Augustus (NCPF, cxix). The surviving text is too short for evidence of any relation to other texts. There are no SDs (the SD printed in NCPF is corrected to a cue-line in MDF 5), references to music, Latin lines, liturgical *incipits*, or notated music in the fragment; and there are no banns or texts that can be associated with it. There are therefore no music cues for this fragment.

9.9   *The Destruction of Jerusalem*

The Coventry cycle was last performed in 1579. Ingram notes that there was no indication at that time that the cycle would be discontinued (*REED.Coventry*, xix), but the fact is that the next civic performance, in 1584, was not of the cycle but of *The Destruction of Jerusalem*. This was apparently a spectacular, and therefore expensive, production, and it was destined not to become an annual event. The city council was evidently uneasy about the possibility of presenting the cycle again, however, and when the commons of the city asked that they be allowed to perform a play in 1591 the Council took a firm line. It was agreed on 19 May that year that the commons might play *The Destruction of Jerusalem, The Conquest of the Danes* or *The History of King Edward IV*, but no other play would be considered (*REED.Coventry*, 332). This had the effect, no doubt intended, of preventing a production of the cycle.[18] In the event, it is impossible to say which

---

[18] In return for their concession in allowing a dramatic event to take place, the Council required that all maypoles be removed by the following Whitsunday, and that no

play was performed in 1591.

The Coventry *Destruction of Jerusalem* of 1584 is assumed to be based on subject-matter treated by Josephus and dramatised in the two French plays of the *Vengeance Nostre Seigneur Jhesucrist*.[19] The author of the Coventry 'tragedy', Mr Smythe of Oxford, was identified by Chambers as John Smythe of St John's College, Oxford (*The Mediaeval Stage* ii, 361), and Craig assumed that Smythe knew the continental versions of the material (*English Religious Drama*, 361).

Although plays taken from Josephus's work on the destruction of Jerusalem are nowhere discussed as related to biblical plays, there are some connections. Mercadé's *Vengeance Jesu-Christ* at Arras follows the *Passion d'Arras* in that manuscript; the material of the *Vengeance*, with which that of *The Destruction of Jerusalem* is presumably cognate, follows narratively from some of the biblical play material; and its subject-matter is not unlike much of the non-biblical material found in the biblical cycles. In fact, the Coventry *Destruction of Jerusalem* is the only English occurrence of this material, and the recovery of its text would be a find of the greatest significance. As it is, only the accounts relating to the play survive for consideration, now the sole evidence of music in the play.

Ingram prints the various guild-records dealing with *The Destruction* in *REED.Coventry*. The Cappers' records (*REED.Coventry*, 303–4) show that the Cappers played a pageant of their own, for John Green was paid 5/-d for 'makynge the booke' (304). What pageant it was we cannot tell, for the players seem to be listed under their own names, not under those of their roles – understandably, perhaps, with a new play. The general expenses include 12d towards the hire of a drum, 3d for the playing of it, 2/6d to six musicians, and 6d for the hire of a trumpet. The inclusion of 'the clarkes' in the payment for supper may or may not refer to singers. The items for instruments are a little curious. In the case of the drum, 3d does not suggest that the performance merited a professional fee, so it was perhaps just a beating of the drum for marching; but it is strange that they hired a trumpet without a player, since any professional player would have his own instrument and prefer to play it. Perhaps this, too, was an amateur performance. It is also entirely possible that 'the trumpet' *was* the player, performing on his own instrument: this is almost certainly the case with the drum, since 12d is a large payment just for hiring the instrument. Perhaps this includes the player's expenses, separate from the 3d fee for the performance. The payment to six musicians, however, is certainly for professionals, although at 5d each they apparently did not have too strenuous a day.

The Carpenters' account book contains no relevant payments, unless that to the Pinners and Coopers means that they contributed to a pageant presented by that company. The Mercers' accounts are more forthcoming, however (*REED. Coventry*, 305–6). They put on their own pageant – (John) Green was paid for

more maypoles be erected in the city.

[19] For a treatment of this subject in drama, see Wright *Vengeance*.

copying their book, too – to which the Girdlers contributed. Diglyn received 7/-d for drumming, a very considerable sum by any standards. There is also a payment of 5/4d for 'mvssike' and, immediately below it, one of 3/4d to 'The Trumppeter'. Whatever part of the story the Mercers played, music was a considerable feature of it: 'music' would suggest minstrelsy at a banquet, perhaps; a substantial sum for entertaining an important royal figure such as Herod.

The Weavers presented a pageant of their own, but the accounts are disappointingly brief (*REED.Coventry*, 306). A payment of 16/-d to John Smythe must indicate a considerable commitment to their pageant, perhaps by the author himself. A payment to singers (307) seems to refer to the annual dinner, not to the play.

The Butchers paid a contribution to the Whittawers (*REED.Coventry*, 307). The Drapers recorded only a global sum of £6/4/-d for the plays (307: it is written as a plural), but this is commensurate with the £8/9/6d expended by the equally wealthy Mercers (306), and it looks as if they had their own pageant.

Easily the fullest of the guild accounts are those of the Smiths (*REED.Coventry*, 307–9), who presented a pageant and, like others, paid John Green for copying their book. Items concerning music include 5/-d to 'the trumpeter for soundynge in the pageant' and, the next payment, 2/6d to 'hym that playde on the flute'; 2d for drink 'at Walkers' for the musicians; 5/-d to the musicians for playing on their instruments in the pageant; 10d to two drum-players; 6/8d to 'Christofer Dyglyne' for his two drums; 7d to the musicians at the second rehearsal and 4d to 'Cristofer Dyglyn' on the same occasion 'in earnest'; and 4d to 'Cocchame', 'in earnest', for playing on his bagpipes, apparently at a later rehearsal on Monday in Whitsun week.

Christopher Diglin is presumably the 'Diglyn' who played the drum for the Mercers, and perhaps it was also he who hired out a drum to the Cappers. The items concerning Diglin have always been taken at face value, but Philip Butterworth has recently suggested another reason for the use of drums, and one that might help to explain the relatively large sums of money paid for them: he suggests very plausibly that drums were used as part of the noise-making equipment for thunder in the production of storms.[20] Alternatively, it may be that he was responsible for organising a considerable amount of dancing.

The Smiths' accounts are especially rich for the production of 1584, which was evidently a spectacular affair with plenty of music and other aural effects: and there is potentially useful material in other accounts, too. Had the text of *The Destruction of Jerusalem* survived there would have been much to discuss concerning music in the play.

---

[20] Butterworth *Theatre of Fire*, 47.

PART 2

Historical Drama 2:
Saint Plays and Miracle Plays

10

The Conversion of St Paul

10.1 Introduction

The Conversion of Saint Paul is the first of the plays found in Digby 133, taking up ff. 37r–50v:[1] there is non-dramatic material on either side of it. The play is reproduced in MDF 3 (1976), with an introduction by D.C. Baker and J.L. Murphy. The standard edition of the Digby plays is LMRP, by Baker, Murphy, and Hall: *St Paul* is on pp. 1–23, with an extensive introduction on pp. xv–xxx.

The play was originally copied as a *libellum* of 12 leaves, but an additional scene – that of Belyall and Mercury – was physically inserted as a gathering of four leaves: the first of these four has been removed, as has the last of the original booklet, but no text is apparently missing on this account (LMRP, xv–xvi).

The editors identify three scribes, as follows (LMRP, xvi–xviii: the letter designations are mine):

Scribe A, the principal scribe, wrote out the main part of the play, apparently ('clearly', according to the editors) in the first quarter of the sixteenth century. His work was added to by the other two scribes.

Scribe B, working apparently 'twenty to thirty years' after Scribe A (LMRP, xvii), added the episode of Belyall and Mercury, now ff. 45–7. In order to arrange the inserted episode, this scribe cancelled a short passage at the end of f. 44v (LMRP, 15) and recopied it at the end of his insertion (f. 47v, printed in LMRP, 18). The editors date his work from 'the 1550s' (LMRP, xviii) or from 'the 1540s–1550s' (LMRP, xxix).[2]

Scribe C, working after Scribe B but at about the same time and 'perhaps twenty

---

[1] The others are *Mary Magdalen, The Killing of the Children* and an incomplete copy of *Wisdom*: see sections 11.1, 9.6 and 16.1, respectively.

[2] The editors' datings of Scribes A and B are contradictory. They may mean that Scribe A worked near the end of the first quarter of the century and Scribe B within a few years on either side of 1550: but even this may be more precise than the evidence really allows. See also note 3, below.

or so years after our manuscript was written' (LMRP, xxix),[3] added the SD *daunce* in three places and probably added the SH *Diabolus*, which clarifies Scribe B's work at the beginning of his insertion, on f. 44r.

The editors regard the language of Scribes A and B as 'East Midland with a number of features found in East Anglia' (LMRP, xix), although they point out that the *x*-spelling is less frequent in this play than 'in *Mary Magdalen* and other distinctly Norfolk texts'. They find no reason to think that the texts are much older than the copies, or that there was any conflict of language between the poets and the scribes (LMRP, xxii).

The evidence indicated to the editors that the play went through two distinct phases (LMRP, xxviii–xxx). The original version may have been a travelling play performed in Cambridgeshire and East Anglia. It could probably be adapted to various sizes of audience and conditions of the playing-location. The directions suggest that the play was originally performed not in a circle but in a more restricted venue such as a street, with the 'sets' placed in a row rather than a circle, since the audience has to move between 'Jerusalem' and 'Damascus'. The play also demands an open space where the conversion itself takes place, and a Heaven scaffold. The editors think that the raised Heaven must have been close to the Damascus stage or waggon. In its second phase the play may have been a town play in Chelmsford, Essex.[4] By then it had acquired the Belyall and Mercury episode, necessitating an additional location in the form of a throne-cart or stage for Belyall. In this form, the play may have been given place-and-scaffold performance. The three directions for dancing had also been added by then.

10.2 Dramatic directions

The dramatic directions of this play are listed in Table 17. Most of Scribe A's directions are in English, with some in Latin; those of Scribe B are all in English; Scribe C's consist only of the word 'daunce'. There is no rubrication. The directions tend to be centred on the page and separated by lines from the surrounding text; additional directions are placed in the margin. The latter are marked as marginal in the fourth column of Table 17. Some of the SDs are, effectively, extended descriptive SHs. This is noted in Table 17. Scribe A also included some headings that clarify the structure of the play: these are noted here because of their relevance to the function of the directions.

---

[3] This dating is not mutually consistent with those for Scribes A and B: see note 2, above.

[4] The connection of this and other play texts with Myles Blomefylde, and the fascinating series of facts leading to this tentative conclusion, are detailed in LMRP, xii–xv. On the possible performance in 1562, see I, 168–74, especially 172–3; and see also Hill-Vasquez 'Possibilities of performance'.

TABLE 17 : DIRECTIONS IN *THE CONVERSION OF SAINT PAUL*

cue-line	f.	scribe	posn.	lang.	Direction if musical : comments
13	37r	C	m	e	*daunce.* Follows the introductory speech of Poeta, and covers Saul's entry.
13		A		e	extended SH
35	37v	A		e	
56	38r	A		e	
84	38v	A		e	includes SH
119	39r	A		e	extended SH
126		A		e	
140	39v	A		e	
154		A		l	SH
					Conclusyon marks the final speech of the first station.
		C	m	e	*Daunce*
161		A		l	Note for end of the first station and beginning of the second.
168	40r	A		e	
182		A		e	Includes SH
210	40v	A		e	Includes SH
244	41v	A		l	
247		A		e	
261		A		e	
268	42r	A		e	Extended SH
291	42v	A		l	(Descent of Holy Spirit)
345	43v	A			*Conclusyo* marks the final speech of the second station.
		C	m	l	*Daunce*
359		A		l	Note for the end of the second station and the beginning of the third.
(411	44v	A		e	Direction cancelled by Scribe B. See under line **501**, below.)
411+	45r	B		e	*Here to enter a dyvel wyth thunder and fyre ....* Start of Belyall episode.
432	45v	B		e	*Here shall entere anoþer devyll callyd Mercury wyth a fyeryng ....* Includes SH.
470	46r	B		e	*Here þei shall rore and crye, and þen Belyal shal saye* Includes SH.

501	47r	B		e	*Here þei shal vanyshe away wyth a fyrye flame and a tempest*
	47v	B		e	Includes SH: corresponds to the SD at line **411**.
599	49r	A	m	l	
648	50r	A			*Conclusyo* marks Poeta's final speech.

10.3 Text references

This play is disappointingly lacking in musical references. It may be that a travel-ling play – for various reasons – was less likely than a locally-initiated one to make use of the resources required for musical performance, or simply that some subjects demanded, and suggested, less by way of musical treatment than others. Neither of these reasons is necessarily enough to account for the lack of musical references used metaphorically, however. The dearth of such references may be due to the dramatist's relative indifference to music, or perhaps to a perception that his audience was not interested in it.

375 [SECUNDUS MILES] A swete dulcet voyce spake hym vnto

This is not a musical reference, but it is of interest as showing the dramatist's concern for vocal sound. The soldier is describing the voice of God speaking to Saul.

661–2 [POETA] Comyttyng yow all to owur Lord Jhesus
to whoys lawd ye syng *Exultet celum laudibus.*

These are the final words of the play, forming what amounts to a 'blessing' ending. It is arguable that this does not even constitute a firm reference to a musical performance here at the end of the play, but it is hard to escape the probability. There is no evidence of a trained choir, so we must assume that the actors were able to lead the singing of *Exultet celum laudibus.*[5]

5 For this cue, see I, 172–3 and 374. The hymn is in AS, 66, 67 and Q; and in LH, 270–1.

10.4 Latin and the liturgy

The editors note that the main source for the play is Acts 9/1–27; that some passages are derived from the office for the feasts of The Conversion of St Paul (25 January) and St Paul the Apostle (30 June); and that the dramatist made use of a sermon by St Augustine. They note also a general debt to the treatment of the story in Caxton's *The Golden Legend*, but see no direct influence from earlier liturgical or spoken plays on the subject (LMRP, xxii). Definite and possible translations from the sources are identified in the notes to the edition, LMRP, 195–7.

1	POETA	Rex glorie, kyng omnipotent

10	[POETA]	Whoo lyst to rede þe booke Actum Appostolorum

The dramatist's acknowledgement of his main source.

215	[DEUS]	Into þe strete, qui dicitur rectus

293–4	[ANANIAS]	Discendet super te Sprytus Sanctus,
		Whych hath wyth hys hye grace illumynyd vs.

This is preceded by **291+sd**, in which the Holy Spirit appears above Saul.

331	[ANANIAS]	In nomine patris et filij et spiritus sancti, Amen.

Saul asks for baptism at **308–10**, which Ananias gives at **325–31**, ending with this, the usual formula. The 'Amen' is a rhyme-word and not, as is common, extra-stanzaic: so it is part of the dialogue, not a cue for the audience (see I, 372–3).

411+13[6]	Inicium omnium peccatorum superbya est

See below, **514**.

425	[BELYALL]	... howse name ys Saulus.

514	[SAULUS]	Initium omnium peccatorum su[per]bia est

---

6 Scribe B broke into Scribe A's work after what is now line **411**, crossing out the remaining 14 lines on that page. These lines were recopied on f. 47v, at the end of the inserted material.

Saul quotes Ecclesiasticus 10/1–15 and Ecclesiastes 10/13 in support of his sermon (LMRP, 196). As will be seen by comparison with line **411+13**, Scribe B made small changes in copying Scribe A's passage.

The following quotations in Saul's sermon, lines **509–71** (except for the use of 'exeunt' in line **532**), are the biblical authority for what he is saying. The quotations are identified by the editors in LMRP, 196–7. None appears to be liturgical, and there is no question of singing them.

520	[SAULUS]	Omnis qui se exaltat humiliabitur.
528	[SAULUS]	Noli tibi dico inaltum sapere sed time.
532	[SAULUS]	Exeunt owt of thy sy3t glotony and lechery
542–3	[SAULUS]	Discite a me quia mitis sum et corde humilis, Et invenietis requiem animabus vestris.
548	[SAULUS]	Quanto maior es tanto humilia te in omnibus
556	[SAULUS]	Omnis fornicator aut immundus non habet hereditatem Christi
560	[SAULUS]	Ex habundancia cordis os loquitur
566	[SAULUS]	Caste viuentes templum Dei sunt
570	[SAULUS]	Oculus est nuncius peccati

The last two items are from Poeta's concluding speech: **662** is the last line of the play.

652–3	[POETA]	As the Bybull sayeth: dim[i]serunt eum summitten[te]s in sporta And Saule, after that, in Jerusalem vera
662	[POETA]	To whoys lawd ye syng Exultet celum laudibus.

10.5 Music and other aural cues

First Station

1_1 **13+md** Function: (b), (h). Scribe C's direction for a dance at the end of the Poet's introductory speech. There is no indication of minstrels, and no information as to the dancers. This belongs to the late revisions of the text.

1_2 **154+md** Function: (c), (h). Scribe C's direction for a dance at the end of the first station. Poeta's following speech, which is the conclusion of the station, is marked as optional – *si placet* – and it is unclear whether Scribe C intended the speech to follow the dance or regarded the dance as the conclusion of the station.

Second Station

2_1 **345+md** Function: (c), (h). Scribe C's direction for a dance at the end of the second station, between Saul's last speech and the Poet's conclusion.

Third Station, with the Belyall episode and the Poet's conclusion

3_1 **662** Function: (g). The singing of *Exultet celum laudibus*. The cast could certainly lead the singing of this hymn, which is not difficult. The Poet seems to expect that the whole audience will join in: see I, 374–3.

Of these four cues, only the last belongs to the play in its original form. As a travelling play, *St Paul* had no need of minstrels or trained singers, and there is no indication that any music was required apart from the final act of audience participation. The mid-century additions, on the other hand, use music quite differently. They demand a minstrel or minstrels, or someone to sing for a dance; and they require dancers as well, presumably professionals, since it is unlikely that the cast could produce entertainment dancing of the required quality.[7]

On the whole, the musical changes in this play support the probability of a travelling play later modified for more elaborate staging: to that extent the text supports Coldewey's theory that *The Conversion of St Paul* was one of the plays mounted in Chelmsford in 1562.[8]

---

[7] These cues presumably do not indicate audience participation: following a general dance there would have to be some arrangement for clearing the area for the next scene, and we should surely have some evidence of this.

[8] See I, section 4.3, especially pp. 172–3.

11

Mary Magdalen

11.1 Introduction

The play of Mary Magdalene is found on ff. 95r–145r of MS Digby 133: it is immediately preceded by non-dramatic material,[1] but is followed by *The Killing of the Children* and an incomplete copy of *Wisdom*, in that order. The play is reproduced in MDF 3, with an introduction by Baker and Murphy. The standard edition is by Baker, Murphy and Hall in LMRP, 24–95, with an extensive introduction on pp. xxx–lii.

The play takes up five octavo gatherings of 16, 16, 8, 4, and 8 leaves, the last leaf of all – which was presumably unused – having been removed 'early in the manuscript's history'. The watermarks show that the gathering of four was originally of eight, as expected, and the editors note that the other four leaves were missing 'before the manuscript was compiled' (LMRP, xxx). The division of the play into two, seen in Furnivall's original EETS edition and confirmed by Coldewey's findings concerning the play's putative performance at Chelmsford in 1562 (see I, 172), occurs after line **924**, where the text reaches the bottom of f. 116r. This is in the middle of the second gathering of 16, at a place which is not any sort of structural division: nor does the division quite coincide with the scribe's change from brown to black ink, which occurs between f. 115v and f. 116r (LMRP, xxx and xxxi). Although Coldewey's theory of two-day performance of the play is convincing, and very possibly correct, therefore, the obvious kind of physical evidence that the dramatist (or scribe) intended it from the start is notably missing. It will nevertheless be convenient to consider the play as a two-day drama.

The watermark suggests a date of c. 1515–25 for the copying of the text: this is compatible with the probable date of the handwriting of the single scribe responsible for this play, which the editors put at c. 1520–30 (LMRP, xxx and xl).

---

[1] *The Conversion of Saint Paul* is considerably earlier in the manuscript.

They consider scribal interference to be considerable, however, and certain linguistic features cause them to date the play itself from the end of the previous century. They note that the writer of *Mary Magdalen* apparently copied a passage from *The Killing of the Children*, which is probably not much older than the copy in this manuscript, dated 1512 (see section 9.6, above): but they do not regard this as conclusive evidence of sixteenth-century composition, since both dramatists might have copied from yet another source (LMRP, xl). It may perhaps be said, however, that a difference of two decades – possibly less – can easily be accounted for by the age of the dramatist, and that an elderly man writing c. 1515–20 might well use some linguistic forms of the 1490s. We are certainly beset by supposition in this matter, and the precise dating of the play must be regarded as problematic.

The play's language is apparently easier to place. The editors list a number of features typical of Norfolk texts (including, to some degree, *The Castle of Perseverance*, *Mankind*, and the Macro *Wisdom*), and cite E.J. Dobson's view that this play and the N-Town plays both came from Norfolk. The editors are less definite than Dobson, but describe *Mary Magdalen* as 'East Anglian, with obvious Norfolk features' (LMRP, xxxvi). At the least this presumably places it on the Norfolk-Suffolk border, if not firmly in south Norfolk.

According to John Coldewey's theory, the play travelled as far as Chelmsford, the county town of Essex, and was performed there in 1562 (see I, 172–4). If Coldewey is right, the play divided in the middle, the halves being played on two successive days around 19 August 1562.[2]

At the end of the play, on the otherwise unused f. 145v, are two solmisation exercises, written vertically near the inner margin. They apparently have no connection with the play,[3] but I have not been able to identify either of the two tunes, which are shown in Example 2. The melodic style suggests that they were composed specially as exercises. The two staves are drawn freehand: each has four lines, with a bar-line at the end following a note with a pause over it. The tunes are written in 'shorthand' black breves – that is, where the body of the note is drawn as a single thick horizontal line – except that the last note of each tune is written as a void breve with a pause. In Example 2 the 'shorthand' breves are notated as black semibreves.

The first tune (a) uses chromatic notes: each semitone interval is notated with an f (for 'fa') against the upper note – except that B-flat is shown by a flat sign – and a sharp (for 'mi') against the lower. The second tune (b) is an exercise in

---

2 Furnivall divided the play after line **924** (LMRP, xlix). This is a good place to break the action, and I follow it here: but, as noted above, there is no evidence whatever for a division at this or any other place in the surviving text.

3 See my comments concerning cue **2₃**, however, in section 11.5.

negotiating large intervals, demanding frequent transposition of the hexachord. The initial sharp sign shows that the note B is to be sung throughout as 'mi' – i.e. B-natural, not B-flat.

Below the lower staff are the words 'Sollf thes[e] ij playnsong[is] & ye (?)xall soollf ony of ye viijᵗʰ tewnys'. The word 'xall', which is not at all clear and may have been altered from something else, is written above 'ye', with a caret following that word. While this rubric suggests that the exercises are to help in singing the psalm-tunes, it is not implied that these are themselves psalm-tunes or other liturgical chants: 'playnsong' simply means an unmeasured melodic line.

Near the outer edge of the paper (which is itself repaired, the new material perhaps hiding some writing), and upside-down in relation to the music, are the words 'and   and Ave': these are probably pen-trials.

EXAMPLE 2 : SOLMISATION EXERCISES FOLLOWING *MARY MAGDALEN*

(a)

is to be sung as

(b)

11.2 Dramatic directions

The play's dramatic directions use both Latin and English: see Table 18, where they are listed. All are in red and, with a single exception, are placed centrally. The statistics for musical directions in relation to the total number of directions in the play are given in Table 19: this shows that out of a total of 100 directions only five are musical, one of those being marginal and therefore perhaps not part of the play as originally written.

Clearly there are far fewer musical directions than we might reasonably expect in a play of this length and subject. The fact that there are apparently so few marginal directions may be relevant here since, as we can see elsewhere, musical directions are often late additions, written marginally.

11.3 Text References

First Day

141 [HEROWDES] No noyse, I warne yow, ...

'Noyse' is here used with its modern, non-musical, meaning.

247 [SECUNDUS SERJAWNT] And so xall ye be dred of hye and low.

Not a musical reference: 'high and low' refers to persons, great and of no importance.

438–9 [BAD ANGYLL] Speke soft, speke soft, I trotte hyr to tene.
I prey þe pertly, make no more noyse.

'Soft' and 'noyse' are here used in their modern, non-musical, meanings.

530–33 [CORIOSITE] But wol yow dawns, my own dere?
MARY Syr, I asent in good maner.
Go ȝe before, I sue yow nere,
For a man at alle tymys beryt reverens.

In the next speech Curiosity seems to comment favourably on Mary's dancing (or perhaps more generally on her attractions, but the line is difficult to interpret) and then goes on to offer her refreshment. Whatever the precise meaning of line **534** it is clear that Mary dances with Curiosity after line **533**.

TABLE 18 : DIRECTIONS IN *MARY MAGDALEN*

cue-line	f.	lang.	direction if musical: comments
First Day			
44	95v	e	
48	96r	e	
113	97r	e	
139	97v	e	
208	99v	e	
216		e	
248	100v	e	
256		e	
264		e	
276	101r	e	
304	101v	e	Includes SH.
333	102r	e	
357	103r	e	Includes SH.
380	103v	e	
397		e	Includes SH.
408	104r	e	Includes SH.
439	104v	e	Includes SH.
469	105r	e	Includes SH.
490	105v	e	Extended SH.
546	107r	e	Includes SH.
559		e	
563	107v	e	Includes SH.
571		e	
587	108r	e	Includes SH.
614	108v	e	Includes SH.
630	109r	e	
640		e	Description of Mary's washing of Christ's feet: see 11.4, below.
691	110v	e	*Wyth þis word seuyn dyllys xall dewoyde from þe woman, and the Bad Angyll entyr into hell wyth thondyr.*
704	111r	e	
725	111v	e	
739		e	
743	112r	e	
775	112v	e	Includes SH.
793	113r	e	Includes SH.

818	113v	e	
823		l	
841	114r	e	
845		e	Includes SH.
868	114v	e	Includes SH.
872	115r	e	Includes SH.
888		e	Includes SH.
902	115v	e	
910	116r	e	
920		e	Includes SH and text.
924		e	Includes quasi-SH for the beginning of
Second Day			
962	117r	e	Includes SH.
992	118r	e	Includes SH.
1004		e	Extended SH.
1022	118v	e	
1030		e	
1046	119r	e	
1060	119v	l	
1095	120r	e	Includes SH.
1124	121r	e	
1132		e	
1142	121v	e	
1177	122r	e	
1178			The SH is written as a Latin direction, *Rex dicitt.*
1210	123r		As 1178.
1227		e	*Syng both.*
1280	124v	e	
1292		e	
1335	125v	e	Includes SH.
1348	126r	e	
1375	126v	l	
1394	127r	e	*Here xall entyre a shyp wyth a mery song.*
1418	127v	e	
1438	128r	e	*Now xall þe shepmen syng.* Marginal, on right: originally placed between lines **1436** and **1437**, and therefore perhaps to follow line **1434**.
1445	128v	e	
1453		e	
1537	130r	e	
1553	131r	e	

1561		e	Includes SH.
1577	131v	e	Includes SH.
1597	132r	l	Includes SH.
1609		e	Includes SH.
1641	133r	l	
1645		l	
1715	134v	l	
1724		l	Includes SH.
1744	135r	l	Extended SH.
1780	136r	e	
1790		l	Includes SH.
1796		l	Includes SH.
1842	137r	l	
1862	137v	l	Includes SH.
1878	138r	l	Includes SH.
1914	138v	l	Includes SH.
1922	139r	e	Includes SH.
1938	139v	e/l	Includes SH (which is the Latin element).
1971	140r	e/l	Includes SH (*Rex* is the only Latin).
1988	140v	l	
2018	141r	e	
2030	142v	e/l	*Her xall she be halsyd wyth angellys wyth reverent song. Asumpta est Maria in nubibus. Celi gavdent, angeli lavdantes felium Dei, et dicit Mari.* NB inclusion of SH, the Latin element.
2038		e	
2044	143r	e	Includes SH.
2072	143v	e	Includes SH.
2084		e	Includes SH.
2092	144r	l	
2100		l	
2108	144v	e	
2122		l	*Gavdent in celis.* Shown to be musical by the text reference at **2122** (see 11.3).
2139	145r	l	Not a direction, but the *explicit* line showing the end of the original play and incidentally giving the play's title: *Explycit oreginale de Sancta Maria Magdalena.*

TABLE 19 : NUMBER OF DIRECTIONS IN *MARY MAGDALEN*

Day	English	Latin	subtotal	musical
1	44	1	45	0
2	37	21*	55	5**

* The three directions with both English and Latin elements appear in both columns.

** Of these five, one is marginal and another is musical only in conjunction with a text reference.

Second Day

933–34 [KYNG OF MARCYLLE]   Ewen as an enporower I am onored ay,
                        Wanne baner gyn to blasse and bemmys gyn to blow.

This reference to the trumpets that the King of Marseille claims is only ten lines after his pomping entry. It is therefore probable that a fanfare has sounded at his entrance, so that his reference is to music that has just been heard.

1139–42   REGINA   To þat lord curtys and keynd,
                        Mahond, þat is so mykyll of myth,
                        Wyth mynstrelly and myrth in mynd,
                        Lett vs gon ofer in þat hye kyngis syth.

Minstrelsy and mirth are here connected in the usual way, although the text does not make clear what kind of minstrelsy might be used during an offering to Mahommet. Minstrelsy during offerings at shrines had certainly been known in earlier times, however,[4] and perhaps the audience of this play might have known of it.

The King's offering is made in his speech at lines **1210–21**. There is no mention of music there, but the Queen's words do not make sense unless some instrumental music occurs during the offering, probably after line **1221**, when the King has finished speaking.

4   See Rastall 'Minstrelsy, Church, and Clergy', 86–8.

1144–7 [PRYSBYTYR]   Loke fast myn awter were arayd.
Goo ryng a bell, to or thre.
Lythly, chyld, it be natt delayd,
For here xall be a grett solemnyte.

The ringing of a bell here parallels passages in the Towneley and Coventry plays of the Purification: this is apparently a tolling bell to mark the beginning of the service, not a peal. There are two problems concerning this bell-ringing, however.

First, the significance of 'two or three' is unclear. Should someone (a clerk?) ring the bell two or three times, or on two or three separate but closely-spaced occasions? Does he mean 'a bell, or two or three bells', and if so is he speaking literally or in a meaninglessly joking way? In practice it is easiest to assume that a single bell should be rung for a short period of time, letting the 'two or three' take care of itself: but the interpretative difficulty remains.

The second problem concerns the placing of the bell-ringing, and whether or not it in fact occurs. The Priest wants the bell-ringing done quickly (**1146**, **1148**), but the text does not indicate that it is done at all. The boy (Clericus) immediately starts a lewd conversation (**1149–77**) which ends with his beating by the Priest (**1177+sd**); and after this the King enters and requires the service to be performed. It is unsatisfactory to assume that the bell-ringing is forgotten in the distraction of the boy's insolence and beating, and there are three opportunities for it in all:

1 Following **1148**. In this case the boy presumably rings the bell while he is making his indecent suggestion to the Priest, line **1149** and perhaps during a few more lines.

2 If the bell is not rung then, it is because the boy has 'misinterpreted' the Priest's instruction to 'Goo ryng a bell', giving it an obscene meaning. In this case he presumably rings it after **1177+sd**, and the ringing covers the entry of the King, stopping in time for the King's lines at **1178–9**.

3 Otherwise, the bell must be rung after **1179** or **1180**, while the Priest prepares for the service but before he tells the boy to bring the service book.

On balance I prefer the second of these. If the boy has wilfully misinterpreted 'Go ring a bell' the scene coheres better than if the boy's lewd comments are wholly gratuitous; placing the bell-ringing after the boy has been beaten at **1177+sd** signals the end of the 'misunderstanding' and a return to the main narrative left at line **1148**; and it covers the King's entry after **1177**.

1222–27 PRYSBYTYR Now, boy, I pray þe, lett vs have a song.
Ower servyse be note, lett vs syng, I say.
Cowff vp þi brest, stond natt to long,
Begynne þe offyse of þis day.

BOY   I home and I hast, I do þat I may,
            Wyth mery tvne þe trebyll to sing.

These lines are followed by the direction for singing. The text does not say unambiguously that the Priest and the boy sing together without help, but **1227+sd** and **1229** give that information (see below). The Priest does say that they will sing the 'servyse be note' – i.e. a liturgical act performed with the written music – and that this is 'þe offyse of þys day'. It does not matter that the boy has already mentioned *saying* the service (line **1150**), because he then read the lesson in lines **1186–201**, evidently spoken and not sung.

The 'song' here cannot be guessed at. Perhaps a parody of the Easter liturgy is intended, if 'þis day' is a reference to the Resurrection events of the previous scene.[5]

The Priest also suggests that he and the boy do not often sing the service: this, at least, is surely the effect of his injunction to the boy to clear his throat (**1224**) and the boy's equally amateurish assurance that he is preparing to sing (**1226**).

The boy does however say that he is going to sing the treble (**1227**), which suggests a separate part, and that they are not singing in unison. This could imply a polyphonic setting, but probably means only that he sings a counterpoint to the Priest's tenor (the plainsong tune).

1228–9 PRYSBYTYR Hold vp. þe dyvll mote þe afray,
                     For all owt of rule þou dost me bryng.

On the incompetence of this performance, and the likely technical reason for its breakdown, see I, 43. The Priest's 'Hold vp!' shows that they stop in the middle of the piece for these lines. Perhaps they try again and get to the end of the piece before **1230**: or perhaps – since he quite illogically starts to show the King and Queen his relics – the breakdown has been too complete for them to sing the piece any further and the Priest feels that changing the subject may save the day. Showing the relics to the strangers present would however be natural at the end of the service, a procedure that would attract more money in the form of offerings and gifts to the church: indeed, this may be part of the dramatist's intention, for throughout this scene he attributes to the worship of Mohammet all the worse features of the medieval Christian Church.

I should be inclined to re-start the piece after **1229**, although the 'business' of bad performance must clearly continue: and indeed this could still be a reason for the Priest's change of subject and subsequent display of relics.

5 Further on this performance, see I, 43–4.

1246 [PRYSBYTYR] þat ye may þer in joy syng

The Priest is giving the equivalent of a blessing at the end of the service, and his use of musical imagery parallels the usual Christian one of heavenly singing. In this play it implies no music.

1586–1605 Note the apparent *lack* of music for this quasi-procession, and for the angel's descent.

2008 [JHESUS] Wyth joy of angyllys, þis lett hur receyve.

As noted so often, joy and music go together where angels are concerned; so although there is no music demanded by **2018+sd**, this line may be regarded as evidence that the dramatist nevertheless intended music there. This occasion is less important than that at **2030+sd**, where Mary is lifted up to be fed, but some music would nevertheless give the right feeling to it and would have the practical function of covering the movement during the feeding of Mary by the angels.

2013 [PRIMUS ANGELUS] O þou osanna, angellys song.

Metaphorical usage. The angel is addressing Christ: the mode of address implies that Christ, like the angelic song, praises the Creator by his very existence.

2021 [SECUNDUS ANGELUS] þou xall byn onoryd wyth joye and reverens

As with **2008**, above, this suggests music. In this case, however, the music is stated in the direction (**2030+sd**).

2037 [MARI] Wyth melody of angyllys shewit me gle and game

Here Mary mentions the music of **2030+sd**. For 'gle and game', see I, 48.

2041–2 [PREST] Wyth grett myrth and melody
Wyth angyllys brygth as þe lewyn.

The Priest, who has observed Mary's lifting-up by the angels, notes the connection between music and 'mirth'.

2096 [SECUNDUS ANGELUS] þis day ȝe xall be reseyvyd wyth angellys
song.

This line refers forward to **2122+sd**: see below.

2122 [SECUNDUS ANGELUS] Now lett vs syng a mery song.

The SD following is for angels singing at the reception of Mary's soul into
Heaven. This is a parallel to scenes of the Assumption of the Virgin, and it
seems unlikely that the dramatist intended only the two angels of the text to
sing: no doubt a whole choir is demanded by this scene.

2138–9 [PRYST] Now, clerkys, wyth woycys cler,
Te Deum Laudamus lett vs syng.

This is the end of the play proper, the last four lines being an addition the
precise significance of which is not clear. The singing of *Te Deum* by the clerks
may suggest that there were many of them present: but it seems unlikely that
the audience would not sing in this final musical part of the performance, and
only a few singers would be needed to start the hymn before the audience
joined in.

11.4   Latin and the liturgy

The playwright(s) evidently felt at home in Latin, and used many small quotations that have the effect of referring to the scriptures without diverting attention
from the main line of thought. In many cases it is not clear why Latin rather than
the English equivalent has been used, although matters of rhyme and metre are
sometimes involved. There are several references that I have been unable to identify, but with this sort of usage that is probably not important.

The play is interesting in its use of liturgy, as it provides thorough-going examples of parody.

175–6 [PHELYSOFYR] Et ambulabunt gentes in lumine [tuo] et reges
In splendore ortus tui.

The editors' note refers to Isaiah 60/3 for this quotation.[6]

---

6   The editors' notes are in LMRP, 197–218.

184–5 SECUNDUS PHYLOSOFYR
              Non avferetur s[c]eptrum [de] Juda et dux de
              Femore eius donec veniet [qui] mitendus est.

The editors' note refers to Genesis 49/10 for this quotation.

342   FLESCH   Clary, pepur long, wyth granorum paradysy

The editors' note identifies *granorum paradisi* as a spice and medicine from Africa. There seems little point in using the Latin name – unless that is how it is most commonly known – except that it provides a rhyme for **344**: but this is probably not vital to the dramatist.

428   SATAN   Spiritus malyngny xall come to þe

434   [SATAN]   How, how, spiritus malyng ...

536–41   It has been suggested that these lines, in which Mary and Curiosity refresh themselves with bread and wine, form a mock Eucharist.[7]

640+sd, 665-73   The episode of Mary washing Christ's feet follows Luke 7/38. The order of the SD is: Mary washes his feet with her tears; she wipes them with her hair; and she anoints him with a precious ointment. Luke 7/38 adds that she kissed his feet after wiping them. As in the Chester episode, the order is changed when Christ speaks of it to Simon the Leper: washing with tears; anointing with ointment; and wiping with her hair. For the order of events and their relation to the Gospel accounts, see I, 273.

661   JHESUS   Recte ivdicasti . ...

The editors' note points to Luke 7/43, from which this is an exact quotation.

691   [JHESUS]   Wherfor I sey to þe Vade in pace.

The editors refer to Luke 7/50 for these words.

697–8   Mary refers to Isaiah's teaching in these lines, the editors citing Isaiah 11/1–2 and perhaps 9/6–7 as her source.

---

[7] Coletti 'Design of *Mary Magdalene*', 319. See also Davidson 'Middle English Saint Play', 82.

705–21 The editors cite Lewis as noting that the Good Angel's speech of rejoicing over Magdalene has the structure of a tripartite hymn to the Trinity.
Lewis did not discover a specific hymn of which this could be a paraphrase, however.[8]

715 [BONUS ANGELUS]   O Lux vera , gravnt vs ʒower lucense

717 [BONUS ANGELUS]   And, Sperytus Alme , to yow most benyne

757 [MARI MAVGLEYN]   thowe I were nevyr so synful, he seyd Revertere

The editors cite Isaiah 44/22: 'revertere ad me, quoniam redemi te'.

761   [MARTHA]   The wyche in Latyn is callyd Savyower.

768–75   Mary's speech of praise is a paraphrase of the Compline hymn *Christe
qui lux es et dies.*

924   [JHESUS]   Wherfor I sey Vade in pace.

Compare Christ's dismissal of Mary at **691** (Luke 7/50); here Christ is
speaking to everyone on stage. According to Coldewey this is the last line of
the First Day, and the dismissal is directed at the audience as well. The
previous use of this formula may be thought to cast doubt on Coldewey's
contention, but it does not invalidate it. If this were spoken to the audience as
well it would undoubtedly be a very effective ending to the day's drama, and
would no doubt elicit an 'Amen' response from all present.

963–92 A devil describes the Harrowing of Hell and then goes back to relate the
story of Christ's death and resurrection. There is apparently no reference to
liturgy.

992   [DYLLE]   I telle yow alle in sum to helle wyll I gonne.

The words 'in sum' seem not be significant, and the alternative reading *in fine*
would not alter that: probably the words are a convenient tag of two syllables
to fill out the line.

1005–10   As the editors point out in their note, Lewis relates these lines to the

---

8 Lewis *Play of Mary Magdalene*, 132.

form of a hymn to the Cross: they cite *Salve crux sancta*, which is not close.[9]

1010+lat [THE THREE MARYS] Domine inclina celos tuos et dessende

This is from the 'record of Davyt', and the editors identify it as Psalm 143/5. They leave this line unnumbered, but the Marys certainly speak it. Note the pronunciation shown by the spelling of 'dessende'.

1111 [JHESUS] Women, I apere to yow and sey Awete.

The editors identify the quotation as Matthew 28/9.

1120 [JHESUS] In nomine Patrys ett Felii et Spiritus Sancti amen.

An extra-stanzaic line, but certainly to be spoken, as it provides a normal ending to a blessing such as Jesus has given his disciples. The disciples should join in the 'Amen'.

1144–5, 1178–83 These lines give the preparations for the service at which the King of Marseille will make his offering to Mohammet. We learn that the Priest's altar will be dressed (**1144**) and that he wishes a bell to be rung (**1145**); that there are more clerks than the one boy present (**1178**); that the Priest recites the service from a book (**1181**); and that the Priest wears vestments. These passages, in fact, are a good example of dramatic writing that does not need directions because of the descriptive or (as here) informative nature of the dialogue.

1186–201 The boy reads the lesson of the day: of its 16 lines, the first 12 are in Latin.
The first line, *Leccyo mahowndys viri fortissimi sarasenorum*, is an obvious parody of the announcement of a reading, just as the last, 'Gravnt yow grace to dye on þe galows', obviously parodies part of a blessing. For the rest, the nonsense Latin is carefully contrived to present certain ideas (the editors explain these in their note in LMRP, 211), while the remaining three English lines replace the deity in the blessing by a variety of unsuitable wildlife, including two devils.

1202–21 The Priest invites the King and his retinue to kneel and make their offering to Mohammet. The King offers a gold coin with a prayer that is largely reminiscent of Christian prayer: the similarity is no doubt deliberate, so that

---

9 Lewis *Play of Mary Magdalene*, 140.

the King can be seen to have his heart in the right place even if he has been brought up to worship Mohammet.

1222–9   The Priest and the boy sing their 'servyse be note': see above, section 11.3.

1230–41   The Priest displays Mohammet's neck-bone and offers it round for the company to kiss; then offers them Mohammet's eye-lid. The benefits to be gained are false and no doubt comic – kissing the neck-bone will enable them to see whatever happens, and the eye-lid will confer blindness for life. This would suggest that a fairly obvious kind of parody might be appropriate for the liturgical singing at **1227+sd**.

1242–8 These lines, the Priest's blessing on the assembled company, are quoted in I, 203. Again, this is a fairly obvious parody, close enough to be recognisable for what it should be, but outrageous in its actual wording.

1471   MARY   Id est Salvator ...

The editors suggest reference to Matthew 1/21.

1483   [Mary]   He seyd In principio erat verbum.

The editors refer to John 1/1 in their note.

1552–3   MARY   Dominus, illuminacio mea, quem timebo?
                            Dominus, protecctor vite mee, a quo trepedabo?

The editors refer to Psalm 27/1 Vulgate 26/1), which adds 'et salus mea' after 'illuminatio mea'.

1609+sd   As noted above (11.3, under **1586–605**), there is a quasi-procession here, with Mary and the two angels going to the King bearing lights: but there is neither reference to, nor direction for, music, either here or at **1597+sd** when the angels descend to her.

1715 [MARY]   In nomine Patrys et Filij et Spiritus Sancti. Amen.

A 'blessing' ending to the scene, with the commonly-used form of Latin words.[10] The 'Amen' is extra-stanzaic, and presumably it should be said by the assembled cast, and perhaps by the audience.

1765 [REGINA]   In manus tuas, Domine.

The Queen's final words as she dies in childbirth. Compare Christ's last words (Luke 23/46) and the verse derived from St Luke's account for use after the office of Extreme Unction;[11] also **2115**, below.

1775 NAVTA   Benedicite benedicite.

1839–42   Peter here baptises the King of Marseille, but 'In þe name of þe Trenite' rather than in the name of the three Persons individually. There is no question of musical performance.

1861 [PETRUS]   Cum Patre et Sancto Speritu.

A briefer form of blessing: the line is written this way to give a rhyme with **1860**, 'Now in þe name of Jhesu'.

1899–900 REGINA O virgo salutata , for ower savacyon
                      O pulcra et casta , cum of nobyll alyans.

The opening of the Queen's three-line address to the Virgin. These sound like quotations from a sung liturgical item or a reading, but I have not been able to identify their source.

1930 [MARY MAVDLEYN] For pavpertas est donum Dei.

The editors refer to 2 Corinthians 13/9, and note that the phrase appears also in *Piers Plowman* B XIV, l. 275.

1939 [REX] Heyll be þou, Mary! Ower Lord is wyth the!

The opening of *Ave Maria* ('Ave Maria, Dominus tecum'), but lines **1940** onwards do not give the rest.

---

[10] When a character only states the intention of blessing someone and then uses this Latin formula, it may be a way of giving the impression of a blessing without actually using the proper form. This would avoid possible problems with an actor not in priest's orders pronouncing the words of blessing.

[11] See MS, 112, and Rastall 'Music and Liturgy in *Everyman*', 308.

1971 [MARI] Ille vos benedicatt, qui sene fine vivit et regnat.

Mary Magdalene's blessing on the King and Queen of Marseille.

2027 MARI Fiat voluntas tua in heven and erth.

This is a clear reference to the Lord's Prayer as reported in Matthew 6/10, as the editors note: 'Fiat voluntas tuas, sicut in caelo et in terra'.

2030+sd Asumpta est Maria in nubibus. Celi gavdent, angeli lavdantes felium
Dei.

I have not been able to identify this.

2101–08 The Priest brings the Host to Mary and she receives it. Apart from line **2104**, the Priest's 'þi sowle to bryng to euyrlastyng lyth' – and even here the rhyme word is not 'life' as we might expect – these lines do not seem to refer to the Mass.

2115-18 [MARI]   In manus tuas Domine!
Lord, wyth þy grace me wysse!
Commendo spiritum meum! Redemisti me,
Domine Devs veritatis!

The editors refer to Psalm 30/6 (AV 31/5), 'In manus tuas commendo spiritum meum; redemisti me, Domine, Deus veritatis', quoted by Christ at his death. See under **1765**, above, and section 12.4, under **Meriasek 2/4329–30**.

2139   [Pryst] Te deum lavdamus lett vs syng!

A note after this line shows that this is the real end of the play, lines **2140–3** being an addition.

11.5 Music and other aural cues

A number of music-cues are fairly obvious in this play, as the previous sections have demonstrated. What is perhaps surprising is the dearth of cues in places where they might have been expected. In comparison with the Mary Play or the N-Town *Assumption*, for example, there is an obvious difference in outlook, even if we assume that a production of *Mary Magdalen* did have music in one or two places where it is not shown in the text. This difference would be explained if *Mary Magdalen* is indeed a travelling play in origin and the other two plays were put on by church communities on their own territory.

First Day

1$_A$ 1– Function: (b), (f). There is no direct evidence of music at the beginning of the play. But if we take the view that the King of Marseille has a trumpet fanfare at the start of the second day, then his remark in lines **933–4** about being honoured as an emperor and being entitled to trumpets (see 11.3 under those lines) suggests that the Emperor should have a fanfare at the start of the First Day.

1$_1$ 533 Function: none. Magdalen and Curiosity dance here (see 11.3). Colin Slim notes that a *basse dance* would have been appropriate in the late fifteenth or early sixteenth century,[12] at the time of the play's composition and the copying of the surviving text. At this period (around 1490–1520) one might expect the loud consort of shawms and trumpet for a *basse dance*. For a putative performance in 1562 the situation is different, since the *basse dance* was not performed in England by then: probably a pavan would be the acceptable equivalent. It would be useful to know more about the minstrels paid at Chelmsford in 1562.[13] By 1562 a softer consort would be more likely – perhaps pipe and tabor, or even flute with either harp or lute.[14]

Second Day

2$_A$ 925– Function: (f), (b) if the second day starts here, or (c), (b) if the play is played straight through. The King of Marseille enters and begins his 'boast'. As he mentions that he is entitled to trumpets (**933–4**), it may be that they are heard at this point (see 11.3).

2$_1$ 1177+sd+ Function: (b), (h). The boy (Clericus) rings a bell for the service. For the placing of this bell-ringing, see 11.3, above, under **1144–7**.

2$_2$ 1221 Function: perhaps (a). Minstrelsy, following the King's speech and dur-

---

[12] Slim 'Mary Magdalene', 462.

[13] See I, 173–4.

[14] This last combination would be rather quiet, however, for an outdoor performance in a playing-place of the size that must have been needed for this play.

ing his offering. The evidence for minstrelsy here is slight, but probably good: see 11.3, above, under **1139–42**. It should be soft minstrelsy, presumably.[15]

It is perhaps strange that minstrelsy should be heard during an offering to Mohammet: certainly the use of music in this play is a little freer than we should expect in a biblical cycle, for instance. It may be explicable in terms of the King's essential goodness: he will, after all, be converted to Christianity with very little trouble. It is also possible that the minstrelsy goes wrong – that is, that it is a parallel to the inadequate musical efforts of the singers. This solution would however degrade the King and Queen, and I prefer to see the minstrelsy as characteristic of those who would do God's will if their ignorance did not prevent it. (It is clear from the closeness of the liturgical parodies to the real thing that the Priest and his Boy know enough of Christianity to be wilful in their adherence to Mohammet.)

2_3 **1227+sd** Function: none. The Priest and his Boy sing the office of the day, apparently with the Boy singing a descant over the Priest's plainsong. As suggested above (11.3, under **1222–7**), this may be a parody of part of the Easter liturgy, if that is the day intended: alternatively, 'þis day' (line **1225**) may refer to the Feast of Mary Magdalene, or whatever was the occasion on which the play was performed.[16]

The performance is a very bad one: the Priest blames the boy, but this only underlines his own incompetence (see 11.3, under **1228–9**). The editors' note for **1229** suggests that 'owt of rule' means 'out of tune, or, at any rate, out of the 'line' of the melody' (LMRP, 211). This is a possible interpretation in the sense that a singer who does this is out of the control of the rulers of the choir.[17] For a modern audience out-of-tune singing is probably easiest to hear. However, I do not think that it was intended – not primarily, anyway. The editors' 'out of the "line" of the melody' is probably closer. Singers used the solmisation system to enable them to sing the right notes – more specifically, to help them sing the semitone intervals in the right place. 'Owt of rule' suggests that the singer has lost his place in the solmisation system. The result of that would be two-fold: first, that he would probably sing at the wrong pitch (singing in a different key would be the modern equivalent); and second, that even if he stayed at the right pitch he would be singing wrong notes (B-flat instead of B-natural, for example). Out-of-tune singing is, for most of us, a corollary to this situation, as is out-of-time singing.[18]

---

15 See the evidence in Rastall 'Minstrelsy, Church and Clergy', 86–8.

16 See I, 169, for the dating of the performances in 1562. A dating of around 29 July and 19 August 1562 seems possible: the feast-day of Mary Magdalene is 22 July; 15 August is the feast of the Assumption of the Blessed Virgin.

17 For the rulers of the choir, see Sandon I, xi.

18 See also I, 43–4. Carter *Dictionary*, under 'rule', defines rule in terms of theory, which would suggest technical error here.

After the singers break down, they perhaps start again after line **1229** and struggle to the end of the piece.

2₄ 1394+sd Function: (b), (h). A 'merry song' at the entry of the ship. The singers are presumably the crew. Although the Boy is the lewd equivalent of the Priest's boy, there is no reason to see the Shipman as an agent of the Devil. The song, although perhaps popular, should not therefore be indecent.

2₅ 1434+sd Function: (a), (d). The direction that appears marginally between lines **1436** and **1437** is placed by the editors after line **1438**, which does not seem to me suitable. The actions are:

1434	The ship sets sail;
1435–6	The Shipman points out Turkey;
1437–8	He points out Satyllye;
1439	The ship arrives at Marseille.

The editors identify Satyllye as Antalya, in southern Turkey (LMRP, 284), but this does not make good sense: perhaps Sicily (Sacyllye) was intended? In this case a song after line **1436** would mark the passage of time on the longest leg of the journey, between Turkey and Sicily – not that most of the audience knew the geography of the Mediterranean well, presumably.

But it may be unwise to try to be specific in placing this song in the text. As the direction is marginal it seems likely that a particular performance, with a particular layout of the playing-place, led a producer to note that the song was sung. Indeed, the marginal direction may be intended as a general indication that the crew sing at various times throughout the voyage. It would certainly be appropriate to have them sing as the ship sets sail, but it might also be appropriate at other times: the staging of this voyage from Palestine to Marseille, which looks so short on paper, might take a considerable time in performance. Without knowing the circumstances of a specific performance there is perhaps little more that can be surmised about this song.

2₆ 2030+sd Function: (a). The angels sing *Assumpta est Maria in nubibus: Celi gaudent, angeli laudantes, Filium Dei*. I have not found this text elsewhere.

2₇ 2122 Function: (f). The angels sing a 'merry song' to celebrate the reception of Mary's soul in Heaven. The direction *Gaudent in celis* suggests that it is not only the two speaking angels that sing, but the whole heavenly host. They sing a song of praise, presumably, in plainsong or polyphony according to the resources available.

2₈ 2139 Function: (i), and originally (g). The clerks present sing the hymn *Te Deum laudamus*. It should be intoned by the priest, or perhaps by one of the clerks. As noted in 11.3, above, the audience probably joins in. This is a set piece for the tableau at the end of the play proper, even if the additional four lines following *Te Deum* are spoken.

12

The Life of Saint Meriasek

12.1 Introduction

Beunans Meriasek, a Cornish play on the life of St Meriasek, survives in a small paper manuscript that is now MS Peniarth 105 in the National Library of Wales, Aberystwyth. The play was edited and translated by Whitley Stokes in 1872, who produced a line-by-line verse translation on facing pages, to which reference is made here; a freer acting translation in prose was published by Markham Harris in 1978.[1] The play is not available in facsimile.

The introductory line reads 'Hic incipit ordinale de vita sancti mereadoci episcopi et confessoris': other titles for the play were introduced by Stokes. The play identifies Meriasek as the son of the Duke of Brittany: he is called Meriadocus in the Latin speech headings but Meriasek in the Cornish text.

A colophon indicates that the copying of the manuscript was completed in 1504 and names the copyist as Dominus Rad[ulphus?] Ton., currently unidentifiable.[2] While most of the play is in Middle Cornish, the first ten pages were copied later than the rest, and the 271 lines that they contain show some late linguistic features: Joyce and Newlyn consider that for linguistic reasons the hand that copied these pages 'can hardly be earlier than *c* 1550'.[3] At some stage after the copying of the main body of the text a corrector has made additions and emendations, including some extra dramatic directions.[4]

---

1 Stokes *Beunans Meriasek*; Harris *Life of Meriasek*.
2 This colophon is reproduced in Stokes *Beunans Meriasek* after p. xvi. It is generally assumed that Ton was the copyist, not the author, because the play itself seems to date from the previous century. Joyce and Newlyn note the burial records of Sir Ric[hard] Tone, a priest, at Camborne in 1547, and say that he 'may have been the scribe': *REED.Cornwall*, 543. This would make Tone quite a young man when he copied the play – not in itself a disqualification – as well as requiring an error in the colophon.
3 Murdoch *Cornish Literature*, 99–100; *REED.Cornwall*, 543.
4 Stokes *Beunans Meriasek*, v–vi. The page presented in reproduction by Stokes, p. 19, suggests that the corrector was the same scribe as the copyist of the main text,

The manuscript contains staging diagrams similar to those for the Ordinalia, one at the end of each of the two days of the play. These show that, like the other surviving Cornish dramas, *Beunans Meriasek* was intended to be performed in a circular playing-place with mansions on the circumference.[5]

The play may not be much older than the copy. Murdoch suggests a date in 'the last decades of the fifteenth century', and the reference to the rose noble (line 2881), which he offers as evidence, would make the composition of the play after 1465, when that coin was introduced.[6]

It is most likely that the play was written for performance in or around Camborne. Camborne parish church bears the only Cornish dedication to St Meriasek;[7] part of the play is set in the area of Camborne, and local place-names are mentioned; and St Mary of Camborne is mentioned several times in the play.[8] Murdoch notes that 'John Nans, who became rector of Camborne in 1501, had previously been provost of Glasney', providing a connection between the presumed performance-place of *Beunans Meriasek* and 'the home of the *Ordinalia*'.[9] Quite what this connection might mean in practical terms is unclear: could Nans have commissioned one of his former colleagues to write the play? Might he have had the ability and the knowledge to write it himself? Or could he have known an existing play in Glasney and asked one of his former colleagues to copy it for him? All we can say, perhaps, is that Glasney College, as the main intellectual centre in the area and with a tradition of dramatic activity, seems the most likely place from which a major dramatic text might emerge in the early years of the sixteenth century.

No playing-place is known in Camborne, but the picture of playing-places now emerging suggests the likelihood that there was one: O.J. Padel gives the probable map-reference in *REED.Cornwall*, 560. Very little by way of documentary record survives from Camborne, although there are several indirect references to dramatic activity in the 16th-century churchwardens' accounts of the parish of St Meriasek and St Martin.[10] The following item could refer to a minstrel playing for dancing at the end of a day's drama:

Item payd to a pyper yn the playe   iiij d.

---

working in a less formal manner and in a blacker ink. In this case the additions were presumably made long before the first ten pages were replaced. These later pages do have some additional material on them, but this is perhaps from yet another late scribe. Further work is needed on the scribes of this manuscript.

5   These diagrams are reproduced in *REED.Cornwall*, 555–6.
6   Murdoch *Cornish Literature*, 100.
7   The dedication to St Meriasek apparently took place in 1329: the dedication to St Martin, leading to a joint dedication to the two saints, occurred later. See Murdoch 'Cornish Medieval Drama', 235.
8   *REED.Cornwall*, 523–4.
9   Murdoch 'Cornish Medieval Drama', 235.
10 *REED.Cornwall*, 475–6; for the item quoted here, see 476.

The sum of 4d certainly suggests no extensive participation in the drama itself. If this payment is to a lone minstrel he was perhaps a bagpiper or a pipe-and-tabor player; or perhaps he was collecting a (rather low) payment for himself and one or more colleagues. There is no evidence for any performance of *Beunans Meriasek*, and this does not suggest a performance of that play, which demands a group of minstrels for the dancing at the end.

12.2   Dramatic directions

The original dramatic directions in *The Life of Meriasek* are in Latin. The principal directions are centred on the page, between blocks of dialogue, sometimes underlined in red, while others are written in the margin. These latter do however sometimes encroach on the centre of the page, just as apparently centred directions can encroach on the margins. In addition, some directions are added to speech headings, specifying where or how a speech is to be delivered.

Another set of directions has been added by the corrector, some in Latin and some in English. A number of them are added to the existing Latin directions or to existing SHs. Because they are later additions they are all, of course, marginal. It is not possible to say how much later than the original directions these are, but – as noted above – they may be written by the main scribe. It seems certain that they are the notes of a stage manager or at least someone involved in a performance: several are notes to warn a stage manager that props or characters should be ready, and these are placed several lines before the actual cue. These added directions seem to refer to one particular performance, since an actor is named in one of them.[11]

The directions for music are listed in Table 20. In the 'position' column, c = 'centred' and m = 'marginal'; in the 'language' column, l and e show the directions to be in Latin or English, respectively. The corrector's additions and emendations are noted when they occur in material listed here.

12.3   Text references

Day 1
1/99–101   PRIMUS SCOLAR[IS]   FIRST SCHOLAR
   Du gveras a b c   God keep A, B, C,
   an pen can henna yv d   The end of the song, that is D.
   ny won na moy yn liuer   I know no more in the book.

11   **1865+sd2**: the point is made in Murdoch 'Cornish Medieval Drama', 215.

TABLE 20 : MUSICAL DIRECTIONS IN *SAINT MERIASEK*

cue-line	posn	lang	Direction : comments
1/291	c	l	*Hic mimi ludent melodiam*
2/3419	m	l	*et cantant omnes tortores*
			Added by the late corrector.
2/3881	c	l	*Descendunt*
	m	e	*organs or syngyng* Added by the late corrector. Gabriel and other angels go to Meriasek with angels' food
2/4509	c	l	*Hic cantant*

This is apparently a metaphorical usage: 'the end of what I can do'. Harris points out (*Meriasek*, 124) that there was a tradition of learning the alphabet by singing it, but our evidence for this is much later than the play.[12]

1/276–7	[PINCERNA DUCIS BRITANIE]	[THE SPENCER OF THE DUKE OF BRITTANY]
	trompys cleryons wethugh wy	Trumpets, clarions, blow ye
	lemen then fest lowenek	Now to the joyous feast!

At the beginning of dinner, with King Conan as the Duke's guest, the Spencer asks Meriasek to seat the assembled company (**273–4**), which Meriasek does (**278–85**): but the order to the trumpets and clarions comes before the seating of guests, and apparently (although there is no direction for it) the company goes to dinner to their sound. The next musical direction, at **291+sd**, could be for this fanfare, but the word 'melody' suggests entertainment while the guests are sitting. In any case, it seems unnecessary for the Spencer to give his order to the trumpets and clarions so early unless they are to play before the seating takes place.

1/921	TEVDARUS	TEUDAR
	Out warnes ty fals jugleer	Out on thee, thou false juggler

'Juggler' is apparently used to designate a low minstrel here, a trickster or illusionist.

---

[12] See above, section 3.4, under **Towneley 12/422–5**.

1/941   [MERIADOCUS]   [MERIASEK]
                 ha my lemmen ath vygeth   And I now will baptise thee.

Meriasek is however unable to baptise Teudar.

1/2511–12   [DUX]   [THE DUKE (OF CORNWALL)]
                 pybugh menstrels colonnek   Pipe ye, hearty minstrels,
                 may hyllyn donsia dyson   That we may be able to dance
                                                                          forthwith.

The end of the first day. The Duke steps out of his role to encourage the audience to return for the second day of the play (which he does not say is on the following day) and to take a drink 'with the play' (no doubt for money); and he then tells the audience that they will be blessed by Christ, Meriasek and Mary of Camborne, before telling the minstrels to pipe up for dancing.

Day 2
2/3767–8   FILIUS   THE SON
                 Maria thymo in nos   Mary to me at night
                 purguir a thueth then preson   Right truly came to the prison
                 gans golov ha mur a tros   With light and much noise.

The 'light and much noise' are not indicated in the text, which gives only dialogue and a few of the corrector's directions (**3658+md–3710+md**). **3658+md** does however state that Mary descends (from Heaven) to the prison 'with two angels', while the woman's son twice remarks on the 'radiance' around him (**3669, 3681**). We may take it, therefore, that the angels bring light with them from Heaven to the prison where the woman's son is; and similarly it is possible that the procession of Mary and the two angels is accompanied by the singing of the angels. At any rate, it seems very unlikely that 'noise' in the modern sense is a part of this rescue operation.

It is also clear that the gaoler has seen the radiance of Mary's appearance, although he does not know what has happened (**3713–14, 3726**); however, he does not mention noise or music.

2/4474–5   [COMES VENETENSIS]   [THE EARL OF VANNES]
                 an cur yma arays   The quire is arranged
                 del goth erbyn den worthy   As behoves to meet a worthy man.

Harris (*Meriasek*, 120), who gives this speech to the Dean, translates these lines 'The chapter is assembled in due order as is seemly ...'. For the problem of translating 'cur', see section 7.3, above, under **Ordinalia 3/1899–900**. Nance's suggested 'choir' (or 'quire') again seems a good solution, although it

405

is not clear whether the word would indicate the people or the building: here, the people must be intended.

2/4504–5	DECANUS	THE DEAN
	Lemen canens an clergy	Now let the clergy sing
	in hanov du a vercy	In the name of God of mercy

The singing occurs at **4509+sd**, during the procession into the church with Meriasek's body.

2/4563–8	[COMES VENETENSIS]	[EARL OF VANNES]
	Pyboryon wethugh in scon	Pipers, blow at once.
	ny a vyn ketep map bron	We will, every son of the breast,
	moys the donsya	Go to dance.

Part of the final speech of the Earl of Vannes, who steps out of role to dismiss the audience. Further on this passage, see I, 375.

12.4 Latin and the liturgy

The play includes many places where a liturgical action might be fitted in, but in most cases it is clear that the action is undertaken only informally. I have generally ignored those occasions on which 'God's blessing on you' is used either as a greeting or in thanks for some service done: the first example below is typical of this kind of 'blessing'.

For the same reason I have not included the occasional informal curse, of which **1/1287** – molleth du in cowethys / God's curse on the company – is an example.

Day 1

1/31	PATER	FATHER
	Beneth du 3ys meryasek	God's blessing to thee, Meriasek!

When Meriasek asks for a formal blessing from his parents (**45–52**) they respond with words that still do not incorporate any of the usual forms:

1/53–4	PATER	FATHER
	Ov mab wek 3ys benneth du	My sweet son, God's blessing to
	ham benneth vy ben3a	And my blessing ever [thee,

1/62–3	MATER	MOTHER
	Ov map benneth varya	My son, Mary's blessing
	dys ham bennath vy neffra	To thee and my blessing for ever.

Although these blessings are not made in the name of the Holy Trinity, they are presumably accompanied by the laying on of hands.

1/118–35 Meriasek states his intention of fasting every Friday.

At **141+sd** Meriasek goes down to the chapel, where he prays to Christ and the Virgin (**142–67**). Although the repetition of the names Ihesu and Marya at the beginnings of lines helps to give a structure to the prayer and is reminiscent of a litany, this prayer does not seem to follow any particular form. (See also the patterning of Meriasek's prayers at **1/546–57, 700–9** and elsewhere, and especially **2/3133–41**.) While most such speeches are given to Meriasek, the Mother prays similarly to the Blessed Virgin (**2/3188–95, 3591–600** and **3615–38**).

1/201–2	MAGISTER	MASTER
	Banneth crist ȝys meriasek	Christ's blessing to thee, Meriasek.
	ham benneth pur colonnek	And my blessing right hearty.

Something like a traditional paternal blessing.

1/216–17	PATER	FATHER
	Meryasek welcum in tre	Meriasek, welcome home,
	ham luen vanneth y rof ȝys	And my full blessing I give to thee.

1/224–5	MATER	MOTHER
	Meriasek bedneth crist ȝys	Meriasek, Christ's blessing to thee,
	ha bedneth ȝe vam neffra	And thy mother's blessing ever.

Parental blessings as before, not in any liturgical form.

Meriasek again asks his parents' blessing at **496–7**, before he goes to take holy orders.

1/502–7	PATER	THE FATHER
	Inter dula du avan	Between the hands of God above,
	ov map gruaff the kemynna	My son, I do commend thee.
	kemer the rovle the honan	Take thine own rule:
	gul nahen me ny alla	Do ought else I cannot:
	ov banneth dis	My blessing to thee!

MATER	THE MOTHER
Amen prest ham banneth vy	Amen ever, and my blessing.

1/529–33 [EPISCOPUS KERNOV]

[EPISCOPUS KERNOV]	[THE BISHOP OF KERNOU]
ry dys ordys me a vyn	Give thee orders I will.
in hanov ihesu lemyn	In Jhesu's name now
sacrys gena betheth suer	Consecrated by me thou wilt be
[*genuflectit*]	[*He kneels*] [surely.
cryst roy dis in pup termyn	May Christ grant to thee alway
omguythe prest in glander	To keep thyself ever in purity!

The direction, which refers to Meriasek, is marginal, added by the corrector. The bishop's words seem to owe nothing to the normal ceremony of ordination to the priesthood.

1/555 MERIADOCUS

MERIADOCUS	MERIASEK
in nomine patris et filij	In nomine Patris et Filii.

The first Latin words used in the dramatic text: significantly, this invocation to the Godhead occurs in the course of Meriasek's healing of the blind man and the cripple.

1/617 In lines **611–17** Meriasek, who is on board a ship foundering in a storm, states his intention of asking Christ's help. In the next two lines, **618–20**, a sailor makes it clear that the ship has landed safely in Cornwall. Meriasek evidently prays after line **617**, therefore, although there is no text for it.

1/1332+md Silvester and the Cardinal, presumably with helpers, bury the martyred Earl and Doctor. There is no text for this, so that it may have been done in dumb-show. The burial is certainly effected very quickly, as the Cardinal requires in lines **1333–4**, so that it is unlikely that a proper liturgical ceremony should be inserted in the play here.

1/1446–7 DOCTOR   Hoc urum malorum
Et nimis rubrorum.

'This urine of evils and bloody retribution'. The Doctor speaks Latin (not very grammatically) to impress the Emperor with his knowledge when he examines the Emperor's urine.

1/1725–6 CONSTANTINUS

CONSTANTINUS	CONSTANTINE
Benedicite pana syght	Benedicite, what a sight
ambuevy haneth in noys	I had this very night!

Constantine's use of the Latin word 'benedicite' in response to his vision of St Peter and St Paul would signal his coming conversion to the audience.

1/1830–1 SELUESTER
Lemmen gruaff the vegethya
in hanov map maria

SILVESTER
Now I do baptize thee
In the name of Mary's Son.

Silvester has stated his intention of baptizing Constantine after the Emperor has done penance for a week (**1818–21**); and Constantine has agreed to this, in addition to giving alms to the poor (**1824–9**). Constantine's prayers to Christ, and his almsgiving, therefore take place while Silvester prepares for the baptism. This baptism is in a much-shortened form.

1/1844–5 CONSTANTINUS
Benedycite pan wolov
revue oma sollebreys

CONSTANTINE
Benedicite, what a light
Was here some time ago!

Constantine has been healed of his leprosy during baptism, and here begins his account of the vision he had of Christ speaking to him.

1/1865+sd1   *ad palacium pape procesc[i]onabiliter*

There is no indication of music in this procession, but it seems likely that processional music would be sung during the Emperor's procession to take Silvester back to the papal residence. This is the end of a major scene.

1/1905 [QUARTUS EXULATOR]
ser parson bona dyes

[FOURTH OUTLAW]
Sir parson, bona dies

The Fourth Outlaw greets the priest in Latin before robbing him: this is however a secular greeting.

1/2175–8 [MERIADOCUS]
pan us dywhy edrega
y raff agis benyga
    in nomine patris et filii
    et spiritus sancti amen

[MERIASEK]
Since you have repentance
I will bless you
In the name of the Father and the
And of the Holy Ghost, amen. [Son

Meriasek blesses the repentant outlaws, using the expected Latin form (see I, 293–4).

Day 2

2/3001–18 The consecration of Meriasek as Bishop of Vannes is effected entirely
during three speeches by the Bishop of Kernou and a second bishop: they seat
him in his chair (**3002**), robe him (**3006+md**), give him a crozier (**3009+md**)
and a mitre (**3010**), and finally bless him **3014–15**) – all without a word of
Latin. The actions are presumably carried out in a decent ceremonial manner,
however.

2/3388–419 The tyrant and his entourage sacrifice to their god. It is not clear
what happens to their gifts, but apparently they are not burned. Most importantly, the Drudge suggests that their god should thank them for the gifts
(**3419**). The torturers sing after the sacrifices are made (**3419+md**): as the
thanksgiving has been turned upside-down, presumably the singing should be
a parody of a suitable song (see 12.5, under **3419+md**).

2/3677 FILIUS	THE SON
Grovs crist benedicite	O cross of Christ, benedicite!

A suitably pious expression of joy, as elsewhere.

2/4047–54 Peter tells Silvester to speak to the dragon, giving him a form of
words that is a shortened version of the Apostles' Creed.

2/4066–7 [SYLVESTER]	[SILVESTER]
syne an grovs theragon scoen	The sign of the cross before us
degeugh aberth maria	Bear ye on behalf of Mary.

The MD that follows this shows that Silvester's first chaplain carries a cross,
so there is a quasi-liturgical procession to the dragon, consisting of Silvester,
his two chaplains (the second bears a lantern), the three dukes and, appar-
ent-ly, both Constantine and the Bishop of Pola; perhaps there are other
servants and chaplains, as well.

2/4154–7 SYLVESTER	SILVESTER
Me agys beseth warbarth	I will baptize you together
oma lemen kyns dybarth	Here now before parting.
in nomine patris et filij	In the name of the Father and the
et spiritus sancti amen	And of the Holy Ghost, amen. [Son

A fuller form of words than that used by Meriasek in baptizing Constantine,
above.

2/4329–30 [MERIADOCUS] [MERIASEK]
   in manus tuas domine   Into thy hands, O Lord,
   spiritum meum commendo   I commend my spirit.

Meriasek's dying words, echoing those of Christ in Luke 23/46. The text is found among the additional verses said following the office of Extreme Unction, and in the versicle and response at Compline.

2/4435–6 [DECANUS] [THE DEAN]
   an vers in manus tuas   The verse *In manus tuas*
   ys leferis heb powas   He said it without pausing.

Part of the Dean's account of Meriasek's death, related to the Earl of Vannes, the Bishop of Kernou and others.

2/4509+sd The clergy sing for the funeral procession into the church. A possible item would be the processional psalm *In exitu Israel*: see I, 290.

2/4537 After this line the body is lowered into the tomb. For the liturgy of this occasion, see I, 290.

2/4541 EPISCOPUS KERNOV BISHOP OF KERNOU
   Arluth neff ren benyga   May Heaven's Lord bless him!

It is tempting to think that the Bishop's benediction over the body has already been said, after line **4534**: but the Bishop has stated his intention of having the body in the grave first and giving his benediction afterwards, which is the proper order. This is indeed the blessing of the body before it is covered, then, and the Bishop orders the covering of the body in the next two lines (**4542–3**). The liturgy of burial has been considerably shortened, therefore, as it is in other plays: see I, 290–3.

The lack of specific liturgical material is surprising, as is the use of informal wordings. The play could be staged with virtually no liturgical ceremonial, the Cornish text being accompanied by minimal dumb-show in most cases. The alternative, which seems to me quite possible but not actually necessary, is to assume that some liturgical ceremony, with the Latin texts said or sung as normal, should be added to the existing text at various places. The fact that most of the evidence for the latter view consists of a rather patchy addition of MDs by the late corrector may suggest that the text and the practice of staging this play did not coincide. As with the additional material in the York cycle, it is impossible to know whether these additional directions make explicit a production tradition that is as old as the text or actually signal a change in production, with specific features being added to the play.[13] A modern-day producer can decide whether to take the whole existing text, including the 'new' directions, or to treat these latter as accretions to an older and simpler drama.

12.5 Music and other aural cues

Day 1

1_A **277** Function: (a). The trumpets play for the guests to enter the banquetting-hall.

1_1 **291+sd** Function: ?(a). The minstrels entertain the guests as soon as they have sat down, probably for the serving of the first course.

1_B **1865** Function: (a), (h). The Emperor's procession to escort Silvester to his palace after Constantine's baptism: liturgical singing would be appropriate, but there is no evidence for it.

1_2 **2486+md** Function: (a), (d). The battle between the Duke of Cornwall and Teudar. The late MD specifies that guns are to be fired.

1_3 **2512** Function: (g). The pipers play for the general dance at the end of the first day.

Day 2

2_1 **3419+md** Function: none. The torturers sing at the end of their offerings to their god. There is no indication as to the nature of their singing, except that the Drudge has just asked his god to thank them all for their gifts: so a parody of a piece that would be suitable for offerings – such as an offertory of the Mass – might be suitable.

2_2 **3658+md** Function: (a). As noted above (12.3), it seems that Mary's angelic companions sing while on their way to rescue the young man from prison. A plainsong item of praise would be suitable.

2_A **3710+md** Function: (a). If Mary is accompanied by angelic music on her way to the young man's prison (cue 2_2), then presumably the angels sing again when she returns with them to Heaven.

2_3 **3881+sd+md** Function: (a). Michael and other angels go to feed Meriasek with heavenly food. The musical accompaniment to this journey is noted as either organs or singing: as the MD is in English, 'organs' probably means the instrument that we call the organ, not just instruments of some kind. It should be noted that in the absence of pageant waggons organ-playing is more difficult to stage in procession than singing is. Organ-music might be best in Heaven, therefore, whereas vocal music could be produced by the angels themselves processing to visit Meriasek.

---

[13] This problem is discussed in relation to the York cycle in section 1.2, above.

2_4 **3947+md** Function: none. The special effects concerned with the dragon include a gun, presumably to shoot out smoke and sparks from the dragon's mouth.[14]

2_B **4073+md, or after 4079** Function: (a). Silvester and his chaplains form a procession to see the dragon. The singing of a prayer for deliverance from evil or danger would be suitable, or perhaps a song of praise.

This cue will depend partly on the blocking for the dukes and Constantine. The First Duke can speak **4073–9** before the procession starts or after it is finished – hence the alternative cue-lines – but not while the procession is in motion if there is singing. (If there is no singing, then of course that possibility is also available.)

2_C **4180+md** Function: (a). The Emperor's procession to escort Silvester to his palace, presumably still with the cross and lantern carried by Silvester's chaplains. A musical procession would again be suitable, with appropriate items of thanksgiving for the taming of the dragon.

2_D **4342+md, 4348** Function: (a). It would be appropriate for the angelic band going to bring Meriasek's soul to Heaven to sing on the journey in both directions. There are suitable items in the Common of Saints, in the section for a confessor bishop.

2_5 **4509+sd** Function: (a). The funeral procession into the church, with the clergy singing *In exitu Israel* or some other appropriate liturgical item: see I, 290–1.

2_E **4537** Function: none. For the possible liturgical items when the body is lowered into the grave, see I, 290.

2_F **4543 or 4547** Function: none. For the possible liturgical items when the body is sprinkled with earth, see I, 290. It is not clear from the text exactly when the singing of such an item might take place: but the positioning of this singing in the play text is not liturgically crucial.

2_6 **4568** Function: (g). The pipers play for the general dance at the end of the play.

---

14 This cue is discussed in Butterworth *Theatre of Fire*, 79–80.

13

The Play of the Sacrament

13.1 Introduction

As a dramatic type *The Play of the Blyssyd Sacrament* is a unique survival from England:[1] it is not a saint play, since the main protagonist is the Blessed Sacrament itself, not a saint; but it is certainly a miracle play. The story involves the desecration of the Host by Jews, various miracles resulting from this desecration, and the conversion of the miscreants. The legend is known from the fourteenth century onwards, and there are dramatic treatments of the theme dating from the fifteenth and sixteenth centuries on the Continent. Although this play is the only known English version (NCPF, lxxiii–lxxv), the episode in which the Jew's hand adheres to the Host has a parallel in the story (**N-Town 40**) of the burial of the Virgin.

The play survives in a composite manuscript, now Dublin, Trinity College MS F.4.20, ff. 338–57. It is preceded by its banns – where the place of performance, Croxton, is named (line **74**) – but otherwise the surrounding material bears no relation to the play. The banns and play take up three paper gatherings, of 8, 8, and 4 leaves: these have now been removed from the main manuscript and are kept separately (NCPF, lxx). The first recto is very dirty and the last leaf is unused, so this copy apparently existed for some time as a separate entity (NCPF, lxxi).

Davis identified three scribes, who evidently worked closely together (NCPF, lxxi–lxxiii). The general style of the scribes suggests a copying date in the early sixteenth century, although the watermarks should date from c. 1530–50 if Briquet's datings of related paper-types are to be trusted (NCPF, lxxi–lxxii). According to the play-text itself, the events dramatised took place in 1461 (line **58** of the banns, and in the *explicit*), which gives a *terminus a quo* for the composition of the play (NCPF, 59 and 89). Davis noted that the considerable scribal interference with the text shows that a period of time elapsed between composi-

---

[1] But see section 14.2, below: miracle plays were not unknown in England.

tion of the play and the writing of this copy. He concluded that the play may have been composed soon after the supposed event in 1461, this copy being written 'half a century or so later' (NCPF, lxxxiv and lxxxv). The evidence for dating is clearly contradictory, however: either the scribes were writing in an old-fashioned way well into the sixteenth century or else the paper used is much earlier than Briquet suspected.[2]

The language of the play and of the banns is East Anglian, which no doubt limits the field of possible Croxtons to those in East Anglia. Davis favoured the one near Thetford because a reference to Babwell Mill (line **621**) points to a location on the Thetford side of Bury St Edmunds, where there was a Franciscan priory.[3] He pointed out that, because of this reference, the Doctor episode at least must have originated in the Thetford/Bury area (NCPF, lxxxiv–lxxxv).[4]

The play is available in facsimile in MDF 5, 93–131, and was edited by Norman Davis in NCPF. The staging of the play is discussed by Darryll Grantley ('Producing Miracles').

13.2 Dramatic directions

Directions are written across the page, and are therefore distinguished from speech headings, which are centred only at the top of a page, being in the left margin otherwise. Both SHs and SDs are highlighted with yellow.

There are no directions in the banns, which are lines **1–80** of the text.

With a single exception (**607+sd**), the play's SDs are in English: there is no obvious reason for the use of Latin for the last of three directions in the Doctor episode. Although the SDs occasionally include directions for speaking, they do not take the place of SHs proper, which are always present when a different character speaks.

There are 34 directions in all: none of them is for music.

---

2 Note that the reference to Evensong in **230–1** does not fix this as a post-Reformation drama.

3 If the mill was owned by the Franciscans the reference may point towards involvement by the friars in the play: but I have not yet found any indication of the ownership of the mill.

4 Further on these banns, see I, 51–2. I am doubtful about the view that *The Play of the Sacrament* is a travelling play (see, for instance, David Mills in *Revels* I, 147), although the statement at the end of the play about the number of players needed does suggest that the text was generally available.

13.3 Text references

Banns

The banns (**1–80**) are spoken by two *vexillatores*, who say what the play is about and advertise the performance 'At Croxston on Monday' (**74**). This means that the banns were intended to be spoken somewhere other than Croxston and within a week of the performance of the play.[5] The banns required at least one minstrel, since the last line (**80**) is

[SECUNDUS] Now, mynstrell, blow vp with a mery stevyn.

This is not certainly a single minstrel, but it is presumably loud music. A shawm, or a pipe-and-tabor, could suitably play dance-music to announce the departure of the performers.

This suggests that minstrelsy announced the beginning of the banns, as well, and that loud music should therefore be heard before line **1**. It is not possible to assume that the same minstrel or minstrels would have performed for the play a few days later, however. That would require separate financing, and unless the play can be shown to demand such minstrelsy it is better to assume that the minstrels were not used on that occasion.

The Play of the Sacrament

834, 837–841 [EPISCOPUS]   Now wyll I take thys Holy Sacrament

...

And beare yt to chyrche with solempne processyon;
Now folow me, all and summe,
And all tho that bene here, both more and lesse,
Thys holy song, *O sacrum Conuiuium*,
Lett vs syng all with grett swetnesse.

The procession is mentioned again in line **844**, so there certainly does now occur what is in effect a Corpus Christi procession, although (as the performance took place on a Monday) it was clearly not Corpus Christi Day. Further on this procession and its music, see 13.4, below. There seems to be a distinction between 'all and summe' who will process and 'all tho that bene here', who will sing: and although *O sacrum convivium* was not a frequently-sung item, it does sound as if the audience were being invited to sing with the cast.

---

5   Line **10** of the banns indicates that a dumb-show of the play was performed simultaneously.

1001–7 [EPISCOPUS]   And in heuyn ther ys both joy and blysse,
                          More then eny towng can tell,
                          There angellys syng with grett swetnesse;
                          To the whyche blysse he bryng vs
                          Whoys name ys callyd Jhesus,
                          And in worshyppe of thys name gloryows
                          To syng to hys honore *Te Deum Laudamus.*

The final lines of the play. It is clear that the Bishop (as the senior cleric present) should then intone *Te Deum*, the whole company joining in. As in other plays, we should assume audience participation here, with the onlookers joining in the hymn led by the cast.

13.4   Latin and the liturgy

Banns
There are no Latin or liturgical elements in the banns.

The Play of the Sacrament
There is a considerable Latin and liturgical content in the play, but it is not evenly spread. The Latin content of the scene between Christ and the Jews would indicate that some of the audience, at least, could be expected to understand Latin and its biblical or liturgical context: but on the other hand the actual liturgical content is in the nature of dramatic paraphrase rather than actual liturgy. There are however two liturgical items to be sung.

230–31 [PRESBITER]   yt ys fer paste none, yt ys tyme to go to cherche,
                          There to saye evynsong, forsothe as I yow tell

323–24 [ARISTORIUS]   Syr Isodyr he ys now at chyrch,
                           There seyng hys evynsong

These two references seem to show that Isadore is reciting the service, perhaps by himself, and not singing it. 'Evensong' was the English word for vespers before the Reformation.

399 [JONATHAS]   He brake the brede and sayd Accipite

404 [JONATHAS]   Comedite Corpus meum.

In this speech (397–404) Jonathas rehearses the events of Christ's institution of the Eucharist. Matthew 26/26 reads 'Accipite et comedite; hoc est corpus meum': the version in the canon of the Mass does not use 'comedite'.

412 [JASON] And how Gabrell apperyd and sayd 'Aue'

Jason rehearses the events of the Annunciation: there is no reason to link this 'Ave' with liturgy rather than the Gospel account (Luke 1/28).

438, 440 [MALCHUS] Because that Phylyppe sayd ...

      ...

      For that he sayd, 'judecare viuos et mortuos'.

For the tradition of the Apostles reciting the Creed, see **Chester 21/335-lat** and section 6.4, above, under **Chester 21**.

448 [JONATHAS] Tinctis Bosra vestibus

Concerning the context of this (mis)quotation from Isaiah 63, see section 6.4, above, under **Chester 20**.

717–18 JHESUS   O mirabiles Judei, attendite et videte
                  Si est dolor similis dolor meus.

Davis amended 'similis' to 'sicut', presumably to bring the quotation to the biblical wording: Lamentations 1/12 reads 'O vos omnes qui transitis per viam, attendite et videte si est dolor sicut dolor meus ...'. The majority of liturgical settings of this verse, of which there are several, use this wording: only the respond 'O vos omnes' uses 'similis', and it does so with 'sicut' as well – 'O vos omnes qui transitis per viam, attendite et videte si est dolor similis sicut dolor meus' (AS, 233; LU, 727). In the speech to the Jews following this quotation Christ amplifies the idea of these lines.

In the next five Latin quotations the Jews follow Christ's lead in using Latin lines together with a paraphrase and amplification of the ideas expressed:

741 JONATHAS Tu es protector vite mee; a quo trepidabo?

Psalm 26/1: the Vulgate and Psalter read 'Dominus' for 'Tu es'.

749 [JASON] Lacrimis nostris conscienciam nostram baptizemus!

Unidentified.

753 [JASON] Ne grauis sompnus irruat.

Unidentified.

756–7 [MASPHAT] O gracyows Lorde, forgyfe me my mysdede!
With lamentable hart: miserere mei, Deus!

Psalms 50, 55 and 56 all begin with these words.

761 [MALCHAS] Asparges me, Domine, ysopo, et mundabor.

Psalm 50/9 reads 'Asperges me hyssopo, et mundabor': but the wording with
'Domine' is found in the antiphon that gives the ceremony of the Asperges its
name (Sandon I, 50; LU, 11 and 13), so the playwright was evidently thinking
of the liturgical context for this verse.

In the following speech Jesus uses Latin lines without a paraphrase:

764–5 [JHESUS] The intent of my commandement knowe ye:
Ite et ostendite vos sacerdotibus meis.

Luke 17/14 reads 'Ite, ostendite vos sacerdotibus'. There is no liturgical item
on this text, apparently.

769 [JHESUS] Et tunc non auertam a vobis faciem meam.

Unidentified, but several similar passages occur in the Psalms and elsewhere,
using the 2nd person: 'Non avertas faciem tuam a me', etc.

778 JONATHAS Oh thow my Lord God and Sauyowr, osanna!

'Hosanna' is too general a form of praise to point to any specific source.

814–16 [EPISCOPUS] O Jhesu fili Dei,
How thys paynfull passyon rancheth myn hart!
Lord, I crye to the, miserere mei

840 For *O sacrum convivium* see 13.3, above: as noted there, the Bishop causes
what is virtually a Corpus Christi procession to return the Host to the church.
The antiphon *O sacrum convivium* was sung in a Corpus Christi procession at
the return to the choir (PS(P), 119v; PS(H), 128).

866–7   EPISCOPUS   Estote fortes in bello et pugnate cum antico serpente,
                     Et accipite regnum eternum, et cetera.

Followed by explanatory paraphrase. The *et cetera* shows that this is not the complete text. 'Estote fortes' is an antiphon, set for the Common of Apostles (AS, 573 and M): what is given here is almost the complete text, in fact, but the ending may change according to the season (see LU, 1118).

900   ARISTORIUS   Holy father, I knele to yow vnder benedycite.

The opening of Aristorius's confession, which ends at **910**: the Bishop gives him penance at **912–19**.

The Jews make confession and ask for baptism in lines **928–51**. The Bishop's blessing (in English) at **952** is apparently not a liturgical form, although the words of baptism may be close: see I, 284 and cf. the wording at **957**, below.

957–9   [EPISCOPUS]   In þe name of þe Father, þe Son and þe Holy Gost,
                     To saue yow from the deuyllys flame,
                     I crysten yow all, both lest and most.

In fact, the Bishop does not seem to use fully liturgical forms. When Aristorius asks for forgiveness at **979** the Bishop only tells him to believe that God will preserve him (**990**).

For *Te Deum* at the end of the play (**1007**) see 13.3, above.

13.5   Music and other aural cues

Banns
1_A **1–** Function: (f). Loud music for the beginning of the banns. This can be inferred from the presence of 1_1, below.
1_1 **80** Function: (g). Loud music for the end of the banns: it is not clear whether a single minstrel is involved, or more than one.

The Play of the Sacrament
2_1 **841** Function: (a). The Bishop and the Jews go in procession to the church. Their singing of *O sacrum convivium* seems to cover the following scene between Aristorius and Sir Isadore as well as the procession from the Jews' house to the church, which apparently happens simultaneously.

The antiphon *O sacrum convivium* was said or sung at the entry into the choir at the end of the procession on Corpus Christi day, so it is appropriate for the processional entry into the church here.[6] It is a largely syllabic chant that would cause no problems to the cast.

2ₐ 867 Function: (h). There is no reason to think that *Estote fortes* is sung rather than said, and in general I think that the Latin lines in this play are not sung. Here, however, it would be appropriate to follow the sung procession with a sung item when the priest lays the Host on the altar; and, as noted above (13.4), the 'et cetera' in the text may indicate that the playwright is following a sense of liturgical propriety according to the season.

The question of whether this is sung or not may have been decided by the circumstances of a particular performance. The note of the characters at the end of the play text, and the assurance that nine players can easily perform the twelve roles, suggests that the play could be performed in a variety of ways, according to the resources available. If the priest is played by a strong actor with a good singing voice, then singing 'Estote fortes' is a good option: if not, it could be said.

2₂ 1007 Function: (g). The end of the play, with the singing of *Te Deum*. The hymn is perhaps intoned by the Bishop, as the senior present, and should be sung by all the cast and the audience (see I, 373).

---

6 See PS(P), 119v; PS(H), 128.

14

Two Prologues

14.1 The Cambridge Prologue

The Cambridge Prologue is found in Cambridge, University Library, Mm.i.18, f. 62R: a facsimile is in MDF 5, 3–5. Like the Rickinghall fragment (section 9.8, above), this prologue consists of two speeches, one in French and the other in English. The manuscript dates probably from the last quarter of the thirteenth century, so that the English part of it is the earliest surviving dramatic text in English.

Although neither of the two speeches is a translation of the other, each constitutes a prologue to a play, in which the audience is addressed and asked to listen quietly (NCPF, cxi–cxii). It is possible that the work is Anglo-Irish in origin, but the linguistic sample is too small for certainty (NCPF, cxiii).

Muir notes that the fragment has always been regarded as the opening of a biblical play, perhaps a Nativity, presenting the emperor Augustus: but she goes on to argue that the French dramatic tradition makes the text more likely to be the introduction to a saint play.[1]

There is no indication of any music, no Latin, and no indication of liturgical content (NCPF, 114–15).

14.2 The Durham Prologue

The source of the Durham prologue, now Durham Cathedral, Dean and Chapter Muniments 1.2. Archidiac. Dunelm. 60, dorse, is a fragment dating from the early fifteenth century. The composition of the text probably did not greatly ante-date this copy.

---

[1] 'Medieval English Drama: The French Connection', 58.

The prologue is edited by Norman Davis in NCPF, 118–19, and there is a facsimile in MDF 5, 27–9. Davis says that the scribe was 'presumably ... a monk or associate of the monastery [of Durham]' (NCPF, cxv): there seems little evidence for this assumption, although the prologue's language does locate its composition in the north-east of England (MDF 5, 27).

The 36-line text is the prologue to a play which, it makes clear, is a miracle of the Virgin. The story concerns a rich knight who, becoming impoverished, fell into the power of the Devil but was rescued from his spiritual plight by the Virgin. Davis mentions the parallel treatments of this story (NCPF, cxvi), and Lynette Muir has discussed it in the context of other English dramatic fragments with French connections.[2]

While a play on a miracle of the Virgin might well have been expected to include music, the Durham Prologue gives no indication of it.

---

2 'Medieval English Drama: The French Connection', 61.

PART 3

Fictional Drama:
Morality Plays

15

The Castle of Perseverance

15.1 Introduction

The Castle of Perseverance is the earliest of the plays usually known as moral plays or moralities. The text is available in facsimile in Farmer *Castle* and Bevington *Macro Plays*, 1–153: the most recent edition, used here, is that by Mark Eccles in Eccles *Macro*, 1–111.

This play is bound with the manuscripts of *Wisdom* and *Mankind*: prior to 1820 these three plays were bound with other, non-dramatic, manuscripts, but the plays alone now make up Washington, DC, Folger Library, Folger MS V.a.354. The manuscripts of *Wisdom* and *Mankind* have a connection with the abbey of Bury St Edmunds, Suffolk (see Eccles *Macro*, xxvii–xxvii and xxxvii), and all three plays were in the collection of Cox Macro, a native of that town, in the eighteenth century. Circumstantial evidence points to East Anglia as the home of *The Castle* also, therefore (Eccles *Macro*, vii). The language is that of the East Midlands: despite some northern vocabulary and a reference to Canwick gallows, near Lincoln, Eccles concluded that the manuscript 'could not have been written by a scribe from Lincolnshire' although 'it may very well have been written by a scribe from Norfolk' (Eccles *Macro*, xi).

The manuscript is the work of one main scribe, working c. 1440, apart from some small amendments and additions made in the fifteenth and sixteenth centuries (Eccles *Macro*, viii–ix). The play itself, and its banns, are somewhat earlier: after reviewing the opinions of earlier scholars Eccles concluded that the play and its banns may have been composed in the period 1400–25, citing a reference to pointed shoes apparently fashionable c. 1382–1425 (Eccles *Macro*, xi). It might be added that a reference to the Castle as 'strenger panne any in Fraunce' (line **1553**) would probably have lost its force after the English victory at Agincourt in 1415, and would have been in bad taste, perhaps, during the resistance led by Joan of Arc in 1429–31.

Allowing for the loss of two leaves in the second gathering (Eccles *Macro*, ix), the play itself must originally have been almost 4000 lines long, taking more than four hours in performance. There is something to be said for Jacob Bennett's view that the last section of the play, lines **3121–649**, was added later and by a different author, for it is a quite separate episode (the Trial in Heaven) and its material is not mentioned in the banns: but Eccles believes that a second author need not be proposed (Eccles *Macro*, xvii–xviii).

The banns, on the other hand, probably are by a second author (*ibid.*). Eccles numbers the lines of the banns and the play consecutively, giving the banns as lines **1–156** of the total text. This is a pity, since the banns were obviously performed on a separate occasion. Unlike those of the Croxton Play (see 13.1), the banns for *The Castle* are clearly for a travelling play, or at least for a travelling script: whereas the Croxton banns are specifically for a performance at Croxton, the banns of *The Castle* simply leave a blank where the name of the place should be.[1] The banns are spoken by two banner-bearers, who are named in the list of the play's characters (Eccles *Macro*, 2): they are accompanied by trumpeters. The First Banner-bearer begins with a call for God's mercy on the king, his subjects, and 'all þe goode comowns of þis towne' that are present. The two speakers then give the audience some idea of the scope and action of the play, although they imply that Mankind's salvation is brought about by the intercession of the Virgin, not through the Trial in Heaven. Finally, they give the date ('þis day seuenenyt') and time (left blank, but probably in the morning: see I, 51) for the performance, which is to take place 'on þe grene': their farewell to the audience twice includes the name of the place where the banns are being read, again left blank in the script. The trumpeters play the banner-bearers off, just as they presumably played them on.

In the discussions that follow, the banns are treated as a text separate from that of the play.

The manuscript of *The Castle of Perseverance* is also famous for its staging plan, which shows a circular playing-place with scaffolds around the perimeter, the Castle itself being in the centre, with Mankind's bed beneath it. This arrangement is presumably generic, since the play was not destined for any one location. The plan has been reproduced many times, and appears as the frontispiece of Eccles *Macro*.

---

[1] Compare the N-Town banns, which use 'N-Town' as a substitute for the actual name to be spoken. None of these three sets of banns makes it clear whether we are concerned with a touring performance or simply with a travelling script. It is obvious that *The Castle* and the N-Town plays were expected to be performed in more than one location, but it is not clear that the same company was involved in more than one venue. Similarly, the script of the *Play of the Sacrament* refers to a particular performance in Croxton, but we do not know that it was not also played elsewhere, by that company or by another. On the information given by banns, see I, 50–3.

15.2 Dramatic directions

The dramatic directions have been discussed by Willis ('Stage Directions') and Henry ('Castle of Perseverance'), as well as by Eccles in his edition. They are mainly in the body of the text, starting at the left margin and separated from the spoken text by lines above and below: but a few are marginal.

All the directions are in Latin except for four in English (Eccles *Macro*, xxiii). Three of these latter are for instrumental music (**455+sd**, **574+sd**, and **646+sd**); the last two are the only SDs written in red, although some SHs are in red and some other SHs are decorated with red (Eccles *Macro*, ix). Eccles considered that the main scribe was responsible for all three of these SDs (*ibid.*). It is however quite possible that they represent a later stage of composition, comparable to the marginal directions added during production elsewhere and sometimes incorporated into the main text by a scribe.[2]

The fourth English SD is undoubtedly a later addition, one of the amendments made after the loss of two leaves from the second gathering. It is not for music.

The directions are listed in Table 21. We see from this that, of 32 directions, several are double directions, usually naming the person to be addressed. Only four are for music, with a fifth for the blowing of a horn, but the three English ones may well have started life as production-notes. This gives a low tally of musical directions, but it should be borne in mind that this play is very short on directions in any case, so that it is impossible to draw conclusions from any statistical analysis. This is in fact a play in which the actions are very largely made clear by the dialogue.

15.3 Text references

Banns

156   [SECUNDUS VEXILLATOR] Trumpe up and lete vs pace.

The demand to the trumpeters to play at the end of the reading of the banns. This may be taken to imply that they also played before the banns were read.

Play

188   [MUNDUS] I dawnse doun as a doo be dalys ful derne.

Eccles quotes similar phrases elsewhere (Eccles *Macro*, 187): the line is clearly metaphorical, and 'dance' has no musical connotations.

---

2 On this issue, as seen in the **Chester** cycle, see I, 26.

TABLE 21 : DIRECTIONS IN *THE CASTLE OF PERSEVERANCE*

Cue-line	f.	lang	Direction if musical : comments
Banns			No directions
Play 455	159r	e	*pipe vp mu*[syk] This is apparently for Mundus: i.e. it belongs to the scene starting at line **456**, not to that just ended.
490	159v	l	
574	160v	e/l	*Trumpe vp. Tunc ibunt Voluptas et Stulticia Malus Angelus et Humanum Genus ad Mundum et dicet.* Includes SH.
614	160v	l	
646	161r	e	*Trumpe vp*
1009	164v	l	Includes SH.
1336	168r	l	Includes SH.
1445	169r	l	
1697	173v	l	This SH is fitted in at the bottom of the page, apparently in the margin.
1705 +lat	172r	l	*Tunc cantabunt Eterne rex altissime et dicet* Includes SH. The singers are apparently the Seven Virtues.
1745	172r	l	
1766	172v	l	
1777	172v	l	
1790	172v	l	
1811	171r	l	
1822	171r	l	
1835	171r	l	
1852	171r	l	*Tunc buccinabit cornu ad Auariciam* The horn is apparently blown by Detraccio, not Mundus, since Auaricia addresses the horn-blower contemptuously (see note to **1853**: Eccles *Macro*, 194).
1863	171v	l	
1898	171v	l	Includes SH.
1968	174v	l	Double SD, including SH.
1981	174v	l	
1990	174v	l	
2198	177v	l	
2377	179v	l	

2409	179v	1	
2556	180r	1	
2920	183v	1	
3228	187r	1	Includes SH.
3560 +sh	190r	1	Gives information that might be transmitted by SD.
3573 +lat	190v	1	Includes SH.
3585	190v	1	Includes SH.
3593	190v	1	
3597 +sh	190v	1	Gives information that might be transmitted by SD.

228   [BELYAL]   In þis brode bugyl a blast wanne I blowe

The 'bugle' Belyal uses is presumably a horn: with it he calls Pride, Anger and
Envy to 'þis grene' (**227**, and cf. **134** in the banns).

240   [CARO]   In myrthe and in melodye my mende is iment.

The close connection of mirth and melody, seen so often in the biblical plays,
is here put into quite another context. Probably we should understand this as
unholy mirth and unholy melody – music used by the vicious.

254   [CARO]   Wyth many berdys in bowre my blastys are blowe

The blowing of a horn is again meant, apparently, although this does not
signal an actual horn-blowing.

328   [BONUS ANGELUS] Of woful wo man may synge

Metaphorical usage.

616   [MUNDUS] Men schul seruyn þe at mel
                    Wyth mynstralsye and bemys blo
                    Wyth metys and drynkys trye.

Mundus is tempting Mankind with the sort of life that he himself enjoys:
minstrelsy at meals suggests a noble household, and therefore wealth.
Mundus's trumpets have already been heard, at **574+sd**.

813–4 [MALUS ANGELUS] Þerfore, goode boy, cum blow
　　　　　　　At my neþer ende.

This is a little obscure, but it is certainly not a musical reference. It could conceivably mean 'Blow your horn behind me', but the reference to his 'nether end' is too specifically indecent. Its primary purpose here is clearly to characterise the Bad Angel and his associates. Iconographical evidence of the kissing of the backside is well-attested (see I, 204–5), although such illustrations do not allow of a distinction between kissing and blowing (but for the Malvern misericord showing blowing with bellows, see I, 207). The implications of the Bad Angel's similar retort at **1276** (see below) are much the same as the more modern 'Kiss my arse', and that is probably intended here.

878–9 [HUMANUM GENUS] Of Mankynde getyth no man no good
　　　　　　　But if he synge si dedero.

Metaphorical usage. On the Latin, see 15.4.

880–2 AUARICIA　　Mankynd, þat was well songe.
　　　　　　　　　　Sertys now þou canst sum skyll.
　　　　　　　　　　Blessyd be þi trewe tonge.

The reference to singing is metaphorical, picking up that of **879**. As **881–2** show, Avarice is pleased with what Mankind has said.

1204–5 LUXURIA　　I may soth synge
　　　　　　　　　　'Mankynde is kawt in my slynge'.

Metaphorical usage.

1212–13 [ACCIDIA]　　Whanne þe messe-belle goth
　　　　　　　　　　Lye stylle, man, and take non hede.

Sloth's advice does not require any mass-bell to be heard here.

1242–3 [HUMANUM GENUS] Mekyl myrþe I moue in mynde,
　　　　　　　　　　Wyth melody at my mowþis met.

Metaphorical usage, connecting mirth and melody.

1276 [MALUS ANGELUS] Goode syre, cum blowe myn hol behynde.

Compare **813–14**, above. Here, where the Bad Angel is speaking to the Good Angel, it is more obvious that the speaker is being contemptuous.

1577 [MALUS ANGELUS] And pleye þe a whyle wyth Sare and Sysse.

Eccles (*Macro*, 192) connects this with other literary references to Sar and Sis, including that in **Chester 7/410** (see 6.3). Like 'pax mery mawd', the references to Sar and Sis seem to refer to the words of a popular song, or at least to a body of popular sub-literary material.

1783 [DETRACCIO] Rappys for to route and rynge.

Not a reference to the ringing of a bell. Eccles offers a more general meaning of 'resound' in his Glossary (Eccles *Macro*, 263).

1796 [DETRACCIO] Ful redy in robys to rynge

As **1783**, 'speak loudly' (see also line **3094**).

1853–4 AUARICIA   Syr bolnynge bowde,
                                Tell me why blowe ȝe so lowde.

This refers to Detraccio's blowing of his horn at Avaricia, **1852+sd**. The speech of Mundus immediately following shows that the vices blame Avarice for letting Mankind escape to the Castle, so we may assume that Detraccio has purposely upset Avarice by blowing his horn loudly (as Avarice here says) and rudely at him.

1897–8 [MUNDUS] Howtyth hye upon ȝene hyll,
                           ȝe traytours, in ȝoure trumpys.

Mundus directs his trumpeters to blow, thus giving the signal for the start of battle. The significance of a 'how' is not merely that of shouting, as Eccles says (Eccles *Macro*, 249), but more specifically of calling comrades together (cf. the shepherds, discussed in I, 348–9, 360–1), as Belial does when he takes on the nature of an herald (**1969**). The references to banners in **1898+sd** (of Mundus) and **1903** (of Belial) emphasise the war-like nature of the trumpet-calls, specified in **1899–900** (see below).

1899–900 BELYAL   I here trumpys trebelen al of tene.
                              þe worþi Werld walkyth to werre

'Trebelen of tene' indicates both a high-pitched sound and one that suggests anger or pain (Eccles *Macro,* 270–1): at any rate, Belial recognises it (and so would the audience, presumably) as the call to battle.

1938   CARO   I here an hydowse whwtynge on hyt.

Eccles glosses 'whwtynge' as 'shouting' (Eccles *Macro,* 276).

2197–8   [BELYAL] Claryouns, cryeth up at a krake,
                     And blowe 3our brode baggys.

Belial encourages another attack. The 'clarions' are probably the same as the trumpets of Mundus: for although they could be a second group, those addressed by Flesh at **2376–7** (see below) would be yet a third, and it is more realistic to assume (for financial and logistical reasons) that only one group of trumpeters is involved. 'At a krake' suggests a loud and sudden noise (Eccles *Macro,* 250). The meaning of **2198** is more difficult: Eccles glosses 'baggys' as 'bagpipes' (Eccles *Macro,* 231: as he says, it clearly has the meaning of 'sacks' when it appears in line **2916**). The blowing of bagpipes in such a case certainly makes sense,[3] but incidentally increases the costs of production to a stage where the music must have been a significant part of the budget. The word 'brode' may therefore simply mean that the bagpipes are of the large, war-pipes, variety, or – perhaps more likely – Belial is drawing attention to the size of the bags and thus indirectly to their significance as symbols of lust.

2217   IRA   I, Wrethe, may syngyn weleawo.

Metaphorical usage.

2334–6   [ACCIDIA] þat had leuere syttyn at þe ale
                     Thre mens songys to syngyn lowde
                     þanne toward þe chyrche for to crowde.

Sloth's description of his adherents calls to mind writings such as that of Manning in *Handling Sin* where singing, dancing and games during the time of church services are specifically denounced.[4] This is the earliest reference to three men's songs in the OED, the next being that in *Promptorium Parvulorum* (Eccles *Macro,* 196). Lines **2334–6** seem to imply that three men's songs are on unholy texts. This is true in the sense that any secular music for alto, tenor and bass (ATB), by definition, did not set sacred texts, but the three men's songs of the fifteenth and sixteenth centuries are not particularly unholy. This

---

3 On the uses of bagpipes, see I, 349–50 and especially n. 134.
4 See Rastall 'Minstrelsy, Church and Clergy', 86.

reference to 'three men's songs' is a little puzzling, then, in its implication of a specific and identifiable body of music that went contrary to the Church's teaching. Probably the passage is a general warning of the potential dangers of all secular song; perhaps, too, three-men's songs were also an improvised genre, of which the written remains are only a part.[5]

2376-7   [CARO]   In bemys bryth
                    Late blastys blowe.

As before, the trumpets of the vices encourage a renewed attack on the Castle (cf. **2198**: in both cases the SD 'Tunc pugnabunt diu' follows).

2607–8   [ABSTINENCIA]   'Make us mery and lete hym gone:
                          He was a good felawe.'

Like other apparent quotations, this could be from a song-text or other popular sub-literary text (cf. the comments under **1577**, above, and under **2611–12**, below).

2611–12   [CASTITAS]   'Make we mery and a ryche fest
                        And lete hym lyn in dedys fodyr.'

Here the source, or a source, of the quotation is given, at **2612+lat**, and it turns out to be Psalm 48/11, not a secular text at all (cf. **2607–8**, above).

2712   [AUARICIA]   And þat schal be þi songe.

Metaphorical usage.

2716   [HUMANUM GENUS]   Certys þat songe is oftyn songe.

Metaphorical usage.

2720   [HUMANUM GENUS]   þat ful songe was neuere songe

Metaphorical usage.

2805   [MORS]   Whanne my blastys arn on hem blowe.

---

5   For improvisation through 'sighting', see I, 95–6. The freemen's songs in the early-seventeenth-century collections of Thomas Ravenscroft are late examples of the genre. For an overview of three-men's song, see Wulstan *Tudor Music*, 55.

Death's 'blastys' are to summon men to their deaths. The lines following show that Death thinks of this in terms of a battle (he mentions his lance at **2807**), so he is probably referring to a trumpet or horn. Possibly the reference is to the Last Trumpet: but if this is an actual reference, rather than a metaphorical one, Death presumably blows a mournful blast on a horn, perhaps heard only by Mankind, before his entrance at **2778**. A horn, rather than a trumpet, would again imply a signal to gather comrades together, an ironic reference to the trumpet-calls to the vices' attacks earlier. The use of 'blow' may refer also to Mankind's statement at **2770–2** that he will follow Avarice 'whyl I may blow [i.e. breathe]' and until 'deth me ouyrthrow'.

3061 [ANIMA]   Of sadde sorwe now may I synge.

Metaphorical usage.

3124 [MALUS ANGELUS] Þi placebo I schal synge.

Metaphorical: in Vespers of the Office for the Dead, 'Placebo' is the first word of the first antiphon, and is used to signify the singing of the office as a whole.

3375 [MISERICORDIA] 'Mercy' schal I synge and say

Metaphorical usage.

3425 [JUSTITIA]   Tyl Deth trypte hym on hys daunce

Metaphorical usage.

3591 [JUSTITIA] Þou devyl bold as a belle

Metaphorical usage. The metaphor may have been chosen partly for its alliteration and rhyme (helle/belle), but its primary purpose is probably to suggest that the Bad Angel is loud and indiscriminate in his speech.

3617 [PATER]   Whanne Myhel hys horn blowyth at my dred dom

Late medieval illustrations of the Last Trumpet show buisines,[6] although the Devil in the Towneley Doomsday, too, refers to a horn (see 4.3), as Pater does here. I see no reason for these two references to change our view that the *buisine* is the instrument proper to the Last Trumpet.

6   Or, before the fourteenth century, oliphants, made from elephant tusks.

3645, 3649 [PATER] þus endyth oure gamys.

> ...

> Te Deum laudamus.

The last line of the play is incidentally interesting for two reasons. First, it shows that 'laudamus' makes a rhyme with blys/is/þis/mys/gamys, which tells us something about the pronunciation of the vowels. Second, God steps out of role here to announce Te Deum, a piece in which he would normally play no part at all in character, since God does not praise himself (see I, 177). Curiously, he does not say that it will be either sung or said: we are left to infer that the usual practice will be followed. This may mean that the issue is open to directorial choice.

Singing is undoubtedly the best option if it is possible. Moreover, it would apparently be sung by everyone present, including Pater and the Vices. If God can step out of his character to announce it, presumably the whole cast (as well as the audience) could sing it as an act of praise by them as actors, not in their dramatic roles. Because the last line is part of a rhyming stanza, it seems to me unlikely that the line itself should be intoned: that would surely not provide a satisfactory conclusion to the stanza;[7] and it would be hard for God to step out of his role in intoning a hymn that should always be intoned by the senior person (i.e. cleric) present. I suggest that God was intended to speak the last line of the play, thus warning the audience of what is about to happen, and that someone else – a cleric? one of the cast? – then intoned the hymn, in which everyone else joined.

15.4 Latin and the liturgy

Latin lines appear throughout *The Castle of Perseverance*, but they are distributed unevenly. As is often the case, Latin quotations supply the authority for things that are said. Citations are therefore at their highest density during the Trial in Heaven scene, and the Good Angel and the Virtues also quote the Scriptures in Latin during their arguments. The Scriptures are not the only authorities quoted, however: Chastity and Business (Solicitudo) both quote unidentified texts (**2303 +lat, 2364+lat**), while Avarice takes a text from Cato (**866**) and Lust quotes a proverb (**503+lat**). It might be expected that the Devil's servants would avoid quoting Scripture, which would not normally be to their advantage: but Folly does misquote Ecclesiasticus (**516+lat**), and the Bad Angel cites part of the Office of the Dead (**3096–7**).[8]

---

7 Modern producers often seem to use this sort of time-saving device, but it would surely not have recommended itself to the Middle Ages.
8 This quotation, based on Job 7/9, is also cited by Satan in **York 37/285–8** and **Towneley 25/305–8** – these are the same passage – and is quoted by Lucifer in

It is not easy to decide, in many cases, whether the Latin should be heard or not. Some quotations are part of the stanzas in which they occur, and can hardly be omitted in performance; but most are extra-stanzaic and may be intended simply as 'footnotes'. Only rarely could the Latin+English pattern be invoked as text-plus-exegesis, and it seems unlikely that any of the texts quoted was sung.

Apart from the singing of Te Deum at the end, where Deus steps out of his role and the hymn seems to be intended as a ceremonial thanksgiving for the play as an event, there is little by way of liturgical content in the play itself. Confession absolves Mankind of his sins with texts that are close enough to a real absolution to be recognisable (**1494–532**), but the dramatic speech is filled out with matters of immediate relevance to the play. Likewise, the flowers thrown down by the Virtues during the attack on the Castle are reminiscent of the Palm Sunday procession, but the event is certainly not modelled on it. As Eccles notes, the flowers are identified as roses, which are symbolic of charity and of the Passion, while Wrath specifically says that he has been hurt by 'a rose þat on rode was rent' (**2220**), i.e. Christ himself (Eccles *Macro*, 195). Some of the language in this part of the play is, indeed, reminiscent of contemporary lyrics: compare **2026**, 'Rode as rose on rys irent', with the line 'Thys rose is raylyd on a rys', from the carol *Of a Rose synge we*.[9]

In the discussions that follow, Eccles's identification follows the quotation: these are found in his notes (Eccles *Macro*, 185–203) under the relevant lines.

Banns
The banns contain no Latin.

Play
361+lat [BONUS ANGELUS] Diuicias et paupertates ne dedris michi Domine

Proverbs 30/8: 'mendicitatem et divitias ne dederis mihi'. As the Good Angel mentions that he can find the relevant quotation in Holy Writ but does not otherwise quote it, this must be spoken as the last line of his speech even though it is extra-stanzaic. There is no reason to think that it might be sung.

410+lat [BONUS ANGELUS] Homo memento finis et in eternum non peccabis

From Ecclesiasticus 7/40: 'memorare novissima tua, et in aeternum non peccabis'. See also **3647–8**, below. The Good Angel has already explained this quotation, and he does not draw attention to the scriptural basis of what he says. This need not be spoken, therefore.

N-Town 26/48.
9 Stevens *Mediaeval Carols*, 13.

503+lat [VOLUPTAS] Non est in mundo diues qui dicit habundo.

Non-scriptural: Eccles cites *Reliquae Antiquae* i, 289, for this proverb.

516+lat [STULTICIA] Sapiencia penes Domini

Ecclesiasticus 1/1: 'Omnis sapientia a Domino Deo est'. As noted above, this must be a deliberate misquotation. Folly mentions that he has a source for his comments, which demands that this quotation be heard.

865+lat [AUARICIA] Labitur exiguo quod partum tempore longo.

Catonis Disticha, 2/17. Avarice cites 'Caton þe grete clerke' as the source of what he has just said. Avarice's last English line, 'þus seyth Caton ...', can be interpreted in two ways, however: as Eccles has punctuated it, with a stop after 'clerke', the 'þus seyth' refers to the English of lines **864–5**; but it could also be read as a comment in English followed by a pithier and authoritative statement, 'þus seyth Caton þe grete clerke: / Labitur ...' On the whole there seems more point to the Latin if it is actually spoken, but this is not a conclusive example.

879 [HUMANUM GENUS] But if he synge si dedero.

Eccles gives sources for this proverb.

1502, 1506, 1515, 1519, 1528, 1532
    [CONFESCIO] Quantum peccasti.
                      Vitam male continuasti.
                      Quicquid gesisti.
                      Vicium quodcumque fecisti.
                      Noli peccare.
                      Posius noli viciare.

Eccles identifies **1528** as John 5/4, 8/11. Confession's speech of absolution is in English, but interspersed with these Latin lines.

1611–12 [CARITAS] Poule in hys pystyl puttyth þe prefe,
                      But charyte be wyth þe chefe.

Eccles identifies the reference as 1 Corinthians 13/1–3, although **1612** strictly refers to verse 13: 'Nunc autem manent fides, spes, charitas, tria haec; major autem horum est charitas'.

1631+lat [CASTITAS] Quia qui in carne viuunt Domino placere non possunt.

Eccles identifies this as a free quotation of Romans 8/8, 'Qui autem in carne sunt Deo placere non possunt'. The sense of the speech is complete without this line being spoken, and it is possible that the Latin is intended only as a 'footnote': but the meaning is considerably impoverished without it, and it seems likely that it should be spoken.

1644+lat [SOLICITUDO] Osiositas parit omne malum.

Eccles cites a number of sources for versions of this saying, including Ecclesiasticus 33/29, which is not close.

1696+lat [HUMILITAS] Cum sancto sanctus eris, et cetera.

Psalm 17/26 (and see also section 17.4 under **Mankind 324–6**). The 'et cetera' suggests the possibility of a liturgical piece being quoted: there is a responsory 'Cum sancto sanctus habitans' (WA, 283), but there seems no reason for a quotation here.

1705+lat [HUMILITAS] Qui perseuerauit usque in finem hic saluus erit.

Matthew 10/22, and cf. 24/13. Neither of these last two quotations (**1696+ lat, 1705+lat**) is necessary to the sense of what Humilitas is saying, although they give explanations at a surface level.

1705+lat+sd Eterne rex altissime

This hymn is set for Vespers in Ascensiontide in the Sarum Use (HS, 101).

2007+lat [HUMANUM GENUS] Omne gaudium existimate cum variis
temptacionibus insideritis.

James 1/2: 'Omne gaudium existimate, fratres mei, cum in tentaciones varias incideritis'. This is a rather general authority for the point that Mankind is making, and it tends to hold up the flow of his speech.

2020+lat [HUMANUM GENUS] Delectare in Domino et dabit tibi peticiones
cordis tui.

Psalm 36/4. This, coming at the end of Mankind's speech, is a rather closer version of what he has just said: in fact, it is virtually part of an English+ Latin pattern.

2094+lat [HUMILITAS] Deposuit potentes de sede et cetera.

> Luke 1/52. Again, the 'et cetera' needs to be explained. The raising of the humble is not particularly relevant, for although Mary's meekness is mentioned at **2089** her raising up is not.

2107+lat [HUMILITAS] Qui se exaltat humiliabitur et cetera.

> Luke 14/11, 18/14. It is hard to know what the 'et cetera' might imply.

2124+lat [PACIENCIA] Quia ira viri justiciam Dei non operatur.

> James 1/2.

2163+lat, 2167 [CARITAS] Ve homini illi per quem scandalum venit.
> ...
> In holy wrytte þis I rede.

> Matthew 18/7. This is a Latin+English pattern, for lines **2164–6** give a loose paraphrase of the Latin. This seems to suggest that the Latin is intended to be spoken, but it is certainly not incontrovertible evidence.

2266–9 [ABSTINENCIA] Certys I schal þi wele aslake
> Wyth bred þat browth us out of hell
> And on þe croys sufferyd wrake:
> I mene þe sacrament.

> Abstinence is speaking to Gluttony: 'the Sacrament' means 'the Eucharist'.

2277+lat [ABSTINENCIA] Cum jejunasset quadraginta diebus et cetera.

> Matthew 4/2: 'cum jejunasset quadraginta diebus et quadraginta noctibus'. Abstinence is now speaking to Mankind. This is a quotation that really does not need to be spoken: it reads much more like a scriptural footnote, for it hardly adds anything to the knowledge or understanding of an audience.

2303+lat [CASTITAS] Mater et Virgo extingue carnales concupiscentias.

> Not known elsewhere.

2364+lat [SOLICITUDO] Nunc lege nunc ora nunc disce nuncque labora.

> Proverb or saying, perhaps most immediately relevant to a religious.

2452+lat [LARGITAS] Maledicti sunt auariciosi hujus temporis.

Not known elsewhere.

2465 [LARGITAS] Rote of sorwe and synne.

Eccles identifies this as 1 Timothy 6/10.

2599+lat [ABSTINENCIA] Mundus transit et concupiscencia ejus.

1 John 2/17. This is not really of immediate relevance to what Abstinence is saying, so the quotation probably need not be heard.

2612+lat [CASTITAS] Et sic relinquent alienis diuicias suas.

Psalm 48/11: 'Et relinquent alienis divitias suas'.

2625+lat [SOLICITUDO] Non descendet cum illo gloria ejus.

Psalm 48/18. This adds little to what Solicitudo is saying, and I think that it is better left unheard.

2638+lat [LARGITAS] Auarus numquam replebitur pecunia.

Ecclesiastes 5/9: 'Avarus non implebitur pecunia'. This, too, does not need to be heard, for the subject has been discussed fully and what Largitas is saying is perfectly clear.

2984–6 [HUMANUM GENUS] Certis a vers þat Dauid spak
                 In þe sawter I fynde it trewe
                 Tesauriʒat et ignorat cui congregabit ea.
                 Tresor, tresor, it hathe no tak.

Psalm 38/7. This quotation is a part of the stanza: and although the Latin line is immediately translated, it must certainly be heard. There is however no question of singing it.

3063 [ANIMA] But Mercy pase alle þynge.

Psalm 144/9. See also **3456+lat**.

3096–7 [MALUS ANGELUS] And bey in inferno
                          Nulla est redempcio

Office of the Dead: 'Quia in inferno nulla est redemptio'. See BS, 2/278. This text appears also in **N-Town 26/48**, **York 37/285–8**, and **Towneley 25/299–302**. Eccles remarks that the biblical source is Job 7/9: 'Qui descenderit ad inferos, non ascendet'.

    This quotation is part of the stanza, and it must be heard: but there is no reason to sing it.

3124 [MALUS ANGELUS] þi placebo I schal synge.

Placebo is the office of Vespers for the Dead: see 15.3, above, under this line.

The Trial in Heaven
3163+lat [JUSTICIA] Vnusquique suum honus portabit.

    Galatians 6/5. Extra-stanzaic, but in the middle of Justice's speech. There is no obvious translation, and it probably should be spoken.

3167+lat [JUSTICIA] Non omne qui dicit Domine Domine intrabit regnum
                                     celorum.

    Matthew 7/21: the Vulgate reads 'Non omnis qui dicit mihi Domine Domine intrabit in regnum caelorum'. The use of 'omne' and the omission of 'in' would suggest that **3167+lat** is an incorrect quotation from memory. Although this line appears in mid-speech (after the fourth line of the stanza) it is in fact extra-stanzaic. There is no real translation of it: rather, it amplifies the speech by making it more specific, and for this reason I should be inclined to have it spoken.

3252–3252+lat [VERITAS] My feythful Fadyr, saunz pere!
                          Quoniam veritatem dilexisti.

    Psalm 50/8. The Latin line is extra-stanzaic: again, it appears after the fourth line of the stanza and makes more specific the statement of an earlier line, in this case **3250**, 'As þou lovyste me, Trewthe, þi dowtyr dere'. In view of the Latin lines in this scene that are part of the stanza and therefore must be spoken, I am inclined to regard lines such as this as spoken lines that could not be fitted into the stanza and were therefore placed at a convenient articulation-point in the stanza.

    Eccles translates the French as 'Without equal' in his Glossary, but 'pere' is surely to be strictly translated as 'father', not as the English word 'peer': that is, it is a reference to God's presence from the beginning of time, since he has no parent.

3265+lat [VERITAS] Aurum sitisti, aurum bibisti.

Untraced. This is again extra-stanzaic but appearing after the fourth line of the stanza, and should probably be spoken.

3271–3 [VERITAS] þou he cried mercy, moriendo,
Nimis tarde penitendo,
Talem mortem reprehendo.

Untraced. These lines are an integral part of the stanza, and must therefore be heard. There is no question of singing them.

3284–6 [VERITAS] Quia veritas manet in eternum,
Tendit homo ad infernum,
Nunquam venit ad supernum.

Psalm 116/2 reads 'veritas Domini manet in aeternum'. This may be part of a liturgical text that quotes the psalm, but if so I have not identified it. This is an integral part of the stanza, and must therefore be heard.

3313+lat MISERICORDIA O Pater misericordiarum et Deus tocius
consolationis, qui consolatur nos in omni tribulacione nostra!

2 Corinthians 1/3–4: Eccles notes that **N-Town 11/73** translates this and that it is quoted also in a meditation ascribed to Augustine.
The Latin is extra-stanzaic, at the beginning of Mercy's speech, but it follows the SH (see Bevington *Macro*, f. 188 of the play). The indications are, therefore, that it should be heard, but there is no reason to sing it.

3339+lat [MISERICORDIA] Si pro peccato vetus Adam non cecidisset,
Mater pro nato numquam grauidada fuisset.

Untraced, although Eccles notes a number of sources in which the idea is used.
These lines are extra-stanzaic, written in the right margin in rather smaller script. But they are translated in the first four lines of the stanza that follows, and the lines rhyme: so it would seem that they were intended to be heard.

3348 [MISERICORDIA] Passus sub Pilato Poncio.

This is presumably a reference to the Apostles' Creed: 'Passus sub Pontio Pilato, crucifixus, mortuus et sepultus'. The inversion of Pilate's name provides the necessary rhyme (see below).

3352–3 [MISERICORDIA] Whanne þou seydyst 'Scitio'.
scilicet, salutem animarum

Line **3352** is the last line of the stanza, with the last three words (3353) in the right margin in smaller script. Eccles refers to John 19/28, 'Jesus ... dixit "Sitio"', and notes that in the Middle Ages this one of the Last Words was regarded as a reference to the health of the soul: hence its appearance as a 'footnote', apparently, in the margin. I am therefore doubtful that **3353**, which Eccles treats as a spoken line although he prints it in its correct place in the margin, should be spoken.

3356 [MISERICORDIA] But seyd 'Consummatum est' was alle.

John 19/30. Part of the stanza, and so to be spoken.

3361 [MISERICORDIA] Aqua baptismatis et sanguis redempcionis.

Not traced. Integral part of the stanza, and therefore to be heard: there is no question of singing it.

3365 [MISERICORDIA] Est causa saluacionis.

Not traced. Integral part of the stanza, and therefore to be heard: there is no question of singing it.

3374–8 [MISERICORDIA] Quia dixisti 'Misericordiam seruabo'.
'Mercy' schal I synge and say
And 'miserere' schal I pray
For Mankynd euere and ay.
Misericordias Domini in eternum cantabo.

Lines **3374** and **3378** are references to Psalm 88/29 and 2, respectively: 'In aeternum servabo illi misericordiam meam' and 'Misericordias Domini in aeternum cantabo'. These quotations are integral parts of the stanza, and should therefore be heard.

3382+lat [JUSTICIA] Justicias Dominus justicia dilexit.

Psalm 10/8: 'Quoniam justus Dominus et justitias dilexit'.
The quotation is extra-stanzaic, but appears after the fourth line of the stanza. It is therefore likely that the Latin is intended to be heard, but if it is really as inaccurate a quotation as it would seem, it is hard to know what point there would be in quoting it – unless, of course, it was for an audience

that knew enough Latin to recognise the import of the quotations but did not know much of the grammar or of the precise quotations. On balance, I think that Justice should speak this line.

3391+lat [JUSTICIA] Quia Deum, qui se genuit, dereliquit.

3400 [JUSTICIA] Sicut justi tui

3404 [JUSTICIA] Quia oblitus est Domini creatoris sui.

Eccles offers Deuteronomy 32/18 for lines **3391+lat** and **3404**: 'Deum, qui te genuit, dereliquisti, et oblitus es Domini creatoris tui'.

Line **3391+lat** is extra-stanzaic, but the other two are integral parts of the stanza: this would suggest that the former line, like the others, should be spoken by Justice, and perhaps it confirms indirectly that other extra-stanzaic Latin lines in this play should be heard by the audience.

'Sicut justi tui' is unidentified. The change of person from the Vulgate in **3391+lat** is the kind of alteration that sometimes happens when a biblical passage is used in liturgy, so these three lines may in fact come from a liturgical source.

3443+lat Letabitur justus cum viderit vindictam.

Psalm 57/11. This is extra-stanzaic, occurring at the end of Justice's speech: it gives the biblical version of the previous four lines.

3456+lat Et misericordia ejus super omnia opera ejus.

Psalm 144/9: 'Et miserationes ejus super omnia opera ejus'. This is extra-stanzaic, occurring at the end of the first stanza of Mercy's speech: it gives the biblical version of the previous four lines.

3469+lat Et misericordia ejus a progenie in progenies et cetera

Luke 1/50, and cf. Psalm 102/17. Extra-stanzaic, at the end of Mercy's speech: it gives the authority for the previous four lines, and as Mercy cites David 'in scriptur', it seems that the quotation could very conveniently be spoken. The 'et cetera' does not seem to have any specific relevance, although it underlines the fact of a quotation.

3478 [VERITAS] So seyth þe gospel.

Truth is citing Matthew 25/41–6.

3521+lat Misericordia et Veritas obuiauerunt sibi, Justicia et Pax osculate sunt.

Psalm 84/11. Extra-stanzaic, at the end of the third stanza of Peace's six-stanza speech. Peace is presenting the biblical justification for her suggestion, made in lines **3518–21**, that the four sisters kiss and decide to save Mankind. The Latin must surely be heard.

3534+lat Hic pax, hic bonitas, hic laus, hic semper honestas.

Eccles compares this with a quotation from St Bernard, but he does not cite a biblical reference.

Extra-stanzaic, occurring after the fourth stanza of Peace's speech: it is not as closely connected with the preceding speech as other quotations, but may nevertheless have been intended for speech by Peace.

3547+lat Et tuam, Deus, deposcimus pietatem ut ei tribuere digneris lucidas et
quietas mansiones.

Eccles finds a version of this quotation in *The Prick of Conscience*, but no reference for its source is given.

Extra-stanzaic, occurring at the end of the fifth stanza of Peace's speech. The quotation relates to the two lines following the Latin, rather than to those preceding it. Probably it should be heard.

3552–3   [PAX]   Tanquam ouis ductus es
Whanne gutte sanguis ran adoun.

Acts 8/32. This is part of the stanza, so there is no question but that it is spoken by Peace. **3552** is not a translation, and therefore makes sense only to someone who understands spoken Latin: but the inclusion of a single Latin word, 'sanguis', in **3553** suggests in any case that at least some of the audience had knowledge of the language.

3560+sh+lat   Ego cogito cogitaciones pacis, non affliccionis.

Eccles cites Jeremiah 29/11, but this quotation is a much-shortened version.

Extra-stanzaic, occurring immediately after the SH for Pater. The placing seems deliberate, so that the Latin is apparently to be heard.

3573+lat   Misericordia Domini plena est terra. Amen!

Psalm 32/5. Extra-stanzaic, occurring at the end of the Father's first stanza. It is followed by the SD/SH 'Dicet filiabus', relating to the rest of the Father's speech: although this may be due to the fact that the SH/SD starts a new page, it seems likely that the SH PATER would be given if the Father had not spoken or sung the Latin.

3597+sh+lat   Sicut sintilla in medio maris.

Eccles traces this back to Augustine, but without giving a precise reference. As it stands, this part-quotation makes little sense to an audience unless they know the whole quotation. It therefore seems most like a footnote reference: but as it occurs after the SH and before the speech proper – it is extra-stanzaic – it should perhaps be heard.

3610 +lat   Ego occidam et viuificabo, percuciam et sanabo, et nemo
                   est qui de manu mea possit eruere.

Eccles cites Deuteronomy 32/39, which this Latin does not however quote very precisely. It is more likely to be a liturgical or other non-Vulgate version, but if it is I have not been able to identify it.

Extra-stanzaic, occurring at the end of the first stanza of the Father's final speech. The Latin is not immediately relevant to the English speech, in that there is no direct translation or paraphrase.

3623+lat   Ecce, requiram gregem meum de manu pastoris.

Eccles cites Ezekiel 34/10 and *Prick of Conscience* 5288–9, but it is the latter that gives the closer wording.

Extra-stanzaic, before the Father's third stanza. The line immediately following the Latin is relevant, and the Latin should probably be heard.

3636+lat   Et qui bona egerunt ibunt in vitam eternam; qui vero mala,
                   in ignem eternum.

Eccles cites the Athanasian Creed and compares Matthew 25/46.

Extra-stanzaic, before the final stanza of the speech. The four lines follow-ing the Latin are a free paraphrase of it: no doubt the Latin should be heard.

3648   [PATER]   Te Deum laudamus!

The last line of the play. Te Deum is a hymn used on occasions of thanks-giving, and frequently at the end of plays.

Many of the Latin lines discussed here are part of the stanza pattern and should certainly be heard, although there is no reason to think that they should be sung

448

rather than spoken; a few would seem to be 'footnotes' only and not to be heard. There is however no way of distinguishing which is which, and on balance I would think it sensible to treat all such lines alike by speaking them.

This raises the interesting question of the audience for whom *The Castle* was written, and their capabilities in relation to the Latin language. On the whole, I believe that the playwrights tended to write for their most educated auditors, on the principle that those who understood the Latin would appreciate it fully, while those who did not would nevertheless derive satisfaction and insight from the knowledge that the English translations did have a Latin authority, be it scriptural or otherwise.

Those Latin lines that indicate a sung performance are included in section 15.5, below; the rest, that should certainly or possibly be spoken, do not appear in the cue-list.

15.5   Music and other aural cues

The Castle of Perseverance has has had some adverse criticism from recent scholars.[10] Whatever the quality of its structure and dramatic effectiveness, however, there is no doubt that its use of musical images and sounds is lively and consistent, with some telling cross-references between the various parties involved (see especially the comments in 15.3).

Banns

1_A 1– Function: (f). A trumpet fanfare can be assumed before the banns begin, on the basis of the fanfare at the end of the banns. There is no evidence as to the number of trumpeters involved: and the minstrels may have formed a shawm-and-trumpet band.

1_1 156 Function: (g). Trumpet fanfare to end the banns.

The Temptation and Repentance of Mankind

2_1 234, or perhaps 230 Function: ?(h). Belial blows his horn to call his supporters together. Although a mid-stanza horn-call at 230 would be perfectly possible, it is perhaps dramatically neater if it happens at 234: and, although this should not be regarded as primary evidence, a horn-call at 234 would signal the end of Scene II.

2_2 455+sd Function: (e), (h). The music that 'pipes up' is attached to Mundus: as noted in 15.2, this cue belongs to the beginning of Scene V, not to the end of Scene IV. There is no indication of the instruments played, although a shawm-and-trumpet band would be appropriate.

---

10 Davenport *Fifteenth-Century English Drama*, 106; Eccles *Macro*, xxvi.

2_3 **574+sd** Function: (b). The SD 'trumpe up' suggests trumpets, but a shawm-and-trumpet band is possible.

2_4 **646+sd** Function: (b) or (e), (h). The minstrels 'trump up' again.

The Siege of the Castle of Perseverance

3_1 **1705+lat+sd** Function: none. The hymn *Eterne rex altissime* is sung by the Virtues.

3_2 **1852+sd** Function: ?(b) or (e). It is apparently Backbiter who blows his horn, loudly and rudely, at Covetousness (see comments in 15.3).

3_3 **1898** Function: (a), (e), (h). The trumpeters (this line shows that there are more than one) blow again, covering the movement of characters around the acting area, showing a change of location, and signalling the end of a scene.

3_4 **2198+sd** Function: (a). Belial's attack is accompanied by clarions and bag-pipes.

3_5 **2377+sd** Function: (a). Flesh's attack is accompanied by trumpets.

The Trial in Heaven

4_1 **3649** Function: (g). End of the play: Te Deum is intoned, perhaps by God, who has stepped out of his role to announce the singing of it. The hymn should be taken up by all the cast and by the audience.[11]

---

[11] Since God has stepped out of character, no doubt the actors playing the vices and their servants could also sing. On the singing of the audience, see I, 373–4.

16

Wisdom

16.1 Introduction

A Morality of Wisdom, Who is Christ, also known as *Mind, Will, and Understanding*, survives in two sources. One, an incomplete text covering the play as far as **752+sd**, is in Oxford, Bodleian Library MS Digby 133; the other, which is complete, appears as the first play in the Macro manuscript (Washington, DC, Folger Library, MS Folger V.a.354).

The complete text is edited by Mark Eccles in Eccles *Macro*, 113–52: it is available in facsimile in Bevington *Macro*, 156–251.[1] The Macro version of *Wisdom* is a late fifteenth-century copy by the main scribe of *Mankind*, an East Anglian, and the play's composition probably dates from the 1460s (Eccles *Macro*, xxvii and xxx– xxxi). This manuscript, like that of *Mankind*, was owned by a monk named Hyngham in the late fifteenth century. Several possible identifications have been offered in the past (see Riggio *Wisdom*, 5; Eccles *Macro*, xxvii–xxviii), but Richard Beadle has shown on paleographic grounds that the man concerned was a certain Thomas Hyngham who was at Bury St Edmunds in the 1470s. This, one of two Thomas Hynghams in the late fifteenth century, was the man who copied the Macro *Wisdom* and most of *Mankind*.[2]

The incomplete version is edited by Baker, Murphy and Hall in LMRP, 116–40. There is a facsimile in MDF 3 (1976), with an introduction by Baker and Murphy. The manuscript is a single gathering, and it is likely that a second and similar gathering contained the rest of the play (LMRP, lxiii). The editors date this manuscript at c. 1490–1500. This would make it a little earlier than the manuscript of *The Killing of the Children*, which was copied by the same scribe, occurs immediately before *Wisdom* in the Digby collection, and bears the date 1512; and rather later than the Macro copy of *Wisdom* (LMRP, lxiv–lxv).

The play has much the same linguistic features in the two versions, and the

---

1   See also Davis's review of Bevington *Macro* (1975).
2   Beadle 'Monk Thomas Hyngham's hand'.

Digby editors believe that the two copies were probably made from a common exemplar (LMRP, lxvi). Milla Riggio, who has recently made an edition that collates the two sources (Riggio *Wisdom*), has demonstrated that the Macro version was 'almost certainly' copied from the Digby manuscript of the play.[3]

A feature of the Macro manuscript that is not found elsewhere, as far as I know, is the marginal crosses that appear next to some SDs and certain speeches in the play. These have been examined by John Marshall, who regards them as 'an informal aid to production' and 'in some way related to stage action and movement'.[4] It seems clear that they were written after the main text and do not represent the playwright's prescriptive instructions: they seem to belong to a slightly later time when a producer was marking those places in which particular actions, movements or changes to the iconography of the play were required.

These do not generally affect any aural aspect of the play. There is however one cross (at line **356**) that Marshall believes indicates a passage in which Lucifer 'not only impersonates Wisdom's voice ... but also adopts the physical demeanour and possibly even the stage location used by Wisdom when delivering [the] lines [that Lucifer parodies]'. Four of the crosses are indirectly related to the dance sequences (at lines **685, 699–700, 717** and **721**), and one comes at the introduction of a minstrel (**757**). These six crosses are discussed in 16.5 and noted in 16.2 or 16.3, as appropriate.

In the Macro version of the play lines **685–784** are marked to be omitted: this cut is shown at line **685** in the Digby version, too, but that copy breaks off before the end of the passage in question. One result of the cut, which is marked in a different (but contemporary) hand and seems to have arisen in an early performance, is that three dances would be omitted, presumably both simplifying the production and cutting the cost.

Wisdom has been given at least two very carefully-thought-out productions in recent years: by John Marshall in Winchester Cathedral in 1981,[5] and by Milla Cozart Riggio at Trinity College, Hartford, Connecticut in 1984. Riggio's book *The Wisdom Symposium*, which followed that performance, contains essays by Riggio herself, Bevington, Gail Gibson, Baker and Alexandra F. Johnston. The play is also the focus of Chapter 4 in Davenport *Fifteenth-Century English Drama* (79–105).

Both of these performances gave full weight to musical and liturgical considerations. Riggio notes that 'Structurally, the play sets liturgical processions in opposition to masque dances', where 'The plainsong in the play symbolizes the wholeness and harmony of God's kingdom' whereas 'three-part music ... and masque dancing signify the breaking of the universal wholeness of God'.[6]

---

3   Riggio *Play of Wisdom*, 6; and, for the evidence, 6–18.
4   Marshall 'Marginal Staging Marks'.
5   For illustrations, see Beadle *Companion*, 306 and 307.
6   Riggio *Wisdom Symposium*, 4. For an informative review of Marshall's production, see Henry '*Wisdom* at Winchester'.

Eccles divides the play into four scenes, which I follow here (Eccles *Macro*, xxxvi):

1) Lines **1–324+sd**: Innocence. Wisdom (Christ) tells Anima of God's love and introduces her to her five wits (senses) and the three powers of the soul (Mind, Will, Understanding).

2) Lines **325–550+sd**: Temptation. The three powers are corrupted by Lucifer.

3) Lines **551–872**: The Sinful Life. The three powers turn to pride, covetousness and lechery, and introduce their followers, who represent maintenance, perjury and lust.

4) Lines **873–1163**: Repentance. The three powers are shown how they have disfigured Anima, who confesses her sins.

Quotations in this chapter generally follow Eccles's text, with corrections incorporated from the Digby version.

16.2 Dramatic directions

Except for four brief directions in Latin, the SDs are in English. In the Digby part-text the SDs are centred and written in red, while SHs are in the right margin.

In the Macro version the SDs start at the left margin, as the text does, but continue to the right edge of the page: some of the SDs have material missing because of trimming of the edge. The copying of Latin texts shows that this use of the margins is peculiar to prose rather than to SDs *per se*. The Macro SDs are also set off from surrounding text by horizontal lines, as indeed each speech is.

Some of the Macro SDs, too, are in slightly smaller script than the surrounding text, and have material squeezed into odd corners in the margin: this suggests that when the dialogue was copied space had been left for SDs to be added later, and that the scribe did not always leave sufficient space. The status of the SDs 'proper' is therefore partly in question, as they may not have been copied together with the dialogue. On the other hand, there are some brief directions for which space seems not to have been left at all, these being squeezed into the nearest available space in the margin. These are almost certainly 'marginal' in the sense that we have met in the York and Chester cycles and elsewhere.

Of the play's eighteen directions, listed in Table 22, no fewer than nine mention musical matters, although only five actually demand a musical performance. We may take into account the fact that several of the directions are multiple, which lowers the proportion of musical content: but even so, the tally is high in comparison with that of many other plays.

TABLE 22 : DIRECTIONS IN *WISDOM*

Cue-line	f.	lang	Direction if musical : comments
Innocence			
1-	98r	e	multiple direction, including SH
16		e	multiple direction, including SH
164	102r	e	*Her enteryd fyve vyrgynes in white kertyllys and mantelys wyth cheuelers and chappelettys and synge* Nigra sum sed formosa filia Jerusalem sicut tabernacula cedar et sicut pelles Salamonis.
324	105r	e	*Here in þe goynge owt þe fyve wyttys synge* Tota pulcra es et cetera *they goyng befor Anima next and her folowynge Wysdom and aftyr hym Mynde Wyll and Wndyrstonynge all thre in wyght cloth of golde cheveleryde and crestyde in on sute.*
Temptation			
325-		e	*And aftyr þe songe entreth Lucyfer ...* Includes SH. Marginal cross against the latter part of this SD.
380	106r	e	Marginal cross against this SD.
518	108v	l	Digby version only. Marginal, and apparently a later addition.
550	109v	e	Marginal cross against this SD.
Sinful Life			
620	110v	l	*Et cantent* Marginal in Macro, following the cue-line, but centralised in Digby. There is a marginal cross against the cue-line.
692	112r	e	*Here entur six dysgysyde in þe sute of Mynde wyth rede berdys and lyouns rampaunt on here crestys and yche a warder in hys honde her mynstrallys trumpes. Eche answere for hys name.*
724	113r	e	*Here entrethe six jorours in a sute gownyde wyth hodys abowt her nekys hattys of meyntenance þervpon vyseryde dyuersly here mynstrell a bagpype.* Marginal cross against this SD.
752	113v	e	*Here entreth six women in sut thre dysgysyde as galontys and thre as matrones wyth wondyrfull vysurs congruent here mynstrell a hornepype.* Marginal cross against this SD.

776	114r	1	Marginal, following the cue-line. Marginal cross against the cue-line.
Repentance			
902	116r	e	Marginal cross against this SD.
912	116v	e	Marginal cross against this SD.
978	117v	1	Apparently marginal: perhaps a later addition.
996	118r	e	*Here þey go owt and in þe goynge þe soule syngyth in þe most lamentabull wyse wyth drawte notys as yt ys songyn in þe passyon wyke* The text follows, written as a speech for Anima. (As this is in prose, however, it extends into the margin, as SDs do.)
1064	119r–v	e	*Here entrethe Anima wyth þe Fyve Wyttys goynge before Mynde on þe on syde and Wndyrstondynge on þe other syde and Wyll folowyng all in here fyrst clothynge her chapplettys and crestys and all hauyng // on crownys syngynge in here commynge in* Quid retribuam Domino pro omnibus que retribuit mihi Calicem salutaris accipiam et nomen Domini inuocabo. Marginal cross at the start of this SD.

16.3 Text references

Innocence

161–4 ANIMA   Than may I sey thus and begynne
Wyth fyve prudent vyrgyns of my reme:
Thow be þe fyve wyttys of my sowle wythinne
'Nigra sum sed formosa, filia Jerusalem'.

Not strictly a musical reference, this speech identifies the five virgins of the SD that follows.

323–4 [ANIMA]   Werfor lawde endeles to þe I cry,
Recomendynge me to þin endles powre durable.

Again, not a musical reference, but it connects Anima's 'lawde' with the song performed in the SD that follows.

Temptation

356 There are no references in this scene, but a marginal cross against line **356** apparently draws attention to Lucifer's parody of a speech previously made by Wisdom (line **277**). Marshall suggests that Lucifer here mimic Wisdom's voice and '[adopt] the physical demeanour and possibly even the stage location used by Wisdom when delivering his lines'.[7]

Sinful Life

613, 617–20　　MYNDE I rejoys of thes; now let ws synge!

　　　　　　　　　　　　　...

　　　　　　　MYNDE A tenowr to yow bothe I brynge.
　　　　　　　WNDYRSTONDYNGE And I a mene for ony kynge.
　　　　　　　WYLL　And but a trebull I owtwrynge,
　　　　　　　　　　The Deuell hym spede þat myrthe exyled!

This passage makes the connection between mirth and music: the relationship is much the same as in the biblical plays, but the appeals to evil (**613**), lust (**616**) and the Devil (**620**) would presumably tell the audience of the essential difference. Considering the use of processional plainsong in scenes 1 and 4, we should probably understand part-music to belong to the forces of evil: in other words, it represents *evil* mirth, confirmed by Will's rather violent way of speaking about his voice-production (**619**). Will sings treble, Understanding the mean (i.e. the middle voice), and Mind the tenor (lowest voice).

685　　　MYNDE　Now wyll we thre do make a dance

This reference is to the dances that the followers of the three powers will perform, at **708+sd**, **734+sd**, and **760+sd**. Marshall notes a marginal cross against this line: he suggests that the statement 'heralds a change in the action from relatively static debate to dance movement', and thinks that the change might have included some dance steps from Mind, Will and Understanding ('Marginal Staging Marks', 80). These three dances were omitted at some time early in the play's history, as noted in 16.1.

700–8　[MYNDE]　... þis ys þe Deullys dance.
　　　　　　　　　Ande here menstrellys be convenyent,
　　　　　　　　　For trumpys xulde blow to þe jugement;
　　　　　　　　　Off batell also yt ys on instrumente,
　　　　　　　　　Yevynge comfort to fyght.
　　　　　　　　　Therfor þey be expedyente
　　　　　　　　　To þes meny of meyntement.

---

[7] Marshall 'Marginal Staging Marks', 80.

Blow! lett see Madam Regent,
Ande daunce, ye laddys! yowr hertys be lyght.

The six disguisers are named as Indignation (i.e. disdain), Sturdiness (i.e. stubbornness), Malice, Hastiness (i.e. rash anger), Wrath (i.e. vengeance) and Discord: Mind himself becomes Maintenance. Mind places the dance of his followers in its moral context by describing it as the Devil's dance (700).[8] He also justifies the use of trumpets by saying that these instruments are used in battle to strengthen the resolve of the soldiers. Presumably he is referring to the battle between Good and Evil.

His argument about the trumpet blowing to Judgement is not so easily explained: but perhaps he regards them as supporting the false witness borne by the followers of Maintenance.

Eccles suggests that Madame Regent was a dance-tune (Eccles *Macro*, 211). But the 'Ande' of **708** suggests that 'lett see Madam Regent', like 'Blow!', is spoken to the minstrels, while the following line is entirely directed at the dancers: and in this case it is hard to know how the trumpeters can show the tune visually, as he seems to be demanding.

Marshall notes that a marginal cross against lines **699–700** may be a warning of an imminent change in movement on the stage.

717 WNDERSTONDYNGE Now wyll I than begyn my traces.

A marginal cross against this line is probably a directorial warning of imminent change in the action, with Understanding trying some dance steps (Marshall 'Marginal Staging Marks', 81).

721 [WNDERSTONDYNGE] The quest of Holborn cum into þis places.

A marginal cross against this line is probably a directorial warning of imminent change in the action, with the Quest of Holborn about to enter (Marshall 'Marginal Staging Marks', 81).

730–4 [WNDYRSTONDYNGE] Here ys þe quest of Holborn, an euyll entyrecte.
They daunce all þe londe hydyr and thedyr,
And I, Perjury, yowr fownder.
Now dance on, ws all! ...

Understanding's followers are introduced as Wronge (i.e. injustice), Sleight (i.e. trickery), Doubleness (i.e. duplicity), Falseness, Raven (i.e violence) and Deceit; Understanding himself is now Perjury.

---

8 On the Devil's dance, see Davidson 'Some Further Thoughts'.

751 [WYLL] Off þe comyn þey synge eche weke by and by.

Metaphorical usage.

757–60 [WYLL] Yowr mynstrell a hornepype mete
þat fowll ys in hymselff but to þe erys swete.
Thre fortherers of loue; 'Hem schrew I!' quod Bete.
Thys dance of þis damesellys ys thorow þis regyn.

Will's followers cannot be identified with certainty, but Eccles thinks that they are probably Rekleshede (heedlessness), Idleness and Surfeit/Greediness as gallants, and Adultery, Mistress and Fornication as 'matrons' (Eccles *Macro*, 212); Marshall considers that Rekleshede, Surfet and Spousebreche (i.e. adultery) are the gallants, partnered by the matrons Idyllnes, Gredynes and Mastres, leaving Will to take on an appropriate new role as Fornycacyon ('Dance and Provenance', 115–16).

Will notes that their minstrel's hornpipe is appropriate to them, being 'foul ... in himself' (presumably because the horn at the end of the instrument symbolises the cuckold) but sweet to the ear – the latter necessary if music is to have the association, evidently intended here, with seduction. A marginal cross against line **757** apparently indicates the entry of the minstrel or the place just before the dance where he begins to play (Marshall 'Marginal Staging Marks', 81).

777 MYNDE Now I schrew yow thus dansaunde!

Reference to the dancing of the followers of Will and Understanding.

Repentance
No references.

16.4 Latin and the liturgy

The sources of *Wisdom* are enumerated by Eccles as follows:

(i) Lines **1–90** are mainly based on the Dominican Heinrich Suso's *Orologium Sapientiae* as translated into English before 1411 by a Carthusian of Beauvale, Nottinghamshire.

(ii) Lines **103–70** and **1117–58** use many of the ideas of the Augustinian Walter Hilton's *Scale of Perfection*, written before 1396 at Thurgarton, Nottinghamshire.

(iii) Lines **401–29** use Walter Hilton's *Epistle on Mixed Life*.

In addition, *Wisdom* draws on Latin treatises then attributed to St Bernard (*Meditationes de Cognitione Humanae Conditionis* and *Tractatus de Interiori Domo*), St Bonaventure (*Soliloquium*), and an anonymous writer (*Novem Virtutes*). These works are used mainly in Scenes 1 and 4, the material in the middle scenes being largely independent (Eccles *Macro*, xxxiii: further on specific quotations of the scriptures and treatises, see the notes in Eccles *Macro*, 203–16).

With a single exception, Latin texts occur only in the first and last scenes (whereas, on the contrary, proverbial material is almost wholly confined to Scenes 2 and 3). Of the Latin quotations, eight are to be found in Hilton's *Scale of Perfection*, while others are in Suso's work and the *Meditationes* (Eccles *Macro*, xxxiii–xxxiv).

I noted above that much of the play is based on the work of a Dominican and an Augustinian, and the play's possible relations with the Dominican order, especially, need to be explored. Milla Riggio and David Bevington, in discussing costuming in Riggio's *Wisdom Symposium*, both mention the black-over-white of Anima's dress without noting that this is the Dominican colour-scheme, shown in the manuscript illustration of Christ as Eternal Wisdom presented as the first plate (facing p. 34).[9] This may suggest a strong Dominican connection for the play, and the possibility that the Latin texts should eventually be sought in the Dominican liturgy rather than in the Sarum use.[10]

17   ANIMA Hanc amaui et exquisiui

Wisdom 8/2. The idea is extended in the four lines following. This line is part of the stanza, and must therefore be heard: there is no reason to sing it.

27   WYSDAM Sapiencia specialior est sole.

Wisdom 7/29. This, too, is part of the stanza and must be heard: there is no reason to sing it.

77   [ANIMA] A, soueren Wysdom, sanctus sanctorum

Part of the stanza, and to be spoken.

79   WYSDOM Fili, prebe michi cor tuum.

---

9 See especially Riggio *Wisdom Symposium*, 10 (where Riggio is in fact discussing the characteristics of *royal* vestment in Anima's costuming) and 20. The illustration, dating from 1473, is from a manuscript of Suso's German works, and shows a male and a female Dominican (the former Suso himself?) standing with the enthroned Christ.
10 Note also lines **488–90**, which seem to be an in-joke at the expense of the Order of Preachers (Dominicans): [LUCYFER] 'But trust not þes prechors, ... Ther is a wolffe in a lombys skyn'.

Proverbs 23/26. This is part of the stanza and must be heard: there is no reason to sing it.

164, 164+sd Nigra sum sed formosa, filia Jerusalem, sicut tabernacula cedar et sicut pelles Salamonis.

The words 'Nigra ... Jerusalem' are quoted by Anima (line **164**), and the whole text appears in the SD following. This is Canticum Canticorum 1/4, not the antiphon for the Common of Virgins (AS, 666), which has a different text. As line **164** is part of the stanza, it must be heard. It would be possible to sing this line and use it as the intonation for the singing of the five virgins, but that would presumably disrupt the poetry of the stanza. I therefore suggest that it be spoken, with the full text sung immediately afterwards.

169–70 [ANIMA] Quod fusca sum, nolite considerare me
Quia decolorauit me sol Jouis.

Canticum Canticorum 1/5, but rather loosely. These lines are part of the stanza, and must be heard: but there is no reason to sing them.

173 [WYSDOM] A, quinque prudentes,...

The 'fyve prudent vyrgyns', first described thus in line **162**, are from Matthew 25/2.

276 [WNDYRSTONDYNGE] Et qui creauit me requieuit in tabernaculo meo.

Ecclesiasticus 24/12. This is a part of the stanza, and must be heard: there is no reason to sing it.

324+sd Tota pulcra es

Presumably the processional antiphon 'Tota pulchra es amica' (PS(P), 123v), with a text taken from Canticum Canticorum 4/7–11 and 2/11–13, not any of the texts beginning 'Tota pulchra es Maria'. Sung by the Five Wits on their exit.

Temptation
394 [LUCYFER] Vt quid hic statis tota die ociosi?

Matthew 20/6. This is a part of the stanza, and must be heard: there is no question of it being sung. Here, as in *The Castle of Perseverance*, we see that the Devil can quote scripture when it suits his purpose.

428   [LUCYFER] Thys was vita mixta ...

Reference to Hilton's *Epistle on Mixed Life*, which lines **405–29** largely follow.

Sinful Life
855 [WNDYRSTONDYNGE] A preuenire facias...

A legal term (explained in Eccles *Macro*, 214).

Repentance
989–96 In this speech Anima states an intention to seek absolution from 'Holy Chyrche'. The procession that follows is Anima's exit for this purpose, so that the act of penitence takes place out of the audience's sight and hearing.

996+sd+lat ANIMA Magna velud mare contricio, contricio tua: quis consoletur
          tui? Plorans plorauit in nocte, et lacrime ejus in maxillis ejus.

Lamentations 2/13, 1/2: Eccles notes that 'Both verses are sung on Holy Thursday' (Eccles *Macro*, 215). In fact, they are sung in reverse order to that given here, and in a slightly different wording: the second on Maundy Thursday at Matins (first lesson) and the first on Good Friday at Matins (second lesson): see LU, 626 and 672. This does not suggest that an existing setting is intended here.

1064+sd Quid retribuam Domino pro omnibus que retribuit mihi? Calicem
          salutaris accipiam et nomen Domini inuocabo.

Psalm 115/12, 13. These verses both exist as antiphons (LU, 965; AS, 222, and GS, 95), but only the second is found in the Sarum use. The antiphons are in different modes (8 and 2, respectively), and inhabit quite different ranges, so that singing them in succession is not musically ideal, although perfectly possible. The SD requires this text to be sung, however: it may be simplest to sing it as two verses of the psalm, to the same chant.

1081   [ANIMA] Magna est misericordia tua!

Psalm 85/13, 107/5. The line is part of the stanza and must be heard: there is no reason to sing it.

1083–4 WYSDOM Vulnerasti cor meum, soror mea, sponsa,
               In vno ictu oculorum tuorum.

Canticum Canticorum 4/9. These lines are part of the stanza and must be heard: there is no reason to sing them. The two lines that follow translate them.

1119–20 [MYNDE] Nolite confirmare huic seculo
Sed reformamini in nouitate spiritus sensus vestri.

Romans 12/2. These lines are part of the stanza, and must be heard: there is no reason to sing them. They are translated in the two lines following.

1127–8 [WNDYRSTONDYNGE] Renouamini spiritu mentis vestre
Et induite nouum hominem, qui secundum Deum creatus est:

Ephesians 4/23, 24. These lines are part of the stanza, and must be heard: there is no reason to sing them. They are translated in the four lines following.

1135 [WYLL] Exspoliantem veterem hominem cum actibus suis.

Colossians 3/9. This line is part of the stanza, and must be heard: there is no reason to sing it. An English paraphrase is given in the two lines following.

1142–3 [ANIMA] Suavis est Dominus vniuersis,
Et miseraciones ejus super omnia opera ejus.

Psalm 144/9. These lines are part of the stanza, and must be heard: there is no reason to sing them.

1151–5 [ANIMA] Justificati ex fide pacem habemus ad Deum.
Now to Salamonys conclusyon I com:
Timor Domini inicium sapiencie.
Vobis qui timetis Deum
Orietur sol justicie.

Romans 5/1; Proverbs 1/7 (and cf. Psalm 110/10, Ecclesiasticus 1/16); Malachi 4/2. These lines are all part of the stanza, and must be heard: there is no reason to sing them.

1163 [ANIMA] Sapiencia Patris, grawnt þat for hys passyon!

This has no liturgical implication.

1163+ [ANIMA] A M E N

Extra-stanzaic, following the last line of the play, and written in the margin (see Bevington *Macro*, f. 121r of this play; the illustration given by Eccles (Eccles *Macro*, facing 151, does not show the margin). In view of the last line (see above), the Amen is presumably to be said by everyone.

16.5 Music and other aural cues

Innocence

1_A 1– Function: (b), (f). Although there is no evidence for it, it is reasonable to suppose that the play might begin, on the entry of Wisdom attired as a king, with music. Unaccompanied plainsong to an appropriate text would be suitable, perhaps one of the 'Wisdom' Magnificat antiphons (AS, 307).

1_1 164+sd Function: (b). 'Nigra sum sed formosa' is sung by the Five Wits at their entrance: as the characters are female their roles should be taken by actors with unbroken voices – i.e. girls or prepubertal boys. The SD seems to suggest that they enter and then sing, but a processional performance of the piece during their entry is perhaps more likely.

I do not know of a setting of this text: it could be sung to a psalm-tone, but perhaps it received a new setting in plainsong style.

1_2 324+sd1 Function: (c). 'Tota pulchra es', as noted in 16.4, above, is probably the processional antiphon (PS(P), 123v). It is sung by the Five Wits in procession as all characters leave the playing area. Note that the song and procession must be finished before Lucifer enters for the next scene, as 324+sd2 shows: 'And aftyr þe songe entreth Lucyfer ...'.

Temptation

No relevant cues.

Sinful Life

3_1 620+md Function: none. Evidently a song of worldly mirth: in view of their immediately past conversation, it should probably celebrate free love. Will, Understanding, and Mind sing treble, mean, and tenor, respectively: that is, it is a three men's song.

The next three cues are included in the material, lines **685–784**, marked by a contemporary hand to be omitted.

3_2 708 Function: none. The dance of Mind's six followers, the music provided by trumpeters. Mind's wish that their 'hertys be lyght' (**708**) suggests a cheerful dance. 'Madam Regent' (**707**) may be the name of the tune, although this seems doubtful: but I have no alternative suggestion as to the significance of this name. See 16.3, above.

3₃ **734** Function: none. The dance of the followers of Understanding, in which Understanding himself joins (**733–4**). Their music is provided by a bagpipe. It would be appropriate for this dance to be recognisable as one danced in the inns of court.

3₄ **760** Function: none. The dance of the followers of Will, accompanied by a hornpipe. For the significance of this instrument, see 16.3.

Repentance

4₁ **996+sd** Function: (c). Anima sings for the processional exit of Mind, Will and Understanding with Anima. As noted in 16.4, above, 'Magna velud mare', does appear in the liturgy, but a new setting (or an existing one that I have not found) seems necessary. The SD specifies a slow performance such as is required in Passion Week. It should be sung unaccompanied.

4₂ **1064+sd** Function: (b). Processional entrance of Anima, the Five Wits, and the Three Powers, all singing 'Quid retribuam Domino'. As noted in 16.4, above, this text exists in the form of two antiphons, but a new setting seems preferable, perhaps to a psalm-tone: it should be sung unaccompanied.

4₄ **1163** Function: (g). There is no evidence for music here, although it is a way of letting the characters leave the playing area in good order. It is possible that the final 'Amen' should be sung rather than said, in which case it must be an impressive musical setting – unaccompanied plainsong, however, not polyphony. Alternatively, a separate and appropriate processional item could be used, following the said 'Amen'. If the Amen is said the audience should probably join in.

17

Mankind

17.1 Introduction

Mankind is one of the Macro Plays, and is edited in Eccles *Macro*, 153–84, with Introduction and Notes: this is the edition normally cited here. Peter Meredith has produced a performing edition that includes 36 lines reconstructed to fill the gap caused by the leaf missing between lines 71 and 72 (Meredith *Mankind*). David Bevington's facsimile (Bevington *Macro*) includes a page-by-page facing transcription, and there is a facsimile also in *Tudor Facsimile Texts* (1907, 1914). The play is discussed by Bevington (*From Mankind to Marlowe*), Davenport (*Fifteenth-Century English Drama*) and others.

The manuscript, ff. 122–34 of what is now Washington, DC, Folger Library, MS Folger V.a.354, consists of a single leaf followed by a gathering of twelve. A leaf that once followed the first, and was presumably contiguous with it, is lost (Eccles *Macro*, xxxvii). One scribe wrote the major part of the play, the last four pages being copied by a second scribe. Like the manuscript of *Wisdom*, that of *Mankind* bears ownership inscriptions of the monk Hyngham and of Robert Oliver, and it also bears the writing of Richard Cake of Bury, senior (*ibid.*). On the basis of the coinage mentioned in the play, Baker dated its composition within a year or two of 1466 (see Baker 'Date of *Mankind*'); Eccles, who notes that there 'is no proof that the play was revised', offers 'between 1465 and 1470' as the date of composition (Eccles *Macro*, xxxviii). Meredith dates it, on various historical grounds, either between 1464 and 1470 or in the period 1471–9 (Meredith *Mankind*, 7).[1]

Mankind is often regarded as a 'popular' play, partly because of the entertaining foolery of the vice characters and partly on account of their collection of money (lines **457–74**) before they will allow Titivillus to appear; in addition, their reference to a tapster (**274–6**) and to 'þe goodeman of þis house' (**467**) led

---

[1] For paleographical and bibliographical discussion of the manuscript, and of those of *Wisdom*, see Beadle 'Monk Thomas Hyngham's hand'.

Eccles to conclude that the play was acted by a travelling troupe and performed in an inn (Eccles *Macro*, xlii). The East Midlands dialect with East Anglian features accords with the Cambridgeshire and Norfolk place-names appearing in the play, and that of Bury (Eccles *Macro*, xxxviii). This reasoning is not conclusive, however, since the collection of money could be a parody for a sophisticated audience, the reference to the 'goodman of the house' might well be ironic, and the 'tapster' is not stated to be on the premises. The mention of a 'yard' outside is unspecific and could indicate all sorts of establishments as the place of performance.

The audience may well be a mixed one, but it is hard to say. Mercy addresses 'ʒe souerens þat sytt and ʒe brothern þat stonde ryght wppe' early on (**29**), and continues to refer to 'sovereigns' and to address Mankind and others as 'brother'. 'Sovereigns' can include prelates as well as secular magnates, while 'brother' is not, of course, limited to religious. There are however reasons for thinking that at least some of the intended audience were religious. Mercy himself is a 'goode fader' (**86**), a clerk (**128, 129**) and Mankind's confessor. New Guise also tells Mercy that he hopes he will become one of 'þe number of þe demonycall frayry' (**153**), which some have seen as a punning reference to the Dominicans (Eccles *Macro*, 218); and another reference to friars (**325–6**) suggests that the play has mendicant involvement. Moreover, Mercy is an able and experienced preacher. His opening sermon, interrupted by Mischief, is not in my view the 'tedious' affair that Eccles thinks (*Macro*, xlv) but a capable and entertaining exposition. Moreover, when the vices at last leave him, Mercy does not return to his original theme but, like any professional preacher with his wits about him, makes the vices the starting-point for a second sermon, this time on idle speech and behaviour (**162–85**).

A Dominican provenance has indeed been suggested for *Mankind*,[2] and this seems to me very likely: the wonder is that no other play has been subject to the same suggestion.[3] There seems little doubt that the play was intended for performance between Christmas and Lent, probably at Shrovetide (Eccles *Macro*, xliv), and there is no reason to suggest that it was performed out of doors – rather the reverse, at that season.[4] It was undoubtedly suitable for all sorts of audience, and may have been a travelling play as Eccles suggested: but the specific references to friars, and the general intellectual content, including the use of Latin, makes it possible, in my view, that it was written and performed for an audience at least partly composed of religious. Meredith, who believes that *Mankind* is not a play for a professional troupe and was probably written for a specific audience and occasion, has also questioned Eccles's view (*Mankind*, 8–11).

Eccles follows Furnivall in dividing *Mankind* into three sections: **1–412**, domi-

---

2   Coogan *Interpretation*.
3   See 16.4, above, for a possible connection with the Dominicans in *Wisdom*.
4   Meredith opts firmly for an indoor setting: *Mankind*, 12.

nated by Mercy; **413–733**, in which Titivillus does his worst; and **734–914**, in which Mercy repairs the damage. I follow these divisions here.[5]

17.2 Dramatic directions

Most directions in *Mankind* are in Latin, only two being in English. The manuscript is not very neatly or spaciously set out, and the directions are usually placed in the margins. A few are modified SHs, and these are placed in the usual SH position, at the right-hand end of the speech-division line: these are therefore marginal, but closer to the main text than the SDs proper.

The directions are listed in Table 23. As this shows, only the first two out of fourteen directions involve music.

TABLE 23 : DIRECTIONS IN *MANKIND*

cue-line	f.	lang	Direction if musical : comments
Mercy			
81	123r	e	*Her þei daunc. Mercy seyth*
161	124r	l	*Exiant simul. Cantent*
400	127r	l	
Titivillus			
424	127r	l	*Clamant*
477	128r	l	includes SH
482	128r	l	includes SH
486	128r	l	includes SH
549	129r	e	
564	129r	l	
672	130v	l	
725	131r	l	Really a SH
Penitence			
798	132r	l	
810	132r	l	
902	134r	l	

5 The discussion of the action in Meredith *Mankind*, 20–38, offers a more detailed, and slightly different, division.

17.3 Text references

Mercy

72–3 [?NEW GYSE] Ande how, mynstrellys, pley þe comyn trace!
Ley on wyth þi ballys tyll hys bely breste!

Eccles glosses 'trace' for this appearance as 'music for a dance' (*Macro*, 271), but it is hard to see what 'the common trace' might be. More likely, 'trace' has its other meaning here (ibid.), of a dance, in which case 'the common trace' simply means 'the obvious dance-steps' for which the minstrels are to play.[6] This is how Meredith understands it (*Mankind*, 45). The dance occurs at **81+ sd**.

These are the first two lines after the gap caused by the missing leaf. The speaker is either New Gyse or Nowadays, and line **73** is addressed to Nowadays or New Gyse, as the case may be. Eccles thinks that line **73** indicates that Nought is being beaten with a rod to make him dance: Meredith regards it as a command to the drummer to beat the head of the drum with the drumsticks until the skin bursts. In any case, the line is clearly not spoken to the minstrels as a group (Eccles *Macro*, 217; Meredith *Mankind*, 45 and 98).

90 MERCY Nay, brother, I wyll not daunce.

No performance is indicated: Mercy here refuses to dance, and the minstrels are not told to play.

91–97 The vices try unsuccessfully to persuade Mercy to dance, using the vocabulary already heard.

175–77 [MERCY] But how þen when þe aungell of hewyn xall blow þe trumpe
Ande sey to þe transgressors þat wykkydly hath wrough,
'Cum forth unto yowr Juge and ȝelde yowr acownte'?

A reference to the Last Judgement.[7]

---

6 The problem is addressed by Nevile 'Dance in Early Tudor England', 233–4. She concludes that a trace may be 'a series of repeated steps, quite possibly moving around the hall in a circular path, ...'.

7 On the question of the Last Judgement being likened to a rendering of financial accounts, Huizinga, in *Waning*, 157, noted the text formerly to be seen over the door of the Audit Office at Lille: 'Lors ouvrira, au son de buysine, / Sa générale et grant chambre des comptes', which is translated 'Then to the sound of the trumpet God shall open his general and grand audit office'.

332–4   [NOWADAYS] We wyll cum gyf yow a Crystemas songe.
    NOUGHT Now I prey all þe yemandry þat ys here
    To synge wyth ws wyth a mery chere:

Eccles (*Macro*, 220) cites Thomas Gascoigne and another preacher who warn against the singing of idle and bawdy songs at Christmas, suggesting that Nought's reference to a Christmas song (which this song is certainly not) is deliberate. The text is given in the lines following, **335–43**: for the text, see I, 59–60, and for the probable method of performance, I, 377. The setting-out of the text explains Nought's remark at **333–4** as to the method of performance. Nought sings each line, the audience (led by New Guise and Nowadays) repeating it after him. Thus the audience, having been told that it is a Christmas song, are led into singing a text the import of which becomes clear only at the second line. Although this is apparently the first surviving example of a song presented in this 'pantomime' way (see I, 377 for a later one), it is fairly obviously a technique that would be known to the audience – indeed, it follows the method of teaching any song to a musically-illiterate group who must pick it up by ear.

Eccles (*Macro*, 220) suggests that 'Hoylyke' may be a pun on 'Holy', with 'hole-like' and 'hole-lick' as possible meanings, or a leek called 'holleke'. The last of these defeats me, but in any case 'hole-lick' is surely the one primarily intended: cf. 'arse lyke'.[8]

The use of 'chorus', which has no significance here in practice (there is no second verse, and no performance), suggests a model. That is, the music is pre-existent and known to the audience.

Titivillus

451–3   MYSCHEFF How, how, a mynstrell! Know ȝe ony out?
    NOUGHT I kan pype in a Walsyngham wystyll, I, Nought, Nought,
    MYSCHEFF Blow apase, and þou xall bryng hym in wyth a flewte.

Eccles follows Smart's suggestion that a Walsingham whistle may be a pilgrim's souvenir from the shrine of Our Lady at Walsingham. Spencer mentions no whistles among the surviving badges and souvenirs from Walsingham, and his discussion of whistles includes nothing that might have come from there: indeed, there seems more evidence for pilgrims' whistles from the continent than from England. He does mention, however, that a horn-shaped whistle found on a London site is inscribed 'ave maria', which suggests that it came

---

8   Ross 'Taboo-Words', 142, and compare I, 204–5 on 'kiss my arse'.

from a shrine of the Blessed Virgin.[9] The line may therefore indicate performance of the play on or near the pilgrim route to Walsingham, which is
consonant with the linguistic area of the play.

Eccles also notes that the rhyme of this stanza requires 'flowte' for 'flewte',
and that *Promptorium Parvulorum* glosses 'flowte' as 'pype'.

Nought apparently plays his pipe after **453**, since the next line is spoken
by (the unseen) Titivillus, showing that Nought's piping has been successful in
bringing that demon before the audience. As Nought now drops out of the
conversation until **471–2** it is possible that he continues to play until the
collection of money is completed.

528   [TITYVILLUS] I xall make hym to dawnce anoþer trace.

Metaphorical usage: 'I shall make [Mankind] take another direction [from
Mercy's]'. For 'trace', see under lines **72–3**, above.

581   MANKYND Ewynsong hath be in þe saynge, I trow, a fayer wyll.

The word 'saying' here seems to preclude the possibility of Mankind's singing
any of the service, and we may therefore assume that line **554**, where he starts
the Pater Noster, is said, not sung.

598   [TITYVILLUS] But I thynke he rydyth on þe galouse, to lern for to
            daunce

Metaphorical usage: 'I think that [Mercy] is hanging on the gallows [for theft],
learning to dance'. 'Dancing' on the gallows was a fairly common idea,
referring to the thrashing around of the legs that accompanied strangulation
by the rope.

Penitence
No references.

---

[9] Spencer *Pilgrim Souvenirs*: his section on the shrine at Walsingham is on pp. 135–48,
and that on the whistles on pp. 207–8 (the latter page for the Marian whistle). See
also Jones 'Walsyngham Wystyll': Jones suggests that the term may have been transferred to birds taught to whistle the ballad-tune 'Walsingham', and that Nought is
therefore saying that he could eat a bird.

17.4 Latin and the liturgy

There is a wide range of Latin usage in the play, from real quotations to the parody Latin of the vices. Although the vices scoff at Mercy, for his real ability in Latin as well as for his knowledge of 'English Latin' (that is, aureate language), they use Latin quotations themselves when it suits them. Despite the 'popular' feel of the play, it is clear that at least some of the audience were very well educated.

Eccles gives the sources for Latin lines in his notes (*Macro*, 216–27), and Meredith likewise (*Mankind*, 100).

Mercy

57   [MYSCHEFF] 'Corn seruit bredibus, chaffe horsibus, straw fyrybusque.'

This is a parody quotation: for the context, see I, 203. Mischief 'explains' it to his listeners (Eccles says 'in the manner of a preacher') in lines **58–9**, because he is picking up statements that Mercy has made in the course of his sermon (and for which Meredith notes the biblical sources).

60   [MYSCHEFF] 'Chaff horsybus et reliqua,'

Again, Mischief 'explains' this line in **61–3**.

126   [NEW GYSE] 'Prauo te', quod þe bocher onto me

Eccles discusses the meaning of this and settles on 'I curse you', which Meredith also gives. Its significance as a Latin speech may be that it is a quotation, but Eccles and Meredith give no source.

129–34   Nowadays taunts Mercy, challenging him to translate an indecent couplet into Latin: see I, 204.

142   [NOWADAYS] Osculare fundamentum!

Nowadays is speaking to Nought: he is apparently still thinking in terms of Latin after the previous conversation, but he is also trying to upset Mercy by his use of Latin in an indecent expression. See I, 204.

228   [MERCY] 'Vita hominis est milicia super terram.'

Job 7/1 (Eccles *Macro*, 219; Meredith *Mankind*, 100). A responsory verse begins with the original wording of this text, 'Militia est vita hominis super terram': but **228** is integral with the stanza, and there is no reason to sing it.

292 [MERCY] 'Dominus dedit, Dominus abstulit; sicut sibi placuit, ita factum est; sit nomen Domini benedictum!'

Job 1/21 reads 'Domino' for 'sibi', as Eccles and Meredith both note; Eccles omits 'sit'. The Book of Job is much used here, and is cited in **286–88**. The scribe originally omitted 'ita factum est', which was added by another hand (Eccles *Macro*, 163; Bevington *Macro*); but this was apparently a simple slip, not a memory of a liturgical version. The antiphon 'Dominus dedit' and the funeral sentence both include the phrase.

309–10 [MERCY]   The blyssynge of Gode be wyth yow and wyth all þes
                                                    worschyppull men!
    MANKYNDE   Amen, for sent charyte, amen!

Mercy makes a 'blessing' exit, although his blessing is not in strict liturgical form.

321 [MANKYNDE] 'Memento, homo, quod cinis es et in cinerem reuerteris.'

Job 34/15: 'homo in cinerem revertetur'. Meredith notes that the text as given in the play comes from the Ash Wednesday liturgy.

324–6 [NEW GYSE] 'Cum sancto sanctus eris et cum peruerso peruerteris.'
        'Ecce quam bonus et quam jocundum,' quod þe Deull to þe frerys,
        'Habitare fratres in vnum.'

Eccles cites Psalm 17/26–7 for the first quotation (**324**), and notes that Sister Philippa Coogan cited discussions of that text in the *Ayenbite of Inwit* and in Bromyard's *Summa Praedicantium*. He cites Psalm 132/1 for the second quotation (**325–6**). Only the second is a liturgical text, but there is clearly no reason to sing either of these. (However, a director might choose to have them sung, as a parody, in which case a parodied psalm-tone would be entirely suitable.)

397 [MANKYNDE] Dauide seyth, 'Nec in hasta nec in gladio saluat Dominus.'

Eccles cites 1 Samuel (1 Regum) 17/47 (in which David is speaking), as does Meredith: 'non in gladio nec in hasta salvat Dominus'.

398–9 Nought picks up the previous quotation, rhyming 'in spadibus' and 'hedybus'.

Titivillus

425–26 [MYSCHEFF] Alasse, alasse! cum hethere, . . .
               Alac, alac! ven, ven! cum hethere wyth sorowe!

The 'Ven, ven!' ('Come, come!', or as Meredith has it also, 'There, there!') is repeated in **433**.

440   [NOUGHT] 3e pley in nomine patris, choppe!

There is no special significance in this phrase, which is common in the liturgy. The vices interlard their speech with the kind of unthinking additions that Mercy warns against: Nowadays swears by 'Cristys crose' in line **442**.

456 [MYSCHEFF] When owr hedys wer togethere I spake of si dedero.

Cf. **Castle 879**: Eccles glosses this (*Macro*, 190) as 'If I give, I expect money in return'.

471–3 NOUGHT   I sey, New Gyse, Nowadays: 'Estis vos pecuniatus?'
                    I haue cryede a fayer wyll, I beschrew yowr patus!
      NOWADAYS Ita vere, magister. Cumme forth now yowr gatus!

'Patus' and 'gatus' are 'latinised' words, easily recognised as 'pate' and 'gate': compare 'spadibus' and 'hedybus', above. The other phrases presuppose knowledge of Latin in the audience, but are not vital if they are not understood.

475–6 TITIVILLUS Ego sum dominancium dominus and my name ys Titivillus.
                 3e þat haue goode hors, to yow I sey caueatis!

Eccles offers Deuteronomy 10/17 and Revelation 19/16 as possible sources for **475**; Meredith suggests 1 Timothy 6/15 in addition. These are clearly related texts, all using the phrase 'Dominus dominantium'. The 'Ego sum' is simple enough to tack on to the beginning of this speech. Eccles notes also that Pilate uses a similar phrase in **Towneley 24/10** ('Dominus dominorum'), and that Pilate also says 'caueatis!' (**Towneley 24/14**).

487   NOUGHT Non nobis, domine, non nobis, by Sent Deny!

Psalm 113(2)/1 (AV 115). Nought is swearing that his purse is empty.

490   TITIVILLUS   ... caueatis!

496 NEW GYSE Then speke to Mankynde for þe recumbentibus of my
jewellys.

Meredith offers 'hitting' for this, but it may be a pun on 'recompense' – i.e.
New Gyse wants compensation for the damage.

512 [NOWADAYS] He ys a noli me tangere.

John 20/17. A 'touch-me-not'.

516 [NOUGHT] For drede of in manus tuas qweke.

Eccles shows that the Latin quotation (Psalm 30/6, Luke 23/46), in conjunction with 'queke' for the sound of choking, refers to hanging.

522 [TITIVILLUS] I blysse yow wyth my lyfte honde: foull yow befall!

A left-handed blessing is a curse, as the second part of the line makes clear:
see I, 202. Eccles cites V.F. Hopper for this.[10]

544 [MANKYNDE] In nomine Patris et Filii et Spiritus Sancti now I wyll begyn.

A common phrase, occurring in the liturgy and probably well understood even
by those who did not know Latin.

551–4 [MANKYND] I wyll here my ewynsonge here or I dysseuer.
Thys place I assyng as for my kyrke.
Here in my kerke I knell on my kneys.
Pater noster qui es in celis.

Eccles cites a Lollard belief, that prayers made in a field were as efficacious
as those made in church, for **552**: but as Mankind puts it the belief is surely
not confined to the Lollards. Evensong is an English name for the evening
office, Vespers, which, like all the offices, begins with the priest reciting the
Lord's Prayer.

Titivillus describes Evensong (which he mentions in **574**) as a 'dyvyn
seruyce' in **566**. Mankind mentions it again, having delayed it, at **581**: and in
the next few lines (**581–88**) he not only turns away from Evensong but says
that he is tired of labour and prayer (**585**). Since Mankind is deliberately
turning away from Mercy's precepts at this stage, labour and prayer may be
mentioned as the monastic ideal here: 'Laborare est orare'.

[10] *Medieval Number Symbolism*, 169.

578 [TITYUILLUS] I xall answere hym ad omnia quare.

Eccles suggests 'with a reason for everything'; Meredith suggests 'At every "why?"' = 'on every point'.

616 [NEW GYSE] A grace was, þe halter brast asonder: ecce signum!

Eccles and Meredith offer no source for this phrase.

666 [MYSCHEFF] And do yt sub forma jurys, dasarde!

'In legal manner' (Meredith).

680–1 MYSCHEFF Here ys blottybus in blottis,
Blottorum blottibus istis.

A humorous mis-use of Latin.

687–93 [MYSCHEFF] Carici tenta generalis
In a place þer goode ale ys
Anno regni regitalis
Edwardi nullateni
On ʒestern day in Feuerere – þe ʒere passyth fully,
As Nought hath wrytyn; here ys owr Tulli,
Anno regni regis nulli!

Eccles convincingly relates this passage to Nought's inability with Latin and with writing: Mischief makes fun of him. Eccles also notes the possibility that this refers to the period between October 1470 and April 1471 when Edward IV was briefly deposed by the Lancastrians: 'in the year of the reign of Edward the nothing' and 'in the year of the reign of the non-king'. Meredith reads these lines similarly.

712 [NOWADAYS] And forbere masse and matens, owres and prime.

An inconsistent list, evidently made for rhetorical purposes and with the needs of rhymes and scansion in mind.

714 MYSCHEFF ʒe must haue be yowr syde a longe da pacem

Eccles interprets this as a dagger, a 'give-peace', and is followed by Meredith.

725 DICANT OMNES Amen!

'Agreed!' This is integral with the stanza, and should be spoken loudly or even shouted.

Penitance

754–5 [MERCY] 'Lex et natura, Cristus et omnia jura
Damnant ingratum, lugent eum fore natum.'

The 'nobyll versyfyer' of line **753** is unidentified: Meredith notes that the text is not biblical.

767 [MERCY] Vanitas vanitatum, all ys but a vanyte.

Ecclesiastes 1/2.

771 [MERCY] My predylecte son, where be ye? Mankynde, vbi es?

Eccles offers no identification for this, but it is presumably a reference to God's calling of Adam in Genesis 3/9.

774–6 [MYSCHEFF] Wyll ȝe here? He cryeth euer 'Mankynde, vbi es?'
NEW GYSE Hic hyc, hic hic, hic hic, hic hic!
þat ys to sey, here, here, here! Ny ded in þe cryke.

Mischief and New Guise mock Mercy.

779–81 NOWADAYS ... domine, domine, dominus!
... a cape corpus,
... non est inventus.

Nowadays continues to mock Mercy: Eccles's note shows that the tags of **780–1** are legal terms.

826 [MERCY] Nam hec est mutacio dextre Excelsi; vertit impios et non sunt.

Apparently based on Psalm 76/11 and Proverbs 12/7, but not liturgical.

830 [MERCY] ȝet for my lofe ope thy lyppys and sey 'Miserere mei, Deus!'

Meredith identifies this Latin phrase as Psalm 50/1, 55/1 and 56/1.

834   [MERCY] Nolo mortem peccatoris, inquit, yff he wyll be redusyble.

Ezekiel 33/11, and later biblical writings. The phrase appears in the antiphon 'Vivo ego' (AS, 158), in the responsory 'Tribularer si nescirem' (AS, 154), and in the verse of the responsory 'Derelinquat impius' (which seems not to appear in the Sarum use). There is no question of singing it here.

850   [MERCY] 'Vade et jam amplius noli peccare.'

John 8/11. Mercy here quotes Christ's words to the woman taken in adultery, words for which 'The holy gospell ys þe awtorite, as we rede in scrypture'. He translates in line **852**: 'Go and syn no more'. This Latin quotation is part of the stanza, and there is no reason to sing it.

862   [MERCY] But whan 3e be go, vsque ad minimum quadrantem 3e
                                        schall rekyn 3our ryght.

Matthew 5/26 is not very close, and may not be the correct identification.

866   [MERCY] 'Ecce nunc tempus acceptabile, ecce nunc dies salutis.'

2 Corinthians 6/2, but also in BS I, 555, 572, 575–6, and 583. There is no reason to sing this 'lessun' rather than speak it.

871   MANKEND O Mercy, my suavius solas and synguler receatory

The use of 'suavius' rather than 'sweet' seems solely to allow more syllables in the line.

882   [MERCY] þe prowerbe seyth, 'Jacula prestita minus ledunt.'

This is indeed a proverb, and neither scriptural nor liturgical.

894   [MERCY] Libere welle, libere nolle God may not deny iwys.

Eccles offers 'Freely to will, freely not to will'; Meredith prefers 'Freely accept, freely reject'.

901–2   MERCY Dominus custodit te ab omni malo
                            In nomine Patris et Filii et Spiritus Sancti. Amen!

Line **901** is Psalm 120/7, and **902** provides the wording that makes it into a formal blessing. Here, at Mankind's final exit in the play, the audience might be expected to join in the Amen.

912–14   [MERCY]   Therefor God grant 30w all per suam misericordiam
Þat ye may be pleyferys wyth þe anellys abowe
And hawe to 30ur porcyon vitam eternam. Amen!

The end of the play. The use of Latin here, which as so often facilitates the rhymes, seems to be also a suitable way of ending the play in a high register.

Eccles discusses 'pleyferys' and refers to Idley *Instructions*, 142. The extra-stanzaic Amen should surely be said by the audience.

17.5   Music and other aural cues

Mercy

1_1 **81+sd** Function: probably none, but it is impossible to be certain because of the missing leaf before **72**. Although the dance itself takes place here, it is possible that the minstrels begin to play after **73**: at least they must make ready to do so, although it would perhaps be impossible for the vices to speak over their actual performance.

The number of minstrels is unknown, but they are certain plural.

1_2 **161+sd** Function: (c). Since 'Content' is added in a different ink (but apparently by the same scribe: see Eccles's note to line **159**), the SD for singing may be a late (?marginal) addition to the play. There is no indication of what they sing: it must certainly be frivolous, and probably indecent.

1_3 **335–44** Function: none. The 'audience' song: Nought leads, and New Guise and Nowadays support the audience: see I, 59–60 and 199–200.

Titivillus

2_1 **453** Function: modified (b), since Titivillus appears only vocally. On the problem of the Walsingham whistle, see 17.3, above. Nought apparently plays a flute of some sort. It is possible that he stops playing as soon as Titivillus speaks, but – for reasons given in 17.3, above – it seems likely that he continues to play until **470**, when the money-collection is complete. There is obviously a good deal of silence, as far as speech is concerned, during the collection, which takes place between lines **462** and **472**: but there must be plenty of improvised business. Background music during this is not necessary (depending on the skill of the other two vices in entertaining the audience), but it might help, especially if it allows some foolery on Nought's part as well.

Penitence

There are no cues for music in the final section: Mercy's frequent recourse to Latin quotations makes music largely unnecessary.

3_1 **902+** Function: apparently none. The audience would perhaps have said the Amen at Mankind's final exit.

3_2 **914** Function: (g). The end of the play is very quiet, with Mercy alone on the stage, but the audience would probably have joined in the Amen.

18

Incomplete and Fragmentary Plays

18.1 Introduction

In this chapter I discuss a number of dramatic fragments, most of which could not now be performed.[1] In some cases the loss of text is clearly a serious one: *Dux Moraud*, for instance, must have been a fine play, and it would no doubt have told us much about the use of music had it survived.

All the fragments discussed here are edited by Norman Davis, the Winchester Dialogues in MDF 5 and the rest in NCPF; and all, with the exception of *The Pride of Life*, are available in facsimile in MDF 5.

18.2 *The Pride of Life*

The Pride of Life is edited by Norman Davis in NCPF, 90–105. The play was written on the back of some fourteenth-century account-rolls of Holy Trinity Priory, Dublin, but probably dates from the first half of the fifteenth century. The manuscript was destroyed in 1922; our knowledge of the play therefore depends on James Mills's edition published in 1891, together with collations made by Mills and others between then and the manuscript's destruction (NCPF lxxxv, lxxxvii).

The play was copied by two scribes, one apparently using an Anglo-Irish exemplar and the other working from dictation (NCPF, lxxxvi, xcvi–xcvii). The incidence of English place-names suggests that the original was English, but this is not certain: the play could have been composed in Ireland (NCPF, xcviii–xcix).

The end of the play is missing, but luckily its theme and action are stated in a prologue. The play is concerned with the certainty of death, and is therefore

---

[1] *The Pride of Life* was reconstructed by Sheila Graham and Alan Philpott, and under the title *Rex Vivus* was performed by The Elizabethans in the late 1970s and early 1980s. The musical direction was by Graham Lyndon-Jones.

closest to the much later *Everyman*: but while commentators have seen The Dance of Death as an almost certain influence on the play, no actual source can be identified (NCPF, lxxix). Briefly, the action of the play is as follows (NCPF, lxxxviii–lxxxix): the King of Life, supported by his knights Strength and Health and his messenger Mirth or Solace, boasts of his power. His queen sends a bishop to remind the King of the imminence of death and to preach the need of God's grace, but the King scorns his advice and challenges Death instead. The surviving text ends here, but the Prologue shows that Death accepted the challenge and overcame the King. In discussing the play I shall divide it into the following sections: Prologue (lines **1–112**); the King (**113–306**); the Bishop and his sermon (**307–450**); and the King's challenge to Death (**451–502**).

Dramatic directions are in Latin and, as is often the case, are partly indistinguishable from speech headings. They are listed in Table 24.

TABLE 24 : DIRECTIONS IN *THE PRIDE OF LIFE*

Cue-line	Direction if relevant : comments
Prologue	No directions
The King	
112	Primarily a SH
The Bishop and his Sermon	
306	Partly a SH
322	*Et cantat*. The Messenger sings, giving the reason that he must do so because he is Solace.
390	Mainly a SH
The Challenge to Death	
450	
470	

There are few text references relevant to this study. Since the Prologue neither mentions the music at **322+sd** nor shows that music occurs elsewhere in the play, it is difficult to gauge the likely extent of music. It does however seem that music was not a primary consideration with the playwright.

The King

229–30 [REGINA] I rede ȝe serue God Almiȝte
        Boþe loude and stille.

Metaphorical reference: 'in all circumstances'.

267   [REX] Mirth and solas he can make

The King is referring to the Messenger, who later names himself as Mirth (**279**) and Solace (**321**: see below). Although this is not a musical reference, therefore, it serves to underline the connection between these qualities and music.

The Bishop and his Sermon

319–22 NUNCIUS Madam, I make no tariyng
         With softe wordis mo;
         For I am Solas, I most singe
         Oueral qwher I go.

This is followed by the SD for the Messenger's singing, and he addresses the Bishop in the next line (**323**). It is apparent, therefore, that the Messenger does indeed 'make no tariyng' on leaving the queen, and that his singing covers his journey to the Bishop.

327 [EPISCOPUS] þe world is nou, so wo-lo-wo,

A metaphorical 'welaway' reference.

It is clear that the musical orientation of the play is small, with little use of musical metaphor. On the other hand, music is used to characterise the Messenger, the bringer of mirth and solace, who is neither a good nor a bad character but merely the deliverer of messages. It would seem, then, that his use of music is primarily good – the bringing of mirth and solace, as in a number of biblical plays – but that it does not necessarily have any religious overtones. The cue is:

3_1 **322+sd** Function (a), (e) and probably (b). The Messenger sings to bring 'solas' during his journey to the Bishop. There is no statement about the type of text involved: it was likely to be of a devotional character, but not necessarily liturgical nor in Latin. A frivolous or bawdy song would clearly be inappropriate. There is no reason to think that there should be any instrumental accompaniment, although that is of course a possibility.

18.3 *Dux Moraud*

Dux Moraud appears in NCPF, 106–13. A facsimile is in MDF 5, 69–[72]. The manuscript is now in the Bodleian Library, Oxford, as MS Eng. Poet. f.2(R), and consists of a parchment roll, originally of the early fourteenth century, on which the play was copied apparently in the second quarter of the fifteenth (NCPF, c–ci). The language of the text places the play in or very close to Bury St Edmunds (NCPF, cx–cxi), but there is nothing to connect it with the abbey.

The text consists of a single actor's part, the character being named as Dux Moraud. The 268 lines of the surviving text suggest a play originally of some 40 minutes in length, but parallel sources of the story show that the play may have continued the story beyond the point reached in the text as we have it (NCPF, cv). It is not easy to categorise the play, which has no parallels in drama: but the theme of Dux Moraud's confession and repentance of his sins places it closest to the moralities. The play concerns Dux Moraud's seduction of his own daughter; their subsequent murder of his wife and of the child born to his daughter; Dux Moraud's repentance and confession; and his renunciation of his daughter and his death at her hands. A possible continuation of the plot concerns the daughter's life as a prostitute and her eventual repentance and death (NCPF, ciii–cv).

The manuscript contains no dramatic directions, and only one musical reference. This, Moraud's '<In es ... al ... > syng' (line 137), is in a context suitable for music – his rejoicing at the death of his child – but is so illegible as to give no information: it may indicate music after 144, but the verbal context is not ideal, and the line is almost certainly a metaphorical statement. It is possible that Dux Moraud's comment 'Now wyl I makyn solas' during the seduction of his daughter (line 76) indicates that music should follow, perhaps after 84; and his

> And perfor I am mery to led
> And gay.
> Damysel, louely of chere,
> Mak we mery here,
> For care, withoutyn duere,
> Is went awey for ay.   **(Dux Moraud 107–12)**

may similarly indicate music or a dance after 112, when he rejoices at the death of his wife: but without texts for the other characters it is impossible to know that this is consonant with the play's musical intentions.

The only certain cue for sound is before 177, when Moraud says that he hears a church bell ringing (lines 177–9) and decides to enter the church. If there is indeed no speech by another character between lines 182 and 183, as Davis thinks

(NCPF, civ), the bell covers Dux Moraud's entry into the church.[2]

There is very little Latin or liturgical content in the play. Dux Moraud's confession (lines **212–29**) does not seem to follow any set form, and consists of a brief recitation of his crimes. At his death, Moraud uses the phrase 'In manus tuas, Domine' (**266**), but without completing the quotation or providing a translation. The impression given is that Latin and liturgy were not prime considerations with the dramatist, although it is impossible to be sure because of the loss of so much text.

It is sad that a cue-list is unlikely ever to be of use: the discovery of the full text of *Dux Moraud* would be a major addition to the repertory. The actual and possible cues are:

1$_A$ 84 Function: (a) or (c). Music while Dux Moraud and his daughter go to her chamber. Without details of staging it is impossible to know if this would be an exit or a matter of movement around the acting area.

1$_B$ 112 Function: probably none. Music, or a dance, for the entertainment of Dux Moraud and his daughter.

1$_1$ 177– Function: (a). The church bell rings, continuing to do so until after **182** while Dux Moraud enters the church.

1$_C$ 268 Function: (a). Comparison with other plays suggests that, Dux Moraud's sins being forgiven before his death, angelic singing should accompany the journey of his soul to Heaven. Whether this would be connected with speech by another character (such as Christ), or whether it would involve no speech, cannot be determined. Certainly it would demand at least a choir of angels in a Heaven. (We might guess that a final homily would be delivered by a doctor-figure, but this would not affect the scene of Dux Moraud's soul entering Heaven, nor the music of that scene.)

18.4 The Reynes Extracts

Oxford, Bodleian Library, MS Tanner 407, is the commonplace book of Robert Reynes of Acle, Norfolk. It was compiled in the late fifteenth century, the latest item in Reynes's hand being, probably, an entry dated 1487. The two dramatic items are edited by Norman Davis in NCPF, 121–3. There are facsimiles in MDF 5, 87–90. Both extracts 'could well be East Anglian' in origin, according to Davis (NCPF, cxxiv).

---

[2] There is no reason to suppose that he comes out of the church before line **183**, as Davis suggests: on the contrary, his decision to confess, his finding of a priest, and his confession must all take place inside the church.

The first item is a speech by a character named Delight (NCPF, 121–2). It seems clear that this is part of a morality play. Delight enjoys 'sporte, myrthe, and play' (line 9), and comments that the sweet singing of birds 'greatly amends' him (30). These ideas are related to views of music found in the biblical plays, but 'sport' and 'play' suggest a rather questionable attitude to life which is confirmed elsewhere in the speech. Delight's enjoyment of 'swet musyciauns in dyuers melody' is set side-by-side with costly clothes and beautiful women 'With ther whyte pappys poppyd vp prately' (49–54): music, then, is presented here as one of the most dangerous worldly pleasures.

There are however no cues for music in this passage.

The second extract (NCPF, 123) is an epilogue, thanking the audience for their attendance and apologising if any offence has been caused. A reference at the end to the costs of production is worth quoting in full, since it shows a feature that we have seen elsewhere.

23–30
> Souereyns alle insame,
> 3e that arn come to sen oure game,
> We pray 3ou alle in Goddys name
> To drynke ar 3e pas;
> For an ale is here ordeyned be a comely assent
> For alle maner of people þat apperyn here þis day,
> Vnto holy chirche to ben incressement
> Alle that excedith þe costys of our play.

The invitation to drink before leaving provides the unusual information that it is a church ale, with the profits (i.e. the money received over and above the costs of the play) being given to the church.

There are neither references to music nor places where music cues might be postulated in this passage. In view of the invitation to drink at the end of *Beunans Meriasek*, in conjunction with minstrelsy and dancing, it is possible that minstrelsy was performed at the end of this play, too (line 30 is the last line): but there is no evidence for it.[3]

18.5 The Winchester Dialogues

Two dialogues appear in Winchester College MS 33, entitled for convenience *Lucidus and Dubius* (ff. 54v–64v) and *Occupation and Idleness* (ff. 65r–73v).

---

3 See I, 375. The lines in *Meriasek* confirm the holding of a church ale to aid the play's finances.

Norman Davis has provided a brief introduction and a transcription for the facsimiles in MDF 5, 133–208. The paper on which the dialogues are written dates from the middle of the fifteenth century, the Anglicana handwriting is from the mid-to-late fifteenth century, and the language is consistent with a mid-century text. In all, it is possible that the dialogues were composed a little before the middle of the century, and they are likely to have been copied soon after 1450 or so.[4]

It is not entirely clear that the dialogues are dramatic, except that there is a dramatic direction in *Occupation and Idleness*. Davis did not think *Lucidus and Dubius* particularly dramatic in character, since it 'proceeds more like a catechism than a debate'; but he considered that *Occupation and Idelness* 'goes beyond the range of simple dialogue form and partakes of the nature of morality plays' (MDF 5, 138). While there is no evidence of performance for either dialogue, therefore, and no obvious intention that *Lucidus and Dubius* should ever be performed, there is some reason to consider them here.

Lucidus and Dubius, as already noted, contains no SDs, and the whole reads as a question-and-answer treatise in which the former pupil (Dubius) questions the master (Doctor Lucidus) on God's intentions regarding his creation, the Fall, and the process of salvation.

There is a single text reference of immediate relevance:

207–14   [LUCIDUS]   It is a place grene and swete,
                      of spysis, trees, and of flouris,
                      with-oute hungere, colde, or hete,
                      with-oute tempest or shouris;

                      ryveris rennynge, songe ful swete,
                      mirthe, ioy with-oute ende,
                      lyf and helthe shul euer mete,
                      age and seeknes shul thennys wende.

This description of Paradise is comparable to Seth's in the Cornish **Ordinalia** 1/766–75, where he remarks on the good fruit, fair flowers, minstrelsy and song, and a fountain and four springs flowing from it (see section 7.3, above). In this case, unlike that in the Ordinalia, the description is not of things actually seen at the time, and so no actual music is intended in performance.

Lucidus and Dubius both use Latin, perhaps derived from both legal and theological language. The Latin content is not large, however, and the piece seems not to expect much knowledge in its auditors – it reads rather like a series of

4   MDF 5, 136–7.

Frequently Asked Questions about Sin and Salvation, although they would not be asked very frequently by uneducated people. Nevertheless, there are a number of Latin lines that give references for explanations made in the text. These are extra-stanzaic and copied in a larger and slightly more formal script than the rest of the text. They are not marked off by the horizontal lines that separate speeches, however, and the inference is that they should be spoken by the character last named.

1/350+   [DUBIUS]   Proprio filio suo non peparsit Deus, sed pro nobis omnibus
tradidit illum.

This is part of Romans 8/32, and provides the complete text of an antiphon (AS, 228). There is however no reason to suppose that it should be sung here rather than spoken.

1/366+   [LUCIDUS]   Pater filium caritate, Iudas cupiditate filium Dei tradidit.
Hec Doctor Subtilis et Magister Sentenciarum.

This appears not to be liturgical, a fact borne out by the attribution to an author. The 'doctor' in question is perhaps Thomas Aquinas.

1/379+   [LUCIDUS]   Vt qui in ligno vicerat, in ligno quoque vinceretur, per
Christum dominum nostrum.

This is not a sung liturgical item, but could be a prayer from the liturgy of the Easter season or of a feast such as the Invention of the Holy Cross. I have not found it in the Sarum Breviary.

1/393+ [LUCIDUS] Hec Magister Sentenciarum

Again, an attribution to an author, although this time the quotation is in English, not Latin.

1/566+ [LUCIDUS] Bonum non solum participanti prodest set eciam obest si
contra interdictum ab eo accipitur in quo non debet.

Apparently not liturgical.

1/593+ [LUCIDUS] Super cathedram Moysi sederunt scribe et Pharisei. Omnia
ergo quecumque dixerint vobis facite. Dicunt enim bonum suple eciam non
faciunt. Magis obedire Deo quam hominibus.

Probably based on Matthew 23/2–3, but apparently not liturgical.

1/610+ [LUCIDUS]   Non enim ipse, Christus per eorum officium ligat et soluit.
Hec Lucidarius siue Lumen Laycorum.

Apparently not liturgical.

There seems no reason to think that any of these texts should be sung rather than
spoken; and there must be some doubt about speaking those lines that attribute
the text to an author, although it would clearly be possible to perform all the
written lines.[5]
There is therefore no evidence in this dialogue that musical performance was
intended.

Occupation and Idleness, as already noted, includes a SD:

2/318+sd   *Tunc venit Doctrina*

This is hardly necessary, as the next speech is given to Doctrine in any case. The
SD actually follows the SH and horizontal line separating the next speech from
the previous one, but is centred in the script column so that it shall not be confused with the spoken text. It is not otherwise distinguished, however, and there
is no reason to suppose that it was a later addition to the piece.
There are no text references to music in this dialogue. The only Latin lines,
apart from brief references to the *Ave* [*Maria*] and the *Pater Noster* (**783–4, 789**),
are those quoted by Doctrine:

2/777–80 [DOCTRINE] For God tauȝt his disciplis all,
                       to þe and to oþer teche wyl y,
                       vigilate ergo, grete and small,
                       nescitis qua hora þat ȝe shul dey.

This is no doubt based on Mark 13/35–7: it is not the verse 'Vigilate et orate'
to the responsory 'In monte Oliveti'. As it is integral to the verse there is no
possibility of singing it.

The rest of the Latin lines are quoted by Doctrine in his discussion of the Blessed
Virgin:

2/829–31 [DOCTRINE] et perelegit eam Deus.
                       Sicut lilium amonge thornes growyng
                       Sic amica mea inter filias;

---

5   On the question of the references for Latin quotations, see I, 80–1.

2/835–8	whan þe angel seide 'Que est ista
	que descendit fro deserte a-doun
	tanquam fumi virgula?'
	Et sicult aurora consurgens,

2/844–7	God seide to his angel anoon,
	'Hec est regina virginum,
	que genuit regem in hire body so clene,
	cui famulantur angely euery day;

2/850–3	God seide to hire, 'Amica veni,
	veni de Libano in flessh and fell.
	Veni coronaberis in heuen most hy
	as quene of heuen and emperes of hell.'

These passages of macaronic verse make use of several Latin texts that have been noticed elsewhere, especially some from the Song of Songs.[6] Clearly there is no question of singing any of them, and they serve simply to give a semblance of authority to what Doctrine is saying.

There is no evidence of musical performance in this dialogue.

---

[6] See especially the texts of the York music, discussed in I, section 3.3: the texts are in Dutka *Music*, 38, 44 and 47, and in Rastall *Six Songs*.

PART 4

Aspects of
Modern Performance

19

Principal Conditions

19.1 Authentic and free production

We can categorise modern productions in various ways, but for the purposes of this chapter I shall divide them into two types:

1 Commercial: a production that aims at financial viability and must draw an audience and entertain it. In this case a producer may try to make the drama 'relevant' to a modern audience, modernising some or all of various elements – language, costumes, manners, music and jokes.

2 Historical: a production that attempts to present the drama in a form that the fifteenth- or sixteenth-century dramatist would have recognised or expected. In undertaking such a production we are likely to learn something of the dramatist's intentions that were not clear before: indeed, we often cannot guess at the effect resulting from this approach.

Of these, (2) should be a prerequisite of (1), but often is not. If a play is approached without the producer having a good idea of what the dramatist intended, modern ideas that are inappropriate to the play may replace elements of the original that have not been understood. The result may still be good drama, for a well-written play can survive a lot of even inappropriate directorial intervention: but ultimately this quick-fix strategy is likely to be dissatisfying in various ways, because of mismatches between authorial and directorial intentions.

In this Part, as in the whole of this book, I assume that our objective is (2), whether the intention is to understand early drama for its own sake, as a prelude to historically-aware ('authentic') performance, or in order to modernise the work for a production designed to be 'relevant' in some way to a present-day audience.[1]

---

[1] In drama, as in music, 100% 'authenticity' is unattainable, which is one reason why I find 'authentic' an unhelpful word in this context. Historical awareness depends on the attitude of those undertaking it, however.

19.2   Producer–director relations

In this section I shall be concerned principally with the relationship between the Producer of an individual play and the Musical Director of the play or cycle. If the play is part of a cycle performance there will usually be an overall Artistic Director, with whom the Musical Director should discuss the broad musical issues, such as the musical strategy for the cycle as a whole and how much money is available for it. Discussions with the Producers of individual plays may go on at the same time, since the overall strategy must both drive and be informed by the decisions of the individual Producers.

The musical director must talk very early on to the producer of the individual play, and these discussions must continue as the play is rehearsed. Matters for discussion will include

(i) Where the musical/aural cues are to be in the play. This is often far from obvious, as I hope this book has demonstrated. There are many cases where a direction is placed in the margin next to a speech in such a way that it cannot be assigned to a particular line. The editor must nevertheless make a decision and place the direction after a particular line. This may or may not be the best placing, or even the most likely one: often the producer or musical director may feel that the direction should take effect elsewhere, changing the relationship between text and music. There are also a few cases where it seems likely that the scribe has made an error in positioning a direction: **York 22₁** is such a cue, for which see section 1.6 under that play, *The Temptation of Christ*. The producer and musical director must agree where such a cue is to take effect.

(ii) The repertory involved: chant or polyphony? vocal or instrumental music? Apart from the artistic considerations involved, as discussed in this book, there are budgetary considerations that might be very important.

(iii) Who shall perform the music: professionals or amateurs? Members of the speaking cast or others? Minstrels/singers in the audience's sight (and there-fore costumed) or behind the waggon and not visible to most of the audience?[2] Again, there are both artistic and budgetary considerations here.

(iv) Any special requirements for casting. Does any member of the cast have to sing, play a bagpipe, etc.? This has to be discussed with the producer very early on in the process. From the musical point of view the situation is simple: if the Virgin Mary is required to sing, then a really good singer must be cast in that role. The producer may not see it in that light, however: he or she may not be fully aware of the importance of music in the play, or the musical consider-ation may be seen as secondary to other and more pressing needs. For

---

[2] The audience watching a 'side-on' waggon play (see 19.3, below) tends to spread so that some can see what is happening behind the waggon. Their position may indicate their level of engagement with the drama. In the case of place-and-scaffold staging, this option is of course not available.

example, there may be – in the producer's view – only one actor who is ideal for the role. If 'ideal' means that the actor looks right, speaks well and moves well, these may beat the musical requirement into a subsidiary place. In a small drama group it may be unrealistic to hope for more.

Musical considerations are often subverted by quite radical deviations from the ideal. One of the most common is that, because there are usually far more women than men in amateur drama groups, roles such as soldiers, angels and even God must be played by women. Of these, not all matter from a musical point of view: angels were often played by boys, so women's voices are in order, although the archangels Gabriel (at the Annunciation) and Michael (at the Harrowing of Hell or the Last Judgement) should be played by men if at all possible.

In this sort of situation some reasonable solution can often be arrived at. The important point to bear in mind is that the problem needs to be avoided if possible, with the producer aware of the musical requirements from the start, and the solution agreed early on – and kept to – if the problem cannot be avoided. The worst scenario is that the producer ignores the musical needs without telling the musical director, perhaps by changing his or her mind in mid-process or by choosing an actor on an inadequate understanding of what is required. To avoid this, the musical director needs to be in regular communication with the producer, and should be easily available for consultation.

(v) Similarly, the musical director must discuss any technological needs very early on. How many singing angels are there, and how much space will they need? What demands does this make on the staging? How will musical events be cued, so that they occur at the right time, if the musicians are not in full view and able to see what is happening elsewhere? Is any special technology such as a speaking-tube required? Producers are often very inventive, and this is helpful when problems need to be solved. It does make regular communication necessary, however, because the producer's solutions may affect music and other matters. For instance, the mechanical problem of raising Christ or the Virgin Mary to the heaven will be of great importance to a producer staging an Ascension or Assumption play, and if this causes problems for the music, that will be seen as a secondary matter. Again, the difficulty for the musical director is being faced with a *fait accompli* that leaves no room for singers or does not allow them to see each other to perform a difficult piece of music. It is a question of solving the musical problems as they are created and incorporating those solutions into all the thinking about the production.

(vi) Costuming: this is not often important to a musical director, but it needs to be considered. If angels are to sing from notation, for example, they may need pockets to carry the music in before that cue; and if a half-mask is to be used, it must be known in advance that the actor can read the music through it. A singing angel should not, of course, wear a full mask, which would impede the actor's ability to sing and to project the voice.

There is another relationship that should be considered here. When several biblical plays are being performed together, as in a cycle, any individual drama group may have its own musical director. This can be very helpful. Early consultation is again needed, however, so that the musical and visual sides of the drama can be discussed between all concerned and the precise responsibilities defined. To give an obvious example: if the overall musical director intends to provide copies of the Sarum or York chant for a cue this must be stated early and the copies produced, or the local director may start teaching a slightly different version of the piece from the *Liber Usualis*. This wastes time and understandably causes distrust and bad feeling. The musical elements in a drama demand, above all, co-operation, mutual trust and understanding between those involved. (See also 19.5, below.)

19.3 Staging

In general, place-and-scaffold staging physically allows more in the way of music than a waggon production does: but precisely what is and is not possible, in the way of machinery, space and so on, depends on the individual circumstances. At the same time, place-and-scaffold staging creates a larger problem of audibility, for several reasons:

(i) The audience is further away, on the edge of the platea;

(ii) A wider arc of projection is needed. If the musicians are on a scaffold at the side of the platea, there are members of the audience at almost 90 degrees on either side of them; and if they perform from the middle of the platea, then the audience is on all sides; and

(iii) There are no nearby buildings to provide acoustic support, as there are in a street performance.

It will be helpful to look first at the acoustics of waggon staging. Two conditions, in particular, need to be considered carefully. First, revivals of waggon staging have tended to erect a light framework on the waggon and to use curtaining, or at most canvas drops, as the back and sides of the acting area, with no roof. Where a raised heaven is needed, often with lifting equipment, the frame of course has to be heavier, but this has not altered the fact that the walling has been of some kind of cloth – indeed, a heavy superstructure is a good reason for keeping weight down as much as possible elsewhere on the waggon. This is however very unhelpful acoustically, because fabric absorbs sound. Whatever the outside acoustic conditions – nearby buildings, or the lack of them – singers and *bas* instruments need all the help they can get in projecting the music to the audience. Inevitably there is a great deal of background noise from a standing street audience, and it is perfectly possible for a group of singers on the waggon to be inaudible only a few yards away.

For this reason I have often wondered if the back and sides of the playing-area on the waggon were not originally more solid than we have assumed. A heavy wooden partition, painted and varnished, at the back and sides of the waggon would go far towards helping singers and instrumentalists, as well as actors, project sound out to the audience.[3] Similarly, and even more importantly, a solid roof over the waggon would make a great difference to the sound.[4]

Second, the matter of acoustics is affected by the side-on/end-on controversy.[5] The matter is however complicated by the question of side walls. Let us consider first the Rogers description of the Chester waggons, which says that the playing area was open on all sides.[6] This, if correct, demands four corner-pillars to support the roof but no side-constructions that would impede the view of an audience. Now let us imagine a performance in which the waggon is in the middle of the street, with audience standing on all four sides. An actor will be tempted to play mainly to the long sides of the waggon, partly because the bulk of the audience is gathered there and partly because the pillars, set closer together if one faces a short side, give poorer sight-lines. It is however difficult to play to both long sides simultaneously, but the actor has two choices.

The first is to play to one long side only. This in effect makes one long side a sort of proscenium theatre, and audience on the other long side will see only the actor's back and will hear very little. A corollary of this situation should be that the back (and perhaps the sides) of the playing area should be solidly walled in: this would improve the acoustics of the waggon and provide a 'backstage' area behind the waggon.[7] However, this could be done only if the waggon were to play to the same side at all stations. Perhaps the Chester waggons were open on all sides precisely because different stations had to be played in different directions, so that first one long side and then the other became the 'front' of the playing

---

3 This may not be important to those immediately round the waggon, but some standing audience may be much further away: and we know that householders on the route often watched the plays from their upper windows.

4 Marshall's discussion of the Chester waggons ('Manner': see especially 28–9) suggests that the sides of the waggons were open to view, but that roofing was usual. In fact, roofing would be more important for acoustic purposes if the audience were on all sides of the waggon.

5 For a recent discussion of this issue, and for further references, see McKinnell 'Medieval Pageant Wagons at York'.

6 See Marshall 'Manner', 17–24 and 28–9.

7 With a waggon open to view on all sides, the actors can make an entry only through the audience or through a trap in the waggon floor. Experience shows that it is occasionally useful to have a third method, which is to enter from a place which is out of sight of the audience: in a 'side-on' presentation this can only be from behind the waggon when the back of the waggon is walled. But this is not often necessary: when one looks at the entrances and exits there are very few indeed that could not be effected through the audience.

area.[8] In this case the sensible plan would be to place the waggon on one side of the street and play to the other: this would eliminate the problem of an audience 'behind' the waggon, provide a 'backstage' area for the cast and, in addition, offer the acoustic advantage of the building on that side of the street.[9]

The actor's second choice is to play to both long sides simultaneously, by facing the short side in the direction of movement.[10] This is the position taken by processional floats on the Continent, although we cannot assume that this mode was also considered suitable for drama. The problem of sight-lines would have to be solved by bringing two pillars back to the middle of the long sides, or even further back, which in turn means that only one end of the waggon can be roofed, the rest forming an unroofed thrust stage. The acoustic disadvantage of this for speech is partly offset by the nearness of the audience on three sides, and partly by the possibility of using the buildings on both sides of the street as sound-boards. On the other hand, the rear of the waggon does need both the roof and a back wall for acoustic purposes, since that end is further away from the waggon's facing audience. With no audience on the rear, short side, that end can be walled with a solid wooden partition as well as being roofed, giving acoustic help to singers and instrumentalists.

To sum up, there seem to be three possible performance-modes on a waggon: first, to have all sides open, and to play from one or other of the long sides from the side of the street; second, to play from the same long side at all stations, in which case the other three sides can be solidly partitioned; and third, to play end-on, in the direction of movement, in which case the back end of the waggon can be roofed and partitioned. Chester may well have used the first of these; it has so far been assumed that York used the second, although the evidence is not

---

8   This must indeed have been the case at Chester, if the first two stations were for the purpose of playing to the clergy at the Abbey gate and to the civic authority at the Pentice, as these are to the left and right of the waggon, respectively. It raises an interesting problem concerning the staging of such events as the Crucifixion, the Ascension and the Assumption. The problem is not insoluble, but an extra dimension is added to present thinking, since such staging must presumably be central in the waggon, and directionally reversible.

9   The Chester waggons, according to Rogers, had a closed 'room' below the deck which the actors could use to change costume, etc. This would mean that the actors did not have to be in view of the audience prior to an entrance from 'behind' or at the side of the waggon.

10   In theory it would be possible to play backwards, i.e. in the direction of the previous station, but this seems unlikely. The processional tradition was certainly to face forwards, in the direction of movement; and facing backwards would demand that the audience, having parted to allow the waggon to pass, should then regroup behind it. Besides, any stage properties or scenery should face forwards so that the next audience can be attracted to the waggon as it arrives.

The Annunciation waggon in Denis van Alsloot's painting of *The Triumphs of Isabella* (1615: see Beadle *Companion*, 52) is shown facing backwards, but this may be so that viewers of the picture can see it properly.

good for that; and the third is a mode that has worked well in York's narrow streets.[11]

In place-and-scaffold staging the situation is simpler. Some music is performed from the platea, most of this (and perhaps all) in procession. Presumably the procession takes place around the perimeter of the platea, so that the audience have not only a close encounter with the procession, if only a brief one, but also experience it as an event that comes and then goes away again, as one does with a procession. **Mary Magdalen 2₄** is an example of this (see 11.5). Here audibility is a secondary concern: it is important to know that there *is* music going on, but the sight of the procession will tell one that anyway. The fact that the music is moving in procession means that the music itself is not of great importance aurally.

Most music is performed as a set-piece tableau, however, in the *sedes* or scaffolds around the perimeter of the platea. As already noted, the problem is likely to be that the wide spread – almost 180 degrees – of the audience, and the distance of the audience at the opposite side of the platea, may make it very difficult to project the music so that it is audible to everyone. The raised position of each scaffold will help, but it would seem also necessary to have at least a solid roof and back wall to any scaffold in which music is performed, and perhaps side walls too. However, if the side walls are solid the musicians may need to be right at the front of the platform.[12]

It will be seen that musicians were likely to have been placed in the audience's sight and generally in an acoustically advantageous place. Certainly placing musicians, whether singers or instrumentalists, behind a waggon is not a good solution acoustically. The trumpeters at the Last Judgement are probably an exception to this, however: clearly, a trumpeter placed behind the waggon will be heard without difficulty by all the audience, so that there is no problem in having an angel on stage miming with a wooden trumpet while a real trumpeter plays out of sight.[13]

Lastly in this section, something needs to be said about where the 'high place' of various plays, from which the angels sing, might be. In waggon staging it was apparently sometimes on top of the waggon itself: in those plays where lifting gear was used to transport someone from earth to Heaven – Christ at the Ascension, the Virgin Mary at her Assumption and for her Coronation – a

---

11 This was demonstrated in the productions by Meg Twycross and others in Stonegate, 1988 and 1992. Even Stonegate seems a little narrow for successful side-on performance.

12 Some research is needed on this. Musicians at the back of a scaffold may find not only that their sound is supported by the walls and the roof, but that it spreads sideways once it is beyond the front edges.

13 It may not be very easy to cue this event, but it is not impossible: and trumpeters, whose movements in playing are not apparent to the audience, have considerable latitude in timing when they mime to the sound of a trumpeter elsewhere.

Heaven on top of the waggon was probably unavoidable. Nevertheless, there are plays that could be staged in other ways: the Shepherds' plays, for instance, require singing angels in a high place, and also demand an angel who speaks to the shepherds, but do not need the angel to move between Heaven and earth. There are some suggestions that a high place at the station itself – a nearby building – was used for this, which would require the organisers to find a suitable building at each station for the appearance of angels. It might have been a viable strategy at Chester, perhaps, with only four or five stations, but was surely too inconvenient a way of providing a Heaven at York.

19.4 The weather

I suggested in section 19.3 that solid walls and roofing on a waggon were desirable as acoustic aids in situations where the audience might not be able to hear musical performances; and that the *sedes* in a place-and-scaffold performance, too, should probably have solid walls and roof to give the necessary acoustic conditions for audibility. But there is another good reason for building solid walls and roofing about the playing-area on a waggon or a scaffold on the edge of a platea: the need to protect costumes, props and musical instruments from the weather. Nor is this only a matter of keeping the rain off valuable instruments that might be damaged by it, for sun and rain are equally inimical to musical instruments, which need protection in both bad weather and good.[14]

It is a curious fact that evidence of a performance being curtailed, postponed or cancelled because of poor weather is very rare. One probable reason for this is that the English climate was favourable to outdoor performance in the period c. 1400–1550, although the picture is a complex one.[15] Lamb notes that the partial recovery of the European climate after the early fifteenth century allowed several varieties of southern fruits to be introduced in England – he mentions apricots, figs, peaches, quince and cherries (Lamb *Changing Climate*, 10) – and that the period 1420–1570 saw a lull in the incidence of sea-flooding, indicating relatively few storms in a period when the sea-level was high (*ibid.*, 174). Lamb's estimates show, broadly, that low temperatures in the mid-fifteenth century rose almost half a degree centigrade by the middle of the sixteenth before falling sharply into the Little Ice Age of the seventeenth; at the same time, rainfall in July and August

---

[14] Costumes, too, are endangered by poor weather, and would be protected by a roof. For the problem of weather-damage in procession, see below. John Grafton's expenses for pageants in York in 1585 include an item 'for 5 visards wee borrowed, and with the rayne were rotte in peeces, ...': *REED.York* I, 423.

[15] Information in this paragraph is from Lamb *Changing Climate*. For an English example of poor weather, see note 14, above; for continental examples, see Meredith and Tailby *Staging Religious Drama*, 299 (Index, under 'weather').

as a percentage of the total annual rainfall shows a distinct dip in the first half of the sixteenth century (*ibid.*, 186, 188). While these statistics do not indicate any sudden and extreme climatic changes, they do suggest that conditions in the period c. 1420–1570 were more conducive to outside performance in England, especially in the summer, than was the case soon afterwards or, for that matter, at the present time.

There is another reason, perhaps the main one, for the lack of comment about the weather in evidence of early performances: audiences have a capacity for standing firm in adverse conditions. This has been severely tested in some recent performances, although not often. The large audience in Dean's Park, York, on the afternoon of 12 July 1998 watched the York *Last Judgement* in a heavy downpour lasting nearly half an hour, while other plays were being performed nearby in the same conditions. In the streets, some people would have been able to shelter in shop doorways or under the shelter of buildings, but in Dean's Park the great majority who did not have umbrellas simply became very wet. Fortunately the day was not too cold, and light drizzle was otherwise the worst weather encountered. All the same, the day showed that an audience will watch a play in much worse conditions than one normally assumes. Some other cycle performances had moved indoors when the weather became too bad, and this was probably necessary: but the question arises just how bad the weather must be before a performance is called off if no indoor alternative arrangements are in place.[16]

If the audience remains in place, damage to costumes and musical instruments still needs to be minimised. Clearly, roofing and solid walls help this, and it should be added that fabric hangings become a liability even in a stiff breeze without any rain. The need for shelter seems to me an important factor in mounting a medieval play out of doors, and I am sure that it always was. For, even if the weather was kinder in the early sixteenth century, we must remember, again, that plays contend not only with rain but with the sun, too.

I have suggested that the actual staging might minimise potential problems with the weather, but this does not apply to the processions between stations in a waggon performance. Costumes might be protected by the wearing of a heavy cloak during the procession, and perhaps these could be stored below the staging deck of the waggon. Again, I am not aware of any evidence for this. As for the instruments, they could be carried in a canvas bag, which was the minstrel's usual way of transporting an instrument, and perhaps carried beneath a cloak in addition. This does however prevent the performance of any music in procession, at least when the weather is bad and perhaps also in strong sunshine. Is this an

---

16 The complete York Cycle in Toronto the same year started off in a downpour and here, too, the audience stayed put. For both occasions, see Palmer's review. The York cycle at Toronto in 1977 and the Chester Cycle at Leeds in 1983 had both been forced to play some pageants indoors: see the reviews by Parry, especially 29, and Carpenter, especially 29.

indication that music was not played in procession? or that the weather was rarely wet enough to make this necessary? or simply that late medieval performers accepted that the weather was a major and unavoidable cause of wear-and-tear on costumes, props and instruments? At present there is no way to tell.

19.5 The performers

Musicians in the late Middle Ages might be professionals or amateurs: the implications of this distinction were discussed in I, section 8.1. To summarise that discussion:

(i) Minstrelsy would normally require professional performers, especially for concerted music. By the middle of the sixteenth century there could have been some competent amateurs available: almost certainly these would have played solos (concerted music and improvisation of any technical difficulty being beyond them).

(ii) Vocal polyphony and difficult plainsong were the province of trained professional church singers. In this group I include choirboys singing angelic chant.

(iii) The easier forms of plainsong, and secular songs, were normally performable by the cast, and in some cases the audience could join in, as noted in I, section 8.6.

The present situation is more complex than that discussed in I, 8.1, and demands that the musical director be entirely clear about the professionalism or otherwise of the performers, in relation both

(a) to what they have to do musically, and

(b) to what effect it should have.

The types of performer usually available for a dramatic performance are as follows:

Minstrels There are a few early-music instrumentalists who earn their living entirely by playing and teaching, but they belong, as they always did, to a very small group. Most minstrels come from a much larger group who are of professional or near-professional standard, earning money by performing but not relying on performance for their living. The amount of money earned varies very much, but it is in addition to a salary that they earn as a teacher, publisher, music critic, solicitor's clerk, or whatever. The main career may not be musical – indeed, usually is not – but it is their chosen way of making a living. The musical part of their lives may be completely separate from this, or it may impinge on it considerably – for instance, by way of time off work needed to perform in concerts or broadcasts, or a special piece of timetabling to enable attendance at evensong every weekday afternoon.

Such performers are not full-time professionals, but cannot be regarded as amateurs, either. For our purposes, however, the distinction may be an academic one. They have to be accounted professionals, because they require a share of the production budget. That being the case, the musical director can use them for music demanding professional performance, as long as the performing standard really is high enough. In practice, a dramatic production will usually employ professionals of this type: I cannot think of a cycle or play in this repertory for which the expense of a full-time professional could be justified. Besides, full-time professionals find it difficult to make time in their rehearsal- and performance-schedules for the rather time-consuming fitting-together of scenes and sections of scenes that characterises the later stages of a dramatic production. Clearly, the way we do things now is less conducive to the use of professionals than it used to be: but both the methods and the type of professionalism have changed.

Singers (i) for polyphony and difficult chant solos. In general, singers for these categories of music will be of the same brand of professionalism as the minstrels just discussed. But there is another group to be added to this type of neo-professional. Much of the practical work in resurrecting medieval drama has had an academic slant, and in university-based productions the available expertise makes it possible to use students as near-professional performers: the quality can be high also when a school is involved. These are however variable, and a musical director should take care to match the demands of the drama to the musical talent available. To be realistic, the use of this kind of talent for music that originally demanded professional musicians is often a mistake. It may be a priority to make use of such resources, of course: a headteacher may demand it because it is educationally good for the pupils concerned and raises the profile of the school, for instance. Nevertheless, objectively the result is often a form of amateurism that in the long run serves the drama relatively poorly. With students in higher education the question can be a borderline one: the results can be of professional quality, but the danger of amateurism is always present. Polyphony and the more florid plainsong should always be left to professional singers, in my view – that is, in effect, the neo-professional type already discussed – with the possible addition of trained students in higher education.

Singers (ii) for relatively simple plainsong in syllabic style. Plainsong of a kind that was usually congregational at the time the plays were written can be en-trusted to amateurs, as can songs in a popular style and other types of basically 'congregational' music such as the metrical psalm in **Chester 3**.

What does 'amateur' mean in this context? I include all actors in this de-finition: I assume that anyone who acts in one of these plays will have certain abilities, even though they may protest (and most of them do) that they have no musical ability whatever. It is rarely true. Modern musical amateurs differ from most of their medieval counterparts in having been educated in a literate society. Their reading ability is therefore more than adequate to the literary task in hand: the disadvantage of this is that, relative to their medieval counterparts, they do not memorise easily. They also differ from their medieval counterparts in having (usually) some knowledge of musical notation, at least to the extent that they can tell when the music goes up or down. Here, too, their memories are likely to be less good than those of their medieval counterparts, but more useful than in literary and textual areas: in fact, modern amateurs – 'non-musicians' – pick up a lot of their music by ear, and their memories are often capacious if not particularly accurate. Moreover, anyone who acts regularly is likely to keep a good facility for memorising lines. The result is that the general run of actors will find it difficult but by no means impossible to pick up, learn thoroughly, and then perform from memory, the kind of plainsong items and popular-style songs that fall to them in late medieval drama. It is worth noting, however, that a song with an English text is always easier to memorise, all else being equal, than one with a foreign text (such as Latin).

To summarise so far, actors as singers, singers as actors, and minstrels roughly coincide with the categories of amateurs, (neo-)professional singers and (neo-) professional instrumentalists as just defined.

Having cleared the ground a little we must consider the types of music in more detail, together with the performers best suited to them.[17]

1 Polyphony needs 'professional' singers. This is normally angelic music (but the same applies to the notated Coventry songs), and must be performed to professional standards.
2 Chant sung by angels, or by Christ, also needs professional quality singers, as in (1). It may be tempting to cut costs here, but this should not be done if possible. Chant, after all, has to be very well sung to be really effective in 'set-piece' performance.
3 Chant sung by individual mortals (the Virgin Mary, principally) must be very well sung: it need not be of 'professional' quality, but neither should it obviously fall much below that standard. In practice, it will normally be wise to cast a 'professional' singer as the Virgin Mary.
4 Chant sung by groups of mortals need not be of professional standard but must be recognisable as a competent act of worship or thanksgiving. The roles in this category include Noah and his family, the shepherds (except for those at Coventry, as (1) above), the apostles at Pentecost and the Souls in Limbo at the Harrowing of Hell. These will normally be ordinary cast members with no musical pretensions: but some of them will almost certainly have good sturdy voices and be able to learn by ear, perform from memory and sing in tune.
5 Other songs performed by 'godly' characters (e.g. the shepherds), as (4).
6 Songs and chant performed by ungodly characters must not be actually incompetent, or they may fail. These performers need to know exactly what they are doing, even when singing a performance that breaks down (as in **Mary Magdalen 2₃**): like circus clowns who fall off the tightrope, they must

---

[17] Rehearsals are discussed in section 20.4, below.

know how to stay on and how to fall. As noted in I, 202, the Gossips' song in **Chester 3**, like others of the type, must be a very good performance of a rather bad performance, because the words must be heard.

7 Minstrelsy must be very good indeed if angelic, and not obviously incompetent (although perhaps loud and raucous) if devilish: cf. (6), above. The performers need to be 'professionals' in all cases, unless perhaps one of the shepherds or shepherds' boys produces a bagpipe for a piece of unscripted 'business'.[18]

18 This may have happened in **Chester 7**: see Rastall 'Some Myrth', 89.

20

The Music

20.1 Repertory

The majority of the music in any play will normally be plainsong, sung in unison by those concerned. Late medieval iconography shows that chant was the music used in Heaven, with only occasional exceptions.[1] A few cues in the plays specify the chant item precisely. Most, however, either do not give a text *incipit* or else specify an *incipit* that is common to two or more items. Where a decision must be made in choosing the chant item, two main criteria should be satisfied:

(i) The text should suit the liturgical occasion or season. It is true that not all of the *incipits* specified in the plays seem particularly appropriate in this way, and we cannot always say that this is due to post-Reformation ignorance of the Latin liturgy. If one comes at the problem from the other direction, however, looking for an appropriate piece to sing at a certain point in the play, then liturgical propriety is a very useful factor.

(ii) Second, the piece chosen should match the abilities of the singers. This is particularly important when an *incipit* offers several pieces in the appropriate liturgical season.[2] A piece of florid responsorial chant may be much too difficult for performance by amateur singers (those members of the cast playing Noah and his family, for instance); conversely, an antiphonal chant in syllabic style will be well below the capabilities of a professional singer playing the role of a singing angel, while the music itself will not be exciting enough for a set-piece performance. Again, not all of the items closely specified in the play texts seem wholly suitable from this point of view, although the general principle must be right.

When these two conditions are fulfilled it is likely that the music will be effective in performance. Some leeway is of course possible: and some choices will not be

---

1   See Rastall 'Musical Repertory'.
2   Witness, as an example, the number of items in the liturgy of the Annunciation (25 March) beginning 'Ave Maria'.

critical – as, for instance, in **Chester 18₁**, where three of the four possible chants are melismatic/neumatic and therefore suitable for a florid angelic set-piece performance (see 6.4, under **18/153+sd**).

There are some cues – in addition to those for which part-music is notated – in which polyphony may be thought suitable. These will normally be important set-piece performances by angels. The choice of piece to be performed depends on various factors. Originally, the use of polyphony no doubt depended partly on the wealth of the guild or other body mounting the performance, and on the outlay that they were prepared to spend on top-class singers. That is still a factor. In addition, the senior singer or other music contact (the precentor, in the case of Chester) must have chosen the piece from the current repertory of his institution, according to the appropriateness of the text and the number and abilities of his singers. This last criterion is of course still applicable, and to some extent so is the 'current' repertory. It is not always easy to know what was the current repertory of the Minster choir in mid-16th-century York, for instance. In general, it is now the musical director's task to decide these issues and choose suitable pieces.

A word of warning is needed here in respect of the use of instruments. There is no direct evidence of melody instruments being used to support church singers in England until after the period in which these plays were performed. There is late evidence for cornetti supporting or replacing the boys in liturgical polyphony, but this is hardly necessary in performances of the plays.[3] If the right singers cannot be found, it is better to choose a setting in fewer parts or to revert to plainsong: and any support for the singers should be in the form of organ accompaniment.[4]

As noted elsewhere, mortals in the plays sometimes sing English songs. What these might be is never obvious, but they should be sung in unison, and well. My own solutions for this problem have been *ad hoc*:[5] but, whatever the solution, it must be acceptable in terms of the musical and literary styles of the time concerned.

Instrumental music can never normally have been a problem in the original

---

3 It is worth repeating here that there was no cross-over between church singers and minstrels, at least until very late and then rarely: see I, 64–5, for James Hewitt and his fellow waits in mid-sixteenth-century Coventry. Any instrumental support was provided by church musicians on the organ.

4 See the discussions of James Hewitt and John Bakyn in volume I, 64–5, 341–2 and 74–5; and especially I, 365.

5 See Rastall 'Some Myrth', 83, 86, 95 and 97. Members of the cast are usually inventive enough to work something out for themselves, and this works well with the Gossips' song in **Chester 3**, for example. The difficulty, in an historical production, is to produce something that is historically credible: and the best way of doing this is to sing existing words of the period to a credible new tune, or to add credible new words to an existing tune of the period. It is rarely the case that original words and tune can be matched, although 'Sweet Jesus is come to us' was a case in point.

productions. Given that minstrelsy had to be soft heavenly music, loud ceremonial music or the sound of the Last Trump, the producers presumably hired
the right minstrels and brought them into one cueing rehearsal.[6] I doubt very much
if they ever discussed what tunes should be played, and no producer would
interfere in the minstrels' working methods. The minstrels would pick a tune and
improvise around it in their normal way; and perhaps, by the middle of the
sixteenth century, some were learning pieces from the polyphonic repertory that
was just becoming available in print in France.[7]

For the musical director there are very few criteria to act on. Considerations of
the symbolisms associated with particular types of instrument are mainly
covered by the needs of particular types of music: one would not use a bagpipe
for heavenly music, for instance, so that its associations of pilgrimage and
lechery are alike irrelevant in that situation.[8] It would obviously be unsuitable for
the minstrels to improvise over a well-known bawdy song, but it is hard to know
where the line should be drawn. Almost anything that the minstrels would play
would be secular in origin, and presumably this did not matter. As before,
considerations of chronology and geography are important in an historical
production: one would not want the minstrels to play seventeenth-century
Spanish music for a production based on information from late-fifteenth-century
York.

20.2 Modes of performance

The mode of performance in any music cue depends on three factors:
1 The dramatic situation, and the level of virtuosity, etc., required for it;
2 The abilities of the performers undertaking the dramatic or musical roles in the
   play; and
3 The possibility, desirability or necessity for the performers to read notated
   music or, alternatively, to perform from memory.
These are not mutually independent: (1) may be modified by (2), for purely
practical reasons, and (3) may be dependent on (1) and/or (2).

---

[6] See I, 172, concerning the performances at Chelmsford in 1562. On loud and soft
     minstrelsy, see I, 47, and Bowles 'Haut and bas'.
[7] Present-day minstrels are gradually learning the art of improvisation on a tune:
     those that cannot improvise should be encouraged to perform instrumental pieces of
     the right period if possible, but otherwise to go to the vocal repertory. In a dramatic
     situation, however, any polyphonic instrumental music must be memorised. It is dif-
     ficult for an instrumentalist to read from notation in procession or during a play, and
     the iconography shows that this was not done.
[8] For these rather contradictory associations, see Rastall 'Some Myrth', 86–9; for a
     more general discussion of instrumental symbolism in the plays, see Dutka *Music*,
     12–13.

As already noted, we should assume that liturgical chant or a secular song, sung in unison, is a perfectly acceptable norm for vocal music, whether it is sung by professionals or amateurs. Those who have acting roles in the drama, whether professionals or amateurs, cannot be cluttered up with books, and therefore must sing from memory.[9] This is obvious enough in the case of the shepherds, the Gossips of **Chester 3**, or Noah and his family, all cases in which the use of books would be a producer's nightmare. It is also true for Gabriel at the Annunciation, for instance, where his movement around the acting area suggests that a book is inappropriate.[10] Simeon is a less clear-cut case: if he is also the priest at the Purification ceremony he can have a liturgical book on the altar, but otherwise he must sing *Nunc dimittis* from memory.

Although we do not use our memories as much as late-medieval people did, seasoned actors and professional church singers alike will probably have no difficulty in memorising even quite extensive musical items. Those who are neither will need considerable rehearsal time (see 20.4, below), and even so may be too unconfident when the time comes. The musical director needs to give some thought to a possible fall-back position. The cast cannot suddenly bring out pieces of paper with the words and music on, because this looks bad and is not consonant with the abilities of late-medieval actors; two stage-hands bringing on a large sheet with the text on may get a laugh, but the same objections apply. Such a prop, too, tends to get in the way of communication, because the cast rely on it and lose eye-contact with the audience. The best solution is to have one or two strong singers, out of sight of the audience and therefore free to read the text and music, supporting the cast unobtrusively. This leaves the actors free to sing from memory and to maintain eye-contact with the audience. This solution works well with larger numbers, especially if the cast concerned are static and can be near the hidden singers, as in the case of Noah and his family or the Prophets in Limbo before the Harrowing of Hell; it cannot be used for small numbers of mobile singers, like the three shepherds, nor for processions, such as that formed when the prophets are led out of Limbo. Whatever the individual circumstances, singers must be given plenty of rehearsal-time to get such music firmly in their minds.

In processions, thought might be given to the possibility of singing the chant rhythmically. There is evidence of chant being rhythmicised in the late Middle Ages and beyond, particularly hymns (in which the strong metric structure encourages rhythmicisation) and processional pieces (in which the rhythm of walking also encourages rhythmic singing).[11] This requires no special ability on

---

9 The exceptions are actors playing (a) a priest in his church/temple and (b) an angel singing in the heaven (see below).

10 We should note also the iconography, in which Gabriel commonly holds a palm in one hand and blesses Mary with the other: he has no hand free to hold a closed book, let alone an open one.

11 See More 'Performance of Plainsong'.

the part of the singers: indeed, amateur singers find it easier to sing chant rhythmically. There is no difficulty with this when reading from an old rhythmicised version of a chant, but rhythmicising an unrhythmicised version is largely a matter of speculation, in which the musical director must simply make the best guess possible.[12] If the procession is a piece of dramatised liturgy the singers can read from books; if not, they should memorise the text and music.

Concerning musical angelic tableaux the situation is relatively simple. Late-medieval iconography shows that angels in heaven did often read from liturgical books or from single parchment membranes. The latter are often for polyphony, but the former certainly show plainsong in many cases.[13] This reflects the fact that angels were musically and textually literate, a situation recognised as demanding a long and hard education in human life.[14] In a play, there is no reason why angels in Heaven should not read from books, and indeed the professional singers who played singing angels in the late Middle Ages presumably brought their own liturgical books for the purpose.

There is another reason why notation might be used, and that is in the performance of improvised polyphony. The simplest form of improvisation over a notated tune is the technique known as strict organum, in which the tune is sung by all voices simultaneously, with fixed intervals between them. Strict organum happens anyway when boys (or women) sing in 'unison' with men, because there is an octave distance between men's and women's voices. Singing at another interval, such as a fourth or fifth above the bass-line, is simply an extension of this idea.[15] Singing in strict organum does not demand performance from notated music: if the chant would be sung from memory, then so can the strict organum.

Another extension of strict organum is 'fifthing'. Fifthing is a note-against-note method of creating a two-part texture by improvising a second voice over the given tune, starting and ending each musical phrase at the octave and proceeding mainly in fifths above the tune at other times.[16] The difficulty of this technique is undoubtedly the matter of moving from the octave to the fifth after the initial note. This is not insuperable, however, especially if the singers are reading from the notated tune, so that professional singers could use the technique in providing angelic music in a play. Christopher Page has suggested that fifthing was also an instrumental technique,[17] which implies that it could be used when performing from memory. There is a possibility, therefore, that as a vocal technique, too, fifthing could be used without the help of notated music. So while

---

12 For an example, see Rastall 'Some Myrth', 98.
13 See the illustrations and relevant discussions in Rastall 'Musical Repertory'.
14 It reflects also the huge liturgical repertory sung by monastic and collegiate choirs, with some pieces being sung only once a year. Although memory played a large part in the education of such singers, the use of notation was also important.
15 See I, 356–7.
16 See Fuller 'Discant and Fifthing'.
17 Page *Voices and Instruments*, 71–2.

angelic vocal music sung as a set piece in a tableau was likely to have been performed from notation, the shepherds, musically competent as they are presented, might perhaps have undertaken fifthing without the help of notation. It remains to be seen if modern singers could learn this technique easily.

A more demanding method technically was the form of improvisation known as 'faburden', described in I, 95–7. This requires performance from the notated tune, and in the Middle Ages could be undertaken only by professionals: that is the case now, taking account of the rather different definition of 'professional' in this context, as discussed in section 19.4. In any case, faburden is suitable only for angelic set-piece performance in a heavenly tableau, or perhaps in dramatisations of high-class liturgical singing.

Before leaving the subject of improvised polyphony it is worth making the point that 'improvised' in this context does not invariably mean that a musical texture was produced at sight. On the contrary, there is some evidence that singers took time to work out their solutions to the presented problem, and that they did so by ear, not on paper. Accepting that a basic musical texture could be produced more or less at sight by following the rules, then, 'improvised polyphony' was a technique that must often have resulted in quite complex decorations and variants through a practical process of trial and improvement.[18]

Notated polyphony is also suitable in the context of angelic set-piece performance, and not normally for any other. The polyphonic settings of texts sung by mortals in the Coventry Shearmen and Tailors' play are unusual in this respect, not least because they must be sung from memory, and indeed are designed to make that possible. While the actors playing the shepherds and the mothers of the Innocents must have been professional singers in the late-medieval sense and need now to be professionals according to my own definition, singing polyphony from memory cannot have been general. Remembering that James Hewitt and his fellow waits at Coventry were also singing-men,[19] it may be that the ability of church singers to perform polyphony without notation was more widespread, even at so late a date, than we know.

I suggested in I, 159, that one way of performing a polyphonic piece was as a solo vocal line with organ accompaniment. My own feeling about this kind of presentation is that the singer might perform without notated music: partly because the sight of a soloist reading from a book seems dramatically dubious, and partly because the Chester *Gloria* sung by the angel to the shepherds (**Chester 7₄**) is closely connected with the angel's speech to the shepherds and seems to demand strong eye-contact. This is hard to rationalise, however, in the context of our imperfect knowledge of singers' day-to-day working methods in the late Middle Ages: but we should note (a) that the *Gloria* was said by many

---

18 On the relationship between improvisation and composition, see Owens *Composers at Work* , Bent *'Resfacta'* and Flynn 'Education of choristers'.

19 I, 64–5, and section 4.5, above.

angels, according to the Bible, not by a single one, and (b) that in the iconography of the period the angels sometimes hold a piece of parchment with the text of the *Gloria* (and sometimes the music, too) and sometimes not. A further consideration concerns the boys who, in the pre-Reformation liturgy, sang the *Gloria* from 'a high place' in the church:[20] while they would normally sing from the book, the *Gloria* is only a very short piece, and the authorities may have felt that it was safer for the boys not to carry books – they were, after all, carrying lighted candles. In view of this the solo angel should probably sing the *Gloria* from memory; and even a group of angels singing the *Gloria* in heaven could perhaps do the same, although there is no need to.

Minstrels mainly performed in a different tradition from church singers, although – as noted in 20.1, above – there may have been some crossover by the middle of the 16th century. In practical terms, minstrels now should be allowed to do what they feel happiest with. It will not be convenient to let them play from notation, however, in any dramatic performance. A musical director is strongly advised not to use minstrels who are unable to perform from memory.

Angelic minstrelsy should be obviously skilful, and should avoid those instruments that have worldly associations – bagpipe, hurdy-gurdy and shawm, for example. Fiddle, harp, lute, dulcimer and psaltery are best if they are available; recorders are acceptable in company with other instruments (but avoid descant recorders), preferably with a firm string bass (harp, lute or fiddle). The Last Trump, really the only loud angelic music, should be virtuosic or at least very impressive.

Music for an ungodly occasion, such as Mary Magdalen's dance with Curiosity (**Mary Magdalen 1₁**: see 11.5 for specific suggestions concerning the instruments and the type of dance), should use suitable instruments: raucous shawms and trumpet for worldly pomp, or the 'lascivious' instruments for sexual licence – flute with harp or lute, perhaps. The worldlings in *Mankind* should use obvious cheap entertainment music with a direct appeal – pipe-and-tabor would be the obvious choice.

20.3 Performance styles

The sound-quality of angelic music should be very good indeed, as medieval literary and theoretical sources indicate. The common denominator of the statements about good singing is that the sound should be high (*alta*), sweet (*suavis*) and clear (*clara*). *Alta* is the word normally used to denote 'loud', but the comment of Isidore of Seville (c. 600) that the voice should be *alta* 'to be sufficient to the sublime', while not entirely unambiguous, does suggest that 'high' is the

[20] See I, 256–7.

correct interpretation.[21] 'High' in this context suggests the head voice, as opposed to the throat (medium) and chest (low) voices, all of these being clearly distinguished from each other. 'Sweet' is perhaps self-explanatory, but 'clear' seems to mean that the voice is projected well and will carry. These do not quite define the tone-quality of the voice, for there is evidence that fifteenth-century singers used a tight production that caused a rather nasal, reedy tone, whereas the sixteenth century saw a looser, more relaxed style.[22] In practical terms, modern singers playing angels should sing with pure voices (i.e. little or no vibrato) and with excellent intonation.[23]

Similarly, we can assume that angelic instrumental music was of very high quality. This does not necessarily mean that the more nasal tone-qualities were unacceptable; but certainly it required a sound that would carry without being unpleasant.

The singing of mortals is clearly of a lesser quality than that of the angels. In the case of godly mortals the singing must equally clearly be of higher quality than the audience could manage, for the cast have practised: but it is important for the audience to be able to identify with the amateur singers. This is less important in the case of ungodly singing, of course. Again, it should be remembered that a semblance of incompetent singing demands considerable skill on the singer's part, and that the words are of great importance in assessing the effect of the performance. To put it more strongly, there can be no excuse for subjecting the audience to a bad musical performance: even a 'bad' performance must be carried out with skill, so that the audience can estimate what the performance *should* have been like.

Lastly, I must mention the question of pronunciation, which has now exercised early-music singers for some years. Actors are encouraged to speak in their own voices, with their own accents: if you put on a mystery play in Yorkshire the actors speak in Yorkshire voices, and a similar effect is heard elsewhere. Musical directors need to be careful that this is not contrasted with a rather precious pseudo-*bel-canto* pronunciation in the music. It would also be inappropriate to sing the Latin with italianate pronunciation. There is, then, much to be said for getting rid of the *bel canto* style and reverting to the earlier vernacular style, including the vowels and consonants that earlier centuries used in England.[24]

---

21 See A.E. Davidson 'Performance Practice of Early Vocal Music', 3.
22 *Ibid.*, 4. Nowhere is it suggested that the singer should cultivate a smoothly-graded voice over the whole range, as *bel canto* dictates: rather, the different characteristics of the three registers were distinguished and developed for musical contrast.
23 Some early-music singers have tended in recent years to sing in the relaxed intervals of just intonation, rather than in the more extreme intervals of Pythagorean tuning. This is not the place to survey the present situation, but even amateur singers are now beginning to interest themselves in the precise intervals to be sung. On questions of tone and vibrato, see Ramm 'Singing'.
24 *Bel canto* is a problem mainly with trained singers ('professionals'), not with the 'amateurs' in my definition. To a large extent, singing in original pronunciation pre

Indeed, if one were to present a play in late-medieval pronunciation, then the music should be treated similarly. Usually plays are spoken in modern (if regional) language, however, so there is no over-riding necessity to sing in an older language. Besides, speaking or singing in the English of (say) the mid-sixteenth century is a skill that is not picked up over a short time. Nevertheless, it is worth avoiding the most obvious solecisms, and one can gain much help from the right books and records.[25] For the English plays it is certainly worth singing Latin texts with English consonants, at least; and if the actors have regional voices it is also worth matching their vowels in the sung texts. Further on this matter, see the next section.

20.4   Rehearsals

Rehearsals need considerable thought and planning, and the musical director should take a 'hands-on' approach. Even in a cycle production where individual plays have their own musical directors, the overall director should work closely with the producers and musical directors of the plays and should be known to the performers. The overall director should be present at the first rehearsal, and should explain clearly to the performers what is required and why. Subsequent rehearsals can then be left to the play's own director, as long as the overall director keeps in close touch, but it is best if at least one more visit is made to a rehearsal to keep enthusiasm going and to pick up any problems. Much, of course, depends on the capabilities and enthusiasm of the play's own musical director and the extent to which s/he is supported by the producer.

In all other situations the musical director will be in personal charge of the music and will therefore be responsible for the rehearsals. In the case of professional musicians the task is usually fairly easy, in that professional singers and minstrels can largely be trusted to deliver the musical performance without much help. In the original productions they needed very little advice: fifteenth- and sixteenth-century church singers spent their working lives in liturgical vestments taking part in liturgical ceremony, so they were used to the situation presented by a play and had the necessary skills. Most modern singers, unless they are very experienced church singers, do not have these skills to the same extent, and are often very nervous about the acting part of what they must do. For this reason the musical director needs to work closely with the producer, and to rehearse the singers carefully so that they know precisely what is expected of them. In so far

vents too precious an effect: the extra consonants break up the flow of sound and the diphthongs cause sound-changes within the syllable, which is precisely what *bel canto* seeks to avoid.

[25] See Copeman *Singing in Latin*, and McGee, Rigg and Klausner *Singing Early Music* (which includes an astonishing *tour de force* by Klausner in a CD of spoken texts). For an excellent briefer discussion, see Wray 'The sound of Latin'.

as the minstrels take part in processions or musical performance during the play, this applies to them also.

With the amateur singers the situation is different: they are likely to be fairly happy with the acting (which they rehearse with the producer), but may be nervous about the singing, even if they sing regularly in a church choir. Their most common problems are worth individual discussion.

(i) Learning music with a Latin text. It is always wise to take time over the text itself, allowing the singers the opportunity to speak the text and to learn what it means. The musical director should provide a good translation, prepared beforehand. If they are to sing in English pronunciation, too, the rules should be clearly stated, because the singers are likely to have learned Italian consonants ('ex-chelsis' rather than the English 'ek-selsis') and Oxbridge vowels ('sah-nctus' rather than the flat first vowel, as in 'hat'). Of course, many people use the older vowels anyway, and vowels may need to be modified only if an approach to original pronunciation is aimed at.[26]

(ii) Plainsong notation. Chant is much more easily performed from its own notation: a four-line staff is easier to read than a five-line staff, and the clef is immaterial if one is going to learn a chant mainly by ear anyway, as is best with amateur singers who will perform from memory. But most people are fazed by incidental features that look alien, and even those who hardly read music anyway may be seriously put off by notation that looks 'different'. If the musical director has the actors' confidence it may be possible to encourage them to the extent that they will learn the chant from the original notation: if not, it is best to give way gracefully and prepare copies with the chant notated in stemless noteheads on five-line staves with a treble clef.

(iii) The use of a Sarum, York or other version of the chant. There will always be some singers who remember a well-known chant in its *Liber Usualis* version, and these may resent the extra difficulties they encounter in rehearsing and memorising a slightly different version of the *Te deum* or *Veni creator spiritus*. There is little that one can do about this, except to be pleasant, encouraging, and firm. Sometimes the item can be presented as a different piece, and interesting for that reason; it always helps to present it as an *authentic* version (the version that was actually sung in York Minster in the early sixteenth century, for instance), if one does not try to denigrate the version that they already know; and having to learn English (and sixteenth-century) pronunciation also helps to give the impression of learning a new piece.

(iv) Singing from memory. Most people are conceptually happy about this but feel inadequate. Plenty of rehearsal time is needed over a long period. It is

---

26 There is an added problem here that can be solved only in an *ad hoc* fashion, and usually by a compromise, with amateurs. The first vowel of 'sanctus' is normally set as a long vowel, and for that reason singers will want to sing the 'ah' sound to it. Persuading them to lengthen the northern 'a' (as in 'hat') for this is always difficult, and the problem is best dealt with as it arises.

always helpful to let the singers have a copy of the words, since those – especially in Latin – are difficult to learn by ear, and most people are happiest if they can see the text. The music, however, whether the singers have the notated music or not, should be learned by ear, with the musical director lining-out to them and making them repeat each phrase many times.

To repeat, singing the music many times over a long period is needed if the musical item is to get 'under the skin' of the singers. A four-phrase hymn-tune, for instance, might be tackled as follows (A, B, C and D are the four phrases): A, A+B; C, A+B+C; D, C+D; B+C+D; A+B (reminder!), A+B+ C+D. It will not be surprising if the first verse, which they have sung through complete, and correctly, at the end of the first rehearsal, will be very unclear in their minds by the start of the second rehearsal. That rehearsal should therefore begin and end with more work on verse 1, with the middle part of the rehearsal devoted to verse 2 (and probably other verses as well): and so on. As the problem here is making the memory work, the singers should be made to concentrate on the matter in hand and not to distract themselves by talking. It is therefore necessary to keep them hard at work: but the corollary is that they should do so for only relatively short periods, and should not be allowed to become mentally tired.

These problems may all be difficulties for a local director, too. The overall musical director must be sympathetic to this, and should build up a good working relationship with the local director accordingly. It may be that the local director needs some discreet assistance before the first rehearsal and at other times; or that an offer from the overall director to teach certain things – such as the pronunciation – will be welcomed by the local director; or, indeed, that the local director would prefer the first rehearsal to be taken by the overall director. However this may be, the overall director needs to be tactful.

Singers are always nervous in this situation, and especially with a musical director whom they do not know well. Five minutes of warm-up exercises – both physical and vocal – help to overcome tension, increase mental receptivity (or, in other words, to break the ice) and start the singing apparatus working. It is impossible to prescribe exercises, as most musical directors will have their own favourites, but the following categories are a reasonable minimum:

1 Physical
  (a) Relaxing: a simple arm-shaking exercise, for example, and exercises for loosening the shoulders and neck.
  (b) Toning: stretching exercises for arms, legs and trunk; exercise of facial muscles; massage of nose, cheeks and ears.
2 Vocal
  A simple vocal exercise to warm up the vocal muscles and practise breath-control. It is important not to work the voice too hard at this stage, so use only the middle of the vocal range. It is good to get the singers listening to what they are doing, at the same time, although this is obviously a

subsidiary function of the exercise and the singers may not even be aware of it.

Some cast-members who have to sing may well be natural performers who know how to *ad lib* lines and 'milk' an audience.[27] For these, singing a song is often not a problem, for they simply use their enthusiasm, natural talent and energy. Actors playing the shepherds, the Gossips of **Chester 3** and the world-lings of *Mankind* are often of this type; and probably, too, the priest's boy of *Mary Magdalen* and others. This makes the musical director's work relatively easy, although close co-operation with the producer is (as always) necessary.

In all these cases it is important to integrate the singers into the main action from the start. They do not usually need to sing in the early rehearsals with the producer, but they must rehearse the action and integrate speech and music.[28] From the beginning, therefore, the musical director should both hold separate music rehearsals and attend the main rehearsals – sometimes with the singers – in consultation with the producer.

For instrumentalists the situation is often, but not invariably, the same. Those with musical 'business' need to discuss with the producer and musical director exactly what is required of them. They should attend some rehearsals, later, with the producer and musical director both present: the reason for this is not only to integrate their music with the stage action and dialogue but also to accustom the other actors to the effect of the music. They can be left to run their own music rehearsals, although the musical director should attend if invited.

The situation is simplest for minstrels undertaking a set-piece performance such as the Last Trump or the heavenly minstrelsy in **Chester 2**. Early discussions should take place about the staging, length of the music, cues, and so on, even if final decisions are not made until a rehearsal with the cast. The only important need is for a technical rehearsal so that both minstrels and cast know how the music fits into the play.

For both vocal and instrumental music, the musical director should attend some parts of the rehearsal that do not concern the musicians. This helps the musical director to get a good grasp of the whole play, which makes it easier for the director to be helpful to the producer in the musical sections.

---

[27] See, for example, I, 370, especially n. 183.

[28] The extent of this depends on the amount of speech they have, of course, and the degree to which it interacts with the speech of other actors. As noted in I, 328–9, the singing and speaking angels in **York 45** seem to have a scene that could be rehearsed entirely separately from the main body of actors, and there are other plays of which this is probably true.

21

Some Possible Extensions

21.1 Introduction

When one reads through a play with an eye to the music cues, it is often the case that there seem to be gaps where cues are missing. For many of these there is evidence of some sort that there ought, indeed, to be a cue there: and it is these that appear as secondary, speculative cues in the cue-lists in the last section of each chapter in parts 1 to 3 of this book. There is a temptation, too, to add cues for which there is no evidence at all, and thus to make a greater use of musical resources than the available information indicates. I have tended to be cautious in this book, and in volume 1, weighing the evidence and attempting to extract basic principles of musical use that could inform our assessment of doubtful cases. How sensible is it to consider extra cues? – and if it should be done, what criteria might be used?

The first criterion is *suitability* – and that is in fifteenth- or sixteenth-century terms, not according to modern ideas. The principles outlined in volume 1 should be kept in mind: they may be used positively, but should not be transgressed. For example, angelic music might be added at a scene-end if a heavenly tableau is representationally appropriate; but an angelic concert would apparently not be appropriate for an angel visiting Joseph (for which see I, 188).

The second criterion is *consistency*. This works at several levels:

(a) In a cycle. I have invoked cyclic consistency for the characters of Eve and Mrs Noah (I, 321 and 326), and for exercising care in the provision of trumpet-music other than the Last Trump in the biblical cycles.[1]

(b) In a play. This is very important. For example,
   (i) if trumpets are used at the end of a set of banns, it would seem unreasonable not to use them also at the beginning, when the attention of the audience needs to be drawn to the banns-criers (for instance, **Sacrament 1$_A$**); and
   (ii) if there is a musical high-spot in the play itself, that may be a very good

---

[1] See Rastall 'Music in the Cycle Plays', 211–12.

reason for not pre-empting it: one would not want the Gossips in **Chester 3** to sing before their scripted drinking song, for instance.

(c) In a scene (or play).

(i) If some Latin tags might have been sung and others not, one should be consistent: all sung, or none. The decision must be based on all of the evidence. There may have been a real choice originally, based on the availability of competent singers among the actors, the financial situation, or the type of staging. In such cases the producer and musical director must discuss the options: it may be a choice between an opulent musical production and a simpler one without music.

(ii) Liturgical ceremony. The given text may be all that is required, or it may be part of a more extensive liturgical scene in which only some items are mentioned for the purpose of making play and liturgy coincident.[2] In some cases – some of the Purification plays, for instance – there is a real choice between leaving the play much as is it and making it into an extensive piece of liturgy with added dialogue (compare with (i), above): and, again, this may sometimes have been an original choice.

(iii) Music for Herod. There is relatively little music for Herod (see **Coventry 1₅**), and it may be thought inconsistent that he have music for his exit but not for his entrance, despite the stated circumstance of going to his rest. The mention of trumpets as well as soft music may suggest both loud music for his exit and soft music to lull him to sleep, in which case this is expensive minstrelsy. It seems sensible, therefore, to make better use of the minstrels by providing Herod with loud music – shawms and trumpet, perhaps – at his pomping entrance for that scene. There is also the question of music for Herod's other appearances in that play, but this is more difficult: the dialogue seems on the whole to preclude it.

These are real problems that go to the heart of our dilemma about providing music in early drama. I have tried to give specific advice in the individual chapters of this book, but the subject is far from exhausted. In particular, the beginnings and endings of plays need more discussion, and I turn to these next.

21.2 Beginnings and endings

The start and end of any play is a possible place for music, but the evidence for it is usually missing. Music at the start or end of a play is not as common as we might think, therefore. The situation is potentially different for cycle plays and independent plays, however, and for processional plays as opposed to those played in a single location.

---

2 See I, chapter 7, for examples.

In processional waggon staging the beginnings and endings of the individual plays are the interface with the procession from the previous station or towards the next one. There is some evidence for minstrels both in procession and at each station, although this is difficult to interpret, to say the least.[3] There is no evidence for singing in procession, although this has proved effective in modern productions. It is possible that some choral items at the ends of plays should be treated as processional, but it is just as likely that they were sung as tableaux. **Chester 23$_1$** is a clear example of this dilemma: Michael leads Elias and Enoch to glory at the end of the play, singing *Gaudete justi in domino*, but it is not clear that he leads them into the procession to the next station: it is just as possible that he leads them to the heaven (wherever that was located), or that they stand in a tableau once the idea of leading the prophets to glory has been established.

In modern performance, some of these matters are decided by the finances: one needs a budget to supply minstrels in procession or at individual stations. Both have worked well, and in the end it must be a production decision whether to have minstrelsy or not. Singing is a different matter, because singing in procession is possible only if the singers are available for the play anyway, whether amateurs or professionals. Some producers of plays in which there is singing do like to use this resource in procession.

Music in procession has a consequential effect on the start of the play when it has arrived at a new station. If the procession is a musical one, the music has itself served to focus attention on the waggon and subsequently on the actors starting the play.[4] In this situation there is rarely any need for music to begin the play.

At the end of a play there is often a moment of stillness before the procession begins. A 'blessing' or 'praise' ending will usually require an 'Amen' response from the audience, a situation often identified in the text.[5] When this happens there is sometimes a musical tableau as well, especially in circumstances such as the end of the cycle. A musical tableau is a common way of signalling the end of a play, especially if it has been a lavish spectacular one with music in it. One question still unanswered is how the actors acknowledged applause: we assume that they did, but it has to be pointed out that they cannot do so if they are processing off the waggon and towards the next station. The more I consider this matter, the more I come to the conclusion that the procession was a separate event, not joined to the end of the play – in other words, that everything to do with the play would finish before the procession started. If this is correct, then all musical events at the ends of plays were static, or at least contained within the

---

[3] See I, 366–7.

[4] This is also true of non-musical noise, such as the racket made by the devils with the Harrowing of Hell waggon at Wakefield in 1980.

[5] See I, 371–3.

immediate playing-area.[6]

For non-processional plays the provision of music can be largely a producer's decision. There is no doubt that music helps to identify the moment when the drama begins and to draw attention to the actor who speaks first. Any music should however be suitable for the character concerned: and it should add to, not substitute for, actions and vocal effects that would be appropriate even without the music. It is a moot point, for instance, whether the entrance of Herod, preceded by a herald pushing his way through the crowd, is enhanced or otherwise by the sound of loud music. Much depends on the production, and it would be interesting to see such an opening scene begun both with and without loud music. On the other hand there are sometimes textual indications that music is not necessary. The opening of **Towneley 14** is an example: Herod tells the assembled company to be quiet, on pain of death, so he has probably not been given a fanfare, which would have the effect of quietening them anyway.

The end of a place-and-scaffold play is in a sense easier to deal with, since the actors do not need to leave the playing-area until after they have acknowledged the applause (if they are going to). It seems to me that many of the non-processional plays deal quite specifically with the problem of ending the play, either with audience involvement in a piece of music such as the *Te deum*, or by an out-of-role address to the audience, sometimes followed by dancing.[7]

21.3 Conclusion

As I hope is clear from this book, the business of providing music for an early English play is a difficult one: there are many decisions to be made, often after much thought and discussion. I hope that the principles suggested, both here and in Volume I, will be helpful in making these decisions.

A musical director must prepare to be flexible as circumstances change: I have known a group of singers pull out of a play on the morning of the performance, although few changes of circumstance are so radical. The various factors governing the provision of music do tend to alter as a production progresses, and a musical director must be flexible in meeting the changing circumstances. It is however important not to let others see this flexibility as a lack of purpose.

Part of this flexibility is due to the musical director's knowledge that there are, and may originally have been, alternative ways of doing things. If a singing actor breaks a leg and has to be replaced by a tone-deaf one, the actor may be able to mime while a singer performs the piece from behind the waggon. One simply

6   This does not mean that I consider the acknowledging of applause to be an important factor, however: as it happens, I do not.

7   See I, 373–6.

moves to the next best solution: but, again, nobody should be led to believe that the music does not matter, nor that the director's overall view of the music is changed.

In short, however flexible one must be in the details, the director should always work within the basic principles, and be seen to do so. As I have tried to make clear in this work, music is an important part of early drama, not an incidental effect, and it is worth giving time and energy to get it right as far as is possible within the limits of available resources.

BIBLIOGRAPHY

This Bibliography lists works cited and other relevant works consulted: and see also the Bibliography of Volume I.

The abbreviations for frequently-cited works are listed on pp. xix–xx, above.

Andersen, Flemming G., Thomas Pettit and Reinhold Schröder. *The Entertainer in Medieval and Traditional Culture*. Odense: Odense University Press, 1997.

Anderson, John, and A.C. Cawley. 'The Newcastle Play of *Noah's Ark*'. *Records of Early English Drama Newsletter* 1977:1. 11–17.

Anderson, M.D. *Drama and Imagery in English Medieval Churches*. Cambridge: Cambridge University Press, 1963.

Attwater, Donald, ed. *The Catholic Encyclopaedic Dictionary*. London: The Waverley Book Co., 1931.

Baker, Donald C. 'The Date of *Mankind*'. *Philological Quarterly* 42 (1963). 90–1.

———. 'The Drama: Learning and Unlearning' in Yeager *Studies*. 189–214.

Bakere, Jane A. *The Cornish Ordinalia: A Critical Study*. Cardiff: University of Wales Press, 1980.

Baldwin, Elizabeth. 'Review of "The Theatre of Saints"'. *Early Theatre* 2 (1999). 114–16.

Batt, Catherine, ed. *Essays in Honour of Peter Meredith*. Leeds Studies in English, new series, 29. Leeds: University of Leeds School of English, 1998.

Beadle, Richard, ed. *The Cambridge Companion to Medieval English Theatre*. Cambridge: Cambridge University Press, 1994.

———. 'The York Hosiers' Play of Moses and Pharaoh: A Middle English Dramatist at Work'. *Poetica* 19 (1984). 3–26.

———. *The Medieval Drama of East Anglia*. PhD dissertation. University of York [UK] Centre for Medieval Studies, 1977.

———. 'Monk Thomas Hyngham's hand in the Macro Manuscript' in Richard Beadle and A.J. Piper, eds. *New Science out of Old Books: Studies in manuscripts and early printed books in honour of A.I. Doyle*. Aldershot: Scolar Press, 1995. 315–41.

———. 'The Scribal Problem in the Macro Manuscript'. *English Language Notes* 21 (1984). 1–13.

———. Unpublished paper on dramatic directions in the York Cycle, Medieval English Theatre meeting at Lancaster, 7 January 1984.

————, ed. *The York Plays*. London: Edward Arnold, 1982.

————, and Peter Meredith. 'Further External Evidence for Dating the York Register (BL Additional MS 35290)'. *Leeds Studies in English*, new series, 11 (1980). 51–8.

Beckwith, Sarah. 'The present of past things: the York Corpus Christi cycle as a contemporary theatre of memory'. *Journal of Medieval and Early Modern Studies* 26 (1996). 355–79.

————. 'Ritual, church and theatre: medieval dramas of the sacramental body' in David Aers, ed. *Culture and History 1350–1600*. Detroit, MI: Wayne State University Press, 1992. 65–89.

Ben-Amos, Ilana Krausman. *Adolescence and Youth in Early Modern England*. New Haven, CT, and London: Yale University Press, 1994.

Beneventan Antiphoner. *Le codex VI.34 de la Bibliothèque capitulaire de Bénévent (XIe–XIIe siècle): Graduel de Bénévent, avec prosaire et tropaire*. Paléographie musicale 15. Solesmes: Abbaye Saint-Pierre, 1937; rpt Berne: Editions H. Lang, 1971.

Bent, Margaret. 'New and Little-Known Fragments of English Medieval Polyphony'. *Journal of the American Musicological Society* 21 (1968). 137–56.

————. '*Resfacta* and *Cantare Super Librum*'. *Journal of the American Musicological Society* 36 (1983). 371–91.

Betcher, Gloria J. 'Makers of Heaven on Earth: The Construction of Early Drama in Cornwall' in Davidson *Material Culture*. 103–26.

————. 'Place names and political patronage and the Cornish Ordinalia'. *Research Opportunities in Renaissance Drama* 35 (1996). 111–31.

Bevington, David. *From Mankind to Marlowe: The growth of structure in the popular drama of Tudor England*. Cambridge, MA: Harvard University Press, 1962.

————, ed. *The Macro Plays: A Facsimile Edition with Facing Transcriptions*. New York: Johnson Reprint Corporation; Washington, DC: The Folger Shakespeare Library, 1972.

————, ed. *Medieval Drama*. Boston MA: Houghton Mifflin, 1975.

Block, K.S., ed. *Ludus Coventriae, or The Plaie Called Corpus Christi*. Early English Text Society, extra series, 120. 1922.

Blomefield, Francis. *An Essay towards a topographical history of the County of Norfolk*. London: 2/1806.

Bolingbroke, Leonard G. 'Pre-Elizabethan Plays and Players in Norfolk'. *Norfolk Archaeology* 11 (1892). 332–51.

Bourne, Henry. *The History of Newcastle upon Tyne: or, the Ancient and Present State of that Town*. Newcastle upon Tyne: 1736.

Bowers, Roger. 'Prowett, Stephen'. *New Grove* 15/317–18.

Bowles, E.A. '*Haut* and *bas*: the grouping of musical instruments in the Middle Ages'. *Musica Disciplina* 8 (1954). 115–40.

Briscoe, Marianne G., and John C. Coldewey, eds. *Contexts for Early English Drama*. Bloomington, IN: Indiana University Press, 1989.

Bryden, John R., and David G. Hughes. *An Index of Gregorian Chant*. Cambridge, MA: Harvard University Press, 1969. 2 vols.

Butterworth, Philip. 'Prompting in full view of the audience: a medieval staging convention' in Alan Hindley, ed., *Drama and Community: People and Plays in Medieval Europe*. Turnhout: Brepols, 1999. 231–47.

———. *Theatre of Fire: Special effects in early English and Scottish theatre*. London: The Society for Theatre Research, 1998.

Carpenter, Nan Cooke. 'Music in the English Mystery Plays' in John H. Long, ed. *Music in English Renaissance Drama*. Lexington, KY: University of Kentucky Press, 1968. 1–31.

———. 'Music in the *Secunda Pastorum*'. *Speculum* 26 (1951). 696–700. Repr. in Jerome Taylor and Alan H. Nelson, eds. *Medieval English Drama: Essays Critical and Contextual*. Chicago, IL: Chicago University Press, 1972. 212–17.

Carpenter, Sarah. Review of the Chester Cycle at Leeds, 1983. *Medieval English Theatre* 5/1 (1983). 29–35.

Carter, Henry Holland. *A Dictionary of Middle English Musical Terms*. Bloomington, IN: Indiana University Press, 1961; repr. Millwood, NY: Kraus, 1980.

Cawley, A.C. 'Medieval Drama and Didacticism' in [Richard Rastall, ed.] *The Drama of Medieval Europe*. Leeds Medieval Studies 1. Leeds: University of Leeds Graduate Centre for Medieval Studies, 1975. 3–12.

———. 'Noah's Ark or, the shipwrights' ancient play, or dirge' in R.L. Thomson, ed. *A Medieval Miscellany in honour of Professor John Le Patourel*. Proceedings of the Leeds Philosophical and Literary Society, Literary and Historical Section, 18/1 (1982). 138–53.

———. 'The Sykes Manuscript of the York Scriveners' Play'. *Leeds Studies in English*, new series, 7–8 (1952). 45–80.

———. 'The Towneley *Processus Talentorum*: a Survey and Interpretation'. *Leeds Studies in English* 17 (1986). 131–40.

———. *The Wakefield Pageants in the Towneley Cycle*. Manchester: Manchester University Press, 1958.

———, and Martin Stevens. 'The Towneley *Processus Talentorum*: Text and Commentary'. *Leeds Studies in English* 17 (1986). 105–130.

Chambers, E.K. *The Mediaeval Stage*. 2 vols. Oxford: Oxford University Press, 1903.

Cheetham, Francis. *English religious alabaster carvings, 1300–1600*. Oxford: Phaidon, 1984.

Clopper, Lawrence M. 'The History and Development of the Chester Cycle'. *Modern Philology* 75 (1978). 219–46.

———. 'Lay and Clerical Impact on Civic Religious Drama and Ceremony' in Briscoe and Coldewey *Contexts*. 103–36.

———. 'Why Are There So Few English Saint Plays?' *Early Theatre* 2 (1999). 107–12.

Coletti, Theresa. 'The Design of the Digby Play of *Mary Magdalene*'. *Studies in Philology* 76 (1979). 313–33.

Coogan, Sister Mary Philippa. *An Interpretation of the Moral Play 'Mankind'*. Washington, DC: Catholic University of America Press, 1947.

Cooper, Frances M.C. 'The Leckingfield Proverbs'. *Musical Times* 113 (June 1972). 547–50.

Copeman, Harold. *Singing in Latin*. Oxford: the Author, 1990; rev. 1992.

Coussemaker, E. de. *Drames liturgiques du moyen âge*. Rennes: Vatar, 1860; repr. New York: Broude Brothers, 1964.

Cox, John D. 'Devils and vices in English non-cycle plays: sacrament and social body'. *Comparative Drama* 30 (1996). 188–219.

Craig, Hardin. *English Religious Drama of the Middle Ages*. Oxford: Clarendon Press, 1955.

———. *Two Coventry Corpus Christi Plays*. Early English Text Society, extra series, 87. 1902; 2/1957.

Davenport, W.A. *Fifteenth-Century English Drama: The Early Moral Plays and their Literary Relations*. Cambridge: D.S. Brewer; Totowa, NJ: Rowman and Little-field, 1982.

Davidson, Audrey Ekdahl. 'The Performance Practice of Early Vocal Music'. *Early Drama, Art, and Music Newsletter* 4/1 (1981). 3–8.

Davidson, Clifford. 'British Saint Play Records: Coping with Ambiguity'. *Early Theatre* 2 (1999). 97–106.

———. 'Carnival, Lent, and Early English Drama'. *Research Opportunities in Renaissance Drama* 36 (1997). 123–42.

———. 'Civic Drama for Corpus Christi at Coventry: Some Lost Plays' in Knight *Stage as Mirror*. 145–164.

———. 'The Devil's Guts' in Davidson and Nichols *Iconoclasm*. 92–144.

———. *Illustrations of the stage and acting in England to 1580*. Early Drama, Art, and Music monograph series, 16. Kalamazoo, MI: Medieval Institute Publications, Western Michigan University, 1991.

———. 'The Lost Coventry Drapers' Play of Doomsday and its Iconographical Context'. *Leeds Studies in English* 17 (1986). 141–58.

———, ed. *Material Culture and Medieval Drama*. Kalamazoo, MI: Medieval Institute Publications, 1999.

———. 'Material Culture, Writing, and Early Drama' in Davidson *Material Culture*. 1–15.

———. 'The Middle English Saint Play and its Iconography' in Clifford Davison, ed. *The Saint Play in Medieval Europe*. Early Drama, Art, and Music monograph series 8. Kalamazoo, MI: Medieval Institute Publications, 1986. 31–122.

———. 'Response [to Clopper "Why ... So Few English Saint Plays?"]'. *Early Theatre* 2 (1999). 113.

———. 'Saints in play: English theatre and saints' lives' in Sandro Sticca, ed. *Saints: Studies in Hagiography*. Binghamton, NY: Medieval and Renaissance Texts and Studies, 1996. 145–60.

————. 'Some Further Thoughts on the "Devil's Dance"'. *Early Drama, Art, and Music Review* 13/1 (1990). 3–7.

————. *Technology, Guilds, and Early English Drama*. Kalamazoo, MI: Medieval Institute Publications, 1997.

————, and Ann Eljenholm Nichols, eds. *Iconoclasm vs. Art and Drama*. Kalamazoo, MI: Medieval Institute Publications, 1989.

Davis, Norman, ed. *Non-Cycle Plays and Fragments*. Early English Text Society, supplementary series, 1. 1970.

————. Review of Bevington *Macro*. *Notes and Queries* 220 (1975). 78–9.

Dennett, J., ed. *Beverley Borough Records, 1575–1821*. Yorkshire Archaeological Society 84, 1933.

Denny, Neville. 'Arena Staging and Dramatic Quality in the Cornish Passion Play' in Neville Denny, ed., *Medieval Drama*. Stratford-upon-Avon Studies 16. London: Edward Arnold, 1973. 125–53.

Dictionary of National Biography, ed. Sir Leslie Stephen and Sir Sidney Lee. 1885–1900.

Dobson, R.B. 'Craft Guilds and City: The Historical Origins of the York Mystery Plays Reassessed' in Knight *Stage as Mirror*. 91–105.

Dorrell, Margaret. 'The Mayor of York and the Coronation Pageant'. *Leeds Studies in English*, new series, 5 (1971). 35–45.

Duffy, Eamon. *The Stripping of the Altars: Traditional Religion in England, 1400–1580*. New Haven, CT, and London: Yale University Press, 1992.

Dunbar, H.F. *Symbolism in Medieval Thought and its Consummation in the Divine Comedy*. New Haven, CT: Yale University Press, 1929.

Dunn, F.I. 'The Norwich Grocers' Play and the Kirkpatrick Papers at Norwich'. *Notes and Queries* 19/6 (1972). 202–3.

Dutka, JoAnna. 'The Fall of Man: the Norwich Grocers' Play'. *Records of Early English Drama Newsletter* 9/1 (1984). 1–11.

————. *Music in the English Mystery Plays*. Early Drama, Art, and Music reference series, 2. Kalamazoo, MI: Medieval Institute Publications, 1980.

————. 'Mysteries, Minstrels, and Music'. *Comparative Drama* 8/1 (1974). 112–24.

————. 'Mystery Plays at Norwich: Their Formation and Development'. *Leeds Studies in English*, new series, 10 (1978). 107–20.

————. 'News from Norwich'. *Records of Early English Drama Newsletter* 20/1 (1995). 19–20.

————, ed. *Records of Early English Drama: Proceedings of the First Colloquium at Erindale College*. Records of Early English Drama. Toronto: Toronto University Press, 1979.

————. *The Use of Music in the English Mystery Plays*. PhD dissertation. University of Toronto, 1972.

Eccles, Mark, ed. *The Macro Plays*. Early English Text Society, original series, 262. London: Oxford University Press, 1969.

Farmer, John S., ed. *The Castle of Perseverance*. London and Edinburgh: The Tudor Facsimile Texts, 1908.

Figueroa, Cristina Mourón, and Begoña Crespo Garcia. 'Theatre, Humour and Women: a "mishmash" full of life' in Higgins *Papers 1997*. 393–421.

Fitch, Robert. 'Norwich Pageants: The Grocers' Play'. *Norfolk Archaeology* 5 (1859). 8–31.

Flynn, Jane. 'The education of choristers in England during the sixteenth century' in John Morehen, ed. *English Choral Practice 1400–1650*. Cambridge: Cambridge University Press, 1995. 180–99.

Forrester, Jean. *Wakefield Mystery Plays and the Burgess Court Records: A New Discovery*. Ossett: 1974.

———, and A.C. Cawley. 'The Corpus Christi Play of Wakefield: A New Look at the Wakefield Burgess Court Records'. *Leeds Studies in English*, new series, 7 (1975). 108–15 and appendices following.

Fuller, Sarah. 'Discant and the Theory of Fifthing'. *Acta Musicologica* 50 (1978). 241–75.

Gallo, F. Alberto. *Music in the Castle*, trs. Anna Herklotz and Kathryn Krug. Chicago, IL: University of Chicago Press, 1995.

Gardiner, Harold C. *Mysteries' End*. New Haven: Yale University Press, 1946.

Gardner, John. *The Construction of the Wakefield Cycle*. Carbondale and Edwardsville, IL: Southern Illinois University Press, 1974.

Gibson, James M., and Isobel Harvey. 'A Sociological Study of the New Romney Passion Play'. *Research Opportunities in Renaissance Drama* 39 (2000). 203–21.

Golden Legend, The, of Jacobus de Voragine, trans. Granger Ryan and Helmut Ripperger. 1941; repr. New York: Arno Press, 1969.

Graduale Sacrosanctae Romanae Ecclesiae. Sablé-sur-Sarthe: Abbatia Sancti Petri de Solesmes, 1974.

Grantley, Darryll. 'Producing miracles' in Neuss *Aspects*. 78–91.

Greene, R.L. *The Early English Carols*. Oxford: Oxford University Press, 1935; 2/1977.

———, ed. *A Selection of English Carols*. Oxford: Clarendon Press, 1962.

Guinle, Francis. 'Songs in Tudor Drama'. *Medieval English Theatre* 16 (1994). 91–115.

Gutenberg, Johann. [42-Line Bible]. Maintz: Gutenberg, c. 1455; facsimile repr. New York: Brussel and Brussel Inc., 1968. 3 vols.

Hamilton, Donna B., and Richard Strier, eds. *Religion, Literature and Politics in Post-Reformation England, 1540–1688*. Cambridge: Cambridge University Press, 1996.

Happé, Peter, ed. *The Complete Plays of John Bale*. Cambridge: D.S. Brewer, 1985–6. 2 vols.

———. 'Cycle plays: the state of the art' in Higgins *Papers 1997*. 69–93.

———. *English Drama Before Shakespeare*. London: Longman, 1999.

———, ed. *English Mystery Plays*. Harmondsworth: Penguin, 1975.

Harris, Markham, trans. *The Cornish Ordinalia: A Medieval Dramatic Trilogy*. Washington, DC: Catholic University of America Press, 1969.

———, trans. *The Life of Meriasek: A Medieval Cornish Miracle Play*. Washington, DC: Catholic University of America Press, 1977.

Harris, Phyllis Pier, ed. and trans. *'Origo Mundi', First Play of the Cornish Mystery Cycle, the Ordinalia: A New Edition*. PhD dissertation. The University of Washington, 1964.

Harrison, Frank Ll., ed. *The Eton Choirbook*. Musica Britannica 10–12. London: Stainer and Bell for the Royal Musical Association, 1956–61.

———. *Music in Medieval Britain*. London: Routledge and Kegan Paul, 1958; 2/1963.

Hays, Rosalind C., C.E. McGee, Sally L. Joyce and Evelyn S. Newlyn, eds. *Records of Early English Drama: Dorset, Cornwall*. Records of Early English Drama. Toronto: Toronto University Press; [Turnhout]: Brepols, 1999.

Helterman, Jeffrey. *Symbolic Action in the Plays of the Wakefield Master*. Athens, GA: The University of Georgia Press, 1981.

Henry, Avril K. '"The Castle of Perseverance": the Stage Direction at line 1767'. *Notes and Queries* 210 (1965). 448.

———. '*Wisdom* at Winchester Cathedral'. *Medieval English Theatre* 3/1 (1981). 53–5.

Higgins, Sydney. *Bibliography of Cornish Medieval Drama*. World-wide web site <http://collectorspost.com/Catalogue/medramacornwall.htm>.

———, ed. *European Medieval Drama 1997: Papers from the Second International Conference on 'Aspects of European Medieval Drama', Camerino, 4–6 July 1997*. Volume I. Camerino: University of Camerino, 1997.

Hill-Vasquez, Heather. 'The possibilities of performance: a reformation sponsorship for the Digby *Conversion of St Paul*'. *Records of Early English Drama Newsletter* 22/1 (1997). 2–20.

Hoffman, C. Fenno, Jr. 'The Source of the Words to the Music in York 46'. *Modern Language Notes* 10 (1950). 236–9.

Hopper, Vincent Foster. *Medieval Number Symbolism*. 1938; repr. New York: Cooper Square Publishers Inc., 1969.

Huizinga, J. *The Waning of the Middle Ages*. New York: St Martin's Press, 1949; New York: Doubleday Anchor Books, 1954.

Hurlbut, Jesse D. 'The Sound of Civic Spectacle: Noise in Burgundian Ceremonial Entries' in Davidson *Material Culture*. 127–40.

Idley, Peter. *Instructions to his Son*, ed. Charlotte D'Evelyn. London: Oxford University Press, 1935.

Index of Middle English Prose. Woodbridge: D.S. Brewer, 2000.

Jack, R.D.S. *Patterns of Divine Comedy: A Study of Medieval English Drama*. Cambridge: D.S. Brewer, 1989.

Johnson, Robert W. 'Noah at Hull'. *The Dalesman* (May 1963). 105–7.

Johnston, Alexandra F. 'The Continental Connection: A Reconsideration' in Knight *Stage as Mirror*. 7–24.

———, and Wim Hüsken, eds. *Civic Ritual and Drama*. Ludus 2. Amsterdam and Atlanta, GA: Rodopi, 1997.

———, and Wim Hüsken, eds. *English Parish Drama*. Ludus 1. Amsterdam and Atlanta, GA: Rodopi, 1996.

Jones, Claude. 'Walsyngham Wystyll'. *Journal of English and Germanic Philology* 35 (1936). 139.

Keane, Ruth M. *The Theme of Kingship in the Chester Cycle*. MA dissertation. University of Liverpool, 1977.

King, Pamela. 'Calendar and Text: Christ's Ministry in the York Plays and the Liturgy'. *Medium Aevum* 67 (1998). 30–59.

———. *Coventry Mystery Plays*. Coventry and County Heritage Series, booklet no. 22. Coventry: Coventry Branch of the Historical Association, c. 1998.

———, and Clifford Davidson, eds. *The Coventry Corpus Christi Plays*. Kalamazoo MI: Medieval Institute Publications, 2000.

———, and Asuncion Salvador-Rabaza. 'La Festa d'Elxe: The Festival of the Assumption of the Virgin, Elche (Alicante)'. *Medieval English Theatre* 8/1, 1986. 21–50.

Knight, Alan E. ed. *The Stage as Mirror: Civic Theatre in Late Medieval Europe*. Cambridge: D.S. Brewer, 1997.

Kolve, V.A. *The Play Called Corpus Christi*. Stanford, CA: Stanford University Press, 1966.

Lamb, H.H. *The Changing Climate*. London: Methuen, 1966.

Lancashire, Ian. *Dramatic Texts and Records of Britain: A Chronological Topography to 1558*. Studies in Early English Drama 1. Toronto: University of Toronto Press, 1984.

Lascombes, André. 'Revisiting *The Croxton Play of Sacrament*: Spectacle and the Other's Voice' in Higgins *Papers 1997*. 111–25.

Lay folk's mass book, The, ed. T.F. Simmons. Early English Text Society, original series, 71. London: N. Trubner, 1879.

Le Patourel, Jean. 'Ceramic Horns' in David Gaimster and Mark Redknap, eds, *Everyday and Exotic Pottery from Europe, c. 650–1900: Studies in honour of John G. Hurst*. Oxford: Oxbow Books, 1992. 157–66.

Leach, A.F., ed. *Beverley Town Documents*. Selden Society 14, 1900.

———, ed. *Report on the Manuscripts of the Corporation of Beverley*. Historical Manuscripts Commission, 54th Report, 1900.

Lepow, Lauren. *Enacting the Sacrament: Counter-Lollardy in the Towneley Cycle*. London and Toronto: Associated University Presses, 1990.

Levine, Laura. *Men in Women's Clothing: anti-theatricality and effeminization, 1579–1642*. Cambridge: Cambridge University Press, 1994.

Lewis, L. *The Play of Mary Magdalene*. Dissertation. Madison, WI: University of Wisconsin, 1963.

Liber Responsorialis pro festis I. classis. Sablé-sur-Sarthe: Abbaye Saint-Pierre de Solesmes, 1895.

Longsworth, Robert. *The Cornish Ordinalia: Religion and Dramaturgy*. Cambridge, MA: Harvard University Press, 1967.

Louis, Cameron, ed. *Records of Early English Drama: Sussex*. Records of Early English Drama. Toronto: Toronto University Press; [Turnhout]: Brepols, 2000.

Lumiansky, R.M., and David Mills. *The Chester Mystery Cycle: Essays and Documents, with an Essay, 'Music in the Cycle', by Richard Rastall*. Chapel Hill, NC: University of North Carolina Press, 1983.

McGee, Timothy J., A.G. Rigg and David N. Klausner. *Singing Early Music: the pronunciation of European languages in the Late Middle Ages and Renaissance*. Bloomington, IN: Indiana University Press, 1996.

McKinnell, John. 'The Medieval Pageant Wagons at York: Their Orientation and Height', in Ostovich and Johnston, *The York Cycle Then and Now*. 79–104.

MacLean, Sally-Beth. 'Saints on Stage: An Analytical Survey of Dramatic Records in the West of England'. *Early Theatre* 2 (1999). 45–62.

Markham, Christopher A., and J. Charles Cox, eds. *Records of the Borough of Northampton*. London: E. Stock, 1898.

Marshall, John. 'The Chester Whitsun Plays: Dating of Post-Reformation Performances from the Smiths' Accounts'. *Leeds Studies in English*, new series, 9 (1977). 51–61.

———. '"Her virgynes, as many as a man wylle": Dance and Provenance in Three Late Medieval Plays'. *Leeds Studies in English*, new series, 25 (1994). 111–48.

———. '"The Manner of these Playes": the Chester Pageant Carriages and the Places Where They Played' in Mills *Staging Chester*. 17–48.

———. 'Marginal Staging Marks in the Macro Manuscript of *Wisdom*'. *Medieval English Theatre* 7/2 (1985). 77–82.

Medieval Drama Facsimiles. Leeds Texts and Monographs. Leeds: The University of Leeds School of English, 1973–. Individual volumes are listed here by editor:
1. The Chester Cycle (MS Bodley 175): Lumiansky and Mills (1973).
2. The Towneley Cycle: Cawley and Stevens (1976).
3. The Digby Plays: Baker and Murphy (1976).
4. The N-Town Plays: Meredith and Kahrl (1977).
5. Non-Cycle Plays and Fragments: Davis (1979).
6. The Chester Cycle (MS Huntington HM 2): Lumiansky and Mills (1980).
7. The York Cycle: Beadle and Meredith (1983).
8. The Chester Cycle (MS H arley 2124): Mills (1984).

Meredith, Peter. '"Item for a grone – iij d" – records and performance' in JoAnna Dutka, ed. *Records of Early English Drama: Proceedings of the First Colloquium*. Records of Early English Drama. Toronto: Toronto University Press, 1979. 26–60.

———. 'John Clerke's Hand in the York Register'. *Leeds Studies in English*, new series, 12 (1981). 245–71.

————. '"Make the Asse to Speake" or Staging the Chester Plays' in Mills *Staging Chester*, 49–76.

————, ed. *Mankind: An Acting Edition*. Leeds: Alumnus, 1997.

————. 'Manuscript, Scribe and Performance: Further Looks at the N.Town Manuscript' in Felicity Riddy, ed. *Regionalism in Late Medieval Manuscripts and Texts*. Cambridge: D.S. Brewer, 1991. 109–28.

————, ed. *The Mary Play from the N.Town Manuscript*. London: Longman, 1987.

————, ed. *The Passion Play from the N.Town Manuscript*. London: Longman, 1990.

————. 'A Reconsideration of Some Textual Problems in the N-Town Manuscript (BL Cotton Vespasian D VIII)'. *Leeds Studies in English*, new series, 9 (1977). 35–50.

————. 'Scribes, texts and performance' in Neuss *Aspects*. 13–29.

————. 'Staging Chester' in Mills *Staging Chester*. 49–76.

————, ed. *The Towneley Cycle*. Leeds: The University of Leeds School of English, 1989; 2/1991.

————, and John E. Tailby, eds. *The Staging of Religious Drama in Europe in the Later Middle Ages*. Early Drama, Art, and Music monograph series, 4. Kalamazoo, MI: Medieval Institute Publications, 1983.

Mezey, Nichole. 'Creed and Prophets Series in the Visual Arts'. *Early Drama,Art, and Music Newsletter* 2/1 (1979). 7–10.

Middle English Dictionary, The. Ann Arbor: University of Michigan Press, 1952– . Also at web-site <http://www.hti.umich.edu/dict/med/>

Mill, Anna J. 'The Hull Noah Play'. *Modern Language Review* 33 (1938). 489–505.

Mills, David. *The Chester Mystery Cycle: a New Edition with Modernised Spelling*. East Lansing: Colleagues Press, 1992.

————. 'The Stage Directions in the Manuscripts of the Chester Mystery Cycle'. *Medieval English Theatre* 3/1 (1981). 45–51.

————, ed. *Staging the Chester Cycle*. Leeds Texts and Monographs, new series, 9. Leeds: The University of Leeds School of English, 1985.

————. '"The Towneley Plays" or "The Towneley Cycle"?'. *Leeds Studies in English* 17 (1986). 95–104.

————. 'Where have all the players gone? A Chester problem'. *Early Theatre* 1 (1998). 129–37.

Montagu, Gwen, and Jeremy Montagu. 'Beverley Minster Reconsidered'. *Early Music* 6/3 (July 1978). 401–15.

Moore, Bruce. 'The Banns in Medieval English Drama'. *Leeds Studies in English*, new series, 24 (1993). 91–122.

More, Mother Thomas [Mary Berry]. 'The Performance of Plainsong in the Later Middle Ages and the Sixteenth Century'. *Proceedings of the Royal Musical Association* 92 (1966). 121–34.

Morley, Thomas. *A Plain and Easy Introduction to Practical Music* [London: 1597], ed. R. Alec Harman. London: Dent; New York: Norton, 1963.

Muir, Lynette R. 'Further Thoughts on the Tale of the Profaned Host'. *The Early Drama, Art, and Music Review* 21/2 (1999). 88–97.

———. 'Medieval English Drama: The French Connection' in Briscoe and Coldewey *Contexts*. 56–76.

Murdoch, Brian. *Cornish Literature*. Cambridge: D.S. Brewer, 1993.

———. 'The Cornish Medieval Drama' in Beadle *Cambridge Companion*. 211–39.

Nance, R. Morton. 'The Plen an gwary or Cornish Playing Place'. *Journal of the Royal Institution of Cornwall* 24 (1933–36). 190–212.

———, and A.S.D. Smith. *The Cornish Ordinalia*, ed. Graham Sandercock. Cornish Language Board, 1982–9. 3 vols.

Neighbarger, Randy L. *An Outward Show: Music for Shakespeare on the London Stage, 1660–1830*. London: Greenwood Press, 1992.

Nelson, Alan H. *The Medieval English Stage: Corpus Christi Pageants and Plays*. Chicago and London: Chicago University Press, 1974.

Neuss, Paula, ed. *Aspects of Early English Drama*. Cambridge: D.S. Brewer; Totowa, NJ: Barnes and Noble, 1983.

———, ed. and trans. *The Creacion of the World*. Garland Medieval Texts, 3. New York and London: Garland, 1983.

Nevile, Jennifer. 'Dance in early Tudor England: an Italian connection?'. *Early Music* 26/2 (1998). 230–44.

New Grove Dictionary of Music and Musicians, The, ed. Stanley Sadie. 20 vols. London: Macmillan, 1980.

Newlyn, Evelyn S. 'Middle Cornish Drama at the Millennium' in Higgins *Papers 1997*. 363–74.

———. 'The Middle Cornish interlude: genre and tradition'. *Comparative Drama* 30 (1996). 266–81.

Norris, Edwin, ed. and trans. *The Ancient Cornish Drama*. 2 vols. Oxford: Oxford University Press, 1859.

O'Mara, Veronica M. 'Saints' Plays and Preaching: Theory and Practice in Late Medieval English Sanctorale Sermons'. *Leeds Studies in English*, new series, 29 (1998). 257–74.

Orgel, Stephen. *Impersonations: the Performance of Gender in Shakespeare's England*. Cambridge: Cambridge University Press, 1996; paperback 1996.

Ostovich, Helen, and Alexandra Johnston, eds. *The York Cycle Then and Now*. *Early Theatre*, special volume. Hamilton, Ontario: McMaster University Press, 2000.

Owens, Jessie Ann. *Composers at Work: the craft of musical composition 1450–1600*. New York: Oxford University Press, 1997.

Page, Christopher. *Voices and Instruments of the Middle Ages: instrumental practice and songs in France, 1100–1300*. London: Dent, 1986.

Paino, Fiorella, and Sydney Higgins. 'Playing the Serpent: Virgin or Mythical Beast?' in Higgins *Papers 1997*. 375–92.

Paléographie musicale 15. See under Beneventan Antiphoner.

Palmer, Barbara D. Review of performances at Toronto and York, 1998. *Shakespeare Bulletin* 18/1 (2000). 35–6.

———. 'Staging the Virgin's Body: Spectacular Effects of Annunciation and Assumption'. *The Early Drama, Art, and Music Review* 21/2 (1999). 63–80.

———. '"Towneley Plays" or "Wakefield Cycle" Revisited'. *Comparative Drama* 21 (1987). 318–48.

Parry, David. Review of the 1977 performance at Toronto. *Medieval English Theatre* 1 (1979). 19–31.

Paxson, James J., Lawrence M. Clopper and Sylvia Tomasch, eds. *The Performance of Middle English Culture*. Cambridge: D.S. Brewer, 1998.

Pearsall, Derek. 'Texts, Textual Criticism and Fifteenth-Century Manuscript Production' in Yeager *Studies*. 121–36.

Pesce, D. *The Affinities and Medieval Transposition*. Bloomington, IN: Indiana University Press, 1987.

Pettitt, Tom. 'Mankind: An English *Fastnachtspiel*?' in Twycross *Festive Drama*. 190–202.

Pickering, Oliver S. 'Poetic Style and Poetic Affiliation in the *Castle of Perserverance*'. *Leeds Studies in English*, new series, 29 (1998). 275–91.

Pilkinton, Mark C., ed. *Records of Early English Drama: Bristol*. Records of Early English Drama. Toronto: Toronto University Press, 1997.

Planchart, Alejandro Enrique. *The Repertory of Tropes at Winchester*. Princeton, NJ: Princeton University Press, 1977. 2 vols.

Poulson, George. *Beverlac, or, The Antiquities and History of ... Beverley*. London, 1829.

Pritchard, V. *English Medieval Graffiti*. Cambridge: Cambridge University Press, 1967.

Processionale Monasticum as usum congregationis Gallicae. Sablé-sur-Sarthe: Abbaye Saint-Pierre de Solesmes, 1893.

Promptorium parvulorum sive clericorum. London: Camden Society 25, 54 and 89 (1843, 1853 and 1865).

Ramm, Andrea von. 'Singing early music'. *Early Music* 4/1 (January 1976). 12–15.

Rastall, G. R[ichard]. 'The Minstrel Court in Medieval England' in R.L. Thomson, ed., *A Medieval Miscellany in honour of Professor John Le Patourel*. Leeds: Proceedings of the Leeds Philosophical and Literary Society, Literary and Historical Section, 18/1 (1982). 96–105.

———. *Secular Musicians in Late Medieval England*. 2 vols. PhD dissertation. Manchester University, 1968.

Rastall, Richard. 'Female Roles in All-Male Casts'. *Medieval English Theatre* 7/1 (1985). 25–51.

———. *A Fifteenth-Century Song Book*. Leeds: Boethius Press, 1973.

———. *The Heaven Singing: Music in Early English Religious Drama I*. Cambridge: D.S. Brewer, 1996; paperback edn., 1999.

———. 'Minstrels and minstrelsy in household account books' in Dutka *REED Proceedings*. 3–21.

————. 'Minstrelsy, Church and Clergy in Medieval England'. *Proceedings of the Royal Musical Association*, 97 (1971). 83–98.

————. 'Music in the Cycle Plays' in Briscoe and Coldewey *Contexts*. 192–218.

————. 'Music and Liturgy in *Everyman*: Some Aspects of Production' in Catherine Batt, ed. *Essays in Honour of Peter Meredith. Leeds Studies in English*, new series, 29. Leeds: The University of Leeds School of English, 1998. 305–14.

————. 'The Musical Repertory' in Clifford Davidson, ed. *The Iconography of Heaven*. Early Drama, Art, and Music monograph series 21 (1994). 162–96.

————, ed. *Six Songs from the York Mystery Play 'The Assumption of the Virgin'*. Newton Abbot: Antico Edition, 1985.

————. '"Some Myrth to his Majestee": Music in the Chester Cycle' in Mills *Staging Chester*. 77–99.

————. *Two Fifteenth-Century Song Books*. Aberystwyth: Boethius Press, 1990.

————. 'Vocal Range and Tessitura in Music from York Play 45'. *Music Analysis* 3/2 (1984). 181–99.

————. 'The [York] Music' in Beadle and Meredith. *York Play*. Medieval Drama Facsimiles 7. Leeds: University of Leeds School of English, 1983. xli–xlv.

Records of Early English Drama. Toronto: Toronto University Press; the last volume shown here co-published in the European Union at Turnhout by Brepols.

REED.Bristol: ed. Mark C. Pilkinton, 1997.

REED.Dorset, Cornwall: ed. Rosalind C. Hays, C.E. McGee, Sally L. Joyce and Evelyn S. Newlyn, 1999.

REED.Shropshire: ed. J. Alan B. Somerset. 1994. 2 vols.

REED.Somerset (including Bath): ed. James Stokes and Robert J. Alexander, 1996. 2 vols.

REED.Sussex: ed. Cameron Louis, 2000.

Remnant, Mary. 'Musical Instruments in Early English Drama' in Davidson *Material Culture*. 141–94.

Revels History of Drama in English 1: Medieval Drama, ed. Lois Potter. London and New York: Methuen, 1983.

Revised Medieval Latin Word-List, The, prepared by R.E. Latham. London: Oxford University Press for the British Academy, 1965; reprinted with Supplement, 1980.

Richardson, Christine. 'The Medieval English and French Shepherds Plays' in Twycross *Festive Drama*. 259–69.

Riggio, Milla Cozart, ed. *The Play of Wisdom: Its Texts and Contexts*. New York: AMS Press, 1998.

————, ed. *The Wisdom Symposium*. New York: AMS Press, 1986.

Robertson, Alec, and Denis Stevens, eds. *The Pelican History of Music I: Ancient Forms to Polyphony*. Harmondsworth: Penguin Books, 1960.

Robinson, John W. 'The Art of the York Realist'. *Modern Philology* 60 (1963). 241–51. Repr. in Jerome Taylor and Alan H. Nelson, eds. *Medieval English*

Drama: Essays Critical and Contextual. Chicago, IL: Chicago University Press, 1972. 230–44.

———. *Studies in Fifteenth-Century Stagecraft*. Early Drama, Art, and Music monograph series, 14. Kalamazoo, MI: Medieval Institute Publications, 1991.

Rogerson, Margaret. 'The Coventry Corpus Christi Play: A "Lost" Middle English Creed Play?'. *Research Opportunities in Renaissance Drama* 36 (1997), 143–77.

Rose, Martial, and Julia Hedgecoe. *Stories in Stone: The Medieval Roof Carvings of Norwich Cathedral*. Huntingdon: Herbert Press, 1997.

Ross, Thomas W. 'Taboo-Words in Fifteenth-Century English' in Yeager *Fifteenth-Century Studies*. 137–60.

Ryan, Denise. '"Item paid ... To him that Rid to throwe graynes": presenting the Innkeepers' Woman in Chester's 1614 Midsummer Show'. *Records of Early English Drama Newsletter* 22/1 (1997). 32–5.

Salisbury, The Use of: See under Sandon.

Sandon, Nick, ed. *The Use of Salisbury*. Newton Abbot: Antico Edition, 1984– .

   I   *The Ordinary of the Mass* (1984).

   II *The Proper of the Mass in Advent* (1986).

   III *The Proper of the Mass from Septuagesima to Palm Sunday* (1991).

   IV *The Masses and Ceremonies of Holy Week* (1996).

   V *The Proper of the Mass from Easter to Trinity* (1998).

   VI *The Proper of the Mass from Trinity to Advent* (1999).

Schell, Edgar. 'Fulfilling the Law in the Brome *Abraham and Isaac*'. *Leeds Studies in English*, new series 25 (1994), 149–58.

Shand, G.B., and Raymond C. Shady, eds. *Play-Texts in Old Spelling*. New York: AMS Press, c. 1984.

Sharp, Thomas. *A Dissertation on the Pageants ... At Coventry*. Coventry: 1825; repr. Wakefield: EP Publications, 1973.

———. *The Presentation in the Temple*. Edinburgh: 1836.

Simpson, Claude. *The British Broadside Ballad and its Music*. New Brunswick, NJ: Rutgers University Press, [1966].

Simpson, Percy, and C.F. Bell. *Designs by Inigo Jones for Masques and Plays at Court*. Oxford: Walpole Society,1924.

Slim, H. Colin. 'Mary Magdalene, Musician and Dancer'. *Early Music* 8 (1980). 460–73.

Smith, Lucy Toulmin. See under Toulmin Smith, Lucy.

Somerset, J. Alan B., ed. *Records of Early English Drama: Shropshire*. Records of Early English Drama. Toronto: Toronto University Press, 1994. 2 vols.

Soule, Lesley. 'Subverting the Mysteries: the Devil as anti-character' in Higgins *Papers 1997*. 135–49.

Spector, Stephen. 'The Composition and Development of an Eclectic Manuscript: Cotton Vespasian D VIII'. *Leeds Studies in English*, new series, 9 (1977). 62–83.

————, ed. *The N-Town Play*. Early English Text Society, supplementary series, 11,12. London: Oxford University Press, 1991.

————. 'Time, Space and Identity in the *Play of the Sacrament*' in Knight *Stage as Mirror*. 189–200.

Spencer, Brian. *Pilgrim Souvenirs and Secular Badges*. London: Stationery Office, 1998.

Stevens, John. *Mediaeval Carols*. Musica Britannica 4. London: Stainer and Bell for the Royal Musical Association, 1952; 2/1958.

————. *Music and Poetry in the Early Tudor Court*. London: Methuen, 1961; corr. and rev. edn Cambridge: Cambridge University Press, 1979.

————. 'Music in Mediaeval Drama'. *Proceedings of the Royal Musical Association* 84 (1958). 81–95.

Stevens, Martin. 'The Missing Parts of the Towneley Cycle'. *Speculum* 45 (1970). 254–65.

————, and A.C. Cawley, eds. *The Towneley Plays*. The Early English Text Society. Oxford: Oxford University Press, 1994.

Sticca, Sandro, ed. *The Medieval Drama*. Albany, NY: State University of New York Press, 1972.

Stokes, James, and Robert J. Alexander, eds. *Records of Early English Drama: Somerset, including Bath*. Records of Early English Drama. Toronto: Toronto University Press, 1996. 2 vols.

Stokes, Whitley, ed. *Beunans Meriasek. The life of Saint Meriasek, bishop and confessor*. London: Trübner, 1872.

Stratmann, Franz Heinrich, ed. *A Middle-English dictionary: containing words used by English writers from the twelfth to the fifteenth century*. New edn, revised by Henry Bradley. Oxford: Clarendon Press, 1891.

Thomson, Leslie. 'The Meaning of *Thunder and Lightning*: Stage Directions and Audience Expectations'. *Early Theatre* 2 (1999). 11–24.

Thomson, Peter. '*Gestus* Revisited: Balaam and Balaak in Chester' in Higgins *Papers 1997*. 127–34.

Toulmin Smith, Lucy, ed. *York Plays*. Oxford: 1885; repr. New York: Russell and Russell, 1963.

Twycross, Meg, ed. *Festive Drama*. Cambridge: D.S. Brewer, 1996.

Tyrer, John W. *Historical Survey of Holy Week, its Services and Ceremonial*. London: Alcuin Club, 1932.

Tyson, Cynthia H. 'Property requirements of *Purificatio Marie*: Evidence for stationary production of the Towneley Cycle' in John R. Sommerfeldt and E. Rozanne Elder, eds. *Studies in Medieval Culture* 8 and 9. Kalamazoo, MI: The Medieval Institute, Western Michigan University, 1976. 187–91.

Uberti, Mauro. 'Vocal techniques in Italy in the second half of the 16th century'. *Early Music* 9/4 (1981). 486–95.

Vroom, Theresia de. 'In the context of "Rough Music": the representation of unequal couples in some medieval plays' in Higgins *Papers 1997*. 151–74.

Wall, Carolyn. 'The Apocryphal and Historical Background of "The Appearance of Our Lady to Thomas" (Play XLVI of the York Cycle)'. *Medieval Studies* 32 (1970). 172–92.

––––––. 'York Pageant XLVI and its Music'. *Speculum* 46 (1971). 689–712.

Weber, Sarah A. *Theology and Poetry in the Middle English Lyric*. Columbus, OH: Ohio State University Press, 1969.

Wells, Robin Headlam. *Elizabethan Mythologies*. Cambridge: Cambridge University Press, 1994.

West, R.H. *Milton and the Angels*. Athens, GA: Georgia University Press, 1955.

White, Paul Whitfield. *Theatre and Reformation: Protestantism, Patronage and Playgoing in Tudor England*. Cambridge: Cambridge University Press, 1993.

Wickham, Glynne. 'The Staging of Saint Plays in England' in Sticca *Medieval Drama*. 99–119.

Wieland, Gernot R., ed. *The Canterbury Hymnal*. Toronto: Pontifical Institute of Mediaeval Studies, 1982.

Willis, James. 'Stage Directions in "The Castell of Perseverance"'. *Modern Language Review* 51 (1956). 404–5.

Wilson, Philip. *The Musicall Prouerbis ... of Lekingfelde*. Oxford: Oxford University Press, 1924.

Woolf, Rosemary. *The English Mystery Plays*. London: Routledge and Kegan Paul; Berkeley, CA: University of California Press, 1972.

Wray, Alison. 'The sound of Latin in England before and after the Reformation' in John Morehen, ed. *English Choral Practice 1400–1650*. Cambridge: Cambridge University Press, 1995. 74–89.

––––––. 'English pronunciation, c.1500–c.1625' in John Morehen, ed. *English Choral Practice 1400–1650*. Cambridge: Cambridge University Press, 1995. 90–108.

Wright, Stephen K. *The Vengeance of Our Lord: Medieval Dramatizations of the Destruction of Jerusalem*. Toronto: Pontifical Institute of Mediaeval Studies, 1989.

Wright, Thomas, ed. *The Chester Plays*. London: Shakespeare Society Publications, 1842 and 1847; reprinted 1853.

Wulstan, David. *Tudor Music*. London: Dent, 1985.

Wyatt, Diana K.J. *Performance and Ceremonial in Beverley before 1642*. PhD dissertation. The University of York [UK], 1983.

Yeager, Robert F., ed. *Fifteenth-Century Studies: Recent Essays*. Hamden, CT: Archon Books, 1984.

INDEX